The **Rough Guide** t

Sicily

written and researched by

Robert Andrews and Jules Brown

with additional contributions from

Ros Belford and Roger Norum

ROUGH
GUIDES

NEW YORK • LONDON • DELHI

www.roughguides.com

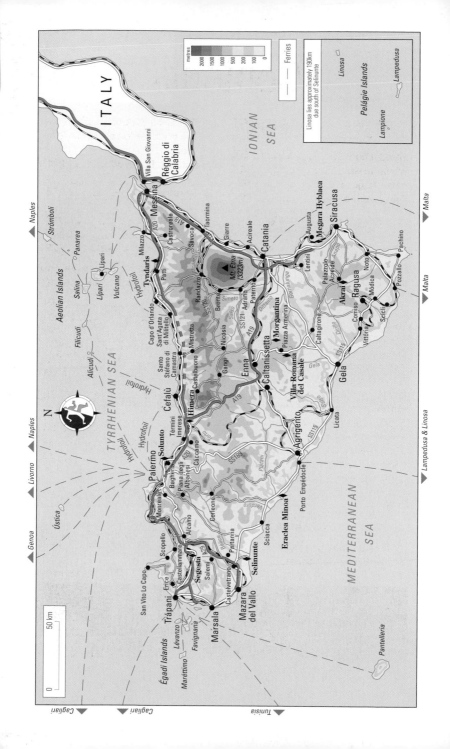

Contents

Introduction to

Sicily

At the centre of the Mediterranean, but on the periphery of Europe, the island of Sicily is a distinct entity from the rest of Italy. Although just 3km from the mainland across the Straits of Messina, it's much further away In appearance, feel and culture. A hybrid Sicilian dialect is still widely spoken, and many place names are tinged with the Arabic that was once in wide use on the island. The food is notlceably different, too: spicier and with more emphasis on fish, fruit and vegetables in the daily diet than in the north. The flora also echoes the shift south – oranges, lemons, olives, almonds and palms are ubiquitous. Above all, though, it's the nature of day-to-day living which separates Sicily from the rest of Italy – experienced outdoors in markets, piazzas and alleys with an operatic exuberance, and reflected in the unique festivals, ceremonies and processions that take place throughout the year.

There's certainly a separate quality in the people, who see themselves as Sicilians first and Italians a very firm second. The island's strategic importance meant it was held by some of the western world's richest civilizations – notably the Greeks, Romans, Arabs, Normans and Spaniards – which, while bequeathing many fine monuments, made Sicily the subject of countless foreign wars, and left it with little economic independence. Centuries of oppression have bred insularity and resentment, and the island was probably the most reluctantly unified Italian region, with Sicilians almost instinctively suspicious of the intentions of Rome. Even today, relations with the mainland are often strained. For many Sicilians, their place in the modern Italian state is illustrated every time they

Fact file

- Sicily is the largest and one of the most densely populated islands in the Mediterranean, with extensive areas of mountains in the north and east, the highest being Mount Etna (3323m) – Europe's largest active volcano. Apart from Etna's sporadic eruptions, Sicily is also prone to seismic upheavals – massive earthquakes destroyed Messina in 1908, and rocked the western part of the island in 1966.

- Sicily has a semi-autonomous status within the Italian republic, with its own parliament and president, and limited legislative powers in such areas as tourism, transport, industry and the environment. There is no separatist movement to speak of, though suspicion of central government runs deep.

- Compared to north Italy, the economy has remained relatively underdeveloped. Though there are pockets of oil-refining and chemical industrial activity, Sicily is mainly agricultural, devoted to the cultivation of wheat, barley, corn (maize), olives, citrus fruit, almonds, wine grapes and some cotton. Tuna and sardine fishing are also important, and the last thirty years or so have seen tourism playing an increasingly crucial role.

- The population – mainly concentrated in the two main cities of Palermo and Catania, on the northern and eastern coasts – is something over five million.

look at a map to see the island being kicked – the perpetual football.

And Sicilians do have a point. There's much that hasn't changed since Unification in the nineteenth century, and what modernization there is has brought associated ills. Pockets of the island have been disfigured by bleak construction projects and unsightly industry, and despite Sicily's limited political autonomy, little has really been done to tackle the more deep-rooted problems: emigration (both to the mainland and abroad) is still high, poverty seemingly endemic, and there's an almost feudal attitude to business and commerce. Both European and central government aid continues to pour in, but much has been siphoned off by organized crime, which, in the west of the island at least, is still widespread. For visitors, however, these matters rarely impinge upon their experience. Mafia activity, for example – almost a byword for Sicilian life when viewed from abroad – is usually an in-house affair, with little or no consequence for travellers.

▼ Santissima Trinità di Delia, Castelvetrano

Catacombs, caves and holes in the ground

Sicily has some of the world's creepiest tourist destinations in the shape of its catacombs and caves, used as burial places for thousands of years and accessible to anyone with a flashlight and a strong nerve. Oldest are the rock-cut tombs of the great necropolis at Pantálica, first used in the thirteenth century BC. Another huge swath of tombs is on view below the Greek temples at Agrigento, while catacombs riddle the ground in the city of Siracusa. But for sheer hands-in-the-air horror, there's no beating the infamous preserved, clothed bodies lining the catacombs of Palermo's Convento dei Cappuccini, or the smaller-scale show in the little village of Sávoca, near Taormina. Bodies were placed here as late as the nineteenth century, and the locals used to pay daily visits, often standing in the adjacent niches to accustom themselves to the idea of the great ever-after.

First-time visitors and regular returnees alike all remark on the island's astonishingly all-encompassing appeal. Its dramatic landscapes range from a mountainous interior and rugged coastlines to remote outlying islands and the volcanic foothills of Mount Etna. Sicily's diverse history, meanwhile, has left it with a surprising abundance of archeological remains and architectural marvels. The island was an important power-base during the Hellenistic period, and the Greek relics, especially, are superb, standing comparison with any of the ruins in Greece itself. The Arab and Norman elements of Sicily's history are vividly manifest on the west and north coasts, while Baroque architecture shows its face in the elegantly restrained cities of the southeast. And if the history leaves you cold, you could simply come – as many do – for the food, the sun, the sea and the beaches. The coastal settlements soak up most of the summer-holiday trade, either at fashionable resorts or simple fishing villages fronted by long swaths of sand, though a number of offshore islands – some quite remote – offer a real chance to escape the crowds.

On location

Setting out on the **movie** trail in Sicily throws up some interesting cinematic bedmates. Francis Ford Coppola's *Godfather* trilogy is the obvious heavyweight – village scenes in Part II (1974) were filmed in Sávoca near Taormina, while *Part III*'s finale (1990) splatters gore across the steps of Palermo's Teatro Mássimo. There couldn't be more of a contrast to the gentilities of *Cinema Paradiso* (1989), filmed by Giuseppe Tornatore in the island's interior, or Michael Radford's *Il Postino* (1994), which used locations on offshore islands Salina and Pantelleria to great effect. These last two films, in particular, were amazing crossover successes, highlighting what many Italian directors had known for years – namely that the glories of the Sicilian landscape offered a unique hinterland for the expression of emotion. To best appreciate the relation of location and mood, see the great Roberto Rossellini's appreciation of the dramatic possibilities of the volcano in *Strómboli: Terra di Dio* (1949), starring a young Ingrid Bergman.

▼ The temple at Segesta

Where to go

Set in a wide bay at the foot of a fertile valley, the capital, **Palermo**, is one of Italy's most visually striking cities, boasting some of the island's finest churches, markets, museums and restaurants. It gets hot and stuffy here in summer, though, which makes escapes out of the city all the more tempting: to the fashionable beach at Mondello, the sanctuary on Monte Pellegrino or the church mosaics at Monreale. East of Palermo, the **Tyrrhenian coast** provides the first opportunity to climb into the hiking and skiing grounds of the Monti Madonie, and it's along here that you'll find one of Sicily's premier resorts, Cefalù, handily situated just an hour from Palermo.

From Milazzo, ferries and hydrofoils depart to the Aeolian Islands, a chain of seven volcanic islands – including Vulcano and Strómboli – that attract sun-worshippers and

adventurous hikers alike. Assorted seasonal holiday towns stretching between Messina – crossing-point to mainland Italy – and the fashionable resort of Taormina, make up the island's Northern Ionian coast, while Sicily's second city, east-coast Catania, broods under the graceful cone of Mount Etna, the most memorable of Sicily's natural attractions.

The finest concentration of historical and architectural sites is arguably in Siracusa, where classical ruins and stunning Baroque buildings decorate Sicily's most attractive city. In the southeast region beyond, beautiful towns like Noto and Ragusa were rebuilt along planned Baroque lines after a devastating earthquake in the seventeenth century, though the unique Neolithic cemeteries of Pantálica survived to provide one of Sicily's most atmospheric backwaters.

After the richness of the southeast towns, many find the simple, isolated grandeur of the interior a welcome change. This is the most sparsely populated region, hiding gems like the well-preserved mosaics at Piazza Armerina, which recall the lavish trappings of Sicily's Roman governors, and the historic mountain stronghold of Enna. Away from the few interior towns, remote roads wind north, back towards Palermo, through little-visited destinations like Prizzi or Corleone whose names chime with the popular image of Sicily as a nest of Mafia intrigue.

Along the south coast, only the ancient temples of Agrigento and the Greek city and beach at Eraclea Minoa attract visitors in any numbers. Further around the coast, Trápani anchors the west of the island, a great

◀ Traditional painted cart, Palermo

The Normans in Sicily

In a long history of invasion and occupation, Sicily's most brilliant period belongs to the **Normans**, the swashbuckling "men from the north" who seized Messina from the Arabs in 1061, and captured Palermo eleven years later. In just over a century, four Norman kings – from Roger I to William II – changed the social and political landscape and bequeathed a lasting legacy of **art and architecture**. Whether in the small, gloriously decorated chapels of Palermo or the vibrant mosaics in the cathedrals of Monreale and Cefalù, the evidence of their glittering wealth and quasi-imperial certainty is clear. And by streamlining administration, imposing the French and Italian languages on what had been a largely Arabic island, and ruling absolutely from a position of strength, the Normans set the framework for the next seven hundred years of foreign domination.

base for anyone interested in delving into the very different character of this side of Sicily. The Arabic influence is stronger here than elsewhere, especially in Marsala and Mazara del Vallo, while Selinunte and Segesta hold the most romantic sets of ancient ruins on the island. It's from ports on the south and west coasts, too, that Sicily's most absorbing outlying islands are reached. On Lampedusa and Linosa, on the Égadi Islands and, above all, on distant Pantelleria, the sea is as clean as you'll find anywhere in the Mediterranean, and you truly feel you're on the edge of Europe.

When to go

▼ Noto balcony

Any of these places can be extremely uncomfortable to visit at the height of a Sicilian summer, when the dusty **sirocco** winds blow in from North Africa; your choice of **when to go** should take this into consideration. In **July and August**, you'll roast – and you'll be in the company of tens of thousands of other tourists all jostling for space on the beaches, in the museums and at the archeological sites. Hotel availability is much reduced and prices will often be higher in response to demand. If you want the heat but not the crowds, go in May, June or September, while swimming is possible right into November. **Spring** is really the optimum time to come, and it arrives early: the almond blossom flowers in February, and there are fresh strawberries in April. **Easter** is a major celebration, a good time to see some of the more traditional festivals like the events at Trápani, Érice and Piana degli Albanesi, though again they'll all be oversubscribed with visitors. **Winter** is mild by northern European standards and is a nice time to be here, at least on the coast, where the skies stay clear and life continues to be lived very much outdoors. On the other hand, the interior – especially around Enna – can get snowed under, providing skiing opportunities south of Cefalù, at Piano Battáglia, or on Mount Etna, while anywhere else in the interior can be subject to (often considerable) blasts of wind and downpours of rain.

▲ Catching tuna during La Mattanza, Favignana

▼ Grocery shop, Lipari Town

Daytime temperatures (°C)

	Jan	Feb	Mar	Apr	May	June	July	Aug	Sept	Oct	Nov	Dec
Palermo (Average)	10.3	10.4	13	16.2	18.7	23	25.3	25.1	23.2	19.9	16.8	12.6
Taormina (Average)	11	10.6	13.1	16.2	20.1	24.1	27.1	27.1	23.7	20	16	12.6

30

things not to miss

It's not possible to see everything Sicily has to offer in one trip – and we don't suggest you try. What follows is a selective taste of the island's highlights – architecture, dramatic landscapes, and even good things to eat and drink. Arranged in five colour-coded categories, you can browse through to find the very best things to see, do and experience. All highlights have a page reference to take you straight into the guide, where you can find out more.

01 **Ortygia, Siracusa** Page **292** • Ortygia's seafront is a great place to enjoy the traditional early-evening *passeggiata*.

02 **Tempio della Concordia, Agrigento** Page **360** • The most captivating of the stunning series of ancient Greek temples which line the ridge below Agrigento.

03 **Mount Etna** Page **263** • The bleak, black upper slopes of Europe's greatest volcano are unforgettable, and, when not swathed in cloud and dust, offer terrific views.

04 **Spaghetti alla Norma in Catania** Page **251** • This hearty local dish is named after one of the most famous operas by local boy Vincenzo Bellini.

05 **Cassata** Page **52** • This ice-cream confection with a soaring sugar and fat content should be approached with care.

06 **Mosaics, Piazza Armerina** Page **341** • Uncovered at a Roman hunting lodge near Piazza Armerina, these brightly coloured mosaics are unrivalled in the Roman world in their quality and extent.

07 **Santa Rosalia celebrations, Palermo** Page **114** • Perhaps the most exuberant of the island's festivities, this involves the whole city in midsummer madness.

08 **The Greek theatre, Taormina** Page **228** • Occupying one of the world's most stunning sites, the theatre offers wonderful views towards Etna and down to the sea, and is still used to stage concerts and dramas.

16

09 **Gola di Alcántara** Page **237** • Wade the deep gorge or else just lounge on the riverside beach here.

10 **Mountain Road, SS120** Page **327** • Drive along the SS120, Sicily's most spectacular transmountain route, for amazing views of sweeping valleys and isolated villages, such as Petralia Sottana.

11 **Caltagirone, La Scala** Page **344** • Famous for its ceramics industry, Caltagirone's most dramatic artistic expression is La Scala, a flight of 142 steps decorated with hand-painted designs.

12 **Pantelleria, island view** Page **425** • Sicily's most chic island, Pantelleria is closer to Africa than Italy, but its unique landscapes attract an increasing number of inquisitive visitors.

14 **Pescheria, Catania** Page **251** • The seething fish market is an intensely colourful and cacophonous experience, bringing you face-to-face with every kind of exotic seafood in the raw.

13 **Selinunte, acropolis and temples** Page **421** • The most romantically sited Greek city in Sicily lies in ruins in a remote corner of the west coast.

16 **Aeolian Islands, hydrofoil or ferry** Page 163 • Island-hopping between the seven Aeolian Islands is easy on a large fleet of hydrofoils and ferries which are in service all year round.

15 **Cappella Palatina in the Palazzo dei Normanni, Palermo** Page **91** • The chapel shows off a dazzling combination of Arab architecture and Byzantine mosaics.

17 **The night-time ascent of Strómboli** Page **196** • The thrilling climb allows a close-up view of the fireworks at the crater.

18 **The Duomo, Siracusa** Page **284** • A fascinating synthesis which encompasses every phase of Siracusa's rich history, the cathedral sits in the heart of Ortygia, the city's old centre.

19 **The procession of the Misteri, Trápani** Page **393** • These realistic, life-sized wooden statues, representing scenes from the Passion, are paraded through the steets of Trápani on Good Friday every year in one of the island's major Easter celebrations.

20 **Alfresco eating** Page **108** • One of Sicily's greatest pleasures is having a meal at an outdoor restaurant, such as the *Santandrea* in Palermo.

21 **Noto** Page **303** • The whole town is a marvel of Baroque building, its honey-coloured stone enhanced by fantastic sculptures.

22 **Marsala wine** Page **413** • Sicily's famous dessert wine has been made in Marsala since the eighteenth century, and is available in wine shops, bars and restaurants across the island.

23 Beach, Eraclea Minoa Page 365 • The sweeping south-coast beach, backed by pine trees and chalky cliffs, is a magnet for locals and visitors during the summer.

24 Castello di Lombardia, Enna Page 322 • Enna's mighty castle guards the steep slopes of this ancient fortified town.

25 **Frutta di Martorana, Palermo** Page **89** • You might find it sickly sweet, but this fruit-shaped candy is an authentic Sicilian experience.

26 **San Giorgio, Ragusa** Page **308** • In Ibla, Ragusa's older quarter, this church is one of the best works of Baroque master-craftsman Rosario Gagliardi.

27 **Riserva Naturale dello Zíngaro** Page **287** • Sicily's first and most beautiful nature reserve offers great walks and plenty of pristine, isolated cove beaches.

28 Diving in Ústica Page **124** • The best place in Italy for undersea exploration, with clear waters and a range of protected fauna.

29 Pantálica Page **297** • This high ravine would be spectacular even without the added interest of thousands of prehistoric tombs that honeycomb its sheer walls.

30 Cloisters at Monreale Page **115** • The delicately sculpted columns here are immaculate examples of medieval craftsmanship.

Basics

operators' details; and see p.46 for more on car rental.

Alternative Travel Group ☎01865/513 333, ⓦ www.atg-oxford.co.uk. Inclusive eight-day guided walking holidays (April–June & Sept/Oct) in the Monti Madonie, from Enna to Cefalù. Prices start at £875 (full-board) plus flights.

Arblaster & Clarke ☎01730/893 344, ⓦwww .arblasterandclarke.com. Deluxe seven-night wine tours, including flights, all meals and tastings, plus an expert guide, from £1499. Also a wine cruise of Italian islands, including Sicily and its offshore islands.

Citalia ☎0870 909 7555, ⓦ www.citalia.co.uk. Packages to Taormina, island tours, self-catering holidays and car rental.

Cook Italy in Italy ☎39.349 007 8298, ⓦwww .cookitaly.com. Siracusa-based cooking holidays from around £1200 for a week. Rates include accommodation, meals, lessons and market trips, but exclude airfares and car rental.

Cresta ☎0870/238 7711, ⓦ www.crestaholidays .co.uk. Short-break or fly-drive holidays, largely based on east coast stays (Siracusa to Taormina) though with options in Agrigento and Palermo, too.

Italiatour in UK ☎0870 733 3000, in Republic of Ireland ☎01/671 7821; ⓦ www.italiatour.co.uk. Specialist Italian operator, offering a week-long escorted "Jewels of Sicily" coach tour, in conjunction with Alitalia flights.

JMC Holidays ☎0870/750 5711, ⓦwww .jmc.com. Beach holidays in a variety of hotels in Taormina and Giardini-Naxos.

Magic of Italy ☎0800 980 3378, ⓦwww .magictravelgroup.co.uk. Holidays in the Aeolian Islands, Cefalù and Taormina, or fly-drive tours throughout Sicily.

Martin Randall Travel ☎020/8742 3355, ⓦ www.martinrandall.com. Small-group cultural tours, led by experts on art, history, archeology and music, to the classic sites of Sicily. From around £2400 for 12 days, including flights, meals and transport.

Prospect Art Tours ☎020/7486 5704. Fully guided twelve-day art and architecture tours, based in four locations (Palermo, Agrigento, Siracusa and near Érice). Tours depart two or three times a year; from £1795, including flights, half-board accommodation, guides and fees.

Ramblers Holidays ☎01707/331 133, ⓦwww .ramblersholidays.co.uk. Half-board walking holidays based in Francavilla (near Taormina), in western Sicily and the Aeolian Islands, from around £450 per week, £650 for two weeks. Weekly departures Feb, March–May, Sept, Oct & Dec.

Sunvil Holidays ☎020/8758 4722, ⓦwww .sunvil.co.uk. Holidays in the best of Sicily's resorts – Cefalù, Taormina and San Vito Lo Capo – as well as city-based stays in Catania, Palermo and Siracusa, and island-based holidays on Lípari.

Flights and packages from the US and Canada

Although there are no direct **flights from the US and Canada to Sicily**, you can fly to the Italian mainland from a number of cities. The main points of entry are Rome and Milan, from where there are plenty of connecting flights on to Sicily. Flying time is around nine hours from New York or Boston, twelve hours from Chicago, and fifteen hours from Los Angeles; from the eastern Canadian cities, flight time is around nine hours, or fifteen hours from the west. For the connection to Sicily add on another hour and a half or so, plus any time spent waiting for the connection itself.

It might be a good idea to travel **via elsewhere in Europe** (particularly Britain or Germany), since there's a broad range of well-priced flights available from all over the US and Canada to various European cities, and there are a wider choice of travel options to Sicily once there. Flying is the most straightforward way to get from Britain to Sicily, and prices are competitive; see "Flights and packages from the UK and Ireland", p.28, for details. Travellers from North America wishing to connect with budget Ryanair flights from London should be aware that the baggage allowances are a lot less generous than on transatlantic flights (see p.27), and that the no-frills flights usually leave from out-of-city airports – allow at least three hours for a connection, and preferably a day.

Alitalia has the widest choice of routes **between the US and Italy**, flying direct every day to Milan and Rome from New York, Boston, Miami, Chicago, San Francisco and Los Angeles. The advantage of choosing Alitalia is the ease of making the connecting flight to Sicily with the same airline. As for American-based airlines, Delta, AA and Continental all fly to Rome or Milan from various US cities. Alternatively, Air France flies from the US to Italy via Paris; British Airways via London; Iberia via Madrid; Lufthansa via Frankfurt or

Munich; Northwest/KLM via Amsterdam; and SAS via Copenhagen.

Generally, the cheapest round-trip **fare** to Palermo or Catania via Rome or Milan, travelling midweek in low season, starts at around US$540, rising to around US$850 during the shoulder season, and to about US$1150 during the summer. Flights from LA, Miami or Chicago usually work out about US$100 on top of these round-trip fares. Local US and Canadian budget airlines can be useful to get to the larger hubs such as New York, where cheap flights are easier to find to Europe.

From Canada, the easiest routing is with Alitalia, which flies direct every day from Toronto and Montreal to Rome/Milan and on to Palermo or Catania, with low-season fares starting at around Can$1400, increasing to around Can$1700 in high season. Air Canada also flies directly to Milan or Rome from Montreal and Toronto, while other airlines to consider are British Airways (via London), Lufthansa (via Frankfurt) and KLM/Northwest (via Amsterdam).

Airlines in the US and Canada

Air Canada ☎1-888/247-2262, ⓦwww.aircanada.ca.
Air France in US ☎1-800/237-2747; in Canada ☎1-800/667-2747; ⓦwww.airfrance.com.
Alitalia in US ☎1-800/223-5730; in Canada ☎1-800/361-8336; ⓦwww.alitalia.com.
American Airlines ☎1-800/433-7300, ⓦwww.aa.com.
British Airways in US and Canada ☎1-800/AIRWAYS, ⓦwww.ba.com.
Continental Airlines ☎1-800/231-0856, ⓦwww.continental.com.
Delta Air Lines ☎1-800/241-4141, ⓦwww.delta.com.
Iberia ☎1-800/772-4642, ⓦwww.iberia.com.
KLM/Northwest US ☎1-800/447-4747, ⓦwww.klm.com, ⓦwww.nwa.com.
Lufthansa in US ☎1-800/645-3880; in Canada ☎1-800/563-5954; ⓦwww.lufthansa-ca.com.
SAS (Scandinavian Airlines) ☎1-800/221-2350, ⓦwww.flysas.com.

Travel agents in the US and Canada

Note that all these numbers below are US-only unless otherwise specified.
Airhitch ☎1-800/326-2009 or ☎212/864-2000, ⓦwww.airhitch.org. For a set price, they guarantee to get you on a flight as close to your preferred destination as possible, within a week.
Airtech ☎212/219-7000, ⓦwww.airtech.com. Standby seat broker; also deals in discount fares and courier flights.
Educational Travel Center ☎1-800/747-5551 or ☎608/256 5551, ⓦwww.edtrav.com. Student/youth discount agent.
STA Travel US ☎1-800/329-9537, Canada ☎1-888/427-5639; ⓦwww.sta-travel.com. Worldwide specialists in independent travel; also student IDs, travel insurance, car rental, rail passes etc.
Student Flights ☎1-800/255-8000 or ☎480/951-1177, ⓦwww.isecard.com. Student/youth fares, student IDs.
TFI Tours International ☎1-800/745-8000 or ☎212/736-1140. Discount fares.
Travel Avenue ☎1-800/333-3335, ⓦwww.travelavenue.com. Full-service travel agent that offers discounts in the form of rebates.
Travel Cuts in Canada ☎1-888/246 9762; in US ☎1-800/592-CUTS. Popular, long-established Canadian student-travel organization.
Worldtek Travel ☎1/800-243-1723, ⓦwww.worldtek.com. Discount travel agency for worldwide travel.

Package holidays and organized tours from US and Canada

There are dozens of companies operating group travel and **tours** in Italy, ranging from all-inclusive luxury escorted tours to smaller specialized groups. However, specifically Sicilian options are less common, though the operators and agencies listed below usually offer tours at least partly based on the island. If you're happy to stay in one (or two) places, you can also, of course, simply book a hotel-plus-flight deal, or, if you're keener to self-cater, rent a villa or a farmhouse for a week or two. Prices vary wildly, so check what you are getting for your money (many don't include the cost of the airfare). Reckon on paying at least US$2000 for a standard ten-day touring vacation without flight, and up to as much as US$5500 for a fourteen-day escorted specialist package with flight.

Specialist tour and package operators in the US and Canada

Adventure Center ☎1-800/228-8747, ⓦwww.adventurecenter.com. Offers a "Sicilian Volcano

Given these prices, you might consider buying a **rail pass** – InterRail and Eurail are the best known – which gives unlimited rail travel throughout Europe, as well as providing discounts on cross-Channel and other ferry crossings. Note that InterRail passes also give discounts on the Eurostar service. For details of all rail passes, including those for use solely within Italy, see "Getting around", pp.43–48. And note that most of these passes have to be bought before you leave home.

Rail ticket agencies

UK and Ireland

Eurostar ☎0870/518 6186, ⊛www.eurostar.co.uk. For Eurostar reservations.
Italian State Railways ☎020/7724 0011, ⊛www.fs-on-line.com. Italian timetables, tickets, fares and passes.
Rail Europe ☎0870/584 8848, ⊛www.raileurope.co.uk. InterRail, Eurostar, Euro-Domino passes.
Travel Cuts ☎020/7255 1944, ⊛www.travelcuts.co.uk. Budget, student and youth travel specialist; InterRail and other passes available.

US and Canada

CIT Rail in US ☎1-800/223-7987 or 1-800-CIT-TOUR; in Canada ☎1-800/387-0711; ⊛www.fs-on-line.com and ⊛www.cit-tours.com. Eurail, Europass and Italian passes.
DER Travel US ☎1-800/782-2424, ⊛www.dertravel.com/Rail. Eurail, Europass and Italian passes.
Europrail International Inc Canada ☎1-888/667-9734, ⊛www.europrail.net. Eurail, Europass and Italian passes.
Eurail US ☎1-866-9EURAIL, ⊛www.eurorail.com. Eurail Pass, Europass and Italian passes.
Rail Europe in US ☎1-800/438-7245; in Canada ☎1-800/361-7245; ⊛www.raileurope.com/us. Official North American Eurail Pass agent.

Australia and New Zealand

CIT World Travel Australia ☎02/9267 1255, ⊛www.cittravel.com.au. Eurail, Europass and Italian rail passes.
Rail Plus in Australia ☎1300/555 003 or 03/9642 8644; in New Zealand ☎09/303 2484; ⊛www.railplus.com.au. Eurail, Europass and Eurostar agents, and Italian rail passes.

Trailfinders Australia ☎1300/780 212, ⊛www.trailfinders.com.au. All European passes.

By bus from the UK

There's no direct **bus service** from the UK to Sicily, which makes travelling this way something of a chore. You have to use the **Eurolines** service from London Victoria to either Rome or Naples (three departures weekly) and then take connecting buses from there to Sicily. Prices are often higher than those of the no-frills airlines – from £86 return to Rome (booked at least a week in advance) or £89 to Naples, with small discounts for under-26s – but it's a hellishly long journey. It takes 32 hours to Rome, 37 to Naples, plus another 6 (from Naples) to 12 hours (from Rome) on to Sicily from Italy. The terminus for SAIS or Interbus **departures in Rome** is Piazza Tiburtina: Interbus (every Mon, Wed, Fri & Sun at 11am) for Messina, Taormina, Catania and Siracusa; SAIS (daily at 8pm and 10pm) for Messina, Catania and Agrigento. The Rome–Sicily leg of the journey will cost you around another £50 return. You can arrange add-on fares from most British and Irish towns to connect with the London departure, though by this time you're looking at a journey well into three days.

If you're still interested, tickets can be purchased from any Eurolines or **National Express** agent.

Bus ticket agencies

Eurolines ☎0870/514 3219, Republic of Ireland ☎01/836 6111, ⊛www.eurolines.co.uk.
National Express agent ☎0870/580 8080, ⊛www.nationalexpress.com.

By car and ferry from the UK

The best **cross-Channel options** for most drivers will be the standard **ferry/hovercraft** links between Dover and Calais or Newhaven and Dieppe. Crossing using **Eurotunnel**, the shuttle train via the Channel Tunnel for vehicles and their passengers only (24hr service, departures every 15min at peak periods), will speed up the initial part of the journey, though overall there are no great savings on time to be made since there's still a long way to go once you reach France.

From the France–Italy border, it's possible, with a bit of luck, to reach the Straits of Messina in a long day if you keep on the autostradas. The shortest crossing over the Straits is from Villa San Giovanni **by ferry**; or, fifteen minutes further south – at the end of the motorway – **by hydrofoil** from Réggio di Calabria. If you want to cut the driving time in Italy, you could use one of the earlier **ferry or hydrofoil crossings from the Italian mainland** to Sicily, from Genova, Livorno or Naples. You can even approach Sicily by travelling **via Corsica or Sardinia**, though obviously this is a somewhat complicated route involving two lengthy crossings – it's not really recommended for just a short trip to Sicily.

Any travel agent can provide up-to-date cross-Channel schedules and make advance **bookings** (which, in season, are essential for cars), or you can book yourself by phone or online. For the Italian crossings, contact the relevant companies or their agents. More details on all these routes are given in the box below.

It's worth noting that on top of the ferry fares and fuel, it'll cost around another £35 per car to use the toll motorways between the French border and Naples, after which it's free until you reach Sicily.

Cross-Channel tickets

Eurotunnel ⊤0870/535 3535, ⊛www.eurotunnel .com. Channel Tunnel services.
Hoverspeed ⊤0870/240 8070, ⊛www.hoverspeed .co.uk. Dover to Calais; Newhaven to Dieppe.
P&O Ferries ⊤0870/600 0600, ⊛www .poferries.com. Dover to Calais.
Sea France ⊤0870/571 1711, ⊛www .seafrance.com. Dover to Calais.

Ferries and hydrofoils from Italy to Sicily

Crossing the Straits of Messina

Drivers buy their tickets at kiosks on the way onto the ferry; foot passengers just walk on and pay the ticket collector on board.

Villa San Giovanni–Messina
FS car ferries, 1–2 per hour, a 25min journey.
Caronte car ferries, every 15–20min (fewer through-out the night), a 20min journey.

Réggio di Calabria–Messina
FS fast ferries, roughly hourly, a 15min journey.
Meridiano car ferries, every 2 hours to Messina port, a 45min journey.
Ústica Lines hydrofoils, 3–5 daily, a 15min journey.

Other crossings from the Italian mainland

Genova–Palermo (with Grandi Navi Veloci): 1 daily, a 20hr journey.
Livorno–Palermo (with Grandi Navi Veloci): 3 weekly, an 18hr journey.
Naples–Aeolian Islands/Milazzo (with Siremar): 2–6 weekly, a 16hr journey.
Naples–Palermo (with Tirrenia): 1 car ferry daily, an 11hr journey; (with

SNAV) 1 catamaran daily (mid-April to early Oct), a 4hr journey.
Naples–Trapani, via Ústica and the Egadi Islands (with Ústica Lines): 1 hydrofoil 4 days a week (June–Sept), a 7hr journey.
Naples–Aolian Islands (Ústica Lines): 1 hydrofoil a day (July–Sept), a 4–5hr journey.

Agents for Italian ferry services

Grandi Navi Veloci (Grimaldi) ⊛www .gnv.it; in UK c/o Viamare ⊤020/7431 4560, ⊛www.viamare.com.
Meridiano in Italy ⊤00 39 0965.810 .410. Timetables on ⊛www.netonline .it/numeri-traghetti.asp.
Siremar in UK c/o SMS Travel

⊤020/7373 6548; ⊛www.siremar.it.
SNAV in UK c/o Viamare (see above); ⊛www.snavali.com.
Tirrenia Line in UK c/o SMS Travel (see above); ⊛www.tirrenia.it.
Ústica Lines ⊤00 39 0923.921.277, ⊛www.usticalines.it.

Red tape and visas

British, Irish and other EU citizens can enter Sicily and stay as long as they like on production of a valid passport. Citizens of the United States, Canada, Australia and New Zealand need only a valid passport, too, but are limited to stays of three months. All other nationals should consult the relevant embassies about visa requirements.

Legally, you're required to register with the police within three days of entering Italy, though if you're staying at a hotel this will be done for you. Although the police in some towns have become more punctilious about this, most would still be amazed at any attempt to register yourself down at the local police station while on holiday. However, if you're going to be living here for a while you may as well do it; see p.62 for more details.

Italian embassies and consulates abroad

Australia Level 43, The Gateway, 1 Macquarie Place, Sydney, NSW ☎ 02/9392 7900; 509 St Kilda Rd, Melbourne, VIC ☎ 03/9867 5744; 12 Grey St, Deakin, Canberra, ACT ☎ 02/6273 3333.

Britain 38 Eaton Place, London SW1X 8AN ☎ 020/7235 9371; 32 Melville St, Edinburgh EH3 7HA ☎ 0131/226 3631; 111 Piccadilly, Manchester M1 2HY ☎ 0161/236 9024.
Canada 275 Slater St, Ottawa, ON K1P 5H9 ☎ 613/232-2401; 3489 Drummond St, Montréal, H3G 1X6 ☎ 514/849-8351; 136 Beverley St, Toronto, ON M5T 1Y5 ☎ 416/977-1566.
Ireland 63–65 Northumberland Rd, Dublin ☎ 01/660 1744; 7 Richmond Park, Belfast ☎ 01232/668 854.
New Zealand 34–38 Grant Rd, Thorndon, Wellington ☎ 04/473 5339.
USA 3000 Whitehaven St NW, Washington DC ☎ 202/328-5500; 690 Park Ave, New York, NY 10021 ☎ 212/737-9100; 2590 Webster St, San Francisco, CA 94115 ☎ 415/931-4924; 500 N Michigan Ave, Chicago, IL 60611 ☎ 312/467-1550.

Information, maps and websites

Before you leave, it's worth checking the various useful websites for information, including that of the Italian State Tourist Office (ENIT) – ⓦ www.enit.it. ENIT offices abroad are also a good source of maps and brochures, though most can easily be picked up later in Sicily. Worth grabbing are any accommodation listings and town plans for the area you're interested in.

Tourist offices

Most Sicilian towns, main train stations and the two principal airports have a **tourist office**, known by one of a variety of acronyms – most often, either an AAPT (Azienda Autonoma Promozione Turistica), a provincial branch of the state organization, or an AAST (Azienda Autónoma di Soggiorno e Turismo), a smaller local outfit. In Italian, ask for the "*ufficio del turismo*". All of these offices vary in degrees of usefulness, and other than in the main cities and tourist areas, staff aren't likely to speak English. But you should always be able at least to get a free town plan and a local listings booklet in Italian, and some will reserve you a room and sell places on guided tours.

Likely summer **opening hours** are Monday to Friday 9am to 1pm and 4pm to 7pm, Saturday 9am to 1pm. If the tourist office isn't open and all else fails, the local Sicilian telephone office and most bars with phones carry a copy of the local *Tuttocittà*, a listings and information magazine which details addresses and numbers of most of the organizations you're likely to want to know about. It also has indexed street maps for local towns and adverts for restaurants and shops.

Italian state tourist offices

Australia Level 26, 46 Market St, Sydney 2000, NSW ☎02/9262 1666, ✉italia@italiantourism.com.au.
Canada 17 Bloor St East, Suite 907, South Tower, Toronto, Ontario ☎416/925 4882, ✉enit.canada@on.aibn.com.
New Zealand apply to the embassy (see p.36).
UK 1 Princes St, London W1R 8AY ☎020/7408 1254, ✉italy@italiantouristboard.co.uk.
USA 630 Fifth Ave, Suite 1565, New York, NY 10111 ☎212/245-5095, ✉enitny@italiantourism.com; 500 N Michigan Ave, Suite 2240, Chicago, IL60611 ☎312/644-0996, ✉enitch@italiantourism.com; 12400 Wilshire Blvd, Suite 550, Los Angeles, CA 90025 ☎310/820-1898, ✉enitla@italiantourism.com.

Maps

The best large-scale **road map** of Sicily is published by the Touring Club Italiano (*Sicilia*, 1:200,000), usually available from the outlets listed below. Otherwise, the Automobile Club d'Italia issues a good, free 1:275,000 road map, available from the State Tourist Offices, while local tourist offices in Sicily often have free road maps of varying quality.

For **hiking**, you'll need at least a scale 1:100,000 map (even better, 1:50,000), though there's not much around – again, check with one of the specialist map shops listed below or with the **Club Alpino**

Italiano, Via E. Petrella 19, 20124 Milan (☎02/2614 1378, ⊛www.cai.it). For specific towns and islands, the maps in the Guide should be fine for most purposes, though local tourist offices also often hand out reasonable town plans and regional maps.

Map outlets

In UK and Ireland

Blackwell's Map Centre 53 Broad St, Oxford OX1 3BQ ☎01865/793550, ⊛www.bookshop.blackwell.co.uk.
The Map Shop 30a Belvoir St, Leicester LE1 6QH ☎0116/247 1400, ⊛www.mapshopleicester.co.uk.
National Map Centre 22–24 Caxton St, London SW1H 0QU ☎020/7222 2466, ⊛www.mapsnmc.co.uk.
National Map Centre Ireland 34 Aungier St, Dublin ☎01/476 0471, ⊛www.mapcentre.ie.
Stanfords 12–14 Long Acre, WC2E 9LP ☎020/7836 1321, ⊛www.stanfords.co.uk. Also at 39 Spring Gardens, Manchester ☎0161/831 0250, and 29 Corn St, Bristol ☎0117/929 9966.
The Travel Bookshop 13–15 Blenheim Crescent, W11 2EE ☎020/7229 5260, ⊛www.thetravelbookshop.co.uk.
Traveller 55 Grey St, Newcastle-upon-Tyne NE1 6EF ☎0191/261 5622, ⊛www.newtraveller.com.

In US and Canada

110 North Latitude US ☎336/369-4171, ⊛www.110nlatitude.com.
Book Passage 51 Tamal Vista Blvd, Corte Madera, CA 94925 and in the historic San Francisco Ferry Building ☎1-800/999-7909 or 415/927-0960, ⊛www.bookpassage.com.
Distant Lands 56 S Raymond Ave, Pasadena, CA 91105 ☎1-800/310-3220, ⊛www.distantlands.com.
Globe Corner Bookstore 28 Church St, Cambridge, MA 02138 ☎1-800/358-6013, ⊛www.globecorner.com.
Longitude Books 115 W 30th St #1206, New York, NY 10001 ☎1-800/342-2164, ⊛www.longitudebooks.com.
Map Town 400 5 Ave SW #100, Calgary, AB T2P 0L6 ☎1-877/921-6277 or 403/266-2241, ⊛www.maptown.com.
Travel Bug Bookstore 3065 W Broadway, Vancouver, BC V6K 2G9 ☎604/737-1122, ⊛www.travelbugbooks.ca.

World of Maps 1235 Wellington St, Ottawa, ON K1Y 3A3 ☎1-800/214-8524 or 613/724-6776, ⓦwww.worldofmaps.com.

In Australia and New Zealand

Map Centre ⓦwww.mapcentre.co.nz.
Mapland (Australia) 372 Little Bourke St, Melbourne ☎03/9670 4383, ⓦwww.mapland.com.au.
Map Shop (Australia) 6–10 Peel St, Adelaide ☎08/8231 2033, ⓦwww.mapshop.net.au.
Map World (Australia) 371 Pitt St, Sydney ☎02/9261 3601, ⓦwww.mapworld.net.au. Also at 900 Hay St, Perth ☎08/9322 5733, Jolimont Centre, Canberra ☎02/6230 4097 and 1981 Logan Road, Brisbane ☎07/3349 6633.
Map World (New Zealand) 173 Gloucester St, Christchurch ☎0800/627 967, ⓦwww.mapworld .co.nz.

Useful websites

Italian **websites** have proliferated in recent years and provide a wealth of information; we've listed a few of the more useful ones for Sicily here.

General Italian sites

ⓦ**www.beniculturali.it** Italian Ministry for Arts and the Environment: museums, monuments, the arts and events, in Italian.
ⓦ**www.bestofsicily.com** Informative site detailing history, the arts, books, food and wine as well as sights and travel.
ⓦ**www.enit.it** Italian State Tourist Office site, with regional accommodation listings, events and other information.
ⓦ**www.initaly.com** Detailed information on the whole country; the Sicily section covers history, culture, festivals, travel and services.
ⓦ**www.sicilia.indettaglio.it** All manner of useful information – from bus routes and zip codes to books and recipes.
ⓦ**www.siciliaonline.it** Amazingly comprehensive site – in Italian – with a searchable database and information on everything from folklore and the weather to transport and festivals.
ⓦ**www.tuttocitta.it** Interactive maps of major cities, and some smaller towns.

Regional information

ⓦ**www.aapit.pa.it** Palermo and regional information.

ⓦ**www.apt.catania.it** Comprehensive information for Catania and its surrounding area.
ⓦ**www.apt-siracusa.it** Official site for Siracusa, with information on accommodation, restaurants and transport connections.
ⓦ**www.apt.trapani.it** Official site for Trápani city and province.
ⓦ**www.isoleegadi.it** The Égadi Islands online, with photos and full listings.
ⓦ**www.netnet.it** Everything about the Aeolian Islands, with links and full accommodation information.
ⓦ**www.pantelleria.it** Useful links to local businesses on Pantelleria, plus practical information and a web cam.
ⓦ**www.parks.it/parco.etna** General and practical information on Etna in English.
ⓦ**www.taormina-ol.it** Hotels and services in the Taormina area.

Transport

ⓦ**www.alitalia.it** Alitalia routes and schedules in English.
ⓦ**www.aziendasicilianatrasporti.it** Bus timetables for all the major Sicilian bus companies.
ⓦ**www.fs-on-line.com** Italian State Railways (FS) timetable information in Italian and English.
ⓦ**www.orariotreni.it** Train timetables and online booking.
ⓦ**www.siremar.it** Siremar ferry timetables for Lampedusa, Linosa, Pantelleria, the Aeolians and the Égadis.
ⓦ**www.snav.com** SNAV hydrofoil and fast ferry timetables between Naples and Palermo and the Aeolians.
ⓦ**www.traghetti.com** Links to most of the principal ferry operators in Italy.
ⓦ**www.usticalines.it** Ústica Lines hydrofoil timetables for Égadis, Pantelleria, Lampedusa–Linosa and the Aeolians.

Miscellaneous

ⓦ**www.camping.it** Excellent site for campers, giving full details of every Sicilian site.
ⓦ**www.gds.it** Website of the newspaper *Il Giornale di Sicilia*, which covers news and affairs across the island.
ⓦ**www.geocities.com/CapitolHill /Lobby/9880/** Excellent site on La Cosa Nostra, with a brief history, famous mobster profiles, Mafia movies and much more.

Ⓦ**www.geo.mtu.edu/~boris/STROMBOLI**
.html Italy's volcanoes in exhaustive detail, with Etna
material to the fore; lots of useful links.
Ⓦ**www.lilibeo.com** Buy Sicilian products
online, from Marsala wine to marmalade, and holiday
homes.

Ⓦ**www.paginebianche.it** Italian phone directory
online.
Ⓦ**www.paginegialle.it** Italian Yellow Pages
online.
Ⓦ**www.press.sicilia.it** Extracts from all sorts of
articles about Sicily.

Insurance

As an EU country, Italy has free reciprocal health agreements with other member
states, but even if you're covered by this, you're strongly advised to take out
separate travel insurance to cover against theft and loss during your travels.
For all non-EU citizens, it's essential to have some kind of travel insurance for
your trip.

Before paying for a new policy, it's worth
checking whether you are already covered. Credit card purchases (including
travel tickets and other holiday-related
items) often are backed by some kind of
insurance; some all-risks home insurance policies may cover your possessions when overseas; and many private
medical schemes include cover when
abroad.

However, you'll almost certainly want
to contact a specialist travel insurance
company, or consider the travel insurance

deal we offer (see box). A typical **travel
insurance policy** usually provides cover
for the loss of baggage, tickets and – up
to a certain limit – cash or cheques, as
well as cancellation or curtailment of your
journey. Most of them exclude so-called
dangerous sports such as scuba diving
and windsurfing, unless an extra premium
is paid. Many policies can be chopped
and changed to exclude coverage you
don't need – for example, sickness and
accident benefits can often be excluded
or included at will. If you do take medical

Rough Guide travel insurance

Rough Guides Ltd offers a low-cost travel insurance policy, customized for
our readers by a leading British broker, provided by the American International
Group (AIG) and registered with the British regulatory body, GISC (the General
Insurance Standards Council). There are five main Rough Guides insurance
plans: **No Frills** for the bare minimum for secure travel; **Essential**, which
provides decent all-round cover; **Premier** for comprehensive cover with a wide
range of benefits; **Extended Stay** for cover lasting four months to a year; and
Annual multi-trip, a cost-effective way of getting Premier cover if you travel
more than once a year. Premier, Annual Multi-Trip and Extended Stay policies
can be supplemented by a "Hazardous Pursuits Extension" if you plan to indulge
in sports considered dangerous, such as scuba diving or trekking. For a policy
quote, call the Rough Guide Insurance Line: free in the UK ☏0800/015 0906 or
☏+44 1392 314 665 from elsewhere. Alternatively, get an online quote at Ⓦwww
.roughguides.com/insurance.

Express. Otherwise, there are ATMs at both airports which you can use on arrival. When receiving change, watch out for a favourite fiddle – giving an old 500 lire coin instead of a €2 coin.

Credit and debit cards

The most painless way of dealing with your money is probably by using **credit**, **charge** or **cash cards**, which, in conjunction with your personal identification number (PIN), give you access to ATMs/cashpoint machines (*bancomat*). Found even in small towns and on some of the more remote islands, these accept all major cards. Make sure you have a PIN number that's designed to work overseas. Cards can also be used for cash advances over the counter in banks and for payment in most hotels, restaurants, petrol stations and some shops. For all these transactions you will pay a fee, usually of around 1.5 percent. Remember that all **cash advances on a credit card** are treated as loans, with interest accruing daily from the date of withdrawal. To block any lost or **stolen card** in Italy, call ☏800.822.056. Be aware that in more remote places, especially islands, it is not unusual for machines to run out of cash, so keep some reserves.

Travellers' cheques

As a useful back-up it's a good idea to take some money in the form of **travellers' cheques**, available from most banks. In Italy, the most widely accepted brands are Thomas Cook and American Express. The usual fee for travellers' cheque sales is one or two percent, though this may be waived if you buy the cheques through a bank where you have an account. It pays to get a selection of denominations. Make sure you keep the purchase agreement and a record of cheque serial numbers safe and separate from the cheques themselves. In the event that cheques are lost or stolen, the issuing company will expect you to report the loss forthwith to their nearest office; most companies claim to replace lost or stolen cheques within 24 hours.

The advantage of having **euro travellers' cheques** is that you shouldn't pay any commission when exchanging them in

Sicily for euros. For other currency cheques, you'll usually – though not always – pay a small commission when you exchange them – around one percent of the amount changed – although some banks will make a standard charge per cheque regardless of its denomination. Both **Thomas Cook** (ⓦwww.us.thomascook.com) and **American Express** (ⓦwww.americanexpress.com) sell euro travellers' cheques, though cheques in sterling or dollars are widely accepted in Sicily too.

Banks and banking hours

The main **banks** you'll see in Sicily are the Banco di Sicilia, the Banca Populare Sant'Angelo, the Cassa di Risparmio, the Banca Nuova and the Banca Nazionale di Lavoro. **Banking hours** vary slightly from town to town, but generally banks are open Monday to Friday, 8.30am–1.20pm and 3–4pm. Outside these times you can change travellers' cheques and cash at large hotels, the airports at Palermo and Catania, and some main train stations.

Money-wiring services

If you run out of money, or there is some kind of emergency, you may need to have **money wired** to you from home, using one of the companies listed below. However, this is never convenient or cheap, and should be considered a last resort. It's also possible to have money wired directly from your home bank to a bank in Sicily, although this is less reliable because it involves two separate institutions. If you go this route, your home bank will need the address of the branch bank where you want to pick up the money and the address and telex number of the bank's head office in Italy, which will act as the clearing house; money wired this way normally takes two working days to arrive, and costs around £25/CA$40/AU$54/NZ$52/$59 per transaction.

Money-wiring companies

Travelers Express/MoneyGram
US ☏1-800/444-3010; Canada

☎1-800/933-3278; UK, Ireland and New Zealand ☎0800/6663 9472; Australia ☎0011800/6663 9472; ⓦwww.moneygram.com.
Western Union US and Canada ⓣ1-800/CALL-CASH; Australia ☎1800/501 500; New Zealand

☎0800/005 253; UK ☎0800/833 833; Republic of Ireland ☎66/947 5603; ⓦwww .westernunion.com (customers in the US and Canada can send money online).

Getting around

A rental car is not essential to **see** Sicily's major towns and sights, but getting around by public transport is not always as easy as it should be. The rail system is slow, few buses run on Sundays and route information can be frustratingly difficult to extract, even from the bus and train stations themselves. Sicily's geography means that it's a push to get right across the island – say Siracusa to Trápani – in one day; though you'll be able to travel most of one of the coastlines easily enough. On the positive side, public transport prices are among the cheapest in Europe.

Each chapter's "Travel details" section has the full picture on transport schedules and frequencies. Note that unless specified, these refer to regular working-day schedules, ie Monday to Saturday; services are much reduced, or even non-existent, on Sundays. Note also that comments such as "every 30min" are approximations – on the railways in particular, there are occasional gaps in the schedule, typically occurring just after the morning rush hour, when the gap between trains may be twice as long as normal.

One thing to bear in mind is that travelling by train is not the best way to see all of the island. Some stations are a fair distance from their towns – Enna and Taormina are two notable examples (though there are usually bus connections) – while much of the west and centre of Sicily is only accessible by bus or car. With this in mind, **rail passes** – like InterRail and Eurail – only really begin to pay for themselves if you intend to see much more of Italy and the rest of Europe on the way.

Trains

Operated by Italian State Railways, Ferrovie dello Stato (FS) **trains** connect all the major towns, but are more prevalent in the east of the island than the west. On the whole the trains *do* leave on time, with the notable exception of those on the Messina–Palermo and Messina–Catania/Siracusa routes that have come from the mainland, which can be delayed by up to three hours – though around an hour late is more normal.

There are five **types of train** in Sicily. **Intercity** trains link the main Italian centres with each other; reservations are obligatory, and a supplement of around thirty percent of the ordinary fare is payable (make sure you pay your supplement before getting on board – you'll have to cough up a far bigger surcharge to the conductor). **Diretto**, **Espresso** and **Interregionale** trains are long-distance expresses, calling only at larger stations. Lastly, there are the **Regionale** services (also called Locale), which stop at every place with a population higher than zero – usually ones to avoid. The last two categories do not permit smoking in any part of the train. Train **tickets must be validated** within an hour of boarding the train, ie punched in machines scattered around the station and platforms. Failure to do this may land you with an on-the-spot fine.

In summer it's often worth making a **seat reservation** (*prenotazione*) on the main routes, something you'll be obliged to do anyway on some trains – check before you get on or you'll pay a large *supplemento* to the conductor. If you don't have time to buy a ticket, you can simply board your train and pay the conductor, though again it'll cost around thirty percent more this way.

As well as the information boards displayed at stations ("Departures" are *Partenze*, "Arrivals" *Arrivi*, "Delayed" *In Ritardo*), it's useful to have a **timetable**. The Sicilian routes are covered by FS's little book, *In Treno Sicilia*, issued twice a year and free from most train stations, and you'll find the main Italy/Sicily routes covered in the national timetables, also available from most stations for a small charge. Pay attention to the timetable notes, which may specify the dates between which some services run (*Si effetua dal… al…*), or whether a service is seasonal (*periódico*), denoted by a vertical squiggle; *feriale* is the word for the Monday-to-Saturday service, symbolized by two crossed hammers; *festivo* means that a train runs only on Sundays and holidays, with a cross as its symbol.

Prices are very reasonable, with tickets charged by the kilometre, while there are **discounts** on normal fares for **children** (fifty percent for 4–12-year-olds) – the under-4s travel free provided they do not occupy a seat. If you're going to be spending a long time in Sicily or Italy, the **Cartaverde** for under-26s, and the **Carta d'argento** for over-60s, come into their own. Valid for one year, these cards give a twenty percent discount on any fare, and are available from main train stations for around €25 each.

For details of Sicily's only **private railway**, the Ferrovia Circumetnea route around the base of Mount Etna, see p.264.

Rail passes

The Europe-wide InterRail and Eurail passes give unlimited travel on the FS network, though you'll still be liable for supplements. The passes can be bought online at ⓦwww.raileurope.co.uk, where you'll also find full details and current prices. Alternatively, contact one of the rail ticket agencies listed on p.34.

The **InterRail pass** is only available to European residents, and comes in over-26 and (cheaper) under-26 versions. The pass is zoned (Italy is grouped with Turkey, Greece and Slovenia), and also gives discounts on rail travel in Britain and Northern Ireland, on the Eurostar service and on cross-Channel ferries. The passes are available for 16 days (one zone only; £159, over-26s £223), 22 days (2 zones; £215, over-26s £303), or one month (all zones; £295, over-26s £415).

The **Eurail Pass** is available in increments of fifteen days, twenty-one days, one month, two months and three months, and is valid for first-class travel. If you're under 26, you can save money with a **Eurail Youthpass**, available in the same increments as the Eurail Pass but valid for second-class travel only. Prices run from US$588 for 15 days (Youthpass US$414) to US$1654 for three months (Youthpass US$1160). A **Eurail Flexipass** is good for ten (US$694, Youthpass US$488) or fifteen (US$914, Youthpass US$642) days' travel within a two-month period.

Passes exclusive to the Italian rail network include the **Euro-Domino** pass, only available to European residents. This is available for between three (£129, Youthpass £97) and eight (£203, Youthpass £152) days' travel within a one-month period. There is a half-price child (age 4–11) fare, and a first-class option available too. For further details, see ⓦwww.b-rail.be/internat/E/passes/eurodomino.

In addition, there are three specific Italian passes: the **Italy Rail Card**, which allows eight, fifteen, twenty-one or thirty days' travel on the FS network; the **FlexiRail Card**, which allows travel for four, eight or twelve days within a one-month period; and the **Chilométrico** ticket, valid for up to five people, which gives 3000km worth of travel on a maximum of twenty separate journeys. However, these passes are similarly priced to InterRail and Eurail passes but with more limited coverage. With all passes, you have to pay supplements on the faster trains.

Buses

Almost anywhere you want to go will have some kind of **regional bus** (*autobus* or pullman) service, usually quicker and more reliable than the train (especially between the major towns and cities), but generally more expensive.

There are three main **companies**, SAIS (ⓦwww.saistrasporti.it), AST (no website) and Interbus (no website), which between them cover most of the island; other companies stick to local routes. Nearly everywhere, services are drastically reduced, or non-existent, on Sunday, something the timetables – and the drivers/conductors – don't necessarily make clear: always double-check. Also, lots of departures (on rural routes especially) are linked to school/market requirements – sometimes meaning a frighteningly early start, last departures in the afternoon, and occasionally no services during school holidays.

Bus terminals can be scattered all over the bigger towns, though often all the buses pull up in one particular piazza, or outside the local train station – if you want the bus station, ask for the "*autostazione*". **Timetables** are worth picking up at every opportunity, and are available from the companies' offices, bus stations or on the bus. You buy **tickets** on the bus, though on longer hauls (and if you want to be sure of a place) try and buy them in advance from the companies' offices. On most routes, it's possible to flag a bus down if you want a ride: the convention, when it stops, is to get on at the back, off at the front. If you want to get off, ask "*posso scéndere?*"; "the next stop" is "*la próssima fermata*".

City buses are always cheap, usually charging a flat fare of between €0.50 and €1. Invariably, you need a ticket *before* getting on. Buy them in *tabacchi*, or from the kiosks and vendors at bus terminals and stops, and then validate them in the machine in the bus. Checks are frequently made by inspectors who block both exits as they get on, though if you're without a ticket you'll usually get off with an earful of Sicilian and be made to buy one; some inspectors might hold out for the spot fine.

Cars

Car travel across the island can be very quick if you use the often spectacular **motorways** (autostradas). Carried on great piers spanning the island, these link Messina–Catania (A18), Catania–Palermo (A19), Palermo–Trápani/Mazara del Vallo (A29) and – though still incomplete – Messina–Palermo (A20). There is also a good new state road between Catania and Gela, while work has just begun on a stretch of autostrada between Gela and Siracusa. The Messina –Catania and Messina–Palermo autostradas are toll-roads. Take a ticket as you come on, and pay on exit; the amount due is flashed up on a screen in front of you.

Traffic is relatively light on the autostradas, which are a pleasure to drive. Elsewhere, the driving experience varies wildly – rural areas are generally hassle-free, while driving in towns can be a nightmare. Although **roads** are pretty good and reasonably well signposted, in small towns they can be very narrow indeed. In addition, one-way systems in old-town areas play havoc with route-finding, reducing many through-town journeys to drive-and-hope marathons. Don't underestimate journey times on the tortuous mountain roads either, and always be prepared for a flock of sheep or idling cows round the next bend.

For **documentation** you need a valid driving licence, an international green card of insurance and, if you are a non-EU licence holder, an international driving permit. It's *compulsory* to carry your car documents and passport while you're driving, and you'll be required to present them if you're stopped by the police – not an uncommon occurrence. You are also required to carry a portable triangular danger sign, which should be provided with rental cars (or available in Britain from most motoring organizations).

Rules of the road are straightforward: drive on the right; at junctions, where there's any ambiguity, give precedence to vehicles coming from the right; observe the speed limits (50kph in built-up areas, 110kph on country roads, 130kph on autostradas); and *don't* drink and drive. Sicilians, needless to say, ignore most, if not all, of these rules as a matter of principle and if you manage to go your entire holiday without being cut up on the inside, jumped at a junction or overtaken on a blind bend, you'll have done well. Speed cameras and traffic-calming humps are becoming more evident, but this doesn't seem to deter Sicilians from travelling at any speed they choose. Driving isn't as horrific as it looks at first, though – the secret is to make it very clear what you're going to do, using your horn as much as your indicators and brakes.

If you **break down**, dial ☎116 at the nearest phone and tell the operator where you are, the type of car and your registration number. The nearest office of the Automobile Club d'Italia (ACI) will send someone out to fix your vehicle, though it's not a free service (and if you need towing anywhere it will cost a fairly substantial amount). Consequently, it might be better to arrange cover with a motoring organization in your country before you leave. Any ACI office in Sicily can tell you where to get **spare parts** for your particular car: see the town and city "Listings" sections for details.

Car rental in Sicily is not particularly expensive by European standards – from around £160/US$225 per week for a three-door, air-con Fiat Punto, with unlimited mileage, from one of the major international firms (addresses are detailed in individual city listings), but usually less from local companies, such as Maggiore (☎www.maggiore.it).

Best of all is to arrange car rental in conjunction with your flight/holiday – most travel agents or tour operators can provide details; as can the **rental companies** (see p.47 for numbers) which can arrange pick-ups in Catania and Palermo. Although the local companies might seem quite casual about such things, it's essential to check that you have adequate **insurance cover** for a rental car. Going by the dints and scratches on almost every car on the road, you want to make sure that if you have a prang, your liability is limited as far as possible – it's worth considering paying the extra charge to reduce the "excess" payment levied for any damage. Italian **fuel prices** are roughly in line with those in the UK, with unleaded petrol (*senza piombo*) slightly cheaper than leaded (*super*).

Never leave anything visible in the car when you leave it, including the radio, and always depress your aerial and tuck in your wing mirrors. When driving in cities, keep your doors locked. Most cities and ports have **garages** where you can leave your car,

a safe enough option. At least the car itself is unlikely to be stolen if it's got a right-hand drive and a foreign numberplate: they're too conspicuous to be of much use to thieves.

As **parking** spaces are rare and small, good parking skills are an asset. The task is easier in early afternoon, when towns are quiet, or at night; if you're hiring, it makes sense to choose a small car. That said, parallel parking is not a familiar concept in Sicily, where the accepted practice is simply to drive your car up on the pavement, or stop where it's most convenient for the driver rather than other road users. This includes the middle of the street, or stopping for a chat with a mate at a major road junction. However, if you park in a *zona di rimozione*, your car will most likely be towed away; and if you've chosen a street that turns into a market by day, you'll be stuck until it closes down. Usually the easiest policy is to seek out the blue lines which signify authorized parking, where you'll need to pay a small sum per hour, usually to an attendant hovering nearby. You'll never be asked to pay between 1 and 4pm, though, when spaces are abundant.

Hitch-hiking (*autostop*) is not widely practised in Sicily and is **not recommended as a means of getting around the island**. It's very definitely not something that women should do on their own, particularly in the more out-of-the-way places; also be warned that cars will sometimes stop to offer you a lift if you're standing alone at a bus stop. If you are hitching, travel in pairs, and always ask where the car is headed before you commit yourself ("*Dov'è diretto?*"). If you want to get out, say "*Mi fa scéndere?*"

However you get around on the roads, **watch the traffic**. Driving in Sicily is almost a competitive sport, and although the Sicilians aren't the world's worst drivers they don't win any safety prizes either. **Pedestrians** will find that far from being unable to step off the pavement – ever – you'll be able to cross quite easily by staring straight at the drivers and strolling boldly across. If in doubt, follow someone old and infirm, or put out your hand policeman-like, but *never* assume that you're safe on a pedestrian crossing – regarded by drivers as an invitation to play human skittles.

Car rental agencies

In the UK and Ireland

Avis ☏ 0870/606 0100, Republic of Ireland
☏ 021/428 1111, ⊛ www.avis.co.uk.
Budget ☏ 01442/276 266, Republic of Ireland
☏ 09/0662 7711, ⊛ www.budget.co.uk.
Europcar ☏ 0870/607 5000, Republic of Ireland
☏ 01/614 2888, ⊛ www.europcar.co.uk.
National ☏ 0870/536 5365, ⊛ www.nationalcar
.co.uk.
Hertz ☏ 0870/844 8844, Republic of Ireland
☏ 01/676 7476, ⊛ www.hertz.co.uk.
Holiday Autos ☏ 0870/400 0099, Republic of Ireland
☏ 01/872 9366, ⊛ www.holidayautos.co.uk
Suncars ☏ 0870/500 5566, Republic of Ireland
☏ 1850/201-416, ⊛ www.suncars.com.
Thrifty ☏ 01494/751 600, Republic of Ireland
☏ 1800/515 800, ⊛ www.thrifty.co.uk.

In the US and Canada

Avis US ☏ 1-800/230-4898, Canada ☏ 1-
800/272-5871, ⊛ www.avis.com.
Budget US ☏ 1-800/527-0700, Canada ☏ 1-
800/472-3325, ⊛ www.budget.com.
Dollar US ☏ 1-800/800-3665, ⊛ www.dollar.com.
Europe by Car US ☏ 1-800/223-1516, ⊛ www
.europebycar.com.
Hertz US ☏ 1-800/654-3131, Canada ☏ 1-
800/263-0600, ⊛ www.hertz.com.

In Australia and New Zealand

Avis Australia ☏ 13 6333, New Zealand
☏ 09/526 2847 or 0800 655 111, ⊛ www.avis
.com.
Budget Australia ☏ 1300/362 848, New Zealand
☏ 0800/652 227 or 09/976 2222, ⊛ www
.budget.com.
Hertz Australia ☏ 13 30 39 or 03/9698 2555, New
Zealand ☏ 0800 654 321, ⊛ www.hertz.com.

Bicycles

A better way to get off the beaten track
is by **bicycle**, especially on the offshore
islands; however, on the Sicilian mainland,
renting is virtually unheard of. Although the
coastal roads are relatively flat for the most
part, the traffic near major towns can be off-
putting, while heading inland and up into the
mountains requires a decent machine and
plenty of stamina: a mountain-bike would
be a good bet, though you can expect to
be a real curiosity in some rural places. In

the Madonie mountains, south of Cefalù,
hiking itineraries published by the tourist
office have brief notes for cyclists, though
you should be prepared to push some of
the way.

An alternative is to tour by **motorbike**,
though again you'll have to bring your own.
Mopeds and **scooters** are easier to find:
virtually everyone in Sicily – kids to grand-
mas – rides these, although the smaller
models are not suitable for any kind of long-
distance travel. They're ideal for shooting
around towns, and you can rent them in
Taormina, Cefalù and other holiday centres
– check the Guide for details. Crash helmets
are compulsory, though you'll see many
Sicilian youths just riding with one slung
over one arm.

Hiking

Serious **hiking** was a fairly rare phenomenon
in Sicily until recently, and there are no long-
distance paths and few marked routes. That
said, some areas have been made more
amenable to walking for pleasure, including the protected coast between Scopello
and Capo San Vito (see p.385 and p.400),
and the Madonie mountains south of Cefalù.
In the latter, rudimentary hiking routes have
been established, making use of existing paths: information and rough maps are
available from the tourist office in Cefalù (see
p.143). We've also detailed some hiking
possibilities in the text. Local tourist offices
will have details of the few mountain refuges
(*rifugi*) for overnight stops in the Madonie and
on Etna (and see "Accommodation", p.48).

Planes

Hardly surprisingly, **flying** isn't a major form
of transport within Sicily. Still, if you're short
on time, taking a plane to the Pelágie Islands
from Palermo, or Pantelleria from either Palermo or Trápani is a distinct – and not too
expensive – possibility. As the alternative is
an overnight ferry ride, this can save you
quite a bit of time.

Flights are with Air One and Meridiana, the
internal arm of Alitalia, and there are tempting **discounts** available: up to fifty percent
off the normal fare if you stay at least a Saturday or Sunday. Local airline and travel
agents will have the latest details, and we've

listed frequencies in "Travel details" for relevant chapters. As well as the Air One and Meridiana services, there are other small airlines – AlpiEagles and Volare/AirEurope – offering services from Catania and Palermo to destinations on the Italian mainland, including Rome, Milan, Venice and Naples.

Ferries and hydrofoils

You'll use **ferries** and **hydrofoils** to get to all the offshore islands: the Aeolians, Égadi and Pelágie islands, Pantelleria and Ústica. There's also a summer hydrofoil service that runs along the northern (Tyrrhenian) coast, from Palermo to the Aeolian Islands, stopping at a couple of towns on the way.

Siremar, SNAV, NGI and Ústica Lines are the main **operators** – local tourist offices have the current schedules, though we give an idea of the timetables in each relevant chapter's "Travel details".

Services are heavily used in summer, making early booking advisable, though you will always get on an Égadi or Aeolian islands ferry if you just turn up. Timetables are pinned up at the dockside or are available from the ferry offices and tourist offices. On the Aeolians, it's worthwhile making sure of your destination arrival time when you buy your ticket, as some routes make extremely wide circuits, which can double your journey time if you're headed in the other direction.

Accommodation

On the whole, accommodation in Sicily is slightly cheaper than in the rest of Italy. There's a whole range of places in all price categories, and on average you'll pay £25–30/US$30–35 a night for two, though more like £35–50/US$50–70 a night in summer in the most popular resorts. If you're watching your budget, a (very) few youth hostels, some private rooms and many campsites are all possibilities.

All types of accommodation are officially graded, their tariffs fixed by law. In tourist areas, there's often a low-season and high-season price, but whatever it costs, the price of hotels and campsites should be listed in the local accommodation booklets provided by the tourist office and posted on the door of the room. Loopholes do exist, however: in summer especially, when demand for accommodation exceeds supply, hotels are prone to add a breakfast charge to the price of the room – make sure you know exactly how much you're going to be paying before you accept the room. Some places – especially in major resorts or on outlying islands – also insist on **half-board accommodation** in the peak summer period (usually August), when the price will include breakfast and one other meal; or you may even be asked to stay for a two- or three-night minimum.

Hotels

Hotel accommodation, while normally abundant in the main towns and tourist areas, tends to thin out in remoter parts, and especially inland. It's worthwhile phoning ahead to book if you're heading for a one-hotel town.

Cheapest hotel-type accommodation is a **locanda**, where rooms will be basic but, on the whole, clean and safe, though nearly always without attached bath/shower. If you want a hot shower, you'll generally have to pay a small extra charge. Occasionally, you'll come across rather elite establishments which have adopted the name *locanda* – these are usually chic, faux-rustic in style. Most common, though, are regular hotels, called either a **pensione** or **albergo** (plural *alberghi*). All come graded with one to five stars, and a double room in a one-star hotel

Accommodation price codes

The hotels listed in this guide have been coded according to price. The price codes represent the cheapest available double room in high season (Easter & June–Aug), usually – but not always – *without* en-suite bathroom or shower. Many cheaper places will also have a few en-suite rooms, for which you'll pay more – usually the next category up in price; higher category hotels nearly always only have en-suite rooms. Out of season, you'll often be able to negotiate a lower price than those suggested here. The categories are:

❶ under €40
❷ €40–55
❸ €55–65
❹ €65–80

❺ €80–100
❻ €100–115
❼ €115–150
❽ over €150

usually corresponds to our ❶ price category. There's usually a choice of rooms, either with or without bath/shower. Most two-star hotels fall into the ❷ and ❸ categories, and once you're up to three-star level and beyond you'll pay prices corresponding to categories ❹ and ❺. In resorts, and especially in summer in places like the Aeolian Islands, four-star and luxury hotels can charge pretty much what they like, which means prices in the ❻, ❼ and ❽ categories are the norm. For the three five-star hotels on the island (in Palermo and Taormina), rates are pretty much as they are anywhere else in the world for such opulence. That said, there are some bargains around out of the summer season, when even the classier hotels drop their room rates by as much as forty percent.

Always ask to **see the room** before you take it ("*Posso vedere?*"), and in the cheaper places check if there's **hot water** available ("*C'è acqua calda?*"). You might want to check if there's air conditioning ("*C'è aria condizionata?*"), which is sometimes available at an extra cost; this can be a godsend in the hottest months, though many prefer the quieter option of a fan. It's worth noting that smaller, cheaper places don't have much in the way of **heating** in the winter – you can freeze in some of the older *palazzi*.

There are few **single rooms** available and, in high season especially, lone travellers will often pay most of the price of a double. Check in the local hotel listings book, which may explicitly state (in English and Italian) that you're only liable for the price of a single room: waving the book at the offending hotel

manager might have some effect. **Three or more people** sharing a room should expect to pay around 35 percent on top of the price of a double room.

In the cheaper places you might be able to negotiate a lower rate if you're staying for any length of time (ask "*C'è uno sconto per due/tre/quattro notti?*").

B&Bs, private rooms, apartments and farm stays

Recent years have seen the growth of "**Bed and Breakfasts**" (as they term themselves), simple rooms usually set aside from the family's living quarters, but you'll usually get some contact with your hosts, at least at breakfast time. Some places going under the name are actually little different from private rooms, with the owners not living on the premises, but you'll invariably find them clean and well maintained. **Private rooms** (*cámere*) for rent in people's houses, often equipped with kitchen, are common in certain resorts, especially Taormina and the Aeolian and Égadi Islands. Ask in local bars, shops and tourist offices, check the text for details and watch for signs. Prices usually fall into our ❶ and ❷ categories for bed and breakfast and private rooms, with variations depending on the season and location.

For longer-term stays, you can rent holiday **apartments** in both Taormina and Cefalù and in other, more remote places, like the Aeolians or even Scopello. Although it's fairly expensive in the summer – the equivalent of over £500/US$700 a month even for a one-bedroom place – there are real bargains to be had in May or late September, and during the winter. Ask in the tourist offices or a local estate agency (*agenzia immobiliare*) and keep an eye out for local advertisements.

Other places for rent include rooms in rural cottages or farmhouses, operated by Agriturist, Via A. di Giovanni 14, 90144 Palermo (℡091.346.046, ⓦwww.agriturist.it). This **agriturismo** scheme has grown considerably in recent years and you'll often find a wide range of activities also on offer, such as horse-riding, hunting and mountain-biking, plus escorted walks and excursions. We've pointed out some possibilities in the text. Rooms usually fall into our category ❷, though as some places will require a minimum stay of three nights, always ring ahead to check. Local tourist offices can usually tell you if there's anywhere suitable in the district, or you can buy magazines listing these properties from newsstands, and Agriturist have produced a book, *Vacanza in Fattoria* (*Farm Holidays*), written in English, which is available from travel bookshops.

Youth hostels, campsites and mountain huts

Official **youth hostels** are sparse, having dwindled to just six, in Castroreale, Érice, Taormina, Nicolosi, Noto and on the island of Lípari. It's hardly worth joining a hostelling organization just to use these (which, out of season, probably won't want to see membership cards anyway), though if you're planning to cross to the Italian mainland it's probably worthwhile: contact your home organization. There are a couple of unofficial hostels as well, in Catania and Trápani

– both detailed in the text. For online information go to ⓦwww.ostellionline.it.

Camping is popular, with approximately ninety officially graded sites dotted around the island's coasts, on a few of the Aeolian Islands, on Favignana (Égadi Islands) and on Lampedusa. At the last count there were only a couple in Sicily's interior, around Mount Etna. Few are open all year round; indeed, campsites generally open or close whenever they want, depending on business. If you want to be sure, it's always worth a phone call; alternatively, check the comprehensive website ⓦwww.camping.it. It's worth bearing in mind that camping isn't going to save you a great deal of money, since most of the sites are large, luxury affairs, often complete with pools, bars, shops and sports facilities. **Charges** are usually between €4 and €7 per person per day, sometimes the same again for a tent and vehicle – often, you'll find a cheap central hotel more of a bargain.

By and large, **camping rough** is a nonstarter in much of Sicily: it's frowned on in the tourist areas and on the offshore islands, and difficult in the interior, where there are scant water supplies and little flat land. Occasional possibilities are detailed in the text; anywhere else you're likely to attract the unwelcome attention of the local police.

In Sicily's hillier regions it's possible to stay in a staffed **mountain hut** (*rifugio*, plural *rifugi*) – particularly in the Madonie and Nébrodi ranges and on Mount Etna. They're operated by the Club Alpino Italiano, and local tourist offices have all the contact details – we've listed some of the best in the text, but you can also check them out online at ⓦwww.cai.it.

Food and drink

There's much to be said for coming to Sicily just for the eating and drinking. Often, even the most out-of-the-way village will boast somewhere you can get a good, solid lunch, while places like Catania and Palermo can keep a serious eater happy for days. And it's not ruinously expensive either, certainly compared to prices in the rest of mainland Italy: a full meal with good local wine generally costs around £12/US$17 a head.

The lists in our language guide (see pp.488–494) will help you find your way around supermarkets and menus, but don't be afraid to ask to look if you're not sure what you're ordering. Also, sample from our lists of specialities, some of which crop up in nearly every restaurant.

The basics of Sicilian cuisine

Historically, **Sicilian cuisine** was held in high regard: one of the earliest of cookbooks, the *Art of Cooking* by Mithaecus, derived from fifth-century BC Siracusa; and in medieval times Sicilian chefs were much sought after in foreign courts, and accorded the same esteem as a French chef today. Contemporary cooking is still excellent, leaning heavily on locally produced basic foodstuffs and whatever can be fished out of the sea.

Primarily, Sicilian food mixes Italian staples – pasta, tomato sauce and fresh vegetables – with local specialities and products of the traditional island industries: red chillies, tuna, swordfish, sardines, olives, pine nuts and capers all figure heavily. The mild winter climate and long summers mean that **fruit and vegetables** are less seasonal than in northern Europe, and are much bigger and more impressive: strawberries appear in April, oranges are available right through the winter, and even bananas are grown on a small scale. Unusual and unexpected foods and fruit are a bonus too: prickly pears (originally imported from Mexico by the Spanish), artichokes, asparagus, medlars and persimmons are ubiquitous, while, in the south and west of the island, the North African influence is evident in the Sicilian version of couscous.

The **Arab influence** is also apparent in the profusion of sweets and desserts available in Sicily – marzipan is used extensively, while *cassata*, the most Sicilian of desserts, derives from the Arabic word *quas-at*, referring to the round bowl in which it was traditionally prepared.

The best time to sample the more unusual dishes and desserts is during a festival, since food plays a central role in Sicilian celebrations. But at any time of year you'll be able to eat dishes that – though apparently common-or-garden Italian/Sicilian – call upon 2500 years of cross-cultural influences, from the Greeks and Romans to the Arabs, Normans and Spanish.

Breakfasts, snacks and ice cream

Most Sicilians start the day in a bar, with **breakfast** consisting of a milky coffee (cappuccino), and the ubiquitous *cornetto* – a jam-, custard- or chocolate-filled croissant. In summer, a brioche filled with coffee or lemon granita (or even ice cream) is popular. Bigger bars or a patisserie (*pasticceria*) will usually have a bit more choice; an *iris* is a pastry ball stuffed with sweet ricotta cheese, an *arancino* is a deep-fried ball of rice with meat (*rosso*) or butter and cheese (*bianco*) filling, and *cannoli* are pastry tubes filled with sweet ricotta cheese and candied fruit. Breakfast in a hotel (*prima colazione*) will be a limp and expensive affair, usually worth avoiding.

Sandwiches (*panini*) can be pretty substantial, a bread-stick or roll packed with any number of fillings. There are sandwich bars in the bigger towns, though often in small villages you can go into an *alimentari* (grocer's shop) and ask them to make you one from whatever they've got on hand. Bakeries too may offer panini or *pane cunzati*, crusty bread rolls filled with pungent combinations such as tuna, tomato, anchovy and capers, as well as pizza slices and calzone.

Bars may also offer *tramezzini*, ready-made sliced white-bread sandwiches with mixed fillings – lighter and less appetizing than your average panino. Toasted sandwiches (*toste*) are common too: in a sandwich bar you can get whatever you like put inside them; in bars which have a sandwich toaster you're more likely to be offered a variation on cheese with ham or tomato.

Other prepared **takeaway food** is pretty thin on the ground. You'll get most of the things already mentioned, plus small pizzas, portions of prepared pasta, chips, even full hot meals, in a **távola calda**, a sort of stand-up snack bar that's at its best in the morning when everything is fresh. The bigger towns have them, often combined with normal bars, and there's always one in main train stations. Otherwise, you'll have to make do with what you can get from a **rosticceria**, something you'll find in every town on the island. The big speciality here is spit-roast chicken (*pollo allo spiedo*); anything else, like Sicilian hamburgers or hot dogs, is best avoided.

You'll get more adventurous snacks in **shops** and **markets** – good bread, fruit, pizza slices and picnic food such as cheese, salami, olives, tomatoes and salads. Some markets sell traditional takeaway food from stalls, usually things like boiled artichokes, cooked octopus, sea urchins and mussels, and *focacce* – oven-baked pastry snacks either topped with cheese and tomato, or filled with spinach, fried offal or meat. In the larger cities, you'll occasionally come across an old-fashioned *focacceria* – takeaway establishments selling only bread-based snacks. For picnics, some tinned and bottled things are worth looking out for too: sweet peppers (*peperoni*), baby squid (*calamari*), seafood salad (*insalata di mare*) and preserved vegetables. You'll find **supermarkets** in most towns; island-wide store chains with food halls are Standa and Upim.

Sicilian **ice cream** (*gelato*) is justifiably famous: a cone (*un cono*) is an indispensable accessory to the evening *passeggiata*, and many people eat a dollop of ice cream in a brioche. Most bars have a fairly good selection, but for real choice go to a **gelateria**, where the range is a tribute to the Italian imagination and flair for display. If they make their own on the premises, they'll be a sign saying "*produzione propria*" though, sadly, this increasingly means they make the stuff from prepacked commercial pastes and syrups. You'll have to go by appearance rather than attempt to decipher their exotic names, many of which don't mean much even to Italians; you'll find it's often the basics – chocolate, lemon, strawberry and coffee – that are best. There's no trouble in locating the finest *gelateria* in town: it's the one that draws the crowds. Sitting down at a bar, on the other hand, is the place to sample a typical Sicilian *cassata*, no relation to the soapy ice-cream cake served in Italian restaurants abroad: the real McCoy is very creamy, packed with ricotta cheese, candied fruit and sometimes chocolate bits, and served with a wafer biscuit.

It's worth noting that it's increasingly rare to find ice cream in restaurants nowadays, unless it's the mass-produced sort (*confezionato*), which soon gets monotonous. Unless they're promenading, most people head for a bar or *gelateria* for their pre- or post-prandial fix.

Pizzas

The whole world knows about **pizza**, and, outside its home of Naples, Sicily is the best place to eat it. Here, as elsewhere in Italy, your pizza comes flat and not deep-pan, and the choice of toppings is often fairly limited – none of the pineapple-and-sweetcorn variations beloved of foreign pizzerias. It's also easier to find pizzas cooked in the traditional way, in wood-fired ovens (*forno a legna*) rather than squeaky clean electric ones, so that they arrive blasted and bubbling on the surface, with a distinctive charcoal taste. However, because of the time it takes to set up and light the wood-fired ovens, these pizzas are usually only served at night, except on Sundays and in some resorts in summer. As well as the usual pizza toppings, you'll find more distinctively Sicilian combinations, using pecorino instead of mozzarella, oregano instead of basil, and lots of anchovies, capers and peperoncini.

Meal prices and reservations

In the accounts of any large town or city in the Guide, recommended restaurants are graded according to the following scale:

Inexpensive: under €15	**Expensive**: €30–50
Moderate: €15–30	**Very expensive**: over €50

These prices reflect the per person cost of a full meal including wine and cover charge – usually consisting of pasta, main course, salad or vegetable, dessert or fruit, and coffee. Obviously, in every restaurant you'll be able to eat for less than the upper price limit if you only have a couple of courses; and in pizzerias you'll rarely get into the Moderate category. The price categories are simply intended as a guide to what you could spend if you pushed the boat out in each restaurant.

Throughout the Guide, we have included telephone numbers for restaurants where it's necessary to **reserve a table** in advance, or for those remote enough to merit a call before you set out. Outside Cefalù, Siracusa and Taormina – and not always there – restaurant staff are unlikely to speak English, so you may have to get someone to ring for you.

Pizzerias, which range from a stand-up counter to a fully fledged sit-down restaurant, on the whole sell just pizzas and drinks, usually chips, sometimes salads. A basic cheese and tomato pizza costs around £2/US$2.80; for something a bit fancier, you'll pay up to £3.50/US$4.90. To follow local custom, it's quite acceptable to cut it into slices and eat it with your hands, washing it down with a beer or Coke rather than wine. Check our list of pizzas on p.488 for what you get on top of your dough.

Meals: lunch and dinner

Full **meals** are much more elaborate affairs. These are generally served in a **trattoria** or a **ristorante**, though these days there's often a fine line between the two: traditionally, a trattoria is cheaper and more basic, offering good home cooking (*cucina casalinga*), while a *ristorante* is more upmarket (tablecloths and waiters). The main differences you'll notice, though, are more to do with opening hours and the food on offer. In small towns and villages, a trattoria is usually best at lunchtime and often only open then – there probably won't be a menu and the waiter will simply reel off a list of what's available that day. In large towns both will be open in the evening, though there'll be more choice in a *ristorante*, which will always have a menu. In either, a pasta course, meat or fish, fruit and a drink should cost £10–14/US$14–20 (fish pushes up the price), though

watch out for signs saying "*pranzo turistico*" or "*pranzo completo*". This is a limited **set menu** including wine which can cost as little as £6/US$8.50, but is usually more in the region of £8–10/US$11–14. **Other types of eating place** include those usually found in tourist resorts that flaunt themselves as a trattoria-ristorante-pizzeria; and restaurant-bars called spaghetterias, which specialize in pasta dishes and are often the haunts of the local youth.

Traditionally, a **meal** (lunch is *pranzo*, dinner is *cena*) starts with an **antipasto** (literally "before the meal"); you'll only find this in restaurants, at its best when you circle around a table and pick from a selection of cold dishes such as stuffed artichoke hearts, olives, salami, anchovies, seafood salad, aubergine in various guises, sardines and mixed rice. If you're moving on to pasta and the main course you'll need quite an appetite to tackle antipasti as well.

As far as the **menu** goes, it starts with soup or pasta, **il primo**, and moves on to **il secondo**, the meat or fish dish. This course is generally served alone except for perhaps a wedge of lemon or tomato. Vegetables and salads (**contorni**) are ordered and served separately, and often there won't be much (if any) choice; potatoes will usually come as fries (*patatine fritte*), but you can also find boiled (*lesse*) or roast (*arroste*), while salads are simply green (*verde*) or mixed (*mista*), usually with tomato. If there's no menu, the verbal list of what's available can be a bit bewildering, but if you don't hear anything you recognize just ask for what you want: everywhere should have pasta with tomato sauce (*pomodoro*) or meat sauce (*al ragù*).

Afterwards, you'll usually get a choice of fruit (*frutta*), while in a *ristorante*, you'll probably be offered other **desserts** (*dolci*) as well. Sicily is renowned for its sweets, an Arab legacy that you can't help but notice in every bar and bakery you pass; most restaurants, though, will only have fresh fruit salad (*macedonia*) and ice cream (or *cassata*) – sometimes there'll be *zuppa inglese* ("English soup", which, disappointingly, is only trifle), *zabaglione* or *torta* (tart, cake) too. In common with the rest of Italy, Sicily has embraced the mass-produced, packaged sweets produced by such brands as Ranieri – *tiramisù*, *tartufo*, *zuppa inglese* are the most common; some of them aren't bad, but they're a poor substitute for the real thing.

It's useful to know that you don't have to order a full meal in trattorias and most restaurants. Asking for just pasta and a salad, or the main course on its own, won't outrage the waiter. Equally, asking for a dish listed as a first course as a second course, or having pasta followed by pizza (or vice versa), won't be frowned upon either.

Something to watch for is **ordering fish**, which will either be served whole (like bream or trout) or by weight (usually per 100g, *all'etto*), like swordfish and tuna – if you don't want the biggest one they've got, ask to see what you're going to eat and check on the price first.

At the end of the meal, ask for **the bill** (*il conto*). In many trattorias this doesn't amount to much more than an illegible scrap of paper and, if you want to be sure you're not being ripped off, ask to have a receipt (*una ricevuta*), something they're legally obliged to give you anyway. Nearly everywhere, you'll pay a small cover charge (*pane e coperto*) per person; service (*servizio*) will be added as well in most restaurants, usually ten percent – though up to fifteen percent or even twenty percent in some places. If service is included, you won't be expected to **tip**; otherwise leave ten

percent, though bear in mind that the smaller places – pizzerias and trattorias – won't expect this.

Vegetarians

Some **vegetarians** might find their food principles stretched to the limit in Sicily. Fish and shellfish are abundant and excellent, while if you're a borderline case then the knowledge that nearly all eggs and meat are free range in Sicily might just push you over the edge. On the whole, though, it's not that difficult if you're committed. Most pasta sauces are based on tomatoes or dairy products, and it's easy to pick a pizza that is meat- (and fish-) free. Most places can be persuaded to cook you eggs in some shape or form, or provide you with a big mixed salad.

The only real problem is one of comprehension: many people don't know what a vegetarian is. Saying you're vegetarian ("*Sono vegetariano/a*") and asking if the dish has meat in it ("*C'è carne dentro?*") is only half the battle: poultry and especially *prosciutto* are regarded by many waiters as barely meat at all. Better is to ask what the dish is made with ("*Com'è fatto?*") before you order, so that you can spot the offending "non-meaty" meat.

If you're a **vegan**, you'll be in for a hard time, though pizzas without cheese are a good standby, and the fruit is excellent. Soups are usually made with a fish or meat broth. However, you'll have absolutely no success explaining to anyone why you're a vegan – an incomprehensible moral concept to a Sicilian.

Drink

Although Sicilian children are brought up on wine, there's not the same emphasis on dedicated **drinking** here as there is in Britain or America. You'll rarely see drunks in public, young people don't make a night out of getting wasted, and women especially are frowned upon if they're seen to be indulging. Nonetheless, there's a wide choice of alcoholic drinks available in Sicily, at low prices; soft drinks come in multifarious hues, thanks to the abundance of fresh fruit, and there's also mineral water and crushed-ice drinks.

Coffee, tea and soft drinks

One of the most distinctive smells in a Sicilian street is the aroma of fresh **coffee**, usually wafting out of a bar (many trattorias and pizzerias don't serve hot drinks). The basic choice is either small, black and very strong (an espresso, or just *caffè*), or weaker, white and frothy (a cappuccino), but there are other varieties, too. If you want to keep your credibility, never ask for a cappuccino after a meal. A *caffelatte* is an espresso in a big cup filled up to the top with hot milk. If you want your espresso watered down, ask for a *caffè lungo*. Coffee served with a shot of alcohol – and you can ask for just about anything in your coffee – is *caffè corretto*; with a drop of milk it's *caffè macchiato* ("stained"). If you want to be sure of a coffee without sugar, ask for *caffè senza zucchero*. Many places now also sell decaffeinated coffee (ask for Hag, even when it isn't); while in summer you'll probably want to have your coffee cold (*caffè freddo*). For a real treat, ask for *granita di caffè* – cold coffee with crushed ice that's usually topped with cream (*senza panna* if you prefer it without cream).

As for **tea**, it's best in summer when you can drink it iced (*tè freddo*), usually mixed with lemon; it's excellent for taking the heat off. Hot tea (*tè caldo*) comes with lemon (*con limone*) unless you ask for milk (*con latte*). **Milk** itself is drunk hot as often as cold, or you can get it with a dash of coffee (*latte macchiato*), and in a variety of flavoured drinks (*frappe*) too.

Alternatively, there are various **soft drinks** (*analcóliche*) to choose from. A **spremuta** is a fresh fruit juice, squeezed at the bar, usually orange, lemon or grapefruit. You might need to add sugar to a lemon juice (*spremuta di limone*), but orange juice (*spremuta di arancia*) is usually sweet enough on its own, especially the crimson-red variety, made from blood oranges. You can also have orange and lemon mixed (*mischiato*). A **succo di frutta** is simply a fruit juice in a bottle, in a range of flavours. A **frullato** is a fresh fruit shake, often made with more than one fruit. The Sicilian speciality **granita** (a crushed-ice drink) comes in several flavours other than coffee. Otherwise, there's the usual range of fizzy drinks and concentrated juices; Coke is prevalent, but the homegrown Italian alternative, Chinotto,

is less sweet – good with a slice of lemon. Tap **water** (*acqua normale*) is drinkable everywhere and you won't pay for it in a bar. But **mineral water** (*acqua minerale*) is the usual choice, either still (*senza gas* or *naturale*) or fizzy (*con gas*, *gassata* or *frizzante*).

Beer, wines and spirits

Beer (*birra*) is usually a lager-type brew which usually comes in a third of a litre (*piccolo*) or two-thirds of a litre (*grande*) bottles: commonest (and cheapest) are the Italian brands, Peroni and Dreher, and the Sicilian Messina, all of which are fine, if a bit weak. If this is what you want, ask for *birra nazionale*, otherwise you'll be given the more expensive imported beers, like Carlsberg and Kronenberg. In some bars and bigger restaurants, and in all birrerias, you also have a choice of draught lager (*birra alla spina*), sold in units of 25cl (*piccola*) and 50cl (*media*), measure for measure more expensive than the bottled variety. In some places you might find so-called "dark beers" (*birra nera*, *birra rossa* or *birra scura*), which have a slightly maltier taste, and in appearance resemble stout or bitter. These are the dearest of the draught beers, though not necessarily the strongest.

With just about every meal you'll be offered **wine** (*vino*), either red (*rosso*) or white (*bianco*), labelled or local. If you're unsure and want the local stuff, ask for *vino locale*: on the whole it's fine, often served straight from the barrel in jugs or old bottles and costing as little as £2–3/US$2.80–4.20 a litre. You may be flummoxed by the *vino locale* not being the colour you've ordered. You'll get whatever they make – in the west, for example, it's often rosé, a tart but refreshing drink; in Marsala, it's amber. Bottled wine is much more expensive, though still good value; expect to pay from around £4/US$5.60 a bottle in a restaurant, though as much as £8/US$11 in places like Taormina. A standard one you see everywhere is Corvo; others to watch for are Settesoli (red and white) from Menfi, in the west; Etna (red and white) from vines grown on the slopes of the volcano; Donnafugata (a crisp, fruity white) from Palermo province; Zucco (a medium-sweet white) from Carini; Montevagno or Salemi (a tangy wine from Sicily's far west);

and Cervasuolo (red and white) from the area around Vittória. One peculiarity is that bars don't tend to serve wine **by the glass**. You'll sometimes find half-bottles, otherwise you'll have to settle for *un quarto* (quarter litre) of *vino locale*.

Sicily produces good **dessert wines**, the most famous being Marsala, sometimes sweetened and mixed with eggs, called *Marsala all'uovo*; but if you're heading to the offshore islands, watch out for *malvasia* (from the Aeolians) and *moscato* (from Pantelleria). In and around Taormina, the local speciality is *vino alla mándorla*, a startlingly addictive almond wine, served ice cold. **Fortified wine** is fairly popular too: Martini (red or white) and Cinzano are nearly always available; Cynar (an artichoke-based sherry) and Punt'e Mes are other common aperitifs. If you ask for a Campari-Soda you'll get a ready-mixed version in a little bottle; a slice of lemon is a *spicchio di limone*; ice is *ghiaccio*.

All the usual **spirits** are on sale and known mostly by their generic names, except brandy which you should call *cognac* or ask for by name. The best Italian brandies are Stock and Vécchia Romagna; for all other spirits, if you want the cheaper Italian stuff, again, ask for *nazionale*. There's the standard selection of **liqueurs**, too, though at some stage try **amaro** (literally "bitter"), an after-dinner drink served with (or instead of) coffee. It's supposed to aid digestion, and is often not bitter at all, but can taste remarkably medicinal. The favourite brand is Averna (from Caltanissetta) but there are dozens of different kinds. Look out, too, for a red liqueur called Fuoco dell'Etna, mostly sold on the east coast, whose effect – fittingly – is of a miniature volcanic explosion. Other strong drinks available, though not especially Sicilian, are *grappa*, almost pure alcohol, made from distilling the grape husks left over from the manufacture of wine, and *sambuca* – a sticky-sweet, aniseed liqueur, traditionally served with one or more coffee beans in it and set on fire at the table, though only tourists are likely to experience this these days.

Where to drink

Bars are less social centres than functional stops, and all very similar to each other – bright, with a chrome counter, a Gaggia coffee machine and a picture of the local soccer team on the wall. You'll come here for **ordinary drinking**, a coffee in the morning, a quick beer, a cup of tea, but, at least in cities, people don't generally while away the afternoon in bars, or spend all night drinking in them (though in villages they are the venue for interminable card games). Indeed, in many places (Palermo included), it's difficult to find an average bar open much after 9pm. Bars have no set licensing hours and children are allowed in; there's often a telephone and you can buy ice cream and sometimes snacks as well as drinks.

Whatever you're drinking, the procedure is the same. It's cheapest to drink standing up at the counter (there's often nowhere to sit anyway), in which case you pay first at the cash desk (*la cassa*), present your receipt (*scontrino*) to the bar person and give your order. If you don't know how much a drink will cost, there's always a list of prices (the *listino prezzi*) behind the bar or *cassa*. When you present your receipt it's customary to leave a small tip on the counter – though no one will object if you don't. If there's waiter service, just sit where you like: it's more expensive to sit down inside than stand up (the difference in price is shown on the price list as *távola*) and it's up to twice the basic price if you sit at tables outside (*terrazza*).

For more **serious drinking**, most people go out and eat as well, at a pizzeria or restaurant, and spin the meal out accordingly if they want a few more beers. Otherwise, the other choice is a **birreria** (literally "beer shop"), where people go just to drink, though often they sell food too. These are where you'll find young people at night, listening to music or glued to rock videos; they're often called "pubs", although they bear little relation to their British namesakes. In tourist areas, bars and cafés (*caffè*) are more like the real European thing and they're open later, but they're more expensive than the common-or-garden bar. Other places to get a drink are the **bar-pasticceria**, which sells wonderful cakes and pastries too, and a **távola calda** in a train station always has a bar.

Communications

As a country of compulsive communicators, Italy presents no problems for staying in touch, whether by phone, mail or electronic media. Despite the ubiquity of mobile phones, public telephones are widely distributed. Most villages have a post office, and recent years have seen the arrival of numerous Internet points, at least in bigger towns and cities.

Mail

Post office opening hours are usually Monday to Saturday from 8.30am to 6.30pm; smaller towns close on a Saturday, and everywhere else, post offices close at noon on the last Saturday of the month. If you want stamps, you can buy them in *tabacchi* too, as well as in some gift shops in the tourist resorts. The Italian postal service is one of the tardiest in Europe – if your letter is urgent, consider paying extra for the express service, or *posta prioritaria*.

Letters can be sent **poste restante** to any Sicilian post office, by addressing them "Fermo Posta" followed by the name of the town. When picking something up take your passport, and make sure they check under middle names and initials (and every other letter when all else fails) as filing is diabolical.

Telephones

Public **telephones** operated by Telecom Italia come in various forms, usually with clear instructions printed on them (in English, too). You can use coins to make a call, though **phonecards** (*schede telefóniche*) are also available in various denominations from *tabacchi* or newsstands. They're accepted in most Sicilian phone booths – in fact some will only take cards. Bars will often have a phone you can use: look for the yellow phone symbol. Alternatively you could find a **Telecom Italia** or other office (listed in the text in the larger towns) or a bar with a *cabina a scatti*, a soundproofed and metered kiosk: ask to make the call and pay at the end. You can do the same at hotels, but they normally charge 25 percent more. Phone **tariffs** are among the most expensive in Europe; they're at their dearest on Monday to Friday between 8.30am and 1pm, but cheapest between 10pm and 8am Monday to Saturday and all day Sunday.

You can make **international calls** from any booth that accepts cards, and from any other booth labelled "*interurbano*". The most convenient – though not usually the cheapest – way of phoning home from abroad is to use a **telephone charge card.**

Using access codes and a PIN number, you can make calls that will be charged to your own domestic account. Contact your service provider before travelling, which provides the card for free. Alternatively, use an **international phonecard** (*carta telefonica internazionale*), available in various denominations from Italian post offices and *tabacchi*; all phones accept them, but before each call you need to dial a special access number and key in the PIN number on the back of the card.

To make a **collect/reversed charge** call (*cárico al destinatario*) dial ☏170 and speak to the (English-speaking) operator.

Cellular phones work on the GSM European standard. You will hardly see an Italian without one, but if you are going to join them make sure you have made the necessary arrangements before you leave – which may involve paying a refundable deposit. You are also likely to be charged extra for *receiving* incoming calls when abroad, while if you want to retrieve messages while you're away, you may have to ask your provider for a new access code.

International telephone codes

For direct international calls from Italy, dial the country code (given below), the area code (minus its first zero, where applicable), and finally the subscriber number.

Australia ☎61
Ireland ☎353
New Zealand ☎64
UK ☎44
USA and Canada ☎1

Calling Sicily from abroad

Dial the access code (☎0011 from Australia, Canada and the US; ☎00 from Britain, Ireland and New Zealand); then ☎39 (for Italy); then the area code *including the first zero* (the major towns are listed below); and then the subscriber number. If calling within Sicily, the area code must always be used, even when dialling locally; all telephone numbers listed in the Guide include the relevant code.

Agrigento ☎0922
Catania ☎095
Cefalù ☎0921
Enna ☎0935
Messina ☎090
Palermo ☎091
Siracusa ☎0931
Taormina ☎0942
Trápani ☎0923

Italian phone numbers

Telephone numbers change with amazing frequency in Italy. If in doubt, consult the local directory – there's a copy in most bars and hotels. Numbers beginning ☎848 and ☎800 are free, and ☎170 or ☎176 will get you through to an English-speaking operator.

Internet access and email

Internet cafés are now common in the major cities, and we've highlighted the more easily accessible places throughout the Guide. One of the best ways to keep in touch while travelling is to sign up for a **free Internet email address** that can be

accessed from anywhere, for example Yahoo (Ⓦwww.yahoo.com) or Hotmail (Ⓦwww.hotmail.com). Once you've set up an account, you can use these sites to pick up and send mail from any computer with Web access.

The media

You'll find the main national **newspapers** on any newsstand: *La Repubblica* is middle-to-left with a lot of cultural coverage; *Il Corriere della Sera* is authoritative and rather right-wing; *L'Unità* is the former Communist Party organ; and *Il Manifesto* is a more radical and readable left-wing daily. Sicily also has its own **local papers**, useful for transport timetables, concerts, film listings and suchlike. In Palermo, the best is the local edition of *Il Giornale di Sicilia*; in Catania, *La Sicilia*; in Messina, *La Gazzetta del Sud*. The most widely read paper, though, is the pink *Gazzetta dello Sport*, essential stuff for the serious sports fan. **English-language newspapers** can be found in Palermo, Catania, Messina, Taormina and Cefalù, at the train station and the main piazza or *corso*, usually a day or two late.

Italian **television** is deregulated, with the three state-run channels, RAI 1, 2 and 3, suffering in the face of a massive independent onslaught, led by the Euromogul and Prime Minister Berlusconi. The output is generally pretty bland, with a heavy helping of Brazilian soaps, American sitcoms and films, and ghastly Italian cabaret shows, though the RAI channels have less advertising and mix some good reporting in among the dross.

The situation in **radio** is even more anarchic, with the FM waves crowded to the extent that you can pick up a new station just by walking down the corridor. Again, the RAI stations are generally more professional, though daytime listening is virtually undiluted, nonstop dance music.

Opening hours and holidays

Basic hours for most shops and businesses are Monday to Saturday from 8am/9am to around 1pm, and from around 4pm to 7pm/8pm, though some offices work to a more standard European 9am to 5pm day. Everything, except bars and restaurants, closes on Sunday, though you might find pasticcerias, and fish shops in some coastal towns, open until lunchtime.

Other disrupting factors are **national holidays** and local **saint's days** (see "Festivals and entertainment" on p.60). Local religious holidays don't generally close down shops and businesses, but they do mean that accommodation space will be tight; check the "Festivals" section at the end of each chapter of the Guide. However, everything, except bars and restaurants, will be closed on the public holidays below.

Churches, museums and archeological sites

The rules for visiting **churches** are much as they are all over the Mediterranean. **Dress modestly** (which usually means no shorts, and covered shoulders for women), and avoid wandering around during a service. Most churches open in the early morning (around 7am or 8am) for Mass and close around noon, opening up again at 4pm or 5pm, and closing at 7pm; more obscure ones will only open for early morning and evening services; some only open on Sunday and on religious holidays. One problem you'll face all over Sicily is that lots of churches, monasteries, convents and oratories are **closed for restoration** (*chiuso per restauro*). We've indicated the more long-term closures in the text, but even if there's scaffolding, you might be able to persuade a workman or priest/curator to show you around.

Museums are generally open daily from 9am to 1pm, and again for a couple of

Public holidays

January 1
January 6 (Epiphany)
Good Friday
Easter Monday
April 25 (Liberation Day)
May 1 (Labour Day)
August 15 (Ferragosto;
   Assumption of the Blessed
   Virgin Mary)
November 1 (Ognissanti; All Saints)
December 8 (Immaculate
   Conception of the Blessed Virgin
   Mary)
December 25
December 26

hours in the afternoon on certain days; likely closing day is Monday, while they close slightly earlier on Sunday, around 12.30pm. **Archeological sites** are usually open from 9am until an hour before sunset (in practice until around 4pm in winter, 7pm in summer). Again, they are sometimes closed on Monday.

You can buy two useful packs called *Le Carte* (a blue pack for the independent museums, green for the state ones) from the main museums. Each contains a series of leaflets in English with information on and photographs of each museum's exhibits, as well as maps of their layout.

Festivals and entertainment

Every day in Sicily is a Saint's Day, celebrated as an onomástico or name day and, for the people called after that saint, ranking above a birthday in importance. The ones you'll notice are the feste, feast days for saints that have a special role for a particular locality. These are still basically unchanged in the smaller towns and villages, though some have evolved into much larger affairs spread over two or three days, and others have been developed with an eye to tourism. The ingredients are the same everywhere: people performing old songs and dances, a costumed procession, special food and sweets, and noisy fireworks to finish with.

Festivals and pilgrimages

You're likely to come across a *festa* at any time throughout the year (check the "Festivals" section at the end of each chapter for exact dates), though there are certain occasions which stand out. **Carnevale** (Carnival, or Mardi Gras time) is a floating festival, five days of celebration in the period just before Lent – which means in practice some time between the end of February and the end of March. Literally, the term means "farewell meat", referring to the last bout of indulgence before the abstinence of Lent, which lasts for forty days and ends with Easter. The best festivities are along the Ionian coast, at Taormina and especially at Acireale, although most Sicilian towns put on a little bit of a show. **Easter week** itself is celebrated all over the island, with slow-moving processions and ostentatious displays of penitence and mourning. Particularly dramatic events take place in the west of the island, at Trápani, Marsala and the Albanian village of Piana degli Albanesi, as well as at Enna in the interior.

Other more unconventional affairs take place at Prizzi in the western interior, and at San Fratello on the Tyrrhenian coast. The biggest island-wide celebration is **ferragosto**, the Feast of the Assumption on August 15, a mid-summer excuse for spectacular fireworks. This is a good time to be in Messina, when the procession of the enormous Giganti on August 14 is followed by the mad scramble of the Vara at ferragosto itself, ending with fireworks over the Straits late at night.

Of the various **pilgrimages** that take place throughout Sicily, the most interesting are in September, notably at Palermo on the fourth, and at Gibilmanna and Tíndari on the Tyrrhenian coast on the eighth.

Among the biggest and best known of the **other popular festivals** are: the Epiphany celebrations in Piana degli Albanesi (Jan 6); the Festa di Sant'Agata in Catania (Feb 3–5); the Sagra del Mándorlo in Fiore, celebrating the almond blossom in Agrigento (first or second week of Feb); the Festa di Santa Rosalia in Palermo (July 11–15); and Il Palio dei Normanni, a medieval-costumed procession and joust in Piazza Armerina (Aug 13 & 14).

Music and cinema

Aside from the festival events, there's a fair selection of cultural events taking place throughout the year. Sicily's archeological remains – particularly its Greek and Roman theatres – provide spectacular settings for **concerts**, usually classical, and there are regular events by local and visiting international orchestras in the theatres at Taormina, Segesta, Siracusa and Tíndari. The **opera** season runs from October to June, the best places to see performances being the Teatro Mássimo in Palermo, or the Teatro Bellini in Catania. Smaller theatres in all the main towns and cities also have music programmes, as well as the dramatic arts. There's no specific Sicilian **rock music** scene. Radio and TV are dominated by mainstream Italian chart music, which is mostly bland Europop, slushy ballads or British and American hits. Some big

Puppet theatre: the story

Popular in Sicily since the fourteenth century, the stories portrayed by **puppets**, or marionettes, are always the same chivalric episodes from the lives of the Paladins, the twelve peers of Charlemagne's court. Basically, it's a tale of the clash between Christianity and Islam and, while each particular **story** unfolds in fairly incomprehensible Sicilian dialect, the **format** is straightforward and unchanged from theatre to theatre. A succession of stiff-legged knights are introduced. The main two, **Orlando** (Roland) and **Rinaldo**, always stand on the left side of the stage and strut around as the puppeteer lists their exploits and achievements; the **Saracens**, with baggy trousers and shields marked with stars and crescents, stand on the right. There may be a love interest, too, perhaps a jousting tournament to decide who gets the hand of Charlemagne's daughter. The main business of each performance is the succession of formal, staged **battles** between the Christian knights and the Saracen invaders. Cross-stage charges by Orlando and Rinaldo, accompanied by drums and shouts, lead to the inevitable clashes of sword and armour, the pile of Saracen dead mounting with each attack. There's often a distraction between bouts as Orlando fights a crocodile, or confronts other monsters and magicians sent to try him. But, whatever the enemy, the engagements are always coloured by great splashes of artificial blood spurted from bodies as each victim tries to outdo the shrieks and groans of the one before. The climax is the representation of some great historical battle, like Roncesvalles, culminating in betrayal and treachery for the boys who face an untimely and drawn-out death on the battlefield.

Most Sicilians know the stories, and a performance in an original theatre is accompanied by a lot of vocal audience participation. If you want more enlightenment, you can see examples of the puppets, stage scenery, handbills and other paraphernalia at the Museo delle Marionette (p.98), the Museo Etnográfico Pitrè (p.102), both in Palermo, or the Museo Vagliasindi in Randazzo (p.266).

international bands do come to Sicily, and, especially during the summer, some of the more enterprising local councils – in Palermo, Messina and Catania – sponsor open-air concerts in public squares or parks.

There are **cinemas** in most towns, though all English-language films are dubbed into Italian. A summer alternative to the indoor movie houses are the open-air film shows that take place in some towns and tourist resorts, detailed in the Guide text. Taormina hosts an important **international film festival** every year in July, with screenings in the Greek theatre.

Theatres and puppet theatres

Regular **theatre** is popular in Sicily: Palermo has thirteen theatres, Catania a few less, and the summer sees open-air performances in many places, including some dramatic productions in the ancient theatres at Siracusa, Tíndari and Taormina. The biggest and most famous theatrical productions are the classical dramas performed at Siracusa (May and June), and the "Pirandello week" performances at Agrigento (July). All theatre performances will, however, be in Italian, although it's well worth getting tickets to the Siracusa and Agrigento performances just for the spectacle.

You should also try to make at least one visit to a traditional Sicilian **puppet theatre** (*teatro dei pupi*). There are still some of the original theatres around in Palermo and elsewhere, as well as a few productions put on for tourists. Check the text for details of where to catch a performance, and see the box above for further details.

Police and trouble

Although Sicily is synonymous with the Mafia, you'll forget the association as soon as you set foot on the island. Cosa Nostra is as invisible to the average tourist as it is ingrained for the islanders, and the violence that sporadically erupts is almost always an "in-house" affair.

Of more immediate concern is **petty juvenile crime**, mainly in the cities and more prevalent here than elsewhere in Italy, barring Naples. Gangs of *scippatori*, or bag-snatchers, will strike in crowded streets or markets, on foot or on scooters, disappearing before you've had time to react. As well as handbags, they whip wallets, tear off visible jewellery and, if they're really adroit, unstrap watches. You can **minimize the risk** of this happening by being discreet: don't flash anything of value, keep a firm hand on your camera, and carry shoulder bags, as you'll see many Sicilian women do, slung across your body. It's a good idea, too, to entrust money and credit cards to hotel managers. If you really want to escape being marked as a tourist, dress smartly and look purposeful at all times. The vast majority of cases occur in Catania and Palermo, and commonly at or on the way to and from the airports. On the whole it's common sense to avoid badly lit areas at night, or deserted inner-city areas by day. Confronted with a robber, your best bet is to submit meekly: it's an excitable situation where panic can lead to violence – though very few tourists see anything of this.

The police

If the worst happens, you'll be forced to have some dealings with the **police**. In Sicily, as in the rest of Italy, they come in many forms. Most innocuous are the **Polizia Urbana** or town police, mainly concerned with directing the traffic and punishing parking offenders. The **Guardia di Finanza**, often heavily armed and screaming ostentatiously through the cities, are responsible for investigating smuggling, tax evasion and other similar crimes, and the **Polizia Stradale** patrol the autostrada. Most conspicuous are the **Carabinieri** and **Polizia Statale**; no one knows what distinguishes their roles, apart from the fact that the Carabinieri – the ones with the blue uniforms – are organized along military lines and are a branch of the armed forces. They are also the butt of most of the jokes about the police, usually on the "How many Carabinieri does it take to...?" level. Each of the two forces is meant to act as a check and counterbalance to the other: a fine theory, though it results in much time-wasting and rivalry in practice. Hopefully, you won't need to get entangled with either, but **in the event of theft** you'll need to report it at the headquarters of the Polizia Statale, the **Questura**; you'll find their address in the local *Tuttocittà* magazine, and we've included details in city "Listings". The Questura is also where you're supposed to go to obtain a Permesso di Soggiorno if you're staying for any length of time, or a **visa extension** if you require one. For other issues, such as being grossly overcharged in a restaurant or hotel, or having a dispute with your landlord, it's more usual to go to the Carabinieri.

In any brush with the authorities, your experience will very much depend on the individuals you're dealing with. Apart from **topless bathing** (permitted, but don't try anything more daring) and **camping rough**, don't expect a soft touch if you've been picked up for any offence, especially

Emergency phone numbers

Police (Carabinieri) ☎112
Emergency services (Soccorso Pubblico di Emergenze) ☎113
Fire brigade (Vigili del Fuoco) ☎115
Road assistance (Soccorso Stradale) ☎116

if it's **drug**-related: it's not unheard of to be stopped and searched if you're young and carrying a backpack, and there is a large, unseen network of plain-clothes police and informers on the lookout for any seemingly suspicious activity. Drugs are generally frowned upon by everyone above a certain age, and universal hysteria about *la droga*, fuelled by the epidemic of heroin addiction that is a serious problem all over Italy, means that any distinction between the "hard" and "soft" variety has become blurred. Theoretically, everything is illegal over and above the possession of a few grams of cannabis or marijuana "for personal use", though there's no agreed definition of what this means and you can expect at least a fine for this. In general, the south of Italy is more intolerant than the north, but, in any case, if you're found with suspicious substances, you can be kept in jail for as long as it takes to analyse the stuff, draw up reports and wait for the bureaucratic wheels to grind – which can be several weeks, and sometimes months. For the addresses of the nearest **foreign consulates** (UK and US in Palermo; Irish, Australian, New Zealand, Canadian in Naples/Rome), see Palermo's "Listings" section (p.111), though bear in mind that staff are unlikely to be very sympathetic or do anything more than put you in touch with a lawyer.

Sexual harassment

Italy has a reputation for **sexual harassment of women** that is well known and well founded, but there's no reason to presume unwarranted intrusion at every turn. If you're travelling on your own, or with another woman, you can expect a certain amount of attention, including tooting and whistling, though bear in mind that local custom dictates that every friend and acquaintance is greeted with a toot. If you follow common-sense rules and don't hang around on your own late at night, the most that should worry you is the occasional try-on. If you're off the beaten track, you're more likely to be subjected to stares (from both sexes). For greater anonymity, dress smartly, and as a deterrent wear or flaunt a wedding ring.

The degree of freedom that Sicilian women enjoy varies from place to place: it's probably greatest in Messina, and smallest in the rural interior. Catania is fairly progressive, while Palermo still lags behind. But the town with the best track record in recent years must be Cefalù, where the women, always known in Sicily for their strong hand in ruling the family, have now extended that role into public life. In this "City of Women", practically all key posts including that of mayor, chiefs of police and magistrates, are held by young women.

Finding work

With an unemployment rate of fifteen to twenty percent, higher than most other Italian regions, Sicily offers few opportunities for finding work.

However, all EU citizens are eligible to work, the two main **bureaucratic requirements** for both working and living in Sicily being a *libretto di lavoro* and *permesso di soggiorno*, respectively a work and residence permit, both available from the Questura (see p.62). For the first you must have a letter from your prospective employers saying they are prepared to take you on, for the second (which is also necessary if you want to buy a car or have a bank account in Italy) you'll need a passport, passport-sized photos and a lot of patience.

Teaching English

The obvious choice is to **teach English**, for which the demand has expanded enormously in recent years. You can do this in two ways: freelance private lessons, or through a language school.

Private lessons generally pay best, and you can charge up to £10–20/US$14–28 an hour – though there's scope for bargaining. Advertise in bars, shop windows and local newspapers and, most importantly, get the news that you're looking for work around by word of mouth, emphasizing your excellent background, qualifications and experience. An advantage of private teaching is that you can start at any time of the year (summer especially is a good time due to schoolchildren and students who have to retake exams in September); the main disadvantage is that it can take weeks to get off the ground, and you need enough money to support yourself until then. You'll find the best opportunities for this kind of work in the tourist resorts and the bigger towns and cities.

Teaching in schools, you start earning immediately (though some schools can pay months in arrears). Teaching classes usually involves more hours per week, often in the evening, and for less per hour, though the amount you get depends on the school. For the less reputable places, you can get away without any qualifications and a bit of bluff, but you'll need to show a degree and a TEFL certificate for the more professional language schools. For these, it's best to apply in writing from Britain (look for the ads in the *Guardian* and the *Times Educational Supplement*, and contact the Italian Cultural Institute at 39 Belgrave Square, London SW1X 8NX (☎020/7235 1461, ⊛www.italcultur .org.uk), preferably before the summer, though you can also find openings in

September. The British Council website (⊛www.britishcouncil.org/work/job) and the TEFL website (⊛www.tefl.com) also both have lists of English-teaching vacancies. If you're looking on the spot, sift through the Italian *Yellow Pages* (*Págine Gialle*) and do the rounds on foot, asking to speak to the *direttore* or his/her secretary; don't bother to try in August when everything is closed. Strictly speaking, you could get by without any knowledge of Italian, but some definitely helps.

The best teaching jobs of all are with a university as a *lettore*, a job requiring fewer hours than the language schools and generally offering a fuller pay packet. Universities need English-language teachers in most faculties, and you should write to the individual faculties at the universities of Messina, Catania or Palermo (addressed to "*Ufficio di Personale*"). That said, success in obtaining a university teaching job usually depends on you knowing someone already in place – as with so many things in Sicily.

Other options

If teaching's not up your street, there's the possibility of **courier work** in the summer, especially around the resorts of Cefalù and Taormina. These are the only places where you might find **bar/restaurant work** too – not the most lucrative of jobs, though you should make enough to keep you in Sicily over the summer. You'll have to ask around for both types of work, and a knowledge of Italian is essential.

Travellers with disabilities

Although most Sicilians are helpful enough if presented with a specific problem you may have, the island is hardly geared towards accommodating travellers with disabilities.

In the run-down medieval city centres and old villages, few budget hotels have elevators, let alone ones capable of taking a wheelchair, and rooms have rarely been adapted for use by disabled visitors. Outside, the narrow, cobbled streets, steep inclines, chaotic driving and parking are hardly conducive to a stress-free holiday either. Crossing the street in Palermo is a major undertaking even if you're fully mobile, while Taormina, the most popular resort, has great accessibility problems for anyone in a wheelchair.

However, there are things you can do to make your visit to Sicily easier. Contacting one of the **organizations** listed below puts you in touch with a wide range of facilities and information that may prove useful; RADAR, for instance, issues a badge enabling disabled drivers to park more freely in Italy. Indeed, if the thought of negotiating your own way around the island proves too daunting, an **organized tour** may be the way to go: it will be more expensive than planning your own trip, but accommodation is usually in higher-category hotels that should have at least some facilities for disabled travellers, while you'll also have someone on hand who speaks Italian to help smooth the way.

Read your travel **insurance** smallprint carefully to make sure that people with a pre-existing medical condition are not excluded, and always pre-warn airline or bus companies, who can cope better if they are expecting you, with a wheelchair provided at airports and staff primed to help. A **medical certificate** of your fitness to travel, provided by your doctor, is also extremely useful; some airlines or insurance companies may insist on it. Make sure that you have extra supplies of drugs – carried with you if you fly – and a prescription including the generic name of the product in case of emergency.

Contacts for people with disabilities

In the UK and Ireland

Holiday Care UK ☎0845/124 9971 or 0208/760 0072, ⊛www.holidaycare.org.uk. Provides free lists of accessible accommodation abroad.

Irish Wheelchair Association Republic of Ireland ☎01/818 6400, ⊛www.iwa.ie. Useful information provided about travelling abroad with a wheelchair.

RADAR (Royal Association for Disability and Rehabilitation) UK ☎020/7250 3222, Minicom ☎020/7250 4119, ⊛www.radar.org.uk. A good source of general advice on holidays and travel.

In the US and Canada

Access-Able ⊛www.access-able.com. Online resource for travellers with disabilities.

Directions Unlimited ☎1-800/533-5343 or ☎914/241-1700. Tour operator specializing in bookings for people with disabilities.

Mobility International USA Voice and TDD ☎541/343-1284, ⊛www.miusa.org. Information and referral services, access guides, tours and exchange programmes.

Society for the Advancement of Travelers with Handicaps (SATH) ☎212/447-7284, ⊛www.sath.org. Non-profit educational organization that actively represents travellers with disabilities.

Wheels Up! ☎1-888/389-4335, ⊛www. wheelsup.com. Provides discounted airfare, tour and cruise prices for disabled travellers, also publishes a free monthly newsletter and has a comprehensive website.

In Australia and New Zealand

ACROD (Australian Council for Rehabilitation of the Disabled) Australia ☎02/6282 4333, ⊛www .acrod.org.au. Provides lists of travel agencies and tour operators for people with disabilities.

Disabled Persons Assembly New Zealand ☎04/801 9100, ⊛www.dpa.org.nz. Resource centre with lists of travel agencies and tour operators for people with disabilities.

Travelling with children

Children are revered in Sicily and will be made a fuss of in the street, and welcomed and catered for in bars and restaurants. It's perfectly normal for Sicilian children to stay up until they drop, and in summer it's not unusual to see youngsters out at midnight, and not looking much the worse for it.

Pharmacies and supermarkets carry most baby requirements, from **nappies** to formula **food**. However, you may not see the brands you are used to at home, and don't expect there to be a full range of (or indeed any) organic food products, especially in smaller towns. Otherwise, food is unlikely to be a problem as most children eat pasta and pizza, both widely available, and whilst specific children's menus are not common, many restaurants are happy to provide a smaller version of an adult meal.

Hotels normally charge around thirty percent extra to put an additional bed or cot in the room. **Self-catering apartments**, or rooms with the use of a kitchen, are quite common, with most Sicilian resorts offering this kind of accommodation. You don't necessarily need to have booked a package holiday to find an apartment or series of rooms – some resorts and islands have these available for touring visitors. Generous **discounts** apply for children at most sights and attractions, and also when travelling on trains (see p.44).

In high summer, the **heat and sun** can be exhausting for children. Make sure they are well covered with sun block, which can be bought in any pharmacy and many supermarkets. Also, do as the Sicilians do and dress your children in bonnets or straw hats, available from most markets, and take advantage of siesta time to recover flagging energy. If you're using public transport, try and travel during the less busy periods – mornings and evenings – and make sure your children drink plenty of water.

Smoking is pretty much the norm everywhere and as Sicilians seem blissfully ignorant of the concept of passive smoking, don't be surprised if your offsprings' admirers blow great wafts of smoke into their faces as they tickle their chins. However, you don't need to be too paranoid – especially in resorts, you can always sit outside at cafés, bars and restaurants and escape the smoke-fugged interiors.

Southern Mediterranean stereotypes certainly still apply in Sicily, with children firmly ensconced in their **gender roles** at an early age: the girls' clothes on sale are all frills and flounces, while the toy, candy and nut trolleys that you find in every piazza have one side devoted to guns and hammers, the other to dolls, tiaras and manicure kits.

Directory

ADDRESSES Usually written as the street name followed by the number eg Via Roma 69. *Interno* refers to the flat number – eg *interno* 5 (often abbreviated as *int.*). Always use postal codes.

BARGAINING This isn't really on in shops and restaurants, though you'll find you can get a "special price" for some rooms and cheap hotels if you're staying a few days, and that things like boat/bike rental and guided tours (especially out of season) are negotiable. In markets, you'll be taken for an imbecile if you don't haggle for everything except food. Ask for *uno sconto* ("a discount").

BEACHES You'll have to pay for access to most of the better beaches (referred to as *lidos*), as well as a small fee to rent a sun-bed and shade and use the showers all day. Elsewhere, on the offshore islands and along the south coast, beaches are free though not always clean; indeed at the end of a busy August day they can look (and smell) like ashtrays. During winter most look like dumps; it's not worth anyone's while to clean them until the season starts at Easter. On the other hand, any beach that's remotely inaccessible should remain in a fairly pristine state. Some beaches, for instance along the north coast, are prone to invasions of jellyfish (*meduse*) from time to time. These are not dangerous, but can cause quite a sting, so take local advice.

CAMPING GAZ Easy enough to buy for the small portable camping stoves, either from hardware stores (*ferramenta*) or camping/sports shops. You can't carry canisters on aeroplanes.

CONSULATES Palermo holds consular agencies for British, US, Dutch, German, French, Belgian and Austrian citizens, and for people of all the Scandinavian countries. Irish, Australian, Canadian and New Zealand consulates are in Naples or Rome (see p.111).

DEPARTMENT STORES There are two main nationwide chains, Upim and Standa. Neither is particularly posh, and they're good

places to stock up on toiletries and other basic supplies; branches of both stores sometimes have a food hall attached.

ELECTRICITY The supply is 220V, though anything requiring 240V will work. Most plugs are two round pins; a travel plug is useful.

ENTRANCE FEES There's usually an entrance fee for museums and archeological sites, although under-18s and over-60s get in free on production of documentary proof of age. Some sites, churches and monasteries, and Palermo's oratories, are normally free to get in; however, there will be a custodian around to open up and show you around, who will expect a small tip.

GAY LIFE Taormina is the only place in Sicily where there is any kind of gay scene, and this is very low-key (see p.232). Although there's no legally sanctioned discrimination against gays, attitudes towards homosexuality (male and female) are much less tolerant here than in Rome or the industrial north. That said, physical contact between men is fairly common in Sicily, on the level of linking arms and kissing cheeks at greetings and farewells – though an overt display of anything remotely ambiguous is likely to be met with hostility. Contact addresses in Sicily of ARCI Gay – part of the cultural wing of the ex-Communist Party's youth section – are in Palermo, at Via Genova 7 (℡091.335.688), and in Catania, as Open Mind, at Via Gargano 33 (℡095.532.685). A useful Italian website (🌐www.gay.it) provides gay-scene news and a few listings for gay-friendly businesses in Sicily.

LAUNDRY Coin-operated laundries are very rare. More common is a *lavanderia*, a service-wash laundry, though these are expensive. Although you can usually get away with it, washing clothes in your hotel room can be problematic – simply because the room's plumbing often can't cope with all the water. It's better to ask if there's somewhere you can wash your clothes.

LEFT LUGGAGE Because of the fear of terrorism, most left-luggage offices in train stations have closed, though there are a few that remain open.

PUBLIC TOILETS These are usually found in bars and restaurants, and you'll generally be allowed to use them even if you're not eating or drinking. You'll find most places very clean, though it's advisable to take your own toilet roll.

RECEIPTS Shops, bars and restaurants are all legally obliged to provide you with a receipt (*una ricevuta*). Don't be surprised when it's thrust upon you, as they – and indeed you – can be fined if you don't take it.

TABACCHI You buy cigarettes (and tobacco) in shops called *tabacchi*, recognizable by a sign displaying a white "T" on a black or blue background. Historically, tobacco and salt were both state monopolies, sold only in *tabacchi* – salt's no longer deemed so important, but cigarettes are still hard to track down anywhere else. You can also buy sweets, stationery and stamps in *tabacchi*.

TIME Sicily (and Italy) is always one hour ahead of Britain, except for one week at the end of September when the time is the same. Italy is seven hours ahead of Eastern Standard Time and ten hours ahead of Pacific Time.

WAR CEMETERIES World War II saw several fiercely contested battles on Sicilian soil; information and a list of Allied cemeteries is available from the Commonwealth War Graves Commission, 2 Marlow Rd, Maidenhead SL6 7DX (☎01628/634221, ⓦwww.cwgc.org).

WATER Safe to drink everywhere, and, if chilled, often indistinguishable from bottled mineral water.

WOMEN'S MOVEMENT For information on the current women's movement in Sicily, contact ARCI Donna, Via di Giovanni 14, Palermo (☎091.301.650).

Guide

Guide

1

Palermo and around

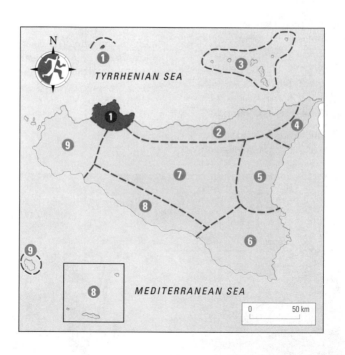

N

TYRRHENIAN SEA

MEDITERRANEAN SEA

0   50 km

CHAPTER 1 # Highlights

* **Frutta di Martorana** Artfully crafted from coloured almond paste, these fruit- and vegetable-shaped candies are a Palermitan tradition. See p.89

* **La Martorana** Catch the superb twelfth-century mosaics of this fine medieval church in the early morning, when they're illuminated by streams of sunlight. See p.89

* **Cappella Palatina in the Palazzo dei Normanni** It's worth braving the scrum for the breathtaking beauty of the Byzantine mosaics, decorated marble floor and carved Arabic ceiling. See p.91

* **Museo delle Marionette** Catch a performance and admire the swashbuckling wooden Sicilian puppets in all their finery. See p.98

* **The festival of Santa Rosalia** Mid-July sees the island's liveliest celebrations, with fireworks, processions and general merry-making. See p.112

* **The cloisters at Monreale** Don't miss the medieval columns with their intricate carvings. See p.117

* **Diving in Ústica** Gin-clear waters and lively underwater action make this one of the best places to dive in Sicily. See p.124

△ Puppets in the museum at Palazallo Acreide

Palermo and around

U
nmistakably the capital of Sicily, Palermo is fast, brash, loud and exciting. Hub of the island since the ninth century AD, it borrows heavily
from the past for its present-day look, showing a typically Sicilian fusion
of foreign art, architecture, culture and lifestyle. In the narrow streets
of Palermo's old town, elegant Baroque and Norman monuments exist cheek
by jowl with Arabic cupolas, while Byzantine street markets swamp the medieval warrens, and the latest Milanese fashions sit in shops squeezed between
Renaissance churches and Spanish *palazzi*. And, ricocheting off every wall, the
endless roar of traffic and wail of police sirens adds to the confusion. Palermo

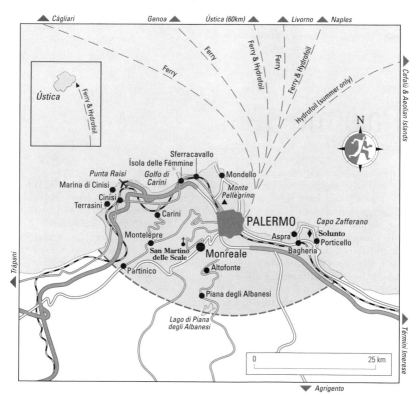

is probably the noisiest city in Italy, and there's pollution in the air, too – a pall of yellow smog hangs over the city, visible from the sea or from the mountains behind on bad days, and in the mottling of dust that covers every car.

It may not be the healthiest place in the world, but it's certainly not dull, with the oppressive summer climate and frenetic street scenes that are redolent of North Africa or the Near East. Indeed, there's little that's strictly European about Palermo, and its geographical isolation has forced the city to forge its own identity, distinct enough to demand that you devote a fair proportion of your stay in Sicily to the capital and its environs. Easily the most populous centre on the island, with around 700,000 inhabitants, it demands at least three or four days to fully explore. Palermo has some of the island's most intriguing sights; also some of its best food and markets, cheapest hotels, and easy access to one of Sicily's finest beaches, at **Mondello**. The other obvious quick retreat from Palermo's bustle is to the heights of **Monte Pellegrino**, the mountain that looms beyond the city to the north.

More substantial targets lie just outside the city's boundaries, most warranting a day-trip. If your enthusiasm has been fired by the city's great Norman heritage, you shouldn't miss the medieval cathedral of **Monreale** and its celebrated mosaics. The **Golfo di Carini**, the curving bay to the west of Palermo, sports a couple of low-key holiday resorts, all with beaches of varying attractiveness and local popularity. Or, heading east along the coast, you can spend an unhurried afternoon at **Bagheria** and its *palazzi*, and take in the nearby Roman site at **Solunto**. Further afield, around 25km south of Palermo, **Piana degli Albanesi** survives as an Albanian Orthodox enclave in a stridently Catholic island. If you feel the pull of the sea, you can always take a day-trip to the offshore island of **Ústica**, though you're likely to want to stay much longer, given the natural attractions of this craggy volcanic slab.

Palermo

In its own wide bay underneath the limestone bulk of Monte Pellegrino, and fronting the broad and fertile Conca d'Oro (Golden Shell) valley, **PALERMO** is stupendously sited. Originally a Phoenician colony, it was taken by the Carthaginians in the fifth century BC and became an important Punic bulwark against the Greek influence elsewhere on the island. Named Panormus (All Harbour), its mercantile attractions were obvious, and it remained in Carthaginian hands until 254 BC. Long considered a prize worth capturing, the city then fell to the Romans, despite a desperate countersiege by Hamilcar Barca, which he directed from the slopes of Monte Pellegrino. Yet Palermo's most glorious days were still to come. In 831 AD the city was captured by the Arabs, under whose rule it thrived as an Islamic cultural and intellectual centre – the river Papineto that now flows beneath the city was said to speak with the Nile and abide by its tides. Two centuries later under the Normans, the settlement continued to flower as Europe's greatest metropolis – famed for the wealth of its court, and unrivalled as a nexus of learning.

By way of contrast, this century has been one of social and economic decline. Allied bombs during **World War II** destroyed much of the port area and over

The Mafia in Palermo

The most glaring symptom of decay in Palermo, the Mafia problem, is intimately connected with the welfare of the city. For years it has been openly acknowledged that a large part of the funds pouring in from Rome and the EU, ostensibly to redevelop the city centre, are unaccounted for – channelled to dubious businessmen, or simply raked off by Mafia leaders. The subtle control exerted by the Mafia is traditionally referred to only obliquely, though it periodically erupts into the news. Mafia issues have had a higher profile than usual in recent years, following the intensification of the struggle to reassert the state's authority in the wake of a number of assassinations of prestigious figures – most notably those of anti-Mafia investigators Falcone and Borsellino in 1992 (see "The Mafia in Sicily", pp.452–458). Since then, the arrest of leading Mafia figures – starting with the arrest of the *capo dei capi* Salvatore Riina in 1993 – has seen the tide turning against Cosa Nostra, helped by the testimony of a succession of informers.

However, the problem is deeply rooted and unlikely to disappear completely, despite the courageous efforts of various individuals. Prominent among these is Leoluca Orlando, mayor of Palermo from 1993–2001, who attempted to combat corruption at municipal level by removing companies suspected of links with organized crime from the tenders list for new contracts. Despite reversals, including disavowal by his own Christian Democrat party, Orlando has continued his fight at a national level, at the head of his own Rete (Network) party.

Fortunately, the Mafia has little relevance for casual travellers, and the closest you'll get to it is through the screaming headlines of local newspapers. Follow the rules and you'll probably avoid having your bag snatched by Vespa-borne delinquents, many of whom are destined to be sucked into the lower ranks of the big Mafia clans.

seventy of the city's churches, turning parts of the medieval town into a ramshackle demolition site – a state of affairs that is now gradually being resolved. Regeneration has been due in no small measure to the efforts of the former mayor, Leoluca Orlando, aided by funds from the European Union (when not siphoned off by illicit means; see box above). Although decay is recognizable in the buildings and some deprivation is apparent, you'll not – unlike in so many other European cities – see beggars and homeless people on the streets. Unemployment is endemic, however, and **petty crime** commonplace. Palermo's underworld exists on many levels and, in a city that absorbs its villains with ease, you'd be well advised to take all due precautions – avoiding the market and back-street areas after dark, and not flashing around bulging wallets or cameras.

Most areas are never anything less than perfectly safe in the daytime, however, and nothing should put you off getting around the city. There are notable relics extant from the ninth to the twelfth centuries, Palermo in its prime, but it's the rebuilding of the sixteenth and seventeenth centuries that shaped the city as it appears today: essentially a straightforward street-grid confused by the memory of an Eastern past and gouged by World War II bombs. Traditionally Palermo has been a city of rich **churches**, endowed by the island's ruling families and wealthy monastic orders, and they're still an obvious draw for visitors, from the hybrid **Cattedrale** and the nearby mosaic-decorated **Cappella Palatina**, tucked inside the Royal Palace, to the glorious Norman foundation of **La Martorana**. And that's not counting the Baroque candidates, like **San Giuseppe dei Teatini** and **Santa Caterina**. Really, though, to see Palermo in terms of an architectural tour would be to ignore much: three significant **museums** – inspiring collections of art and archeology – splendid markets, back-street puppet theatres, and a wealth of excellent restaurants.

Arrival

Palermo's Falcone Borsellino **airport** (☎800.541.880, ⓦwww.gesap.it) is at
Punta Raisi, 31km west of the city. From just outside the Arrivals terminal,
regular Prestia & Comandè buses (1–2 hourly, 6.30am until the last flight arrival;
45min journey) run right into the centre, stopping by the Politeama Theatre

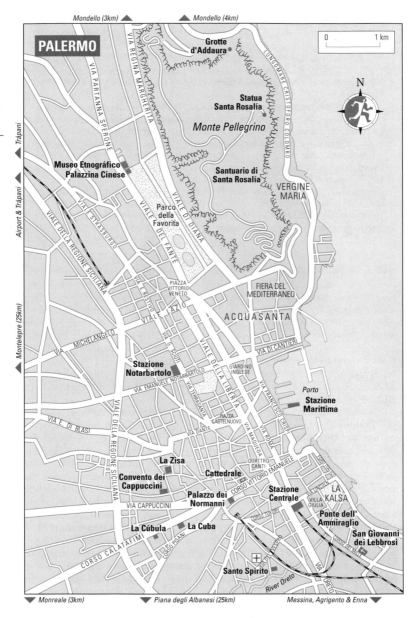

Mondello (3km) ▲   ▲ Mondello (4km)

PALERMO

Grotte
d'Addaura

Statua
Santa Rosalía

Monte Pellegrino

VIA REGINA MARGHERITA

VIA PARTANNA SPERONE

Museo Etnográfico
Palazzina Cinese

◄ Trápani

◄ Airport & Trápani

◄ Montelepre (25km)

Santuario di
Santa Rosalía

VERGINE
MARIA

N

VIALE D'DIANA

Parco
della
Favorita

VIALE DEL FANTE

VIALE DELLA REGIONE SICILIANA

VIA STRASBURGO

VIA F.RESTIVO

PIAZZA
VITTORIO
VENETO

FIERA DEL
MEDITERRANEO

VIALE LAZIO

ACQUASANTA

VIA MICHELANGELO

VIA G. SCIUTI

VIALE DELLA LIBERTA

VIA DI CANTIERI

Stazione
Notarbartolo

VIA EMANUELE NOTARBARTOLO

VIA TERRASANTA

GIARDINO
INGLESE

VIA FRANCESCO CRISPI

VIA VINCO CRISPI

Porto
Stazione
Maríttima

VIA E. DI BLASI

VIALE DELLA REGIONE SICILIANA

PIAZZA
CASTELNUOVO

VIA DANTE

VIA ROMA

VIA MAQUEDA

La Zisa

Convento dei
Cappuccini

VIA CAPPUCCINI

Cattedrale

QUATTRO
CANTI

CORSO VITTORIO EMANUELE

Stazione
Centrale

VIA LINCOLN
VILLA
GIULIA

LA
KALSA

Palazzo dei
Normanni

CORSO TUKORY

Ponte dell'
Ammiraglio

La Cúbula   La Cuba

CORSO PISANI

CORSO CALATAFIMI

San Giovanni
dei Lebbrosi

VIA ORETO

Santo Spirito

River Oreto

0   1 km

LUNGOMARE CRISTOFORO COLOMBO

▼ Monreale (3km)   ▼ Piana degli Albanesi (25km)   Messina, Agrigento & Enna ▼

Palermo's bus terminals

AST, Piazza Lolli (℡091.680.0031) for Bagheria, Capaci, Carini, Partinico and Santa Flavia; Corso Re Ruggero (℡091.680.0030) for Castelbuono, Corleone, Lercara Friddi, Módica, Montelepre and Ragusa.

Cuffaro, Via P. Balsamo 13 (℡091.616.1510) for Agrigento.

Gallo, Via P. Balsamo 16 (℡091.617.1141) for Siracusa and Sciacca.

Interbus, Via P. Balsamo 26 (℡091.616.7919) for Catania and Siracusa.

Prestia & Comandè, Stazione Centrale (℡091.580.457) for the airport and Piana degli Albanesi.

Randazzo, Via P. Balsamo (℡091.814.8235) for Cáccamo, Piazza Armerina, Polizzi Generosa and Santa Flavia.

Russo, Piazza Marina (℡0924.31.364) for Balestrate, Castellammare del Golfo, Partinico and San Vito Lo Capo.

SAIS, Via P. Balsamo 16 (℡091.616.6028 or 091.617.1141) for Caltagirone, Caltanissetta, Catania, Cefalù, Enna, Gangi, Gela, Messina, Petralia, Rome, Piazza Armerina and Términi Imerese.

Salemi, Via R. Gregorio 44 (℡0923.981.120) for Castelvetrano, Marsala, Mazara del Vallo and Salemi.

Segesta, Via P. Balsamo 26 (℡091.616.9039) for Álcamo, Messina, Partinico, Trápani and Rome.

Stassi, Salita Partanna, off Piazza Marina (℡091.585.699) for Corleone.

Virga, Piazza Verdi (℡091.418.021) for San Martino delle Scale.

on Piazza Ruggero Séttimo, and ending at Stazione Centrale, in front of the *Albergo Elena*; buy your ticket (€5) on the bus. Note that the last departure on the return journey is at 11pm. Taxi fares for the same trip are around €40. Alternatively, you could take the regional train from the airport's new Departures terminal, a five-minute walk from arrivals, to the Stazione Centrale (roughly hourly, 5.40am–11.40pm; 1hr journey). Note that though Catania rather than Palermo is the island's main airport, facilities here are good, including bars, money exchange (Mon–Fri 9am–4pm, plus cash machines), and an English-speaking **tourist office** (Mon–Fri 8am–midnight, Sat & Sun 8am–8pm; ℡091.591.698). For details of car rental at the airport, see "Listings", p.111.

   Trains all arrive at and leave from Stazione Centrale (℡091.603.1111 or 091.603.3121) in Piazza Giulio Césare, at the southern end of Via Roma. Some (from Trápani/Álcamo) stop first in the northwest of the city at Stazione Notarbártolo; sit tight and you'll end up at Stazione Centrale.

   Local, provincial and long-distance, island-wide **buses** operate from a variety of terminals all over the city, of which there are full details in the box above. Handily, though, the **main bus arrivals** and ticket offices are in the streets around the train station – mainly Via Balsamo and Via Gregorio – while other major termini are Piazza Marina, down by the old port, and Piazza Lolli, off Via Dante from Piazza Castelnuovo – both mostly used by AST services to and from Palermo province.

   Palermo is a grand place in which to arrive by sea. All **ferry** services – from Ústica, the Aeolians, Genova, Livorno, Naples and Cágliari (in Sardinia) – dock at the **Stazione Maríttima**, just off Via Francesco Crispi, from where it's a ten-minute walk (straight up Via Emerico Amari) to Piazza Castelnuovo and the modern city centre. The terminal building has a convenient, inexpensive left-luggage office (daily 7am–7.30pm; €2 per day), great for stowing big bags

Useful bus routes

AMAT city buses
From the ranks outside Stazione Centrale
#101 and #102 to Piazza Politeama (Piazza Castelnuovo) and Viale della Libertà.
#109 to Piazza dell'Indipendenza (for Palazzo dei Normanni and buses to Monreale).
#139 to Piazza Marina/Corso Vittorio Emanuele and Stazione Maríttima.

From Corso Vittorio Emanuele
#104 and #105 run along the corso.

From Via Roma
#101 to Via Príncipe di Belmonte and Giardino Inglese.

From Piazza Sturco/Piazza Politeama
#806 to Parco della Favorita/Mondello.

Circular minibuses
Linea Gialla to Orto Botanico, La Kalsa, Via Alloro, Quattro Canti, Ballarò and Corso Tukory.
Linea Rossa to Via Roma, Vucciria, Via Libertà, Piazza Politeama, Teatro Mássimo and Via Maqueda.

Taxi ranks
There are **taxi ranks** at:
- Piazza Giulio Césare ☎091.616.2001
- Piazza Castelnuovo ☎091.588.133
- Piazza Giuseppe Verdi ☎091.320.184
- Piazza Indipendenza ☎091.422.703
- Piazza San Domenico ☎091.588.876
- Piazza Matteotti ☎091.303.237
- Via Malta ☎091.616.2000
- Via Roma ☎091.588.876

7.20am–8.20pm), run from the train station and regularly ply the most-frequented tourist destinations, including the markets: see box above for the routes. Tickets for these cost €1 for two hours' travel, or €3.30 for the day, and are available from AMAT ticket kiosks. Other city buses run from 4am until midnight (11.30pm on Sundays). You'll find main **city bus ranks** outside the train station, in Piazza Castelnuovo, along Corso Vittorio Emanuele, and along the southern stretch of Viale della Libertà.

Taxis and other transport
Taking a horse-drawn carriage, a **carrozza**, is a swanky way to see the city. They tout for business alongside Piazza Pretoria or by the cathedral: an hour-long trip costs around €50, though it's worth bargaining. Don't consider getting around the city **by car**: one short afternoon driving in congested Palermo could take years off your life. However, we've given details of car rental companies in "Listings" (see p.111), should you want to have your own transport once you're out of the city. If you're adept on two wheels, **biking** presents an easier alternative. As long as you realize the rules of the road – he who hesitates is lost, and go for the gap – weaving your way in and out of the traffic can be an exhilarating way to save time and legwork. You can get free daily rental (plus helmet and lock), in exchange for a hefty deposit, and for the more adventurous, **scooter** rental is also available. Details of scooter and bike rental outlets are given in "Listings" (p.111).

Accommodation

Palermo is the easiest Sicilian city in which to find good, cheap **accommodation**. Prices here are the lowest on the island. In the city itself, but not on the coast, July and August are counted as low season; in June and September, and also around the time of Palermo's annual festival (July 11–15), you'd be wise not to leave it too late in the day if you want the better rooms; turning up before noon is best, or ring ahead and reserve. Note that if you do go for a cheaper option, English-speaking staff are rare, and at night and in the early morning things can get very noisy. If you're a light sleeper, then ear plugs are a must – unless you're inured to rubbish lorries, barking dogs, thumping radios and raucous coughing and spitting.

The tourist office can provide information about **renting a room** in an apartment or house, which can be less expensive and more comfortable than staying in a basic hotel. One good option is Marjolein Wortmann, a friendly Dutch woman with two fairly quiet rooms to rent, right in the centre near Via Roma, at Vicolo Madonna del Cassaro 7 (☏091.325.780, ⓔmarjolein_wortmann@hotmail.com; ❷).

Hotels

Nearly all the reasonable budget **hotels** in Palermo – known variously as *alberghi, pensioni* or *locande* – are to be found on and around the southern ends of Via Maqueda and Via Roma, roughly in the area between Stazione Centrale and Corso Vittorio Emanuele. Here, there are often several separate places in the same block, usually cheaper the higher the floor. Beyond the corso, the streets begin to widen out and the hotels tend to get more expensive.

Stazione Centrale and around

Alessandra Via Divisi 99 ☏091.616.7009, ⓕ091.616.5180, ⓦwww.albergoalessandra. it. Simple rooms, most with TV and shower in a well-maintained building; a safe choice for single women. It's on the corner with Via Maqueda, though, so rooms overlooking that street are noisy. ❸

Elena Piazza Giulio Césare 14 ☏091.616.2021, ⓕ091.616.2984. Not the best place around, but it's cheap, opposite Stazione Centrale and right on the airport bus stop, so late-night arrivals need not fear walking the dark old-town streets. Three- and four-bedroom units are also available, and you'll save €10 if you forego a private bath. ❸

Italia Via Roma 62 ☏091.616.5397. A friendly, family-run place on the fourth floor, high above the traffic noise. The 18 rooms are reasonably sized and squeaky clean, with shared bathrooms up the corridor. No credit cards. ❸

Orientale Via Maqueda 26 ☏091.616.5727, ⓦwww.albergoorientale.191.it. One of the most atmospheric old-town hotels, an eighteenth-century palazzo with a marble courtyard and columns, and two cavernous double rooms (nos. 6 and 7, where Mussolini once stayed) complete with a long balcony overlooking Via Maqueda. Other doubles are plain, and look down onto the courtyard and the Albergheria market, while singles are half-price. No credit cards. ❸

Rosalia Conca d'Oro 3rd floor, Via Santa Rosalia 7 ☏091.616.4543, ⓕ091.617.5852. Charming rooms and a welcoming owner make this a sought-after choice, though it can be noisy. It's conveniently close to Stazione Centrale, and the seven rooms fill quickly. No credit cards. ❶

Sausele Via V. Errante 12 ☏091.616.1308, ⓕ091.616.7525, ⓦwww.hotelsausele.it. Close to the station, clean and secure, this modern, well-managed Swiss-run hotel is air-conditioned and has lots of rooms, though it can be noisy at night. Take the first right off Via Oreto, south of the station. ❹

Sicilia Via Divisi 99 ☏ & ⓕ091.616.8460. Pleasantly run and recently renovated, this represents good value, with air-conditioned rooms; those around the small downstairs courtyard are quieter. A good choice for women, and free parking available nearby. ❷

▲ *Ferries to Cagliari, Genoa, Livorno, Ústica*

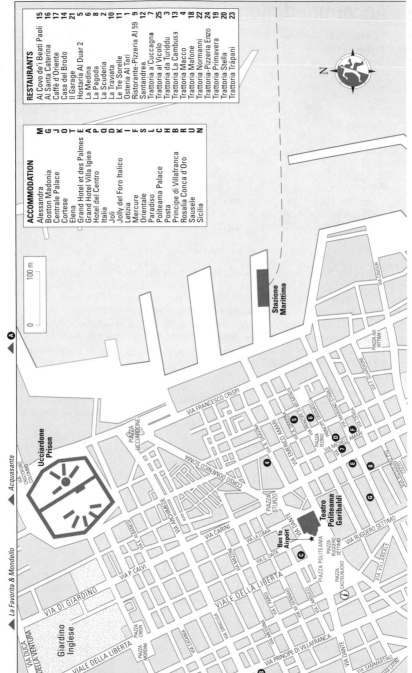

ACCOMMODATION

Alessandra	M
Boston Madonia	G
Centrale Palace	J
Cortese	O
Elena	T
Grand Hotel et des Palmes	E
Grand Hotel Villa Igiea	A
Hotel del Centro	P
Italia	Q
Joli	D
Jolly del Foro Italico	K
Letizia	I
Mercure	F
Orientale	S
Paradiso	L
Politeama Palace	C
Posta	H
Principe di Villafranca	B
Rosalia Conca d'Oro	R
Sausele	U
Sicilia	N

RESTAURANTS

Al Covo de'i Beati Paoli	15
Al Santa Caterina	16
Caffè d'Oriente	17
Casa del Brodo	14
Il Garage	21
Hostaria Al Duar 2	5
La Medina	6
La Pagoda	8
La Scuderia	2
La Traviata	10
Le Tre Sorelle	11
Osteria Al Tari	1
Ristorante-Pizzeria Al 59	9
Santandrea	12
Trattoria a 'Cuccagna	7
Trattoria al Vicolo	25
Trattoria da Turiddu	3
Trattoria La Cambusa	13
Trattoria Macco	4
Trattoria Mafone	18
Trattoria Normanni	22
Trattoria-Pizzeria Enzo	24
Trattoria Primavera	19
Trattoria Stella	20
Trattoria Trápani	23

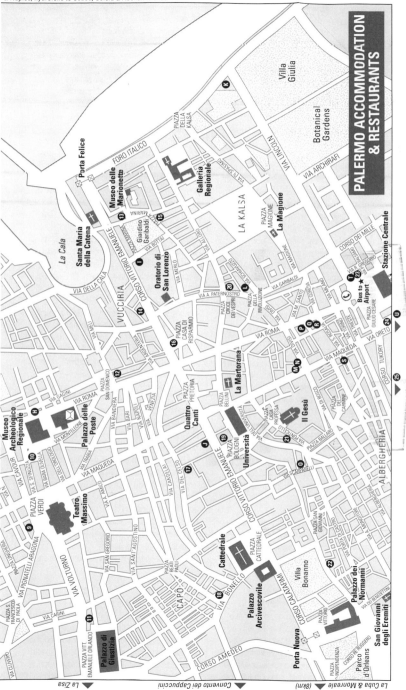

PALERMO ACCOMMODATION & RESTAURANTS

PALERMO AND AROUND

Corso Vittorio Emanuele and around

Centrale Palace Corso Vittorio Emanuele 327 ☎091.336.666, ℱ091.334.881, ⓦwww.centralepalacehotel.it. A few steps away from the Quattro Canti, this renovated *palazzo* makes a soothing base, overseen by courteous staff. Lovely rooms have high ceilings, quality furnishings and a choice of streetside, balcony or atrium view. Take breakfast in the cool Baroque salon, or dinner in the serene panoramic roof terrace-restaurant. Garage parking available. ❻

Hotel del Centro Via Roma 72 ☎ & ℱ091.617.0376. A basic hotel, though useful as a fallback if all else is full. Pleasant management, rooms with private bathroom, and space usually available. ❹

Cortese Via Scarparelli 16 ☎ & ℱ091.331.722. The advantages here are friendly management, nicely decorated rooms, some with views over the noisy Ballarò market, and locked parking space. However, the hotel sits well off the main drag and is not particularly salubrious (the unlit side streets that lead to the building can be rather intimidating at night). Follow the signs from Via Maqueda that point left down Via dell'Università. ❷

Jolly del Foro Italico Foro Italico 22 ☎091.616.5090, ℱ091.616.1441, ⓦwww.jollyhotels.it. The only hotel in the centre with a pool, the *Jolly* – one of a chain, which is apparent from the bland room decoration – overlooks the sea and the Foro Italico. ❼

Letizia Via Bottai 30 ☎ & ℱ091.589.110, ⓦwww.hotelletizia.com. On a road running between Corso Vittorio Emanuele and Piazza Marina, this attractive and friendly establishment has rooms full of character and very nice period furniture; by far the best choice in this area. There's safe street parking and free Internet for guests, too. ❻

Paradiso Via Schiavuzzo 65 ☎091.617.2825. The windows of this first-floor *pensione* overlook the Piazza della Rivoluzione, in a good location not far from Via Roma. One of the cheapest in town. No credit cards. ❶

The modern city

Boston-Madonia Via Mariano Stabile 136 ☎091.580.234, ℱ091.335.364, ⓦwww .hotelsmadiona.it. Located in a complex of five separate hotels on a main street at the top end of Via Roma in the modern city, most of the rooms here have some personality, though service can be a bit hit-and-miss. Only two singles available. Garage parking also available. If they're not to your liking, four other, similarly priced, hotels are just a lift ride away. ❹

Grand Hotel et des Palmes Via Roma 396 ☎091.602.8111, ℱ091.331.545, ⓦwww.thi.it. One of central Palermo's monuments, this magnificent building – complete with rooftop terrace – is where Richard Wagner stayed and finished composing *Parsifal* in 1882. Glamorous in its public rooms, though some bedrooms can be disappointingly basic, and overpriced. Garage available for €15. ❽

Joli Via Michele Amari 11 ☎091.611.1766, ℱ091.616.1765, ⓦwww.hoteljoli.com. Classy rooms in a pleasant, quiet neighbourhood make this a good choice. It sits right on Piazza Florio, handy for both the port and the modern city. ❺

Mercure Via Mariano Stabile 112 ☎091.342.991, ℱ091.611.6822, ⓦwww.metha.com. Palermo's newest chic hotel, this is industrial minimalist design at its finest. The identical rooms all have sleek tiled baths, and some offer great views. It's popular with business travellers, which makes weekends here refreshingly quiet. ❼

Politeama Palace Piazza Ruggero Séttimo 15 ☎091.322.777, ℱ091611.1589, ⓦwww.hotelpoliteama.it. An excellent location for this fairly modern hotel, right opposite the Politeama Theatre. All the comfortable rooms are soundproofed, which deals effectively with the manic traffic outside. Quite popular with older tour groups. ❽

Posta Via Gagini 77 ☎091.587.338, ℱ091.587.347, ⓦwww.hotelpostapalermo.it. Much favoured by actors, this courteously run, modern hotel has character, charm and a dash of 1970s styling and is a good bet for women travelling on their own. The street runs parallel to Via Roma, between Piazza San Domenico and Via Cavour. Garage parking available. ❺

Principe di Villafranca Via G. Turrisi Colonna 4 ☎091.611.8523, ℱ091.588.705, ⓦwww.principedivillafranca.it. Furnished to the hilt with antique Sicilian furniture and early twentieth-century art, this luxury hotel has a great location – it's far enough out of the centre to give some peace and quiet, and is a good, safe area to park in. ❽

Out of the centre

Grand Hotel Villa Igiea Via Belmonte 43 ☎091.543.744, ℱ091.547.654, ⓦwww.cormorano .net/sgas/villaigiea. At Acquasanta, 3km north of the city, this classic Art Nouveau building, originally a villa of the Florio family (the first people to can tuna), was designed by Ernesto Basile in 1900. It's still sumptuous and for the seriously wealthy. ❽

Campsites and youth hostels

There are two **campsites** outside Palermo. Both are at Sferracavallo (see below), 13km northwest of the city, and are reachable on bus #616 from Piazza Vittorio Veneto at the northern end of Viale della Libertà in the modern city (take #101 from the station, or #106 from Piazza Ruggero Séttimo up this long avenue to save a walk). Given the price of Italian campsites, however, and the distance involved, it's probably worth sticking with a central budget hotel. If you're driving and heading out of town, other campsites within range are stretched along the Golfo di Carini, to the west of Palermo (see p.120).

There are two **youth hostels** near Palermo: the *Casa Marconi*, at Via Monfenera 140 (℡091.657.0611, ⓦwww.casamarconi.it), is on the expensive side and a bit of a bus trek, but it's spankingly modern and has private rooms only (❷); you'll need to book ahead as it fills quickly. To get there, take bus #246 from the station to the end of the line at the hospital, cross on to Via G. Basile and turn left into Via Monfenera. The *Baia del Corallo* hostel, at Via Plauto 27 (℡091.679.7807, ⓔostellodipalermo@libero.it; doubles ❶, dorm beds €18), is even further out in Sferracavallo, 30 minutes or so from Palermo. It's convenient for the beach, but not much else, and you'll need two bus connections to get there: from Stazione Centrale, take bus #101 to the stadium (or the metropolitana train to Tommaso Natale) and then the #628, and get off at the *Hotel Bellevue* stop just after Sferracavallo.

Camping Trinacria Via Barcarello ℡091.530.590. Right across from the sea, with a pizzeria on the premises, and some small, basic bungalows that sleep two to four people. ❷

Camping dell'Ulivo Via Pegaso ℡091.533.021. A fair bit cheaper than the *Trinacria*, and quite basic, though there are also similar bungalows here. ❶

The City

Historical Palermo sits compactly around one set of central crossroads, the **Quattro Canti**, which is at the core of four distinct quarters. The **Albergheria** and the **Capo** quarter, the latter beyond the cathedral, lie roughly west of Via Maqueda; the **Vucciria** and old harbour of La Cala and **La Kalsa** lie to the east, closest to the water. In the past there was little contact between the inhabitants of each quarter, which had their own dialects, trades, palaces and markets; even intermarriage was frowned upon. Today these areas, together with the more modern stretch along **Viale della Libertà**, hold all of Palermo's most enduring monuments and buildings. It's a fairly undisciplined mess, with sixteenth- and seventeenth-century town planning conspiring with late nineteenth-century ambition and twentieth-century bombs to lend an eclectic look to the city – tight alleys, stately piazzas and contemporary office blocks mixed to distraction. But each quarter retains something of its medieval character in a web-like system of streets, where decaying buildings often mask gardens or chapels containing outstanding works of art, or even stabling for a goat – a world away from the din of the urban assault course outside.

Given that cars, let alone buses, can't get down many of the narrow streets in the old city centre, you'll often have no choice but to walk or cycle around most of what is detailed below – although for certain specific sights, don't hesitate to jump on a bus. Certainly, you'll need some form of transport to reach Palermo's **outskirts**: it's no fun at all slogging up and down the long thoroughfares of the modern city.

N

@ **Stazione Marittima**

VIA CAVOUR

VIA T. GUARDIONE

PIAZZA XIII VITTIME

VIA FRANCESCO CRISPI

VIA BENEDETTO GRAVINA

VIA EMERICO AMARI

VIA MASSIMO D'AZEGLIO

VIA PRINCIPE DI BELMONTE

VIA GRANATELLI

PIAZZA FLORIO

VIA MARIANO STABILE

VIA PRINCIPE GRANATELLI

VIA MARIANO STABILE

VIA CERDA

PIAZZA UCCIARDONE

CORSO DOMENICO SCINÀ

Ucciardone Prison

VIA DUCA DELLA VENTURA

VIA CRISTOFORO COLOMBO

▲ *Acquasanta*

▲ *La Favorita & Mondello*

VIA E. ALBANESE

VIA ARCHIMEDE

VIA CARINI

VIA LA LUMIA

VIA P. CALVI

VIA DI GIARDINO

Giardino Inglese

VIALE DELLA LIBERTÀ

VIA CATANIA

PIAZZA MORDINI

PIAZZA CRISPI

PIAZZA MORELLI

VIA SIRACUSA

VIA MESSINA

VIA VII GENNAIO

VIA E. PARISI

VIA G. DAITA

VIA MAZZINI

VIA CARDUCCI

VIALE DELLA LIBERTÀ

PIAZZA STURZO

VIA DANTE

Teatro Politeama Garibaldi

★ **Bus to Airport**

PIAZZA POLITEAMA

PIAZZA RUGGERO SETTIMO

VIA RUGGERO SETTIMO

PIAZZA CASTELNUOVO

VIA VILLAFRANCA

VIA VILLAFRANCA

ⓘ

Villino Basile

VIA PRINCIPE DI VILLAFRANCA

VIA DANTE

@ VIA SAMMARTINO

VIA LATINI

▲ *Museo Mormino*

▲ *Villa Malfitano*

& Villa Malfitano

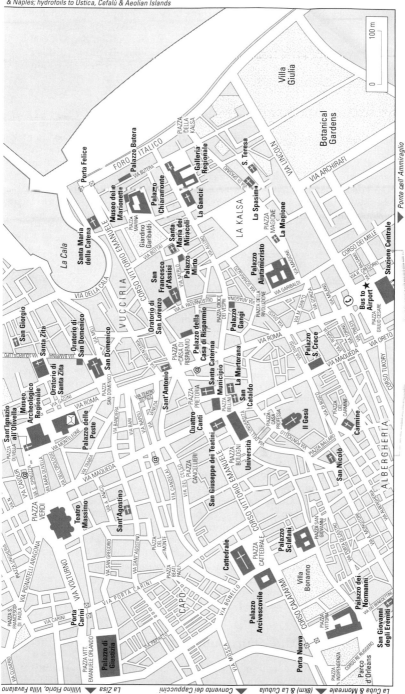

▶ *Ponte cell' Ammiraglio*

Villino Florio, Villa Favaloro ▲ La Zisa ▲ ▲ Convento dei Cappuccini ▲ La Cuba & Monreale ▲ (8km) & La Cubula ▲

If you want to cut down on **admission charges**, go for the two reduced-price tickets (€8), valid for two days and available from participating museums: one covers La Zisa, La Cuba, Monreale cloisters and San Giovanni degli Eremiti, the other the Museo Archeológico, Galleria Regionale Siciliana and Palazzo Mirto. Finally, bear in mind that information in English is scarce at most of the sights.

Around the Quattro Canti

In the heart of the old city – ten minutes' walk from the train station – is Piazza Vigliena, better known as the **Quattro Canti** or "Four Corners". Erected in 1611, this is not so much a piazza as a set of Baroque crossroads that divide central Palermo into quadrants. It's worth strolling around to check the tiered statues – respectively a season, a king of Sicily and a patron of the city in each concave "corner", where, in previous centuries, the heads of convicted rebels were hung from poles. You'll pass this point a good few times as you explore, and only a few seconds away from here are some of Palermo's most opulent piazzas and buildings, including four of the city's most extraordinary churches.

On the southwest corner (entrance on Corso Vittorio Emanuele), the early seventeenth-century **San Giuseppe dei Teatini** (Mon–Sat 7.30am–noon & 5.30–8pm, Sun 8.30am–12.30pm & 6–8pm) is the most harmonious of the city's Baroque churches. The misleadingly simple facade conceals a wealth of detail inside, from tumbling angels holding the holy water on either side of the door to the lavish side chapels and encrusted ceiling. There's plenty of contrasting space, though, with 22 enormous columns supporting the dome, mostly restored after bomb damage in 1943. Outside, adjacent to the church, is the main building of the **Università**, a dull nineteenth-century restoration job replacing what was originally a convent adjoining San Giuseppe. There are generally plenty of students around here, and a couple of good bars in the little piazza across from the entrance.

Piazza Pretoria: the Municipio and Santa Caterina

Cross Via Maqueda to **Piazza Pretoria**, where you'll see the gleaming-white nude figures of its great central fountain, a racy sixteenth-century Florentine design, protected by railings to ward off excitable vandals. The piazza also holds the restored **Municipio**, now plaque-studded and pristine, and, towering above both square and fountain, the massive late sixteenth-century flank of the church of **Santa Caterina** (enter from Piazza Bellini), the antithesis of the quietly magnificent San Giuseppe over the road. This is Sicilian Baroque at its most exuberant: every inch of the enormous interior is covered in wildly decorative, pustular relief work, deep reds and yellows filling in between sculpted cherubs, Madonnas, lions and eagles. One marble panel (in the first chapel on the right) depicts Jonah about to be devoured by a rubbery-lipped whale, with a Spanish galleon above constructed from wire with string rigging. Given this overwhelmingly theatrical design, it's difficult to argue with Vincent Cronin's image of a " … frenzied mind … throwing out powerful and extravagant images before tumbling over the verge of madness".

Piazza Bellini: the churches of San Cataldo and La Martorana

Just around the corner from the Pretoria fountain, **Piazza Bellini** is largely a car park by day, with vehicles jammed together next to part of the

Frutta di Martorana

When Palermo's religious houses were at their late medieval height, many supported themselves by turning out remarkable sculpted confectionery – fruit and vegetables made out of coloured almond paste. La Martorana was once famous for the quality of its almond "fruits", which were sold at the church doors, and today most Sicilian *pasticcerie* continue the tradition: in Palermo these creations are known as *frutta di Martorana*. It's always worth looking in cake-shop windows, which usually display not only fruit but also fish and shellfish made out of the same sickly almond mixture. The best time to see the displays is in October, before the festival of Ognissanti (All Saints).

city's old Roman wall, and beneath two more wildly contrasting churches. The little Saracenic red golf-ball domes belong to **San Cataldo**, a squat twelfth-century chapel on a palm-planted bank above the piazza (Mon–Sat 9.30am–12.30pm; €1). Other than the crenellations around the roof, it was never decorated, and in the eighteenth century the chapel was even used as a post office: it still retains a good mosaic pavement in an otherwise bare and peaceful interior.

The understatement of this little chapel is more than offset by the splendid interior of **La Martorana** opposite (Mon–Sat 8am–1pm & 3.30–6.30pm, Sun 8.30am–1pm), one of the finest surviving buildings of the medieval city. A Norman foundation, it was paid for in 1143 by George of Antioch, King Roger's admiral, from whom it received its original name, Santa Maria dell'Ammiraglio. After the Sicilian Vespers, the island's nobility met here to offer the Crown to Peter of Aragon, and under the Spanish the church was passed to a convent founded by Eloisa Martorana – hence its popular name. It received a Baroque going-over and its curving northern facade in 1588, but happily this doesn't detract from the great power of the interior; enter through the slim twelfth-century campanile, an original structure that retains its ribbed arches and slender columns. A series of spectacular **mosaics** are laid on and around the columns supporting the main cupola – animated twelfth-century Greek works, commissioned by the admiral himself, who was of Greek descent. A gentle Christ dominates the dome, surrounded by angels, with the Apostles and the Madonna to the sides. The colours are still strong, a golden background enlivened by azure, grape-red, light-green and white, and, in the morning especially, light streams through the high windows, picking out the admirable craftsmanship. Heavy Baroque marble and frescoes by the entrance do their best to dampen the effect, but even here there's some respite: on both sides of the steps, two more original mosaic panels (from the destroyed Norman portico) have been set in frames on the walls: a kneeling George of Antioch dedicating the church to the Virgin, and King Roger being crowned by Christ – the diamond-studded monarch contrasted with a larger, more simple and dignified Christ. The church is a popular location for Palermitan weddings, spectacular events that often culminate in newlyweds releasing a dozen white doves from the steps of the church.

The Albergheria

The district bounded by Via Maqueda and Corso Vittorio Emanuele, just northwest of Stazione Centrale – the **Albergheria** – can't have changed substantially for several hundred years. There are proud *palazzi* on Via Maqueda itself, notably the eighteenth-century **Palazzo Santa Croce**, on the corner of Via Divisi. But behind is a warren of tiny streets and tall, blackened and leaning buildings: it's an atmospheric district to wander around, and much of the central area is taken up by a street market, which conceals several fine churches too. It's a poor neighbourhood, too, as a stroll down shored-up **Via Ponticello**, a block before the university, proves – the bomb damage of World War II has never been made good.

Also on Via Ponticello, the church of **Il Gesù**, or **Casa Professa** (daily 7–11.30am & 5–6.30pm), was the first Jesuit foundation in Sicily, whose glorious Baroque swirl of inlaid marble and relief work and gaudily painted ceiling – topped by a green-and-white-patterned dome – took over a hundred years to complete. Continuing down the road will lead you to **Piazza Ballarò**, which, together with the adjacent **Piazza del Cármine**, is the focus of a raucous daily fruit and vegetable **market**, alive with the cries of vendors from early in the morning. Here gleaming fish curl their heads and tails in the air, squashes come as long as baseball bats and vine leaves trail decoratively down from stalls. There are some very cheap snack and drinking places here, too, where you can sidle in among the locals and sample sliced-open sea urchins, fried artichokes, *arancini* and beer. Above all the activity looms the bright majolica-tiled dome of the seventeenth-century church of the **Cármine** (Mon–Sat 8.30am–1.30pm), a singular landmark amid the dirty and rubbish-strewn alleys, with a spacious interior and adjoining cloister and convent. You enter from Piazza del Cármine.

San Giovanni degli Eremiti

Any of the long streets west of Piazza del Cármine lead to Via dei Benedettini, which marks the westernmost edge of the quarter. Over the busy road, behind iron gates, is the Alberghería's most peaceful haven, the deconsecrated church of **San Giovanni degli Eremiti** (Mon–Sat 9am–7pm, Sun 9am–1pm; €4.50) – St John of the Hermits. Built in 1132, this is the most obviously Arabic of the city's Norman relics, its five ochre domes topping a small church that was built upon the remains of an earlier mosque (part of which, an adjacent empty hall, is still visible). It was especially favoured by its founder, Roger II, who granted the monks of San Giovanni 21 barrels of tuna a year, a prized commodity controlled by the Crown. Apart from some worn frescoes, the interior reveals little of interest, though. A path leads up through citrus trees to the church, behind which lie some celebrated late thirteenth-century cloisters – perfect twin columns with slightly pointed arches surrounding a wilted garden.

Immediately behind the church, on Corso Re Ruggero, the **Palazzo d'Orleans** is also set in its own garden: once home to the exiled Louis-Philippe of France in 1809, it's now the official residence of Sicily's president.

The Palazzo dei Normanni

Turn left out of San Giovanni and it's a few paces to the main road, where, if you turn right and veer left up the steps, you'll climb out of the clamorous traffic to gaze on the vast length of the **Palazzo dei Normanni**, or Palazzo Reale. A royal palace has always occupied the high ground here, above medieval Palermo. Originally built by the Saracens in the ninth century, the palace was enlarged considerably by the Normans, under whom it housed the most magnificent of medieval European courts. Sadly, there's little left from those times in the current structure. The long front was added by the Spanish in the seventeenth century, and most of the interior is now taken up by the Sicilian regional parliament (hence the security guards and limited access).

Of the Royal Apartments, it is now only possible to make a guided visit to the **Sala di Ruggero** (Mon, Fri & Sat 9am–noon; free), one of the earliest parts of the palace and covered with lively twelfth-century mosaics of hunting scenes. It's a brief visit, best done first, before you descend a floor to the beautiful **Cappella Palatina** (Mon–Fri 9am–noon & 3–5pm, Sat 9–11.45am; free), the undisputed artistic gem of central Palermo. The private royal chapel of Roger II, built between 1132 and 1143, its intimate interior is immediately overwhelming, with cupola, three apses and nave entirely covered in **mosaics** of outstanding quality. The oldest are those in the cupola and apses, probably completed in 1150 by Byzantine artists; those in the nave are from the hands of local craftsmen, finished twenty odd years later and depicting Old and New Testament scenes. The colours are vivid and, as at Monreale and Cefalù, it's the powerful representation of Christ as Pantocrator that dominates the senses, bolstered here by other secondary images – Christ blessing, open book in hand, and Christ enthroned, between Peter (to whom the chapel is dedicated) and Paul. Aside from the mosaics, the chapel has a delightful Arabic ceiling with richly carved wooden stalactites, a patterned marble floor and an impressive marble Norman candlestick (by the pulpit), 4m high and contorted by manic carvings.

The Cattedrale and the Capo

From the Quattro Canti, the busy southwestern stretch of **Corso Vittorio Emanuele** is dotted with secondhand bookshops and run-down eighteenth-century *palazzi*. There is no preparation for the sudden, huge bulk of the **Cattedrale** (daily 8am–6pm; free; Ⓦwww.cattedrale.palermo.it): set back in gardens on the right of the corso, it's a more substantial Norman relic than the Royal Palace. Founded in 1185 by Palermo's English archbishop Gualtiero Offamiglio (Walter of the Mill), the Cattedrale was intended to be his power base in the city. Yet it wasn't finished for centuries, and in any case was quickly superseded by the glories of William II's foundation at Monreale (see p.115).

The Cattedrale is an odd building in many ways, due to the less-than-subtle late eighteenth-century alterations that added the dome – completely out of character – and spoiled the fine lines of the tawny stone. Still, the triple-apsed eastern end (seen from a side road off the corso) and the lovely matching towers are all twelfth-century originals; and, despite the fussy Catalan-Gothic facade and arches, there's enough Norman carving and detail to give the exterior more than mere curiosity value. The same is not true, however, of the inside, which was modernized by Fuga, the Neapolitan architect responsible for the dome. It's grand enough, but cold and Neoclassical, and the only items of interest are the fine portal and wooden doors (both fifteenth-century) and the royal **tombs**, Palermo's pantheon of kings and emperors. As you enter, two crowded chapels to the left contain the mortal remains of some of Sicily's most famous monarchs: among others, Frederick II (left front) and his wife Constance (far right), Henry VI (right front) and Roger II (rear left) – Roger's tomb was brought back shortly after he died from the cathedral at Cefalù, where he had requested that he be laid. In a reliquary chapel to the right of the choir, the remains of St Rosalia (see p.114) are housed in a silver casket, close to an urn containing the arm of St Agata.

Perhaps more rewarding than the rest of the overblown interior is the **treasury**, or *tesoro* (Mon–Sat 8am–6pm; €2), to the right of the choir: highlight of the collection is the twelfth-century jewel- and pearl-encrusted skullcap and three simple, precious rings removed from the tomb of Constance of Aragon in the eighteenth century.

Entrance to the treasury also lets you into the **crypt**, home to twenty-three impressive marble tombs (all numbered), many of which are Roman sarcophogi with interesting decoration. No. 12 is a Greek sarcophagus boasting an imposing effigy by Antonello Gagini, and no. 16 is the tomb of the founding archbishop.

Palazzo Arcivescovile and the Porta Nuova

Over the road, at the western end of the Cattedrale, stands the **Palazzo Arcivescovile**, the one-time archbishop's palace, entered through a fifteenth-century gateway. Inside, the Museo Diocesano brings together art from the cathedral and from city churches destroyed during World War II. The museum is currently closed, but you should be able to take a look in the courtyard. A little way up Via Bonello (left out of the palace) there's usually some activity in the open-air **Mercato delle Pulci**, an antique/junk market in Piazza Peranni displaying chandeliers galore.

Back on the corso, the road runs up to the Royal Palace, on the northern side of which lies the commanding **Porta Nuova**. Erected in 1535, it commemorates Charles V's Tunisian exploits, with suitably grim, turbaned and moustachioed figures adorning the western side. Through the gate, the long road, now Corso Calatafimi, heads southwest to Monreale.

Il Capo

On foot, circle around the apses of the Cattedrale and stroll up into the **Capo** quarter. One of the oldest areas of Palermo, it's another tight web of run-down streets, unrelieved by space or greenery, save for the graceful **Piazza del Monte**, tree-planted and with a couple of restful neighbourhood bars. There's not much to see other than a few surviving sculpted portals in the decaying palaces, but it's an instructive tour if you've seen only grand buildings up to now. One alley, Via Porta Carini, climbs past shambolic buildings and locked, battered churches to reach the decrepit **Porta Carini** itself, one of the city's medieval gates. There are market stalls packed into Via Porta Carini, and the entire area is reminiscent at times of an Arab souk, though with a decidedly Sicilian choice of wares.

The market extends on either side of Via Porta Carini, west to the edge of the Capo district and east, along **Via Sant'Agostino** – the closer you get to Via Maqueda, the more it's devoted to clothes and shoes rather than food. Keep an eye out for **Sant'Agostino** (Mon–Sat 7am–1pm & 4–5.30pm, Sun 7am–noon), built by the Chiaramonte and Sclàfani families in the thirteenth century. Above the main door (on Via Raimondo) there's a gorgeous latticework rose window and, inside through the adjacent side-door, some fine **stuccoes** by Serpotta. Another door leads to a quadrangle of calm sixteenth-century cloisters. Otherwise, turn the corner, and along Via Sant'Agostino, behind the market stalls, the church sports a badly chipped, sculpted fifteenth-century doorway attributed to Domenico Gagini – one of a whole dynasty of talented medieval sculptors who covered Sicily with their creations.

Along Via Maqueda and Viale della Libertà: the modern city

North of the Quattro Canti, you leave most of the interesting medieval alleys behind, and the streets off to the left of Via Maqueda gradually become wider and more nondescript as they broach the area around Piazza Verdi, site of the late nineteenth-century **Teatro Mássimo**. It's a monumental structure, all dome and columns, supposedly the largest theatre in Italy and beautifully cleaned up after years of closure (see box below). You don't have to attend a performance to appreciate its majestic, heavily gilded interior as **tours**, with an English-speaking guide (Tues–Sun 10am–4pm, every 30min; €3), take place throughout the year, except during rehearsals. There's an abundance of pink marble, rich reds, blues and golds in the echoing Sala Pompeiana where the nobility once foregathered and, in the auditorium, a domed ceiling, constructed in the shape of a flower head, which lifts its petals to the skies when things get too hot.

The theatre marks the dividing line between old and new Palermo. Beyond here there's little that's vital, though plenty that is grand and modern. Via Maqueda becomes **Via Ruggero Séttimo**, which cuts through gridded shopping streets and passes the enclosed Piazza Ungheria on its way to the huge double square that characterizes modern Palermo – known as **Piazza Politeama**, it's made up of Piazza Castelnuovo to the left and Piazza Ruggero Séttimo to the right. Dominating the whole lot is Palermo's other massive theatre, the late nineteenth-century **Politeama Garibaldi**. Built in overblown Pompeiian style, and topped by a bronze chariot pulled by four horses, the theatre also houses the city's **Galleria d'Arte Moderna** (entrance on Via Turati; Tues–Sat 9am–8pm, Sun 9am–1pm; €3.10). There's some attractive work here, all twentieth-century Sicilian stuff, best of which is the sculpture, including a small bronze study of an exhausted horse (by Enrico Quattrociocchi), and Gerbino's sympathetic statuette of his greatcoated, heavily bearded father – though Michele Catti's autumnal scenes of Palermo are good, too. Watch out, as well, for the international touring exhibitions that often visit.

PALERMO AND AROUND | The City

The Teatro Mássimo: the glory and the Realpolitik

In May 1997, almost a hundred years to the day after its inauguration and after 23 years of closure, the Teatro Mássimo was reopened by Palermo's then-mayor, Leoluca Orlando. It had been boarded up for just over a year longer than its original construction period, during which time it had been vaunted as an emblem of the new Sicily, a monument to rival Europe's great opera houses in Paris and Vienna. Its construction was entrusted to Giovanni Battista Basile, whose strictly Neoclassical design was possibly influenced by Charles Garnier's contemporary plans for the Paris Opéra, and the first stone was laid in 1876. The architect did not live to see the end of the project, however, and the work was finished by his son, Ernesto Basile. After its inauguration, the opera house became the focus of high society, and saw an illustrious procession of musical performers grace its vast auditorium, with director Franco Zeffirelli's (now a senator) productions in the 1950s ranking among the theatre's greatest moments. By the time it closed for radical repairs in the 1970s, however, the building was in a sorely neglected state, and in true Sicilian style its renovation became bogged down in political and financial problems. It did, however, open its doors briefly to Francis Ford Coppola, who shot the long climactic opera scene of *The Godfather: Part III* here, using the theatre's sweep of steps to great effect.

It was with a sense of triumph, therefore, that Leoluca Orlando – having thrown all his influence behind the effort to coincide the reopening with the theatre's centenary – presided over the gala ceremony, at which the celebrated Claudio Abbado conducted and thousands attended (mostly watching from a screen outside). The acoustic quality of the theatre alone is so superior to that at the Politeama (which hosted the opera season during the period of closure), while the spruced-up exterior injects impressive style into Palermo's cityscape.

93

Along Viale della Libertà

Many of the city buses stop in between the two large piazzas, and you might want to hop on one if you're heading any further north, along the wide **Viale della Libertà**, as it's about 1km to the modern city's other attractions.

At Viale della Libertà 52, the **Museo Mormino** (Mon–Fri 9am–1pm & 3–5pm; €4) houses a beautifully presented collection of artefacts and paintings in the sumptuous Banco di Sicilia building. On the **first floor**, there's a wide representation of colourful Italian majolica from the sixteenth to the eighteenth centuries, and an extensive collection of Greek vases. Look out for the splendid small Etruscan mirror with a relief of Silenus as you enter the gallery, and the third-century BC terracotta statue of a young boy in case B. There are also maps and coins aplenty, but you'll probably get more from the horde of attractive nineteenth-century paintings in the second-floor rooms, including seascapes and tuna fishing as portrayed by Antonino Leto, and the charming paintings of women by Ettore de Maria Bergler.

From here, you're close to the **Giardino Inglese**, one of the city's few parks, though actually not much more than a palm-planted garden. For real expanses of parkland you'll have to take the bus a couple of kilometres further north to the Parco della Favorita (p.102).

A couple of blocks east of the Giardino Inglese is Palermo's notorious **Ucciardone prison**, connected by an underground passageway to the maximum-security bunker where the much-publicized *maxi processi* (maxi-trials) of Mafia suspects were held in the 1980s. The gloomy Bourbon prison has been called "the best-informed centre in Italy for gossip and intelligence about the operations of organized crime throughout the world", not least because it's home to a good percentage of the biggest names in the Italian underworld at any one time. It's reported that Mafia affairs are conducted here almost undisturbed, by bosses whose food is brought in from Palermo's best restaurants and who collaborate with the warders to ensure that escapes don't happen – something that might increase security arrangements and hamper their activities. Following the murders of Mafia investigators Falcone and Borsellino in 1992, a large group of prisoners were transferred from here to the Asinara high-security prison in Sardinia in an attempt to shake up the criminal intelligence network; there's even talk of a new prison being built in the city, though this is extremely unlikely to happen soon, if ever.

East to the water

On the east side of the prison, Via Cristóforo Colombo runs down to the water, past a selection of neglected Baroque *palazzi*, to the seventeenth-century **Arsenale** (closed to the public). The exterior – erected by Mariano Smirighio – is worth a look, if you fancy the stroll. To the north of here, 1km or so away, is the fairly attractive but foul-smelling port of **ACQUASANTA**, overlooking which is Ernesto Basile's **Villa Igiea**, an Art Nouveau building erected in 1899 for the wealthy Florio family. It's now a luxury hotel (see p.84), though if you have a drink in the bar you can poke around inside a little – the dining room, in particular, is a fantastic creation. Buses #721 and #731 from Piazza Crispi (near the Giardino Inglese and Ucciardone prison, and reachable on #101 from the train station or Piazza Politeama) run out as far as the villa.

Via Roma, the Vucciria and around

Running from the Stazione Centrale to Piazza Sturzo (below Piazza Ruggero Séttimo), **Via Roma** is a fairly modern addition to the city. Parallel to Via

Maqueda, and connected to it by a series of narrow alleys, it's nothing like as interesting as its neighbour in its lower reaches, its buildings consisting mostly of tall apartment blocks concealing hotels. The only real diversion is **Via Divisi**, off to the east – a narrow street whose pavements are chock-full of stacked bikes from a series of cycle shops. The surrounding area also groups its commodities: ironmongery, wedding dresses, baby clothes and ceramics all have their separate enclaves. The rest of Via Roma is all clothes and shoe shops, and there's nowhere to linger until you cross Corso Vittorio Emanuele.

Just up from the corso is the church of **Sant'Antonio**, raised on a plat-form, to the side of which steps lead down into the sprawling **market** of the **Vucciria** quarter. Winding streets, lit by naked light bulbs even at noon on a summer's day, radiate out from a small enclosed piazza, wet from the ice and waste of the groaning fish stalls – swordfish heads stuck to marble slabs and huge sides of tuna from which fishmongers carve bloody steaks. There are a couple of excellent little restaurants tucked away in the alleys (best at lunch-time), some very basic bars where the wine comes straight from the barrel, and all manner of food (fresh octopus, for example) and junk on sale. This is also *the* place to buy great porcelain pasta bowls, espresso cups and coffee-makers. Other than early morning, when the action is at its most frenzied, lunchtime is a good time for a wander, when the stallholders take a break for card-playing sessions conducted around packing cases, or simply fall asleep amongst their produce.

San Domenico and around

The northern limit of the market is marked by **San Domenico** (Mon–Fri 9am–11.30pm, Sat & Sun 5–7pm), a large church set back off Via Roma and fronted by a statue-topped marble column. The fine eighteenth-century facade, with its double pillars and slim towers, is lit at night to great effect, while inside a series of tombs contains a horde of famous Sicilians. Parliamentarians, poets and painters, they're of little interest to foreigners except to shed light onto Palermitan street-naming. Outside, on the north side of the church at Piazza San Domenico 1, is the small **Museo del Risorgimento** (ring for entry; Mon, Wed & Fri 9am–1pm, closed Aug; free), an illuminating historical collection pertaining to the nineteenth-century Italian anti-Bourbon revolt. To visit the adjacent cloister, ring ☏091.329.588.

More worthwhile, however, is to head behind the San Domenico church along Via dei Bambini 16 to the **Oratorio del Rosario di San Domenico** (Mon–Fri 9am–1pm & 2–5.30pm, Sat 9am–1pm), one of many such small chapels in the old part of the city which contain the best of Palermo's Baroque decoration. This sixteenth-century oratory, built and still maintained by the Knights of Malta, was adorned by the acknowledged master of the art of stucco sculpture, **Giacomo Serpotta** (see p.463), who lined the walls with allegorical figures. Born in Palermo in 1656, Serpotta devoted his entire life to decorating oratories like this, a tradition continued by his son, Procopio (some of whose work can also be seen in the Oratorio di Santa Caterina behind the main post office). Here, the somewhat dusty figures of *Justice*, *Strength* and suchlike (resembling fashionable society ladies, who often served as models) are crowned by an accomplished and well-lit altarpiece by Van Dyck.

Further up Via Roma, on the left, is Palermo's main post office, the gargantuan **Palazzo delle Poste**. Built by the Fascists in 1933, it's an oblong concrete block, with a wide swath of steps spreading up to a colonnade of ten unfluted columns that run the length and height of the building itself. The pink-coloured paint on the walls has somewhat softened the severe effect, especially at night when floodlights impart a rosy glow. But the empty pretension of the post office is put to shame by what hides behind it, around the corner in Piazza Olivella. Here, the church of **Sant'Ignazio Martire all'Olivella** (Mon–Sat 9–10am & 5–6pm, Sun 9.30am–noon) displays an opulent Baroque touch in its great chandeliers and rich side chapels; next door, the cloisters and surviving buildings of a sixteenth-century convent – once the property of the church – now house the city's excellent archeological museum.

Museo Archeológico Regionale

If you've been touring the best of western Sicily's ancient sites (or are intending to do so), the **Museo Archeológico Regionale** (Mon 8.30am–1pm, Tues–Sat 8.30am–6.45pm, Sun 9am–1.30pm; call ☎091.611.6805 to check hours as they are liable to change; €4.50) is a must, gathering together artefacts found at all the major Neolithic, Carthaginian, Greek and Roman settlements in a magnificent collection that culminates with items from the site at Selinunte. The exhibits are displayed on two main floors, together with a top floor that is usually roped off, but can be visited in the company of a museum attendant. The main exhibits in the collection are labelled in English, and you can pick up a free illustrated booklet on them, also in English, on the way in.

The entrance to the **ground floor** is through the smaller of two cloisters, which displays anchors and other retrieved hardware from the sea off the Sicilian coast. There are **Egyptian and Punic** remains in rooms to either side, and beyond, the larger, thickly planted cloister is devoted to **Roman** sculpture, notably a giant Emperor Claudius on the left, enthroned in the style of Zeus. Rooms at the far end contain numerous early Greek carved stelae and assorted inscribed tablets (including one from Roman Taormina recording expenses charged by the town's magistrates).

Beyond here, the material is almost entirely **Greek**, beginning with the assembled stone **lion's-head water-spouts** from the so-called Victory Temple at Himera (fifth century BC), the nineteen fierce animal faces tempered by braided fur and a grooved tongue that channelled the water, and leading on to the high spot of the museum, the adjacent **Sala di Selinunte**. This gathers together the rich **stone carvings** (or metopes) from the various temples (known only as Temples A–G) at Selinunte on the southwest coast – a vital stop if you intend to visit the site itself (see p.421); the sculpted panels from the friezes that adorned the temples are appealing works of art, depicting lively mythological scenes. The earliest and least impressive, single panels from the early sixth century BC, sit under the windows on the right and represent the gods of Delphi, the Sphinx, the rape of Europa, and Hercules and the Bull. The reconstructed friezes opposite, from Temples C and (more fragmentary) F, catch the eye more: vivid works from the fifth century BC, like Perseus beheading Medusa with a short sword, his legs in profile but his head and torso facing directly out in archaic style. The most technically advanced tableaux are those in the frieze at the end of the room, from the early fifth-century BC Temple E, portraying a lithe Hercules fighting an Amazon, the marriage of Zeus and Hera, Actaeon savaged by three ferocious dogs, and Athena and the Titan. There's additional interest in the female heads, three on either side of the door, taken from Temple E. The remaining rooms on the ground floor deal with mainly **Etruscan** funerary art, the most notable exhibits being several third- to second-century BC sarcophagi painted with graphic battle scenes.

You have to retrace your steps to the small cloister for the stairs up to the **first floor**, which also has plenty of interest: lead water pipes with stopcock retrieved from a site at Términi Imerese (p.135), some 12,000 votive terracotta figures, and a few delicately carved stone heads found at Solunto (p.123). There's more Greek sculpture (including a fragment of the frieze from the Parthenon) and a reconstructed Roman mosaic pavement as well. Worth a look are the newly restored, Punic aedicules (mini-temples), from Lilybaeum (modern Marsala) gaily depicting funerary banquets, and a bronze fourth-century warrior's body armour and helmet from Greece. But pick of the lot here are two rich **bronze sculptures** – the naturalistic figure of an alert and genial ram (third century BC) from Siracusa, once one of a pair (the other was destroyed in the 1848 revolution), and a glistening, muscular study of Hercules subduing a stag, found near Pompeii.

The **second floor** holds a range of Neolithic items, including casts of the incised drawings from Addaura, on Monte Pellegrino, and Lévanzo (see p.405), shelves full of Greek and Etruscan amphorae, and frescoes from Solunto (see p.123). But the most impressive sight on this floor is the room full of beautifully preserved Roman mosaics – the largest of which measures nearly ten metres in length – excavated from Piazza della Vittória in Palermo: one, from the second century AD, depicts the triumph of Neptune; another, from the third century AD, shows Orpheus with a lyre, surrounded by amenable beasts.

Across Via Roma: to La Cala

There's an immediate change in style and surroundings once you cross back over Via Roma and head towards the water. The area around the docks suffered gravely during the last war, particularly the late sixteenth-century church of **Santa Zita** (Mon–Fri 9am–1pm & 3–5.30pm, Sat 9am–1pm), on quiet Via Squarcialupo, which was badly bomb-damaged. It's since been restored, and inside you'll see some flamboyant polychrome marbling and good sculpture by Antonello Gagini. The marvellous oratory behind Santa Zita, the **Oratorio del Rosario di Santa Zita** (Mon–Fri 9am–1pm & 2–7pm, Sat 9am–1pm) contains some of the wildest flights of Giacomo Serpotta's rococo imagination – a dazzling confusion of allegorical figures, bare-breasted women, scenes from the New Testament, putti galore, and, at the centre of it all, a rendering of the Battle of Lepanto. Take time to absorb the details of this tumultuous landscape, especially the loving care with which he depicted individual figures – the old men and women, melancholy boys perched on the ledge – and notice Serpotta's symbol on the left wall: the golden snake. Striking wealth indeed when you step outside and consider the area around.

Via Squarcialupo continues down to **Piazza XIII Víttime**, where five tall V-shaped steel plates splinter out of the ground, commemorating the officials who lost their lives in Palermo's enduring struggle with the Mafia. It replaces a monument commemorating thirteen Palermitani shot by the Bourbons in the 1860 revolt, which now lies along Via Cavour. The whole of the area around is rather forlorn: to the south, the shored-up buildings just back from the water have ground floors given over to car repair workshops, the rooms open to the road and stuffed full of every kind of vehicular wreckage.

South of this area lies the thumb-shaped inlet of the old city harbour, **La Cala**. Once the main port of Palermo, stretching as far inland as Via Roma, La Cala started to decline during the sixteenth century, when silting caused the water to recede to its current position. All the heavy work eventually moved northwest, to docks off the remodelled postwar streets (site of the Stazione

Maríttima); La Cala's function as harbour to the few fishing-boats that still work out of Palermo is now outweighed by its duty as marina for the yachts of the well-heeled. It's interesting to stroll around the maritime clutter at least once, and there are excellent views over the little harbour to Monte Pellegrino in the distance.

Along Corso Vittorio Emanuele: from Quattro Canti to the water

There's a markedly different character to the quarter south of La Cala, bounded by Via Roma and the corso. Heavily bombed during the war, this area holds some of the poorest streets in the city, although a slow renovation is now in evidence. Towards the water along **Corso Vittorio Emanuele**, high narrow streets peel off to the left and right, mostly dark and forbidding. One, Via A. Paternostro, cuts away to the right to the thirteenth-century church of **San Francesco d'Assisi** (Mon–Fri 8am–6pm, Sat & Sun 8am–noon & 4.30–6pm), whose well-preserved portal, picked out with a zigzag decoration, is topped by a wonderful rose window – a harmonious design that is, for once, continued inside. All the Baroque trappings have been stripped away to reveal a pleasing stone interior, the later side chapels showing beautifully crafted arches – the fourth on the left is one of the earliest Renaissance works on the island, sculpted by Francesco Laurana in 1468. To the side of the church, at Via Immacolatella 5, the renowned **Oratorio di San Lorenzo** (Mon–Fri 9am–noon; subject to closure due to excavations) contains another of Giacomo Serpotta's stuccoed masterpieces, intricately fashioned scenes from the lives of St Lawrence and St Francis.

Back on the main road, the corso runs straight down to the water, with the harbour of La Cala to the left, overlooked by the church of **Santa Maria della Catena**, named after the chain that used to close the harbour in the late fifteenth century. The corso ends at the Baroque gate, the **Porta Felice**, begun in 1582 as a counterbalance to the Porta Nuova, visible way to the southwest. From here, you can judge the extent of the late medieval city, which lay between the two gates.

Just before Porta Felice, make two quick rights onto Via Butera, then Vicolo Niscemi, and at no. 5 you'll find the engaging, fully renovated **Museo delle Marionette** (Mon–Fri 9am–1pm & 4–7pm; €3; ring bell for entrance), Palermo's definitive collection of puppets and painted scenery. A traditional Sicilian entertainment, puppet theatres have all but died out on the rest of the island, though you can still catch performances here in Palermo (see p.111 for details). Based around French and Sicilian history and specifically the exploits of the hero Orlando (Roland), performances nearly always depict the large, dashing knights in clanking armour – Orlando, Rinaldo and friends – combating Saracen invaders, usually culminating in a great battle. With a commentary often delivered in dialect, you don't follow the lines so much as the short, sharp action – frenetic battle scenes awash with blood and cries, as Orlando single-handedly slays the enemy and saves the day. It's all great fun, and in summer the museum puts on free **shows** (Spettácolo dei Pupi): check at the museum (☎091.328.060) or tourist office (see p.77) for times. As well as the indigenous puppets, you'll see glittering dragons from Rangoon and full-frontal Korean nudes, together with Punch and Judy in their traditional booth.

Back on Via Butera, a little further down the street is the newly restored **Palazzo Butera**, whose seventeenth-century facade faces out over the Foro

Italico. Once the home of the Branciforte family, at one time the wealthiest family in Sicily, it was gradually partitioned and sold off, and is now only open for conferences or groups of visitors (call ☎091.611.0162 to arrange an appointment).

The whole area beyond the Porta Felice was flattened in 1943, and has since been rebuilt as a fairly ugly promenade, the **Foro Italico** (also known as Foro Umberto I), complete with small amusement park, from where you can look back over the harbour to Monte Pellegrino. This is one of the liveliest places in the city on summer evenings, when the locals take to the street armed to the teeth with ice cream from one of the several *gelateria* palaces lined along here.

Piazza Marina

Double back through the gate and bear left into **Piazza Marina**, a large square that skirts around the tropical **Giardino Garibaldi**, famed for its enormous banyan trees, laden with aerial roots. It's another popular venue for the city's elderly card-players, who gather around green baize tables at lunchtime for a game. Reclaimed from the sea in the tenth century, subsequently used for jousting tournaments and executions, and now surrounded by *palazzi* and pavement restaurants, every corner of the piazza is worth exploring. The second largest of Palermo's palaces, the **Palazzo Chiaramonte**, flanks the east side of the square: dating from the fourteenth century, the palace was the home of the Inquisition from 1685 to 1782, before becoming the city's law courts – a function it only abandoned in 1972. Today, it is the administrative centre for the university and is open to the public for occasional art exhibitions only.

On the other side of Piazza Marina, the southwest corner is marked by the sixteenth-century church of **Santa Maria dei Mirácoli**, a lovely Renaissance structure. Via Merlo runs west of here, and at no. 2 is the **Palazzo Mirto** (Mon–Sat 9am–7pm, Sun 9am–1pm; €2.60), a late eighteenth-century building that's one of the few in the city to retain its original furniture and fixtures, thus giving a rare insight into *palazzo* life. Though nothing is labelled and only the first floor is open to the public, it's worth going in for the exquisite ceilings, the intimacy of the Chinese Room, imposing *baldacchino* and the tapestries, still in good colour, in the Salone degli Arezzi. The courtyard boasts an overblown Baroque fountain, lacking only in gushes of water.

La Kalsa and the Galleria Regionale

Balarm, the immense city of beauty, the wondrous splendid sojourn, the world's vast metropolis, adorned in elegance… Balarm has buildings of such beauty that travelers come from afar for the well-known marvels of its architecture.

The "Balarm" in the laudatory above penned by al-Idrisi, court geographer to the Amir of Sicily, is of course Palermo, written at a time when **La Kalsa** (from the Arabic, *khalisa*, meaning "pure") was its cultural and intellectual heart. Planned and built by the Saracens, it is one of the oldest quarters in Palermo, brimming with history, and still contains a great number of monuments and buildings. It is finally surfacing from the poverty and decay it suffered after World War II, and its centre has now been grassed over and planted with trees, providing a welcome respite from the narrow confines of the surrounding streets and alleys. The programme of concerts, films, theatre and exhibitions of the summer KalsArt festival, and at Lo Spasimo throughout the year (see p.100

and p.110), has rejuvenated the area in the evenings, and on summer nights many of its historical buildings and monuments are open to the public, often with free tours (in English) guided by local students. Out of season, however, it's still an area where it pays to be cautious after dark.

The Galleria Regionale

For a daytime visual feast, the **Palazzo Abatellis**, Via Alloro 4, comes up trumps, a fifteenth-century building that still retains elements of its Catalan-Gothic and Renaissance origins, notably in its doorway and courtyard. Revamped since the war, it now houses the **Galleria Regionale** (Mon–Sat 9am–1pm, Tues–Fri also 2.30–7pm, Sun 8am–12.30pm; €4.50), with its excellent medieval art collection.

The **ground floor** contains sculpture, beginning with an intricately carved twelfth-century Arab doorframe that once adorned a Palermitan mansion. Beyond, room 4 holds works of the fifteenth-century sculptor **Francesco Laurana**: his white marble bust of *Eleonora d'Aragona* is a calm, perfectly studied portrait. Room 5 is devoted to the work of the Gagini clan, mostly statues of the Madonna, though Antonello Gagini is responsible for a rather strident *Archangel Michael*, with a distinct military manner. The only non-sculptural item is a magnificent fifteenth-century **fresco**, the *Triumph of Death*, by an unknown (possibly Flemish) painter. It's a chilling study, with Death cast as a skeletal archer astride a galloping, spindly horse, trampling bodies slain by his arrows. He rides towards a group of smug and wealthy citizens, apparently unconcerned at his approach; meanwhile, to the left, the sick and the old plead hopelessly for oblivion.

There are three further frescoes, this time thirteenth- and fourteenth-century Sicilian and rather crude, above the steps up to the **first floor**, which is devoted to painting. This section is unusually comprehensive, with no shortage of excellent Sicilian art, the earliest (thirteenth- to fourteenth-century) displaying marked Byzantine characteristics, including a fourteenth-century mosaic of the *Madonna and Child*, eyes and hands remarkably self-assured. Later fifteenth-century paintings and frescoes are all vivid and imaginative in their portrayal of the *Coronation of the Virgin*, a favourite theme. This floor also contains some notable highlights, not least a collection of works by the fifteenth-century Sicilian artist **Antonello da Messina**: three small, clever portraits of SS Gregory, Jerome and Augustine (with a rakish red hat); and an indisputably powerful *Annunciation*, a placid depiction of Mary, head and shoulders covered, right hand slightly raised in acknowledgement of the (off-picture) Archangel Gabriel. There's a second view – looking down – of the *Triumph of Death*, and some important Flemish works too, such as a **Mabuse** triptych of the *Virgin and Child*, crammed with detail and surrounded by some extraordinarily ugly cherubs.

La Gancia and Lo Spasimo

There's more work by the Gagini family (sculpted fragments and reliefs) in the fifteenth-century church of **La Gancia** – or Santa Maria degli Angeli – next door to the gallery. When restoration work is complete (call ☎091.616.5221 for hours), check out the interior, which is covered in understated marble decoration and boasts a ceiling of brown stars.

From here, Via Alloro runs southwest, past a succession of ailing *palazzi*, before feeding into a confusing jumble of squares, principally Piazza Aragona and **Piazza Croce dei Vespri** (marked by a cross for the French who died in the 1282 Sicilian Vespers rebellion). Here stands the huge entrance to the **Palazzo Valguarnera Gangi**, where Visconti filmed the ballroom scene in *The Leopard*; you may be able to get in by smooth-talking the porter. Close by, to the south, is

Piazza della Rivoluzione, from where the 1848 uprising began and which is marked by an oddly elaborate fountain. From this last piazza, **Via Garibaldi** leads south, marking the end of the route that Garibaldi took in May 1860 when he entered the city (he marched north, up Corso dei Mille and into Via Garibaldi). Here, at Via Garibaldi 23, the immense, battered fifteenth-century **Palazzo Aiutamicristo** keeps bits of its original Catalan-Gothic structure.

Piazza Magione and around

Little Via Magione leads around the south side of the palace to the lovely church of **La Magione** (daily 9.30am–7pm); standing in isolation at the edge of the Piazza Magione, it's approached through a pretty palm-lined drive and garden. It was originally built in 1151 for the Cistercians, but subsequently given to the Teutonic knights as their headquarters by Henry VI, and is a fine example of Arab-Norman architecture. Its real treasures are housed in the cloister and adjacent corridor (€2). The cloister itself was built in a similar style to the cathedral at Monreale, and houses a rare Judaic tombstone re-carved into a basin for holy water. In the room between the cloister and the chapel, there's a well-maintained fresco of the crucifixion which originally hung at the altar of the chapel, though far more interesting and rare is a plaster preparation of the fresco, opposite. The only example of a fresco model in Sicily, its near-mathematical sketch lines show the care and detailed planning that went into the creation of such works. Alongside, supporting two small stone arches, a small Arab-Norman column is carved with a Koranic inscription in Kufic Arabic, a first-millennium angular script used for inscribing on hard surfaces and extant throughout much early Islamic art. Several before-and-after photographs on the wall opposite the column show the facade of the church before it was restored to its original Arab-Norman design at the beginning of the 1900s.

Back on **Piazza Magione** itself, you'll find a grassy open park popular with Palermo's young in the evenings: it's safe and well-lit and makes a good spot to sit down with a bottle of wine. To the southeast of the piazza, past Via della Vetriera, where murdered judge Paolo Borsellino was born and bred, lies the former church and convent of Lo Spasimo, on Via dello Spasimo. The church itself, **Santa Maria dello Spasimo** (daily 8am–midnight), now roofless except for the Gothic apse, was variously used as a theatre, barracks, plague hospital and rubbish tip, and is now a popular concert venue (see p.110). Its most famous painting, *Lo Spasimo di Sicilia*, painted by Raphael and installed here in 1520, is now on show in the Prado in Madrid. To the side of the church is a small building (ask an attendant for the key if it's locked) which houses a large model of Palermo in wooden bricks; the garden above and beyond it on the bastions is a useful spot for listening in to concerts if the nave is full.

On the other side of the piazza down a small street in the north corner, lies the **Parco Letterario Giuseppe Tomasi di Lampedusa**, Vicolo della Neve all'Alloro, a cultural centre and wine bar with a small museum and bookshop, that hosts concerts and readings, and runs evening guided tours of the area in Italian and English (tours usually Thurs–Sun 6.30pm & 9pm; Ⓦwww.parcotomasi.it; €6.50). Even if you're not interested in Lampedusa himself, the centre has a nice cobbled garden where you can relax over a granita or a glass of Sicilian red.

Villa Giulia

A few minutes' walk from the piazza along Via Lincoln is Palermo's best central park, **Villa Giulia**, an eighteenth-century garden that provides a welcome escape from the traffic. Attractions include aromatic gardens, a children's train,

ringing of the vesper (evensong) bell was the signal to drive the French out of Sicily; most were eventually slaughtered by the oppressed islanders.

The Convento dei Cappuccini

Of all the attractions on the edge of Palermo, the **Convento dei Cappuccini** (daily 9am–noon & 3–5pm; €1.50) is the most intriguing, reachable by taking bus #327 or walking from Piazza Indipendenza to Via Pindemonte, and following signposts for a couple of hundred metres. For several hundred years this monastery retained its own burial ground, placing its dead in catacombs under the church. Later, responding to requests and bequests from rich laymen, many others began to be interred here, right up until 1881. The bodies (some 8000 of them) were preserved by various chemical and drying processes – including dehydration, the use of vinegar and arsenic baths, and treatment with quicklime – and then placed in niches along various corridors, dressed in the suit of clothes that they had previously provided for the purpose. The rough-cut stone corridors are divided according to sex and status, with different caverns reserved for men, women, the clergy, doctors, lawyers and surgeons. Suspended in individual niches and pinned with an identifying tag, the bodies are vile, contorted, grinning figures, some decomposed beyond recognition, others complete with skin, hair and eyes, fixing you with a steely stare. Those that aren't arranged along the walls lie in stacked glass coffins, and, to say the least, it's an unnerving experience to walk among them. Times change, though, as Patrick Brydone noted in his late eighteenth-century *A Tour Through Sicily and Malta*:

> Here the people of Palermo pay daily visits to their deceased friends ... here they familiarize themselves with their future state, and chuse the company they would wish to keep in the other world. It is a common thing to make choice of their nich, and to try if their body fits it ... and sometimes, by way of a voluntary penance, they accustom themselves to stand for hours in these niches ...

Of all the skeletal bodies, saddest are the many remains of babies and young children, nothing more than spindly puppets. Follow the signs for the sealed-off cave that contains the coffin of two-year-old Rosalia Lombardo, who died in 1920. A new process, a series of injections, preserved her to the extent that she looks as though she's asleep – after over seventy years. Perhaps fortunately, the doctor who invented the technique died before he could tell anyone how it was done.

Eating

You can eat well and cheaply in Palermo, either snacking in bars and at market stalls or sitting down in a score of good-value pizzerias and restaurants throughout the old town. Basic foodstuffs are particularly good here: snacks like *arancini*, pastries and ice cream, as well as more substantial pizzas are among the best you'll taste in Sicily, if not Italy. Fish is a feature on menus in more expensive trattorias and restaurants that advertise *cucina casalinga* or *cucina siciliana*; the local speciality is *pasta con le sarde*: macaroni with fresh sardines, fennel, raisins and pine kernels. It's worth noting that eating places tend to close early, especially in the central old town, where if you turn up at 10pm the waiters are likely to be packing up around you. For the most popular places, go before 8pm, or be prepared to wait in line.

Breakfast, snacks and cakes

Almost any bar or *pasticceria* is a good bet first thing in the morning, with **breakfast** pastries fresh from the bakeries. But for something more substantial than just *cornetti* head for one of the following places:

Pasticceria Alba Piazza Don Bosco 7. Wonderful pastries.

Caffé Ateneo Via Maqueda 170. Central café-bar, opposite San Cataldo church on the corner of Via dell'Università, bursting with *arancini*, pastries and the like.

Bar Costa Via G. d'Annunzio 15 (off Viale della Libertà, north of Piazza Boccaccio). High-class *pasticceria* in the north of the modern city, which specializes in lemon crème.

Ferrara Piazza Giulio Césare 46. Just to the left as you exit the train station, this has a good range of fast-food snacks as well as complete lunches.

Franco U Vastiddaru Piazza Marina 1. Though you pay for the location here, the pizzas, salads, burgers and fries are quite decent. Stand up to eat or take to the outdoor garden, where you'll meet mostly tourists.

Bar Mazzara Via Generale V. Magliocco 15 (corner of Piazza Ungheria). Lampedusa is supposed to have written parts of *The Leopard* here in this smart snack bar/*pasticceria*. Ice cream and *arancini* also available, as is a great array of marzipan goodies.

Panineria Via Trabia 35 (off Via Maqueda, close to Teatro Mássimo). Good sandwiches, either toasted or filled rolls; pizza slices, too.

Caffé San Domenico Piazza San Domenico. Outdoor tables close to the Vuccíria market for your early-morning coffee and *cornetto*.

Pasticceria Scimone Via Imera 8 and Via V. Miceli 18b (both north of Via Mosca). Excellent *pasticceria* whose wares can also be eaten at *Trattoria La Cambusa* (see p.107).

Bar Spinnato Via Príncipe di Belmonte 115. Classy *pasticceria* and bar with great ice cream. Pianist plays outdoors in summer.

Ice cream

One of the city's prime glories is its *gelaterie* (ice-cream shops), and you might want to follow local custom and experiment with a morning *brioche con gelato* (ice cream in a bun). You can buy ice cream just about anywhere, but Palermo has some classic shops and cafés – famed all over Italy – especially in the newer, northern part of the city.

Da Ciccio Corso dei Mille 73. Round the corner from the train station, this tiny, inexpensive place is usually packed.

Cofea Via Villareale 18. Superb ice cream. Try a granita too.

Ilardo Foro Italico I 12 (at the end of Via Alloro towards the water). The *Ilardo* has been in business for decades and is well known for its very good (and luridly coloured) ice cream. Open from 4pm till late evening. Closed Oct–May.

San Francesco Piazza San Francesco. Just to the side of the *Antica Focacceria San Francesco*

Food markets

Some of the best snacks are on sale in Palermo's markets, mostly traditional takeaway food – chopped boiled octopus (*purpu* in Sicilian), *arancini*, cooked artichokes, as well as bread, fruit and vegetables. In every market, you'll also find stalls selling *pani cu' la meuza* – bread rolls filled with sautéed beef spleen or tripe, which either come unadorned (*schiettu*, meaning "nubile") or topped with fresh ricotta and caciocavallo cheese (*maritatu*, "married").

The best-known market is at Vuccíria, off Via Roma between Corso Vittorio Emanuele and the San Domenico church, but there's also food on sale at the Ballarò market in Piazza del Cármine (p.90) and along Via Sant'Agostino (p.92). The Ballarò market, in particular, has a few very basic *hosterie* – wooden tables scattered around the market stalls – where you can accompany your snack with a beer or two.

(see below) and run by the same people, this is a good old-town place with tables in the square, open till 4am.

Stancampiano Via Notarbartolo 51. Not very central – in the modern north of the city – but well known for its award-winning ice cream.

Pizza places

Although you can buy slices throughout the day in bars and cafés, proper restaurants usually only serve **pizza** at night, because it takes hours to set up and light the wood-fired ovens. However, there are a couple of exceptions to this rule in Palermo, and several places do serve pizza at both lunch and dinner on Sundays. Some of the outlets listed below also serve other food, too: on the whole, though, the best pizzas are served in those places that pre-pare nothing else, save perhaps salad and the odd bowl of pasta. Since these restaurants are the cheapest option for a sit-down meal, the most popular get packed at the weekends, full of young people intent upon a night out rather than just a meal. At all of the places below, you'll be able to eat and drink inexpensively, with pizza, salad and wine rarely coming to more than €15 a head.

Al 59 Piazza Giuseppe Verdi 59. Alfresco dining in a large, covered bamboo terrace with a central fountain, opposite the Teatro Mássimo, a fine place to while away an evening. Plenty of pasta available too. Closed Wed. Open late.

Antica Focacceria San Francesco Via A. Paternostro 58 (off Corso Vittorio Emanuele and opposite the church of San Francesco). Splendid old-time pizzeria (open since 1834) with marble-topped tables and floor, cast-iron sur-roundings and authentic Sicilian fast food, from fresh pizza slices (€2) to other oven-baked snacks. See above for *gelateria*.

Antica Pizzeria Belmonte Via Príncipe di Belmonte 81. In the heart of the modern shopping district, there's nothing very old about the *Antica Pizzeria*, but it's a good place to eat – and near lively central bars.

Bellini Piazza Bellini. Housed at the back of the Teatro Bellini, the large pizza ovens are in

business most of the day. At night, sit at outdoor tables underneath La Martorana church – one of the city's more romantic locations. Arrive before 8.30pm to avoid the crowds. Closed Wed & Dec–Jan.

Pizzeria Italia Via Orologio 54 (off Via Maqueda, just before Teatro Mássimo). One of the best in central Palermo. It's crowded, noisy and the pizzas are superb – try the "Palermitana", made with anchovies, breadcrumbs, pine nuts, cheese and olive oil, or tasty creations using classic Sicilian ingredients like aubergine, pork sausage, capers and olives. Eves only. Closed Mon.

Trabia Via Trabia 35, off Via Maqueda, just before Teatro Mássimo. This quick stop is more of an adjunct to the fast-food/sandwich/ takeaway joint next door than a restaurant, but still a useful spot for *forno a legna* pizzas, mixed salads and house wine. Open till around 11pm.

Restaurants

There are several budget eateries around Stazione Centrale, not all of them the tourist traps you might expect. Other **restaurants** are scattered all over

---

Meal prices

The restaurants listed are graded according to the following price categories:
Inexpensive: under €15   **Moderate**: €15–30
Expensive: €30–50   **Very expensive**: over €50
These prices reflect the per person cost of a full meal including wine and cover charge; see p.53 for more details.

the city, and many excellent local places serving *cucina casalinga* are hidden in gloomy old-town streets: you might want to take a taxi late at night if you feel unsure about walking there. At the other end of the scale, Palermo also has several top-notch restaurants worth considering if you want to taste the very best Italian food, and although prices in these are high, they're considerably less than equivalents elsewhere in Italy. **Non-Italian food** is becoming more common in Palermo, though some places have a mediocre menu and a short life; we've listed the best options below. Finally, it's worth bearing in mind that some of Palermo's best restaurants are way **out of the centre**, known to locals for their classic Sicilian cookery but fairly inaccessible for most visitors. If you've got a car, or someone to drive you, try one of those listed below; always ring first to check opening times.

Stazione Centrale and around

Trattoria-Pizzeria Enzo Via Maurolico 17/19 (very close to Stazione Centrale; turn left as you exit the station). Perhaps the city's best bargain for full-blown meals, the *Enzo* serves hefty portions of pizza, pasta and basic meat and fish at low prices – you'll be hard pressed to spend over €9, even with wine. No credit cards. Closed Fri. Inexpensive.

Trattoria Trápani Piazza Giulio Césare; opposite the station, next to the *Albergo Elena*. This basic family-run trattoria is a good bet for lunch, with filling, tasty food. Closed Sun. Inexpensive.

Trattoria al Vicolo Piazza San Francesco Saverio ☏091.651.2464. A good atmosphere and local specialities in a small but smart place in the Albergheria district, accessible from Corso Tukory (fifth on the right as you head west) or Piazza Cármine. Closed Sun. Moderate.

Corso Vittorio Emanuele and around

Caffè d'Oriente Piazza Cancellieri 8 ☏091.326.832. Also known as *Caffè Arabo*, this is an authentic slice of Tunisia in a sequestered nook close to the Quattro Canti (up Via Monte Vergine from Corso Vittorio Emanuele). With seats inside and in the piazza, there's a wide selection of rich and filling rice and couscous dishes, some outstanding salads, marzipan sweets and *frullati* to finish. Belly-dancers do their stuff at weekends, and narghiles are on hand for a postprandial smoke. You can also sit at the bar here – like the restaurant, open till late. Closed Mon. Moderate.

Trattoria La Cambusa Piazza Marina 16. Excellent old-town restaurant specializing in fish and also serving *semifreddo* – ice cream with brittle almond topping. Closed Mon. Moderate.

Casa del Brodo Corso Vittorio Emanuele 175. In business for over a century, this place attracts both locals and tourists to its two small rooms. *Bolliti di manzo* and *lingua in salsa verde* are the specialities and there's also a good tourist menu, which includes a selection of antipasti but not drinks. Moderate.

Al Covo de'i Beati Paoli Piazza Marina 50. In a great location right on Piazza Caribaldi, with outdoor tables, though you may have to wait for one, especially on weekend evenings. The pizzas are good and service is brisk. Closed Mon in winter. Moderate.

Il Garage Piazza Ecce Uomo just across from Il Gesù ☏333.490.6356. A great little hole-in-the-wall restaurant, whose affable Tunisian owner cooks very good homemade fish, lamb and couscous dishes. Also makes a great beer or wine stop. It's quite hard to find, but ask anyone in the vicinity for "Mario" and they'll direct you. Inexpensive.

Trattoria Mafone Piazza Papireto 15. Also known as *da Massimo*, this neighbourhood trattoria sits a few short blocks behind the cathedral, with tables in the piazza. The menu is almost exclusively seafood, with a great speciality of *fettucine da Massimo*, a filling pesto dish with fresh clam and shrimp. Closed Mon. Moderate.

Trattoria Normanni Piazza della Vittória 25. Just off Piazza dell'Indipendenza, this reliable place attracts mainly locals. The speciality, *spaghetti ai Normanni*, is a terrific concoction of shrimps, aubergines, fresh tomatoes and grated peanuts. Arrive early to be sure of a table outside. Closed Sun. Moderate.

Trattoria Primavera Piazza Bologni 4 ☏091.329.408. Bright and lively neighbourhood trattoria, between the cathedral and Quattro Canti, serving genuine Sicilian food; there's a nice little summer terrace too. A short list of pastas, fresh fish and meat (home-made sausage) are served up to an enthusiastic local clientele, though service isn't the greatest. Reservations advised on weekend evenings. No credit cards. Closed Mon & Sun evening. Moderate.

Al Santa Caterina Corso Vittorio Emanuele 256 –258. You can eat on a balcony overlooking the corso at this large first-floor restaurant, housed in a sixteenth-century *palazzo*. There's an extensive menu and loud pop music. Closed Wed. Moderate.

Santandrea Piazza Sant'Andrea ✆091.334.999. Chic and popular restaurant, a stone's throw away from Piazza San Domenico and the Vucciria market from which most of the ingredients are obtained. Menus don't exist, and dishes are seasonal and generally delicious, if somewhat pricey. Home-made desserts are fantastic and there's a good wine list. Book early if you want to sit outside. Closed Tues & Jan. Expensive.

Trattoria Stella *Hotel Patria*, Via Alloro 104 (corner of Via Aragona). The hotel is no more (though you'll see the sign over the entrance), but the restaurant spills out into a lovely late-medieval courtyard, a super place to spend the evening, though it can get crowded. Specializes in barbecued lamb and fish; the *calamaro imbottito grilleè* is a favourite. Closed Mon in winter, Sun evening July & Aug. Moderate.

The modern city

Hostaria Al Duar 2 Via Ammiraglio Gravina 31. There's regular Italian food at this friendly restaurant near the northern end of Via Roma, but the best bet is the superb-value *Completo Tunisino* – a huge pile of Tunisian food, which comes as several different courses and ends with couscous. Closed Wed. Moderate.

Trattoria a' Cuccagna Via Príncipe di Granatelli 21a, off Via Roma before the Teatro Politeama. This long-established, wood-panelled restaurant, whose walls are crammed with local memorabilia, serves authentic Sicilian food, including *escalope al marsala*. Expensive.

Trattoria Macco Via B. Gravina 85, off Piazza Sturzo. At the top of Via Roma, this pleasant trattoria specializes in Sicilian dishes – swordfish

involtini and spaghetti with *ricci*, for example. Good local wine. Moderate.

La Medina Via Príncipe di Belmonte 31, opposite Piazza Florio. Newly redecorated in classical Arab decor with beautiful inlaid mosaics on the walls, this spacious restaurant does everything well from Tunisian to Italian to continental, though its specialities are *brick della casa* and couscous. Moderate.

La Pagoda Via M. Stabile 28 (between Via Roma and Via Ruggero Séttimo). Apart from the usual pasta and pizzas there are a few unusual foreign dishes on offer here – *risotto Thailandese* for one. Closed Mon. Inexpensive.

La Traviata Piazza Olivella 18. Quiet restaurant nestled in a quiet alleyway just steps from the Museo Archeológico, it serves good pasta dishes for around €6 and a big selection of pizzas. Moderate.

Le Tre Sorelle Via Volturno 110 ✆091.585.960. Popular new trattoria, not far from the Teatro Mássimo, whose €12 seafood menu changes daily. Closed Sun. Moderate.

Restaurants out of the centre

La Scuderia Viale del Fante 9 ✆091.520.323. Classic Sicilian and Italian cuisine at a restaurant near the stadium at La Favorita. The food is terrific, the prices less so; advance reservations are advised. Closed Sun & Aug. Expensive.

Osteria Al Tari Piazza G. le Cascino 45 ✆091.546.436. In the shadow of Monte Pellegrino, in the north of the city, this is a lovely local restaurant serving authentic Sicilian food. Closed Sun. Moderate.

Trattoria da Turiddu Via Ugo La Malfa ✆091.636.0085. This fantastic fish restaurant is a long ride north of the centre by taxi – on the road to the airport, before Sferracavallo. But the trip is rewarded by a set meal (there's no menu) that encompasses plate after plate of marvellous fish and seafood. Closed Tues. Moderate.

Drinking, nightlife and entertainment

After dark and over much of the city, Palermo's frenetic lifestyle stops, pedestrians flit quickly through the shadows, and the main roads are given over to speeding traffic and screaming police sirens. You may find the empty streets off-putting if you're on foot, but keeping to the main thoroughfares should minimize the possibility of problems. The city centre's few **bars** tend to close at around 9pm, though **birrerias** stay open later, and in summer life continues unabated until the small hours at **Mondello** (see p.113). Palermo's newer parts, around Viale della Libertà, see more street-life, with an energetic *passeggiata* and cruising cars blasting away like mobile discotheques. If none of this is your scene, then there is more cultural **entertainment** to be had back in the city centre, where music, theatre and dance performances, and arts events, are staged. Along with the larger mainstream venues, there are a good number of bars and clubs which put on live music and entertainment.

To find out **what's on** in Palermo, check the listings in *Lapis* or the daily *Il Giornale di Sicilia* (see p.79).

Bars and birrerias

Places to **drink** in – as opposed to a coffee stop – drift in and out of fashion, and you'll have to follow the crowds to find the current favourite. Many of them are in the northern quarters of the city, some of them a bus- or taxi-ride away, and the only central street geared up to evening drinks being the traffic-free **Via Príncipe di Belmonte**, which has a glitzy selection of bars and *pasticcerie*. Worth checking, though, are the bars along Via Candelai, a favourite haunt of students.

American Bar Grande Albergo Sole, 5th floor, Corso Vittorio Emanuele 291 (near the Quattro Canti). Stunning roof-terrace bar, from where you can gaze across the rooftops to the city's church domes and the mountains behind. Excellent place for a sunset drink and well worth the slightly inflated prices.

Champagneria del Mássimo Via Spinuzza 59. Charming wine bar with outdoor seating near the Teatro Mássimo; it's a lively spot on summer nights and stays open till late.

La Corrida Piazza Olivella 9. One of a line of bars opposite the archeological museum, this late-opening place is good for a snack and a sit-down.

Drunks Via Candelai 28. An aptly named rock-n-roll pub humming with the local university crowd. Beers on tap are €1.50, and there's a long list of strong cocktails: try the deadly Nelson – bourbon, vermouth and crema cacao – but not on an empty stomach. Open until 2am.

Bar Fiera Vecchia Piazza della Rivoluzione. Favoured by the young, this handsome aluminium and dark wood bar serves a great variety of cocktails. There's also a restaurant upstairs.

Il Golosone Piazza Castelnuovo. A popular place for drinks and fancy *paste* (including *frutta di Martorana*), owned by the same people who run the *Bar Spinnato* (see p.105).

Caffè del Kàssaro Corso Vittorio Emanuele 390 (near Quattro Canti, with another entrance in Via San Salvatore). Draught and bottled beers, panini, tables outside, and rock, blues and funk music. Open late in summer.

Kursaal Kalhesa Foro Italico 21. Set deep in the rock of the *foro*, this slick café and wine bar (*enoteca*) is furnished with traditional Sicilian furniture and has a huge fire in winter, with English and European newspapers to browse through. There's also live music (see below) and Internet available (€6.50 per hr). Closed Mon.

Lord Green Pub Via E. Parisi 30, at the corner of Garzilli. A nice neighbourhood place with a slight edge to the crowd; stays open till late.

Bar Marcuso Via Príncipe di Belmonte 84. Beer, milkshakes, pizza slices and a good-humoured atmosphere, with seats outside.

The Navy Via Cala 46. The only place for a beer on the harbour, the decor is rather staid, though at times reminiscent of an English pub, with a nautical theme and British beers.

Parco Letterario Giuseppe Tomasi di Lampedusa Vicolo della Neve all'Alloro ⓦwww.parcotomasi.it. Just off Via Alloro, this cultural centre dedicated to the Sicilian author offers a large wine list, with antipasti, panini and good granita as well. A cool and quiet place to stop, afternoon or evening, with outdoor seating.

Pinguino Via Ruggero Séttimo 86. Famous *spremute*, milkshakes and a range of non-alcoholic cocktails, a popular stop for those with late-night munchies. Closed Mon.

Tabuca Piazza Marina 6. Small, quiet and refined drinking spot with tables outside in summer.

Villa Boscogrande Via Tommaso Natale 91. Way out in the northeast of the city, towards Sferracavallo, this *palazzo* was the setting for parts of Visconti's film of *The Leopard*; smart and expensive. Bus #628 from Piazza de Gásperi.

Clubs

Unlike drinking establishments, many of which are close to the centre, Palermo's **clubs** are almost exclusively found in the new, northern section of the city, especially on and around Viale Regione Siciliana. Apart from a few fleeting exceptions, they're expensive discos, chock-full of fashion victims and – unless you're very keen – rarely worth the long journey out there. Still, for anyone determined to party in Palermo itself, here's a list of the better places, but check posters and newspapers for the current popular venues. In summer, the scene switches to Mondello and Isola delle Femmine, while the beach at the Riserva Naturale Capo Gallo in Sferracavallo, about 30 minutes north of the city (℡091.671.6066, ⓦwww.riservamontepellegrino.palermo.it), is popular with student groups for ad hoc weekend parties until dawn. Note that for the discos, you may have to pay to "join" the club before they'll let you in.

Agricantus Via XX Settembre 82 ℡091.309.636.
Bloom Viale Regione Siciliana 6469 ℡091.688.9727.
Cuba Libre (aka Pay One) Via dei Nebrodi 55 ℡091.527.265.

Dancing Club Viale Piemonte 16 ℡091.348.917.
Julip's Viale Lazio 51 ℡091513.621.
Kandisky Discesa Tonnara 4 ℡091.637.5611.
Skylab Piazza Báida ℡091.673.7830.

Live music

There's no major **rock music** venue, and top British and American bands rarely make it further south than Naples, though the *Comune* regularly stages open-air rock events featuring local acts in the summer, usually in the Giardino Inglese and other green spaces – watch out for posters around the city for details.

The Teatro Mássimo on Piazza Verdi (℡091.605.3111, ⓦwww.teatromassimo.it) is the first choice for performances of **classical music** (Oct–June), ranging from opera and ballet to concerts and recitals; in summer it moves to the Teatro del Parco di Villa Castelnuovo, Viale del Fante 70b (℡091.605.3301), for concerts and outdoor performances of ballet and operetta. The central Teatro Politeama Garibaldi on Piazza Ruggero Séttimo (℡091.605.3315) and Teatro Golden, Via Terrasanta 60 (℡091.305.217), put on a pretty decent programme of concerts throughout the year; for the Golden, take bus #103 from the Politeama, or walk west along Via Dante and turn right at Piazza Virgilio. For folk music and dance performances, the Teatrino Ditirammu del Canto Populare, Via Torremuzza 6 in La Kalsa (℡091.617.7865, ⓦwww.teatrinoditirammu.it), is an intimate venue with seating for just 52. Throughout the year, Lo Spasimo, on Via dello Spasimo in La Kalsa (℡091.616.1486) runs an excellent series of concerts, both classical and jazz, many of them free, while the KalsArt festival (ⓦwww.kalsart.it; mid-June to mid-Sept) is a huge cultural extravaganza of live music, theatre and cinema events that take place at a number of venues in the La Kalsa district. Various local musical associations also coordinate musical events, among them ALEA, who have their office at Piazza G. Meli 5 (℡091.322.217), and the Associazione Siciliana Amici della Musica, at Piazza Marina (℡091.584.679).

For other **jazz** venues, the Teatro Golden has occasional gigs, and *Kursaal Kalhesa* (℡091.616.2282, ⓦwww.kursaalkalhesa.it) at Foro Italico 21 has jazz on Thursday nights.

Theatre and cinema

Palermo and its surroundings have a stack of other **theatres**, worth checking out if you speak Italian; the season generally runs from November to May. In particular, the Teatro Siciliano Zappalà, at Via Autonomia Siciliana (℡091.543.380, ⓦwww.teatrofrancozappala.it), features traditional theatre productions in Sicilian dialect. Mainstream theatres include the Teatro Biondo, Via Teatro Biondo 11, off Via Roma (T 091.582.364 or 091.743.4341, W www .teatrobiondo.it) and Teatro Lelio, Via Furitano 5a (T 091.681.9122), which favours national drama companies. For avant garde theatre, Teatro Libero, Salita Partanna 4, Piazza Marina (T 091.617.4040, W www.teatroliberopalermo.it), and fits the bill.

Cinemas show the latest films dubbed into Italian – it's rare to find films in their original language with subtitles. The main central screens are right next to each other at 160–166 Via Emerico Amari: ABC (T 091.329.246) and Imperia (T 091.611.3388).

Puppet theatre

The best theatrical experience, and something you should do at least once in Sicily, is visit a **puppet theatre**. There are tourist performances at the Museo delle Marionette (see p.98), but it's better to get to one of the surviving backstreet puppet theatres for a genuine experience: search out Cuticchio Mimmo, at Via Bara all'Olivella 52, close to the Museo Archeológico (T 091.323.400, W www.figlidartecuticchio.com; summer daily, off-season Sat & Sun 6.30pm; €6); Teatro Ippogrifo, Vicolo Ragusi 6, off Corso Vittorio Emanuele, not far from the Quattro Canti (T 091.329.194; one performance daily at 5.30pm; €10); for shows at Monreale, see p.119. You're best off confirming timings at the theatres or the tourist office.

Listings

Airlines Air Malta, Via Cavour 80 T 091.625.5848; Air Sicilia, Via G. Sciuti 180 T 091.702.0310; Alitalia, Via Mazzini 59 T 091.601.9111 or 848.865.643; British Airways, Falcone Borsellino airport T 091.702.0329 or 848.812.266; KLM, c/o Guccione, Via A. Gravina 80 T 091.581.146; Med Airlines, Falcone Borsellino airport T 091.702.0239; Meridiana, Via XII Genaio 1g T 091.702.0254; SAS, Via Cavour 80 T 091.611.1233; Tunis Air, Piazza Castelnuovo 12; T 091.611.1845.

American Express c/o Giovanni Ruggeri, Via Emerico Amari 38 T 091.587.144 (Mon–Fri 9am–1pm & 4–7pm, Sat 9am–1pm).

Banks and exchange Banks are open Mon–Fri 8.30am–1pm; many branches also open 2.45–3.45pm; most will exchange all travellers' cheques or cash for a nominal commission and accept all major credit, debit and charge cards. Central banks include: Banco di Sicilia, Via Roma 185 and Via Cavour 131/a; Cassa di Risparmio, Piazza Cassa di Risparmio 2, Via Libertà 185; and Banca Nazionale del Lavoro, Via Roma 291. There are exchange offices at both the airport (Mon–Fri 9am–4pm) and the main post office's BancoPosta, Via Roma 322 (bank hours).

Bike rental You can get free bike rental at Via Príncipe Belmonte, at the Giardino Inglese and Piazza Unità d'Italia. Otherwise, *Kursaal Kalhesa*, Foro Italico 21 T 091.616.2828, has bikes for €8 per day; Totò Cannatella, Via Papireto 14a T 091.322.425, charges €13.

Bookshops There's a large selection of English books from Feltrinelli, Via Maqueda 395, opposite the Teatro Mássimo (Mon–Sat 9am–8pm); from Mondadori, on the corner of Via Roma and Piazza San Domenico (also open until 8pm); and Libreria Flaccovio, Via Ruggero Séttimo 37.

Car rental Avis (Punta Raisi airport T 091.591.684; Via E. Amari 91 T 091.586.940); Eurauto (for camper vans: Via Príncipe Paternò 119 T 091.201.529); Europcar (airport T 091.591.688; Via Cavour 77a T 091.301.825); Hertz (airport T 091.213.112; Via Messina 7e T 091.323.439); Holiday Car Rental (airport T 091.591.687; Via E. Amari 85a T 091.325.155); Maggiore (airport T 091.591.681; Stazione Notarbartolo T 091.681.0801); Sicily By Car (airport T 091.591.250; Via M. Stabile 6a T 091.581.045).

Car repairs ACI, Viale delle Alpi 6 T 116.

Consulates UK, Via Cavour 117 T 091.326.412; USA, Via Vaccarini 1 T 091.305.857; Netherlands, Via Roma 489 T 091.581.521. Other major consulates are in Naples or Rome, including: Australia, Via Alessandria 215, Rome T 06.852.721; Eire,

Piazza di Campitelli 3, Rome ☎06.697.9121; New
Zealand, Via Zara 28, Rome ☎06.440.2928.
Emergency numbers General emergencies
☎113; Carabinieri ☎112; road accident ☎116
or 091.656.9511; fire brigade ☎115; ambulance
118; *Ufficio Denunce* (for lost property or theft)
☎113 or 091.210.324.
Ferry and hydrofoil companies Grandi Navi
Veloci, at the port at Calata Marinai d'Italia
☎091.587.404, ⓦwww.grimaldi.it (for Livorno,
Rome and Tunis); Siremar, Via Francesco Crispi
118 ☎091.749.3111, ⓦwww.gruppotirrenia
.it/siremar (for Ústica); Tirrenia, at the port on Via
Molo ☎091.602.1111 (for Naples,
Genova and Cágliari); Ústica Lines, Via Cap. di
Bartolo 55 ☎091.844.9002, ⓦwww.usticalines
.it (for Naples, Ústica, Cefalù and the Aeolian
Islands).
Gay info ARCI Gay, Via Genova 7 ☎091.335.688.
Hiking Club Alpino Italiano, Via Garzilli 59
☎091.329.407; Club Alpino Siciliano, Via A. Paternostro 43 ☎091.581.323. For maps and details of
mountain refuges, see "Maps" below.
Hospital Policlínico, Via del Vespro 127
(☎091.655.1111). For emergency first aid, see
"Emergency numbers".
Internet access *Aboriginal Café*, via S. Spinuzza
51 (Mon–Sat 11am–3am, Sun 6pm–3am; €3.50
per hour); Galtourist, Stazione Maríttima (Mon–Fri
9.30am–1.30pm & 2.30–7pm, Sat 9.30am–
12.30pm, closed Jan & Feb; €6 per hour); Inter-
natational Point, via dei Candelai 11 (Tues–Sun
7pm–3am; €2 per hour); *Kursaal Kalhesa*, Foro
Italico 21 (daily 11am–late; €6.50 per hour);
Internett@mente, Via Sammartino 3a (Mon 3–8pm,
Tues–Sat 10am–8pm; €3.50 per hour).
Left luggage Stazione Centrale by track 8 (daily
6am–10pm; €3.50 for 5 hours); Stazione Maríttima (daily 7am–7.30pm; €2 for 12 hours).
Maps Detailed maps for hiking in the Monti Madonie from the Istituto Geográfico, Via Danimarca
25 ☎091.511.401; Cartoleria de Magistris, Via A.
Gagini 23 ☎091.589.233.

Newspapers English and European newspapers
and magazines are sold at the station, at *Kursaal
Kalhesa*, Foro Italico 21, and newsagents at the
top of Via Ruggero Séttimo. Local listings are in the
daily *Giornale di Sicilia*.
Parking Garages are: Di Giandomenico, Via Oreto
18, behind Stazione Centrale; Central Garage,
Piazza Giulio Césare 43, near station; Via Guardione 81, near Stazione Maríttima, behind Via Crispi;
Via Sammartino 24, town centre, off Via Dante;
Politeama, Via Parisi 6d, off Viale della Libertà near
Piazza Castelnuovo; Via Archimede 88, off Viale
della Libertà, also central. €8–15.50 per night to
leave a car; usually less when arranged through
your hotel.
Pharmacies All-night service at Lo Cascio, Via
Roma 1; Di Naro, Via Roma 207; and Pensabene,
Via Marina Stabile 177. Other chemists operate a
rota system, with the address of the nearest open
chemist posted on the door of each shop.
Post offices Main post office is in the Palazzo
delle Poste at Via Roma 322; poste restante at
counters #15 and #16 (Mon–Sat 8am–6.30pm).
There is also a branch at the Stazione Centrale
(same hours, except closed Sat).
Scooter rental Rent a Scooter, Via San Meccio
10 (near Piazza Ungheria) ☎091.336.804; or
Motorent, Via E. Amari 91 (☎091.602.3455)
Supermarkets UPIM, Via Roma (corner of Piazza
San Domenico); Standa, Via Libertà 30 (junction
with Via Archimede); GS, Piazza Marina (parking
available); all open Mon–Sat until 8pm.
Telephone offices ASTT is on Piazza Giulio
Césare, directly opposite the train station (daily
9am–10pm).
Travel agents CTS, Via Garzilli 28 (off Via Dante,
between Piazza Lolli and Piazza Castelnuovo)
☎091.611.0713 (Mon–Fri 9am–1pm & 3.30–
7pm); or Pietro Barbaro, Via Príncipe di Belmonte
51/55 ☎091.333.333 (Mon–Fri 9am–1pm &
4–6pm, Sat 9am–1pm).
Women's movements ARCI Donna, Via di
Giovanni 14 ☎091.345.799.

Around Palermo

Any respite from Palermo's noise is welcome, and it's worth taking the time
to get out of the city at least once. The easiest trips, to **Mondello** and **Monte
Pellegrino**, can fill in a few spare hours whenever you like, though Palermitans
tend to pack both destinations to the gills on summer Sundays. The other

retreat, to the cathedral town of **Monreale**, demands more serious attention; you could see it in an afternoon, but consider a full day (and possibly a night) to get the most out of it and the surrounding valley. Less demanding is a jaunt west to the small family resorts that line the **Golfo di Carini**, a change in pace from the frenetic action at Mondello. Side-trips east, to **Bagheria** and **Solunto**, won't occupy more than half a day out from the city, and you could always see them as a stop on the route out of Palermo, along the Tyrrhenian coast. Travelling south from the capital, you can also make a stop at the Albanian settlement of **Piana degli Albanesi**, couched on an upland plain in thoroughly pleasant surroundings – the Easter celebrations here are justly renowned.

Bus and train services to all these places are good; details are given in the text and "Travel details", p.128. For a real change of air, though, jump on a ferry or hydrofoil to the island of **Ústica**, as little as an hour and a quarter from the city. With good, clean swimming and a lazy feel, you may end up staying longer than planned.

Mondello

Regular buses run the 11km to **MONDELLO**, the most scenic route passing through Acquasanta and then skirting the coast below Monte Pellegrino as far as Valdesi. From here, a marvellous two-kilometre sandy **beach** curves round to the small resort, tucked under the mountain's northern bluff. The beach is the main attraction, though Mondello does have a tiny working harbour, a jetty from which you can try your luck fishing, and the remnants of a medieval tower. Come in the day and you can split your time nicely between the beach and **eating** on the seafront, a major occupation here. There's a line of trattorias – some with outdoor terraces – where the temptingly fresh fish is displayed in boxes. Or you can grab some excellent snack food from the waterfront stalls – *pasta con le sarde*, deep-fried vegetables, shrimps and whitebait – and then hit the beach.

Stay late and summer nights at Mondello are fun, the venue for Palermo's *passeggiata*. The bars in the main square, Piazza Mondello, are packed, the roads around blocked with cruising cars full of the local youth, and open-air discos add a bit of excitement. In winter it's more laid-back and rarely busy, but the restaurants and snack stalls are still open and it usually stays warm enough to swim until well past the end of the season.

Practicalities

From Piazza Sturzo or Viale della Libertà, buses #806 and, in summer, #833 head to **Mondello**, a half-hour ride through the city's northwestern suburbs. The last bus back leaves around 11.30pm, and a taxi back to the centre costs about €30. There's a kiosk on the seafront in summer, with scraps of **tourist information** to hand out (open daily until late).

None of the **restaurants** along the front are particularly cheap, but you can put together inexpensive meals by eating from the snack stalls or buying portions of fresh, sliced *pólipo* (octopus) served at stand-up counters at the front of several restaurants.

If you do want to sit down and eat, good places along the front include *Da Calógero*, Via Torre di Mondello 22 (closed Mon Oct–June), close to the tower, which serves plates of mussels and other seafood dishes from €4, as well as *ricci di mare* – black, prickly sea urchins, which you can have with spaghetti. The slightly grander *Totuccio*, at no. 28 (closed Mon), has a first-floor balcony overlooking the sea, and serves similar food including dishes such as *zuppa di vóngole*. In the piazza, *Siciliando* (closed Wed) has a huge selection of pizzas, reasonably priced pasta dishes and an upstairs terrace (the best places are usually reserved; call ahead on ☎091.454.422), while the fancier *Sympathy* (☎091.454.470; closed Fri) beyond the piazza at Via Piano di Gallo 18, a continuation of the *lungomare*, has a few tables outside, attracts a local, well-heeled crowd and is more expensive; the house speciality is *fettuccine alla Michele* at €10. If you feel like really splashing out, the area's swankiest restaurant is the Disneyesque castle just offshore – the *Charleston* (☎091.450.171), which offers one of the best (expensive) dining experiences in Sicily, with the multi-course menu costing a cool €55, excluding wine. In the same complex, you can rent windsurfing equipment or spend the afternoon diving or snorkelling.

There are several **hotels** in Mondello, but all are impossibly full in summer and (mostly) very expensive. If you do fancy staying, ring first. *La Torre*, just at the end of the beach road (☎091.450.222, ☎091.450.033, ⓦwww.latorre .it; ⑤), is a modern establishment set apart from the beach and harbour, with good-sized rooms, and a terrace bar with views straight out to sea. Alternatively, the *Conchiglia d'Oro*, Via Chloe 9 (☎091.450.032, ☎091.450.359; ⑤), is set further back from the beach, but has a pool: it's quiet enough and very popular with families.

Monte Pellegrino: mountain and sanctuary

North of the city and a clear landmark visible from the port area, the massive bulk of **MONTE PELLEGRINO** splits Palermo from the bay at Mondello. The mountain was occupied as far back as 7000 BC: Paleolithic incised drawings were found in the Grotta d'Addaura on Pellegrino's northern slopes and there are casts of some of the best in Palermo's Museo Archeológico. Today, Monte Pellegrino is primarily a target for Sunday picnickers and pilgrims, here to visit the shrine of the city's patron saint, **St Rosalia.** William II's pious niece, Rosalia, renounced worldly things and fled to the mountain in 1159; nothing more was heard of her until the early seventeenth century, when a vision led to the discovery of her bones on Pellegrino. Pronounced sacred relics, the bones were processed around the city in a successful attempt to stay the ravages of a terrible plague, a ceremony that is re-enacted every July 15 and September 4, with a torchlight procession to the saint's sanctuary.

The half-hour **ride to the mountain** is extremely impressive (bus #812 from Piazza Sturzo or Teatro Politeama, though the frequency is erratic), providing wide views over Palermo and its plain. You enter the **Santuario di Santa Rosalia** (daily 7am–7pm) through a small chapel, built over a deep cave in the hillside where the bones of Rosalia were discovered in 1624. Inside, the water trickling down the walls is supposedly miraculous, while a bier contains a reclining golden statue of the saint. Goethe thought the statue "so natural and pleasing, that one can hardly help expecting to see the saint breathe and move". Certainly the saint's expression is realistic, though she seems rather smug, too – an effect perhaps induced by the huge pile of banknotes stacked up beside her, offerings from the faithful.

A small road to the left of the chapel leads to the cliff-top promontory – a half-hour's walk – where a more restrained statue of St Rosalia stares over the sprawling city. Another path, leading up from the Santuario to the right, takes you to the top of the mountain – 600m high, and around a forty-minute walk. Elsewhere, the trails that cover Monte Pellegrino are dotted with families picnicking, while kids play on rope swings tied to the trees. Heading back, wait until the heat drops and descend by the **Scala Vecchia**, a stepped path that twists from the road by the sanctuary all the way down to Le Falde, near the site of the city's exhibition ground, the Fiera del Mediterraneo. On the way, you can make a short diversion to the Castello Utveggio (built in 1932, now a management school) for more marvellous views, and regain the road at the bottom to pick up a bus back to the city centre.

Monreale

Beach and mountain are all right for a couple of hours' escape from the city, but the major excursion is to **MONREALE**, a small hill-town 8km southwest of Palermo that commands unsurpassed views down the Conca d'Oro valley, with the capital shimmering in the distant bay. Norman Lewis called the valley "the greatest and most glorious orchard and market garden in the world", noting that although "there was nothing of gold about it except the roofs of houses on nearby slopes, it frothed, bubbled and exploded with the voluptuous greenery of millions of trees and plants". This panorama from the "Royal Mountain" alone is worth making the trip for, though the real draw is not this, but the mighty Norman cathedral, hidden further in among the houses.

Buses #309 and #389 run frequently from Piazza dell'Indipendenza (outside the Porta Nuova, reached by bus #109 from Palermo's train station) through the western suburbs and up the valley, taking around twenty minutes. Bus #389 drops you right in Piazza Monreale by the Duomo; #309 leaves you in the centre of town, from where it's a few minutes' walk along Corso Pietro Novelli and Via Roma up to the cathedral.

The Duomo

Flanking one side of the town atop a sea-facing shelf of land, the **Duomo** (daily: May–Oct 8am–6.30pm; Nov–April 8am–12.30pm & 3.30–6.30pm) presides magisterially over the town and Conca d'Oro valley. The rather severe, square-towered exterior, though handsome enough, gives no hint of what's inside: the most extraordinary and extensive area of Christian medieval mosaicwork in the world, the apex of Sicilian-Norman art. Keep coins handy to switch on the lights inside if they aren't already on, though the chances are you won't be the only visitor here, as it's a regular coach stop. Bear in mind that, despite the continual influx of tourists, the same rules apply as in other Italian churches: miniskirts, shorts and bare shoulders are frowned upon, and you may not be allowed in if dressed inappropriately.

The cathedral and the town that grew up around it in the twelfth century owe their existence to young King William II's rivalry with his powerful Palermitan archbishop, the Englishman Walter of the Mill. Work had started on Walter's fine cathedral in the centre of the city in 1172. Determined to quickly break the influence of his former teacher, William endowed a new monastery in his royal grounds outside the city in 1174, and its abbey church – this cathedral – was thrown up in a matter of years. Already exempt from taxes and granted other privileges, the church consolidated its position when Monreale was made an archbishopric in 1183, two years before Walter's cathedral was

△ The Cathedral, Monreale

finished. This unseemly haste had two effects. A highly personal project, Monreale's power lasted only as long as William did: though he wanted to create a royal pantheon, he was the last king to be buried there; and later, when Roger II's tomb was removed from the cathedral at Cefalù, it went to Walter's cathedral in Palermo. But the speed with which the Duomo at Monreale was built assisted the splendid uniformity of its most famous feature, its interior art – a galaxy of coloured mosaic pictures bathed in a golden background.

The **mosaics**, almost certainly executed by Greek and Byzantine craftsmen, are a magnificent achievement, thought to have been completed in just ten years. Despite the sheer size of the decorated interior (102m by 40m), the gleaming mosaics form a circular and reinforcing picture from which it's possible to read the Testaments straight from the walls. Once inside, your eyes are drawn immediately over the wooden ceiling to the all-embracing half-figure of Christ in benediction in the **central apse**. It's an awesome and pivotal mosaic, the head and shoulders alone almost 20m high, face full of compassion, curving arms with outstretched hands seemingly encompassing the whole beauty of the church. Underneath sits an enthroned Virgin and Child, attendant angels and, below, the ranks of saints – each subtly coloured and identified by name. Interesting here is the figure of Thomas à Becket (marked "SCS Thomas Cantb", between Silvester and Laurence), canonized in 1173 (just before the mosaics were begun), and presumably included as a political show of support by William for the papacy – an organization for which Walter of the Mill's lay supporters, the nobility, held no brief. The two **side-apses** are dedicated to SS Peter (right) and Paul (left), the arches before each apse graphically displaying the martyrdom of each – respectively, an inverse crucifixion and a beheading. The **nave mosaics** are no less remarkable, an animated series that starts with the Creation (above the pillars to the right of the altar) and runs around the whole church, while the darker **aisle mosaics** depict the teachings of Jesus. Most scenes are instantly recognizable: Adam and Eve; Abraham on the point of sacrificing his son; positively jaunty Noah's-ark scenes showing the ship being built, recalcitrant animals being loaded aboard, Noah's family peering out of the hatches; the Feeding of the Five Thousand; and the Creation itself, a set of glorious, simplistic panels portraying God filling His world with animals, water, light … and Man.

It's difficult to keep your eyes off the walls, but it's worth roaming the whole building. Above the two thrones (royal and episcopal) are more mosaics: William receiving the crown from Christ (less graceful than a similar picture, of Roger, in La Martorana; see p.89) and the king offering the cathedral to the Virgin. Both William I and William II are buried here in side chapels, the cathedral's progenitor in the white marble sarcophagus to the right of the apse.

The southwest corner of the cathedral gives access to the **tower** (daily 9.30am–6pm; €1.50), well worth the entry fee. One hundred and eighty steps take you up to the roof, for views of the cloisters (see below), from where you continue around the church and upwards, leaving you standing right above the central apse – an unusual and precarious vantage-point. Back inside, tickets for the collection of reliquaries in the **treasury** (daily 9.30am–noon & 3.30–6pm; €1.50) are sold at the end of the left aisle.

The apse and cloisters

Although all its real artistic attractions are inside, the cathedral's solid exterior merits a closer look too, particularly the enormous triple **apse** (signposted "*absidi*") – a polychromatic jumble of limestone and lava, supported by slender columns and patterned by a fine series of interlacing arches. You have to circle the cathedral to see this, down a street to the left of the entrance. And it's certainly worth visiting the **Chiostro dei Benedettini**, or cloisters (Mon–Sat 9am–7pm, Sun 9am–1pm; €4.50), part of William's original Benedictine monastery. The formal garden is surrounded by an elegant arcaded quadrangle, 216 twin columns supporting slightly pointed arches – a legacy of the Arab influence in Sicilian art. Look closely at the carved capitals of the twelfth-century columns and you'll see that no two are the same: on one, armed hunters do battle with winged beasts; another has two men lifting high a casket of wine; elsewhere are flowers, birds, snakes and foliage; while around the whole facade of the arches, geometric shapes dip and dance from column to column. A single column in the southwest corner even forms a little fountain, in its own quadrangle. Entrance to the cloisters is from Piazza Gugliemo, in the corner by the right-hand tower of the cathedral.

The rest of town

After you've seen the cathedral, there's a lot to be said for just strolling the dense latticework of steep streets – especially in the early afternoon when few people are about. Several Baroque churches (mostly locked) are hidden here and there; the **Chiesa del Monte**, in Via Umberto I, has stuccoes by Serpotta. At some point, wander into the grounds of the new convent (built in 1747) behind the cathedral cloisters for the fine views from the **belvedere**, straight down the valley. The convent itself displays Pietro Novelli's fine seventeenth-century painting of St Benedict handing out bread to assorted monks and knights. Elsewhere, the modern **Istituto Statale d'Arte per il Mosaico** (200m south of the car park to the right, past the Carabinieri barracks) is open during term time for anyone interested in watching mosaic-restorers at work. Otherwise, it's easy to while away time in the couple of bars in Piazza Vittorio Emanuele, overlooking a fountain and palm trees.

Practicalities

Information is available from the **tourist office** (Mon–Sat 8.30am–1.30pm & 2.30–6.30pm; ☏091.656.4501), in the cathedral square. There's limited **accommodation** – try the quaint *La Ciàmbra* B&B, Via Sanches 23 (☏091.640.95.65 or 335.842.58.65, ⓦwww.laciambra.com; ❷), wedged into a web of narrow gardened streets behind the Duomo's apse, or the pleasant, family-run *Carrubella Park*, Via Umberto I 233 (☏091.640.2187; ❺), with good views.

There's a good selection of **places to eat** in the streets just off the Piazza Duomo, though it can be pricey. A good choice is *Dietro L'Angolo*, at Via Piave 5 (a minute's walk from the Duomo towards the belvedere), with spectacular views of the valley from its terrace, and spaghetti dishes at around €7. Back up towards the Duomo and heading left down a side street before reaching the apse, *Mizzica*, Via Cappuccini 6 (closed Tues), is a popular choice, with a tourist menu at €14, while *Bricco & Bacco*, Via B. D'Acquisto 13, is a fairly standard brasserie-cum-wine-bar offering €13 menus. Along Via Roma from the cathedral, the *Trattoria da Peppino* (closed Thurs) is tucked away down a side street off Piazzetta Giuseppe Vaglica, with decent meals and pizzas in the evenings for around €13. Further out of town on Via Circonvallazione (the Palermo road), *La Fattoria* (The Farm) is a large garden restaurant, that is a favourite with Palermitani on Sundays and with coach parties all week. Its prices are very low (most dishes range from €3.50–6) and the house speciality, *pennette Caruso*, is particularly good; it's 3km by road from the centre, a stop on the bus route from Palermo, but far closer if you walk down the hill from the Duomo, below the main town car park. If you're in Monreale on a summer evening, stop by the Sanicola theatre, Via Benedetto di Aquisto 33 (℡091.640.9441), for one of its frequent **puppet shows** (Mon, Wed & Sat at 5.30pm & 9pm; €5).

Around Monreale: San Martino delle Scale and Báida

Seven kilometres out of Monreale, on a hill above the road to San Martino, you'll see the finely preserved twelfth-century Norman castle on the right, known as the **Castellaccio**. Once a fortified monastery built by William II, it's now run by the Sicilian Alpine Club as a mountain refuge, though if there's anyone at home they'll let you in to look around the castle. It's worth the twenty-minute scramble up for the views, which stretch over to the impressive white monastery at nearby **SAN MARTINO DELLE SCALE**. An ancient religious settlement, it's been taken over in recent years as a summer hill resort – holiday homes and Sunday-trippers are much in evidence. But the Benedictine monks are still there, and it's worth visiting their **Abbazia di San Martino** (Mon–Sat 9am–noon & 4.30–6.30pm, Sun 9–11am & 5–6.30pm) – supposedly founded by Gregory the Great in the sixth century – to see the frescoes by Pietro Novelli, a grand fountain and sculptures by Marabitti, and the eighteenth-century marble staircase, all in the abbey; the church itself is monumental but rather bland. The *Messina*, halfway between the abbey and the Castellaccio, at Via della Regione 108 (℡091.418.149; ❷), is a decent place to **stay** and also offers pizzas at €4.50 and other cheap meals.

You can reach San Martino from Monreale on the local #2 **bus**, or on the Virga buses that run three to four times a day from Palermo's Piazza Verdi (by the Teatro Mássimo), running through the wooded "Paradise Valley". At the eastern end of the valley, a road leads from the village of Boccadifalco (about 5km out of the capital) 2km north to **BÁIDA**, a tenth-century Saracen village (*baidha* is Arabic for "white"). Here, you'll find a convent built in the fourteenth century by monks from the Castellaccio, and an interesting church, which retains an ochre facade from its fifteenth-century construction, together with an earlier apse, and a statue of St John the Baptist, wrought by Antonello Gagini; ask for the custodian at Via del Convento 41. Báida is a pretty village, ringed by hills, and again there are direct buses from Palermo, most convenient of which is the #462 from Piazza Príncipe di Camporeale (itself reached by #122 from Stazione Centrale, or #110 from Piazza dell'Indipendenza).

West: the Golfo di Carini and inland

If you're looking for a **beach** to while away a few hours, then the small succession of holiday resorts along the **Golfo di Carini** are perfectly adequate, and certainly less exhaustingly trendy than Mondello. In fact, given their proximity to the capital, these small fishing ports are surprisingly undeveloped. Better still, they're sheltered by the huge mass of Monte Gallo to the east and protected from the waste ejected into the sea from the city by virtue of their location, tucked safely around the corner of the headland.

The coast: Sferracavallo to Terrasini

The nearest, adjacent towns of **SFERRACAVALLO** and **ISOLA DELLE FÉMMINE** are the best bet, and while the latter is uncomfortably close to a cement factory on one side, it's quickly forgotten once you're inside the town. The *isola* in question is a tiny offshore islet. Both towns run to pricey hotels and less-exclusive **campsites** – the closest official camping spots to Palermo: the two in Sferracavallo are listed on p.85; in Isola delle Fémmine (actually 1km west of town) the single site is only open in the summer months – *La Playa* (℡091.867.7001), which lies close to a sandy beach. For a decent **restaurant**, you need only head to the beach road where you'll have your pick from nearly a dozen places. *Ristorante Cutino*, Via Palermo 10 (closed Tues) in Isola delle Fémmine, is highly recommended, specializing in seafood with a €27 menu. There's similar good food at the *Scogliera Azzura*, Via Nazionale 10, right on the seafront, which is also a hotel that's very popular with families (℡ & ℻091.867.78.74; ❷).

Regular local **trains** stop in Isola delle Fémmine, which is also served by bus #628 from Viale del Fante (Stadio), near La Favorita (bus #101 or #107 from Stazione Centrale).

The train stops at other resorts on or just in from the coast, and there are more summer campsites around, at Capaci and Cinisi. The western promontory, **Punta Raisi**, is home to Palermo's airport, said to be controlled by the Mafia, who freight stocks of heroin, processed in factories deep in rural Sicily, out to the United States.

Further west, **TERRASINI**, forty minutes out of Palermo, is typical of the small ports along the gulf, with a sandy beach, several trattorias and a clutch of expensive tourist hotels. There's also a private collection of Sicilian painted carts in the **Museo Etnográfico**, hidden away on Via Carlo Alberto dalla Chiesa (June–Sept Mon–Sat 9am–8pm; Oct–May Mon–Sat 9am–12.30pm, Sun 9am–12.30pm & 4–7pm; €1.50): look out for the signposts near the main piazza, which point left from the main road as you head down to the sea; it's a right turn at the end of a cul-de-sac. On the waterfront, theatrical and musical performances are held in the courtyard of the **Palazzo d'Aumale** between July and September.

Inland: Carini, Montelepre and Partinico

The inland town of **CARINI** (reachable from Palermo either by train or an AST bus from Piazza Lolli), 5km from the coast, has a clutch of sixteenth-century churches, and what would be a first-rate **castle** were it not in a pitiful state of decay, closed and forgotten. The battlemented fortress dates from Norman times and was subsequently held by some of Sicily's leading feudal dynasties: in 1508 a famous murder occurred here, immortalized in an anonymous contemporary poem considered to be the highest example of Sicilian popular versifying, *La Baronessa di Carini*.

Montelepre

A very minor road climbs 11km south of Carini to the small town of **MONTELEPRE** (direct AST bus from Palermo), notable only for its history. To Sicilians, Montelepre is instantly familiar as the birthplace and home of the notorious bandit **Salvatore Giuliano** (1922–50), who hid out in the hills and caves around here, slipping into town at night to see family and friends. Not only was he hunted by the Carabinieri, but platoons of hand-picked soldiers combed the *maquis* for him and, as his ambitions and legend grew, so did his charisma, enhanced by such madcap gestures as writing to President Truman and offering the annexation of Sicily to the United States, in a last-ditch attempt to sever the island from the Italian State. Known to his comrades as Turiddu, he was a folk hero to the Sicilian people, embodying their hopes and frustrations more than any other individual in recent history. He was betrayed and killed, his body found in a courtyard in Castelvetrano, in the south, on July 5, 1950. No one knows exactly what happened or who was responsible for his death, though his deputy, Gaspare Pisciotta, chose to confess to the crime. Many doubt that he was the one who pulled the trigger, and Pisciotta himself was on the verge of making revelations at his trial that would have implicated high-ranking Italian politicians, when he too was assassinated in his cell at Ucciardone prison. Whatever the truth, there's a pungently Sicilian flavour to the affair, full of betrayal and counterbetrayal, heroes and villains, and Giuliano's legend has since grown to Robin Hood dimensions, nowhere more so than in his home territory around Montelepre. As his biographer Gavin Maxwell was told: "They should change the name of that village, really – anything else but Montelepre would do. No one can look at it straight or think straight about it now – it just means Giuliano."

The house in which Giuliano lived, **Casa Giuliano**, Via Pietro Merra 189 (daily 9am–1pm & 3.30–7.30pm; free), is now a museum run by Giuliano's nephew, though there is more Giuliano memorabilia on display at the **hotel** and **restaurant** dedicated to the man himself, further down the same road. A modern construction built to look like a castle, *Castello di Giuliano*, Via Pietro Merra 1 (☎091.894.10.06, ⓦwww.castellodigiuliano.it; ❷), has a number of nicely done rustic/medieval-style rooms, and the attached restaurant serves a plentiful menu of good seafood dishes, including *pesce fantasia allo chef.*

Partinico

Montelepre is only one of a whole arc of villages to the southwest of Palermo where poverty and desperation have long been ingrained. Outlawry is deeply rooted, not just in its romantic guise of banditry, but in the more sinister network of mutual interests and organized criminality that bind politicians and mafiosi together. As gripping a story as Giuliano's, is that of **Danilo Dolci** and his campaign for relieving some of the burden weighing down the people of **PARTINICO**. Around 10km southwest of Montelepre on the SS113 (and 1hr by train from Palermo), this dreary and distressingly poor town is only distinguished for its connections with this social reformer, the "Sicilian Gandhi", who founded his first self-help and education centre here and campaigned tirelessly to have a dam built locally – something that was resisted at every turn by the Mafia and their political clients, who controlled the existing water supplies. For more on Dolci, and the villages along the Golfo di Castellammare – with which Partinico properly belongs – see pp.382–385. If you're driving this way, you might relish a break at the *Mamma Rosa*, at Piazza Stazione 5 (closed Tues) – a surprisingly good, if somewhat pricey, pizzeria-**restaurant** with veranda seating, which is located outside the village next to the train station.

East: to Bagheria and Solunto

You're likely to see both **Bagheria** and the ancient ruins at **Solunto** as easy half-day trips from the capital; regular **buses** (AST from Piazza Lolli) and frequent local **trains** swing out of Palermo and cut eastwards, across Capo Zafferano, stopping in both towns. It's a considerably more pleasant journey than it was in the eighteenth century, when the road – as described by Dacia Maraini in her memoir *Bagheria* – was not only foully potholed, but lined "with the heads of bandits impaled on pikestaffs ... dried by the sun, infested by flies, often with chunks of arms and legs with blackened blood sticking to the skin ..."

Bagheria

It's **BAGHERIA** that provides the first spark of interest on the run out through Palermo's uninspiring eastern suburbs. Just 14km from the city, it quickly established itself as a seventeenth- and eighteenth-century summer retreat, the Palermitan nobility sitting out the oppressive heat in a series of Baroque country villas scattered across town. The whole, in the words of Maraini, evoked "the atmosphere of a summer garden enriched by lemon groves and olive trees, poised between the hills, cooled by the salt winds". Most of the villas are still privately owned, however, and you'll need to find someone in the grounds (or ring the bell) to be allowed in.

Access to the notorious **Villa Palagonia** (Ⓦwww.palagonia.it; daily 9am–1pm & 4–7pm; €4) is easier: it's on Piazza Garibaldi, at the end of Via Palagonia, a good ten minutes' walk from the train station (left out of the station onto Corso Butera, then left onto Via Palagonia). Buses drop you in Corso Umberto, from where it's a straight walk. Known for its eccentric menagerie of grotesque gnomes, giants, gargoyles and assorted mutants, the villa was the brainchild of Ferdinand, Prince of Palagonia, a hunchback who – in league with the architect Tommaso Napoli – took revenge on his wife's lovers by cruelly caricaturing them. The garden walls are still amply furnished with the deformed monsters, though only 64 of the original 200 statues remain, and now in a rather deteriorated state. Nonetheless, they add entertainment to a wander around the well-stocked garden. Climbing an impressive stairway watched over by a menacing eagle that surmounts the pediment, the villa itself holds the **Salone degli Specchi** – its ceiling covered with mirrors, sadly in want of repair – and some good marbling.

From Corso Umberto, on the south side of Villa Palagonia, Via Trabia brings you to the more restrained Villa Trabia and **Villa Valguarnera** (also by Napoli), which comes as something of a relief after this madness, the latter displaying Bagheria's most sumptuous facade, pink and festooned with a royal coat of arms, Attic statues by Marabitti, and views out towards the sea. Villa Valguarnera's oval courtyard was one of the settings used in the Taviani brothers' film *Kaos*. Just when you thought you'd left the weirdness behind, **Villa Butera**, at the end of Corso Butera, has within its grounds a collection of wax figures in Carthusian apparel. Legend has it that their creator, Ercole Branciforti, had promised the erection of a Carthusian abbey in return for the granting of a prayer, and took the crafty way out when the prayer was answered.

A little further out from the centre (back to the train station and over the level crossing, 300m to the right), the **Villa Cattólica** (Tues–Sun 9.30am–7pm; €4.50) contains a good gallery of twentieth-century art and has regular exhibitions and a permanent exhibition of Bagheria's most famous son, Renato Guttuso (1912–87), whose brilliant use of colour and striking imagery made him one of Italy's most important modern artists.

Practicalities

If you fancy **staying the night** here, *Da Franco Il Conte* (Ⓣ091.966.815, Ⓕ091.969.515, Ⓦwww.dafrancoilconte.it; ❷) is a decent lodging with a pizzeria attached. For **food**, try the atmospheric *Ostaria Zza Mario*, off Via Goethe at Via Parenó 7, close to the Villa Palagonia (no credit cards; closed Mon). It's the oldest restaurant in town, has no menu and serves wine from the cask. For **ice cream** and other desserts, head for the *Bar Valentina* at Corso Umberto 4.

Solunto and around

One stop beyond Bagheria (get out at Santa Flavia–Solunto–Porticello station), is the Greco-Roman town at **SOLUNTO**. Cross over the tracks and walk down the main road towards the sea; after 300m there's a signposted left turn, from where it's another twenty minutes' walk up the hillside to the **site** (Mon–Sat 9am–7pm, Sun 9am–2pm, last entry 1hr before closing; €3), beautifully stranded on top of Monte Catalfano. Ancient Solus, a Phoenician settlement, was originally founded in the eighth century BC, resettled in the fourth century BC, and later Hellenized, finally surrendering to Rome after the First Punic War, when its name was changed to Solentum. The visible ruins mostly date from the Roman period, notably the impressive remains of wealthy houses that line the hillside. One, with a standing column, was built on two floors, the stairs still visible, and retains a complete geometric mosaic floor. The main street, Via dell'Agora, leads past more houses and shops to the *agora* itself, a piazza with nine clay-red-coloured recessed rooms at the back. Above it sit the fragmentary ruins of a theatre and a smaller odeon, deliberately sited so as to give marvellous views away to the coast. Beyond the *agora* are the remains of a water cistern and storage tanks – necessary, as Solentum had no natural springs. It was, and is, a glorious spot: the fishing villages below are split by a small bay, and guarded at one end by the medieval **Castello di Sólanto**.

Porticello and Aspra

With your own transport you can return to Palermo along the coastal route from Santa Flavia, through **PORTICELLO** village, where there's a decent **hotel**, the *Baia del Sole*, close to the beach at Via Raffaello Sanzio 39 (☎091.957.590; ❷); ring ahead, as it's popular. There's also a good local **restaurant**, *La Muciara*, Via Roma 103, with a wide range of fresh fish, impeccable service and a rather grand wine list, all at moderate prices. Past the stuck-out thumb of Capo Zafferano, it's about another 5km to **ASPRA**, from where you can see the whole of the Gulf of Palermo ahead of you. From here, one road runs the 2km or so south to Bagheria; another goes west, back into the city.

South: Piana degli Albanesi

Less than an hour's bus ride south of the capital is the upland plain where **PIANA DEGLI ALBANESI**, founded by fifteenth-century Albanians uprooted from their homes in flight from the Turkish invasions, sits placidly above a pleasant lake, a million miles from the manic goings-on in Palermo. The six thousand inhabitants here follow the Orthodox rite (though they acknowledge the authority of the pope), and proudly retain many of their old traditions. Piana is most spectacular at Easter, when the small town is full to the brim with people here to admire the handsome costumes – black with gold brocade on Good Friday, brightly coloured on Easter Sunday. If you can't make it then, try to come on Sunday mornings when there are traditional Orthodox services in one of the three churches lining the steeply sloping main street, **Via Giorgio Kastriota**. In truth, though, at most times of the year there's little point coming just to see the town. Apart from the street and building signs – in Albanian as well as Italian – there's little to spark your interest, save the **Museo Cívico** (Tues–Sun 9am–1pm, Tues, Thurs & Sat also 3–7pm; free), an ethnographical museum at the bottom of the hill, illustrative of former rural life and displaying traditional costumes and jewellery.

There's a bit more to the immediate surroundings. Three kilometres south of the town, the artificial **lake** lies in a beautiful setting, surrounded by mountains, a good venue for a picnic and a lazy siesta. If you want a decent walk, you could go on a bit further (4km from Piana, to the right of the lake) to the mountain pass southwest of town, **Portella della Ginestra**, scene of one of the most infamous episodes in recent Sicilian history. On May 1, 1947, when the Albanians and villagers from neighbouring San Giuseppe Jato had assembled for their customary May Day celebrations, gunfire erupted from the crags and boulders surrounding the plain, killing eleven and wounding 55, many of them children. This massacre was the work of the bandit Giuliano, whose virulent anti-Communist feelings were exploited by more sinister figures high up in the political and criminal hierarchy: only two weeks previously, the people of Piana degli Albanesi, together with most other Sicilians, had voted for a Popular Front (left-wing) majority in the regional parliament. The cold-blooded killings erased at one stroke the bandit's carefully nurtured reputation as defender of the poor and friend to the oppressed (see "Sicily's history", p.448, and Montelepre, p.120).

Practicalities

To get to Piana degli Albanesi, there are several **buses** (Mon–Sat), run by Prestia & Commandé, from Stazione Centrale in Palermo; the last one back leaves at 4pm. Buses stop at the top of Piana, in Piazza Vittorio Emanuele: follow the road downhill and you'll pass all three of the town's churches, with the museum (and a tourist office in the same building) at the bottom on the right.

For **food**, the only central choice is the moderately priced *Trattoria San Giovanni*, Via G. Matteotti 34 (closed Tues), a rustic, plant-filled spot whose windows overlook the town; from the piazza, take any road to the right, cross the bridge and it's up on your right. There are a couple of bars selling panini on Via Giorgio Kastriota, and another restaurant, *La Montagnola*, lies on the outskirts, which you'll pass on the bus on the way into Piana.

Altofonte

The route to Piana takes you through crowded **ALTOFONTE**, once the extreme southerly end of Roger II's royal park and still enjoying a grand view of the Conca d'Oro bowl. The **Chiesa Madre** in Piazza Umberto gives onto the remains of the cupola-topped royal chapel from this period, though it's been considerably changed since then; ask at the sacristy if you want to see it.

Ústica

A turtle-shaped volcanic island, a lonely 60km northwest of Palermo, **ÚSTICA** is one of the more appealing destinations away from the capital, ideal for putting your feet up for a few days. Colonized originally by the Phoenicians, the island was known to the Greeks as Osteodes, or "ossiary", a reference to the remains of 6000 Carthaginians they found here, abandoned to die on the island after a rebellion. Its present name is derived from the Latin *ustum* – "burnt" – on account of its blackened, lava-like appearance. Exposed, isolated and never a particularly attractive place to live, Ústica had a rough time throughout the Middle Ages, its sparse population constantly harried by pirates who used the island as a base. In the Bourbon period the island was commandeered as a prison for political enemies, and even as late as the 1890s the few inhabitants were nearly all exiled prisoners: Antonio Gramsci, the great theorist of the Italian Communist Party, was once interned here.

Today, tourism has rescued the island without altogether spoiling it, and Ústica's fertile nine square kilometres are just right for a day's ambling. Though lacking sandy beaches, the island's greatest draw is the surrounding limpid waters, ideal for **snorkelling** and **skin-diving**, activities that attract an international meeting of scuba enthusiasts every June to September; if you want to have a go, Profondo Blu, at the harbour (☎091.844.9609, ⓦwww.ustica-diving.com), organizes trips and rents equipment. Part of the coastline has been designated Italy's first Natural Marine Reserve, where "fish-watching" is a popular activity (since "fish-catching" is forbidden): **boat trips** to tour the many grottoes that puncture the rugged coastline are plentiful (see below). Another interesting option for seeing Ústica by sea is a weekend sailing charter from Palermo; Starsail (☎091.327.241, ⓦwww.starsail.it) runs all-inclusive trips starting at €230 per person.

Arrival

Ferries and **hydrofoils** operate daily from Palermo (from the Stazione Maríttima), the cheapest passage being €10.60 one way by ferry (journey time 2hr 30min), or €16.20 by hydrofoil (1hr 15min); summer departure times from Palermo are currently 8.15am, 3.30pm and 7pm. You can buy tickets from Siremar, Via Francesco Crispi 120 (☎091.749.3111); see "Travel details" for more information.

You arrive at **ÚSTICA TOWN**, the island's only port: the town centre is up the flight of steps leading from the harbour. You'll emerge in the main square, which is really three interlocking squares – piazzas Cap. V. di Bartolo, Umberto I and Vito Longo. In the topmost of the three, Piazza Cap. V. di Bartolo, on the left-hand side of the church, is the Monte dei Paschi di Siena **bank** with ATM (Mon–Fri 8.20am–1.20pm) and, next door, the R&S Militello **ticket agency** (☎091.844.9002) for ferries and hydrofoils; there's also a ticket office at the harbour, open just before sailings, and a **pharmacy** at Piazza Umberto I 30. Ostea, just down from Piazza Umberto I at Via S. Francesco al Borgo 9 (☎ & ⓕ091.844.8112, ⓦwww.ostea.it; May–Sept daily 9.30am–1pm, 5–8.30pm; Oct–April Mon–Sat 9.30am–1pm), runs a **tourist office** which also provides **Internet** access (€4 per hour); for online information, check ⓦwww.usticaonweb.it.

Renting a **boat** from the quay should cost around €13 per person for three hours, though be sure to agree a price beforehand, or try *Tranchina* (see below), which also rents out **mopeds**, though these are hardly necessary as there's an efficient **minibus** service (pay on board) that plies Ústica's one circular road every hour or so. In any case, it doesn't take much more than two or three hours to walk round the entire island.

Accommodation

Ústica Town holds most **places to stay**, though the island is not particularly cheap; in summer hotels fill up quickly, and in winter only a few remain open. However, there are plenty of opportunities to **rent rooms:** try Ostea (see above) or the locals themselves; the *Bar Centrale*, also in Piazza Umberto, is a good place to ask for *cámere*.

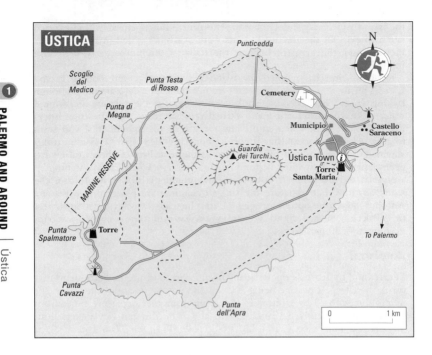

Ariston Via della Vittória 5 ☎091.844.9042. Smart, central hotel with eleven rooms and impressive sea views. Diving trips can be arranged. Half- or full-board only between June and Sept, and sizable reductions in winter. ❺

Caminita Vittorio Via Tufo 1 ☎091.844.9212. This individual rents out two attractive self-contained rooms (with kitchenette and bathroom), one with a sweeping view down over the town to the sea. It's just a few minutes from the square: at the church, turn right along Via Calvario and Via Tufo is the sixth on the left. No credit cards. ❷

Hotel Clelia Via Magazzino 7 ☎091.844.9039, ⓦwww.hotelclelia.it. Recently refurbished, this basic little *pensione* has a roof-terrace restaurant with sea views and Internet access for guests. Rates drop considerably out of season. ❹

Hotel Giulia Via San Francesco 16 ☎ & ⓕ091.844.9007, ⓦwww.giuliahotel.com. Open

year-round, with eleven perfectly acceptable, two-star rooms right off the main plaza. ❻

Hotel Grotta Azzurra Località San Ferlicchio ☎091.844.9048, ⓦwww.framonhotels.com. Part of the ubiquitous *Framon* chain, this smart, pricey hotel sits over its own bay, with a pool and sun terraces cut into the rocks below. It's a 5min walk from the centre: as you climb from the port, follow the road around to the left; open June–Sept only. Rates drop by half in June and Sept. ❽

Tranchina *Da Umberto* restaurant, Piazza Umberto I 1 ☎091.844.9542, ⓦwww.isoladiustica.com. Umberto and his son Gigi rent out rooms in over 30 apartments and houses around the island, some with great sea views and some more rustic buildings in the middle of the island overlooking a few grazing cattle. They also hire out scooters and can arrange boat tours of the island. ❹

Around the island

The **town centre** is a small, bright place, built on a steep slope, its low build-ings covered in murals. Most of what passes for entertainment here – chatting in the open air, having a coffee in the couple of bars, impromptu games of soccer – takes place in and around the three central squares, which merge into each other, tumbling down the hill from the church. Historical interest can be found at the **Museo Archeológico**, housed in the Torre Santa Maria to the south of the town (usually Mon–Sat 5–7pm; €2.50) a low-key assortment, mostly comprising crusty anchors, amphorae, oddments from shipwrecks in the area and Bronze Age objects from Faraglioni.

What you don't get from the town centre, however, is a view of the water and, consequently, a sense of Ústica as an island, so perhaps the first thing you should do is climb up to the remains of the **Castello Saraceno**, above the town: from the top of the square to the right of the church, the path runs left of the fancy cross at the end of Via Calvario. This easy twenty-minute walk leads to an interesting old fort, pitted with numerous cisterns to catch the precious water, and provided with rock-cut steps, which give you a good initial view of the island's layout.

From here you can see Ústica's highest point, the **Guardia dei Turchi** (244m), at the summit of a ridge that cuts the island in two, and topped by what looks like a giant golf ball – in fact a meteorological radar system. You can also climb up here from the town, in about an hour or so: take Via B. Randaccio to the right of the church, turn left at the top and then right, and you'll come to the Municipio, where you turn left along Via Tre Mulini for the summit – keep straight ahead on the cobbled path, cutting off to the left when you reach the stepped path. If you're interested you can ask around the town's bars for donkey hire (about €15 an hour).

Once you've exhausted the possibilities in town, walking around the island is the most attractive move. There's a **coastal path** for at least half of the route, which you pick up by keeping straight on past the Municipio and then bearing off the road to the right, down past the cemetery. The path hugs the cliffs along the island's north side as far as the **Marine Reserve**, whose northernmost point is at **Punta di Megna** (where the path and road converge). If you're equipped, there's excellent snorkelling at Punta di Megna and at the offshore rock of **Scoglio del Médico**, where the clear water is bursting with fish, sponges, weed and coral. The road then keeps to the west coast as far as the old *torre* (tower) at **Punta Spalmatore**, where you'll find some of the island's best bathing spots; try below the *torre*, or – below the nearby lighthouse – at **Punta Cavazzi**, where there's a *piscina naturale*, a perfect, sheltered pool of seawater that can get uncomfortably crowded in high season.

The more cultivated southern coast is best seen by boat as the road runs inland here. If you're walking, veer away from the coast at Spalmatore, following the inland road past the Punta Spalmatore tourist village. After about ten minutes you'll pass the *Trattoria Baia del Sole*, a fine place for lunch (see below), and further along you rejoin the main road back across the eastern half of the island to the port.

Eating and drinking

There are several places to eat on and around the central squares, and most of the hotels have **restaurants**, often with roof terraces and sea views. Many restaurants close during the winter, though the ones listed below should all remain open year-round. Of the **bars**, the *Oasi Bar*, serving snacks as well as drinks, is dead central in Piazza Vito Longo, as is the *John Bar* in Piazza Umberto I.

Trattoria Baia del Sole Zona Spalmatore. In a rustic restaurant with fine sea views on the western side of the island, La Signora presents you with superb food that's all home-made – including the antipasti (preserved tuna and olives, *melanzane sott'olio*, goat's cheese) and *pasta con le sarde* made with locally caught sardines and fennel picked from the surrounding hills. The local wine is a tart rosé, which complements the salty food well. If you ring ☏091.844.9175, they'll come and pick you up from anywhere on the island. No credit cards. Moderate.

Trattoria Giulia Via San Francesco 13. The simple trattoria attached to this *albergo* is open to non-guests and specializes in couscous. No credit cards. Inexpensive.

Trattoria Da Mario Piazza Umberto I 21. In this small and simple, box-like restaurant on the square, with tables outside in summer, Mario

cooks and dispenses dishes such as spaghetti with fresh crabmeat, roast squid and local wine. It's excellent, and open throughout winter, too. Moderate.

Le Terrazze Via Cristóforo Colombo 3. A piz-zeria-ristorante on the other side of the port, with terrace views of the sea and surrounding hills. Closed Mon, Tues, Thurs & Fri in winter. Moderate.

Festivals

January
6 Orthodox Epiphany procession at **Piana degli Albanesi**; traditional costumes and the distribution of oranges. Similar goings-on at **Mezzojuso** to the southeast.

Easter
Holy Week Traditional Orthodox processions and celebrations at **Piana degli Albanesi**, best on Good Friday and Easter Sunday; and also at **Mezzojuso**.

April
23 Costumed processions at **Piana degli Albane-si** to celebrate St George's Day.

Last week Annual World Windsurfing Festival at **Mondello**; races, food, drink and entertainment.

July
11–15 The festival of St Rosalia – who saved the city from plague – in **Palermo**. A procession of the saint's relics, fireworks and general mayhem.

August
21 A colourful horseback parade, *la cunnatta*, at **Marineo**, on the Corleone road.

September
4 Pilgrimage to Monte Pellegrino in **Palermo** in honour of St Rosalia, patron saint of the city.

Last week Annual International Tennis Tourna-ment in **Palermo**.

October/November
Last week in October and first week in November A week of ecclesiastical music concerts at **Monreale** cathedral.

Travel details

Trains

Palermo to: Agrigento (12 daily Mon–Sat, 6 daily Sun; 2hr); Bagheria (2–3 hourly; 10min); Caltanis-setta (7 daily Mon–Sat, 4 daily Sun; 1hr 40min–2hr); Capaci (hourly; 40min); Carini (hourly; 45min); Castellammare del Golfo (hourly; 1hr 20min); Castelvetrano (7 daily Mon–Sat, 1 daily Sun; 2hr 15min); Catania via Caltanissetta (5 daily Mon–Sat, 1 daily Sun; 3hr 30min); Cefalú (hourly; 45min–1hr); Enna (8 daily Mon–Sat, 3 daily Sun; 2hr 15min); Isola delle Fémmine (hourly; 20–25min); Marsala (5 daily; 2hr 40min); Mazara del Vallo (5 daily; 2hr 30min); Milazzo (hourly; 2hr 30min–3hr 10min); Messina (hourly; 3hr–4hr 25min); Solunto (1–2 hourly; 15min); Términi Imerese (every 30min; hourly 25min); Trápani (hourly; 3hr 15min).

Buses

Palermo to: Agrigento (hourly Mon–Sat, 5 daily Sun; 2hr 15min); Bagheria (hourly Mon–Sat; 1hr); Các-camo (2 daily Mon–Sat; 1hr); Caltagirone (3 daily Mon–Sat, 1 daily Sun; 3hr); Caltanissetta (13 daily Mon–Sat, 8 daily Sun; 1hr 40min); Carini (hourly; 40min); Castelbuono (3 daily Mon–Sat; 1hr 50min); Castellammare del Golfo (5 daily; 50min); Catania (hourly; 2hr 40min); Cefalù (3 daily Mon–Sat; 1hr); Corleone (hourly Mon–Sat; 1hr 30min); Enna (6 daily Mon–Sat, 4 daily Sun; 1hr 35min–2hr); Gela (4 daily Mon–Sat, 3 daily Sun; 2hr 30min–3hr); Messina (7 daily Mon–Sat, 4 daily Sun; 3hr 10min); Piana degli Albanesi (6 daily Mon–Sat; 1hr); Piazza Armerina (5 daily Mon–Sat, 4 daily Sun; 2hr 5min–2hr 20min); San Martino delle Scale (2 daily Mon–Sat; 30min);

San Vito Lo Capo (2–5 daily; 2–3hr); Siracusa (4 daily Mon–Sat, 5 daily Sun; 3hr 15min); Términi Imerese (6 daily Mon–Sat; 40min); Trápani (hourly; 2hr).

Ferries

Palermo to: Cágliari (1 weekly; 14hr 30min); Genoa (1 daily; 20hr); Livorno (3 weekly; 17hr); Naples (2 daily; 11hr); Salerno (1 weekly; 8hr 30min); Tunis (1 weekly; 9hr); Ústica (June–Sept 1 daily; Oct–May 6 weekly; 2hr 20min).

Hydrofoils

Palermo to: Aeolian Islands (June–Sept 2 daily; Oct–Dec 3 weekly; 3hr–8hr); Cefalù (June–Sept

3 weekly; 1hr 10min); Naples (1 daily; 4hr); Ústica (June–Aug 3 daily; Sept–May 2 daily; 1hr 15min).

Ústica to: Favignana (June–Sept 3 weekly; 2hr); Naples (June–Sept 3 weekly; 4hr); Palermo (June–Aug 3 daily; Sept–May 2 daily; 1hr 15min); Trápani (June–Sept 3 weekly; 2hr 30min).

Planes

Palermo to: Genova (1 daily; 1hr 40min); Lampedusa (3 daily; 1hr); Milan (11 daily; 1hr 40min); Naples (5 daily; 55min); Pantelleria (1 daily; 45min); Rome (21 daily; 1hr 5min).

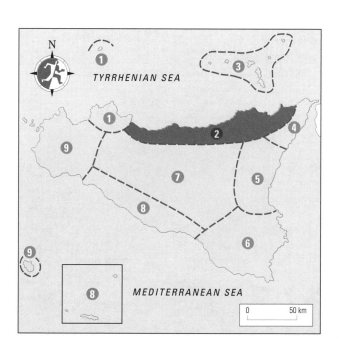

2

The Tyrrhenian coast

N

TYRRHENIAN SEA

MEDITERRANEAN SEA

0   50 km

CHAPTER 2

Highlights

* **Castello at Cáccamo** Perched high on a spit of land, this impressive Norman castle can be seen for miles and offers great inland views. **p.137**

* **Monti Madonie** Walks in the mountains are especially beautiful in spring, when wild flowers are superabundant, and in autumn when the leaves turn. **p.139**

* **Gibilmanna** Stupendous view from the sanctuary over the lush countryside and snaking road to the Tyrrhenian sea. **p.145**

* **Wild mushrooms** Sample the delicious varieties of funghi cooked up at the *Nangalarruni* restaurant in Castelbuono. **p.145**

* **Tíndari** Spend time with the lizards exploring the Roman remains of Tyndaris, loftily located by the sea. **p.151**

△ Dawn in the Monti, Madonie

THE TYRRHENIAN COAST | Highlights

The Tyrrhenian coast

Practically the whole of Sicily's northern shore, the **Tyrrhenian coast**, is dedicated to holidaying. At its best it's an eye-catching succession of cliff and cove, sandy strips and citrus groves, but all too often these are eclipsed by a monotonous ensemble of new villas and hotel developments. In summer, the beaches can get as congested as the road that runs through the numerous small coastal towns and villages, but out of season, you'll find that there's plenty of room to breathe.

At any time of year, the major distraction is **Cefalù**, a beach resort *par excellence*, whose medieval cathedral contains some of the best mosaicwork you'll find on the island. Its fine beach and rocky setting provide the sort of views that attract artists in droves, and it's one of Sicily's few package-tour destinations from Britain. Consequently, you'll find hotel space difficult to come by in summer, though it's worth battling with the crowds to spend at least a day here. Cefalù aside, the attractions of the Tyrrhenian coast are best enjoyed en route to Palermo or Messina. A good half-day's wandering can be spent in and around the old spa town of **Términi Imerese**, including a trip out to the blustery hill-top stronghold of **Cáccamo**, which holds the biggest and best-preserved of Sicily's Norman castles. Everywhere, too, the Tyrrhenian coast is dotted with ancient archeological remains, the most complete of which is the cliff-top site of Greco-Roman **Tyndaris** in the east.

If it's **beaches** you're after, then some of the best lie beyond the off-putting industrialization around the fortified town of **Milazzo**, or just below Tyndaris at **Oliveri**; other more crowded swathes lie around small resorts like **Sant'Agata di Militello** and **Capo d'Orlando**, which also make lively stop-overs. Away from the coast, you soon leave the crowds behind in the dramatic **Madonie** and **Nébrodi** mountains. There are some good hikes in the hills between **Castelbuono** and **Piano Battáglia**, while further east you can make other inland excursions to some venerable old hill-towns, especially **Mistretta**, **San Fratello** and **Castroreale**, little touched by the mayhem on the coast.

The Tyrrhenian coast is more accessible than much of the Sicilian seaboard. There's a good **train** service all the way along, making it easy to stop off in any of the seaside resorts that take your fancy, or at places from which regular **buses** link inland destinations, though a car is useful for continuing into Sicily's interior. **Driving** can be slow along the coast itself, especially where there's still no autostrada – specifically the 40km between Cefalù and Sant'Agata, through which the traffic files at a snail's pace along the twisting SS113. Where the A20 autostrada does exist, it's a toll-road. For a more leisurely mode of travel, Ústica Lines operates a useful (though limited) summer **hydrofoil** service between Palermo and the Aeolian Islands, taking in Cefalù.

N

THE TYRRHENIAN COAST

Naples ▲

Ferry & Hydrofoil

Stròmboli

Panarea

A e o l i a n   I s l a n d s

Salina

Lipari

Vulcano

Filicudi

Alicudi

T Y R R H E N I A N
S E A

Hydrofoil

Hydrofoil

Hydrofoil

Hydrofoil

Ferry & Hydrofoil

Réggio di
Calabria

Messina

A20

Barcellona

Milazzo

Castroreale

Novara di
Sicilia

Tindari
Oliveri

Tyndaris

San Biagio

Patti

Floresta

SS120

Naso

Frazzanò

SS116

San Marco
d'Alunzio

Capo d'Orlando

Sant' Agata
di Militello

San
Fratello

Mistretta

Capizzi

M o n t i   N è b r o d i

Santo Stefano
di Camastra

Castel di Tusa

Geraci Siculo

SS117

Tusa

Piano Battaglia

Halaesa

Castelbuono

Gibilmanna

Pizzo
Carbonara

Pizzo
Antenna
Grande

Piano Zucchi

Cefalù

M o n t i   M a d o n i e

Collesano

Himera

Piano
Zucchi

Tèrmini
Imerese

Càccamo

S. Leonardo

A19

Cesarò

SS289

SS120

Randazzo

SS185

Giardini-Naxos

Taormina

Reggio di Calabria

Catania & Acireale ▶

Adrano ▶

Nicosia ▶

Gangi ▶

Enna ▶

Palermo ▶

Palermo ▶

25 km

0

Términi Imerese, Cáccamo and ancient Himera

The first stop out of Palermo is **Términi Imerese**, though if you're driving keep an eye open for the **Chiesazza** on the left, after the exit for Altavilla Milicia. Built by Robert Guiscard in 1077, this ruin of a Norman church was once annexed to a Basilian monastery. The autostrada is the best vantage-point from which to view the remains, which appear stranded by the side of the road – don't bother working your way round to take a closer look.

Términi Imerese

Fifteen kilometres further on, **TÉRMINI IMERESE** has the magnificent backdrop of Monte Calógero, and a seafront marred by some of the only industry you'll see this side of Milazzo. Términi was originally settled by Greeks from Zancle (Messina) in the seventh century BC, and subsequently grew in importance as it absorbed the influx of survivors from the destroyed city of Himera, 13km to the east (see p.138). Later, as Therma Himeraia, it flourished under the spa-loving Romans, and today the town is still famous for its waters, reputed to be good for arthritis and pasta-making. Otherwise, the main attractions are some noble Baroque churches, and a good museum holding finds from the site of ancient Himera. Términi makes a useful base for trips to this site, and inland to Cáccamo – both easy bus rides away.

Términi: the upper town

If you're not here to take the waters, head for the **upper town**, which holds Términi's main sights, a few laid-back eateries and the town's centre. At the top of the steep cobbled steps and lanes sits a spacious and sleepy piazza, dominated by the pink-fronted **Duomo**, a monumental seventeenth-century creation that's been heavily restored over the years. The inside reveals some eighteenth-century sculptures by **Marabitti**, best of all his *Madonna del Ponte* in the fourth chapel on the right, and – unusually – there's plenty of information in English.

Beyond the Duomo extends the palm-fringed **belvedere**, which offers an extensive panorama over the lower town, port and sea that's partly disfigured by the industrial tangle below. A few metres below the Piazza Duomo, the excellent **Museo Cívico** (Tues–Sat 9am–1pm & 4.30–6pm, Sun 9am–12.30pm; free) is housed in a building that contains elements dating back to the fourteenth century. In the restored chapel, you can see work by Antonello Gagini and, best of all, a triptych of the *Madonna with Child and Saints*, attributed to Gaspare da Pésaro – there's another fifteenth-century *Madonna* on the stairs, this time a glittering and tender fresco. Other rooms in this well-displayed collection hold paintings, and prehistoric and archeological material (including finds from Himera); look out for the marble bust of an elegant second-century Roman matron in room 4. You can pick up a free guidebook, with information in English, at the entrance.

Back across the piazza and down Via Iannelli, the small fifteenth-century church of **Santa Caterina d'Alessandria** has a pointed arched doorway surmounted by a crude relief. The church is generally locked up, but if you're lucky you'll get to see some frescoes of the saint's life inside, with captions written in the local dialect. A few steps around the corner from here, the shady vegetation of **Villa Palmieri** shelters the remnants of a public building from

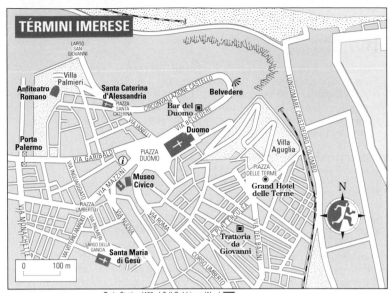

Train Station (400m) & Il Gabbiano (1km) ▼

the Roman era, and there are the remains of an **Anfiteatro Romano** at the far end of the park, off Via Garibaldi – just up from the Porta Palermo, the former entrance to the city.

Although there's not much else to detain you, the steep, cracked streets below the Duomo are pleasant to explore. Below Piazza Umberto I, on Largo della Gancia, there is a fine Renaissance wooden panel hidden behind the altar in **Santa Maria di Gesù**. Dating from around 1400, it shows St George slaying the dragon.

The lower town: practicalities

Términi's **lower town** has less of specific interest, its narrow streets playing host to a congested mass of traffic, people and grocery stores. Still, it's here that you'll **arrive**, and where you'll find both the town's hotels – including the thermal spa – and a trattoria.

The **train station** is 400m southeast of the town centre, and sells tickets either at the station newsstand or at the machines in the waiting room (credit cards only): alternatively, you can buy them on the train, but they'll cost a few euros more. To get to town, turn right outside the station, walk past Piazza Crispi and down Corso Umberto e Margherita to reach Via Roma, the stepped street that climbs to the upper town. Local and long-distance **buses** arrive and depart from immediately outside the station. The **tourist office** (Mon–Fri 8am–2pm, plus Mon & Wed 3–6pm; ☎091.812.8253) is situated in the upper town, close to the museum, just off Via Mazzini at Chiassuolo Maltese.

If you're going to see Cáccamo or Himera (or both), you'll probably need to **stay the night**, and the only budget option is *Il Gabbiano*, at Via Libertà 221 (☎091.811.3262, ℻091.811.4225, ⓦwww.hotelgabbiano.it), a nice find after the lengthy walk (turn left out of the train station, walk parallel to the lines for about 15min, and the hotel is on the right). The rooms in the renovated annexe, with shared facilities (❷) are much cheaper than those in the better-equipped main building (④). The town's only alternative is the reasonably priced *Grand Hotel delle Terme* (☎091.811.3557, ⓦwww.grandhoteldellaterme.it; ④), with its lovely roof-top pool. The hotel dominates Piazza delle Terme at the point where Términi's thermal waters issue forth at a constant 42°C, and non-residents can stop in and have a look at the stone and mosaic thermal baths beneath the hotel, where some of the original structure is still visible, or use the modern spa (from €10 for facials, mud baths and massages). The nearest **campsite** is the *Himera*, 15km east of town at Buonfornello, with a pool, a disco and small apartments for rent (☎091.814.0175): to get there, take a bus from outside the train station.

Eating places in Términi are similarly few and far between. In the upper town, the old-fashioned *Bar del Duomo*, on Via Belvedere (closed Wed), has upstairs seating under a colourful wooden roof, where you can have inexpensive set meals with fresh fish from €6, and pastries on offer downstairs, while the *Trattoria del Gelato*, at the end of the belvedere, is the place for ice cream. Otherwise search out signposted *Da Giovanni* in the lower town (no credit cards), a welcoming trattoria, buried within the network of alleys off Piazza Terme at Via Nogara 4. There's no menu, but the owner will reel off the options.

Cáccamo

Buses from Términi's train station run regularly to **CÁCCAMO**, 10km south. Set amid green hills, it's the first of many inland towns hereabouts worth visiting. Cáccamo's remarkable **castello** (daily 9.30am–noon & 1.30–6.30pm; free) is the main draw, and the first thing you see as you approach – a chalk-white array of towers and battlements dominating the town and commanding the heights above the deep San Leonardo river valley. Built in the twelfth century, but much modified, the 130-roomed castle presents an imposing front, but the heavily restored and bare interior doesn't merit much more than a cursory wander. The steep path up leads through three gateways to the main keep; one of the oldest sections contains the Sala della Congiura, the chamber where the barons' plot against William I ("the Bad") was hatched in 1160.

When you've had your fill of the castle, take time to stroll around the jumble of houses and squares that make up the town. It's not much more than an overgrown village, disturbed only by the weight of traffic along the one main street. At some stage you'll wind up at the secluded Piazza del Duomo behind the castle crag. Here sits an enclave of faded buildings presided over by Cáccamo's **Chiesa Madre** (Mon–Sat 8am–1pm; tip expected), dating in part from 1090 though rebuilt during the fifteenth century, and now heavily Baroque in character. The reliefs around the sacristy door are attributed to Francesco Laurana, the Renaissance sculptor who has left his mark all over the region, particularly in Palermo. Look out, too, for the seventeenth-century tablet depicting St George and the Dragon over the main portal. To the left of the cathedral, the **Chiesa dell'Anime del Purgatorio** (Mon–Sat 8am–1pm; tip appreciated) is more of an attraction. Its walls are covered with pretty blue, white and gilded stucco decoration, but the *pièce de résistance* is the **catacombs**, revealed only when the custodian peels away part of the floor in front of an altar. Follow him down the crumbling steps to view the fully clothed and collapsing bodies lying in niches in the walls. Residents of the town made their last journey here between the seventeenth and mid-nineteenth centuries.

There's a decent enough **hotel** at the back of the town, *La Spiga d'Oro*, Via Margherita 74 (☎091.814.8968; ❷); it has an inexpensive restaurant, though you're liable to get your breakfast pastries from a plastic bag. The hotel is a ten-minute walk up from the *castello*, though the bus from Términi stops just below. For a **meal** right by the castle, there's the medieval-looking *A Castellana* (closed Mon), a reasonably priced pizzeria-*ristorante*. If you're heading **for Palermo**, there's a handy early-afternoon bus to the capital from Cáccamo, and there's also a lunchtime departure **for Cefalù**; otherwise the last bus back to Términi leaves at around 6pm (Mon–Sat).

Ancient Himera

The site of Greek **Himera** is a short train ride from Términi Imerese – if you're driving, take the Buonfornello exit from the autostrada. Himera was the first Greek settlement on Sicily's northern coast, founded in 648 BC as an advance post against the Carthaginians, who controlled the west of the island, and allegedly dedicated to Athena. The town inevitably became a flashpoint, and in 480 BC the Carthaginian leader Hamilcar landed a huge force on the coast nearby, with the intention of taking Himera and very probably the rest of Sicily at the same time. Pitted against the combined armies of Akragas (Agrigento), Gela and Syracuse, the invading force was demolished and Hamilcar himself perished – either assassinated by Greek spies before the battle, or killed when he threw himself onto the pyre afterwards, depending on whose version you read. The outcome of the battle marked a significant upheaval of the classical world – and, in the case of Sicily, a new balance of power, with the Greeks in the ascendant. But their glory was short-lived: in 409 BC Hamilcar's nephew, Hannibal, wreaked his revenge and razed the city to the ground, forcing the surviving citizens west to what is now Términi Imerese.

All that's left of the important Chalcidinian settlement that once stood here is one ruined monument: a massive **Tempio della Vittória** erected to commemorate the defeat of the Carthaginians. It's a conventional Doric construction, with six columns at the front and back, and fourteen at the sides. Interestingly, the two stairwells on either side of the entrance to the *cella*, or sanctuary, suggest the involvement of craftsmen from Akragas in its construction, though it's known that the physical labour was carried out by the captured Carthaginians themselves. Despite the paucity of the actual remains, and the proximity of the modern road and rail network, the solitary ruin does have a powerful appeal. It's said to stand on the very site of the 480 BC battle, and after the victory some of the rich Carthaginian spoils were pinned up inside.

The acropolis lay to the south of the temple, inland, and, though excavations have uncovered a necropolis and some smaller temples, much work remains to be done at the site. Only the western area is open, below which is an extensive, well-designed **museum** (Mon–Sat 9am–6pm, Sun 9am–1pm; €2), housing some of the items dug up from the area. The collection is repetitive, consisting mostly of large, cracked vessels, though there are good plans of the site as you come in and, on a lower floor, a big well-maintained mosaic and a few of the striking lion's-head water-spouts that drained the temple's roof. One strangely moving window displays the grave of a married couple, the wife sleeping curled up next to her husband's skeleton, her leg resting on his, their mouths agape. The Museo Cívico in Términi (see p.135) and the Museo Archeológico Regionale in Palermo (see p.96) also house a number of assorted findings from the Himera site. Moderately priced **meals and refreshments** are available at *Baglio Himera*, opposite the temple.

Hiking and skiing in the Monti Madonie

By car, Buonfornello is also the autostrada exit you need to take for an excursion into the **Monti Madonie**: keep on the coastal SS113 and head south at Campofelice di Roccella. By **bus** (from Palermo or Términi) you can get as far as Collesano, beyond which you have to hitch or walk the 15km southeast to **Piano Zucchi**, whose surrounding slopes are filled with skiing Palermitani in winter. In spring and autumn it's just as attractive for the pleasant hiking, and if you want more than a few hours in the hills you can **stay** at the *Rifugio Orestano* (☎0921.662.159; ❶); **meals** are also available here. For this and the *Marini* listed below, it's always wise to book ahead.

Ten kilometres further south, **Piano Battáglia** is the best base for visiting the highest of Sicily's peaks after Mount Etna, and the only other resort (apart from Etna) equipped for winter sports. It's a very un-Sicilian-looking place, with Swiss-type chalets and even alpine churches, and the area is equally popular for summer picnics as it is for winter skiing. As well as **hikes** to the two highest peaks, Pizzo Antenna Grande (1977m) and Pizzo Carbonara (1979m) – see below – there's a good choice of less ambitious walks along the region's numerous paths, and one to Castelbuono (see p.145). If you want to stay at Piano Battáglia, there's a handful of **hostels** around, best of which is the *Rifugio Marini* (☎0921.649.994), which offers private rooms (❶) and full board – worth taking, as there's nowhere else in the area to eat, and no shops – and also rents out **skiing equipment**. The large, cheerful pine-clad *Hotel Pomieri* (☎0921.649.998; ❷), 4km to the southwest of Piano Battáglia, offers a more upmarket alternative. Otherwise, there are plenty of **freelance camping** possibilities in these hills during the summer.

From Piano Battáglia you can continue south along good minor roads to Polizzi Generosa or Petralia Sottana, though without a car you'll have to walk – 16km and 25km respectively. Alternatively, you can head back down towards the coast, bypassing Collesano and following the minor road due north for Cefalù – close on a fifty-kilometre hike.

The hike to Pizzo Carbonara from Piano Battáglia

This fairly strenuous walk (4–5hrs there and back) takes you through contrasting countryside of beechwoods and bare, limestone peaks, with rewarding views whether you make the summit or not. From *Rifugio Marini*, cross the plain to come out onto the road; turn right and immediately left, winding uphill to reach a small footpath ascending steeply along the main valley. Continue for an hour and round the spur, turning into the river valley. The level path enters a small wood; on leaving this you'll see a zigzag path rising on the opposite bank. Continue along this for twenty minutes and you'll find yourself looking down on Piano Zucchi; otherwise, leave the path and cut up the head of the valley to reach the open uplands, dotted with deep depressions and beechwoods. Continue in the same direction until wooden crosses mark the rounded summit of Pizzo Carbonara – head for it by any convenient route. On a very clear day you can see Etna's peak from here.

Cefalù

Despite the barrage of modern building outside the town centre, **CEFALÙ** remains a fairly small-scale fishing port, partly by virtue of its geographical position – tucked onto every available inch of a shelf of land underneath a fearsome crag, **La Rocca**. Roger II founded a mighty cathedral here in 1131, and, as befitting one of Sicily's most influential rulers, his church still dominates the skyline: the great twin towers of the facade rear up above the flat roofs of the medieval quarter, and the whole structure is framed by the looming cliff. Naturally, it's the major attraction in town, but most visitors are also tempted by Cefalù's fine curving sands – the main reason why the holiday companies have moved in in such great numbers during recent years. It's still not quite as developed as Sicily's other package resort, Taormina: the crowds are manageable, even in summer, and outside July and August you could do worse than make Cefalù your base for a few days, especially if you're attracted by the hiking possibilities in the hills to the south. Palermo, too, is less than an hour to the west by train.

The Duomo

It's worth making a beeline for the **Duomo** (daily: summer 8am–noon & 3.30–8pm; closes 7pm in winter) first thing in the morning if you want to avoid the tour-coach hordes. Apocryphally, it was built in gratitude by Roger who found refuge at Cefalù's safe beach in a violent storm, though it's more likely that the cathedral owed its foundation to his power struggle with Pope Innocent II. Shortly after his coronation, Roger had allied instead with Anacletus, the anti-pope, whose support enhanced the new king's prestige. Roger's cathedral benefited from Anacletus's readily granted exemptions and privileges, its conception at once rich and showy, something that's obvious over 850 years later. Quite apart from the massive, fortress-like exterior, with twin towers linked by a double row of arches, inside (covering the apse and presbytery) are the earliest and best preserved of all the Sicilian church mosaics, dating from 1148.

Most of the rest of the Duomo's interior is thoroughly plain, with all the former Baroque decoration finally stripped away after years of "restoration", which enhances the impact of the **mosaics**. They follow a familiar pattern: Christ Pantocrator, right hand outstretched in benediction, open Bible in the left, dominates the central apse; underneath is the Madonna flanked by archangels; then the twelve Apostles, in two rows of six. Forty years older than those at Monreale (p.117), these mosaics are thoroughly Byzantine in concept: Christ's face is elongated, the powerful eyes set close together, the outstretched hand flexed and calming; the archangels have their heads tilted towards the Madonna. Check out the Gagini statue of the Madonna in the chapel to the right of the sanctuary, then head back outside for an exterior view of the triple apse – hemmed in by the soaring cliff. Next door, the twelfth-century cloister is worth a look for its original twin columns, carved with anthropomorphic figures.

Note that you may be turned away if you are wearing shorts or baring your shoulders, though women may be lent shawls upon entering.

The rest of town

Cefalù's ageing, tangibly Arabic tangle of central streets provides an immediate incentive for some strolling around. Piazza Duomo itself is always lively, especially in the early evening. Just around the corner, at Via Mandralisca 13, the

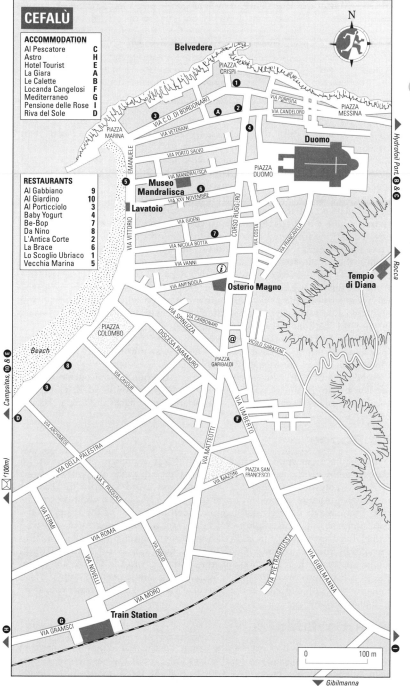

CEFALÙ

ACCOMMODATION
Al Pescatore	C
Astro	H
Hotel Tourist	E
La Giara	A
Le Calette	B
Locanda Cangelosi	F
Mediterraneo	G
Pensione delle Rose	I
Riva del Sole	D

RESTAURANTS
Al Gabbiano	9
Al Giardino	10
Al Porticciolo	3
Baby Yogurt	4
Be-Bop	7
Da Nino	8
L'Antica Corte	2
La Brace	6
Lo Scoglio Ubriaco	1
Vecchia Marina	5

Belvedere

PIAZZA CRISPI

VIA PORPORA

VIA CANDELORO

PIAZZA MESSINA

VIA C.O. DI BORDONARO

VIA VETERANI

VIA PORTO SALVO

VIA MANDRALISCA

EMANUELE

Duomo

PIAZZA DUOMO

PIAZZA MARINA

Museo Mandralisca

VIA XXV NOVEMBRE

Lavatoio

VIA GIOENI

CORSO RUGGERO

VIA COSTA

VIA FRANCAVILLA

VIA VITTORIO

VIA NICOLA BOTTA

VIA VANNI

Tempio di Diana

Rocca

VIA AMENDOLA

Osterio Magno

VIA CARBONARI

VIA SPINUZZA

PIAZZA COLOMBO

Beach

DISCESA PARAMURO

VICOLO SARACENI

@

PIAZZA GARIBALDI

Campsites, ⑩ & ⓔ

VIA CAVOUR

VIA ARCHIMEDE

VIA UMBERTO

VIA DELLA PALESTRA

VIA S. PASQUALE

VIA MATTEOTTI

PIAZZA SAN FRANCESCO

VIA MAZZINI

VIA FERMI

VIA ROMA

VIA GIGLIO

VIA NOVELLI

VIA PIE TRAGROSSA

VIA GIBILMANNA

VIA MORO

Train Station

VIA GRAMSCI

G

0	100 m

Gibilmanna

Museo Mandralisca (daily: Easter–Sept 9am–7pm; Oct–Easter 9am–noon; €4) houses a small collection of quality objects. On the first floor you'll find its most famous exhibit, the wry and powerful *Portrait of an Unknown Man* by the fifteenth-century Sicilian master **Antonello da Messina**; however, it suffers from a lack of sensitive framing and presentation, and a rope keeps you well at a distance. Look out, too, for the quirky Greek *krater* (fourth century BC) showing a robed tuna-fish salesman, knife in hand, disputing the price of his fish. Shell devotees should head for room 4, where you'll find over twenty thousand of them.

From the museum, walk down towards the water and the little harbour off Piazza Marina. When it's quieter, say at lunchtime, this part of Cefalù repays long dawdles through its alleys with views of rows of washing stretched between houses, and fishermen mending nets in the high-vaulted boathouses along Via Vittorio Emanuele. At the latter, you'll also see a relic of Saracen occupation – the **lavatoio**, a wash-house at the bottom of a curving staircase, with cold water pouring forth into the basins. Back past Piazza Marina, a left turn off Via C. di Bordonaro brings you to Piazza Crispi, where a **belvedere** gives onto the old Greek walls of Cefalù, mostly covered and incorporated into a sixteenth-century bastion. Frankly, though, these sights are no more than excuses to poke around this atmospheric area: each of the parallel streets off narrow Corso Ruggero is lined with attractive buildings in various stages of well-tended decay. One of the most impressive is the **Osterio Magno**, on the corner of Via Amendola and the corso, the surviving part of a medieval palace, now renovated with wood and steel and regularly used for art exhibitions (free). Meanwhile, the long sandy **beach** beyond the harbour beckons. It's one of Sicily's best, though jam-packed in summer, and offers marvellous views over the red roofs of the town and sheltered swimming in clear waters. The best swimming spots are west of town, where there are free showers.

If you have time, it's also worth walking east, around the headland beyond the Duomo, to the tourist port where the summer hydrofoils dock. It's a pretty bay, full of fishing-boats and with some strange rock stacks inviting a clamber on the far side of the port.

La Rocca

A much more energetic pastime is to climb the mountain above town, **La Rocca**, following the steps at the side of the Banco di Sicilia in Piazza Garibaldi. A steep twenty-minute climb takes you to the so-called **Tempio di Diana**, a megalithic structure adapted in the fifth century BC by the addition of classical doorways, their lintels still in place. Keep to the left of the temple and a path continues upwards, right around the crag, through pinewoods and wild fennel. Further on, it dips in and out of a surviving stretch of medieval wall to the sketchy **fortifications** at the very top, which look down to the coasts on either side of the headland. You can then cut down to the temple and rejoin the path back into town, the whole walk taking a little over an hour – much longer if you stop and stare at the extensive views. Take water with you, as it's a strenuous climb.

Practicalities

The **train station** is south of the town centre, ten minutes' walk from the main Corso Ruggero; all local **buses** leave from the square outside the station. If you're not staying, leave your bags at the **left-luggage** office inside the station (daily 7am–9pm). The summer **hydrofoil** service to and from Palermo and the Aeolian Islands (see "Travel details" on p.157) docks in the tourist port to the east of town, a twenty-minute walk away around the headland; the boat leaves Cefalù for the Aeolians at around 8.10am and calls again for Palermo at around 7.50pm. The **tourist office** is at Corso Ruggero 77 (summer Mon–Sat 8am–9pm, Sun 9am–1pm; winter 8am–2pm & 3–7pm; ☎0921.421.050, ⓦwww.cefalu-tour.pa.it), where you can pick up free maps, accommodation lists and local bus timetables, as well as the **listings** brochure "*Cefalù – Where to go, What to do*", with details of the city's daily summer concerts and theatre performances: for more information on cultural events, check ⓦwww.cefaluinforma.it.

Accommodation

Staying over can prove expensive in summer (if you can find space in any of the hotels), though it's easy and pleasant enough outside peak season. There's a dearth of budget accommodation, but don't be tempted by the rather unsavory accommodation touts at the train station: ask instead at the tourist office about renting private **rooms**, or self-catering apartments, though there's usually a minimum stay of seven nights. Note that in high season, July and August, hotel prices can rocket. From October to Easter, most hotels close; of those listed below – including all the central budget choices – only the *Al Pescatore*, *Locanda Cangelosi* and *Pensione delle Rose* stay open all year.

The nearest **campsites** are next to each other, 3km west of town beyond the beach, just off the SS113 (and behind the *Club Med* complex); both are closed in winter.

Pensioni and hotels

Astro Via Nino Martoglio 8 ☎0921.421.639, ⓕ0921.423.103, ⓦwww.astrohotel.it,. Close to the beach and nicely furnished, but pricey, this is a few minutes' walk west of the train station, reachable from Via Moro/Via Gramsci or Via Roma. ❺

Le Calette Via Vincenzo Cavallaro 12 ☎0921.424.144, ⓕ0921.423.688, ⓔcalette@pn.itnet.it. On the other side of the headland, overlooking the tourist port, this villa-style hotel is beautifully sited in its own little cove. All rooms face the sea and those on the second floor have large balconies, though the proximity of the rail-line can mean rude dawn awakenings. Otherwise, facilities are top-notch. ❻

Locanda Cangelosi Via Umberto I 26 ☎0921.421.591. Just off Piazza Garibaldi, this is the cheapest place in town by some way, but it only has four rooms, so get there early or call ahead. It's basic, and the management isn't particularly friendly, though there is a fridge available for guests. A couple of rooms have balconies overlooking the noisy street. No credit cards. ❶

La Giara Via Veterani 40 ☎0921.422.518, ⓦwww .hotel-lagiara.it. *La Giara* is very central, close to the Duomo, and offers clean rooms and a handsome terrace. Outside of August, when half- or full-board is necessary, it's reasonably priced. ❹

Mediterraneo Via Gramsci 2 ☎0921.922.573, ⓕ0921.922.606. Handily placed right opposite the train station, this modern hotel lacks character, but represents good value and offers friendly service. Rates fall at the lower end of this scale. ❺

Al Pescatore Località Caldura ☎ & ⓕ0921.421.572. Around the headland via the SS113, this is excellent value, with amenable service and sea-facing balconies. Watch for the sign: it's difficult to spot. ❻

Riva del Sole Viale Lungomare 25 ☎0921.421.230, ⓕ0921.421.230, ⓦwww .rivadelsole.com. Right on the seafront, this upmarket place might seem a little pretentious, but it has nice rooms and a good restaurant. Ask for a room "*con una vista del mare*" and you'll get the sea views, though it can be incredibly noisy. Half-board only June–August. Closed Nov. ❺

Pensione Delle Rose Via Gibilmanna ☎ & ⓕ0921.421.885. Good-value *pensione* offering half-board only in July and August. Some rooms have spacious terraces, and breakfast is abundant, with cheese and salami as well as rolls and jam. The main drawback is its distance from the centre, a 15–20min walk along the continuation of Via Umberto I. ❹

Hotel Tourist Viale Lungomare ☎0921.421.750, ℱ0921.923.916, ⓦwww.touristhotel.it. Though it's a bit of a walk (15min) along the shore road, this is a good bet if you're looking to get away from the clamour of partying Cefalù. The rooms are somewhat soulless, but many have terraces and enviable sea views. ❺

Camping

Costa Ponente ☎0921.420.085. Well equipped, with a swimming pool open July and August, and beach nearby. La Spisa buses stop outside. Easter–Oct.

San Filippo ☎0921.420.184. Adjacent to the Costa Ponente, with minimal facilities, though there is a shop. Easter–Oct.

Restaurants

There are dozens of **places to eat** scattered around town, though many are overpriced and mundane; the best places are detailed below, most of them offering good-value tourist menus. Anyone on a tight budget, and vegetarians who will appreciate the choice, could do worse than to sample the self-service *antipasto al buffet* in the restaurants along the waterfront – you get a plateful for around €5. For an explanation of the restaurant price categories, see p.53.

L'Antica Corte Corso Ruggero 193 ☎0921.423.228. A simple, elegant restaurant with seating in a quaint, cobbled alley. Pizzas are on offer as well as a full menu: try the fettuccini with anchovies or the stuffed swordfish. Moderate.

Baby Yogurt Corso Ruggero 158. For a quick fill-up, you can try out yoghurt in every conceivable form, including sandwiches. Inexpensive.

Be-Bop Via Nicola Botta 4. A pub-like joint, that serves decent hot and cold snacks, sandwiches, crêpes and ice cream. Live jazz and South American music at weekends. Inexpensive.

La Brace Via XXV Novembre ☎0921.423.570. You dine here to classical music in a room formed by two stone arches. The aubergine pasta is good, along with the swordfish *involtini*. Well on the tourist trail, it fills up quickly, and you'll need to book in summer at weekends – the Dutch owner speaks English. Closed Mon & mid-Dec to mid-Jan. Expensive.

Al Gabbiano Lungomare G. Giardina. One of the best along the central seafront, this has a good *antipasto al buffet*, spicy *zuppa di cozze* and pizzas in the evening. There's a summer garden at the back. Closed Wed in winter. Moderate.

Al Giardino Lungomare G. Giardina. A 15min walk west along the seafront, this lively restaurant has a summer terrace, huge pizzas and good *penne al'arrabbiata*. Inexpensive.

Da Nino Lungomare G. Giardina. Similar food and prices to neighbouring Al Gabbiano, but pizzas are also served at lunchtime in summer. Closed Tues & Nov. Moderate.

Al Porticciolo Via Carlo Ortolani di Bordonaro 66 and 92 ☎0921.921.981. Two atmospheric, low-vaulted little *ristoranti* attracting a smart crowd, with outdoor seating: no. 92 is slightly more upmarket, but both have surprisingly reasonable prices. Pizzas also served. Closed Wed in winter. Moderate.

Lo Scoglio Ubriaco Via C.O. di Bordonaro 2–4. At the bottom of the corso, this slick place adorned with photos and messages from stars and VIPs has a sea-facing terrace and serves pizzas as well as pasta and main dishes. The name means the "Drunken Rock". Closed Tues in winter. Moderate.

Vecchia Marina Via Vittorio Emanuele 73 ☎0921.420.388. Good fish restaurant, one of whose walls incorporates a mighty fish tank. Sicilian dishes served, and a decent wine list, too. Set menu at €19. Closed Tues & Nov/Dec. Moderate.

Listings

Banks Banco di Sicilia, on Piazza Garibaldi and Corso Ruggero; Banca Populare Sant'Angelo, Via Roma 7; Monte dei Paschi di Siena, Piazza del Duomo 13. All Mon–Fri 9am–1.20pm & 2.45–3.45pm.

Car rental Barranco, Via Umberto I 13 ☎0921.421 .525; Cerniglia, Via G. Matteotti 35 ☎0921.424 .200; Liberto, Via G. Matteotti 19 ☎0921.421.957.

Hiking Regular excursions around Piana Battáglia and Castelbuono. Contact the local branch of the Club Alpino Italiano for details, c/o Ferramenta Matassa, Via Spinuzza 7 ☎0921.422.250.

Hospital Contrada Pietrapollastra ☎0921.920.111.

Internet access Bacco Online, Corso Ruggero 38 (Mon–Sat 9am–1pm & 4–8pm; €5 per hour).

Pharmacies Battáglia, Via Roma 13; Cirincione, Corso Ruggero 144 (Mon–Fri 8.30am–1pm & 4–8pm). There's a rota system for evening and late-opening pharmacies posted in the window.
Police Carabinieri Discesa Paramuro ℡0921.421.105.
Post office Via Vazzana 9 (west along Via Della Palestra, then left again). Changes foreign currency (cash only). Mon–Sat 9am–1pm & 4–7pm.
Scooter rental Scooters for Rent, Via G. Matteotti 13 ℡0921.420.496 or 338.230.9008; €20–30 per half-day, €25–60 per day.

Supermarket Sidis, Via Cannizzaro (Mon–Sat 9am–1pm & 5–8.30pm, plus Sun 9am–1pm mid-June to Sept).
Taxis Ranks at Piazza Stazione ℡0921.422.554; Piazza Duomo ℡0921.421.178.
Telephone offices Agenzia S. Mauro, at Via Vazzana 7, for international calls.
Travel agents Pietro Barbaro, Corso Ruggero 82 ℡0921.421.595; Turismez, Via Umberto 1 ℡0921.420.601, ⓦwww .turismezviaggi.it.

Into the hills: Gibilmanna, Castelbuono and hiking

There are some good half-day excursions to be made into the leafy, green and flower-filled **Monti Madonie**, south of Cefalù, and for once the public transport services make them easily accessible. Pick up hiking itineraries from Cefalù's tourist office, together with a useful map of paths in the area.

Your first stop might be the **Santuario di Gibilmanna** (daily 9am–1pm & 3–5pm; free), just 14km from town (buses from Cefalù's Via Umberto I) in a spot made sacred by the Arabs, who recorded miraculous deeds by the Madonna on the hillside. The sanctuary is the goal of pilgrimages, which culminate on September 8 each year, though there are usually people around throughout the summer, picnicking amid the cypress trees, praying, or admiring the superb view from the belvedere. There's a **museum** beside the sanctuary (daily 10.30am–1pm & 3–6pm; €1) containing artefacts from churches, convents and monasteries in the area, and a restaurant and bar nearby. The only **accommodation** lies 1km beyond the shrine at the agriturismo *Fattoria Pianetti*, surrounded by mountain and woodland walks (℡0921.421.890; no credit cards): half-board (❷ per person) or full-board (❸ per person) is compulsory. You stay in little cottages beyond the farmhouse; the dining room is open to non-residents at weekends (book ahead), and pony treks are available in summer.

Castelbuono and Geraci Sículo

Another good road, turning inland about 8km east of Cefalù, climbs further into the mountains, running up the green valley and dipping over the first range of hills to **CASTELBUONO**, a 40min ride (the town is also on a regular bus route from outside Cefalù's train station). Castelbuono is a comely town, spread across the lower reaches of the surrounding mountains and sheltering behind the squat fourteenth-century **Castello Ventimiglia** (summer daily 9am–1pm & 4–10pm; winter Tues–Sun 9am–1pm & 4–8pm; €1.50): inside, there's a small stuccoed chapel, the work of Giácomo Serpotta. Castelbuono's steep, crooked streets – dotted with elaborate fountains and shady piazzas – encourage a stroll. Best of the churches is the fourteenth-century **Matrice Vecchia** (daily 11am–1pm & 5–7pm), fronted by a pretty loggia and containing extensive sixteenth-century frescoes of the *Passion of Christ* in the crypt.

145

On foot from Castelbuono to Piano Battáglia

To manage this strenuous seven-hour, twelve-kilometre hike easily in a day, you'll have to base yourself at the snug Club Alpino Siciliano refuge, the *Francesco Crispi* (☏0921.672.279; €37.50 per person full-board, or €15 for just a bed), two hours' strenuous walk above Castelbuono, in the Milocca forest; follow the steep winding road out of town for half an hour beyond the posh *Hotel Milocca* (☏0921.671.944; ❹), a fully equipped three-star with a pool and ponies for hire.

From the refuge, keep on the jeep path, leaving the woodlands after half an hour to reach Piano Pomo. Carry on to a small plain surrounded by four minor peaks, with crosses on each of the summits. There's a wire fence on the left, which you should climb over, and then continue over stony ground in the same direction for fifteen minutes until the large rounded peaks appear: 1km ahead (due west) is Pizzo Antenna (1977m), topped with an antenna; further away to the left (southwest) is conical Monte Ferro (1906m). Take the wooded Zotofonda Valley between these two and you'll reach Piano Battáglia (p.139) in around three hours.

If you're intent upon other serious walks in the hills, the tourist office in Cefalù has details of the local refuges, as well as contoured 1:50,000 maps of the region; alternatively, try the tourist office in Castelbuono (see below). For campers, there's no shortage of places to pitch a tent.

The **tourist office**, Via Umberto I 79 (summer Mon–Sat 9am–1pm & 4–8pm; winter Mon–Sat 9am–1pm & 3–7pm; ☏0921.671.124), can supply maps, and there a few good **accommodation** options: the inexpensive *Ariston*, Via Vittimaro 2 (☏0921.671.321; no credit cards, ❶), is a good bet in town, or head 2km out of town on the SS286 to the *Bergi* agriturismo ranch (☏0921.672.045, ⓦwww.agriturismobergi.com; ❶), with spacious accommodation and a cavernous room for meals. For more luxury, there's the five-star *Relais Santa Anastasia*, 3.5km before Castelbuono (☏0921.672.233, ⓦwww.santa-anastasia-relais.it; ❼), a restored tenth-century abbey with pool, jacuzzi and fitness centre. For **lunch**, don't miss the wild-mushroom dishes at the highly-recommended *Nangalarruni*, Confraternite 5 (closed Wed), with its brick and fresco decor. It also has a good tourist menu at €13 and the sweet, local *digestivo*, Elisir di Fontana, is definitely worth a sip or two. The **Internet**, a rare luxury in these parts, can be surfed at Planet Web, Via Vittorio Emanuele 46 (☏0921.677.193).

Beyond Castelbuono there's good **hiking** country: head up the road (SS286) towards Geraci Sículo, and half an hour's walk gives you splendid views back over the town and castle. There's a superb hike from Castelbuono to Piano Battáglia (see box above), or you could keep on the road as far as **GERACI SÍCULO** itself, 25km from Castelbuono, sitting under the brow of its hill and marked by a ruined eleventh-century castle. Buses come this way, too, from Cefalù three times a day, passing through Castelbuono, and you can complete the transmountain route by staying on until Gangi, another 25km.

East to Capo d'Orlando: more routes inland

The best stretches of the Tyrrhenian coast all lie **east of Cefalù**: clean sand and stony beaches, backed for the most part by extensive groves of orange and lemon trees. The train stops at several small seaside resorts – **Castel di Tusa**,

Sant'Agata and Capo d'Orlando – where there's reasonable hotel accommodation. There are buses south, too, into the hills – the **Monti Nébrodi** – from various points on the coast; short runs worth making if only for a breath of fresh air away from the popular beaches. If you're driving, you can easily park on certain stretches of the highway and make your way down to the more remote beaches, though motoring along this road can be hairy in the summer, especially as the railway intersects the road at several points, bringing traffic to a standstill for up to fifteen minutes while trains pass.

Castel di Tusa

Some 25km east of Cefalù, the village of **CASTEL DI TUSA** is smaller and quieter than most along this stretch, with the remnants of a defensive castle, some good rocky beaches and a unique place to stay. There's a **campsite** here, *Lo Scoglio*, Strade Statale 113, km 164 (☎0921.334.345; May–Sept), though a better option is the town's only **hotel**, the *L'Atelier sul Mare*, close to the sea on Via C. Battisti (☎0921.334.295, ⓦwww.ateliersulmare.com; ❸–❺). Founded by local artist Antonio Presti, the hotel's rooms are designed by different artists: one is adorned with Arabic and Italian poetry and sports a mammoth window to the sea, with a shower that works like a car wash, while another has furnishings that emanate a red glow at night. Non-residents can see round the rooms on a guided tour daily at noon.

Three kilometres up the road (there's no bus), on the way to the inland village of **TUSA**, are the sparse ruins of **Halaesa** (daily 8am–1hr before sunset; €2), a fifth-century BC Sikel settlement that enjoyed some success under Rome until despoiled by the Praetor Verres. The name derives from the Greek *alaomai*, meaning to wander aimlessly, and refers to the original settlers here, the peripatetic Alesini, who had tried settling just about everywhere else. You can just about make out the chequered layout of the streets, remains of the *agora*, and – at the highest point – foundations of two third-century BC temples, with lofty views down over the Tusa valley.

Santo Stéfano and Mistretta

Frequent trains from Palermo/Cefalù stop at **SANTO STÉFANO DI CAMASTRA**, a coastal resort known for its colourful ceramic work. Santo Stéfano is awash with gift shops, with plates, jugs and decorative pottery piled high along the sides of the roads – haggle hard for the best bargains. There's an eclectic range of ceramics displayed in the spacious **Museo della Ceramica** (Mon–Fri 9am–1pm & 4–8pm; closes 7pm in winter; free), towards the sea in the Palazzo Trabia, Via Palazzo. Upstairs are beautifully restored rooms with colourful ceilings, and an impressive ceramic kitchen range. If you need a **place to stay**, the only option is *La Playa Blanca*, Via Fiumara Blanca (☎0921.331.248, ⓦwww.laplayablancahotel.com; ❹), a fine place right on the water, located on the road just east of town. There's also the usual selection of **fish restaurants** and **pizzerias**, catering to Italian holidaymakers.

Just to the west of Santo Stéfano, a high viaduct flies off 16km inland to the first and biggest of the **Nébrodi** hill-villages, **MISTRETTA** – reached by bus from Santo Stéfano. The handsome old centre of eighteenth- and nineteenth-century buildings is unspoiled by modern construction; a seventeenth-century cathedral has the hoary look of a medieval monument; and the population is largely composed of brown-suited pensioners milling around their veterans' associations. If you can, visit during the Saint's Day's **festivities** (the Festa della Madonna) on

September 7–8, when the Madonna delle Luci is paraded around accompanied by figures of Mytia and Kronos, allegedly the founders of the village.

Mistretta also holds one of the few **accommodation** options in the Nébrodi hills, an alternative in high season to taking your chances down on the noisy coast. The sole hotel is the *Sicilia*, at the top of the main corso at Via Libertà 128 (☎0921.381.463; closed ten days in Sept; ❶), which also runs a **pizzeria** with outside seating. For snacks, though, call in at the *Gran Bar*, halfway up the corso – it's an old-fashioned place perfectly in keeping with Mistretta's prevailing sepia tone.

The road from here rolls on over the range to Nicosia, 28km south (see p.327), accessible by a regular daily bus which afterwards doubles back into the mountains to the small village of Capizzi, isolated amid vernal woods and meadows.

Sant'Agata and San Fratello

Back on the coast, **SANT'AGATA DI MILITELLO** is one of the livelier Tyrrhenian resorts, busy and noisy in summer with mainly Italian tourists. Its wide landscaped promenade supports a little funfair, there's a very long pebbled beach, and the remains of a dumpy castle now house a pizzeria. The small fishing fleet working off these shores means you get excellent fish in the local restaurants and, if you want **to stay**, there's the standard two-star *Parimar*, Via Medici 1 (☎0941.701.888; ❷), a good fifteen-minute walk from the centre of town, or the slightly cleaner and nicer *Roma Palace* (☎0941.703.516, ℻0941.703.519; ❹). In summer, **hydrofoils** connect Sant'Agata with the Aeolian Islands; the Covemar agency at Via Medici 383 (☎0941.701.318) sells tickets.

Several buses a day from Sant'Agata slink south over the mountains to Cesarò, the first part of the meandering route taking in **SAN FRATELLO**, just 15km from the coast. This large village was once populated by a Lombard colony, introduced to Sicily by Roger II's queen, Adelaide di Monferrato, and still retains Gallic-Italian traces in the local dialect. The best time to come here is on the Thursday and Friday of Holy Week, before Easter, for the **Festa dei Giudei** (Feast of the Jews) – a unique Carnevale-type celebration in the post-Lent period, when locals adorn themselves in red devils' costumes, masked and hooded, complete with black tongues and horses' tails (a reminder of their traditional trade of horse-raising), to the cacophonic accompaniment of trumpets, bells and drums. Needless to say, the ecclesiastical authorities take a dim view of these proceedings, but have to make do with having the Easter Sunday church congregations in suitably contrite and sober mood.

For a pleasant picnic spot, head for the Norman church of **Santi Alfio, Filadelfio e Cirino**, isolated on top of a hill at the entrance to the village (follow the rough track from the cemetery). The church is dedicated to three brothers horribly martyred by the Romans: the first had his tongue torn out, the second was burnt alive, and the third hurled into a pot of boiling tar.

San Marco d'Alunzio and Frazzanò

Seeing any more of the coast between Sant'Agata and Capo d'Orlando, or the hills beyond, isn't really on without your own transport. Buses are too few and far between to be much good for day-trips, although regular services do leave Sant'Agata for **SAN MARCO D'ALUNZIO**, 5km away and a couple of kilometres inland. An impressively sited village, called Aluntium by the Romans, San Marco had already been established in Greek times, and its principal point of interest, the **Tempio di Ércole**, recalls that era – an evocative shell that was converted into a Norman church by Robert Guiscard. It has since been deconsecrated, though something of its mystique remains, thanks to its imposing position high above the coast. Later religious monuments, many built from the local red marble, particularly the **Chiesa di Santa Maria della Grazie**, with a *Madonna* attributed to **Domenico Gagini**, and the **Chiesa Matrice** with an unusual triumphal arch, make San Marco somewhere you could easily spend a couple of hours roaming around; there are also the fragmentary remains of a **castle** where members of the Hauteville family (Sicily's Norman rulers) once resided.

A short drive east along the coastal road brings you to the turnoff for **FRAZZANÒ**, 14km up in the mountains, beyond which lies the Basilian church and monastery of **San Filippo di Fragalà**, a fortress-like structure built by Count Roger in the eleventh century. With high walls enclosing a courtyard, this is sadly abandoned and falling apart, but you can tiptoe over the crumbling floors and peer into the narrow cells, examine the faded Byzantine frescoes on the walls of the church, and enjoy the views from the ramparts. If there's no one around to let you in, try round the back for an open door.

Capo d'Orlando and Naso

Occupying a headland that was the site of a historic defeat for the Aragonese king, Frederick II, at the hands of a group of rebellious barons in 1299, **CAPO D'ORLANDO** is a slick holiday town today, surrounded by good rocky and sandy beaches. It's the last major resort on this stretch of coast and if you're sufficiently charmed by the **swimming**, which is best on its eastern side (around the San Gregorio area), you might well want **to stay**. The cheapest choice is the 1960s-style *Nuovo Hotel Faro*, Via Libertà 7 (⊕0941.902.466, ⓦwww .nuovohotelfaro.com; ❸), with spacious rooms and balconies fronting the sea, though half-board is compulsory in August. Turn right out of the station and walk along Via Crispi, head for the sea at Piazza Matteotti, and the hotel's a few blocks to the right. For **information**, ask at the kiosk on the seafront (summer daily 9.30am–12.30pm & 4.30–9.30pm) or the regular **tourist office** at Via Piave 71, on the corner of Via Losardo (Mon–Sat 9am–1pm & 4.30–7.30pm; ⊕0941.912.784).

Inland from Capo d'Orlando, the oddly named town of **NASO** ("Nose") sits at the end of a twelve-kilometre bus ride, where you can see (just before entering the town, up a steep lane on the left) the partly ruined **Convento dei Minori Osservanti** – fifteenth-century, with an interesting tomb of the same period decorated with allegories of the six virtues. The road continues up, another 33km, to **Floresta**, lying on a grassy plain and, at 1275m, claiming the distinction of being Sicily's highest village, then down to Randazzo and the foothills of Mount Etna.

Roman remains at Patti, Tíndari and San Biagio

East of the cape, the coast is more built-up, as the unremarkable towns merge into one long conurbation. **Patti**, however, 30km on, possesses the remains of a fourth-century AD **Roman villa** – east of the town, close to the train station and under an autostrada viaduct. The extensive site (daily 9am–1hr

△ Fishermen and lobster, Capo d'Orlando

before sunset; €2.10, or €2.60 for a combined ticket with Tyndaris) contains a few poorly maintained mosaics and the ruins of a bathhouse. At the top of the town, Patti's **Cattedrale** has a powerful *Madonna* by Antonello de Saliba and, in the right transept, the tomb of Adelasia, much-loved first wife of Roger I, with the date of her death inscribed at the bottom, 1118.

Tíndari

Patti's villa is one of a series of classical remains dotted along this stretch of coast. The area's most complete collection lies at **TÍNDARI**, 11km to the east (around three buses daily from Patti's main square). Originally founded in 396 BC, **Tyndaris**, as it was known, was one of the last Greek settlements in Sicily, built and fortified by settlers from ancient Syracuse as a defence against Carthaginian attacks along this coast. Almost impregnable on its commanding height, the town prospered even under Rome, when it was given special privileges in return for its loyalty.

As the bus climbs the hill to the site, however, the first thing you see, glistening from its cliff-top position, is the **Santuario di Tíndari** (daily 6.45am –12.30pm & 2.30–7pm), a lavishly kitsch temple erected in the 1960s to house the much-revered *Madonna Nera*, or Black Madonna. A plaque underneath this Byzantine icon boasts *Nigra sum, sed hermosa* ("I am black, but beautiful"), a

reference to the esteem in which she has been held for a thousand years since the icon appeared from the east to perform a series of miracles, such as producing a soft mattress in the nick of time to save a child who was hurtling to the rocks below. Pilgrims throng to the sanctuary to pay their respects, especially around the Black Madonna's feast day on September 8. Buses stop in the car park over 1km from the sanctuary, from where minibuses leaving every ten minutes or so shuttle up to the litter of cabins and stalls at the foot of the church (return tickets €0.60). There's a great view from the sanctuary, overlooking a long tongue of white sand and the Marinello lagoons below.

The **archeological site of Tyndaris** (daily 9am–7pm; €2) lies at the end of a path that starts in front of the sanctuary. Most of the visible remains are Roman, including some houses and shops along the main street, the *decumanus* – one of them (probably a *caldarium*, or bathhouse) with traces of plumbing still surviving – and an impressive **basilica** at the eastern end. Strictly an entrance to the *agora* lying beyond (in the area now covered by tourist shops), this building was restored in the 1950s, using modern materials, though it still retains a certain grandeur. You can just about make out the manner of its construction, bridging Greek and Roman building techniques, and designed in such a way that the central gallery could be shut off at either end and used for public meetings, with the market traffic diverted along the side passages.

The *decumanus* has streets running off it, and at the bottom of one is the **Casa Romana**, a Roman house in good condition, with mosaic floors. At the other end of the main street, the **teatro**, cut into the hill, boasts a superb view over the sea, as far as the distant Milazzo promontory. A part of the stage remains from the original third-century BC Greek edifice, but most of the rest is Roman, dating from the Imperial Age when the theatre was converted for use as a gladiatorial arena. Later, it was partly dismantled to furnish stone for the **city walls** that once surrounded the settlement, of which a good portion remain. You'll have seen some of them on the road up, including the ancient city's **main gate**, built to the same "pincer" design as the one at the Euryalus castle outside Siracusa (see p.287).

The site's **museum** (currently closed) contains some of the best finds from the excavations, including a massive stone head of Augustus. There's also a reconstruction of the theatre's scene-building, and some eighteenth-century watercolours showing how the basilica looked before its overhaul.

Ask at the ticket office by the entrance to the archeological site (℡338.992.84.53) for information on the **classical dramas** and **concerts** staged here in the evenings during July and August; tickets generally cost around €15.

San Biagio

If have your own transport, you could drive a further twenty minutes along the coastal road east of Tíndari to the more modest Roman remains at **SAN BIAGIO**, right on the SS113. The excavations of a first-century AD **Roman villa** here (daily 9am–1hr before sunset; €2.10) revealed interesting evidence on the construction of baths, but above all it's the vivid mosaics that make this worth stopping for – one in particular depicting a fishing scene at sea.

Practicalities: seeing the sites

There are two **train stations** within reach of the main sites: Patti–San Piero Patti station is the stop for Patti; for Tyndaris you can either take a bus from Patti station direct to the site, or stay on the train for a few more kilometres to Oliveri–Tíndari, from where it's about a three-kilometre (uphill) walk.

Without a vehicle, it's easy to get stranded in these parts. If you do stay, there's plenty of decent and peaceful **swimming** to be enjoyed, and there are a couple of **campsites** at Patti and one at Oliveri. Best of these is the *Marinello* (☎0941.313.000), quiet and within a few steps of a good sandy beach; it's located off the coast road between the two towns, at the end of a track. Patti also has some decent enough beachside **hotels**; *Villa Romana*, on Via Praia (☎0941.361.268; ❶), a few metres from the sea, offers the best value.

Inland: to Castroreale

From San Biagio, two choice inland routes branch off into the Monti Nébrodi, the first of which, the SS185, is the only road in the province connecting the Tyrrhenian and Ionian coasts, leading to Giardini-Naxos (see p.234). This is one of the finest routes on the island, climbing gently into the hills through some handsome countryside to **NOVARA DI SICILIA**. You could make a convenient lunch-break at this small town, in the *Pineta* **trattoria**, just off the main square (Largo Bertolami), which serves inexpensive meals. The dense woods above, with expansive views over the sea, are a favourite spot for the locals, who come out here on a Sunday, armed to the teeth with picnic hampers and portable stoves, though there are enough shady nooks and glades to find your own space. The road climbs to 1270m before descending, in sight of Etna's dramatic slopes, to Francavilla and Castiglione (see p.238).

Castroreale

Back on the coast and heading east, you can make a detour at the uninspiring Barcellona to the Peloritan hill-town of **CASTROREALE**, 8km to the south and one of the oldest cities in Sicily. Favoured by Frederick II of Aragon, who came here for the hunting, the town enjoys magnificent views over the hills and out to sea. At its highest point is a tower, the one remaining fragment of Frederick II's fort, built in 1324 and subsequently ruined by earthquakes.

The rest of Castroreale is creakingly medieval, and it's enough just to stroll along the quiet, sloping streets, dropping in at the couple of basic bars for a drink. If you feel like **staying**, there's an excellent agriturismo, *Green Manors*, just outside town (☎091.811.3262, 🖷091.811.4225, 🖥www.greenmanors.com; ❼), run by a Belgian-Italian family and dishing up some of the best meals around.

To get to Castroreale by public transport, take a bus from the bus station at Barcellona (3 daily Mon–Sat; last departure at 2.30pm); if you're arriving by train, hourly buses connect the *autostazione* with Barcellona's train station, some way out of the centre (tickets from the bar in the station). Alternatively, it would not be inconceivable to walk up, by following the Longano River valley inland for about three hours – the steep bit's at the end.

Milazzo

If it weren't for the industry besieging **MILAZZO** – the first major town on this coast after Términi – it wouldn't be a bad-looking place. A long plane- and palm-tree-lined lungomare looks across the sparkling sea, while behind the town a rambling old castle caps Milazzo's ancient acropolis. Most people, though, are put off by the unsightly oil refinery that occasionally produces a yellow smog overhead, and only stop long enough to get out again, taking the first ferry or hydrofoil to the Aeolian Islands (see Chapter Three), for which Milazzo is the major point of embarkation. But Italian tourists know the town well, and regularly crowd the beaches and campsites strung along **Capo Milazzo**, the finger of land behind the town.

The Town

If you're in a hurry, Milazzo is easy enough to handle. You could be on an outward-bound ferry or hydrofoil within an hour of arriving; see below for all the details. But there's enough in and around town to make it an enjoyable overnight stop, before or after your Aeolian trip, with one major sight – the castle – that stands comparison with any in Sicily.

Historically, the site's strategic importance made it one of the most fought-over towns in Sicily. The Greeks arrived in 716 BC, after which the town was contested by successive armies, from the Carthaginians to the Aragonese. It even became a base for the British during the Napoleonic Wars, while fifty years later Garibaldi won a victory here that set the seal on his conquest of Sicily. None of this is evident from the fairly nondescript modern streets behind the port, but a fifteen-minute walk north along Lungomare Garibaldi and up through the **old town** offers a pleasing change in aspect. Here, the views open out over bay and plain, while the higher you climb, the older and more decrepit the buildings become – some churches and *palazzi* on the approach to the castle are little more than precariously balanced shells.

To appreciate the citadel's size, walk round to the north side, where the formidable defences erected by the Spanish still stand almost in their entirety. The massive walls are magnificent, pierced by a suitably imposing tunnelled gateway. The **castello** itself (guided tours hourly Tues–Sun: March–May 10am–noon &

ACCOMMODATION
California	A
Central	C
Cosenz	B
La Bussola	D
Riviera Lido	E

RESTAURANTS
Al Gámbero	2
Il Covo del Pirata	4
La Casalinga	3
Pizzeria da Tonino	1

MILAZZO

0   200 m

3–5pm; June–Sept 10am–noon & 5–7pm; Oct–Feb 3–5pm; €3.10) is steeped in military history: built by Frederick II in the thirteenth century on the site of the Greek acropolis and on top of Arab foundations, it was enlarged by Charles V, and restored by the Spanish in the seventeenth century. Inside the castle walls is the **Duomo Antico** (presently closed for restoration), a central Norman keep, the old Sala del Parlamento and the remains of the Palazzo dei Giurati, later used as a prison.

Milazzo has a couple of other churches worth looking at. Directly opposite the castle's entrance, the Dominican **Chiesa del Rosario**, together with its convent, was formerly a seat of the Inquisition, while below, in the new town, the silver-domed **Duomo Nuovo** has some excellent Renaissance paintings in the apse: four panels of SS Peter, Paul, Rocco and Thomas Aquinas; between the last of these, an *Adoration of the Child* by Antonello de Saliba, and an *Annunciation* by Andrea Giuffrè above that. Large, graceful chandeliers adorn the nave.

Capo Milazzo

The thin promontory north of town is the focus of most of the summertime activity. A couple of fine hotels, three or four well-equipped campsites and a decent restaurant or two are grouped around the headland of **Capo Milazzo**, 6km out of town; it's a twenty-minute bus ride away on #2 from Piazza della Repubblica (start of the lungomare) or #6 from the port or Piazza della Repubblica. There are plenty of good **beaches** all around here, but the sandiest is close to the centre of town, on Milazzo's western, less-developed side (at the end of Via Colombo).

Practicalities

Buses (including the Giuntabus service from Messina) stop right on the quayside. The **train station** is a good 3km south of the centre, but local buses run into town every twenty to thirty minutes during the day, dropping you on the quayside or further up in Piazza della Repubblica. Buy tickets (€1) from the bar inside the train station, or take a taxi (around €10).

Milazzo's **tourist office** is at Piazza Duilio 20 (Mon–Sat 9am–1pm & 3–6pm; July & Aug also Sun 10am–noon & 6–8pm; ☎090.922.2865), just back from the harbour. There's **Internet** access nearby at Mailboxes Etc., Via Dei Mille 7 (Mon–Fri 8.30am–1pm & 4–8pm; €6 per hour).

For **ferries** and **hydrofoils** to and from the Aeolian Islands, see the box on p.165; shipping agencies in Milazzo are listed opposite.

Accommodation

There are plenty of reasonably pleasant **hotels** handy for the port; though if you have a car and the inclination to get out of town, one of the nicest spots is the *Riviera Lido* (☎090.928.3456, ℱ090.928.7834; ❺), with its own beach on the promontory on the Strada Panoramica.

Less-exalted choices in town include the *Central*, Via del Sole 8 (☎090.928 .1043; ❷), a cheery little place with nice large rooms. The *California*, opposite, at Via del Sole 9 (☎090.922.1389; ❷), is drearier and darker, though you get a room with bathroom for the price (singles share). If these are full, next best choices are the *Cosenz*, in Via E. Cosenz (☎090.928.2996; ❷), or the more upmarket *La Bussola*, at Via XX Luglio 29 (☎090.928.2955, ⓦwww.hotelabussola .it; ❺), with a buffet breakfast included in the price. None of the first three accepts credit cards. Of the **campsites at Capo Milazzo**, the huge *Villaggio*

Turistico Cirucco (℡ & ℻090.928.4746; mid-June–Oct) and the *Riva Smerelda* (℡090.928.2980; May–Oct) both also have bungalows for rent, too (both ❷).

Eating and drinking

Milazzo's *passeggiata* is one of the liveliest in Sicily, with baby buggies, vespas and cars clogging Lungomare Garibaldi, and a swarm of couples and families dropping in for ice cream at the bars along the way. One noteworthy spot for a **drink**, just downhill from the castle on Via Duomo Antico, is the *Caffè Antico*, whose outdoor terrace has distant views of the coast.

Of the **pizzeria–restaurants** right by the port, *Al Gámbero* is quite popular and moderately priced, though not particularly distinguished. Local favourites for fish are *La Casalinga* (closed Sun evening Sept–July), on Via Riccardo D'Amico, off Lungomare Garibaldi, where the speciality is spaghetti with crab sauce, and *Il Covo del Pirata*, Lungomare Garibaldi 47–48 (closed Wed Sept–July), which can be fairly pricey, though it serves cheaper pizzas as well. Best place for these, however, is *Pizzeria Da Tonino*, Via Cavour 27 (closed Mon in winter), right in the centre and with low prices. Out of town, on the cape, two places to try are the classy fish restaurant *Villa Esperanza*, Via Baronia 191, set in a large garden (℡090.922.916; closed Mon and Nov), and *La Baia*, on Via Sant'Antonio, for pizzas.

Getting to the Aeolians

Sailings to the Aeolians operate daily and are frequent enough to make it unnecessary to book (unless you're taking a car), although bear in mind that there is a reduced service between October and May. Inconveniently, the ferry companies only sell one-way tickets, so if you're going just for the ride, you'll have to rush off the boat on one of the Aeolians to buy a return ticket back to Milazzo before the ferry leaves port. For schedules and prices **from Milazzo**, see the box on p.165.

The **shipping agencies** are all down by the Milazzo harbour and open usual working hours as well as before all departures – Siremar for ferries and hydrofoils, Ústica Lines for hydrofoils only, and NGI for ferries only. You can pick up useful ferry/hydrofoil **timetables** from any of the agencies below. If you need to leave a car in Milazzo, there's a convenient choice of **garages** (including a couple on Via G. Rizzo) – expect to pay around €10 per day.

Navigazione Generale Italiana (NGI) Via dei Mille 26 ℡090.928.3415.
Siremar Alliatour, Via dei Mille 45

℡090.928.3242.
Ústica Lines Catalano, Via dei Mille 33 ℡090.928.7821.

Festivals

February/March
Carnevale celebrated in **Cefalù** with three days of events, including a costumed children's procession on the last day.

Easter
Holy Week On the Thursday and Friday, bizarre happenings at **San Fratello**, the Festa dei Giudei, with processions and devils' costumes. Processions, too, in **Barcellona**.

May
Festival in **Milazzo** dedicated to San Francesco di Paola.

June
Start of the theatrical performances and concerts at the castle in **Milazzo**; runs through to August.

May
Start of the theatrical season at **Tyndaris** with events in the ancient theatre; runs through to August.

August
15 Procession of boats along the coast in honour of Madonna di Porto Salvo at **Capo d'Orlando**.

September
A medieval procession, La Castellana, in **Cáccamo**, composed of five hundred characters representing all the notables in the town's history from the eleventh to the nineteenth centuries.

Check with tourist office in Palermo for dates (sometimes held in Aug).
7–8 Procession with Madonna delle Luci and her guardians at **Mistretta**.
8 Informal pilgrimage to the sanctuary of the Black Madonna at **Tyndaris**. Pilgrimage, too, at **Gibilmanna**, south of Cefalù.

October
Horse fair in **San Fratello**.

November
Historical fair held in **Sant'Agata di Militello**.

Travel details

Trains

Cefalù to: Messina (1–2 hourly; 2hr 20min–3hr); Milazzo (1–2 hourly; 1hr 35min–2hr 25min); Palermo (hourly; 45min–1hr).
Milazzo to: Cefalù (hourly; 1hr 35min–2hr 25min); Messina (1–2 hourly; 35min–1hr); Palermo (hourly; 2hr 30min–3hr 10min).
Sant'Agata di Militello to: Barcellona (1–2 hourly; 1hr–1hr 20min); Capo d'Orlando (1–2 hourly; 15min); Messina (1–2 hourly; 1hr 25min–2hr 20min); Milazzo (1–2 hourly; 50min–1hr 20min); Oliveri–Tíndari (hourly; 55min); Patti (1–2 hourly; 40min).
Términi Imerese to: Cefalù (1–2 hourly; 30min); Messina (1–2 hourly; 2hr 30min–3hr 25min); Palermo (every 30min; 35min); Sant'Agata di Militello (1–2 hourly; 1hr 10min–1hr 30min); Santo Stéfano di Camastra (hourly; 1hr 10min).

Buses

Barcellona to: Castroreale (3 daily Mon–Sat; 30min).
Cáccamo to: Palermo (2 daily; 1hr 15min); Términi Imerese (2–6 daily Mon–Sat; 15min).
Castelbuono to: Campofelice (1 daily Mon–Sat; 1hr 10min); Cefalù (8 daily Mon–Sat, 2 daily Sun; 40min); Collesano (1 daily Mon–Sat; 50min); Gangi (3 daily Mon–Sat, 2 daily Sun; 1hr 20min); Geraci (3 daily Mon–Sat, 2 daily Sun; 50min); Isnello (1 daily Mon–Sat; 25min); Palermo (3 daily Mon–Sat; 1hr 50min–2hr); Términi Imerese (1 daily Mon–Sat; 1hr 30min).
Cefalù to: Castelbuono (11 daily Mon–Sat, 2 daily Sun; 40min); Gangi (4 daily Mon–Sat, 1 daily Sun; 2hr); Geraci (4 daily Mon–Sat, 1 daily Sun; 1hr

25min); Gibilmanna (3 daily; 30min); Palermo (2 daily; 1hr); Petralia (1 daily; 1hr 30min).
Milazzo to: Messina (hourly; 50min).
Patti to: Tíndari (3–5 daily; 20min).
Sant'Agata di Militello to: Cesarò (1 daily; 1hr 30min); San Fratello (1 daily; 20min).
Santo Stéfano di Camastra to: Mistretta (3–6 daily; 40min); Nicosia (1 daily Mon–Sat, change at Mistretta; 2hr 50min).
Términi Imerese to: Cáccamo (2–6 daily Mon–Sat; 15min); Castelbuono (1 daily Mon–Sat; 1hr).

Ferries

Ferry timetables change seasonally, so if time is of the essence, it's always worth checking with the tourist office or ferry company for the most up-to-date schedules.
Milazzo *June–Sept* to: Alicudi (2 daily; 6hr); Filicudi (2 daily; 4hr 55min); Ginostra (5 8 weekly; 6hr); Lípari (6–9 daily; 2hr); Naples (6 weekly; 16hr 30min); Panarea (6–10 weekly; 4–5hr); Rinella (6–8 weekly; 3hr 40min); Santa Marina (6 daily; 3hr–3hr 40min); Strómboli (6–10 weekly; 5hr 10min–7hr); Vulcano (3–6 daily; 1hr 30min).
Milazzo *Oct–May* to: Alicudi (2 weekly; 6hr 5min); Filicudi (2 weekly; 4hr 55min); Ginostra (2 weekly; 6hr); Lípari (8 daily; 2hr); Naples (2 weekly; 16hr 30min); Panarea (2 weekly; 4–5hr); Rinella (2 weekly; 3hr 40min); Santa Marina (8 daily; 3hr–3hr 40min); Strómboli (2 weekly; 5hr 10min–7hr); Vulcano (8 daily; 1hr 30min).

Hydrofoils

Hydrofoil timetables change seasonally so, if time is of the essence, it's always worthwhile checking with the tourist office or hydrofoil company for the most up-to-date schedules.

Cefalù *June–Sept* to: Strómboli, calling at all Aeolian islands (1 daily, 5hr); Palermo (1 daily; 1hr 10min).

Milazzo *June–Sept* to: Alicudi (4 daily; 2hr 55hr); Filicudi (4 daily; 2hr 20min); Ginostra (3 daily; 1hr 45min–2hr 30min); Lípari (hourly; 45min–1hr); Panarea (6 daily; 1hr 45min–2hr 10min); Rinella (7 daily; 1hr 40min); Santa Marina (hourly; 1hr 20min–2hr); Strómboli (6 daily; 1hr 25min–2hr 20min); Vulcano (hourly; 45min).

Milazzo *Oct–May* to: Alicudi (5 weekly; 2hr 55min); Filicudi (5 weekly; 2hr 20min); Ginostra (1 daily; 2hr 30min); Lípari (hourly; 45min–1hr); Panarea (3 daily; 1hr 30min); Rinella (hourly; 1hr 40min); Santa Marina (hourly; 1hr 20min–2hr); Strómboli (3 daily; 1hr 25min–2hr 20min); Vulcano (hourly; 45min).

Sant'Agata di Militello *July–Sept* to: Lípari (1 daily; 1hr 10min); Vulcano (1 daily; 1hr).

The Aeolian Islands

③

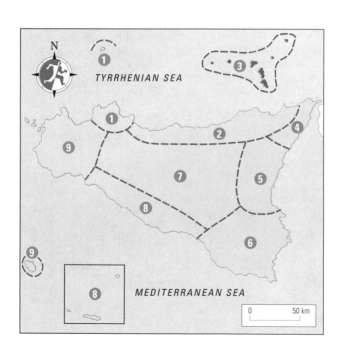

CHAPTER 3 # Highlights

✳ **Museo Eoliano, Lípari**
An essential stop for anyone in the Aeolian Islands, this holds numerous prehistoric works as well as one of Sicily's best collections of Greek antiquities. **p.166**

✳ **The view from Quattrocchi, Lípari**
One of the all-time great panoramas from Lípari's western coast, this encompasses the faraglioni and the island of Vulcano. **p.177**

✳ **The mud baths of Vulcano** Wallowing in this murky, smelly soup might not be to everyone's taste, but it's a memorable experience, and good for you to boot. **p.178**

✳ **Pollara, Salina** The beach here is one of the best in the archipelago, offering utter serenity and crystal-clear waters. **p.186**

✳ **The ascent of Strómboli** The night-time is the best time to appreciate fiery explosions from the crater here. **p.191**

△ View from Quattrocchi, Lípari

3

The Aeolian Islands

The **Aeolian Islands**, or Isole Eolie, are a mysterious apparition when glimpsed from Sicily's northern coast – sometimes it's clear enough to pick out the individual white houses on their rocky shores; at other times they're murky, misty and only half-visible. D.H. Lawrence, on his way to Palermo by train in bad weather, thought they resembled " … heaps of shadow deposited like rubbish heaps in the universal greyness". The sleepy calm that seems to envelop this archipelago masks a more dramatic existence: two of the islands are still volcanically active, and all are buffeted alternately by ferocious storms in winter and waves of tourists in summer. But their unique charm has survived more or less intact, fuelled by the myths associated with their elemental and unpredictable power. Volcanoes have always been identified with the mouths of hell, and it was here that Jupiter's son, Vulcan, had his workshop. One of the islands is named after this god of fire and metalworking, while another takes its name from Liparus, whose daughter Ciane married Aeolus, ruler of the winds and master of navigation; Aeolus, in turn, lent his name to the whole archipelago. These winds were kept in one of the Aeolians' many caves, which were presented to Odysseus in a bag to bring on his travels. His curious crew opened the bag and, as a result, blew his ship straight back to port.

The more verifiable **history** of the islands is equally eventful. The first settlers exploited the volcanic resources here, above all the abundance of obsidian, a hard glass-like rock that can be worked to produce a fine cutting edge and was traded far and wide, accruing enormous wealth to the archipelago. The islands were drawn more closely into the Greek ambit by the arrival, at about 580 BC, of refugees from the wars between Segesta and Selinus (Selinunte). Welcomed by the inhabitants, these errant Greeks organized themselves into two groups: those who cultivated the land and settled the smaller islands, and those who defended their settlements from Etruscan pirates and, in turn, preyed on other shipping. The land was held in common, and the loot divided – this system was so successful that their contributions to the sanctuary at Delphi rivalled even those of great Syracuse. Those Greeks based on the fortified citadel of Lípari later allied themselves with Carthage, who made Lípari their base during the First Punic War. For its pains, Greek Lípari was destroyed by the Romans in 251 BC and the islands became part of the Roman province of Sicily, paying a hefty tribute to Rome as well as taxes on its exports of obsidian. The islands subsequently changed hands several times before being abandoned to the frequent attacks of wide-ranging North African pirates, culminating in the terrible slaughter that took place in 1544 at the hands of Khair ed-Din, or Barbarossa, who

THE AEOLIAN ISLANDS

Naples

Strombolicchio

Strómboli

Strómboli

Ginostra

Lisca Bianca

Bottaro

Le Formiche

Basiluzzo

Dáttilo

Panarea

San Pietro

Punto Milazzese

Acquacalda

Porticello

Canneto

Santa Marina di Salina

Lingua

Lipari

Lipari

Canale di Salina

Terme di
San Calógero

Malfa

Salina

Pollara

Rinella

Bocche di Vulcano

Vulcano

Porto di Levante

Filicudi

La Canna

Valdichiesa

Filicudi Porto

Capo Graziano

N

Milazzo

Réggio di Calabria

& Messina

Alicudi

Alicudi Porto

Cefalù & Palermo

0

20 km

consigned all the survivors of the massacre to slavery – a figure estimated to have been as high as 10,000. Italian unification saw the islands used as a prison for political exiles, a role that continued right up to World War II, with the Fascists exiling their political opponents to Lípari. The last political detainee to be held here was, ironically, Mussolini's own daughter, Edda Ciano, in 1946.

Emigration, especially to Australia, had reduced the Aeolian population to a mere handful of families by the late 1950s, when the arrival of the first hydrofoil signalled salvation by a nascent tourist industry. Agriculture has largely been abandoned, and the economic revival today is based purely on tourism (though Lípari's pumice industry still flourishes), with hotels sprouting on previously barren ground, and running water and electricity installed almost everywhere. Nonetheless, enough primitive splendour has remained for the islands to attract a procession of film crews, the movies ranging from Rossellini's *Strómboli: Terra di Dio* (1949), mostly remembered for the director's off-screen romance with the star, Ingrid Bergman, and Antonioni's *L'Avventura* (1960), filmed on the rocks at Panarea's Lisca Bianca, to Nanni Moretti's *Caro Diario* (*Dear Diary*, 1994), shot on all the islands, and Michael Radford's *Il Postino* (1994), filmed on Salina. Recently listed as a UNESCO World Heritage site, the Aeolians also appeal to hiking enthusiasts and geologists, with good waymarked paths on nearly all the islands.

The highlights

Each Aeolian island has a distinct identity, though all are embraced by beautiful, clean sea of a limpid quality rarely found along the coast of Sicily. Sandy **beaches** are sparse, and tend to be ash-black, but by renting a **boat**, easily done at every Aeolian harbour, there's access to any number of secluded coves, hidden caves and quiet snorkelling waters. **Scuba diving**, too, is popular, with schools on several islands. Other attractions include a series of remarkable **archeological** sites – notably on Lípari, Panarea and Filicudi – and, quite simply, the fruits of the islands' agricultural and fishing industries. **Aeolian food** is some of the most distinctive in Italy, with the traditional crops of capers and olives flavouring most dishes, *malvasia* grapes providing one of Sicily's more ancient wines, and fresh swordfish, tuna and squid in abundance.

During the summer months at least, you'll not be alone, especially on the popular, central islands. **Vulcano**, with its mud baths, hot springs and smoking main crater, is closest to the mainland and too well known for its own good. **Panarea**, the smallest and most elite Aeolian, also attracts a well-heeled crowd that descends on its few hotels and beaches every August. The only two with any room are the main island, **Lípari**, and less popular **Salina** – the former sporting the most sights and facilities of all the islands, the latter making a calmer alternative base, with little glitz or hubbub. For something completely different, a trip up to **Strómboli**'s seething crater is an unforgettable experience; the island itself is also becoming increasingly trendy with the chic set, as well as with enthusiastic groups of volcano-climbers. But for a taste of what it was like twenty – or a hundred – years ago, make the effort to get out to the two remotest of the Aeolian Islands, **Filicudi**, with a tiny but surprisingly high-quality choice of accommodation and restaurants, and **Alicudi**, the wildest of the group. The islands are easy to explore using the frequent ferries and hydrofoils traffic that ply between them, and whose arrival is often the high point of the day. **Out of season** is a different matter altogether, and in most islands that can mean up until early June and after early September. With many facilities closed and activities drastically curtailed, there's a refreshing absence of other tourists, and accommodation rates accordingly plummet. You may find glorious sunshine in winter, but if the weather turns, you're in danger of being stuck here for days – the archipelago is frequently lashed by storms between October and March, and cut off from the mainland by heavy seas.

Getting to the Aeolian Islands

Access is easiest and cheapest **from Milazzo** (see p.153), with year-round ferries and hydrofoils connecting the port with all the islands. Most ferries and hydrofoils from Milazzo call first at Lípari, which is connected by ferry and hydrofoil to all the other islands, though some stop in at Vulcano first. Schedules and ticket prices from Milazzo are detailed in the table overleaf.

There are also fairly regular hydrofoil services in summer **from Palermo**, **Cefalù** and **Messina**; see "Travel details" at the end of the relevant chapters, and contact local tourist offices and travel agents for current information. Note that routes from Palermo and Cefalù stop in Filicudi and Alicudi first. There are also irregular summer services to Lípari and Vulcano from Tyrrhenian ports – usually from **Capo d'Orlando** or **Sant'Agata Militello** if they're operating at all (see p.148 and p.149). From **mainland Italy**, there are connections from Réggio di Calabria (some via Messina) and Naples; from Naples, Strómboli is the first port of call. Lastly, in summer occasional cruises run to the islands from Vibo Marina, on the Calabrian coast. See "Travel details" (p.203) for a rundown of the main services.

You'll find it useful to get hold of **timetables** from the tourist offices in Milazzo or Messina, or from the ferry and hydrofoil companies themselves: Siremar (ⓦwww.siremar.it), Ústica Lines (ⓦwww.usticalines.it) and NGI (ⓦwww.ngi-spa.it) are the main operators. Car-carrying **ferries** (*navi* or *traghetti*) take about twice as long as **hydrofoils** (*aliscafi*), but are nearly half the price, and the hydrofoils are more prone to cancellation in bad weather, particularly on routes to the more distant islands. Few services are full and there's rarely a problem getting tickets at the harbourside office before departure, except in August, when you should buy tickets a few days in advance.

Getting around

Lípari is the hub of the Aeolian ferry and hydrofoil system, and you may need to return there to catch onward services to one of the other islands. Once there, most of the islands are small enough to be easily negotiable **on foot**, and if you're planning on **hiking**, or climbing the craters on Vulcano and Strómboli, take strong shoes or boots. Both Lípari and Salina are equipped with good **public transport** links, and are the only two islands you might consider taking a car to, but it's hardly necessary. Two wheels would be more apt, and you can **rent bicycles** (€5–15 per day), **mopeds and scooters** (€15–50 per day) on the islands; agencies are noted in the text. There are also **garages** in Milazzo to store your car if you need to (see p.156). For a pricey alternative, Air Panarea's **helicopter** service, at Via I Ditella on Panarea (ⓉO090.983.4428, ⓦwww.airpanarea.com), can take you anywhere in the islands – including night tours of Strómboli – as well as Naples and Rome.

Ferries and hydrofoils from Milazzo

The following table shows the frequency of services from Milazzo and gives the (rounded-up) price for the relevant one-way journey: return tickets are double, children go for half-price, and tickets are a few euros cheaper from October to May. Taking a car from Milazzo to Lipari costs between €17 and €40, depending on its size (an average four-door costs €25); bicycles are €4; vespas around €7; hydrofoils allow bicycles only. Note that you'll need to pay an extra €1 on top of the prices quoted below, as part of a tax levied on all journeys to the islands from the Sicilian mainland.

Milazzo to:	Ferries (navi/traghetti)			Hydrofoils (aliscafi)		
	June–Sept	Oct–May	Price	June–Sept	Oct–May	Price
Alicudi	5 weekly	4 weekly	€12.80	2 daily	1 daily	€21.30
Filicudi	5 weekly	4 weekly	€12.70	2 daily	1 daily	€17.50
Ginostra (Strómboli)	6–7 weekly	4 weekly	€12.50	3 daily	1 daily	€16.20
Lipari	7 daily	4 daily	€6.30	hourly	hourly	€11.30
Panarea	6–7 weekly	4 weekly	€7.60	6 daily	2 daily	€13.30
Salina (Santa Marina)	4 daily	4 daily	€7.90	hourly	hourly	€12.80
Salina (Rinella)	6–8 weekly	4 daily	€8.30	7 daily	9 daily	€12.80
Strómboli	6–7 weekly	4 weekly	€10	6 daily	2 daily	€16.20
Vulcano	4 daily	4 daily	€5.80	hourly	hourly	€10.50

Accommodation

In high season (Easter, July & Aug), **accommodation** is scarce and expensive, and if you want to stay at these times, you'd be wise to phone and book some weeks in advance, particularly for Strómboli. You may also find that many places insist that you pay for **half-board** (*mezza-pensione*), which covers dinner, bed and breakfast: with restaurant prices relatively high, this is usually a fairly good deal.

Outside high season, many hotels and *pensioni* drop their prices by up to fifty percent. Also, **renting apartments** or **private rooms** can turn out to be an economical option; we suggest several places which offer rooms in the Guide – otherwise, ask around and look for *cámere* signs, or apply to *agenzie immobiliari* (rental agencies) in Lípari. There's a **youth hostel** on Lípari, and **campsites** on Lípari, Vulcano and Salina – but camping rough is illegal.

Prices and facilities

Prices on the islands verge on the exclusive side. **Restaurants** can be expensive, since much of the food (as well as much of the water on some islands) has to be imported; service and cover charges on Lípari and elsewhere can touch fifteen to twenty percent. In many places, there's not always the option of a cheap pizzeria either, so if money is tight expect to do some self-catering.

All the islands are connected by **telephone**, and there are phone kiosks at every harbourside, even in remote areas, though almost everyone sports mobile phones. The **Internet** is still quite rare, with only three islands offering public access. There are **banks** and/or ATMs on every island but Alicudi, and you can change money at some post offices, travel agencies and major hotels, though the rates aren't as good. **Water** is scarce and you will be asked to use the minimum. **Electricity** has only slowly come to some islands and, if you're spending any time on Alicudi, Filicudi or Strómboli, a torch isn't a bad investment.

Lípari

LÍPARI is the busiest, the most popular and the most diverse island in the Aeolian archipelago. Arriving by sea at its main town – also called Lípari – gives a pleasant foretaste of what is to come: a thriving little port, dominated by an impressive castle on an acropolis which effectively divides the town into two. The road that circles the island from here takes in several much smaller villages, some good beaches and excellent views out to its neighbouring islands, all of which are within easy reach.

Historically, it has always been Lípari that has guided the development of the Aeolians. In classical times, after obsidian had been superseded by metals, the island's prosperity was based on its sulphur baths and thermal waters, which still attract many visitors today. Its alum, too, was much prized, and was found more abundantly here than anywhere else in Italy. Today, with a population of over

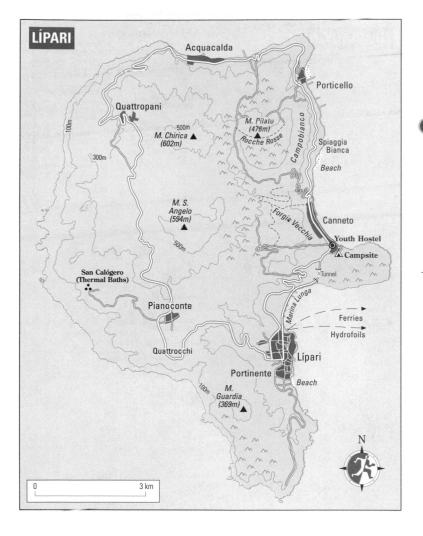

10,000, the economy is bolstered by a thriving pumice industry in the north of the island, though the main money-spinner is inevitably Lípari's natural beauty, which brings in tourists by the boatload.

Lípari Town

LÍPARI TOWN's sights are concentrated in its citadel, or **upper town**, protected by the sturdy walls of the **castello**. Most of what remains of this formidable structure is sixteenth-century Spanish in style, though it incorporates fragments of earlier medieval and even Greek buildings. Until the eighteenth century, this was the site of Lípari town, and still

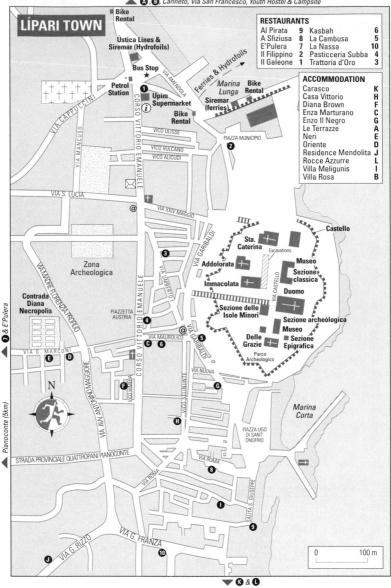

Canneto, Via San Francesco, Youth Hostel & Campsite

LÍPARI TOWN

Bike Rental

Ústica Lines & Siremar (Hydrofoils)

Bus Stop

Petrol Station

Upim Supermarket

Bike Rental

Marina Lunga

Bike Rental

Siremar (ferries)

Ferries & Hydrofoils

PIAZZA MUNICIPIO

VICO ULISSE
VICO VULCANO
VICO ALICUDI

VIA AMENDOLA

CORSO VITTORIO EMANUELE

VIA CAPPUCCINI

VIA MANCUSO

VIA S. LUCIA

VIA XXIV MAGGIO

VIA GARIBALDI

Zona Archeologica

Contrada Diana Necropolis

VIA MADRE FLORENZA PROFILIO

PIAZZETTA AUSTRIA

VIA G. MARCONI

CORSO VITTORIO EMANUELE

VIA UMBERTO

VIA MAUROLICO

VIA NUOVA

VIA ROMA

VIA SCILIUTE

VIA AVV. ANTONIO MAGGIORE

VICO RAFFAELA

STRADA PROVINCIALE QUATTROPANI PIANCONTE

VIA ROMA

VIA G. FRANZA

VIA G. RIZZO

SALITA S. GIUSEPPE

PIAZZA UGO DI SANT' ONOFRIO

Marina Corta

Castello

Sta. Caterina

Excavations

Museo

Addolorata

Sezione classica

Immacolata

Duomo

VIA CASTELLO

Sezione delle Isole Minori

Sezione archeólogica

Delle Grazie

Museo Sezione Epigrafica

Parco Archeológico

N

Pianoconte (5km)

& E'Pulera

&

0   100 m

RESTAURANTS

Al Pirata	9	Kasbah	6
A Sfiziusa	8	La Cambusa	5
E'Pulera	7	La Nassa	10
Il Filippino	2	Pasticceria Subba	4
Il Galeone	1	Trattoria d'Oro	3

ACCOMMODATION

Carasco	K
Casa Vittorio	H
Diana Brown	F
Enza Marturano	C
Enzo Il Negro	G
Le Terrazze	A
Neri	E
Oriente	D
Residence Mendolita	J
Rocce Azzurre	L
Villa Meligunis	I
Villa Rosa	B

contains the **Duomo** (daily 9am–1pm), along with the dilapidated ruins of several Baroque churches, giving the place a forgotten, spectral air. The most impressive approach to the upper town is from Via Garibaldi, from which long steps cut right through the thick walls, bringing you up to the Duomo itself: scattered all about are the **excavations** of superimposed layers of occupation, from the Neolithic to the Roman age, a continuous record covering almost two thousand years. It's a unique sequence, providing archeologists with heaps of finds that have enabled them to date other Mediterranean cultures.

Museo Eoliano

You won't make much sense out of the wide trench exposing fragments of Bronze Age and Iron Age huts without going into the superb **Museo Eoliano** (daily 9am–1.30pm & 3–7pm; €4.50), housed in buildings scattered around the Duomo and which contains one of Europe's most important prehistoric and classical collections.

To the right of the Duomo, the seventeenth-century bishop's palace contains the main **Sezione Archeológica** of the museum. Its displays are laid out chronologically, starting upstairs with Neolithic to Bronze Age discoveries. Here, for example, is revealed the early exploitation of obsidian, made into blades and exported all over the western Mediterranean – glass cases contain mounds of shards, worked flints, adzes and knives. These give way to finds from ancient burial sites, where you can trace the development of the various Aeolian cultures through their pottery: from the earliest, extremely plain examples to later work, adorned with motifs and other ornamentation. Downstairs covers the Iron Age to classical times, and again it's easy to follow the social and economic progress of the islands – burial techniques become more sophisticated, while the Bronze Age tools displayed here are more elaborate and more useful than anything seen previously, with scalpels, razors and fine blades all on show. There's vivid figurative work, too, such as the lid of a mid-sixth-century BC *bothros*, or sacred repository of votive articles, embellished with a reclining lion.

The other principal section of the museum, the **Sezione Classica**, on the left side of the Duomo, holds classical and Hellenic material retrieved from various necropoli. Some of this is imaginatively displayed, such as the eighth-century BC burial urns from Milazzo preserved in sections of lavic wall. There are also re-creations of both a Bronze Age burial ground and of the Lípari necropolis (eleventh century BC), where bodies were either buried in a crouching position in large, plump jars or their cremated remains placed in bucket-shaped jars (situlae). Most eye-catching of all, perhaps, are the towering banks of amphorae, each 1m or so high, dredged from the ocean under Capo Graziano (p.197), many still encrusted with barnacles.

The upstairs rooms of the Sezione Classica hold the most treasured items, including shelves of **decorated vases** – some from Paestum showing a variety of satyrs, gods, queens, clowns and courtiers, from the first half of the fourth century BC. Later polychromatic works are identified as those of an individual known as the Lípari Painter (300–270 BC) and his pupils and rough contemporaries. On vases, jars and bowls, the decorations and pictures explore an extraordinary variety of themes – sacrifices, bathing scenes, mythical encounters and ceremonies. Other funerary goods here are less simple to categorize, but are often more affecting: toy vases and statuettes from a young girl's grave, and delicate clay figurines of working women using mortar and pestle or washing children in a little bath.

The museum, though, is best known for what comes last in the Sezione Classica, namely the oldest and most complete range of Greek **theatrical masks** in existence. Many are models, found in fourth-century BC graves, and covering the gamut of Greek theatrical life from the tragedies of Sophocles and Euripides to satyr plays and comedies. The latter are particularly well represented, with masks of Hades and Herakles bearing unnerving, gruesome grins. One room has a good collection of small terracottas grouped in theatrical scenes, while there are also statuettes representing actual dancers and actors – nothing less than early Greek pin-ups of the period's top stars. On the way out, spare a glance for the series of etchings by the English sea captain, W.H. Smyth, showing views of the Aeolians and other Sicilian scenes in 1823.

Having scoured the main sections of the museum, you may be daunted to discover that there's still more to come, but in truth the final two sections warrant not much more than a skip through. Across the road from the archeological section, a building houses the **Sezione delle Isole Minori**, covering the prehistory of the minor islands and including some lovely vases from Salina, finds from sites on Panarea and Filicudi, and a wealth of vulcanological material. Around the back of the archeological section, the **Sezione Epigrafica** contains a little garden of tombs and engraved stones, and a room packed with more inscribed Greek and Roman tombstones and stelae. Most people head straight for the **Parco Archeológico** instead (Mon–Sat: April–Sept 9am–7pm; Oct–March 9am–4pm; free). Situated at the end of the road, it also has some Greek and Roman tombs, and a modern Greek-style theatre where concerts and plays are performed between July and September. There's a nice view over the rooftops and the Marina Corta from here.

The rest of town

There's little else specific to see in Lípari, though the lower town does provide occasional reminders that the citadel wasn't the only part of the settlement inhabited in classical times. A **Zona Archeológica** (usually locked), off the main corso, preserves the remains of various buildings and houses; rather easier to appreciate is the **necropolis**, visible off Via G. Marconi, where Greco-Roman tombs stud a sunken field. The finds from here, called the Contrada Diana necropolis, are held in the Sezione Classica of the museum.

Other than this, the main activity is mooching around the town's small, packed streets, with their lively array of chic boutiques and souvenir emporia interspersed with *alimentari* and fishing-tackle shops. The best place to while away an afternoon is at the **Marina Corta**, where the constant coming-and-going of hydrofoils, taxis, bikes and people can be observed from the cool haven of parasol-covered bars. The pedestrianized **Corso Vittorio Emanuele** is usually awash with people, while Piazza Municipio (also called Piazza Mazzini), just north of the *castello*, has more fine sea views. A good time to be around is on August 24, when the town's main **festival** takes place – dedicated to St Bartholomew and an excuse for all sorts of high jinks.

Practicalities

Hydrofoils and **ferries** dock at the Marina Lunga (sometimes called Porto Sottomonastero), which has a small **left-luggage** office (daily 8am–8pm; €3 for 12 hours). A fifteen-minute walk south of here is Marina Corta, a smaller harbour used for excursion boats, with virtually everything

Lípari is not a bad place to book a boat excursion, since it's close enough to the main group of islands to allow a decent day-trip. You could, of course, simply use the scheduled ferry and hydrofoil services to visit the neighbouring islands, but if you're staying in Lípari and want to do an all-day trip visiting and swimming off Panarea, then seeing Strómboli by night, one of the agencies in town (see "Listings", p.174) can oblige for around €35. Day-trips to Panarea or Vulcano, allowing plenty of swimming, are around half that price. Alternatively, a group might bargain with one of the fishermen down at the Marina Corta for a boat trip around Lípari – prices are negotiable, depending on numbers and season.

Marina Lunga is the departure point for full-day boat excursions to one of Lípari's best beaches at Vinci, a secluded cove on the southwestern shore, where gentle sand abuts crystal-clear water. Return tickets cost €5, with numerous departures a day – try the Gruppo Arancio stalls at both Marina Lunga and Marina Corta (☎368.767.0342 or 334.329.5486); the last return is currently 7.50pm.

of note lying between these two marinas. The **tourist office**, at Corso Vittorio Emanuele 202 (July & Aug Mon–Fri 8.30am–1.30pm & 4–10pm, Sat 8.30am–1.30pm; Sept–June Mon–Fri 8.30am–1.30pm & 4.30–7.30pm; ☎090.988.0095, ⓦwww.aasteolie.info), can provide a useful hotel list for all the Aeolian Islands, a local bus timetable, and other brochures and leaflets. For details of ticket offices for **ferry and hydrofoil departures**, see "Listings" (p.174).

Accommodation

There's more choice of **accommodation** in Lípari than any of the other islands, though you can still find yourself stuck for a room in high season. Outside peak summer season, most places have reductions of up to forty to fifty percent and, in July and August especially, it makes sense to listen to the offers of **rooms** as you step off the boat. You'll pay around €25–40 per person in August, €20 at other times of the year, and, though you may be asked to spend a minimum of two nights (or a week in summer), it can still work out cheaper (and nicer) than a *pensione*, given that you'll nearly always get something with a shower, kitchen, and balcony or terrace. Alternatively, look for notices in shop windows, or ask around in the harbour bars and shops. Other budget choices include the **youth hostel** and the island's only **campsite** – both out at Canneto, 3km north of town (see p.175). All Lípari's hotels and some rented rooms have pages on the islands' website, ⓦwww.netnet.it – as do all the hotels on the other islands.

Carasco Porto delle Genti ☎090.981.1605, ⓕ090.981.1828, ⓦwww.carasco.it. Superbly located three-star hotel with its own rocky cove, pool and sparkling views. Excellent facilities (and some good off-season discounts). Mid-April to mid-Oct. ⑧

Casa Vittorio Vico Sparviero ☎ 090.981.1523 or 338.392.3867. Open year-round, the nine rooms and apartments – some with kitchenettes – are clean and plain, though the ground-floor rooms don't get much sun; there is also a roof terrace. From October on singles drop to €20. ⑤

Diana Brown Vico Himera 3 ☎ 090.981.2584 or 338.640.7572, ⓦwww.dianabrown.it. Centrally located in a tiny lane parallel to Corso Vittorio Emanuele, the twelve rooms have air-conditioning, fridges and kettles, and several have full kitchen facilities. Spotlessly clean with a great roof terrace, the place is run by a jovial South African expat; breakfast for €5 per person. ⑤

Enza Marturano Via Maurolico 35 ☎368.322.4997. Four bright, immaculate and modern rooms with views, ranged around a communal lounge/kitchen, with a terrace overlooking the corso; off season you

△ Boat, Lípari

can get singles here for €15. Call ahead if possible: otherwise, the owner usually greets the early-morning boats (and lives at Via Umberto I 13). No credit cards. ❸

Enzo Il Negro Via Garibaldi 29 ℡ 090.981.3163, ✉ enzoilnegro@libero.it. Eight rooms – all with TV and private bathroom – just up from the hydrofoil port, with a splendid roof terrace. ❺

Residence Mendolita Via G. Rizzo ℡ 090.981.2374, ℻ 090.981.2878, Ⓦ www .mendolita.it. Attractive terraced villas and apartments south of the town centre, near the Portinente beach. They're operated in conjunction with the excellent *Filippino* and *E'Pulera* restaurants (see below) and the half-board price (around ❻ per person in Aug) gets you a meal in either. The cheaper options go fast. ❻

Neri Via G. Marconi 43 ℡ 090.981.1413, ℻ 090.981.3642, Ⓦ www.pensionineri.it. Down an alley off the corso after no. 85, this fine old mansion, quiet and well kept, has wrought-iron balconies, with breakfast (included in rates) served on a lovely terrace, though there's no restaurant. Some rooms look straight onto the necropolis; travellers' cheques as well as credit cards accepted. March to mid-Nov. ❼

Oriente Via G. Marconi 35 ℡ 090.981.1493, ℻ 090.988.0198, Ⓦ www.hotelorientelipari.com. Just down from the *Neri* and similar in quality and facilities, this English-managed place is stuffed with knick-knacks and sports a patio garden and air-conditioned rooms; full bar attached. ❼

Rocce Azzurre Via Maddalena 69 ℡ 090.981.3248, ℻ 090.981.3247, Ⓦ www.hotelrocceazzurre.it. Adjacent to its own little pebble beach, 10min south of the centre, this secluded hotel is popular with families. There's a sun terrace built over the rocks and you can arrange diving/snorkelling here, too. At least half-board (from ❻ per person) is the rule in Aug. ❼

Le Terrazze Via Francesco Crispi 135 ℡ 090.981.2386 or 338.585.8821, Ⓦ www.eoliecasevacanze.it. These rented rooms and apartments, some with cooking facilities, lie a 10min walk north of the Marina Lunga, towards Canneto, and right across from the sea. Scooters and cars are available to rent. After September, rooms drop to €32, making this one of Lipari's best out of-season deals. No credit cards. ❺

Villa Meligunis Via Marte 7 ℡ 090.981.2426, ℻ 090.981.0149, Ⓦ www.villameligunis.it. A converted *palazzo*, this elegant central four-star has excellent views of the citadel and sea from its rooftop restaurant, which sports a pool alongside. Well-run with all the amenities, and great discounts off-season. There is also an equally luxurious eighteenth-century annexe with apartments. ❽

Villa Rosa Via Francesco Crispi 134 ℡ 090.981.2217. Right next door to *Le Terrazze* (see above), this place has very similar rooms, plain but comfortable with attached bathrooms, and right in front of the sea. Fridges and cooking facilities are provided. No credit cards. ❹

Eating

The town has numerous **restaurants and pizzerias**, many of them open-air. Some offer tourist menus at €10–15, though these can be poor quality, and even the cheaper places levy exorbitant fifteen- to twenty-percent service charges. The restaurants below with telephone numbers require reservations in high season: for an explanation of the price categories, see p.53.

For self-catering, there's a UPIM **supermarket** (Mon–Fri 8am–9pm, Sat 9am–9.30pm) and various *alimentari* and bakeries on the main corso – *Il Fornaretto* **bakery**, at no. 117, sells fine bread, as well as pizza slices and *calzone* to go (closed Wed afternoon & Sun). *Giovanni D'Ambra Pasticceria*, Vico Morfeo 50, just by the hydrofoil port, has excellent baked goods and Aeolian sweets.

La Cambusa Via Garibaldi 72. Small, popular place with tables on the street and quite reasonable prices for its Sicilian specialities. Closed Nov–Easter. Moderate.

E'Pulera Via Diana ℡ 090.981.1158. Run by the daughter of the *Filippino* family, this romantic courtyard-garden restaurant specializes in rich and filling Aeolian food: swordfish *involtini*, caper salads, home-made pasta, almond biscuits, *malvasia* wine. Super cooking, well worth the prices, and it stays open till late (kitchen closes at midnight). It's 2min behind the *Neri pensione* (see above); turn left at the end of Via G. Marconi. Closed lunchtimes & Oct–Mar. Expensive.

Il Filippino Piazza Municipio ☎090.981.1002. Lípari's top restaurant, in business since 1910. It's in the upper town and has a shaded outdoor terrace and high prices, but the food and atmosphere make it well worthwhile – the *zuppa di pesce* is particularly good, as is the grouper-stuffed *ravioloni*. The massive wine list is a veritable encyclopedia of Italian vintages. Closed mid-Nov to Dec and Mon Jan to mid-April. Very expensive.

Il Galeone Corso Vittorio Emanuele 220. Streetside pizza joint at the top end of the main corso, just around the corner from the ferry port. Choose from one of twenty tasty pizzas – and from other dishes too, or try the €11.50 *menù turistico*. Closed Nov–Jan and Wed outside summer. Inexpensive.

Kasbah Via Maurolico 25 ☎090.981.1075. Chic restaurant with a long garden, where fish is prepared in original ways – try the *tagliata di tonno*, tuna breaded and cooked with almonds and tomatoes, or the original *pizza siciliana*. Closed Mon & Nov–March. Expensive.

La Nassa Via Giuseppe Franza 36 ☎090.981.1319. Local favourite just 5min from the Marina Corta, with excellent seafood, a semi-formal atmosphere and folk art on the walls. Closed Oct–March. Expensive.

Trattoria d'Oro Via Umberto I 32. Back-street trattoria with decent, though not sensational, food and often long waits. There's a short à la carte menu, or a €16 fixed-price menu including dessert, cover charge and service. Moderate.

Al Pirata Salita S. Giuseppe, Marina Corta ☎090.981.1796. Classy, often busy, place enjoying the town's best harbourside location, but secluded and serene. Home-made pasta and fresh seafood are on the menu. Closed Nov–April. Expensive.

Pasticceria Subba Corso Vittorio Emanuele 92. One of the island's best, going for seventy years and serving up coffee, cakes and pastries from breakfast time until late in summer (closes 7/8pm in winter); nice outdoor seating. No credit cards. Inexpensive.

A Sfiziusa Via Roma 29. Budget-priced trattoria back from the hydrofoil port that's good for pasta and fresh fish of the day; squid and prawns are frozen, though. Closed Sun Oct–April. Inexpensive.

Drinking and nightlife

Best **bars** for lounging around in are those with outdoor seats at the Marina Corta – *Il Gabbiano*, *La Vela*, *Café du Port* and *Al Pescatore* (also a restaurant) – where the beers and snacks are pricey but the vantage-point is the best in town. *Chitarra*, across the square beneath the church, also has harbourside seats and **live music** most nights after 10pm, while *Bar La Precchia*, 191 Vittorio Emanuele, occasionally has a DJ spinning lounge music out front. Lípari goes to bed fairly early, though in summer at least you can extend the night by drinking at the *Megaton Bar*, Via XXIV Maggio 51, on the way to the castle (open until 2.30am; closed Fri Oct–June). Alternatively, out of town, there's **dancing** at *White Beach* on the lungomare in Canneto, and at *Sangre Rojo* disco (☎338.290.9524) in Quattropani, whose loud pop music attracts huge crowds (both open late and summer only).

Listings

Banks and exchange Change money and travellers' cheques at Banca Antonveneta, on Via Ten. M. Amendola, just off the corso; at Banca Mercantile Italiana, Banca di Roma or the Monte dei Paschi di Siena, all on the corso (all with ATMs); or at Cassa di Risparmio, on Piazzetta Austria (ATM). Hours are generally Mon–Fri 8.30am–1.30pm & 3–4pm, Sat 8.30am–12.00pm. There are exchange facilities at Costa-Meligunte Travel, Eoltravel and Menalda Tours, all on the corso, but the rates aren't as good. You can also change cash or American Express travellers' cheques at the post office (see p.175).

Bike and scooter rental Expect to pay from €15 per day for a bike, and around €50 for a scooter, excluding fuel (much less outside peak season); you'll have to leave your passport, credit card or a hefty deposit as security. Rental outlets include: Da Tullio, Via Amendola 22, Marina Lunga ☎090.988.0540; Da Marcello, Via Sottomonastero, Marina Lunga ☎090.981.1234; and Roberto Foti (see "Car rental", below).

Boat excursions Navigazione Regina, Marina Corta, Marina Lunga and lungomare in Canneto ☎ 090.982.2237; Gruppo Arancio, Marina Lunga and Marina Corta ☎ 368.767.0342; Pignataro Shipping, Marina Corta ☎ 090.981.1417; Roberto Foti (see "Car rental", below) arranges excursions to Strómboli, including the ascent on foot, for €50 per head including the guide.

Boat rental Rubber dinghies rent from €60 a day, plus deposit (fuel extra). Operators include Da Massimo, with a kiosk on Piazza Marina Corta ☎ 360.549.627; and Roberto Foti (see "Car rental" below).

Bookstore Mimmo Belletti, Corso Vittorio Emanuele 203, sells a large selection of English newspapers and books as well as local maps and guides (summer daily 8am–midnight; winter daily 8.30am–2pm & 4.30pm–9pm).

Car rental Roberto Foti, Via F. Crispi 31 ☎ 090.981.2352, with offices also at Via Roma 47 and at Canneto; from €40 per day.

Diving Many of the larger hotels can put you in touch with a diving school, or contact the Diving Centre La Gorgonia, Salita S. Giuseppe, Marina Corta ☎ 335.571.7567 or 090.981.2060, Ⓦ www.lagorgoniadiving.it. Roberto Foti (see "Car rental", above) also rents out scuba gear.

Emergencies Hospital ☎ 090.98.851; first aid ☎ 090.988.5267; Carabinieri ☎ 090.981.1333.

Ferry and hydrofoil companies NGI, Via Ten. M. Amendola, near Marina Lunga ☎ 090.981.1955; Siremar, dockside offices at Marina Lunga, hydrofoils ☎ 090.981.2200 and ferries ☎ 090.981.1312; Ústica Lines, dockside office at Marina Lunga ☎ 090.981.2448.

Internet Internet Point, Corso Vittorio Emanuele 185 (daily 9am–1pm & 4–8pm); Net Café, Via Garibaldi 61 (daily 9am–1pm & 4–10pm). Both charge about €3 for 30min.

Pharmacy Cincotta, Via Garibaldi 60 ☎ 090.981.1472; Internazionale, Corso Vittorio Emanuele 128 ☎ 090.981.1583; Sparacino, Corso Vittorio Emanuele 95 ☎ 090.981.1392. Pharmacies open late according to a rota system, detailed on the doors of the shops.

Post office Corso Vittorio Emanuele 207 (Mon–Fri 8.30am–6.30pm, Sat 8.30am–1.20pm).

Showers The barber shops in the square at the Marina Corta and on Via Maurólico have public showers.

Telephones Public phones on Via Garibaldi; outside the UPIM supermarket on the corso; Piazzetta Austria; and at Marina Corta and Marina Lunga.

Around the island

Buses leave Lípari town (from Marina Lunga, opposite the service station) approximately every hour for the **rest of the island** (every 20min in summer for Canneto, less regular on Sundays and outside July and August). Nowhere is more than thirty minutes' ride away; pick up a timetable from the bus operators, Urso Guglielmo (☎ 090.981.1262), at Via Cappuccini 29, above the Marina Lunga. Buses run in two directions: clockwise to Quattropani (€1.55); and anticlockwise to Canneto (€1.30), Porticello and Acquacalda (both €1.55) buy tickets on board. If you're really pushed for time, but want to get a flavour of Lípari's island scenery, Urso buses run a ninety-minute **tour of the island** (*giro dell'isola*) three times a day (currently at 9.30am, 11.30am & 5pm; €3.70) from July to the end of September; reservations essential, and a minimum of eight people.

Marina Lunga is also the site of the island's only **petrol stations** (Agip and Esso), as well as two or three **scooter– and bike-rental** outfits; see "Listings" (p.174) for details. There are **taxis** available on the Marina Corta.

Canneto

It's around 3km north of Lípari town to the nearest village, **CANNETO**, with the bus swooping through a tunnel to reach the bay on the other side of the headland from town. A long stony beach fronts the village, itself little more than a long succession of bars and trattorias, mostly closed outside summer. If you're after more secluded swimming, stay on the bus until it reaches a stop beyond the far northern end of the lungomare, at a steep rise. From here, a stepped path runs up, around and down to the **Spiaggia Bianca**, an expansive sand-and-pebble beach that is popular with locals and tourists alike, and worth the effort to reach. Refreshments and parasols are available in summer.

Canneto itself has a leisurely air, with parasols and dinghies for hire on the long shore, and a few good accommodation options including a couple of **hotels**: the *Odissea*, on the road parallel to the seafront at Via Nazario Sauro 14 (☏090.981.2337; closed Oct–May; ❼), offering en-suite rooms with partial sea views; and the discreetly luxurious *Casajanca*, Marina Garibaldi 109 (☏090.981.2337; ❽), whose comforts hardly merit the sky-high rates in summer, but are a real bargain outside the peak season. You can get a better deal at the *Giallorosso*, on the corner of Marina Garibaldi and Via Risorgimento (☏090.981.1298; Easter–Oct; no credit cards, ❹), where the rented **rooms** – some with air-conditioning, all with private bathrooms – overlook the sea. Canneto also has the archipelago's only **youth hostel**, in a house right at the southern end of the seafront (☏090.981.1540; March–Oct; no credit cards). With limited capacity and few vacancies in summer (early booking is advisable), there are no dormitories here, but mini-apartments, each with cooking facilities, for €20 per person, €13 outside summer. It's just a few metres down from the island's only **campsite**, the *Baia Unci* (☏090.981.1909; March–Sept), a nice, clean place, with its own simple bar and restaurant. The bus from Lípari stops outside hostel and campsite.

Among the **restaurants** in Canneto, try *La Bussola* for moderately priced pizzas and full meals, or the wood-panelled *del Pescatore*, for their solid €14 *menù turistico* – both lie at the southern end of the strip. The village also has a small supermarket and a couple of *alimentari*. You can **rent scooters** from Roberto Foti, Marina Garibaldi 16 (☏090.988.0825).

Campobianco and Monte Pilato

Buses continue north of Canneto, through the Cave di Pomice at **CAMPOBIANCO**, where the various pumice workings have left huge white scars on the hillside; the ground all around for 2 or 3km looks as if it's had a dusting of talcum powder. More uses for this volcanic debris are being found all the time, and it's presently used in such diverse products as toothpaste, light bulbs, construction materials, jeans (for bleaching) and fertilizer. Years of accumulation of pumice sediment on the sea bed below have turned the water a piercing aquamarine colour – very enticing and instantly accessible by sliding the 30m or so down the brilliant white mountains of dust formed by the quarrying. This is nothing new to the islanders and other cognoscenti, who've been doing it for years; indeed the pumice-chute was used for one of the closing scenes in the Taviani Brothers' epic film *Kaos*.

Above Campobianco, a path leads up the slopes of **Monte Pilato** (476m), thrown up in the eruption from which all the pumice originally came. The last explosion occurred in around 700 AD, leading to the virtual abandonment of Lípari town and creating the obsidian flows of Rocche Rosse and Forgia Vecchia, both of which can be climbed. Although it's overgrown with vegetation, you can still make out the outline of the crater at the top, and you may come across the blue-black veins of obsidian. Despite obsidian's quite different appearance, it is almost identical in composition to pumice, and it's the presence of obsidian on Lípari that makes the island's beaches sparkle.

Porticello and Acquacalda

There's a bus stop above the stony beach at **PORTICELLO**, from where a road (and a quicker, more direct path) winds down to a small bay, which sunbathers share with the Heath Robinson–style pumice-work machinery that connects the white hillside with the pier. Somewhere, you feel, should be someone cranking a handle on a very large wheel to set it all in motion. There's no shade here, and the pebble beach soon reaches scalding temperatures, though the water is a tempting colour. A couple of vans sell cool drinks and snacks.

There are seven or eight buses a day out here from Lípari, all of which terminate a couple of kilometres further on at **ACQUACALDA**. You could walk between the two villages in about half an hour, if you wanted some aerial views of the azure waters and pumice quarries, and pick up the return Lípari bus in either place. Acquacalda itself is just a one-street village – not a very attractive one – with more pumice machinery, a long, usually deserted stone beach and a couple of waterfront bars selling panini and other snacks. There's also a homely **trattoria** – *Da Laura* – which has a terrace overlooking the sea and Salina across the water; it's at the top of the road coming into the village from Porticello. Another, more enticing option is *Aurora*, a seafood restaurant with seating smack on the beach. Both are closed in winter.

Quattrocchi to Quattropani

Heading west from Lípari town, you can walk to the vantage-point for one of the Aeolian Islands' most stunning vistas. Climbing the 3km through lush and fertile country, you'll know you're at **QUATTROCCHI** when Vulcano and the spiky *faraglioni* rocks, which puncture the sea between the two islands, sweep into view to the south. The curious name of this spot ("Four Eyes") is said to derive from the fact that newly wedded couples traditionally come here to be photographed, so gracing every shot of this memorable place with two pairs of eyes.

Keep on the road to **Pianoconte**, a fragmented village that has a trio of popular restaurants, best of which is probably *La Ginestra* (☎090.982.2285; closed Mon), with a shady veranda and pizzas in the evening.

Just before the village, a sideroad slinks off down to the old Roman thermal baths at **San Calógero**. It's a particularly pleasant route to follow on foot, across a valley and skirting some impressive cliffs, the baths right at the end of the road. Lengthy excavations here have unearthed a great deal of archeological material, particularly from the Mycenaean age (fifteenth century BC), and even if the spa-hotel is closed (as it usually is) you should be able to look around the site, including the steamy chamber where the hot water issues, and walk down the path to the sea below.

The bus from Lípari (through Quattrocchi and Pianoconte) ends its run at **QUATTROPANI**, a dispersed settlement with a pleasing church and more fine views. There are twelve buses a day here (seven on Sun), though if it isn't too hot you could walk the 5km or so, round the winding road, to complete the island circle at Acquacalda, and catch the bus back from there.

Vulcano

Only a few minutes south of Lípari by ferry or hydrofoil, separated by the kilometre-wide channel Bocche di Vulcano, is the island of **VULCANO**. Closest of the Aeolians to the Sicilian mainland, it's the first port of call for services from Milazzo, and you don't have to disembark to experience the sulphurous, rotten-egg smell which, with the wind in the right direction, hits you before you've even reached the small port – disconcerting if you're not expecting it. The island's **Gran Cratere** hangs menacingly over its inhabited northern tip, its plume of vapour a constant reminder of its silent power, though this very old volcano is in the last, smoking, phase of its life and unlikely to spring anything more harmful than the nasty smell.

That said, the volcano was threatening enough to dissuade anyone from living here before the eighteenth century, since when there have been some hasty

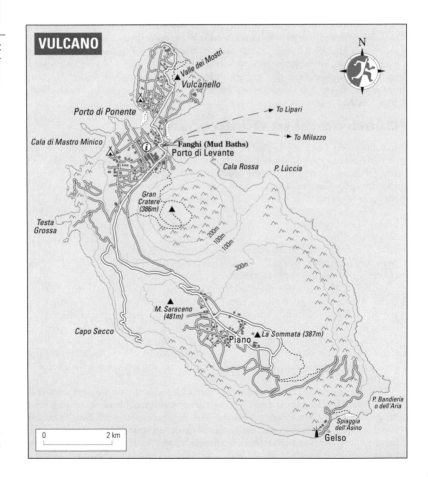

evacuations, and subterranean activity here is still monitored round the clock. In the nineteenth century a Scot called Stevenson bought the island to exploit the sulphur and alum reserves, but all his work was engulfed by the next major eruption. Although the volcano's last gasp of activity occurred between 1886 and 1890, its presence permeates the island, giving Vulcano a more primeval flavour than any of the other Aeolians. Everything here is an assault on the senses, the outlandish saffron of the earth searing the eyes, as violent as the intense red and orange of the iron and aluminium sulphates that leak out of the ground in the summer, to be washed away with the first autumn rains.

However, none of the day-trippers who come to bronze themselves on Vulcano's beaches are discouraged, while numerous villas and some sprawling luxury hotels make this among the most exclusive of the Aeolian Islands. Don't let this put you off: if you can't find a place to stay here, or can't afford the prices, Vulcano still offers a good day out, with some of Sicily's stranger volcanic enticements and one of the best **beaches** in the entire archipelago.

Around the island

Ferries and hydrofoils dock at **PORTO DI LEVANTE**, a little harbour in the lee of the Gran Cratere, backed by a couple of streets of restaurants, villas and shops. This is where most of the facilities are located (see "Practicalities", p.180), while straight ahead from the landing dock and to the right you can't miss Vulcano's famed **fanghi**, or mud baths (Easter–Oct daily 7am–9pm; €1.50), situated below a spiky, multicoloured *faraglione*. More exactly it's one pool, containing a thick yellow soup of foul-smelling sulphurous mud, in which people come to wallow, caking every inch of their bodies with the stuff, and flopping belly-up into the gloop. This surreal performance is all part of a long tradition – specifically for skin and arthritic complaints – though the degree of radioactivity here makes it inadvisable to immerse yourself for any length of time, and unsuitable for young children or pregnant women. Avoid contact with the eyes (it stings like hell) and remove contact lenses as well as any silver or leather jewellery, which will be ruined just by coming into contact with the sand hereabouts. When you've had enough of the mud, hobble over to rinse yourself off in the nearby sea, where in some places the water itself bubbles up very hot – you need to take care in order not to get scalded. There's a fair beach here, though unless you have a cast-iron stomach, the aromas wafting over from the mud bath may preclude tucking into a leisurely packed lunch. For slightly cleaner fun, the **Piscine Geotermiche**, on the Gelso road, around the corner from the tourist office (April–Oct 9am–6pm; €14), has three whirlpools fed by the therapeutic geyser water. Just back from the beach on Via Porto di Ponente, the **Centro Informatico Vulcanologico** (Mon–Fri 10am–1pm & 5–7.30pm) provides information on the local geology.

Porto di Ponente and Vulcanello

A narrow neck of land separates Porto di Levante from **PORTO DI PONENTE**, a fifteen-minute walk past the *fanghi*. Here, a perfect arc of fine black sand lines a bay looking onto the towering pillars of rock that rise out of the channel between Vulcano and Lípari – the setting for some unforgettable sunsets. There are a couple of seafront cafés here, and some fairly elite hotels set back from the sands.

From the beach, the only road heads north through the trees to **Vulcanello**, the volcanic pimple thrown up out of the sea in a famous eruption in 183 BC, and joined to the main island by another flurry of activity a few centuries later. The walk takes less than an hour. The birth of Vulcanello excited enthusiasm in the high society of the time: it was witnessed by some of the greatest luminaries of the second century BC, and described by Pliny, Livy and Strabo. On the north side of Vulcanello, the **Valle dei Mostri** – literally the "Valley of the Monsters" – is an area of lavic rock formations, blackened and sculpted by the elements.

The Gran Cratere

Above all else, leave yourself time for the walk up to Vulcano's main crater, the **Gran Cratere**, just to the south of the Porto di Levante. Follow the road immediately to the left of the dock and walk up it for 500m or so (signposted "Al Cratere") until you're directed off the road to the left and up the slope. It only takes an hour to reach the crater, though it's a tough climb and totally exposed to the sun, so do it early or late in the day, and do it in strong shoes. The only vegetation consists of a few hardy gorse bushes on the lower slopes, nibbled at by goats whose bells echo across the scree. The first part of the path ascends a virtually black sand dune before reaching the harder volcanic crust, where it runs above the rivulets caused by previous eruptions. Reaching a ledge with views over all the other Aeolian Islands, you look down into the vast crater itself, where vapour emissions – acrid and yellow – billow from the surrounding surfaces. It's a rewarding, if slightly alarming, climb, nerves not exactly steadied by the admonitory notices at the start of the climb that plead "Do not sit down, Do not lie down".

South to Gelso

From Porto di Levante, a road (and bus service) runs 15km south, past **Monte Saraceno** (481m, with views as far as Alicudi and the Sicilian coast), to the hamlet of **GELSO**, stranded on Vulcano's south coast. "*Gelso*" is Italian for "mulberry" and they're cultivated here, along with capers. Three buses daily run to Gelso between mid-June and mid-September (currently at 10.15am, 11.30am and 4.30pm); at other times, unless you want to do it on foot, you'll have to hitch (though there's little traffic), cycle or hire a **boat**: fishermen at Porto di Levante will usually run you there and back for a reasonable rate, giving you enough time for lunch at one of the island's excellent, moderately priced **trattorias** (though these are normally closed in winter). If you time it right (the last bus back is currently at 5pm), you might take a dip at the tiny patch of black sand here, or better still at the **Spiaggia dell'Asino**, a larger cove accessible from a steep path which you'll have passed on your way into Gelso (there's a bus stop). It's a great spot for a swim, and there are umbrellas, deck chairs and pedalos to rent in summer.

Practicalities

Disembarking from ferry or hydrofoil at Porto di Levante, walk straight ahead, between the rocks, for the *fanghi* and Porto di Ponente; or left, along the harbour in front of the *Hotel Faraglione*, to the traffic island for the crater and village. The **tourist office** is housed in a geodesic dome just up from the port

(June–Sept Mon–Sat 8am–2pm; ☎090.985.2028). The Siremar **ticket agency** (☎090.985.2149) is on the terrace, a few metres above the traffic island, with the NGI office just beyond (☎090.985.2401); Ústica Lines (☎090.985.2230) operates from the Thermessa agency, at one end of the *Hotel Faraglione*. There's a **bank**, Banco di Sicilia (summer only: Mon–Fri 8.30am–1.30pm & 2.45–3.45pm) with an ATM at Porto di Levante, and you can also change money at the Thermessa agency.

Buses run from the dockside to Piano (7 daily Mon–Sat, 2 daily Sun). You can rent pretty much anything on Vulcano, from a scooter to a yacht, though perhaps the best bet is a **boat**, so that you can visit Gelso and the caves and bays on the island's west side. Talk to the boatmen hanging around the port, or, for self-steering vessels, contact Centro Nautico Baia Levante (☎090.982.2197 or 339.337.278) or Da Tonino (☎335.585.9790), at Porto di Ponente (by the *Mari del Sud* hotel); expect to pay upwards of €80 in August (less at other times), depending on the type of boat. You can also join a round-island **cruise** (€11) or tour of the other Aeolians (€15–50) with Vulcanomare, Via Reale 39 (☎090.985.3064). For **bikes**, Da Paolo and Sprint, opposite each other on Via Porto Levante, rent out mountain bikes (€5.20 a day), and mopeds and scooters (around €25 in high season, €15 in low).

Accommodation

You could climb the crater and Vulcanello, and bus across the island and back all in a day-trip, but if you want to stay on Vulcano, always ring first, and expect prices to erupt in summer.

There are fairly reasonable rooms to let at **Porto di Levante**, though the sulphurous smell here can be utterly pervasive. Best choices are the five air-conditioned mini-apartments at *Residence Natoli*, Via Porto Levante 4 (☎090.985.2059; ❹), each with cooking facilities and sharing a pleasant veranda. Alternatively try one of the two cheaper hotels: the *Torre* (☎090.985.2342; no credit cards, ❹), in the piazzetta at Via Favaloro (off the crossroads near the mud bath), which has plain rooms, or the more cheerful *La Giara* (☎090.985.2229; ❺), on Via Provinciale. The *Hotel Faraglione*, right on the harbour-front beneath the rock (☎090.985.2054; ❺), has nice views and an outdoor *pasticceria*-bar (half-board compulsory in August; ❺ per person). *Al Togo* (☎090.985.2128, ⓦwww.altogohotel.it; ❹) has simple rooms and a small pool, though it's a ten-minute hike from the port, off the Gelso road. If you're planning on spending most of your stay here in and out of the mud, plump for the *Rojas Bahia* (☎090.985.2080; ❽), with a number of decent rooms 30m from the thermal pool (sixty percent cheaper off-season).

On the **Porto di Ponente** side, prices are considerably higher, with the exception of the *Residence Lanterna Bleu* (☎090.985.2178; mid-Jan to mid-Dec) – a series of one-bedroom (❹) apartments with kitchen, which drop in price by up to fifty percent outside July and August. Alternatively, there's *Orsa Maggiore* (☎090.985.2018, ⓦwww.orsamaggiorehotel.com; mid-April to mid-Oct; ❼), a spacious, modern hotel 1km from the beach, with a nice pool deck, and bicycles and scooters for rent (half-board compulsory in August; ❺ per person). Two top-of-the-range places, both close to the black-sand beach and comfortably equipped, are *Les Sables Noirs* (☎090.9850, ⓦwww.framon –hotels.com; mid-April to mid-Oct; ❽) and the *Eolian* (☎090.985.2151, ⓦwww.eolianhotel.com; March–Oct; ❽) – early-season discounts at both can be a real steal for accommodation of this standard. At the northern-most point of the island in **Vulcanello**, the tranquil and modern *Arcipelago*

(☏090.985.2002, 🌐www.hotelarcipelago.it; April–Oct; ⑥) has cheerful rooms and a large pool with smashing blue vistas. Just south of here and very close to the beach, lies the largest of Vulcano's **campsites**, the busy *Togo-Togo* (☏090.985.2303, 🌐www.campingtogotogo.it; April–Sept), also with bunga-lows available (around €85 for up to four people). There's a much smaller site, *Eden Park* (☏090.985.2120; 🌐www.isolavulcano.it; May–Sept), on the south side of the bay and slightly inland, where campers can pitch on real grass; they also have small rooms with bath and kitchen that are pricey in August (⑦), but somewhat cheaper in other months.

Eating

Food on Vulcano is mostly either exorbitantly priced with snobby service, or of poor quality, despite the battery of restaurants to choose from along the road that bends around from the port. Try *Da Maurizio* (Easter–Oct), just beyond the Siremar agency, with a nice shady garden and good food, though unless you stick to the tourist menu you could easily spend over €25. For cheaper **pizzas**, *Il Palmento* (Easter–Nov), just up from the mud baths, is not bad, and has a €15 tourist menu. A less expensive and often better option is to get takeaway bits and pieces from the Italmec **supermarket** across the road (open until midnight in August). The best place for a romantic **drink** is *Cantine Stevenson*, whose outdoor candlelit tables are good for night-time people-watching, while *Ritrovo Rimigio* has tables on an attractive terrace overlooking the dock at Porto di Levante, and serves good pastries and ice cream, too: both stay open well after midnight in summer.

Elsewhere on the island, pricier restaurants include *Baia di Ponente*, in the *Les Sables Noirs* hotel (see above) overlooking the sea at Porto di Ponente, and *Belvedere*, loftily situated at Piano, between the port and Gelso. At Gelso itself, you'll find authentic but cheaper fare at *Da Pina* trattoria, on the seafront, offering simple seafood salads and delicious pasta dishes. All places are open in the summer (roughly Easter to Oct).

Salina

SALINA's ancient name, *Didyme*, or "twin", refers to the two volcanic cones that give the island its distinctive shape. Both volcanoes are long extinct, but their past eruptions, combined with plenty of water – unique in the Aeolians – have endowed Salina with the most fertile soil of all the islands. The slopes are verdant, and the island's tree cover contrasts strongly with the denuded crags of its more westerly neighbours. Look out on your wanderings for the exotic **caper** flowers, and the abundant **vines** that carry the *malvasia* grape – both are vigorously cultivated here and sold from houses and farms all across Salina. You'll come across these two traditional Aeolian specialities on every island, but, while caper production is still flourishing, *malvasia* wine has fallen victim to the general depletion of agriculture. Salina is one the few islands where you can still try the authentic, sulphurous taste of this sweet and strong honey-coloured wine in its place of production: much of what you'll drink on the other islands either comes from Salina or is imported from the Sicilian mainland.

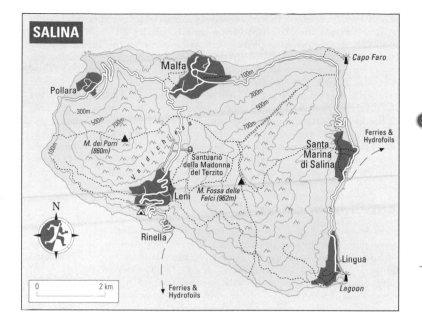

Salina's central position in the archipelago makes it ideal as a base for exploring the others. It's not as in thrall to tourism as Lípari, Vulcano or Panarea, giving it a quieter, more relaxed air. But it sees itself as the height of sophistication compared to, say, Filicudi, and indeed Salina is big enough to support a bus service, several distinct villages, and plenty of accommodation and restaurants. Yet it's still very much part of the relaxed ebb and flow of traditional Aeolian life, ultimately dependent – as all the islands are – on the comings and goings of the ferries and hydrofoils.

Santa Marina di Salina

The main island port is **SANTA MARINA DI SALINA**, on the east coast, visually unexciting but a relaxed enough spot to persuade you to linger. Most of its identikit structures are concrete, including the long lungomare that reaches north from the harbour, fronting a stone beach from which people splash about in the sea. There's a main street, **Via Risorgimento** – a rarity in these parts – which runs parallel to the water, one block back, and here are shops that sell more than just the bare necessities of life – boutiques, even. A couple of the gift shops sell a decent map of the islands.

The Siremar (☎090.984.3004) and Ústica Lines/NGI (☎090.984.3003) **agencies** are just back from the dockside, and open thirty minutes before sailings. **Buses** to all points on the island stop just outside the offices; there's a timetable posted up by the port (pay on board). The hub of the service is Malfa (see p.185) and you may occasionally have a short wait there for an onward connection, but basically there are twelve daily buses from Santa Marina to Malfa, Leni and Rinella, and seven daily to Pollara. There's a similar regular service to Lingua, though you could comfortably walk there from Santa Marina (about 20min). For **motorbike rental**, walk left off the dockside and, about 300m after the Agip **petrol station** on the road to Lingua, Antonio Bongiorno (℡090.984.3308 or 090.984.3409) has daily bike rental for €5, vespas for €30, and two-seater buggies for €50, though these are negotiable. Note that the island's only other petrol station is at Malfa.

Other services include a **post office** (Mon–Sat 8.10am–1.20pm), at Via Risorgimento 130, next to the church, where you can change cash, a couple of **banks** at Via Risorgimento 158 (summer only Mon–Fri 7.30am–1.30pm & 2.45–3.45pm) and another on the seafront just beyond the Ústica Lines office (Mon–Fri 8.40am–1.20pm); both banks have ATMs (there's also a bank in Malfa; see p.185). There are a couple of **telephone** booths on the front (near the ticket agencies), a couple more in the Villa Comunale by *La Cambusa* restaurant, and one by the church.

Accommodation

Santa Marina has little in the way of budget **accommodation** – there's more availability down the road in Lingua (see below). Most economical are **private rooms**, advertised in shops and bars; try *Catena de Pasquale* at Via Francesco Crispi 17 (℡090.984.3094; no credit cards, ❸), on the street at the top end of Via Risorgimento, a ten-minute walk from the port – turn left just beyond the *Carpe Diem alimentari*. Some of the rooms are dowdy, but moderately priced meals are available. Better value is the **hotel** *Punta Barone* (℡090.984.3172; April–Sept; ❹), right by the sea at the northern end of the village, a ten-minute walk from the port; it's attractively perched over the rocks with nice, quiet rooms and a restaurant (half-board compulsory in July and August; ❹ per person). The best hotel on the island, however, is *Mamma Santina*, Via Sanità 40 (℡090.984.3054, ℻090.984.0351, ℠www.mammasantina.it; ❽), signposted to the left off Via Risorgimento, with great views, a glistening swimming pool and exquisite furnishings in the top-floor rooms. It has been furnished wall-to-wall with gorgeous Mediterranean-coloured tiles by the affable owner Mario, an architect and top-class chef, who also heads the superb restaurant (add €25 per person for half-board); on arrival, call to be picked up from the port. Prices drop by fifty percent from September to May, and **apartments** are available for longer stays. Nearer to the port (left up the hill), the hotel *Bellavista* offers brightly tiled rooms with verandas and views, at rates that tumble by up to forty percent outside August (℡090.984.3009; April to mid-Oct; no credit cards, ❽).

Eating and drinking

Self-caterers will revel in the choice offered by the two or three **alimentari** along Via Risorgimento. Of the two named *Carpe Diem*, the further one (no. 28), is the best and makes up excellent sandwiches, with a convenient fruit-and-vegetable store next door.

The village boasts several top-notch **restaurants**. *Porto Bello* (closed Nov & Wed in winter), immediately by the dock, serves excellent local antipasti, pasta with capers and tomatoes, slabs of swordfish, and good wine, while *Da Franco*, superbly sited at the top of the village, a twenty-minute walk from the centre (up Via Risorgimento, left up Via F. Crispi, right at the top and keep following the signs) has terrific local food and fish (open all year, except a few days in Dec). In either, a large meal will cost around €30, and from both outdoor ter races you can watch the necklace of lights come on across the water on Lípari.

Another great option is the moderately priced restaurant at the hotel *Mamma Santina*, whose sublime *spaghetti all'erbetta* is cooked with fourteen herbs and spices, while the house speciality is a tasty *trancia di cernia*. The restaurant at *Punta Barone* is also worth checking out for moderately priced, simple, hearty Aeolian cooking.

For **drinking**, *La Cambusa*, next to the port, is good during the day, with a pleasant terrace bar and assorted pastries on offer, while *Nni Lausta*, close to the port at Via Risorgimento 188, is a good bet in the evenings, serving cocktails and beers until late (closed Nov–March). It has a lounge and patio upstairs (not always open), with pasta and fish meals also on offer.

Lingua

Three kilometres south, **LINGUA** is a pleasant spot, connected to Santa Marina by bus, though the undulating road makes a fine stroll, weaving around the coves in between the two settlements. Lingua itself is not much more than a lungomare, backed by a tiny cluster of hotels and trattorias facing the shore of Lípari. At the end of the road is the salt lagoon from which Salina takes its name, and there's a narrow **beach**. Facing the lagoon, a small **ethnographic museum** (May–Oct daily 9am–1pm & 5–8pm; Nov–April hours variable) holds examples of rustic art and island culture – mainly kitchen utensils and mill equipment, much of it fashioned from lavic rock.

A good choice here for **accommodation** is *A Cannata* (☏090.984.3161, ⓦwww.acannata.it; ❺), set a few metres back from the sea near the church: some of the rooms have a terrace with wonderful views of Lípari, and the home-cooked food is exceptional (there are pizzas, too). Half-board is compulsory in August (❸ per person). Both *Il Delfino* (☏090.984.3024, ⓦwww.ildelfinosalina.com; ❻), right on the lungomare, and *Il Gámbero* (☏090.984.3049; April–Oct; ❺), at the end of the promenade by the lagoon, have a good choice of attractive rooms set back from the sea; half-board is obligatory at both in August (both ❺ per person). Either side of August, the room-only rate at both these places is more like ❸, and it drops well below ❶ in the cooler months. Each has a **restaurant**, where fish predominates. *Il Gámbero* has a shaded terrace where you can sip a melon, fig or kiwi granita, and provides diners with a free ride from Santa Marina or take their shuttle bus, usually found hanging out around the harbour. There's also an *alimentari* for self-caterers on the road above *A Cannata*, to the left.

Malfa and Pollara

Back the other way, Salina's only road climbs from Santa Marina and traces the coast north, turning west at **Capo Faro**, where there's a signposted holiday village on the cliffs. The road then winds in through the outlying districts of **MALFA**, easily the island's biggest town, spilling down from the wide terrace outside its peach-coloured church to a tiny *mole* at the bottom. There's a good beach, stony but picturesquely backed by ruined fishermen's houses, and the *Santa Isabel* bar-restaurant, with a terrace overlooking the cove, is a good place to pause. The bus stops up by the church, and again a few hundred metres below, above the harbour. The two are connected by a devilishly twisting road, across which cuts a more direct series of paths.

Malfa has the island's fanciest **hotels**, overlooking the sea: there's the romantic *Signum*, Via Scalo 15 (☎090.984.4222, ⓦwww.hotelsignum.it; ❼), with very nice terraced rooms and poolside views of the sea, and further along at no. 8, the equally posh *Punta Scario* (☎090.984.4139, ⓦwww .hotelpuntascarico.it; April–Oct; ❻), where half-board is obligatory in August (❺ per person). Both hotels offer good off-season discounts and are reached from footpaths starting just below the CRAI supermarket on the main road. Outside town, 3km along the road to Santa Marina, *Capo Faro* (☎090.984.4330, ⓦwww.capofaro.it; ❽) is a converted vineyard château with a large pool and tennis courts; its sparkling rooms boast flat-screen TVs and great views, though you'll need a car here to avoid relying on the buses. The *Punta Scario* (summer only) and *Signum* provide the town's best **restaurants** (reservations recommended) - try *Signum*'s mouthwatering *maccheroncini ricotta*. *Ritrovo Papiro*, a bar in the upper village, sells warm panini and has a single computer with **Internet access** (summer open 24hrs; off-season 6am–9pm; €4 for 30min). Just above the bar, the Banca Antonveneta (Mon–Fri 8.20am–noon & 2.35–3.35pm) has an ATM, and there's a **scooter rental** shop next door, with scooters and mopeds for €25 a day, less outside high season. The bus stops opposite the shop, on its way into and out of the village. The island's only **disco** is at the Salina Bowling Club (summer only), 6km out of Malfa, on the road to Leni, with rocking dance fests several nights a week, though you'll need your own transport to get there.

Just out of Malfa, a minor road (and several buses a day) snake off west to secluded **POLLARA**, raised on a cliff above the sea and occupying a crescent-shaped crater from which Salina's last eruption took place some 13,000 years ago. Scenes from Michael Radford's film, *Il Postino*, were shot here and on the narrow **beach** at the base of cliffs below the village, which itself is the best reason for coming to Pollara – with its pristine seclusion and crystalline waters, this is one of the best beaches in the archipelago, though there is a risk of being hit by falling rocks from the vertical cliff. Lunchtime is the best time to visit, when there's some shade – in the morning, the whole bay is in deep shadow, and there is little protection from the sun in the afternoon. A steep path winds down to the beach from below the church where the hourly bus from Malfa stops (last bus back at 6.30pm), and where a caravan provides the sole refreshments (summer only). If you want to stay, *Casa Fenicia* (☎090.984.3952; ❷), left just off the Pollara road before the massive billboard, has clean, quiet rooms year-round.

Inland: Madonna del Terzito and the peak

Trails cut right across Salina, in particular linking Santa Marina with the peak of **Monte Fossa delle Felci**, the sanctuary of **Madonna del Terzito**, Leni and the south coast at Rinella. Although the distances aren't great, climbing up from the coast at Santa Marina or Rinella is to be avoided at all costs, since the inclines are punishing. You'll do infinitely better to take the bus to the sanctuary – any between Santa Marina/Malfa and Leni/Rinella pass right by – and start there, saving yourself the first 300m of climbing. Don't go overloaded, wear strong shoes, and take plenty of water.

Whichever route you take, the walking is very pleasant, since most of inland Salina has been zealously protected: pines are abundant, and wild flowers much in evidence higher up, while the scampering and slithering of geckos and snakes keeps you on your toes. The paths, terraces and viewpoints are all well maintained, with no vehicles allowed. Hunting and shooting are banned, too, which helps keep the bird numbers high.

The sanctuary to the peak

In the central plain of **Valdichiesa**, the road passes within 100m of the seventeenth-century sanctuary of **Madonna del Terzito**, set in the saddle between the two peaks of Salina – a green and fertile location, with fine views over the sea. A signposted track to the left of the church takes you to the summit of **Monte Fossa delle Felci**, the easternmost of the peaks and the archipelago's highest, at 962m. It's a steady climb through preserved forest and mountain parkland, which takes the best part of two hours – only in the latter stages does it become tougher, with a final 100m clamber over rocks to reach the stone cairn and simple wooden cross at the top. The views are magnificent.

Little green signposts on the way point out alternative approaches and **descents**, from Malfa and Leni particularly, so you don't have to retrace your steps completely on the way down. You can also head straight down to Lingua or Santa Marina; however, while the tracks are never anything less than clear, the descent is very steep, and soil erosion and the crumbling volcanic underlay can make getting a grip a tricky business. Count on another two hours back down, whichever descent you follow.

Rinella

Most ferries and hydrofoils also call at the little port of **RINELLA**, on the island's south coast, 15km from Santa Marina and not a bad place to base yourself for a couple of days. **Buses** meet the boat arrivals on the quayside (and call here several times a day otherwise). Notices at the port advertise **rooms** for rent, and there's a good **hotel**, *L'Ariana* (☎090.980.9075, ⓦwww .hotelariana.it; ❹), above the port to the left, with comfortable, renovated rooms and a decent restaurant. Though lacking seafront rooms, the smaller, tidy *Principe di Rinella* (☎090.980.9308; April–Sept; ❸), via S. Gaetano 5, is a good alternative, with nice wood trim throughout. Rinella also has the island's only **campsite**, one of the nicest in the Aeolians: *Tre Pini*, 200m up the road from the port (☎090.980.9155, ⓦwww.trepini.com; April–Oct), has a bar-restaurant and tiny one-bedroom bungalows (❷ in July & Aug), and you can also **rent scooters** from here (as well as from the port). There are two or three local **bars** with views by the port, and a good **pizzeria**, *Da Marco* (open weekends only in winter). The Siremar (☎090.980.9170) and Ústica Lines (☎090.980.9233) **ticket offices** are next to each other on the quayside.

Rinella's main drawback is that it's at the very bottom of a remarkably winding, steep road, which makes you rather dependent on the buses. Still, you could climb at least as far as **Leni**, the little village 3km higher up the slope, whose church you can see peeking out from the shelf of land from the coast below.

Panarea

PANAREA, to the east, is the smallest island of the Aeolian archipelago, at just 3km by 1.5km, and the prettiest, surrounded by clusters of outlying islets that provide some of the best swimming hereabouts. It's almost Greek in aspect, sporting freshly painted white houses at every turn, their terraces decked with plants and flowers, and swept narrow lanes shaded by fruit trees. Inhabited since Neolithic times, Panarea also holds one of the region's most important archeological sites, easily accessible on the dramatic **Punta Milazzese**.

No cars can squeeze onto the island's narrow lanes to disturb the tranquillity, though electric carts and heavily loaded three-wheelers are common. Indeed, Panarea's cosy intimacy has made it into something of a ghetto for the idle rich, one-upping Vulcano on the exclusivity scale. In August, every room and

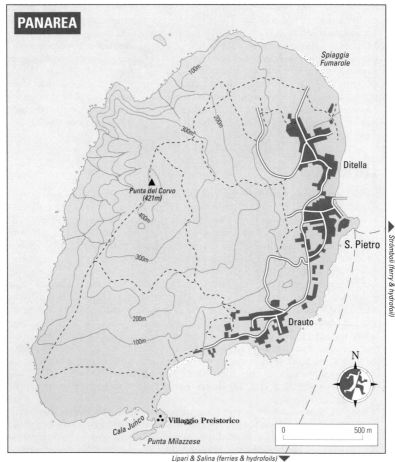

PANAREA

Spiaggia Fumarole

100m

200m

300m

Punta del Corvo
(421m)

400m

Ditella

300m

S. Pietro

Strómboli (ferry & hydrofoil)

200m

100m

Drauto

N

Cala Junco

Villaggio Preistorico

Punta Milazzese

0   500 m

Lipari & Salina (ferries & hydrofoils)

every inch of sand is taken, as wealthy northern Italians descend for a month of diving off blinding white yachts and wading knee-deep in the crystalline water. Though restaurant prices here are the highest of all the Aeolians, out of peak season you can find reasonably priced accommodation, and it's certainly worth a couple of lazy days' pleasure. Note that there are no streetlamps, so be sure to carry a torch at night.

Around the island

Panarea's population divides itself between three hamlets on the eastern side of the island – Ditella, San Pietro and Drauto – though, as they meld into one another and there are no street names as such, it's a distinction that hardly helps the visitor. For what it's worth, boats dock at the port of **SAN PIETRO**, tucked onto gentle terraces and backed by gnarled outcrops of rock. It's here that you'll find most of the accommodation, restaurants and facilities (see "Practicalities", p.190).

Make your way through the tangle of lanes, head south and it's a gentle thirty-minute stroll above the coast to the mainly stone beach below **Drauto**. Just beyond here, the path descends to a better, more popular, sandy beach – the only one on the island – overlooked by the *Trattoria-Bar Alla Spiaggetta* (closed Oct–March), which serves drinks as well as moderately priced lunches and dinners.

Steps at the far end of the beach climb up and across to the headland of **Punta Milazzese**, ten minutes further on, where a Bronze Age village of 23 huts was discovered in 1948; the oval outlines of the foundation walls are easily visible. This beautiful site, occupying a hammerhead of land overlooking two rocky inlets, is thought to have been inhabited since the fourteenth century BC, and pottery found here (displayed in Lípari's museum; see p.169) shows a distinct Minoan influence – fascinating evidence of a historical link between the Aeolians and Crete that goes some way to corroborating the legends of contact between the two in ancient times. There are super views: across to Vulcano and Lípari, west to Salina, and beyond to Filicudi, where the outline of Capo Graziano is just visible.

Steps descend from Punta Milazzese to **Cala Junco**, a delightful stony cove whose aquamarine water, scattered stone outcrops and surrounding coves and caves (these others accessible only by boat from San Pietro; see "Practicalities", below) make it a popular spot for snorkelling. Beyond the point, a waymarked path (look for the red-and-white signposts) wends into Panarea's interior, passing below the island's highest peak, the craggy **Punta del Corvo** (421m), before descending back to San Pietro – a rewarding hike of two to three hours.

North of San Pietro, passing through **Ditella**, you'll see evidence of volcanic activity in the steaming gas emissions (*fumarole*) on the gradual ascent to Calcara, where the track ends at the local tip. The stone beach near here (signposted "Spiaggia Fumarole") is another attractively isolated spot.

The offshore islets

Above all, be sure to make a trip out to Panarea's own archipelago, the largest and youngest islet of which is **Basiluzzo**, formerly inhabited but now only used for caper cultivation. Next down in size, and nearest to Panarea, **Dáttilo** points a jagged, pyramidal finger skyward and has a minuscule beach; there's better swimming at **Lisca Bianca**, the stark setting of Antonioni's *L'Avventura*, where the tranquil water is sheltered by **Bottaro** opposite. Nearby **Lisca Nera** and **Le Formiche** (The Ants) are mere wrinkles on the sea surface, though a constant hazard to shipping. You'll need to arrange **boat rental** at San Pietro (see "Practicalities", below).

Practicalities

San Pietro's harbourside is a line of trendy bars, restaurants with terraces, fishermen touting boat rides, and the Siremar (☎090.983.007) and Ústica Lines (☎090.983.344) **agencies** almost next door to each other. There's also a **cash machine** here, but no bank. In the warren of alleys behind are a *tabacchaio*, a little supermarket, two or three *alimentari*, a gift shop, bakery, more trattorias and a couple of pizza places.

Boat rental to Panarea's offshore islets can be arranged at the jetty at San Pietro, either at the seafront kiosks or look for signs advertising "*Noleggio barche*" in nearly every bar, shop and restaurant; expect to pay from €60 for a motorboat in summer (petrol about €10 extra per day). A **boat trip** to the isles and back costs around €15 per person: if you want to stay for a while, make sure your boatman understands what time to pick you up. *Eolo Sub* (☎347.672.0020, Ⓦ www.calabriadiving.com) by the *Hotel Cincotta* (see below) organizes excellent **diving** trips along the archipelago.

If you're looking to **stay** in Panarea, bear in mind that July and August are very busy, and that between October and Easter most places close. It's always worth asking around for **rented rooms**, which cost around €50 per person in August, and considerably less out of season. On the harbourside, *Trattoria da Francesco* (☎090.983.023; ❷) has ten en-suite rooms (half-board only in Aug at ❺ per person), while up from the port, several houses on Via San Pietro rent rooms; just look for the signs. If you want to be nearer Punta Milazzese and the beach, keep going as far as Drauto, where the *Trattoria La Sirena* has five rooms (☎090.983.012; Easter–Sept; ❸).

Of the **hotels** at San Pietro, cheapest are the *Tesoriero* (☎090.983.098, Ⓦ www .hoteltesoriero.it; mid-March to Sept; ❹) and the *Casa Rodà* (☎090.983.006; April–Sept; ❻), both on Via San Pietro, and both around fifty percent cheaper in low season. At no. 15 along the same road, the *Quartara* (☎090.983.027, Ⓦ www.quartarahotel.com; April–Oct; ❽) is the island's newest hotel, run by a cheerful family: its fashionable rooms have elegant wood furniture, and there are two jacuzzis out back. On a hill to the left of the port, there's the dominating *Raya* (☎090.983.013, Ⓦ www.hotelraya.it; mid-April to mid-Oct; ❽), with the less imposing but equally eminent *Cincotta* (☎090.983.014; Easter–Oct; ❽) nearby: both are superb, with wonderful terraces and facilities, and reasonable rates outside high season. Away from the port, at Drauto, the *Girasole* (☎090.983.018, Ⓦ www.panarea.com/girasole; mid-March to Sept; no credit cards; ❼) is a plainish family-run hotel with attractive terraces. All Panarea's more expensive hotels provide a little three-wheeler at the dockside to transport you and your luggage.

For **meals**, *Da Francesco* (March–Nov), with moderate prices, is as good as any by the harbour, while *O Palmo*, just up from the port, has a garden restaurant serving decent food and evening pizzas. Walking north towards Ditella, after ten minutes or so you'll reach *Da Paolino* (Easter to mid-Oct), set in a family house whose terrace has fine views of Strómboli. You can have a very unpretentious meal of pasta and salad here for less than €20 – try the rich *mille baci* pasta with greens – and the fish is whatever the family has caught that day, or just stop by for a glass of local wine. Back down the road past the *Quartara*, you'll get great *carne asado* and *chorizo* at *Antonio il Macellaio*, run by the eponymous Argentine butcher; you'll pay dearly for your steak here, but it's full of flavour. The *Bar del Porto* (June to mid-Oct) is good for a harbourside snack, serving salads and panini. For **nightlife**, the terrace of the *Raya* is all the rage, where a sophisticated dance party lasts for hours on summer nights, while *Bridge Club* down at the harbour provides a more sedate evening.

Strómboli

The most spectacular of all the Aeolians, **STRÓMBOLI** is little more than a volcanic cone thrust out of the sea. This most active outlet of the volcanic belt throws up showers of sparks and flaring rock at regular intervals of about twenty minutes, though only visible at night – occasionally from as far away as the Calabrian coast. It was Strómboli's crater from which Professor Lindenbrook and his colleagues emerged in Jules Verne's *Journey to the Centre of the Earth*.

Over the last hundred years, there have been a handful of eruptions – the two largest being in 1930, when serious damage to many homes sparked a spate of emigration from the island, and, more recently, in December 2002, when a landslide of 10,000 cubic metres of volcanic rock spewed into the sea, sending a ten-metre-high tsunami wave to the Calabrian and Sicilian coastlines, inundating waterfronts and even breaking a Milazzo tanker in half. On the island itself, the lava primarily made its way down the uninhabited face, though some volcanic dust ended up on rooftops in both the main town and Ginostra. Although no one was injured, the 2002 blow-up reminded the world that Strómboli is very much alive and kicking.

Still, undaunted, people have always lived under the skirts of this volcano, and the straggling parishes of San Vincenzo, San Bártolo and Piscità (often grouped together simply as Strómboli), and the solitary community of **Ginostra**, in the far west side of the island, exist in a charmed world, their white terraced houses adorned with bougainvillea and wisteria, remote from the fury of the craters above. Plumbing is at best rudimentary, especially in Ginostra, which is dependent on wells for its water supply, and some houses still have no electricity at all. But despite this, Strómboli, too, has become something of a chic resort, its excellent black-sand beaches overlooked by two or three first-class hotels and some swish bars and open-air discos.

Strómboli town

The main settlement of **Strómboli** spreads between the lower slopes of the volcano and the island's beaches for a distance of around 2km. It's an utterly straightforward layout of two largely parallel roads and steep, interconnecting alleys, though the profusion of local place names keeps visitors on their toes.

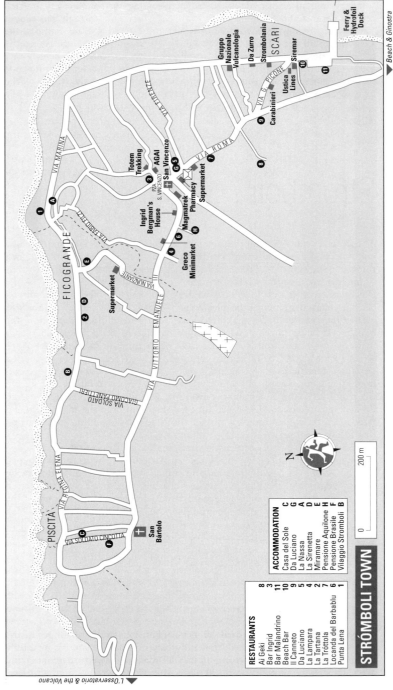

STRÓMBOLI TOWN

◀ L'Osservatorio & the Volcano

▶ Beach & Ginostra

RESTAURANTS

Ai Geki	8
Bar Ingrid	3
Bar Malandrino	11
Beach Bar	10
Il Canneto	9
Da Luciano	5
La Lampara	4
La Tartana	2
La Tróttola	7
Locanda del Barbablu	6
Punta Lena	1

ACCOMMODATION

Casa del Sole	C
Da Luciano	G
La Nassa	A
La Sirenetta	D
Miramare	E
Pensione Aquilone	H
Pensione Brasile	F
Vilaggio Stromboli	B

0   200 m

Ferries and hydrofoils dock at the quayside known as **Scari**, which, in summer, is thick with electric carts and accommodation touts; if you haven't already got a room booked, you should succumb (see p.194 for more). From here, the lower coastal road, Via Marina and Via Regina Elena, runs around to the main beaches of **Ficogrande**, a long black stretch overlooked by several hotels and, further on, **Piscità**, the island's best ashy beach. It's around 25 minutes' walk from the port to here. The other road from the dock cuts up into what could loosely be described as "the village", where, as Via Roma, it runs past a few white-painted shops and restaurants to the church of **San Vincenzo**, whose square offers glorious views of the offshore basalt stack of Strombolicchio. Beyond the square, the road changes its name to Via Vittorio Emanuele III, and it's another fifteen minutes' or so walk along here to the second church of **San Bártolo**, above Piscità, just beyond which starts the path to the crater. Once you've got this far, you've seen all that Strómboli village has to offer. The only "sight", apart from the churches, is the house in which **Ingrid Bergman** lived with Roberto Rossellini in the spring of 1949, while making the film *Strómboli: Terra di Dio*. A plaque records these bare facts on the pink building, just after San Vincenzo church, on the right, before you reach the *Barbablu* restaurant.

As well as the black sand beaches north of the dock, there's also a sand-and-stone stretch **south of Scari**, past the fishing boats. Clamber over the rocks at the end of this beach and there's a further sweep of generally empty lava-stone beach, which looks very inviting: its relative isolation attracts a fair bit of nude sunbathing, even though there's no shade and the rocks become scalding hot.

Practicalities

The offices of Siremar (☎090.986.016) and Ústica Lines (☎090.986.003) are both on the harbourside road, as is the bar *da Zurro* (☎090.986.283), where you can buy tickets for the summer-only Lauro fast-ferry service to Naples and the other islands. The port area also has several **agencies** offering crater climbs, cruises and boat trips, all charging the same kind of prices; the biggest is the English-speaking Strombolania (daily: July & Aug 5.30am–11pm; Sept & June 7am–8pm; ☎090.986.390), beneath the *Ossidiana* hotel at the harbour, which can also arrange boat, bike and apartment rentals. A screen outside the office monitors activity at the volcano mouth through a video link (though it's rarely very spectacular on account of the billowing smoke). Beyond the Strombolania office, the Gruppo Nazionale Vulcanologia has a cabin (irregular hours) with background information on the volcano – a useful stop if you're thinking of making the **ascent to the crater**, for which you are legally required to be accompanied by a qualified guide. The two main guide operators are the AGAI (Associazione Guide Alpine Italiane), which has an office below Piazza San Vincenzo (usually open April–Oct daily 10.30am–12.30pm; ☎090.986.211 or 347.014.7141), and Magmatrek, on Via Vittorio Emanuele just off the piazza (☎090.986.5768 or 333.906.6053, ⓦwww.magmatrek.it), where the local climbing guru, Zazà, and his welcoming Australian wife run treks, dish out information and screen films about the history of the volcano. Totem Trekking, opposite the church, sells and rents out hiking equipment and accessories. Guides usually supply helmets and dust masks, but if you're making the ascent at night you'll need your own torch. Finally, various shops in the village sell a good **map** of Strómboli (€2.50) showing local hiking trails, with a commentary in English.

The main **boat trips** offered are tours around the island, calling at Ginostra and Strombolicchio (3hr; €15); and trips out at night to see the Sciara del Fuoco by boat (2hr 20min; €15). One excursion, leaving at 7pm, includes a halt at Ginostra followed by a cruise to the Sciara del Fuoco, returning at midnight. Most trips start and finish at the beach at Ficogrande, where you can buy tickets from stands like Paolo Sforza (℡090.986.145 or 338.431.2803), or the friendly Società Navigazione Pippo (℡090.986.135 or 338.985.7883), which also has a stall in front of the *Beach Bar* at Scari. Both also **rent boats** for about €40 for half a day, or €70 for a full day.

Most other facilities are in the village: **supermarkets** are on Via Roma and Via Nunziante (both Mon–Sat 8.30am–1pm & 4.30–8pm, open later and Sun in Aug), while Piazza San Vincenzo is home to the **pharmacy** (℡090.986.713; daily 9am–1pm & 4.30–8.30pm), **post office** (Mon–Fri 8am–1.30pm, Sat 8am–12.30pm), which can also change cash, and a grocery store with **ATM**. For **Internet** access, there's Totem Trekking (daily 10am–1pm & 4–10pm, closed Mon morning Sept–June, and reduced hours in winter; €3.50 for 30min), and the **bookstore** down towards the San Bártolo church (daily 10.30am–1pm & 5.30–7.30pm; €3 for 15min), which sells a few English titles.

Accommodation

Provided the price – around €25 per person in summer – and location are OK, getting a **room** from one of the touts at the dockside is as good a way as any – there's no obligation to stay, if you don't like what you see once you get there. Prices are generally higher on the coastal road, and half-board may be obligatory in August, when you'll need to book in advance.

Pensione Aquilone Via Vittorio Emanuele 29 ℡ & Ⅎ090.986.080. Up an alley opposite the Greco minimarket, this is a friendly place, with plain, rather monastic cells ranged around a rose garden and lemon grove. The beds are comfortable enough though, and the en-suite bathrooms are clean. *Mezza-pensione* weighs in at ❹ per person in peak season, and there's also a cosy mini-apartment round the back with cooking facilities for €100 per day. March–Oct. ❹

Pensione Brasile Via Soldato Cincotta, Piscità ℡ & Ⅎ 090.986.008. Tranquil spot at the far end of town, with friendly management and fourteen clean, modern rooms with or without bath. Obligatory half-board (❸ per person) mid-June to Aug. April–Oct. ❸

Casa del Sole Via Soldato Cincotta, Piscità ℡090.986.017. Further down the same road as the *Brasile*, this is a cheapie in a nice old building within metres of the sea. You can share five-bed rooms for €20 per person, a double for €42 per room, or a single for €20 (off-season only). There's no restaurant, but kitchen facilities are available, and there's a sun terrace. Simple four- to six-bed apartments are also available all year; rooms only Easter–Oct. No credit cards. ❷

Da Luciano Via Roma 15 ℡ 090.986.088. Nearest place to the harbourside on the main street,

this is nothing special, but one of the more realistically priced options, with views of the sea and much lower prices outside August. No credit cards. ❺

Miramare Via Vito Nunziate 3, Ficogrande ℡ 090.986.047, Ⅎ 090.986.318. Small, smart hotel on the coast road, overlooking Ficogrande beach, with panoramic terraces and restaurant. April to mid-Oct. ❼

La Nassa Via Fabio Filzi and Via Marina, Ficogrande ℡ 090.986.033. Good, clean rooms near the sea at budget rates, with en-suite bathrooms and private terraces, all with sea views. Apartments also available for weekly rentals. No credit cards. April to mid-Oct. ❹

La Sirenetta Via Marina 33, Ficogrande ℡ 090.986.025, Ⅎ 090.986.124, ⓦ www.lasirenettahotel.it. Very swish hotel with elegant restaurant and nightclub and its own pool, opposite the black sands of Ficogrande beach. Minimum seven-day stay in mid-Aug. The room rates drop considerably outside July–Sept. April–Oct. ❽

Vilaggio Strómboli Via Regina Elena ℡ 090.986.088. A 2km walk from the harbour, with simple rooms jutting up against the breaking waves, this pleasant, quiet place is one of the nicest seaside stays; also has a good terrace restaurant. ❹

Eating and drinking

Assuming you're not tied to your accommodation for meals, there's plenty of choice, with most places sporting outdoor terraces and even sea views. The best **restaurants** serve the freshest seafood and blend Aeolian cuisine with modern elements. Moderately priced places along Via Roma/Via Vittorio Emanuele III include *Il Canneto* (closed mid-Sept to Easter), whose waiters reel off a list of daily pastas and fish: spaghetti with clams, or coloured with squid ink, followed by fresh fish, with salad, wine and coffee – the bill might touch €30 a head, though you could eat for less. There's a jollier atmosphere at the popular *La Lampara* (closed in winter), higher up past the church, where pizzas are also available on a large raised terrace. Pizzas are also served at *La Tróttola* (closed Mon–Fri in winter) and *Da Luciano*, both standard places on Via Roma where you can eat reasonably well for under €25, while *Ai Geki* (or *Gechi*), at the end of an alley off Via Roma (☎090.986.213; open all year), has veranda seating and reasonable prices, with pastas at around €9.50. If you want to push the boat out, try the superb dishes on offer at the chic *Locanda del Barbablu*, Via Vittorio Emanuele 17 (☎090.986.118; evenings only; closed Oct–April), with a discreet garden, or down by the sea at Ficogrande, where *Punta Lena* (☎090.986.204; closed Nov–May) enjoys a marvellous position at the water's edge, and serves sumptuous fishy preparations. A full meal will cost around €60 for two here, excluding drinks.

As far as the **bars** go, the ones down at the harbour see a lot of action during the day, particularly the *Beach Bar* and the larger *Malandrino*, where you can pick up pizzas and other snacks. At night, there's no better spot than *Bar Ingrid*, in the square by San Vincenzo church, a lively place, open until 2am, that does a roaring trade in vodka shots served in curious little test tubes. At Ficogrande, *La Tartana* (closed mid-Sept to Easter), at one end of the beach near the *Sirenetta* hotel – of which it is a part – attracts the in-crowd and serves grills during the day and cocktails and beers until 2am. **Dance** venues come and go here, but there is always something going on in town – ask in the bars, look out for posters and follow your ears to find the scene.

Around the island by boat

Boat tours of the island set off two or three times a day from the harbour and Ficogrande beach, costing around €15 a person (see "Practicalities" on p.193). The boats circumnavigate the entire island in two to three hours, calling at Ginostra (see p.196) – where you get half an hour to scramble around the hamlet – before rounding the western headland and idling slowly past the dizzy **Sciara del Fuoco**.

Rising sheer out of an incredible deep-blue sea water, the *sciara* is a huge blistered sheet down which thousands of years' worth of volcanic detritus has poured, scarring and pockmarking the hillside. Menacing little puffs of steam dance up from folds in the bare slope, where absolutely nothing grows. No one docks on the pristine shoreline, since it's too unpredictably dangerous. Come at night by boat, and through the Stygian gloom you'll see orange and red flashes from the crater above as the volcano goes through its pyrotechnic paces.

Most boat trips also take in Strómboli's basalt offspring, **Strombolicchio**, a couple of kilometres out. The colours here, too, are noteworthy, this time the varied streaks of ochre, green, blue, white, brown and black rock that tumble away through the crystal water as you circle the hulking, rusting, encrusted monolith up close. You can even climb the two hundred or so precipitous steps leading up this battlemented rock to the lighthouse on its top, a lonely vantage-point.

The volcano

Guides for the **ascent of the volcano** are readily available in the village (see "Practicalities", p.193), and it is illegal to climb the volcano without one. Most excursions leave from Piazza San Vincenzo at 5.30 or 6pm and are back by midnight (around €20 a head, cheaper in low season); night climbs start soon after midnight, allowing you to reach the viewing platform at around 3am, wait a couple of hours for the dawn, and return at around 7am (about €30). The full force of the eruptions is best appreciated at night, though the walking is inevitably trickier, and you'll miss the superb views out to sea. Whatever time you choose to make the ascent, it's worth booking in advance in summer – but be prepared for the hike to be postponed because of bad weather.

The **route** starts a few minutes' walk beyond San Bártolo church, where a fork bears left, heads through the houses and then climbs upwards to the first orientation point, *L'Osservatorio*, a bar-pizzeria (closed in winter) with a wide terrace and a view of the volcano. The ascent is not particularly dangerous, provided you stick to the marked paths, but you'll need good shoes, a sun hat and plenty of water (two litres per person, minimum) in hot weather. You should also remove contact lenses on account of flying grit at the top. If you intend to see the volcano at night, take a sweater (it gets cold and windy up there) and waterproofs. Don't, under any circumstances, come down in the dark without a guide, and keep an eye on the weather.

On the way you'll pass the frighteningly sheer volcanic trail that channels all the lava outflows, known as the **Sciara del Fuoco**, plunging directly into the sea. At the top, the fiery explosions can vary in intensity, but it's always a fairly impressive performance, the noise alone something like an express train thundering directly below you. Ignore the warning signs at your peril.

Ginostra

Without seeing its name on ferry timetables, you might not even be aware of the existence of **GINOSTRA**, the hamlet on the west side of the island. However, its very remoteness makes it an appealing destination for lovers of isolation, and for the contrast with the touristy atmosphere of Strómboli town. From the minuscule harbour – far too small for ferries or hydrofoils, and only just big enough for the launch which carries passengers to and from the inter-island service – zigzag steps climb into a supremely peaceful cluster of typical white Aeolian houses on terraces. Donkeys are tethered to posts outside homes; ancient exterior stone ovens lie idle; cultivated hedges and volcanic stone walls snake up the hillside – all bathed in a refreshing simplicity, with few diversions for thrill-seekers. There is a bar-**restaurant**, *L'Incontro*, at the top of the steps, and the classier *Puntazzo* further up the hill (☎090.981.2464; closed mid-Oct to May), with fairly high prices but terrific local food and wine. Surprisingly for such a sleepy backwater, it can get full in summer, so book ahead.

Accommodation is limited to the tiny *Locanda Petrusa* (☎090.981.2305; May–Sept; no credit cards, ❸), which is under the same management as

L'Incontro and has three large rooms with their own terraces and a shared bathroom; half-board is obligatory in July and August (❹ per person). Otherwise, ask around for **rooms** to let, but make sure you bring a torch, since nights here are profoundly black.

Weather permitting, there are **hydrofoils** back to Strómboli town twice a day in summer (once daily in winter). A century ago, there was a land route in the form of a maintained **path** that skirted the shore and traversed ridges and valleys. Years of neglect and natural assault by the elements has done for most of the path, though some survives – and where it doesn't it's possible to scramble the rocks and follow the line of the coast. Experienced climbers/hikers could do the route back to Strómboli in around four hours, though if you're at all interested you'd do well to engage the services of a guide; ask at *L'Incontro*. However, you don't need to go very far, following the coast anticlockwise, to find spots where you can swim off the rocks and from stony patches of beach.

Filicudi

FILICUDI, the bigger of the two minor, westerly islands, is closer to the main pack, and an hour by hydrofoil from Lípari. Its small harbour is dominated on one side by a modern hotel that's closed for eight months of the year. When combined with the ungainly straggle of concrete buildings along the front, this isn't the greatest of introductions to what turns out to be many visitors' favourite island. Once you've climbed away from the port, the rest of the pretty island is relatively easily accessible on foot. Paths crisscross the slopes, lined with scraggy volcanic boulders interspersed with great flowering cacti whose pustular blooms erupt upon the elephant-ear leaves. There are no sand beaches to speak of, and while the offshore waters are becoming increasingly popular with the yachting and diving set, the island is still a long way from being overdeveloped.

Around the island

The island's road runs east from **FILICUDI PORTO**, executing a sharp turn at the start of the path up to the archeological site, the **Villagio Preistorico** at Capo Graziano, where the remains of a dozen or so oval huts mark the place that gave its name to the local Bronze Age culture that immediately preceded Panarea's Punta Milazzese, from the eighteenth to thirteenth century BC. Discovered in 1952, the small site is always open and is a calm but unspectacular spot. Finds from the site are on show at the museum in Lípari (see p.169), and at Filicudi's new portside **Museo Archeológico** (daily July to mid-Sept 9.30am–1pm & 3–6pm; free), a rather haphazard collection of amphorae, anchors, lamps and other island treasures. From Filicudi Porto's stone **beach**, a path leads around the southern and western sides of the cape where, with a bit of determined scrambling, you can reach quiet rocky coastal stretches with sublime swimming.

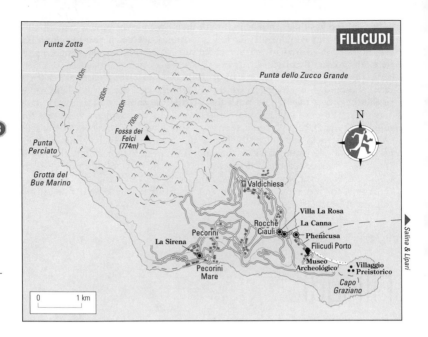

To head west, to the rest of the island, it's quicker to climb the stepped path to the left of the hotel at the port, which in ten heart-busting minutes leads to the **Rocche Ciauli** district of the island, where the road forks. Turning right (north) it's a further twenty minutes up the switchback road to the dispersed central village of **VALDICHIESA**, past stepped terraces and clusters of white houses. The church itself – set back on a terrace with splendid views – is in a terribly sorry state: paint peeling from the doors, walls riven by cracks and with a derelict campanile, inhabited by pigeons and lizards, and topped by a small dome gently subsiding beneath its own weight. Above church and village lie the heights of **Fossa dei Felci** (774m), reached by vague paths that climb through the terraces. A signposted path from the turning below Valdichiesa leads to **Zucco Grande**, an abandoned village about fifty easy minutes' hike away – this is one of the most rewarding hikes on the island. Filicudi's mountain slopes are all painstakingly lined with stone terracing, a monument to former agricultural activity but now serving only to reduce soil erosion.

The road peters out shortly beyond the church, though a path leads off to the right where the road ends at the little shrine and telephone box. This cuts south, down the hillside, through abandoned houses and along walls and banks of volcanic stones, until it drops to **PECORINI**, no more than a few houses grouped around a church. Here, you meet the left (east) road-fork from Rocche Ciauli, which continues on its sinuous way, around the valley and down to the little harbour of **PECORINI MARE**. A short cut, by vertiginous donkey track, starts to the side of the church up in Pecorini and takes just fifteen minutes down to the harbour. Pecorini Mare is another scrap of a hamlet with a small dockside, a Carabinieri post, a boutique, a "Saloon", which sells beer and other drinks and gelati, a couple of trattorias, and a **diving** outfit, Apagon (℡090.988.9955, Ⓦwww.apogon.it; €30 with equipment rental). The water either side of the dock is limpid and surprisingly warm, though the uncompromising stony beach makes lying around uncomfortable. If you don't want to walk the 4km to Pecorini Mare or get here by boat or scooter, Franco (☎347.757.9516) runs a minibus from Filicudi Porto, charging about €5 a head if you join a group, more if there are too few takers.

By boat

You could see a lot more of Filicudi by **renting a boat**, giving you the chance to explore the island's uninhabited northern and western coasts; it's about €15 a head in high season, falling to €8–10 at other times, and you usually need a minimum of 2–3 people. There's usually someone at the harbour touting for custom, but, if not, try asking at one of the nearby shops and restaurants. For **boat trips** around the island, Edoardo Taranto (☎090.988.9835) runs two-hour trips for €20 per person; alternatively, ask at *La Canna* (see below), or see any of the fishermen at Filicudi Porto or Pecorini Mare.

To the west of Filicudi Porto, **Punta Perciato** has a fine natural arch, while the nearby **Grotta del Bue Marino** ("Seal Grotto") is a wide rocky cavity 37m long by 30m wide, its walls of reddish lava barely visible in the pitch black of the interior: the last seal to have lived here, however, was shot thirty years ago by a local fisherman. Near the island's northwest coast, the perpendicular **Canna** is a startling sight, a rugged and solitary obelisk 85m tall, the most impressive of all the *faraglioni* of the Aeolian Islands.

Practicalities

At Filicudi Porto, the Siremar (☎090.988.9960) and Ústica Lines (☎090.988.9984) **agencies** are on the dockside, both open before departures. Next door is a **pharmacy** (☎090.980.9053; Thurs & Sat 9.30–11.45am), while further along there's a **phone box**, **general store**, **ATM** and two or three **restaurants**, none of which accepts credit cards: the *Capo Graziano* also sells home-made *gelato*, and the small *pasticceria* at *Da Nino sul Mare* has some of the best fresh doughnuts (*ciambelle*) this side of the Atlantic. The port is a positive metropolis compared to the rest of Filicudi.

Accommodation facilities are scattered around the island, and need to be booked in advance in summer. The weathered *Phenicusa* (☎090.988.9946, Ⓦwww.phenicusahotel.com; June to mid-Sept; ❼), overlooking the port, is the most obvious spot, and has its own restaurant (full board is compulsory in July and Aug at ❻ per person). Rooms are only functional but there are terrific views from the sea-facing ones (for which there is a small supplement), and breakfast is served on the sun-soaked terrace. For more atmosphere and even better views, however, you couldn't do better than the relaxed, family-run *La Canna*, Via Rosa 43 (☎090.988.9956, Ⓦwww .lacannahotel.it; ❺), at the top of the steps to Rocche Ciauli, where ten lovely bright rooms with tiled bathrooms open onto a spacious terrace with a magnificent view over the bay below. The price includes breakfast (good coffee and home-made bread and preserves), and an extra €20 a head will get you an excellent dinner – pasta, fresh fish, local caper salads and plenty of home-produced wine and fruit. There's a small pool, and they'll pick you up from the dock if you have heavy luggage. In July and August half-board is compulsory (❻ per person). Immediately above *La Canna*, at the Rocche Ciauli road junction, *Villa La Rosa* (☎090.988.9965,

Ⓦwww.villarosa.it; closed Nov; ❻) is a bar-restaurant-grocery with rooms and a nice outdoor terrace; half-board is compulsory in July and August (❹ per person). In summer, the bar becomes a late-night disco. If everywhere is full, it's worth asking around for **rooms**: Vincenzo Anastasi (Ⓣ090.988.9966, or ask at *La Canna*) has apartments for rent. Alternatively, consider staying in Pecorini Mare, where *La Sirena* (Ⓣ090.988.9997, Ⓦwww.pensionelasirena .it; ❺), run by an English expat, has beautifully furnished sizable rooms right by the sea as well as a number of rather nice houses to rent; half-board is required in August (❹ per person). Its **restaurant** is worth a visit even if you're not staying, with decent prices for the fresh seafood dishes (from €10) and some great seats right on the waterfront. At Filicudi Porto, the best restaurant is *A Tana* (closed Oct–May), a few minutes' walk up the seafront from the port, where you can sup on *pasta con cozze e vóngole* on a lovely terrace directly overlooking the beach. A full meal here costs under €25.

The island's **post office** is in Pecorini, up by the church (Mon–Sat 8.20am–1pm), but there is nowhere to change money on Filicudi. You can **rent boats** from the main harbour at Filicudi Porto (from €60 a day plus petrol) and from Marcopolo in Pecorino Mare (Ⓣ340.786.4385, Ⓦwww .marcopolofilicudi.com; €40 a day plus petrol). Alternatively, Guiseppe (Ⓣ090.988.9011) runs fishing trips and guided tours of Filicudi. **Scooters** can be rented from Centro Nautico (€25 per day), just up from the Siremar ticket agency (Ⓣ090.988.9960) in Filicudi Porto.

Alicudi

Ends of the line in Europe don't come much more remote than **ALICUDI**. Two and a half hours from Milazzo by hydrofoil, or five by ferry, the island forms a perfect cone, a mere Mediterranean pimple, and its precipitous shores are pierced by numerous caves. Up the sheer slope behind the only settlement, **Alicudi Porto**, terraced smallholdings and white houses cling on for dear life, decorated with tumbling banks of flowers. Indeed, Alicudi's ancient name of Ericusa was the word for the heather that still stains its slopes purple in spring. Its rocky isolation has been formerly exploited by the Italian government, who used the island as a prison for convicted Mafiosi, but now it's virtually abandoned by all but a few farmers and fishermen, giving the place a supremely relaxed pace.

It's this quietude, of course, that attracts tourists; not many, it's true, but enough for there to be some semblance of facilities in the village to cater for visitors. You'll be asked by locals if you're a foreigner, meaning *from Italy* – which is about as far-flung as can be imagined here. Life is simple, though not lived entirely in isolation. Electricity arrived at the start of the 1990s, so now there's TV, too. There are two general stores, plenty of fancy boat hardware, even a car or two parked at the dock (though, since there are no navigable roads, it's not clear whether this is bravado or forward planning on behalf of the owners). You have to walk to reach anywhere and the network

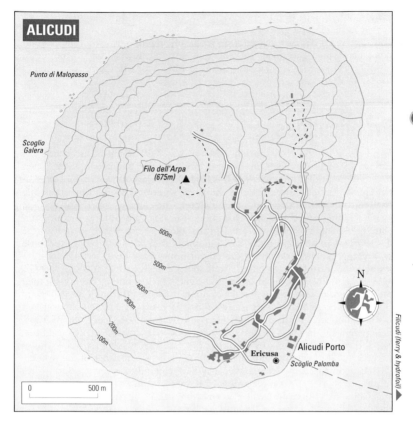

of volcanic stone-built paths behind the village is extremely steep and tough – all the heavy fetching and carrying is still done by donkey or mule, whose indignant brays echo across the port all day.

The island

Things to do are simply enumerated. The most exhausting option is the hike up past the castle ruins to the island peak of **Filo dell'Arpa**, which (at 675m) requires a fair bit of effort. The path runs up through the village houses from the port and there's a proper stone-built track most of the way. Unfortunately, the track looks as though it was created by a malevolent giant emptying a bag of boulders from the top and letting them fall where they will. Go in something other than very soft shoes and take plenty of water. There's absolutely no shade, and it will take at least two hours to get up, though the magnificent views make it worthwhile.

Otherwise, you'll probably get all the exercise you need clambering over the rocky **shore** to the south of the port. The path soon peters out beyond the island's only hotel and the power station, but the rocks offer a sure foothold as they get larger the further you venture. The water is crystal clear and, once you've found a flat rock big enough to lie on, you're set for more peace and quiet than you'd bargained for. The only sounds are the echoed mutter of offshore fishermen, the scrabbling of little black crabs in the rock pools and the lap of the waves.

Practicalities

From the dock, walk to the left past the beached fishing-boats and in the almost cave-like dwellings in front of you are the Siremar **agency** (open before departures; ☎090.988.9795), Ústica Lines (☎090.988.9370) and – in the arched terrace above – one of the island's **general stores** (the other one is along the path to the *Ericusa*; see below). The Siremar office also doubles as a telephone office (officially summer Mon–Sat 9am–1pm & 4–9pm, Sun 9am–noon; winter Mon–Sat closes 7pm), though it's not always open. If you're desperate to make a call, seek out Signora Russo, who has the white house with green railings and shutters directly in front of the dock.

The *Ericusa* **hotel** is a five-minute walk south along the shore (☎090.988.9902, Ⓦwww.alicudihotel.com; June to mid-Sept; ❸), a modern, twenty-roomed place with sea views, terrace and restaurant (half-board minimum in July & Aug at ❸ per person). **Apartment or room rental** is a feasible option and usually quite straightforward: *Italo Palermo* (☎090.988.9681 or 368.335.1265; no credit cards, ❸) has apartments with one two rooms, kitchen facilities, hot showers and verandas overlooking the sea. Alternatively, try *Casa Mulino* (☎090.988.9681, Ⓦwww.alicudicasamulino.it), or ask in either of the stores.

Unless you **eat** at the *Ericusa*, you may have to fend for yourself. Both stores sell bread, cheese, cured meats, olives, beer, ice cream, and whatever fruit and vegetables arrived on the boats. Alternatively, call in on Signore Silvio during the day, who lives up the hill behind the Siremar office (anyone can point you in the right direction). He cooks dinner on request – spaghetti, fresh fish, salad, fruit and wine – for around €20 a head, served on his lovely bougainvillea-covered terrace in the company of whoever else happens to turn up.

Incidentally, if you're staying the night, bring a **torch**. The village is asleep and pitch-black by 10pm and the steps are treacherous.

Festivals

Easter
Holy Week Procession of the saints in **Lípari**.

July
17 Festival of Santa Marina in **Santa Marina di Salina**, Salina.
23 Festival of St Mary of Terzito at the **sanctuary of Madonna del Terzito** on Salina.

August
10 Festival of San Lorenzo in **Malfa**, Salina.
24 Procession of San Bartolomeo's statue and relics in **Lípari town** accompanied by fireworks. Celebrations, too, on **Alicudi**.

Travel details

For ferry and hydrofoil services from Milazzo to the Aeolians, see the table on p.165; and for services from the Tyrrhenian coast or Messina, see "Travel details", Palermo, p.128 and p.239 respectively.

Hydrofoils and ferries from mainland Italy

Ústica Lines hydrofoils from Réggio di Calabria June–Sept 5 daily; Oct–May Mon–Sat at 1.25pm to: Lípari (1hr 35min–3hr); Vulcano (1hr 25min–3hr 20min); Rinella, Salina (2hr 30min); Santa Marina, Salina (2hr–4hr).

Ústica Lines hydrofoils from Naples July–Sept daily at 8.30am to: Strómboli (4hr); Panarea (4hr 35min); and Lípari (5hr).

Siremar ferries from Naples April–June & Oct Tues, Fri & Sun 9pm; July & Aug Mon, Tues & Thurs–Sun 9pm; Sept Sun–Tues, Thurs & Fri 9pm; Nov–March Tues & Fri 9pm to: Strómboli (8hr); Ginostra (9hr); Panarea (10hr 20min); Santa Marina, Salina (11hr 30 min); Rinella, Salina (11hr 35min); Lípari (12hr 35min); Vulcano (13hr 40min).

Inter-island ferries

Lípari June–Sept to: Alicudi (5 weekly; 3hr 15min–3hr 50min); Filicudi (5 weekly; 2hr–2hr 40min); Ginostra (7 weekly; 3hr); Milazzo (7 daily; 2hr); Naples (5 weekly; 14hr); Panarea (1–2 daily; 1hr 45min–2hr); Salina (2 daily; 50min); Strómboli (1–2 daily; 3hr–4hr 15min); Vulcano (3 daily; 25min). **Lípari** Oct–May to: Alicudi (4 weekly; 3hr 15min); Filicudi (4 weekly; 2hr); Ginostra (4 weekly; 3hr); Milazzo (4 daily; 2hr); Naples (2 weekly; 11hr 35min); Panarea (4 weekly; 1hr 45min–2hr); Salina (2 daily; 50min); Strómboli (4 weekly; 3hr–4hr 15min); Vulcano (2 daily; 30min).

Inter-island hydrofoils and fast ferries

Lípari June–Sept to: Alicudi (6 daily; 1hr–2hr 45min); Cefalù (1 daily; 2hr 10min); Filicudi (6 daily; 1hr); Ginostra (3 daily; 1hr–1hr 25min); Messina (5 daily; 1hr 50min–2hr 10min); Milazzo (hourly; 45min–1hr); Naples (1 daily; 6hr); Palermo (2 daily; 3hr 30min); Panarea (4 daily; 1hr); Réggio di Calabria (5 daily, 1hr 55min); Salina (hourly; 20min); Sant'Agata Militello (1 daily; 1hr 10min); Strómboli (4 daily; 1hr 15min–1hr 45min); Vulcano (hourly; 10min).

Lípari Oct–May to: Alicudi (1 daily; 1hr 30min); Cefalù (3 weekly; 2hr 10min); Filicudi (1 daily; 1hr); Messina (1 daily; 1hr 30min); Milazzo (hourly; 40min–1hr); Palermo (3 weekly; 3hr 30min); Panarea (3 daily; 25min); Réggio di Calabria (1 daily; 2hr); Salina (hourly; 20min); Strómboli (3 daily; 1hr); Vulcano (hourly; 10min).

Buses

Lípari town to: Acquacalda (9 daily Mon–Sat, 4–8 daily Sun; 30min); Canneto (every 30–60min Mon–Sat, 4–16 daily Sun; 10min); Cave di Pomice (9 daily Mon–Sat, 4–8 daily Sun; 20min); Pianoconte (10 daily Mon–Sat, 3 daily Sun; 20min); Quattrocchi (10 daily Mon–Sat, 3 daily Sun; 15min); Quattropani (10 daily Mon–Sat, 3 daily Sun; 30min).

Santa Marina di Salina to: Malfa, Leni & Rinella, Via Santuario Madonna del Terzito (12 daily; 30min); Pollara (7–8 daily; 25min); Lingua (hourly; 5min).

The northern
Ionian coast

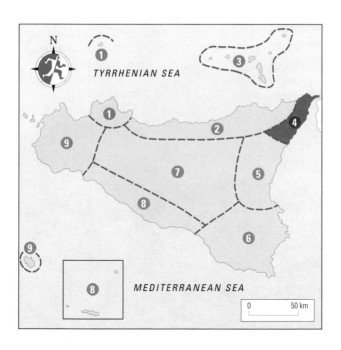

CHAPTER 4

Highlights

✳ **Ferragosto in Messina**
Giant puppets and daz-
zling fireworks over the
Straits are the highlights
of this spectacular mid-
August party, which
overtakes the whole
town. **p.216**

✳ **Fish supper in Ganzirri**
A few kilometres north of
Messina, you can dine
simply but sumptuously
on seafood alongside
the lakes or facing the
Straits. **p.217**

✳ **Teatro Greco,
Taormina** Superbly
sited with views

towards Etna and over
the sea, this is an atmo-
spheric venue for con-
certs, films and
dramas. **p.228**

✳ **The *passeggiata* in
Taormina** Join Taormi-
na's glittering evening
parade, which contin-
ues until late into the
evening, with a choice
of bars and restaurants
along the way. **p.231**

✳ **The Gola di Alcán-
tara** Explore the swirl-
ing waters of this deep
gorge to the south of
Taormina. **p.237**

△ Passegiata, Taormina

4

The northern
Ionian coast

emmed in by the mountains, the **northern Ionian coast** is Sicily's most visually exotic strip, crammed with some of the most brilliant displays of colourful vegetation you'll see anywhere on this flower-filled island. Perhaps not surprisingly, it's crowded by an almost unbroken ribbon of development and is one of Sicily's most popular resort areas, with both Italian and foreign tourists lured by the stunning views down to a turquoise sea.

Just across the busy Straits from mainland Italy, **Messina** has a noisy, modern aspect, and as its streets and squares have only scant remains of the town's long history, your initial impulse may be to move on quickly. Apart from its own meagre merits, however, there are some enticing spots within easy reach of here, to the mountains behind, or around the cape to the beaches on the Tyrrhenian side. Otherwise, keep on south, where you'll find some unspoiled **hill-villages** amid the woods and craggy uplands of the **Monti Peloritani**. These seem as secure today from the tourist hordes as they were in the past from piratical raids, and two or three of the villages are distinguished by impressive Norman churches built by Count Roger in the eleventh century to consolidate his grip on the island. Further down, the only road penetrating any distance inland takes in the **Alcántara valley** and its spectacular gorge, before heading up to the gnarled old town of **Castiglione di Sicilia**.

There are sandy **beaches** – and resorts aplenty – all the way down the coast, and you'd do well to avoid the area in July and August if you want a bit of elbow room. Even outside these months there's a fairly high level of satura-tion-tourism in the area's most illustrious resort, **Taormina**. Undeniably pretty, it was a simple hill-village as little as fifty years ago, set apart from others in the Peloritani range only by virtue of its fine ancient theatre. Now it's a high-profile, high-class tourist centre, packed in summer but still retaining enough small-town charm to merit at least a day-trip.

4

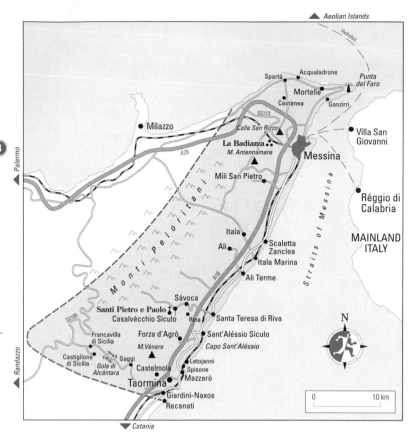

Messina and around

MESSINA may well be your first sight of Sicily, and from the ferry it's a fine one, stretching out along the seaboard, north of the distinctive hooked harbour from which the city took its Greek name – Zancle (Sickle). The natural beauty of its location, looking out over the Straits to the forested hills of Calabria, is Messina's best point; Shakespeare (who almost certainly never laid eyes on the city) used it as the setting for his *Much Ado About Nothing*. Yet the city itself presents a duller view from close quarters, with only a few buildings of any historical or architectural interest dotted along traffic-choked streets that are used as a racetrack by drivers who rank among the most reckless in Sicily. The unedifying appearance is not entirely Messina's own fault: the congestion is largely the result of the surrounding mountains, which squeeze the traffic along the one or two roads that link the elongated centre with the northern suburbs. Messina's modern aspect is more a tribute to its powers of survival in the face of a record of devastation that's high even by Sicily's disaster-prone standards.

Crossing the Straits of Messina is one of the most evocative entries into Sicily. Two ferry services (*traghetti*) operate from **Villa San Giovanni**, 12km north of Réggio di Calabria: the state-railway-run FS (☎892021) and a private firm, Caronte (☎800.627.414).

If you're **driving**, the Caronte, with more frequent crossings, makes better sense: follow signs from the Villa San Giovanni autostrada exit, a straightforward run through town, stopping at the first ticket kiosk (well-marked) where you can park at leisure and sort out your ticket (from €19 for a car one way; returns valid for sixty days cost from €31, three-day returns from €20). If you miss this kiosk there's a second after passing under the railway, but it can be a bit of a scramble here, with nowhere to park. The queue for boarding begins soon after: the average wait is ten minutes, and even in the peak times of August and rush hour, it won't be much more than 25.

Travelling **by train**, you might want to stay on it if you're crossing at night (though you'll probably be woken by the clanking din as the train is loaded onto the FS ferry), but by day it's quicker to leave the train at Villa San Giovanni station and skip the shuttling operation. Following the signs for the ferries, descend directly from the platform to sea level, where there is an FS ticket office (single tickets cost €0.80). Overhead signs tell you which bay leads to the first departure, or follow everyone else. There are enough FS ferries (1–2 an hour) to make it unnecessary to walk the 500m to the Caronte ferries. **Journey time** for crossings is 25 minutes on FS and 20 minutes on Caronte ferries. A bar on board serves snacks (including some good *arancini*), coffee and refreshments. Drivers might as well leave their vehicles, though look sharp as the ferry approaches Messina, as disembarkation is a rushed affair (and a suitable introduction to driving in Messina).

From Réggio di Calabria to Messina, there are three to five daily Ústica Lines hydrofoil services (☎090.364.044, ⓦwww.usticalines.it), as well as FS fast-ferry (*nave veloce*) crossings (roughly 7am–11pm; Mon–Sat hourly, six only on Sun), both of which take about 15 minutes. In addition, Meridiano Lines runs a ferry every couple of hours, taking 45 minutes. All services leave from the port, a couple of hundred metres back from Réggio Lido station, and tickets, from the kiosk at the terminal, cost €2.80. There's also a fast-ferry service, operated by FS, direct from Réggio's airport (six daily; 35min; about €9), timed to coincide with flight arrivals. Take the free SOGAS shuttle bus from Arrivals to the boat. For information on hydrofoil and ferry tickets for the **return journey**, see "Listings", p.216.

This atmospheric entry into Sicily may be superceded if plans to build the world's longest suspension **bridge over the Messina Straits** go ahead. Spearheaded by Berlusconi, but fiercely opposed by the environmental lobby and seismologists, the bridge will span the two-mile straits, suspended from pylons as high as the Eiffel Tower, and carrying a 12-lane motorway and a two-track railway. Seismologists fear that the bridge will be unable to resist a severe earthquake, while environmentalists claim that its pylons will affect the delicate water table that feeds the lakes of Faro and Ganzirri. However, with both the Calabrian and the Sicilian Mafia set to make a killing on construction contracts, the battle lines are drawn.

The greatest damage has been caused by the unstable geological belt on which Messina stands, responsible for a series of catastrophic **earthquakes**. The most notable of these occurred in 1783 and 1908; on the latter occasion the shore sank by half a metre overnight and around 80,000 people lost their lives. The few surviving buildings, along with everything that had been painstakingly reconstructed in the wake of the earthquake, were subsequently the target of Allied bombardments, when Messina achieved the dubious distinction of being the most intensely bombed Italian city during World War II.

Today, the wide remodelled streets and low reinforced buildings guard against future disasters of a natural kind, but make for a pretty uninspiring spectacle. The few monuments that remain – chiefly, the **Duomo** and the nearby **Chiesa Annunziata dei Catalani** – though worth investigating, won't occupy more than a couple of hours' worth of ambling. Take more time to see the treasure-trove of art contained in the **Museo Regionale**; one of Sicily's best collections, it helps to make up for what the rest of the city lacks. Otherwise, Messina's pleasures are to be found in kicking around its portside promenade and absorbing the scintillating views across the Straits. If you're here in summer, you'll see the passage of the tall-masted *felucche*, or **swordfish boats**, patrolling the narrow channel, attracted to these rich waters from miles up and down the Italian coasts. You can enjoy their catch the same day in a good choice of restaurants either in town or a little way north, at **Ganzirri**, where lakeside fish restaurants provide welcome relief from Messina's motor madness. Beyond, and around the corner of **Punta del Faro**, the city's main lidos line the coast at **Mortelle**, where you can swim, eat and drink to your heart's content; the beaches, bars and pizzerias here are where the city comes to relax.

Arrival, information and city transport

It takes a good hour to reassemble **trains** from the mainland at Messina's **Stazione Maríttima**. If you're changing trains or stopping at Messina, you might as well disembark and walk 100m on to the **Stazione Centrale**, at Piazza della Repubblica, where most of the **local and long-distance buses** also arrive and depart. Note that **buses to Milazzo for the Aeolian Islands** leave from the nearby Giuntabus office, Via Terranova 8, at the junction with Viale San Martino, with a stop in Piazza Duomo. For further details of buses **out of the city**, see "Listings", p.216.

Drivers and pedestrians using **ferries** from Villa San Giovanni or Réggio di Calabria also disembark at the Stazione Maríttima, though Caronte ferries pull in further up, on Via della Libertà, ten minutes' walk north along the harbour. This is slightly more convenient for the slip road to the Palermo (A20) and Catania (A18) **autostradas**: drivers arriving off the FS ferries should head up Viale San Martino (well signposted). **Hydrofoils** (from the Aeolian Islands or Réggio di Calabria) dock at the terminal (signposted "*aliscafi*") in the port area.

Messina has three different **tourist offices** with overlapping responsibilities; all should be able to provide a town map, a hotel list for the whole province including Taormina and the Aeolians (though not necessarily up-to-date) and information about getting to the Aeolians. There are two offices close together outside the train station, on the right: the excellent city Ufficio Informazioni Turistiche, on Piazza della Repubblica (Mon–Thurs 8.30am–1.30pm & 3–5pm, Fri 9am–1.30pm; sometimes opens Sat mornings; ☎090.672.944), and, just beyond, at Via Calabria 301, the provincial tourist office (Mon–Sat 8.30am–6.30pm; ☎090.674.236, ✉aziendaturismo@aziendaturismomessina.it). Most of Messina's hotels are scattered around this area, and it's just a short walk to Piazza Cairoli, where there are banks, shops and a third, local, tourist office upstairs at no. 45 (Mon–Wed 8am–2.30pm & 3–6.30pm, Thurs &

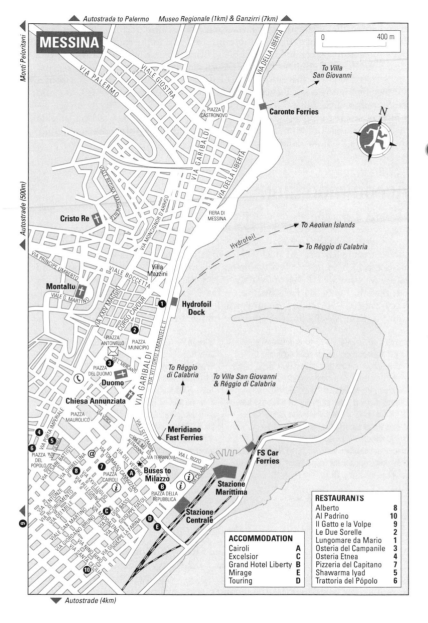

Fri 8am–2.30pm only; ℡090.293.5292). The independent **website** Ⓦwww
.messinacitymap.com has city-wide listings of transport services and tourist
attractions, and includes a detailed street map.

Walking is the best option for getting around Messina's central core; you
could get to the city's museum on foot, but it's quite a trek (about 45min from
the station) along the traffic-congested shore road, so for this – or for venturing

anywhere further – take the city's new, single **tram line** (#28). It runs between Annunziata in the north (for the museum) to Gadzi in the south, with frequent departures from Piazza della Repubblica, Piazza Cairoli and Piazza Municipio. Also from Piazza Repubblica and Via Garibaldi, bus #79 goes to Ganzirri, and buses #80 and #81/ (barrato) go to Ganzirri and Mortelle (other bus routes are specified in the text). Tickets, available from most *tabacchi*, cost €0.90 (valid for 90min) and €2.60 (valid all day).

Taxi ranks are found at Piazza Cairoli (☎090.293.4880), Via Calabria, outside Stazione Centrale (☎090.673.702), and at the Caronte terminal (☎090.44.492); there's also a 24-hour radio taxi (☎090.6505).

Accommodation

Messina's cheaper **hotels** are near the station, though they're not very scintillating choices. This is one Sicilian city where business travellers take precedence over tourists, and the best reasonably priced accommodation is actually outside the centre, in Ganzirri (see p.217). The **youth hostel** is 30km west at Castroreale (see p.153), so not really a viable option, and the only **campsite** you'll find in the Messina area, *Il Peloritano* (☎090.348.496), is situated inconveniently far out beyond Punta del Faro on the northern coast (bus #81/ to Rodia, from Via Calabria). Otherwise, to camp you'll have to go as far west as Milazzo, or south to Sant'Aléssio, both about forty minutes away.

Cairoli Viale San Martino 63 ☎ & ℱ 090.673.755. Large, old-fashioned, central hotel right next to Piazza Cairoli, and the best budget deal in the centre of town, certainly for a room without bath. ❹
Excelsior Via Maddalena 32 ☎090.293.1431. Central, modern hotel, primarily for business travellers but useful if everywhere else is full. ❹
Grand Hotel Liberty Via I Settembre 15 ☎090.640.9436, ℱ090.640.9340, ⓦwww .framon-hotels.com. Very swish, Art Nouveau-style hotel right opposite the train station, popular with business travellers. ❼

Mirage Via N. Scotto 3 ☎090.293.8844. Down an alley three blocks to the left (south) of Piazza della Repubblica; rather shabby, with small rooms, but adequate. Rooms without bath ❷, with bath ❸.
Touring Via N Scotto 17 ☎090.293.8851. Just up from the *Mirage*, its flashy entrance gives way to bare but spacious rooms, each with TV and telephone. Rooms without bath are a fair bit cheaper and the communal bathrooms are fine. Try and avoid rooms on the ground floor where the desk clerk's TV and the hot-drinks machine can be noisy. No credit cards. ❷ without bath, ❹ with bath.

The City

Messina's most important monument, the **Duomo** (Mon–Sat 7am–7pm, Sun 7.30am–1pm & 4–7.30pm), is symbolic of the city's phoenix-like ability to re-create itself from the ashes of its last disaster. Standing defiantly at the bottom of its spacious piazza, it's the reconstruction of a twelfth-century cathedral erected by Roger II, one of a series of great Norman churches that included the sumptuous cathedrals of Palermo and Cefalù. Formerly, the building dominated medieval Messina, and was the venue for Archbishop Palmer's marriage of Richard the Lionheart's sister Joan to the Norman-Sicilian, William II. Devastated by the earthquake in 1908, it was rebuilt in the years following World War I, only to fall victim to a firebomb in 1943 that reduced it once more to rubble. What you see today is mostly a faithful copy, which took years to complete, with few elements remaining of the original fabric.

The Romanesque facade is its best aspect, the lower part mostly authentic and dominated by a richly decorated, late-Gothic **central portal**, extravagantly pointed, with good detail, and flanked by two smaller contemporary doors. Almost everything in the undeniably grand **interior** is a reproduction, from the marble floor to the elaborately painted wooden ceiling. Two rows of sturdy columns line the nave, topped by cement capitals faithfully copied from originals, some of which survive in the Museo Regionale. The **mosaicwork** in the three grand apses holds most interest, though it pales into insignificance beside the island's other examples of the genre, and only the mosaic on the left – of the Virgin Mary with St Lucy – is original. All the same, try to find someone to switch on the lights, as the mosaics then take on a majesty that's entirely lost in the gloom that normally shrouds the cathedral's interior. There's little else here that predates the twentieth century, apart from some salvaged tombs, most handsome of which is that of Archbishop de Tabiatis from 1333, on the right of the altar and heavily graffitied. The **tesoro** (same hours; €3) holds precious reliquaries, the bejewelled *Manta d'Oro* – a holy adornment for sacred images, of a kind more commonly used in Orthodox rites – and a collection of skilfully crafted silverware.

Back in the piazza, the detached **campanile** claims some attention, particularly when the hours strike – best of all at noon, when you get the full mechanical performance. The belltower, like the cathedral, is something of a fake, looking much older than its sixty years, though it can safely claim to be the largest astronomical clock in the world. On the side facing the cathedral two dials show the phases of the planets and the seasons; above them a globe shows the phases of the moon; while facing the piazza, the elaborate panoply of moving gilt figures, activated on the hour, half-hour and quarter-hour, range from representations of the days of the week and the four Ages of Man to Dina and Clarenza, the two women who saved the city from a night attack by the Angevins during the Wars of the Vespers. There's a lion, too – Messina's ancient emblem – that unleashes a mighty roar over the city at midday, quite alarming if you're not expecting it.

In front of the cathedral and its belltower is the **Fontana di Orione**, a fountain daintily carved in the mid-sixteenth century by Montorsoli, a Florentine pupil of Michelangelo. It depicts Orion, the city's mythical founder, surmounting a collection of cherubs, nymphs and giants, and surrounded by four figures (representing the rivers Nile, Ebro, Camero and Tiber) reclining along the balustrade.

Just back from the Duomo, the truncated section of the twelfth-century **Chiesa Annunziata dei Catalani** (call Be' Domenico ℡090.668.4211 for access) squats below pavement level, Messina's only surviving example of Arab/Norman church-building. The blind arcading around the apses and the Byzantine-style cupola are the perfect antidote to the ugly cement facade surrounding its three portals, and the interior is suitably simple, with the transept and apse true to their original construction. In front, a martial statue by the sculptor Andrea Calamecca (Calamech) stands half-hidden under the trees, showing a proud Don Giovanni of Austria, victor of the Battle of Lépanto (the victorious Christian fleet sailed from Messina in 1535).

From here, it's a short stroll to the **harbourside**, with its combination of constant activity and compelling vistas over the Straits. It's Sicily's deepest natural harbour and a port of call for freighters and cruisers of all descriptions, as well as for frequent NATO warships. But the greatest traffic consists of ferries, endlessly plying back and forth, which – until the much-talked-about bridge across the Straits comes into being – are Sicily's chief link with the mainland.

The rest of Messina's unremittingly modern centre won't take up much of your time, though the area around **Piazza Cairoli** is the place for shopping and bustling evening promenades. You'll feel less cramped, however, when you head out north, to the city's marvellous museum and beyond.

The Museo Regionale

Messina's **Museo Regionale**, at Via della Libertà 465 (Mon & Fri 9am–1.30pm, Tues, Thurs & Sat 9am–1.30pm & 4–7.30pm, Sun 9am–12.30pm, closed Wed; last entry 30min before closing; €4.50), is a repository for some of Messina's greatest works of art, many of them carefully rescued from earthquake rubble, and includes what is perhaps Sicily's finest collection of fifteenth- to seventeenth-century art. A much bigger museum building is being built next door, and the collection will be transferred there (for an update call ☎090.361.292): until then, the layout of the museum is as described below. To get here by bus, take tram #28 to the last stop, Annunziata. The museum lies on the left, immediately after the Regina Margherita hospital.

It's the earlier rather than the later material that claims your attention, basically the items in the first few rooms. The collection starts with some lovely Byzantine work, larded with a good helping of Gothic, well evident in a fourteenth-century triptych of the *Madonna with Child between SS Agatha and Bartholomew*, and a remarkably modern-looking wooden crucifix from the fifteenth century, with a sinuous, tragic Christ. The highlight is **room 4**, where there are marvellous examples of fifteenth-century art, notably an ethereal statue of the *Madonna and Child*, attributed to Francesco Laurana, and the museum's most famous exhibit, the *St Gregory* polyptych, by Sicily's greatest native artist, **Antonello da Messina** – a masterful synthesis of Flemish and Italian Renaissance styles that's a good example of the various influences that reached the port of Messina in the fifteenth century (for more on Antonello, see p.100 and p.142). The statue of *Scilla*, the classical Scylla who terrorized sailors from the Calabrian coast (as described in Homer's *Odyssey*), is on display in **room 6**; it's an alarming spectacle, with contorted face and eyes awash with expression. Sculpted by Montorsoli in 1557, it was once adjoined to an imperious figure of Neptune in the act of calming the seas, a copy of which stands on the seafront just up from the hydrofoil terminal. Of the museum's remaining works, the most noteworthy in the suitably darkened **room 10**, are a couple of large shadowy canvases by **Caravaggio**, commissioned by the city in 1609, the best of which is the atmospheric *Raising of Lazarus*. The last room on the ground floor has a monstrous ceremonial carriage from 1742, hauled out for viceregal and other high-ranking visits. Though faded and tarnished, its gilt bodywork is still awesomely grandiose, showing an impressive array of detail. Upstairs is a collection of mainly ecclesiastical silverware, an art at which Messina once excelled.

Eating and drinking

Messina has a good choice of **restaurants**, either inexpensive and fast – as befitting a port and transit point – or offering a more relaxed atmosphere. If you're here in summer, you should try and sample the **swordfish**, freshly caught and a local speciality; May and June are the best months for this, before the water gets too warm. Specific areas in which to look for restaurants are around Piazza Cairoli, Piazza del Pópolo and the streets in-between, where rough-and-ready trattorias rub shoulders with a bunch of more serious eating places. The same area is best for **bar life**, with a number of lively birrerias staying open late, though most close in summer when everyone's at Ganzirri (see p.217) or Mortelle (see p.218).

Cafés, bars and birrerias

Abbate Via Garibaldi 62. A wine-shop cum bar with wines from Sicily, Piemonte and Tuscany, and gastronomic delights such as crostini with game pate. Closed Wed pm.

Billé Piazza Cairoli 7. Superb and rather refined *pasticceria* with *frutta di mándorla*, ice cream, pastries, chocolates and more. It's where the piazza joins Via T. Cannizzaro. Closed Tues.

Dolce Vita Piazza del Duomo. Sharp little café-bar with a few outdoor tables beneath the campanile. Good snacks, sandwiches and imported beer.

The Duck Via Pellegrino. English-style pub, popular with US sailors from the nearby base. Stones bitter on tap and a range of German bottled beers. Rolls and chips also on the menu. Closed Mon & mid-July to mid-Sept.

Irrera Piazza Cairoli 12. In business since 1910, serving cakes, *frutta di martorana* (marzipan fruits) and pastries of renowned quality. Closed Mon.

Bar del Panorama Viale Principe Umberto (next to the Santuario Cristo Re). Known as the *Bar del Pappagallo* – a fixture here for 38 years – it serves the best ice cream and granitas in town, along with traditional snacks like *arancini*. A great view to boot.

Pisani Via T. Cannizzaro 45. One of Messina's most famous pastry shops, renowned for its *pignolata* – a sugary confection covered with brown or white icing with a doughy filling.

Restaurants

Osteria del Campanile Via Loggia dei Mercanti 7. Nice little trattoria to the rear of the Duomo, with a filling *maccheroni alla Norma* and surprisingly good pizzas, though service can be slow. There are a few outdoor tables too. Closed Sun except July & Aug. Moderate.

Pizzeria del Capitano Via dei Mille 88. Excellent pizzas in this no-frills place close to Piazza Cairoli, with fast service and low prices. Cheap pasta is also on offer. Closed Mon. Inexpensive.

Le Due Sorelle Piazza Municipio 4 ☎090.44.720. With only five tables, this is a small and select trattoria, but also innovative and memorable. Specialities such as *paella marinara* and *couscous con pesce* cost about €10 each, but are well worth the splurge. Booking advised. Closed Mon. Expensive.

Osteria Etnea Via Martino 38. Abundant portions and low prices make this tidy little place near Piazza del Pópolo popular with locals. The menu's long and service is brisk. No credit cards. Closed Sun. Inexpensive.

Il Gatto e La Volpe Via Ghibellina 154. This little trattoria has an old-style brick interior and different local specialities every day. Closed Sun eve. Moderate.

Lungomare da Mario Via Vittorio Emanuele 108, with an entrance also on Via Garibaldi. A fine choice for a fish lunch, opposite the hydrofoil dock, though noisy if you sit outside. Closed Wed Sept–July. Moderate.

Al Padrino Via S.Cecilia 54–6. Specializes in traditional Sicilian fare, such as *maccu* (mashed fava beans), along with innovative dishes like aubergine stuffed with hand-made pasta and ricotta. Closed Sat eve and Sun. Inexpensive.

Da Piero Via Ghibellina 121. A Messina institution serving great local seafood. Try the *involtini di pesca spada*. Closed Sun and Aug. Moderate.

Trattoria del Pópolo Piazza del Pópolo. Good-value traditional neighbourhood trattoria where you can eat outside, enjoying the rare calm of this corner of the city. Service is friendly, and the pasta and fish dishes are excellent. Closed Sun & mid-Aug. Moderate.

Shawarma Iyad Via M. Giurba 8. Kebabs and other oriental dishes share menu space with pasta and pizza at this simple trattoria off Piazza del Pópolo, with some outdoor seating. Closed Tues. Inexpensive.

Nightlife and entertainment

Messina by night can be extremely beautiful, especially from the high **Via Panoramica** (which changes its name along its route west of the centre from Viale Gaetano Martino to Via Príncipe Umberto and Viale Regina Margherita) – from here, with the city at your feet, there's a long, sparkling view across to mainland Italy. From the centre, the closest sections of this route are the Viale Príncipe Umberto and Viale Regina Margherita stretch, where there are bars and pizzerias around two floodlit sanctuaries (Cristo Re and Montalto) and plenty of scope for some pleasant evening strolling. In summer, free **classical concerts** are often held here behind the Cristo Re (details from any tourist office).

Ferragosto

If you're in Messina in midsummer, you might catch the festivals around the Feast of the Assumption, or **ferragosto**. Although all the villages on both sides of the Straits hold festivals around this time, with some pretty spectacular fireworks lighting up the sky on any one night, Messina's festivities are grander, beginning around August 12, when two plaster giants (*giganti*) are wheeled around town, and finally stationed near the port opposite the Municipio. These are said to be Messina's two founders, Mata and Grifone, one a white female, the other a burly Moor, and both mounted on huge steeds. On ferragosto itself, August 15, another towering carriage, the Vara, is hauled through the city centre. It's an elaborate column supporting dozens of papier-mâché cherubs and angels, culminating in the figure of Christ stretching out his right arm to launch Mary on her way to Heaven. This unwieldy construction is towed on long ropes, pulled by hundreds of penitents – semi-naked if they're men, all in white if they're women – and cheered on by thousands of people along the way. The whole thing is a sweaty and frenetic performance, finishing up at Piazza del Duomo, where flowers are thrown out to the crowds, many of whom risk being crushed in the mad scramble to gather these luck-bearing charms. Late at night, one of Sicily's best **firework displays** is held on the seafront near Via della Libertà.

Back down in the centre, free concerts of **classical**, **jazz**, **rock and world music** are staged in Piazza del Duomo in July and August, also the period when **free films** are shown (usually at 8.30pm), generally in the Villa Mazzini public gardens near the hydrofoil dock or nearby off Via della Libertà around the Fiera di Messina, though the venue may change. Watch out for posters giving details of all of these, or ask at the tourist office – and arrive early, as these events tend to get crowded. In summer, most evening life takes place half an hour away around the lake at Ganzirri (see p.217) and at Mortelle (see p.218), where there are, respectively, a better selection of fish restaurants and more open-air films.

Listings

Airlines For all air tickets, contact Albertours, Piazza della Repubblica 25 ☎090.712.035.

Airport Nearest at Réggio di Calabria, for internal services and summer charters only. Info on ☎0965.643.291.

Ambulance ☎118.

Banks and exchange There's a bureau de change at the train station (daily 7am–9pm), and banks with cashpoints (ATMs) outside in Piazza della Repubblica and in and around Piazza Cairoli.

Bus companies AST, from Via del Vespri near Piazza della Repubblica ☎090.662.244 (for Ali Terme, Barcellona, Forza d'Agrò, Itala, Tíndari and Patti); Cavalieri, Via Primo Settembre 137 ☎090.771.938 , with departures from Autosilo Cavallotti, near the train station (for Réggio di Calabria airport); Giuntabus, from Via Terranova 8 ☎090.673.782 (for Milazzo and the Aeolian Islands); Interbus, from Piazza della Repubblica

☎090.661.754 (for Randazzo and the coast south to Taormina and Catania); SAIS, from Piazza della Repubblica ☎090.771.914 (for Palermo, Rome, Catania and Catania airport); TAI, from outside the Banco d'Italia near the train station ☎090.675.184 (for Capo d'Orlando, Patti and Tíndari).

Car rental Avis, Via Garibaldi 109 ☎090.679.150; Maggiore, Via Vittorio Emanuele II 75 ☎090.675.476; Sicilcar, Via Garibaldi 187 ☎090.46.942.

Car repairs ACI, Via de Fante ☎090.358.428.

City buses For information on all local routes call ATM on ☎090.228.5279.

Ferry tickets All tickets across the Straits are on sale at kiosks at the respective terminals; for Villa San Giovanni, call ☎892.021 (FS) or ☎800.627.414 (Caronte).

Hospital Ospedale Piemonte, Viale Europa ☎090.222.4238.

Hydrofoil tickets To Réggio di Calabria and the Aeolians, on sale at the hydrofoil terminal; call Ústica Lines on ☎090.364.044, ⓦwww.usticalines.it.
Internet Via Centonze 74, three streets up from Piazza Cairoli (daily 8am–10pm), charge €2.50 for 30min. You can also telephone from here.
Pharmacy There's an all-night service on a rotating basis: consult any pharmacy window to find out current *farmacie notturne*, or call ☎090.717.589.
Police Carabinieri, at Via Monsignor d'Arrigo ☎112; road accidents ☎113; anything else, at the Questura, Via Plácida 2, or Via XXIV Maggio ☎090.49.907 or 090.43.353.
Post office Main office at Largo S. Giacomo (Mon–Sat 8.15am–6.30pm).
Ticket agency Theatre tickets, including for Taormina's Teatro Greco and Tíndari's teatro, at Lisciotto Viaggi, Piazza Cairoli 13 ☎090.719.001; or from Associazione Teatro Sicilia, Via Sant'Agostino 23 ☎090.674.593.
Travel agency Lisciotto Viaggi, Piazza Cairoli 13 ☎090.719.001.

Around Messina

There are several mountain or coastal destinations less than thirty minutes from the centre of Messina by bus or car, all well worth a visit. If you're driving, you might wish to follow the high-level Via Panoramica north rather than the congested coastal road, which is the route the **bus** takes; though make a point of taking this lower road – an extension of Via della Libertà – at least once, passing fishermen's houses that back onto short sandy strips, in areas that must once have justified their idyllic names of Paradiso, Contemplazione and Pace. In Pace, look out for the British cannons lining the esplanade, pulled out of the Straits where they were sunk during the Napoleonic Wars.

Ganzirri and Punta del Faro

The #79 and #81 buses make a stop in **GANZIRRI**, 10km north of Messina's centre, which (in summer especially) becomes the hub of milling crowds hanging around the excellent bars and attending Italian **pop concerts** held nightly throughout August.

There's mussel-farming on Ganzirri's lake, and you can eat plenty of fresh shellfish, swordfish or whatever else has been hauled in that day by the many boats operating around here. Most of the **trattorias** are squeezed into the wedge of land between lake and sea, and you can eat outside at nearly all of them. Prices tend to be high, but for very reasonably priced, exquisitely cooked **fish** dishes, seek out *Lilla Currò*, signposted up a lane on the right side of the lake (closed Mon). Keep going along this road (keeping right, towards Faro) for the area's best **pizzeria**, *Mito dello Stretto* (closed Thurs in winter), with a terrace right on the Straits, while further still you'll find the cosy *Mínico Il Pescatore* (signposted *Il Pescatore*, just before the church; closed Thurs), which offers a good-value fixed-price menu (€20) of seafood dishes from Sferracavallo, west of Palermo. The #79 bus stops right outside.

Here, **Punta del Faro** (also called Capo Peloro) is the very tip of Sicily, the nearest point to Italy where the lighthouse (the *faro*) is dwarfed by the towering pylon supporting the massive cables that tether the island to the mainland. Here, too, was where the legendary **Charybdis** once posed a threat to sailors – along with Scylla on the opposite shore – still remembered in the locality's name of Cariddi.

For a decent **pensione**, the *Donato*, at Via Caratozzolo 8 (☎090.393.150; no credit cards, ❹), offers excellent value, its tastefully decorated rooms – all with bath – undisturbed by the scream of Vespas, and just 50m from the sea. It's signposted off the lake, just beyond *Lilla Currò*.

Mortelle and Acqualadrone

A couple of kilometres further up the road, on the Tyrrhenian coast, **MOR-TELLE** is the focus in summer for Messina's bronzed youth, who throng the orderly lidos and fine sandy **beaches**, filling the air with the drone of a thousand motorbikes. There is no lack of sleek bars and pizzerias here, and Mortelle is also the site of screenings of **open-air films** in July and August, nightly at 8.30pm and 10.45pm, at the Arena Green Sky (opposite the *Due Palme* pizzeria); tickets cost around €5. Westwards from Mortelle is a succession of sandy beaches and beach towns, best of which is **ACQUALADRONE** (bus #80 from Messina's Stazione Centrale).

Inland

Inland from Messina, the ridge-top of the **Monti Peloritani** offers the best vantage-point of the Tyrrhenian and Ionian coasts and also has some good walking in the woods. To reach the ridge, take the old Palermo road from Via Garibaldi in the city (bus #71 from Via Garibaldi). On the way, you can stop off at the old monastery of Santa Maria della Valle, better known as **La Badiazza** (always open). Secluded in a deep gully, this old Benedictine monastery lies at the end of a twenty-minute walk along a dirt road that leads off to the right just before Via Palermo passes under the autostrada. The monastery dates from the twelfth century, but was reconstructed after a fire in the fourteenth century and later abandoned. Today, recently restored, it has regained its fortress-like appearance and looks quite capable of withstanding a corsair raid.

You can wander through the pinewoods around here, but they are thicker further up the SS113 (Via Palermo); from there you can take a left turn at the crossroads at **Colle San Rizzo** (where the bus stops), then it's another 10km south to reach the panoramic **Monte Antennamare** sanctuary, a shabby building in a sublime spot (1124m high). Back at Colle San Rizzo, you could make a round trip by descending north to Castanea, another wooded area favoured by hunters, and down to the Tyrrhenian coast at Spartà, on the Messina road.

The coastal route to Taormina and the hills

There's no shortage of beaches on the coastal strip **south of Messina** if you delve in between the closely packed houses that line this stretch. They're nothing special near the city, but once beyond the suburbs there are a few low-key seaside resorts that would do for an hour or two if you are desperate for a swim. Along the coast, it's best to take the **train**, which traces the shoreline pretty much all the way: on a clear day there are sparkling views across to Calabria, while the ragged cliffs rearing above the tracks are covered with acres of prickly pears. The slower buses, on the other hand, stick to the backstreets of the successive towns and villages – a largely unedifying ride and excruciatingly slow. This is also true for **drivers**, though the toll autostrada (the A18) is a fast alternative, plunging through some fairly dramatic scenery as it cruises above the sea. You don't have to stick with the coast for the entire journey, though: there are some short trips to be made **into the hills** on the way, for which good **bus services** exist from some of the coastal resorts – you might even consider walking, if you've the time.

Mili San Pietro to Ali Terme

Messina's ungraceful suburbs extend almost as far as the autostrada turn-off at Tremestieri. Shortly beyond, a minor road leads off inland from Mili Marina to **MILI SAN PIETRO**, a nondescript little place 2km up the road (from Messina, take hourly bus #8 from Piazza della Repubblica or anywhere central). As the village swings into view, the grey cupolas of the monastery-church of **Santa Maria** are just visible below the road on the right. The Basilian monastery of which this was a part was founded by Count Roger in 1082, but is now abandoned – irreverently occupied by assorted farmyard animals and permeated by their pungent rural smells. The church survives – just – its exterior displaying some nice interlaced blind arcading on one wall and a semicircular apse. But the inside is derelict and not particularly interesting, although it's said to contain the burial place of Roger's son, Jordan; ask at the church in the centre of the village for the key.

Further down the coast by 7 or 8km, **Scaletta Zanclea** is a popular resort with an impressive eleventh-century **castle** at its highest point, containing some heraldic knick-knacks. The key is kept at the *Comune*. The next village down, Itala Marina, has an inland parent, **Itala**, 2.5km up the road from the coast, just beyond which – over the bridge on the road to Croce – is the church of **San Pietro**. Built by Roger in 1093, in thanksgiving for a victory over the Arabs, the building has features in common with Santa Maria in Mili San Pietro, and provided the model for the church near Casalvécchio Sículo built eighty years later (see p.222). This domed, red-brick construction has been restored and is still in use; indeed the best time to see it is before the 11am service on Sunday morning – otherwise, contact the priest for the key; find him on Itala's main street, at no. 26.

If you're stuck for **somewhere to stay** along this stretch, **ALI TERME** – a village known for its sulphur baths – has three hotels: the antique but gratifyingly inexpensive *Terme Granata Cassibile* (℡0942.715.029; ❶), which has shared bathrooms; the *Terme Marino Giuseppe* (℡090.715.031; ❸), a bit classier; and the smaller, more modern *La Magnolia* (℡0942.716.377; ❾; half-board obligatory in August), on the seafront.

Santa Teresa di Riva and Sávoca

Ten kilometres south of Ali Terme, **SANTA TERESA DI RIVA** is the first recognizable resort on this stretch, with an extensive beach and a few trattorias. Though the town itself is nothing to shout about, it's a useful jumping-off point for the foothills of the **Monti Peloritani**: **buses** leave from here for Sávoca and Casalvécchio Sículo; ask the driver of the Messina–Catania bus to put you off on the seafront (Lungomare Santa Teresa), and Sávoca is signposted to the left, the bus stop for the village one block back from the sea on the corner of a crossroads. Sávoca is also accessible by direct bus from Taormina (see "Travel details", p.239).

Sávoca

It's a winding four-kilometre run up to **SÁVOCA**, a peaceful village, evocatively situated: houses and three churches perch on the cliffsides in clumps, with a tattered castle (originally Saracen) topping the pile. Two pincer-like streets, Via San Michele and Via Chiesa Madre, reach around to their respective churches, the grandest being the square-towered thirteenth-century **Chiesa Madre**. Sitting on a tiny ridge between two opposing hills, it's a fine vantage-point from which to look down the valley to the sea and across the surrounding hills. Spare a glance, too, at the house next door, lovingly restored and displaying a fifteenth-century stone-arched double window; the house is one of many in the village that have had a face-lift as outsiders move in to snap up run-down cottages as second homes. These days, Sávoca is within the Taormina commuter belt and most of the people who live here work elsewhere – something that's to its advantage: during the day the streets and hillside alleys are refreshingly empty, and the medieval atmosphere still intact.

Signs in the village point you to the **Cappuccini monastery**, whose catacombs (Tues–Sun: April–Sept 9am–1pm & 4–7pm; Oct–March 9am–noon & 4–7pm; scheduled for restoration, call ☎0942.761.007 for details; donations requested) contain a selection of gruesome mummified bodies. These are the remains of local lawyers, doctors and the clergy: two hundred to three hundred years old, they stand in niches dressed in their eighteenth-century finery, the skulls of less-complete colleagues lining the walls above. An added grotesque touch is the green paint with which the bodies have been daubed, the work of vandals and hard to remove without damaging the cadavers. Ask the custodian and you'll probably be shown the church **treasury** as well, which has a small collection of liturgical books and seventeenth- and eighteenth-century bibles. More offbeat delight is at hand in the village's *Bar Vitelli*. An appealing wood-panelled, eighteenth-century stone-flagged building, it (and the village) were used as the scene of Michael Corleone's betrothal to Apollonia in Coppola's film *The Godfather*. A few words of Italian might nudge the woman behind the bar into recounting her memories of the shoot – she's something of an expert on all the *Godfather* films. There are numerous mementoes of other episodes in the bar's past inside, and tables under the pergola outside.

In summer, the signora at the *Bar Vitelli* will probably persuade you to sample her delicious lemon granita, which she makes daily. Sávoca also has a *paninoteca* for **snacks** below the Capuchin monastery and a popular **trattoria**, *La Pineta*, with a panoramic terrace, near the bar, but there's nowhere to stay – a shame really, but you could easily see the village (and the rest of the route, described below) on a day-trip from Taormina or Messina, provided you time the buses right.

Casalvécchio Sículo

The only road beyond Sávoca (and served by the same bus from Santa Teresa) careers another 2km along the ridge to **CASALVÉCCHIO SÍCULO**, which, if anything, has even better views of the valley from its terraces. There's not much to detain you here, except the quiet village atmosphere, but walk

△ Olives

through Casalvécchio and, after about 500m, a rough road drops away to the left (signposted), snaking down into a lush, citrus-planted valley. It's about a twenty-minute hike to the Norman monastery of **Santi Pietro e Paolo**, gloriously situated on a high bank above the river. Built in the twelfth century, its battlemented facade and double domes are visible from a distance through the lemon groves and, though considered Sicily's best example of Basilian (Greek) architecture, the church betrays a strong Arabic influence, particularly in the polychromatic patterns of the exterior. If it's locked, there should be someone around in one of the adjacent buildings with a key.

Either head back up to the main road and wait for the return bus to pass, or continue downhill for a longer **walk**, beyond the monastery to the River Agrò. It's about another hour's tramp, alongside the wide (and mostly dry) river bed to Rina, back towards the sea. The main (SS114) coastal road is signposted from Rina, and in another twenty minutes, through a small tunnel, you're back in Santa Teresa, on the Messina–Catania bus route.

Forza d'Agrò and Sant'Aléssio

The only other worthy diversion into the hills is just a few kilometres south, where the turn-off at **Capo Sant'Aléssio** gives the first views of Taormina. The cliffs here support a sturdy castle and, though you can climb up to it, you can't get in – it's been for sale for years.

Four kilometres inland of here, atop a corkscrew road, is **FORZA D'AGRÒ** (reached by AST bus from Messina and Taormina) – like so many Sicilian villages, a breezy place defiantly crumbling all around its mostly elderly inhabitants and with little left of the Norman **castello** that crowns it. It's a memorable clamber up to the top: the streets become ever more perilous, and the stone cottages increasingly neglected and held together by rotting spars of wood. One push, it seems, would bring the whole lot down. The lower parts of the village are better maintained, but not much – hi-fi stores and clothes shops are tucked into tiny cottage interiors, and a couple of churches are locked and decrepit.

Still, it's close enough to Taormina to attract the tour buses, which deposit their passengers in the village square, where there are a couple of bars to help idle the time away. And there's a fine, moderately priced **restaurant** too, known to both tourists and locals: *L'Abbazia*, where specialities include mixed vegetable grill made with local mushrooms, aubergine, peppers and radicchio, which you can eat on a terrace with great views (☎0942.721.226; closed Mon lunch; moderate–expensive). There's even **somewhere to stay** if you are so inclined, the *Souvenir* on Via Belvedere (☎0942.721.078; no credit cards, ❹), where half-board is compulsory in August (€55 per person).

Sant'Aléssio Sículo

If you're energetic enough, you can make the descent on foot from Forza d'Agrò back down to the main coastal road and Capo Sant'Aléssio, where you can pick up the Messina–Catania bus. One kilometre north of the cape, there's a train station at **SANT'ALÉSSIO SÍCULO** village, a small resort with a wide beach and a few cheap accommodation possibilities. There's a **campsite** here, *La Focetta* (☎0942.751.657; June–Sept), and another close to Capo Sant'Aléssio, the *Forza d'Agrò Mare* (☎0942.751.158; May–Sept), at Località Buzzurratti.

Taormina

TAORMINA, high on Monte Tauro and dominating two grand, sweeping bays below, is Sicily's best-known resort. The whole town is devoted to – and dependent on – the top-notch international tourism that parades through its streets from April to October. You'd be wrong, though, to avoid Taormina because of this: it's certainly expensive to stay here, but the veneer of exclusivity is only skin-deep, and at heart the small town still can't seem to believe its good luck. There's enough left of its hill-village charm to make it a worthy stop, especially if you hole up at one of the cheaper nearby beach resorts. And, although Taormina itself has no beach (all local beaches are a steep climb downhill), the outstanding remains of the classical theatre and the sheer beauty of the town's site amply compensate. Among many passing travellers besotted by Taormina, Goethe and D.H. Lawrence are the two big names touted by the tourist office; Lawrence was so enthusiastic about Taormina's prospect and climate that he lived here (1920–23), in a villa at the top of the valley-cleft behind the theatre.

Despite the intrusion of contemporary tourists, Taormina retains much of its late medieval character. The one main traffic-free street is an unbroken line of intimate piazzas and fifteenth- to nineteenth-century *palazzi*; its churches are unobtrusive and attractive; and there's an agreeably crumbly castle and rows of flower-filled balconies. The downside is that at New Year, Easter and between June and August it can get supremely crowded: the narrow alleys are filled shoulder-to-shoulder with tourists, while the beaches below town simply seethe. April, May or September are better, but to avoid the crowds completely come between October and March, when the views of Etna are incomparably clearer, and the spring brings flamboyant displays of all kinds of flowering plants.

Locally, there are several good **walks** to be done, including a trip up to the neighbouring village of **Castelmola** and the mountain behind it. Most people, though, are content with the excellent **beaches** that punctuate the coastline below Taormina; all the details are given in "Around Taormina" (see p.233). You'll not avoid the crowds in any of these places, but it's worth noting that the nearest town to Taormina, Giardini-Naxos, might be a more realistic base for your beach-going – cheaper and less pretentious than Taormina in every way.

Arrival, information and getting around

Trains pull up at Taormina–Giardini station on the water's edge, way below town – one of Italy's most attractive stations, in Sicilian-Gothic style with Art Nouveau decoration. There's also a **tourist office** here (Mon–Sat: summer 8.30am–2pm & 4.30–7.30pm; winter 8.30am–2pm & 3–6pm; ☎0942.52.189). It's a *very* steep thirty-minute walk from here up to Taormina: turn right out of the station and, after 300m, turn left through a gap in the buildings, signposted "*Centro*". Much better (certainly if you have luggage) is to arrive by bus – from Messina or Catania – or take one of the fairly frequent local buses up the hill, roughly every 30 minutes from outside the train station. Taormina's **bus terminal** (information on ☎0942.625.301), where they all stop, is on Via Luigi

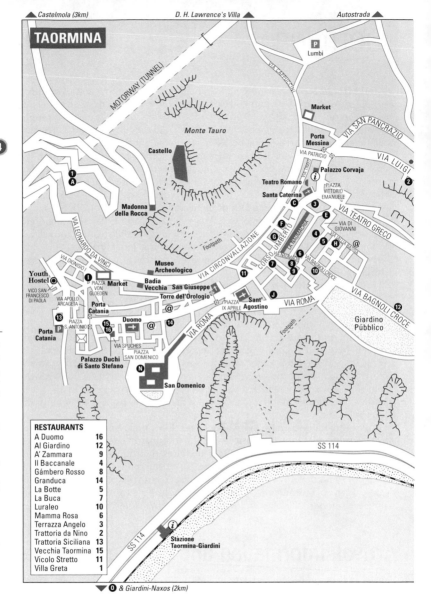

TAORMINA

MOTORWAY (TUNNEL)

Monte Tauro

Castello

Madonna
della Rocca

Footpath

P
Lumbi

Market

Porta
Messina

VIA PATRICIO

VIA MATRICIA

VIA SAN PANCRAZIO

VIA LUIGI

Palazzo Corvaja

Teatro Romano

Santa Caterina

PIAZZA
VITTORIO
EMANUELE

VIA DI
GIOVANNI

VIA TEATRO GRECO

Museo
Archeologico

VIA CIRCONVALLAZIONE

CORSO UMBERTO

VIA BAGNOLI CROCE

VIA LEONARDO DA VINCI

VIA DIONISIO

Youth
Hostel

VICO SAN
FRANCESCO
DI PAOLA

VIA APOLLO
ARCAGETA

Porta
Catania

PIAZZA
VON
GLOEDEN

Market

Badia
Vecchia

San Giuseppe

Torre dell'Orologio

PIAZZA
IX APRILE

Sant'
Agostino

VIA ROMA

VIA BAGNOLI CROCE

Giardino
Púbblico

Porta
Catania

PIAZZA
S. ANTONIO

Duomo

VIA SPUCHES

PIAZZA
SAN DOMENICO

VIA ROMA

Footpath

Palazzo Duchi
di Santo Stefano

San Domenico

SS 114

RESTAURANTS

A Duomo	16
Al Giardino	12
A' Zammara	9
Il Baccanale	4
Gámbero Rosso	8
Granduca	14
La Botte	5
La Buca	7
Luraleo	10
Mamma Rosa	6
Terrazza Angelo	3
Trattoria da Nino	2
Trattoria Siciliana	13
Vecchia Taormina	15
Vicolo Stretto	11
Villa Greta	1

SS 114

Stazione
Taormina-Giardini

▼ ⓞ & Giardini-Naxos (2km)

Pirandello. Alternatively, a **taxi** ride from the train station to the town costs
€15, and from €70–80 from Catania airport. If you want to park a car, you'll
be charged at least €4.50 in peak season to leave it for two hours (around €15
for 24hr) in the **Porta Catania** multi-storey car park, situated below Piazza
S. Antonio, and connected to it with a flight of steps. **Lumbi car park**, at the
top of town (both car parks are signposted off the Taormina Nord autostrada
junction) is a lengthy walk up steps to Via Cappuccini; the circular free minibus

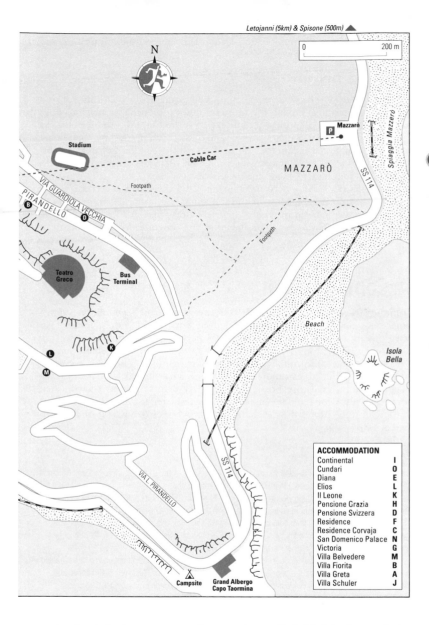

N

0   200 m

P Mazzarò

Stadium

Cable Car

MAZZARÒ

Footpath

VIA GUARDIOLA VECCHIA

PIRANDELLO

B

D

Footpath

Teatro
Greco

Bus
Terminal

Beach

Isola
Bella

K

L

M

SS 114

VIA L. PIRANDELLO

SS 114

Spiaggia Mazzarò

ACCOMMODATION

Continental	I
Cundari	O
Diana	E
Elios	L
Il Leone	K
Pensione Grazia	H
Pensione Svizzera	D
Residence	F
Residence Corvaja	C
San Domenico Palace	N
Victoria	G
Villa Belvedere	M
Villa Fiorita	B
Villa Greta	A
Villa Schuler	J

Campsite   Grand Albergo
Capo Taormina

service (see below) can save you the ten-minute climb. Slightly cheaper is the **Mazzarò car park** below (see p.233), alongside the cable car off the coast road, where you'll be charged €4 for 1–3 hours or €7 all day.

The main street, **Corso Umberto I**, runs right through town, from Porta Messina to Porta Catania at the other end. The useful English-speaking **tourist office** is in the crenellated Palazzo Corvaja, off Piazza Vittorio Emanuele (Mon–Sat 8.30am–2pm & 4–7pm; ☎0942.23.243, ⊛www.gate2taormina.com).

Pick up a free map, accommodation listings and bus and train timetables, and programmes for summer events in the theatre.

Getting around

You'll walk nearly everywhere in town, though there is a **minibus service** from the bus terminal linking the more far-flung parts of Taormina, including the Lumbi car park. The most useful service is the one from the terminal to Madonna della Rocca, which passes several of the main hotels, operating every forty-five minutes from 8am to 7.15pm. **Taxi** ranks are in Piazza San Pancrazio and Piazza Vittorio Emanuele, where prices are posted; as a general guide, it's about €10 from here to Madonna della Rocca.

The **cable-car** service between Taormina and the beach at Mazzarò, next to the Mazzarò car park, is useful and fun, operating from 8.30am until about 2am in summer, 8.15pm in winter (tickets €1.60 single, €2.70 return); alternatively, a regular bus from the bus terminal runs down to Mazzarò daily from 6.30am to 7.30pm.

Accommodation

Without a **reservation**, finding a **bed** between June and September is a time-consuming business – only a handful will be both available and affordable, so start looking early. Late arrivals can usually persuade the tourist office to ring round for available rooms, though this way you don't get to see them first.

It's worth bearing in mind that in the frantic summer months, everywhere (these places included) can more or less charge what they like, often by simply slapping on an obligatory breakfast charge: it's a good idea to take the first reasonable place you're offered and check the rest later. If everywhere is full, or you prefer to be nearer the beach, try Giardini-Naxos (see p.234) or Mazzarò (see p.233).

Hotels

Continental Via Dionisio I 2a ☎0942.23.805, ℱ0942.23.806, ⓦwww.continentaltaormina.com. At the top of town, with sweeping views across to Etna and the bay from the impressive bar-roof terrace. Rooms are modern and air-conditioned. **❼**

Residence Corvaja Corso Umberto I 19 ☎0942.628.808 or 348.610.0676. It's advisable to look over the rooms here before booking, as they vary considerably – some are large, some are gloomy, and some have balconies looking onto the corso. Cooking facilities available. **❺**

Cundari Via Nazionale 9 ☎0942.53.287. This is a good-value choice if you want to stay around the train station rather than in Taormina itself. Take a note of the bus times at the station and you're just ten minutes away from the centre of town. It's very clean and basic, with some rooms en suite. No credit cards. Closed Jan. **❷**

Diana Via di Giovanni 6 ☎0942.23.898. This tiny *locanda* has just four rooms (all with bath/shower)

and some of the cheapest prices in town. No credit cards. **❷**

Elios Via Bagnoli Croce 98 ☎ & ℱ0942.23.431. A smartish two-star *pensione* with nice rooms, all with shower, and a view-laden roof terrace, but occasionally fierce management. **❺**

Pensione Grazia Via Iallia Bassia 20 ☎ & ℱ0942.24.776. A budget option in a street behind the public gardens. Basic but clean rooms, and positively mothering management. No credit cards. **❹**

Il Leone Via Bagnoli Croce 126 ☎ & ℱ0942.23.878. Around 300m from the bus station, the balconies here overlook the bay below, making this one of the better budget places. Small, plain, kitchenless apartments also available for lets. No credit cards. **❷**

Residence Salita Dente 4 ☎0942.23.463, ℱ0942.23.464. Tucked into one of the town's central, medieval streets, the cheapest rooms here are good value, though they don't have the views that the more expensive rooms with bath enjoy. **⑥**

San Domenico Palace Piazza San Domenico 5 ⑦0942.613.111, ⑤0942.625.506, ⑩www.thi.it. Taormina's finest hotel, stunningly situated in a fifteenth-century convent. Views and facilities are unsurpassed – there's a heated pool and tennis courts – and prices steep (over €350 per night for a standard room in high season), though it does appear at discounted rates on high-class packages from the UK. **⑧**

Pensione Svizzera Via L. Pirandello 26 ⑦0942.23.790, ⑤0942.625.906, ⑩www .pensionesvizzera.com. Just up from the bus terminal, the orange-pink hotel sports a pleasant shady terrace and some good views over the coast north of town, and there's a shuttle service to a private beach. Rooms are fully equipped, and nearly all have balconies with sea views. **⑥**

Victoria Corso Umberto I 81 ⑦0942.23.372, ⑤0942.623.567. Housed in one of the main corso's converted *palazzi*, close to Piazza IX Aprile, this has a pleasant top-floor breakfast room and offers a bird's-eye view of the corso from the roof terrace. All rooms have shower/WC, and off-season prices plummet. **⑥**

Villa Belvedere Via Bagnoli Croce 79 ⑦0942.23.791, ⑤0942.625.830. Large cliff-side hotel in an attractive turn-of-the-century building, with gardens and a pool. Rooms at the front are easily the best, though you're paying more for the views and terrace. Out of season, prices are much lower. **⑧**

Villa Fiorita Via L. Pirandello 39 ⑦0942.24.122, ⑤0942.625.967. A three-star rating, comfortable, airy rooms with expansive views, a garden and a swimming pool, which isn't bad at all for these prices. It's close to the cable-car station (and only just creeps into this category, with uniform prices all year). **⑦**

Villa Greta Via Leonardo da Vinci 41 ⑦0942.28.286, ⑤0942.24.360. A truly delightful *pensione* managed by a friendly family, who also offer decent half- and full-board rates. The comfortably furnished rooms have shower and terrace, with superb views over town, bay and volcano; the little restaurant (see p.231) has an outdoor terrace. It's a steep 15min walk above Taormina on the Castelmola road; the bus passes right outside. **⑤**

Villa Schuler Piazzetta Bastione (entrance also on Via Roma) ⑦0942.23.481, ⑤0942.23.522, ⑩www. villaschuler.com. With scintillating bay views from the tranquil, palm-shaded terrace, and an extensive garden at the back, this makes a luxurious oasis at quite reasonable prices. Closed mid-Nov to early March. **⑦**

Apartments

It can also be worth enquiring at the tourist office about **furnished apartments**, usually rented out by the month in summer only, but sometimes for negotiable periods out of high season. There are dozens all over town, all with bathroom and kitchen facilities, and prices start at around €500 a week for two people – though you should be able to negotiate lower rates in winter. There are some very central one- or two-room apartments for rent from *Residence Circe* (⑦0942.23.168), at Corso Umberto 78; *Il Leone* and *Villa Schuler* also have apartments to let; check above for details. The tourist office has a full list of possibilities, including apartments by the sea at Mazzarò.

Youth hostel and campsites

Taormina has an official mini-**hostel** just up from Piazza Sant'Antonio, on Vico San Francesco di Paola, the *Ostello Ulisse* (⑦0942.23.193, ⑩www .ostellionline.org; closed Jan to early Feb and Nov to early Dec). Dorms have four, six or ten bunkbeds, costing €14.50 per night including breakfast, but space is very limited – as are facilities (though there is a small kitchen and veranda) – so a call beforehand is essential. The nearest **campsite**, *San Leo* (⑦0942.24.658), on the cape below town next to the *Grande Albergo Capo Taormina*, is open all year, but it's only worth it if you're desperate to be close to town; you can reach it on any bus running between Taormina and the train station. Otherwise, head further afield to sites at Letojanni (p.234) and Giardini-Naxos (p.234).

Around the town

Whenever you visit Taormina, you shouldn't miss the **Teatro Greco** (summer daily 9am–7pm, winter daily 9am–4pm; €4.50), signposted from just about everywhere, at the end of Via Teatro Greco. Vincent Cronin (in *The Golden Honeycomb*) thought the theatre was " ... deluged to distraction with multiple beauty ... sited by connoisseurs", and certainly it's a considered choice, the theatre carved out of the hillside and giving a complete panorama of southern Calabria, the Sicilian coastline and snow-capped Etna – a glorious natural backdrop for the audience.

Despite its name, the existing remains are almost entirely Roman. Founded by Greeks in the third century BC, it was rebuilt at the end of the first century AD, a period when Taormina enjoyed great prosperity under Imperial Roman rule, and the reconstruction completely changed the theatre's character. The arched apertures, niches and columns of the impressive Roman scene-building, for example, must have obscured the views of Etna, which presumably were a major reason for the theatre's original siting. Likewise, Imperial Roman drama was strictly gladiatorial, so the stage and lower seats were cut back to provide more room and a deep trench was dug in the orchestra to accommodate the animals and fighters. Still, it all adds to the interest, and you'll want to scramble up and down the seats of the *cavea*, as well as poke around the high-vaulted rooms on either side of the scene-building – all of which is best done in the early morning or near closing time if you want to avoid the high-season crowds. You can't fault the acoustics either, and in summer (July & Aug) the theatre hosts an **international arts festival** including film, theatre and music; tickets and information are available from the tourist office.

Relics of Roman Taormina can be seen in the **Museo Archeológico** at the **Badia Vecchia** (Tues–Sun 9am–1pm & 4–8pm; €1.70), near where Via Circonvallazione meets Via Leonardo da Vinci. This surviving remnant of a fifteenth-century abbey, with the swallow-tailed battlements and twin Gothic windows characteristic of Taormina, is one of the old town's most graceful buildings, and worth a glance whether or not the interior is open.

Back on the corso, and right at its northern end, the fine fourteenth-century **Palazzo Corvaja** – home to Taormina's tourist office – is decorated with inlaid black and white lava and encompasses an attractive courtyard. A staircase here gives access to the main hall, where the Sicilian "parliament" met in 1410 to choose a successor to the Aragonese line, and which now houses an entertaining exhibition of often wacky folklore, the **Museo Siciliano d'Arte e Tradizioni Popolari** (Tues–Sun 9am–1pm & 4–8pm; €2.58). Many of the assorted items have a religious connotation, such as, in the first room, the waxworks of the Madonna and a nativity scene of cork and wax showing the Napoleonic general Gioacchino Murat paying homage to the infant Jesus against an Italian city backdrop. A corridor off this room holds the museum's quirkiest exhibits – twenty-five panel paintings, mostly from the 1860s, showing various people being saved by miraculous intervention from such terrible fates as falling onto a stove or being attacked by cats – while the main room has bits and pieces of Sicilian carts colourfully painted with scenes from *Cavalleria Rusticana*, among other themes, with a wax head of St John the Baptist thrown in for good measure.

Opposite the Palazzo Corvaja, the church of **Santa Caterina** on the corso has been built almost on top of a small, brick-built odeon, known as the **Teatro Romano** (originally used for musical recitations): peer down at it through the railings from outside and then enter the church to take a closer look at bits of the theatre exposed in the floor of the nave.

There's little else that's vital in town and, really, Taormina's attractions are all to do with strolling along the flower-decked streets and sheer-stepped alleys, and window-shopping in the converted ground floors of Corso Umberto's fifteenth-century *palazzi*. A few other vestiges of Roman and medieval Taormina can be taken in during your wanderings through town, however. Heading south, back along the corso, turn off a side street to the left (Via Naumachia) to find, on the left, the niched wall of **La Naumachia**, a Roman water cistern and gymnasium. It's a long (122m), refreshingly shop-free expanse – though a restaurant and barber's have staked their pitches here. Bang in the middle of Corso Umberto I, **Piazza IX Aprile** is identifiable by its restored twelfth-century **Torre dell'Orologio**, a clocktower you can walk right through. The views here, from a terrace overlooking Etna and the bay, are splendid, and the inviting outdoor cafés make much of their position – though be warned that they are expensive places to sit and drink. Both churches in the square, low-key and unassuming, indicate how small-scale Taormina was until fairly recently. Squat fifteenth-century **Sant'Agostino** is now a library, while **San Giuseppe** tops the steps at the back of the piazza, its seventeenth-century facade adorned with plaques depicting skull and crossbones.

Through the clocktower is the oldest part of Taormina, and the narrow corso is awash with stately *palazzi*, now neatly displaying antiques, shoes, clothes and local lace in their lower windows. The battlemented **Duomo**, originally built in the thirteenth century, though restored since, isn't of vast interest. Typically subdued in design, it's fronted by a pretty seventeenth-century fountain. Steps to the right lead to a patchy, enclosed Roman mosaic, badly faded, just above Piazza del Duomo.

Head the other way, behind the square and cathedral, and a street drops down to the impressive convent of **San Domenico**, now a luxury hotel (see p.227) and containing a contemporary cloister (which you can't get into) and a restored church hall adjoining it (which hosts the odd concert). Though you'd never know to look at it, the convent was badly bombed during World War II, when it was commandeered as the headquarters of Field Marshal Kesselring.

At some point, it's worth fetching up at the **Giardino Púbblico** (dawn–dusk) on Via Bagnoli Croce. The shady gardens were endowed by a Scot, Florence Trevelyan, who settled in Taormina in 1899 having been "invited" to leave England in the wake of a romantic liaison with the Prince of Wales, the future Edward VII. She also contributed the curious *apiari* ("beehives") – pavilions, variously resembling rustic log cabins and stone- or brick-built pagodas and now holding caged birds, plants and a children's play area. Elsewhere, the park is furnished with a motley collection of memorials, bits of artillery and a mini-submarine, among other items, and has panoramic viewpoints which make ideal spots for a sit-down or picnic; there's also a quiet little bar (March–Oct) perched on the edge of the drop, with outstanding views.

Out of the centre: D.H. Lawrence's villa and the castello

A left turn out of the easternmost town gate, Porta Messina, leads you down Via Cappuccini and Via Fontana Vecchia, before dropping down to Piazza Franz Pagano. Follow the road around and a left fork – Via David Herbert Lawrence – announces that you've reached the villa in which **D.H. Lawrence** lived for three years in the 1920s. It's on the right-hand side of the road, a pink-and-cream-coloured building, now a private house, and marked by a simple plaque reading: "D.H. Lawrence, English author, lived here 1920–1923".

This is of fairly specialist interest (after all, there's nothing to see except the back of a house) and, for a more rewarding walk, consider hiking up to the tumbledown medieval **castello** above Taormina, where the panoramas take in the town and theatre as well as the coastline. There's a very steep path that leads up from the Circonvallazione, past the cliff-top cross of **Madonna della Rocca**, the climb taking around half an hour.

Eating and drinking

As with accommodation, there are few food and drink bargains in Taormina, and unless you're careful you'll go through money like water. Many **restaurants** offer a limited-choice *pranzo turístico*, usually around €15 a head, but these rarely include a drink. The quality of the food can sometimes be a bit of a lottery, too, especially in peak season, when everywhere is run off its feet, and you may need to book ahead. The restaurants listed below may not be the very cheapest in town, but they do offer consistently good value. A good alternative for lunch is to buy some fast food Sicilian-style at a **rosticceria** like *La Fontana*, on the corner of Via Timeo and Via Patricio, just west from the Porta Messina, where you can load up with delicious takeaway *arancini, caponata, parmigiana, lasagne* and so forth (closed Mon). See also "Listings" for **market** and **supermarket** shopping; and p.53 for an explanation of the restaurant price categories.

Restaurants

Terrazza Angelo Corso Umberto I 38 ☎0942.24.411. One of the town's best locations, with two terraces to sit out on, and views down to the Naumachia. It's touristy but smart, with fairly reasonable prices, and pizzas on the menu. Closed Thurs in winter. Moderate.

Il Baccanale Piazzetta Filea 3 ☎0942.625.390. Just off Via Bagnoli Croce, in the old centre, this rustic little place has outside tables and decent Italian and Sicilian specialities, including grilled sardines and delicious stuffed *calamari*. Closed Thurs in winter. Moderate.

La Botte Piazza Santa Domenica 4 ☎0942.24.198. An accommodating restaurant that promises *cucina tipica Siciliana*, and has outdoor seating in summer. A wood-fired oven produces better pizzas than in most competing places; alternatively, circle the impressive antipasto table along with the local clientele. Closed Mon in winter. Moderate.

La Buca Corso Umberto I 140 ☎0942.24.314. Either eat in the cavern-style dining room or in the attractive terrace garden beyond. There's a decent list of pastas and pizzas, and a memorable *zuppa di pesce*, but pricey house wine. Closed Thurs. Moderate.

A Duomo Vico Ebrei 11 ☎0942.625.656. Fine restaurant with a serious commitment to local ingredients and local dishes such as *maccu* (mashed fava beans), stuffed sardines and lamb or kid stew. Lovely terrace outside and a simple, pretty interior. Moderate.

Gámbero Rosso Via Naumachia 11 ☎0942.24.863. Inconsistent in quality – sometimes excellent, occasionally disappointing – this has outdoor tables on the steps and others, off the main thoroughfare, round the back. Choosing one of the relatively expensive fish dishes pushes the prices up considerably, but there is a pizza menu too. Closed Thurs in winter. Moderate.

Al Giardino Via Bagnoli Croce 84 ☎0942.23.453. Fresh pasta and first-class antipasti served in this trattoria opposite the Giardino Púbblico. There are good-value fixed-price menus (€11.50), and service is amiable and enthusiastic. Closed Tues. Moderate.

Granduca Corso Umberto 170 ☎0942.24.983. A restored fifteenth-century *palazzo*, whose slightly forbidding dining room (serving sophisticated fare) and more relaxed garden (for pizzas) both enjoy stunning views over the bay below town. Moderate for pizzas; expensive for a full meal.

Luraleo Via Bagnoli Croce 27 ☎0942.62.016. Touristy, but serves good antipasti and risotto, with a calm outdoor eating area. Closed Wed in winter. Moderate.

Mamma Rosa Via Naumachia 10 ☎0942.24.361. Straightforward pizzeria-*ristorante*, with great antipasti, decent pizzas and cheap local wine. Fairly good value for Taormina. Closed Tues in winter. Moderate.

Trattoria da Nino Via Luigi Pirandello 37
℡ 0942.21.265. Basic, reliable trattoria away
from the main drag, offering the usual repertoire
of pastas, grills and salads. Closed Fri Sept–July.
Moderate.

Trattoria Siciliana Salita Ospedale 9
℡ 0942.24.780. Outside the Porta Catania, across
from the post office, this is a pleasant place to
eat, raised above the square on a terrace. It's
well thought of locally for its Sicilian specialities, including fresh tuna, though it also serves
simpler and less expensive dishes. Closed Wed.
Moderate.

Vecchia Taormina Vico Ebrei 3 ℡ 0942.24.359.
Probably Taormina's best pizzeria, so expect a
crowd. Closed Wed, also lunchtime July–Aug.
Inexpensive.

Vicolo Stretto Vicolo Stretto 6 ℡ 0942.23.849.
Reached up the slimmest of alleys off the corso,
by Piazza IX Aprile (and easy to miss), this wonderfully chic restaurant has a good spaghetti with
zucchini and other tasty Sicilian dishes. Closed
Mon in winter. Expensive.

Villa Greta Via Leonardo da Vinci 44
℡ 0942.28.286. This attractive *pensione* dining
room is open to non-guests and has alfresco terrace seating in summer. Seafood (of course) is the
speciality, and the wine's from their own vineyard.
Moderate.

A' Zammara Via Fratelli Bandiera 15
℡ 0942.24.408. One of the best places to try Sicilian dishes such as *maccheroni alla Norma*. Eat
outside in a garden of orange trees or in the rusti-
cally furnished interior. Moderate.

Bars and cafés

Arco Rosso Via Naumachia 7. A rarity: a proper
little bar, tucked just off the corso, which sells
good local wine by the glass or bottle, doesn't
charge the earth for it, and sees its fair share of
locals, too. Closed Wed.

Marrakech Piazzetta G. Garibaldi. Elegant tea-
room and late-night café with Arabic decor and
a young American-European crowd. It's one of a
cluster of sophisticated drinking holes at this end
of town (between Piazza San Domenico and the
corso), this one with outdoor seating. Cocktails
cost around €5. Closed Mon in winter.

Mediterraneo Café Via Giovanni di Giovanni.
Trendy bar and crêperie with jazzy sounds playing
until late and live music most Wednesdays. Fruit
vodkas a speciality. Closed Tues in winter.

Mocambo Piazza IX Aprile. Seats on the corso
in Taormina's most prestigious spot, and comfy
armchairs and sofas inside this rather genteel
teashop cum-*gelateria*.

Nero d'Avola Vico Spuches 8. Great *enoteca*
(wine bar) serving lots of interesting wines and
snacks.

O'Seven Largo La Farina 6. Just off the corso,
Taormina's inevitable "Irish" pub is very popular, with
drinking until late, and panini and pizza served.

Re di Bastoni Corso Umberto 170. Popular place
for all kinds of drinks plus sandwiches and salads.
Paintings on the dark orange walls lend a bohemian,
folksy feel, and there's occasional live music. Try the
strawberry caipirinhas. Closed Mon in winter.

Shatulle Piazza Paladini. Currently the main focus
of Taormina's gay and lesbian scene, with seats
outside and crowds spilling into the piazza.

Time Out Via San Pancrazio 19. Outside
Porta Messina, and with a pleasant garden, this
is the scene of a lively crowd until 3am most
nights, and offers panini and chips as well as
draught Guinness and other beers. Closed Wed
in winter.

Wunderbar Caffé Piazza IX Aprile. Once the haunt
of Garbo and Fassbinder, this remains the most
favoured spot in town for the see-and-be-seen brigade, with outdoor seats beneath the clocktower.
But even a coffee here comes with a startlingly
high tab, so sip slowly.

Nightlife and festivals

Taormina's **nightlife** may seem dauntingly exclusive at times, but it isn't really
– just dauntingly dear and in fact rather tame. Be prepared to pay heavily for
drinks in the few discos and video-bars, all of which are as good, or bad, as
each other. At some point you'll probably want to sit and **drink** in one of the
pavement cafés. Again, though, they're not cheap – in Piazza IX Aprile, the
prime spot, a small beer will set you back €3–4, and a cappuccino not much
less. The favourite entertainment in Taormina is also free: joining the town's
swanky *passeggiata* along the corso. Alternatively, if you've overdosed on the
town's glitzy glamour, take a bus down to Giardini-Naxos (see p.234) for a
waterfront stroll – by no means the worst way to spend an evening.

In summer particularly, Taormina enjoys late hours, with people milling around the streets until long after midnight. There are several **bars and birrerias** to repair to – the *Marrakech, Mediterraneo, O'Seven, Re di Bastoni* and *Time Out* cafés listed above all stay open into the small hours. As for Taormina's **discos**, most are only open in the summer and charge €5–10 for entry (usually including your first drink). Those listed below are among the best. Taormina also has a (fairly discreet) **gay scene** – check out *Bar Ziggy* at *Le Perroquet* (see below), or hang out at *Shatulle* (see above) on Piazza Paladini.

Festival time is always fun in Taormina, since it's not difficult to pack the narrow central streets with revellers. Main annual occasions are **Taormina Arte** (ⓦwww.taormina-arte.com) from July to August, featuring theatrical, film and musical performances at the theatre, and the festivals and parades staged at **Christmas** and **Carnevale**. A procession of traditional, decorated Sicilian carts, or **Sfilata del Carretto Siciliano**, usually takes place at the end of June, but lack of funding has meant that this rare opportunity to view the famous painted carts has been cancelled in recent years, though it may be revived in the future. In summer, ask in the tourist office about **performances** in the Teatro Greco, enabling you to appreciate the auditorium for the purposes for which it was designed. Ticket prices start at €4.20 for film, €20.70 for theatre, and €15.60 for music and ballet, while prices for rock, jazz and world music concerts vary for each performance. The local *Comune* also stages a season of events in the Giardino Púbblico, including traditional dance, song and puppet shows (admission free), and in the Palazzo Duchi di Santo Stefano, near Porta Catania; get details from the tourist office, or look out for posters around town.

Clubs

Bella Blu ☎0942.24.239. Via Guardiola Vecchia. Smart, fashionable and expensive.
La Giara Via La Floresta ☎0942.23.360. As above, but with a terrace.
Panasia Beach Via Nazionale, Contrada Spisone ☎0924.23.170. Lido by day and a cool club by night, with four huge divans on the sand to chill out on.
Le Perroquet Piazza San Domenico ☎0942.24.462. Taormina's main gay club, with a bar, *Ziggy*, open daily, and discos on Fri and Sat in summer.
Séptimo Via San Pancrazio 50 ☎0942.625.522. Commercial house for terminal fashion victims. Closed Mon–Fri & Sun in winter.
Tout Va Via L. Pirandello 70 ☎0942.23.824. Off-putting doorman but far more relaxed and with younger crowd than most of Taormina's clubs. Closed Mon–Fri in winter.

Listings

Airport Etna/Interbus buses run hourly (four on Sun) to Catania airport from the bus terminal, calling at the train station and Giardini-Naxos, and with a stop also at Catania's train station.
Banks and exchange The lowest rates are at the Banco di Sicilia, Corso Umberto I 91 (Mon–Fri 8.30am–1.30pm & 2.45–3.45pm).
Bike rental Push-bikes available from *Villa Schuler* (see "Accommodation", above) and Etna Rent, in Giardini-Naxos (see p.235).
Bus information Interbus at bus terminal ☎0942.625.301.

Car rental Avis, Via S. Pancrazio 7 ☎0942.23.041; California, Via Bagnoli Croce 86 ☎0942.23.769; City, Piazza Sant'Antonio 5 ☎0942.23.161; Italia, Via Pirandello 29 ☎0942.23.973; Sicily By Car, Via Apollo Arcageta 4 ☎0942.21.252; Tauro, Via Apollo Arcageta 12 ☎0942.24.700.
Excursions and travel agents For trips around Etna, Alcántara and further afield to Palermo, Siracusa and Piazza Armerina, contact: SAT, Corso Umberto I 73 ☎0942.24.653, ⓦwww.sat-group.it; CST, Corso Umberto I 101 ☎0942.626.088; SAIS, Corso Umberto I 222 ☎0942.625.179; or the tourist office (see p.223).

First aid Call ☎0942.53.745, or ☎0942.625.419 at night.

Internet access *Las Vegas* at Salita Alexander Humbolt, opposite Corso Umberto I 186 (daily 10am–1pm & 2.30pm–midnight), and Corso Umberto I 214.

Laundry Service wash at Piazza del Duomo, with items priced individually.

Market There's a daily indoor morning market (Mon–Sat) off Via Cappuccini, for fruit and veg, and a weekly Wednesday market at Parcheggio von Gloeden, below town, for household items.

Newspapers English-language papers from shops along the corso and in the news kiosk at the train station.

Petrol stations Agip, Esso and IP on Via L. Pirandello.

Pharmacy There are English-speaking pharmacists at the British Pharmacy, on the corner of Piazza IX Aprile ☎0942.625.866, and Ragusa, on Piazza Duomo ☎0942.28.022. Late-night openings operate according to a rota system, indicated on the pharmacy doors.

Police Carabinieri, at Piazza Badia 4 ☎0942.23.232.

Post office Piazza Medaglia d'Oro (Mon–Sat 8.30am–6.30pm; closes at noon last day of month).

Scooter rental Mopeds and scooters can be rented from California, Italia, and Tauro – see "Car rental" above. From €25 a day.

Supermarket SMA supermarket outside the Porta Catania (and to the right) on Via Apollo Arcageta.

Telephones Make telephone calls from kiosks in Via S. Pancrazio and on the corso near Piazza del Duomo.

Around Taormina

The **coastline below Taormina**, north and south, is immensely appealing – a mixture of grottoes, rocky coves and good sand beaches – although much of it is either sectioned off as private lidos (which you have to pay to use; prices vary from around €6 to €15 a day) or simply gets very packed in summer. Little communities – not quite villages – have developed around the bay to the north; easiest to reach, by bus or cable car, are the small, stony stretches around **Mazzarò**. For decent expanses of sand you'll have to travel to **Giardini-Naxos**, around a fifteen-minute bus ride south of Taormina, and very much a separate town, with its own holiday trade and nightlife. Indeed, rooms here are plentiful, and you might well want to stay in one of the numerous *pensioni* right by the beach, rather than up in Taormina.

For an alternative day out from Taormina, away from the crowded streets, it's an idea to head **inland**, up into the hills surrounding the nearby village of **Castelmola**.

North: Mazzarò, Spisone and Letojanni

The closest beaches to Taormina are the extremely popular pebbled coves at **MAZZARÒ**, easily reached by a **cable-car** (*funivia*) service – €1.60 each way (€2.70 return), every fifteen minutes from Via L. Pirandello in Taormina (until about 2am in summer, 8.15pm in winter). There's also a steep **path**, which starts just below the cable-car station.

The coast here is protected as a marine-life sanctuary, so the water is remarkably clear, and the snorkelling magical. You can also rent pedal boats to explore the local grottoes. Of the two beaches, the southernmost is usually the most packed, fronting its much-photographed islet, the **Isola Bella**, while the little bay to the north (Spiaggia Mazzarò) is emptier and shelters a very reasonable seafood restaurant, the *Trattoria Il Barcaiolo* (Easter–Oct), whose terrace looks out over beached fishing-boats. There are a dozen small **hotels** here, too, ranged along the main road and above the beaches, though get the tourist office to ring for you first from Taormina: cheapest is *La Marina*, in Piazzale Funivia (☎0942.24.739; closed Nov–Feb; ❺), near the cable-car station (half-board only in Aug at €100 per person). Recommended, though devilishly expensive in summer, is one of Taormina's top hotels, the *Villa Sant'Andrea*, Via Nazionale 137 (☎0942.23.125; ❾), a gracious early-nineteenth-century villa right on the beach, with water lapping under the balconies. Expect to pay over €350 for a room here in peak season.

Spisone and Letojanni

The beach bars and restaurants at **SPISONE**, north again, are also accessible by path from Taormina, this time from below the cemetery in town (off Via Guardiola Vecchia). It's around half an hour's walk, though there are also buses that make the trip from Taormina's bus terminal, passing Isola Bella and Mazzarò on the way.

From Spisone, the coast opens out and the beaches get wider. **LETOJANNI**, 5km from Taormina, is a little resort in its own right, with some rather more ordinary bars and shops, and a few fishing-boats on a sandy beach. There's a superb **restaurant** here, *Da Nino*, at Via L. Rizzo 29 (☎0942.36.147; closed Tues in winter), attracting fans from Taormina and beyond – a great place to eat fish, well worth the steepish prices.

In summer, Letojanni gets as busy as anywhere else on this stretch, but it's not a bad place **to stay** out of season: *Da Nino* has twelve rooms with or without bath (❶), while, a few doors along on the seafront, *Da Peppe*, Via Vittorio Emanuele 345 (☎0942.36.159; March–Oct; ❺), is a *pensione* with artistic touches in the rooms; it also has a good restaurant over on the beach, presided over by Peppe from behind a bushy beard. There are also two nearby **campsites**: *Paradise International* (☎0942.36.306; May–Oct), about 1km north up the coast, and the larger but equally well-equipped *Eurocamping Marmaruca* (☎0942.36.676), 3km away in the same direction. Regular buses head back to Taormina, passing Spisone and the Isola Bella, and trains link the village with Taormina–Giardini station.

South: Giardini-Naxos

Roomier and better for swimming are the sands south of Taormina, principally at **GIARDINI-NAXOS**. The wide, curving bay – easily seen from Taormina's terraces – was the launching point of Garibaldi's 1860 attack on the Bourbon troops in Calabria and, equally significantly, the site of the first Greek colony in Sicily. An attractive and obvious stop for ships sailing between Greece and southern Italy, there was a settlement here by 734 BC, named Naxos after the Greek island from which the colonists came, though it was never very important. The **excavations** (daily 9am–1hr before sunset; €4) lie right on the cape, Capo Schisò, the entrance in between two restaurants. The remains are very low-key – a long stretch of ancient, lava-built city wall, two covered kilns and a sketchy temple – but it's a pleasant walk through the lemon groves, and there's a small but mildly interesting **museo archeológico** on the site, which houses some of the finds – mainly fragments of amphorae and masks, together with maps of the area of Greek colonization – while another building close by has a collection of anchors and more amphorae, all dredged up from the sea. To visit the site, walk or take the bus from Taormina to Naxos/Recanati and follow the signs ("*Scavi*").

Giardini itself, the sprawling town backing the beach, is an excellent alternative to Taormina as a source of accommodation and food. Prices tend to be a good bit cheaper, and in high season, if you've arrived by train, it's probably worth trying first; again, though, starting early in the day is a good idea. The **beach** itself is among the most popular in the whole of Sicily, large parts of it partitioned off and maintained as private lidos, where you can rent sun loungers, umbrellas and watersports gear. Nearly all have associated bar-restaurants, too, so provided you've come with enough cash there's little incentive to leave the sands all day.

Around the cape, the next bay south is largely taken up by the holiday village of **Recanati**. This is the end of the line for buses from Taormina and, though the beach here is fairly long, it's not at all an attractive target. Almost without exception, every building is either a package-tour hotel or a block of holiday apartments, and it's a long walk to Giardini for a decent bar or restaurant.

Practicalities

Buses run every thirty minutes to Giardini from Taormina's bus terminal, the last one at midnight in summer, and 10.30pm the rest of the year. The last bus back to Taormina is at 12.15pm in summer, 10pm in winter, from the stop outside the bar-restaurant *Da Angelo*, opposite the Chiesa Immacolata, on Via Tysandros by the seafront. **Taxis** back to Taormina cost from €16–20.

Via Tysandros runs right around the bay, with the **tourist office** at no. 54 (Mon–Fri 8.30am–2pm & 4–7pm, Sat 8.30am–2pm; ☎0942.51.010, ⓦwww .aastgiardininaxos.it). Beyond the tourist office, Via Tysandros becomes Via Schisò, curving round as far as the headland and fishing harbour, while Via Naxos runs behind, and parallel to, much of Via Tysandros/Via Schisò. There are **banks** at Via Tysandros 78, Via Naxos 239 and on Corso Umberto.

You can **rent bikes and cars** in Giardini-Naxos from Etna Rent, Via Casarsa 27, a turning off Via Dalmazia (☎0942.51.972), with prices at €7.80 per day or €49 per week for a mountain bike; from €32 per day or €200 per week for a scooter; and €53.30 per day or €260.80 per week for a small car.

Accommodation

If you're looking for a **place to stay**, you could do worse than start at the tourist office, which recommends centrally located budget hotels. Good initial choices include: *Otello*, Via Tysandros 62 (☎0942.51.009; ❹), which has small, plain rooms, most with balconies but not all overlooking the sea; *Villa Sant'Antonio*, Via Filicudi 8 (☎0942.51.475; ❷), a quiet place overlooking orchards at the southern end of town; or *La Sirena*, Via Schisò 36 (☎0942.51.853; ❹), also at this end of town close to the *scavi* and pier; at least half-board is required in August (€70 per person), but check the room first, as some are sub-standard. A grade up, there is the central, German-run *Villa Mora* at Via Naxos 47 (☎0942.51.839; ❹), and the *Del Sole*, Via Naxos 98 (☎0942.51.159; ❺), which has a roof garden, while you can enjoy some of Giardini's best views from the *Panoramic*, at the far end of the seafront strip at Via Schisò 22 (☎0942.51.159; ❹), though it's fairly characterless, and a mite tatty round the edges. Half-board is obligatory in August at the last two options. There are loads of other possibilities, from *pensioni* to smart hotels, and if these are full, or don't appeal, just take a walk along the seafront and see which of the others have room, as well as looking out for "*camere*" signs above the trattorias. Another option if you intend to stay in the area for some time is to take a **furnished apartment**. Like Taormina, they're cheaper in winter and rented by the month-only in summer, but the prices here are a good bit more realistic – ask in Immobiliare Naxos (☎0942.51.184), Via Vittorio Emanuele 126; staff speak English.

The **campsite** *Maretna* (☎0942.52.794; mid-March to mid-Oct) is fairly central, off Via San Giusto, but is poorly equipped and has almost no shade; get off the bus from Taormina at the Chiesa Immacolata, cross the train tracks and turn left. A better choice would be to catch any bus for Catania, getting off after about five minutes (ask for San Marco, near Calatabiano) and walk a couple of kilometres towards the sea: two campsites sit within a few minutes of each other on Via San Marco, the best being the *Almoetia* (☎095.641.936), equipped with restaurant, a market and plenty of shade, and the prices aren't bad.

Restaurants and bars

Giardini's **pizzerias** and **restaurants** are consistently better value than those in Taormina. Of the cheaper places, best is the inexpensive *ristorante*-pizzeria attached to the *Lido d'Angelo*, on Via Tysandros, with a lovely terrace over the beach, while fine pizzas, a big antipasto table and fresh pasta are on offer at the moderately priced *Fratelli Marano*, Via Naxos 181. The moderate *Arcobaleno*, Via Naxos 169 (closed Thurs in winter), also serves pizzas and has plenty of grilled fish specials. *La Conchiglia*, Via Naxos 221, has Sicilian meat specialities, including *agnello* (lamb) at moderate prices, and less pricey but still high-quality pizzas, but if you want to escape the constant din of the passing traffic, try the slightly more upmarket but still reasonably priced *La Cambusa* (aka *Terrazza sul Mare*), at the end of Via Schisò by the pier, where you can eat pizzas and good seafood at outdoor tables right on the beach (closed Tues in winter).

Of the **bars** along the front, *Café Chantal*, Via Tysandros 116, has good snack lunches in kitsch pink surroundings with late-night drinking, while the nearby *Bar Pancrazio* (closed Wed in winter) is popular with a young crowd, who hang out on the pavement in front. The drinks here are cheap, English is spoken, and ice cream and panini are available too. Alternatively, you'll find good ice cream and granitas at the *Bar Europa*, Via Naxos 195, which closes at about 11pm.

Inland: Castelmola and Monte Vénere

After taking in Taormina's castle, you could always just continue to follow the road (or the marked path) further up to **CASTELMOLA**, 5km above and seemingly sprouting out of the severe crag beneath it. It's around an hour's climb on foot to the village, making it best tackled in the morning or evening, but there are also regular buses to and from Taormina. It's a tiny place, with just one cobbled road, some lean-to houses and the remnants of a long-demolished castle, though modern building has destroyed some of the place's charm, as do the view-seeking tourists with cars who make drink-stops here in summer. There's a fine **bar** in the Lilliputian piazza, with a roof terrace and a yellowing newspaper cutting chronicling the visit of Earl Mountbatten (a cousin of the Queen, and Prince Philip's uncle) in the mid-1950s. Most of the bars in town serve a splendid *vino alla mándorla* (almond wine), the sweet local brew. The *Bar*

Turrisi also specializes in frankly phallocentric decor, designed to give tourists a shock or a smirk. Among the **restaurants** here, most highly recommended is *Il Maniero*, occupying a tower once part of the castle on Salita Castello, with phenomenal views. It might be worth phoning first, as it quickly fills up (T0942.28.180; closed Wed & Jan–Feb).

If you fancy spending the night up here, or using this as a base instead of Taormina, there is one reasonably priced **hotel**, the *Panorama di Sicilia*, Via de Gásperi 44 (T0942.28.027; ❷), and one more expensive, the *Villa Sonia*, Via Porta Mola 9 (T0942.28.082; ❽). Both have grand views.

Another couple of hours' walk beyond are the heights of **Monte Vénere** (885m) – take the path behind Castelmola's cemetery – where usually the only other people around are the shepherds. **Returning to Taormina**, through Castelmola, you can vary your route back. At the crossroads just out of Castelmola, a road leads off around Monte Tauro and across the other side of the valley: keep bearing right and you'll eventually end up on Via Fontana Vecchia, which finishes up in town – around a two-hour stroll. Less of a hike is the path (signposted "Taormina"), which leads steeply down behind the castle, entering town on Via Cappuccini.

The Alcántara valley

Four buses daily (but fewer in winter, and just one on Sundays; €4.30 return) leave from Taormina–Giardini train station and from Taormina itself for the green hills south of town and the pretty **Alcántara valley**. It's an hour's ride all told, the bus heading a few kilometres down the coast and then turning inland, with stops at several villages, some crowned with ruined medieval castles.

The Gola di Alcántara

Beyond the uninviting dormitory suburb of Gaggi, the valley is immediately more attractive, the road snaking into the hills and the railway line carried over a viaduct which crosses the Alcántara River (the name, Alcántara, is a corruption of the Arabic word for bridge). For the most part it's fertile, green countryside, with gentle hills supporting a profusion of citrus groves, olive trees and wild flowers, while the road runs over and alongside the river past isolated farms.

Twenty minutes beyond Gaggi, get the bus driver to let you off at the **Gola di Alcántara** (daily: May–Sept 7.30am–8pm; Oct–April 7.30am–7pm; €2.50), a vast geological cleft in the hillside. It's highly commercialized at the top, with a car park, bar and restaurant, and access is by guided tour only. There's a lift to the bottom of the gorge, where you can slosh along the river for 400m in swirling pools (€15, including salopette rental). To continue under the waterfall and into the gorge itself costs €20 including the hire of a wet suit. The last bus back to Taormina leaves at 2.25pm Monday to Saturday, 12.30pm on Sunday.

Francavilla and Castiglione

You could walk from the gorge, or pick up the next bus on to **FRAN-CAVILLA DI SICILIA**, 4km away, alongside the river and overlooked by the few surviving walls of its hillside castle. This was the site of one of the bloodiest battles fought in Sicily, when the Austrian army (given logistical support by the British) engaged with the Spanish in 1719, to no obvious result apart from the loss of some 8000 lives. There's a path up to the ruins, and although much of the town is newly built there's a fair amount of interest in the couple of old central streets, and in walking up to the **Convento dei Cappuccini** that peers over town and river (take the signposted right turn as you approach the village). A modest little **museum** here (daily 11am–1pm & 3.30–7.30pm; donation requested) shows how the monks – now reduced to fewer than five – passed their time in baking, brewing and crafting, and you can buy some of their honey or grappa-like concoctions to take away.

You might want **to stay** in Francavilla, both for the scenery and the fact that it has the area's only hotels: the *Centrale*, on the main road through town, is currently closed for renovation, but is the better option, so phone ☎0942.981.052 to see if it is open; alternatively, there's the fancier *D'Orange d'Alcántara* (☎0942.981.374, ⓦwww.hoteldorange.itgo.com; ❹) on the way in from the Gola di Alcántara on Via dei Mulini, though it's often block-booked in summer by package tourists.

Five kilometres above Francavilla, and across the border in Catania province, the numerous church spires and the lofty, ruined rock-built castle of **CASTIGLIONE DI SICILIA** make an inviting target as the bus labours up the switchback road. It's easy to spend a couple of hours just wandering the quiet streets of this old mountain settlement, which meander up as far as a small piazza at the top of town, where there's little more than a barber with a sign in English offering "individual hair styling", and a flight of steps leading up to the shattered castle, or **Fortezza Greca** (always open), which offers grand panoramic views.

A short walk beyond the piazza, and well signposted all over town, you'll find an excellent pizzeria and restaurant, the *Belvedere d'Alcántara*, whose rooftop terrace takes full advantage of the soaring views. If you're heading back to Taormina, you can either hang around for the return bus to Giardini (it leaves from outside the bar at Via Regina Margherita 174, back down the hill from the piazza), or – better – walk down the hill to Francavilla, an easy hike, and pick up a bus from there. The walk takes around an hour, and at the bottom of the crag, on the way into Francavilla, you cross a sturdy medieval bridge. Just beyond here, at the back of the factory at the side of the road, is the sad ruin of a **Byzantine church**, one of several in the area left to rot.

Beyond the Alcántara valley: some day-trips

There are a handful of **round-trip** alternatives from Taormina if you want to make a day of it. Infrequent buses from Castiglione head to Catania (p.244), or two a day go on to Randazzo to the west (see p.266). Alternatively, it's around 9km through Castiglione to Linguaglossa (p.267), where you can pick up the round-Etna railway – a journey described in the next chapter. One last possibility for those with their own transport is to return to Francavilla, from where the SS185 climbs up into the Monti Peloritani and to Novara di Sicilia, and then down to the Tyrrhenian coast. Both town and route are covered on p.153.

Festivals

January
1–6 New Year celebrations in **Taormina**. Puppet shows, folk-singing and concerts, ending on Twelfth Night.

February & March
Carnevale Carnival celebrations in **Taormina** and **Giardini-Naxos**. processional floats, fireworks and music for three days.

June
Last week Sfilato del Carretto: puppet shows, a parade of painted carts and folk-singing in **Taormina**'s most traditional festival (though this has been cancelled in recent years).

July
First week International Film Festival in **Taormina**, with screenings in the Teatro Greco.
1 onwards Dance, drama, film and music; all performances held in the Teatro Greco in **Taormina**; runs until early August.

August
12–14 Procession of the giganti in **Messina**.
15 Ferragosto procession and fireworks in **Messina**.

December
20 onwards Christmas and New Year celebrations in **Taormina**. Puppet shows, folk-singing, parades and concerts.

Travel details

Trains

Messina to: Catania (1–2 hourly; 1hr 30min–2hr); Cefalù (12 daily; 2hr 15min–2hr 45min); Milan (13 daily; 15–17hr); Milazzo (1–2 hourly; 35min–1hr); Naples (9 daily; 5hr 50min–6hr 25min); Rome (15 daily; 7–9hr 15min); Palermo (up to 13 daily; 3hr 15min–5hr); Taormina (1–2 hourly; 40min–1hr).
Taormina to: Catania (1–2 hourly; 45min–1hr); Messina (1–2 hourly; 40min–1hr); Siracusa (hourly or every 2 hr; 3hr).

Buses

Messina to: Ali Terme (1–3 hourly Mon–Sat, 3 daily Sun; 45min); Barcellona (10 daily Mon–Sat; 1hr); Capo d'Orlando (9 daily Mon–Sat; 1hr 15min–1hr 50min); Catania (1–2 hourly Mon–Sat, 10 daily Sun; 1hr 35min); Catania airport (9–14 daily Mon–Sat, 4 daily Sun; 1hr 45min); Forza d'Agrò (2 daily Mon–Sat; 1hr 35min); Giardini-Naxos (4 daily Mon–Sat, 1 daily Sun; 50min–1hr 50min); Itala (13 daily Mon–Sat, 3 daily Sun; 50min); Letojanni (2–3 hourly Mon–Sat, 11 daily Sun; 1hr–1hr 30min); Milazzo (fast service 1–2 hourly Mon–Sat, 4 daily Sun; 50min); Palermo (6–7 daily Mon–Sat, 4 daily Sun; 3hr 15min); Patti (10 daily Mon–Sat; 1hr–1hr 30min); Randazzo (2 daily Mon–Sat; 2hr); Rome (4 daily; 9hr); Sant'Aléssio (2–3 hourly Mon–Sat, 12 daily Sun; 1hr–1hr 15min); Santa Teresa di Riva (1–3 hourly Mon–Sat, 12 daily Sun; 55min–1hr 10min); Scaletta (1–2 hourly Mon–Sat, 3 daily Sun; 35min); Taormina (14 daily Mon–Sat, 3 daily Sun; 1hr 15min–1hr 45min); Tíndari (3 daily Mon–Sat; 1–2hr).
Taormina to: Castelmola (3–4 daily Mon–Sat, 2 daily Sun; 10–15min); Castiglione (21 daily Mon–Sat; 12 daily Sun; 1hr 15min); Catania (7 daily Mon–Sat, 5 daily Sun; 1hr 5min); Catania airport (7 daily Mon–Sat, 5 daily Sun; 1hr 25min); Forza d'Agrò (1 daily Mon–Sat; 30min); Francavilla di Sicilia (5 daily Mon–Sat, 1 Sun; 55min); Giardini-Naxos (1–3 hourly; 10min); Gola di Alcántara (5 daily Mon–Sat, 1 daily Sun; 1hr); Isola Bella (roughly every 30min in summer, hourly or less in winter & Sun; 10min); Letojanni (roughly every 30min in summer, hourly or less in winter & Sun; 25min); Mazzarò (roughly every 30min in summer, hourly or less in winter & Sun; 12min); Messina (14 daily Mon–Sat, 3 Sun; 55min–1hr 40min); Recanati (every 15–30min in summer, less in winter & Sun; 20min); Sávoca (2 daily Mon–Sat;

45min); Spisone (every 30min in summer, hourly or less in winter & Sun; 15min).

Taormina–Giardini train station to: Castiglione (3 daily Mon–Sat; 55min); Francavilla di Sicilia (7 daily Mon–Sat, 1 daily Sun; 40min); Gola di Alcántara (6 daily Mon–Sat, 1 Sun; 40min); Randazzo (2 daily Mon–Sat; 1hr).

Ferries

Messina to: Villa San Giovanni (FS every 45min, Caronte every 20min, every 40–60min at night; 20–35min).

Hydrofoils and fast ferries

Messina to: Lípari (4 daily June–Sept, 1 daily Oct–May; 1hr 40min–3hr); Panarea (3 daily June–Sept; 2hr 5min–2hr 50min); Réggio di Calabria (approx hourly; 15min); Santa Marina Salina (5 daily June–Sept, 1 daily Oct–May; 2hr 10min–2hr 35min); Strómboli (3 daily June–Sept; 1hr 30min–3hr 15min); Vulcano (5 daily June–Sept, 1 daily Oct–May; 1hr 20min–3hr 10min).

5

Catania, Etna and around

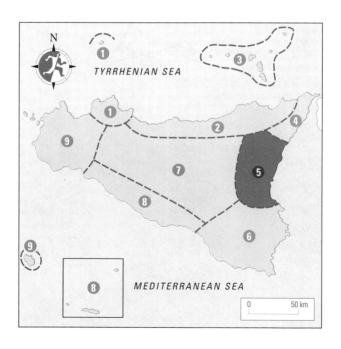

CHAPTER 5 # Highlights

* **Pescheria, Catania**
Not for the squeamish,
this raucous fish market
brings you face-to-face
with every kind of exotic
seafood. **p.251**

* **Spaghetti alla Norma**
Catania's signature dish,
made with ricotta and
aubergines, is named
after one of opera mae-
stro Vincenzo Bellini's
most popular works.
p.251

* **Performance at Teatro
Mássimo Bellini, Cata-
nia** Taking its name from
Catania's most famous
native son, this is the
ideal venue for a night at

the opera, ideally to see
one of the works by the
man himself. **p.255**

* **Carnevale at Acireale**
Sicily's masked
Carnevale celebrations
don't come much more
colourful than the five-
day splurge in this
Baroque coastal town
north of Catania. **p.260**

* **The ascent of Etna** The
smoking cone of Etna
dominates much of
eastern Sicily, and invites
an ascent of its black-
ened upper slopes, not
least for the awesome
views. **p.268**

△ Spaghetti alla Norma

5

Catania, Etna and around

Bang in the middle of the Ionian coast, **Catania** is Sicily's second largest city and the point of arrival for most of the island's foreign visitors, who land at the airport just outside. But unlike other stops on the mostly pretty, indented shoreline, Catania is by no means a prime tourist destination: there's heavy industry here, a large port and some depressing suburbs, glimpsed as you edge in on the train. Still, it's an intensely vibrant city with a uniformly grand architecture bestowed upon it after the late seventeenth-century earthquake that wrecked the whole region. Making full use of the local building material (lava), the eighteenth-century architect Giovanni Vaccarini gave Catania a lofty, noble air, and despite the neglect of many of the churches and the disintegrating, grey mansions, there's still much of interest. Delving about reveals lava-encrusted Roman relics, surviving alongside some of the finest Baroque work on the island, while the street-life and thronged piazzas and pubs make this Sicily's liveliest city, which, particularly in summer, can boast the island's most exuberant evening promenades.

Excursions from the city take in the villages around the town of **Acireale**, all small-scale resorts with good swimming from the rocks and fresh fish in the trattorias. But the most rewarding expedition is to drive or take a bus a few kilometres north to **Mount Etna**, Europe's highest volcano. Still active (the last eruption occurred in October 2002), its massive presence dominates the whole of this part of the coast. The towns and villages around, like Catania, are built from the lava it periodically ejects. A road and a small single-track railway, the **Circumetnea**, circumnavigate the lower slopes, passing through a series of hardy towns, like **Randazzo**, almost foolishly situated in the shadow of the volcano and surrounded by swirls of black volcanic rock. Reaching the top, or at least the lower craters below the summit, is possible too, either on foot or by mountain bus – both are heady experiences.

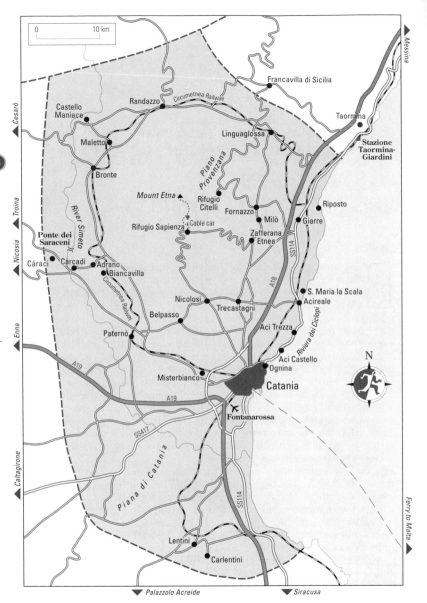

Catania and the coast

First impressions don't say much at all for **CATANIA** – on an initial encounter possibly the island's gloomiest spot. Built from black-grey volcanic stone, the central streets can feel suffocating, dark with the shadows of tall grimy Baroque churches and *palazzi*. The influence of Etna is pervasive: in the buildings, in the brooding vistas you get of the mountain at the end of Catania's streets – even the city's main thoroughfare is named after the volcano.

But fight the urge to cut and run, as Catania is one of the most intriguing of Sicily's cities, with a **history** to match. Some of the island's first **Greek colonists**, probably Chalcidinians from Naxos, settled the site as early as 729 BC, becoming so influential that their laws were eventually adopted by all the Ionian colonies of Magna Graecia. Later, the city was one of the first to fall to the **Romans**, under whom it prospered greatly and, unusually for Sicily, Catania's surviving ancient relics are all Roman. In the early Christian period Catania witnessed the martyrdom of **Agatha**, who, having rejected the improper advances of the praetor, Quintianus, was put to death in 252. She was later canonized (becoming the patron saint of Catania) and it was her miraculous intervention that reputedly saved the city from complete volcanic destruction in the seventeenth century. Even with the saint's protection, Catania has had its fair share of disasters: Etna erupted in 1669, engulfing the city in lava, and the **earthquake** of 1693 devastated the whole of southeastern Sicily.

Given these repeated catastrophes, the **modern city** is overshadowed in terms of historical monuments by Palermo. Still, there are some remarkable Baroque churches – dating from the eighteenth-century rebuilding of the city – and the stumpy remnants of its medieval castle. Catania is also Sicily's only large urban centre outside the capital: first and foremost, a businesslike, commercial place, with the island's busiest market and some of its best traditional food. In any case, if you want to visit Etna and are relying on public transport (drivers usually choose to see it from the prettier towns and villages hereabouts), you'll have to leave from Catania itself.

Catania is a major transport terminus, not only for buses and trains south to Siracusa, but also for travel west, including services to Enna, Agrigento and Palermo. Before moving on, it's worth taking day-trips out to the nearby towns and villages: there's a diverting **coastal route north**, through small bathing resorts, to Baroque **Acireale**; while **south** of Catania you can make a quick escape to the good beaches fronting the gulf, behind which lies the flat and sparsely populated **Piana di Catania**, the fertile plain that traditionally fed the city. At the plain's southern extremity sits **Lentini**, close to the site of one of the earliest Greek colonies to be founded in Sicily.

Arrival, information and city transport

The **airport**, Fontanarossa, is 5km south of the city and is the entry point of Air Malta and British Airways flights to Sicily (for flight information call ☏095.340.505). A white building across from the Arrivals hall holds all the car rental agencies (see "Listings", p.258). To get into the city by public transport, take the Alibus (every 20min 5am–midnight) from right outside, which runs to the central Piazza Stesícoro (on Via Etnea) and to Stazione Centrale in around twenty minutes; tickets (€0.80) are available from the AST booth on your left as you leave the Arrivals hall. A taxi from the rank outside the airport will cost €15–20 for the same journey. Note that buses to and from Siracusa, Taormina, Ragusa, Agrigento, Enna and Palermo also stop at the airport, and there are direct services, too, from the airport to Messina and Milazzo (for the Aeolian Islands).

Catamarans from Malta dock on the Molo Centrale, just off Via Dusmet, from where it's a short walk to Piazza del Duomo and Stazione Centrale; if you are really laden with luggage, bus #4/27 also runs past the dock into the centre and terminates at Stazione Centrale.

All main-line trains use **Stazione Centrale** in Piazza Giovanni XXIII (information on premium rate line ☎892.021), northeast of the centre, which

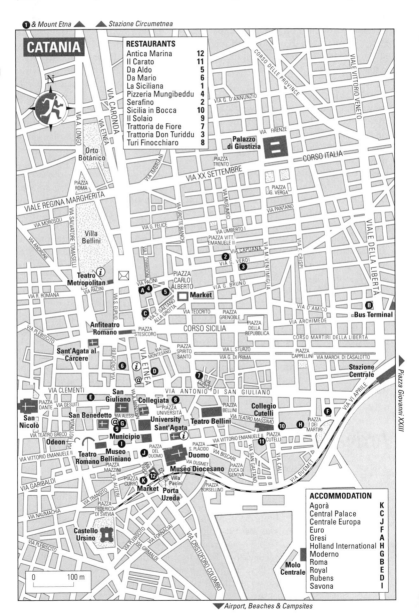

① & Mount Etna ▲   ▲ Stazione Circumetnea

CATANIA

RESTAURANTS
Antica Marina 12
Il Carato 11
Da Aldo 5
Da Mario 6
La Siciliana 1
Pizzeria Mungibeddu 4
Serafino 2
Sicilia in Bocca 10
Il Solaio 9
Trattoria de Fiore 7
Trattoria Don Turiddu 3
Turi Finocchiaro 8

ACCOMMODATION
Agorà K
Central Palace C
Centrale Europa J
Euro F
Gresi A
Holland International H
Moderno G
Roma B
Royal E
Rubens D
Savona I

▼Airport, Beaches & Campsites

has **left-luggage** facilities (daily 7am–10pm). You could walk into the city from here, though if you're aiming for Piazza del Duomo or Via Etnea it's quicker to jump on a bus; see "City transport" below. All other **buses**, both regional from Catania province and island-wide, also stop in Piazza Giovanni XXIII, at the bus station on the far side, across from Stazione Centrale. The square is large and very busy with fast-moving traffic, so keep your wits about you. Night arrivals would do well to take a taxi into the centre (around €6–8), since the station area isn't the most salubrious in town.

For arrivals and departures on the narrow-gauge Etna train, the **Stazione Circumetnea** is at Via Caronda, at the northern end of Via Etnea. For information on the service, call ☎095.541.250; there are more details about the round-Etna train on p.264.

Note that **driving in Catania** is a stressful experience, not just because of the congested and often chaotic traffic, not to mention the complicated one-way systems, but also the difficulty of **parking**. If you have a car, the best advice is to ask your hotel where to leave it, otherwise park wherever you can find space. Note that you can only stay for an hour in the zones marked with a blue line, and you'll need to buy a ticket (*bigletto ditta sostare*; €0.52 per hour) from a newsagent or news kiosk.

For all **departure information**, including full details of getting to the airport, bus companies, ferry and catamaran operators, and "travel agents", see "Listings", p.258.

Information

There's a small **tourist office** (daily 9am–7pm; ☎095.730.6255) inside Stazione Centrale on platform #1, which provides accommodation listings and free maps. The main office is at Via D. Cimarosa 10, signposted off Via Etnea and down Via Pacini (Mon–Fri 9am–8pm, Sat & Sun 9am–2pm; ☎095.730.6211 or 095.730.6233, ⓦwww.apt.catania.it), and is the starting-point for **free guided tours** of the city on literary, musical and architectural themes (Thurs–Sun at 9am; 3–4hr). In addition there are small offices at the port (Tues–Thurs 8am–2pm; ☎095.730.6209) and at Via Etnea 63 (Tues, Fri & Sat 2–8pm; ☎095.730.6222), and a useful **information office** run by the *Comune*, sited around the corner from the Duomo at Via Vittorio Emanuele 172 (daily 8am–8pm; ☎095.742.5573, ⓦwww.comune.catania.it). There is also an information desk at the airport (Mon–Sat 8am–9pm, Sun 8am–2pm; ☎095.730.6266 or 095.730.6277), again with free maps, accommodation lists and bus timetables.

City transport

You'll need little more than a map and your own two feet **to get around the city**. Most of the sights are confined within a small area, the centre of which is Piazza del Duomo – just a twenty-minute walk from the train station. From here, Via Etnea steams off north, lined with the city's most fashionable shops and cafés; fish market and port lie behind to the south; the best of the Baroque quarter, to the west.

You'll rarely need to use the AMT **city buses** (information ☎095.751.7111 or ⓦwww.amt.ct.it) in Catania itself, though they'll save you a walk into the centre from the station – and you'll have to jump on one to get to the airport and the campsites. There are **stops** immediately outside Stazione Centrale: buses #1/4, #4/7 and, on the other side of the piazza, #432 and #448 run into the centre, along Via VI Aprile and Via Vittorio Emanuele to

Piazza del Duomo, Via Etnea and Piazza Stesícoro. Another central pick-up point is Piazza Borsellino (below Piazza del Duomo), where there's a stop for the airport Alibus (#4/57) and for #4/27L (for the campsites and beaches). **Tickets** are valid for any number of journeys within ninety minutes and are available from *tabacchi*, the newsagents inside Stazione Centrale, or the booth outside it. The same outlets also sell tickets (€2), valid for one day's unlimited travel on all local AMT bus routes. All tickets must be punched inside the bus on the first ride.

The city has a new **Metropolitana** underground system (℡095.534.323) which operates every 15 minutes between 7am and 8.20pm (tickets €0.80 for any number of journeys within 90min, available from the *tabacchi* at the train station). It's a limited route running from the main Stazione Centrale (beyond Platform 11) south to Catania Porto and north and northwest as far as Catania Borgo, the terminal for the Stazione Circumetnea on Via Caronda. All tickets must be punched at machines before boarding the train. There are **taxi** ranks at Stazione Centrale, Piazza del Duomo and Via Etnea (Piazza Stesícoro); call ℡095.330.966 or 095.338.282 for 24-hour service.

Finally, if you're planning to **rent a car** on arrival, consider renting from agencies in the city to avoid the surcharge on airport rentals. Also parking in the city is extremely difficult, so it's a good idea to rent in Catania itself on the day you leave; see "Listings" (p.258) for addresses and numbers.

Accommodation

Finding a vacant hotel room in summer, particularly August, can be very difficult; it's always as well to reserve in advance if you possibly can. There's little choice, particularly near the train and bus stations, although as long as you plan ahead you'll be able to stay fairly close to the main sights. Bear in mind, however, that parts of central Catania have a reputation for petty crime and violence – be careful if you're out on your own at night. If you're happy with security at your hotel, leave your valuables there before going out.

Campsites are all a bus ride out of the city: there's one to the north, while buses #4/27L from Piazza Borsellino, and in summer bus #D from Piazza Duomo, Piazza Borsellino, Piazza Stesícoro and Via Etnea, all head to the long beach south of Catania where there are three more big sites along Viale Kennedy. All have bungalows available, too (two-berth from ❸ in summer, ❶–❷ in winter; four-berths also available), though you'll need to reserve well in advance.

Hotels

Centrale Europa Via Vittorio Emanuele 167 ℡095.311.309, ℻095.317.531. This small two-star enjoys an unrivalled location right on Piazza del Duomo, with the downside of noise in some rooms. Rooms with a view are at a premium but don't cost any extra. En-suite rooms come into the next price category. ❹

Euro Piazza dei Mártiri 8 ℡095.531.007. A practical one-night stop in a B&B, not too far (about 400m) from the train station, with just two comfortable, spacious rooms and separate, spotless bathrooms – it can be extremely noisy, though. No credit cards. ❶

Gresi 3rd floor, Via Pacini 28 ℡ & ℻095.322.709. Close to the Villa Bellini, this is a mite pokey and the plumbing is occasionally idiosyncratic, but it's kept spick-and-span, some rooms have frescoed ceilings, and there's a welcome lift. No credit cards. ❹

Holland International Via Vittorio Emanuele 8 ℡095.533.605, ℗www.hollandintrooms.it On the first floor of an ageing *palazzo*, on the way into town from Stazione Centrale (at the eastern end of the street). Run by a Dutchman who speaks good English and knows the region well, it's clean and welcoming and boasts rooms with frescoed ceilings as well as a comfortable, if eccentrically decorated lounge overlooking Piazza dei Mártiri. Rooms with bath nudge into the next price category. ❷

Moderno Via Alessi 9 ☎095.326.250, ℱ095.326.674, ⓦwww.albergomoderno.it. In a quiet cul-de-sac off Via Crociferi, this comfortable but not very *moderno* hotel is as well placed as anything in the city centre. Facilities include air-conditioning and – very welcome – heating in winter. They also have singles. ❺

Roma Via della Libertà 63 ☎095.534.911. Boxy, functional rooms (including singles) close to Stazione Centrale; a useful fall-back for late-night arrivals. No credit cards. ❸

Royal Via Antonio di San Giuliano 337 ☎&ℱ095.715.3551, ⓦ www.hotelroyalcatania .it. Occupying a Baroque *palazzo*, this hotel has a good location with views, west of Via Etnea where the street starts to climb in steps. Rooms are quiet, comfortable and well equipped. ❽

Rubens Via Etnea 196 ☎095.317.073, ℱ095.321.277. Small hotel with seven rooms, all with bathroom, air-conditioning and fridges, and a friendly owner who speaks excellent English. A good-value choice if you want to stay on the main Via Etnea, though it's always busy, so book ahead. ❹

Savona Via Vittorio Emanuele 210 ☎095.326.982, ℱ095.715.8169. Well placed, close to Piazza del Duomo, this recently renovated hotel makes a safe, clean, comfortable and surprisingly quiet central base. ❺

Hostel and campsites

Agorà Piazza Currò 6 ☎095.723.3010, ⓦwww .agorahostel.com. Easy-going hostel offering dorms with 6 and 8 bunkbeds each at €16–20 per person, and two doubles costing €45–50 per room; all prices include breakfast. It's centrally located near the markets and opposite the site of a Roman bathhouse, but there's some noise from passing trains. Below is a restaurant and wine bar housed in a natural cave with one of Catania's underground streams running through it. Good-value meals, Internet access and washing facilities all available, and there are regular live and DJ'd music evenings.

Internazionale La Plaja Viale Kennedy 47 ☎095.340.880. Popular, monster-sized campsite near the beach, with a disco. Horse-riding also available.

Jonio Via Villini a Mare 2, Ognina ☎095.491.139. Smaller-scale than most of the local sites, and quite a way north of the city centre, at Ognina (see p.259). From Stazione Centrale, take bus #448.

Villagio Souvenir Viale Kennedy 71 ☎095.341.162 or 095.533.001. The cheapest and smallest campsite south of the city, more open in aspect than its counterparts. May–Oct.

Villagio Turístico Europeo Viale Kennedy 91 ☎095.591.026. Similar setup to *La Plaja*, with even more facilities and considerably higher pitch-rates. Mid-May to mid-October.

The City

You could see the whole of central **Catania** in a busy day's strolling, but the city really deserves more of your time if you can spare it. The vigorous street activity in the swarming markets and along the main Via Etnea is well worth staying to enjoy, not to mention the nightlife.

Something to be aware of as you potter around the crumbling backstreets of the Baroque town is the relatively high incidence of **petty crime**. Catania has a well-deserved reputation for pickpockets and, while the main streets are safe enough, don't flash money and cameras around too obviously in the more run-down areas or the markets, and avoid badly lit roads at night.

Around Piazza del Duomo

Catania's main square, **Piazza del Duomo**, at the bottom of Via Etnea, is a handy orientation point: from here, most things of interest are only a few minutes' walk away. It's also one of Sicily's most engaging piazzas, rebuilt completely in the first half of the eighteenth century by the Palermitan, Giovanni Battista Vaccarini, who was made Catania's municipal architect in 1730. He surrounded the square with elegant buildings, like the **Municipio** on the northern side, finished in 1741, providing some relief from the grandeur by adding the central **elephant fountain**: an eighteenth-century lava elephant supporting an Egyptian obelisk on its back. This has become the city's symbol and features an inscription, *Agatina MSSHDEPL* – apparently an acronym for "The mind of St Agatha is sane and spontaneous, honouring God and liberating the city" (and also visible on the cathedral's facade).

The Duomo

Cross over to the piazza's eastern flank for Vaccarini's grandest project, the **Duomo** (daily 7.30am–noon & 4–7pm). Originally founded by Count Roger in the eleventh century, it was built on the site of a Roman baths (there are plans to open them to the public; call ℡095.310.777 for details). Of the medieval church, only the apses, beautifully crafted from volcanic rock, survived the 1693 earthquake; you can see them through the gate at Via Vittorio Emanuele 159. Vaccarini's heavy Baroque touch is readily apparent from the imposing facade, on which he tagged granite columns filched from Catania's Roman amphitheatre.

The interior is no less grand, adorned by a rich series of **chapels**: the Cappella di Sant'Agata (to whom the Duomo is dedicated) is to the right of the choir, and houses the relics paraded through the city on the saint's festival days; next to it, entered through a fine sixteenth-century doorway, is the Cappella della Madonna, with a Roman sarcophagus which holds the ashes of the Aragonese kings – Frederick II, Louis and Frederick III. It's worth looking in the sacristy too, for a fresco depicting the disastrous 1669 eruption of Mount Etna, completed only eight years after the event, while a wander through the rest of the church reveals the uncovered medieval foundations and ancient columns. The tomb of the composer Bellini, a native of the city, is set in the floor before the second column on the right as you enter, inscribed with a phrase from his opera, *La Sonnámbula*.

To the right of the Duomo, check out the **Museo Diocesano** (Tues–Sun 4–7.30pm; €4.20), a collection of religious art and silverware, including sculpture from the fifteenth century and a gallery of paintings going back to the fourteenth century. Arranged on four floors, the museum houses a fair amount, including items recovered from the pre-1693 cathedral and, on the ground floor, the ornate silver *fercolo*, or cart, brought out on St Agatha's Day to carry the saint's relics; however, much has quite a specialist appeal, and you can take in most of it at a brisk pace.

East along Via Vittorio Emanuele II

Via Vittorio Emanuele II cuts across the piazza, its eastern arm running towards the sea. Opposite the Duomo, the church of **Sant'Agata** (same hours as Duomo) is another of Vaccarini's creations, though this time the pale grey Rococo interior dates from after his death: capitals, iron balconies, even the chandeliers and aisle lights, are a profusion of ruffs, curls and spidery ornamentation. The church entrance is just off the main road, on Via Raddusa. Slightly further on is the little **Piazza San Plácido**, with an eighteenth-century church of the same name and a house, at Via Vittorio Emanuele 140, that was the home of early nineteenth-century Catanese erotic poet Domenico Tempio. It's now desperately neglected, though you can still make out the fairly raunchy figures of men and women playing with themselves, supporting the balcony above the blackened doorway. Further east, past the **Collegio Cutelli**, now a school but distinguished by Vaccarini's round courtyard, Via Vittorio Emanuele ends in **Piazza dei Mártiri** – marked by a statue of St Agatha atop a Roman column, looking over the harbour.

From the market to the Castello Ursino

Back in Piazza del Duomo, head for Catania's open-air **food market** – at its best early in the day – either by walking down through the towering late seventeenth-century **Porta Uzeda** and bearing right, or by going south across the piazza and nipping down the steps behind a marble fountain. This takes you right into the action – usually over by the early afternoon, but until then almost frightening in its intensity. A medieval warren of narrow streets spreads around the **fish market** (the **Pescheria**), slabs and buckets full of twitching fish, eels and shellfish, some of which – mussels and sea urchins – you might be offered, cut open, to try. There are endless lanes full of vegetable and fruit stalls, as well as bloody butchers' tables, and an excellent little trattoria, the *Antica Marina* (see p.256).

The roads wind from here through a dilapidated neighbourhood to an open space (Piazza Federico di Svevia) punctured by the **Castello Ursino**, once the proud fortress of Frederick II. Originally the castle stood on a rocky cliff, over the beach, but following the 1669 eruption, which reclaimed this entire area from the sea, all that remains is the blackened keep. The **Museo Cívico** (Tues–Sat 9am–1pm & 3–6pm, Sun 9am–noon; around €4 when there's an exhibition, otherwise free) is housed inside and makes excellent use of the bare interior. Wooden walkways run the breadth of the castle, looking down into the foundations and basement rooms, while the walls of the central chambers are hung with retrieved mosaic fragments, stone inscriptions and tombstones. The ground floor is usually taken up with temporary exhibitions, while the permanent exhibits include such extraordinarily delightful items as a Greek terracotta statuette of two goddesses

---

Spaghetti alla Norma

Spaghetti alla Norma – cooked with tomato and aubergine/eggplant (*melanzane* in Italian) – is served in most local restaurants. Here's how to prepare it:

Ingredients (serves 4)

Two aubergines/eggplants, cut into 1/2 inch (1cm) slices (if in Sicily, buy the violet globe-shaped Tunisian aubergines)

Two tablespoons (30ml) olive oil

Two cloves of garlic, peeled and crushed with the back of a knife

One tablespoon tomato purée

1lb (454g) fresh plum tomatoes, chopped roughly (use tinned if unavailable)

10oz (300g) spaghetti

Grated hard ricotta salata cheese (alternatively, use parmesan, an aged pecorino, or feta)

Two tablespoons chopped basil leaves

Salt

Black pepper

Spread aubergine/eggplant slices on a plate, sprinkle with salt and leave for thirty minutes; this removes the bitter oils. Wash the slices under cold water, dry, and then fry on both sides in a large frying pan until golden brown (use a low heat). Put to one side.

Gently fry the garlic cloves in two tablespoons of olive oil for two minutes, then add chopped (or tinned) tomatoes, one tablespoon tomato purée, and a pinch of salt and pepper, and sauté for thirty minutes, or until the sauce reduces slightly. Add half the chopped basil leaves to the sauce and stir.

Cook the spaghetti in boiling water until *al dente*, drain and place in bowls. Spoon the tomato sauce on top of the spaghetti, add slices of fried aubergine and top with grated ricotta and the remainder of the basil leaves. Eat with a robust red wine.

△ Catania fish market

being pulled in a sea carriage by mythical beasts, and a seventeenth-century French pistol, inlaid in silver and depicting rabbits, fish and cherubs.

Beyond the spruced-up gardens fronting the castle, the houses hereabouts are in a fairly ruinous state and you might as well head back towards the centre (following Via Anteri). Straddling Via Garibaldi, the arcaded **Piazza Mazzini** was constructed from 32 columns, presently scaffolded, which originally formed part of a Roman basilica.

Via Crocíferi and the Teatro Romano

Just north of Piazza Mazzini is perhaps the most interesting section of the city – a tangle of churches, narrow eighteenth-century streets and archeological remains that begins as you cross over Via Garibaldi and walk up to Via Vittorio Emanuele II. Everything close by is big and Baroque, and the narrow, pedestrianized **Via Crocíferi** – which strikes north from the main road under an imposing arch – is lined with some particularly arresting religious and secular buildings, little changed since the eighteenth century; excavations along here have revealed sections of Roman mosaic paving. Amble up Via Crocíferi and you can peer in the courtyards of the *palazzi* (one with a plantation of banana trees) and poke around the churches – best of which is **San Giuliano**, about halfway up on the right, which has a facade by Vaccarini and an echoing elliptical interior.

Back at the bottom of the street, opposite San Francesco church, the house where the composer Vincenzo Bellini was born in 1801 is now open as the **Museo Belliniano** (Mon–Sat 9am–1pm, also Tues & Thurs 3–6pm, Sun 9am–12.30pm; free), an agreeable little collection of photographs, pianos, original scores, his death mask and other memorabilia. Bellini composed his first work at age 6, and was only 33 when he died in Paris; his body was transported back to Sicily to be buried. He notches up several tributes around the city, including a piazza, and Catania's main theatre and park all named after him, as well as the ultimate accolade – a pasta dish, *spaghetti alla Norma*, named after one of Bellini's operas (see box on p.251 for the recipe).

To the west, along Via Vittorio Emanuele, is the **Teatro Romano** (Mon–Sat 9am–1.30pm & 3–7pm, Sun 9am–1pm; €2.10), at no. 266, a surprisingly large chunk of Roman hardware to have survived the city's eighteenth-century refit. Built of lava in the second century AD, on the site of an earlier Greek theatre (it's marked "Teatro Greco" on some signs and maps), much of the seating and the underground passageways are preserved, though all the marble which originally covered it has disappeared; adjacent, there's a smaller **Odeon**, which was used for music and recitations, built between the second and third centuries AD. If the gate is locked you can get a view of it by walking around the block and doubling back on the higher Via Teatro Greco.

San Nicolò

The other way down Via Teatro Greco, west, leads to **Piazza Dante**, a pretty crescent of houses, some of whose ground floors contain little workshops – of cabinetmakers, metalworkers – open to the pavement. Opposite is the unfinished facade of **San Nicolò**, its grim eighteenth-century exterior studded by six enormous, lopped columns. This is the biggest church in Sicily (105m long), its stark interior undecorated save for the sculpted choir stalls and a meridian line drawn across the floor of the transept, embellished with zodiacal signs. There are free guided tours, usually taking place in the morning, though you can see most of what there is to see on your own; however it's doubtful whether you'll be able to climb up to the dome – a shame, as it offers one of the best views over the city.

The church is part of the adjoining Benedictine convent, with equally impressive dimensions – it's the second largest convent in Europe after Mafra in Portugal. Officially you can't get in, but there's a gate to the left of the church, through which are the remains of some **Roman walls** and, behind, the massive conventual buildings: from here, you can at least see part of the Baroque exterior, rich in sculpted ornamentation. If you can persuade someone to open the gate into the convent itself, there are two lovely courtyards beyond, the first containing an overgrown cloistered garden.

Along Via Etnea

Most of the other city sights are ranged around the long and busy **Via Etnea**, which runs north from Piazza del Duomo and out of the city. Following its full length would eventually lead you right to the foothills of Mount Etna – and from the street's northern end there are much-trumpeted views of the peak in the distance. Mostly, you'll be concerned with the southern stretch of Via Etnea, the liveliest section lying between Piazza del Duomo and the Villa Bellini: an out-and-out shopping street, good for browsing and a coffee at one of the popular, brightly polished bars.

The west side

Nearly all the notable buildings and churches are on the **west side** of Via Etnea. Past the Municipio, the first square off the street (Piazza dell'Università) holds the main building of the **University**, founded by the Aragonese kings in the fifteenth century. The earthquake postponed its completion until the 1750s, and Vaccarini – again – was responsible for the attractive courtyard.

Further on, **Piazza Stesícoro** marks the modern centre of Catania, an enormous square split into two by Via Etnea, and a useful point to pick up buses. The western side is almost entirely occupied by the sunken, black remains of Catania's **Anfiteatro Romano** (daily 9am–1.30pm & 3–7pm; free), dating back to the second or third century AD. Although much is still concealed under the surrounding buildings, it's the grandest of Catania's Roman remains. Built from lava blocks, the amphitheatre could hold around sixteen thousand spectators – quite a formidable size – the ranks of seating supported by long **vaults** which you can wander along under Piazza Stesícoro. A diagram here shows the original dimensions of the theatre, from which it's evident that the section you're walking through represents only one tiny excavated corner.

Much more modest is the twelfth-century church of Sant'Agata al Cárcere (Tues–Sat 4–7pm, Sun 10am–noon), above its own square nearby (reached from Via Cappuccini). With strong defensive walls, it was built on the site of the prison where St Agatha was confined before her martyrdom at the hands of the Romans, and a custodian will let you into the third-century **crypt** – now bright with electric candles. More sinister is the chapel's medieval stone doorway, topped by evil, grinning, sculpted heads and ape-like creatures.

Back on Via Etnea it's not far to the **Villa Bellini**, just beyond the post office: a large, ornamentally laid-out public garden that provides a welcome touch of greenery and even the occasional concert from the bandstand in the summer. The stand-up drinks bar here is where the local police hang out, whiling away time between meal breaks – on the bar are pinned rather touching photos of the regulars, posing stiffly in uniform on horseback or motorbikes. There's more seclusion, too, in the **Orto Botánico** (Mon–Sat 9am–1pm; for a guided tour call ☎095.430.901), a botanical garden at the northern end of the park, across from Piazza Roma.

The east side

There's precious little on the **east side** of Via Etnea worth the legwork, though the streets marching towards the station and the sea hold some good cafés and restaurants. The highlight of the area is the long, rectangular **Piazza Carlo Alberto**, home to the rumbustious *Fera o Luni* **market** (daily except Sun, when an antiques fair takes over), replete with fruit and vegetables, household gear and clothes. This is a great spot for all kinds of shopping and souvenir-hunting, and once the stalls have gone it's the venue for spontaneous games of football and general hanging-out.

South of the traffic-ridden Corso Sicilia, the warren of streets is largely closed to cars in the evenings, which is the best time to explore the local bar-life and eateries. The only specific sight here is **Piazza Bellini**, a strange conglomerate of buildings from some diverse architectural periods. A wide flight of steps leads up to a crumbling church, there's a Fascist-built office block and – overshadowing the lot – the bulky **Teatro Mássimo Bellini**. Finished in 1890, its elaborate facade leans over the square, and during the opera and concert season (winter & spring) you can usually take a quick look inside before the performances begin; programme details are available from the box office inside.

Eating, drinking and nightlife

You'll rarely do better for **eating** than in Catania: fresh fish is a speciality, and there are some good restaurants about, from budget places in the markets to expense-account jobs in the modern city. The presence of students means that the **bars** and **nightlife** are fairly lively, too, while Catania hosts one of Sicily's best religious **festivals** every February.

Markets, snacks and fast food

Catania's two main **markets** are in Piazza Carlo Alberto (see above) and in the streets through the Porta Uzeda (see p.251), great places to wander and munch from a variety of fresh-fruit stalls, stand-up cafés and snack bars. Outside these areas, and at other times, there's an abundance of places to get **breakfast** and other **snacks**, the best of which are listed below. Around San Martino's Day (November 11), the Catanese make *crispelle* – fritters of flour, water, yeast and ricotta or anchovies – and the Festa di Sant'Agata in February (see p.258) also sees a whole panoply of food stalls selling traditional sweets and snacks. During summer, kiosks along Via Umberto I offer a thirst-quenching Catanian speciality: soda water and crushed lemon with or without salt (*seltz e limone con/senza sale*).

Astoria Via S. Euplio 30. Near the Villa Bellini and tourist office (parallel to Via Etnea), with a choice selection of *cannoli, arancini*, ice cream, pastries and exotic teas. It's one of the few cafés in town with outdoor tables, too, and thus not a bad place for a beer in the early evening. Closed Sun.

Al Caprice Via Etnea 30–36. Wide choice of snacks, sandwiches and *távola calda* meals (grilled meats and chicken), with indoor seating and waiter service. It is also a *gelateria catanese*, with two dozen varieties of ice cream.

Centrale Via Etnea 123. A busy *távola calda*, at Piazza Stesícoro, with a full range of snacks.

Café Charmant Via Etnea 19. Half a dozen tables overlooking Piazza dell'Università; the smart staff nip out with coffee, snacks and ices, and there's a cheap *menu turístico* if you fancy something more filling.

Étoile d'Oro Via Dusmet, through the arch in Piazza del Duomo and right. The only place in Catania open 24hr, and a magnet at night for a real cross-section of the city, including police,

255

mafiosi and assorted lowlifes. Pastries, snacks (usually freshly cooked) and drinks always available. Closed Sun.

Café Fontana Largo Paisiello 14. Esplanade café in the modern square opposite the tourist office, named for the *modernista* fountain hidden under the steps at the far end of the square. A rare, relatively calm place to sit outside during the day for a drink and snack. Closed Sun.

Friggitoria Stella Via Monsignor Ventimiglia 66. A good place to sample *crispelle* as well as other traditional fried snacks, this back-street establishment has been going for years and is well thought of locally. Closed Sun.

Savia Via Etnea 302. Opposite the main entrance to the Villa Bellini, this is one of Catania's finest stand-up café-bars, open since 1899 and always busy with folk digging into *arancini*, pastries and the like. Closed Mon.

Scardaci Via Etnea 158, and above Villa Bellini on Via Santa Madalena. Great stop for an ice cream on the evening *passeggiata*, with a fantastic range of flavours in cones or cups, as well as *frullati* and *cornetti*. Also serves the best *cannoli* (ricotta-filled pastry tubes) in Catania. Closed Sun afternoon & Mon afternoon.

Spinella Via Etnea 300. Next-door rival to the *Savia*, though smaller and less frantic; snacks, pastries and ice cream.

Tertulia Via Rapisardo 1. Café/bar/bookshop behind the Teatro Bellini, that stays open till the early hours, popular with artists and intellectuals. Hosts art exhibitions and activist meetings too.

Restaurants

The consistently best deals are found in **restaurants** in and around either of Catania's two markets, though these won't necessarily be open at night. It's surprisingly difficult to find a central pizzeria, but with many places cooking good-quality Sicilian and Catanese dishes – *spaghetti alla Norma* (see p.251) is the local pasta – you shouldn't have too hard a time. For an explanation of the restaurant price categories, see p.53.

Da Aldo Piazza G. Sciuti. A popular place at lunchtime for quick grills (*cucina alle brace*), the house speciality; it's first left off Via Pacini, down Via al Carmine, coming from the Carlo Alberto market. No credit cards. Closed Sun & evenings. Inexpensive.

Antica Marina Via Pardo 29 ☎095. 348.197. Traditional market trattoria, if a little smartened up, serving excellent fish. Closed Wed. Moderate.

Il Carato Via Vittorio Emanuele II 81 ☎095.715.9247. Sicilian dishes with a creative twist from one of Catania's most inspired chefs. Has a wonderful wine list too, as befits a place that began life as an *enoteca*. Closed Sat lunch and Sun. Moderate.

Trattoria de Fiore Via Coppola 24. In the heart of an area dense with restaurants, this offers good basic cooking such as *spaghetti alla zucca* (with pumpkin sauce), and there are outdoor tables. No bottled wine. No credit cards. Closed Mon. Moderate.

Da Mario Via Penninello 34. Down some steps at the top end of Via Crociferi, this quiet and tidy trattoria lacks the fizz and furore of some of Catania's other eateries, but offers low prices for its local specialities. Closed Mon. Inexpensive.

Pizzeria Mungibeddu Via Corridoni 37. On the outskirts of the *Fera o Luni* market (Piazza Carlo Alberto), just off Via Pacini, this back-street pizzeria – also known by its non-dialect name of *Mongibello* – is good for takeaway food or meals at one of the few tables. No credit cards. Closed Mon. Inexpensive.

Serafino Via Musumeci 43. Reasonable prices, good antipasti and great seafood are the draws here. Semi-rustic decor, and a busy but relaxed atmosphere. Closed Mon. Moderate.

Sicilia in Bocca Piazza Pietro Lupo 16–18 ☎095.746.1361. Not far from the Teatro Mássimo Bellini, and off Via Ventimiglia, this is a lively place, where you can watch the crustacea as you choose your fish amidst earnest conversation as to their individual merits; the antipasti are good, too. There's another branch in the warehouse basement of an old *palazzo* with seating outside as well, on Via Dusmet, near Piazza del Duomo (closed Mon). Closed Wed. Moderate.

La Siciliana Viale Marco Polo 52a ☎095.376.400. Renowned as one of eastern Sicily's best restaurants, though it's way up in the north of the city – take bus #7/22 up Via Etnea from Piazza Stesicoro. The pasta dishes and desserts, particularly, are marvellous, but a full meal costs around €40 a head. You'll need to reserve a table and dress up. Closed Sun evening & Mon. Very expensive. .

Trattoria Don Turiddu Via Musumeci 50. Across the road from *Serafino* (see above), this is a rowdier alternative, and is usually overflowing with zealous seafood lovers. There's no menu: just choose your main course at the entrance, help yourself to antipasti, and tuck in alongside the regular local clientele. Closed Sun & Aug. Moderate.

Turi Finocchiaro Via E. Reina 13 ☎095.715.3573. Very popular central pizzeria

and restaurant – just off Piazza dell'Università, set back in a courtyard, with a second entrance on Via Cestai. Help yourself from the antipasto table; this, and the pasta, meat and (fewer) fish dishes are all thoroughly Sicilian in execution – which means vegetarians are well served here. Closed Wed & lunchtime. Moderate.

Nightlife: bars, pubs and clubs

Unusually for Sicily, Catania's streets teem until late, especially in summer, and the city can boast the island's best choice of **bars and pubs** – some with live music. In addition, the *Comune* operates *café concerto* periods during the summer, when the old-town streets and squares between Piazza dell'Università and Piazza Bellini are closed to traffic between 9pm and 2am. The bars here all spill tables out onto the squares and alleys, and live bands keep things swinging until the small hours. Drinks are relatively pricey (€3–4 for a beer), but it's one of the nicest evening diversions in Sicily.

La Cartiera Pub Via Casa del Mutilato 8. Young, studenty Catanese bar, off the northeastern side of Piazza Bellini, with various beers on tap and in bottles. Sells food as well. Closed June–Sept.

La Collegiata Via Collegiata 3. This large pub-pizzeria on two levels overlooks Piazza dell'Università; the terrace is a pleasant place for a night-time drink, with the floodlit churches of Via Crociferi as a backdrop.

Guliven's Via Crociferi 69. Elegant and intimate pub-*panineria* on this historic street, with outdoor tables by the steps of the adjacent church, and occasional karaoke. Closed Mon eve except in summer.

Nievski Via Alessi 15–17. Down the steps from Via Crociferi, this "*pub alternativo*" is a great place for organic food at lunchtime, and beers at night. It has Internet access and is the centre for all kinds of concerts and events too. Closed Sun lunch & Mon.

The Other Place Pub Via E. Reina 18. Amazingly, exactly like a pub, with a youthful crowd spread at tables across two floors. It's just off Piazza dell'Università, and there are tables (and pizzas served at them) outside in summer. Closed Mon.

Picasso Piazza Ogninella 4 & **L'Altro Picasso** Piazza Scammacca 1b. Adjacent old-town bars with interior art displays, at their best during *café concerto* season, when the tables here offer the best ringside view of all the action.

Waxy O'Connor's Piazza Spírito Santo. Hugely popular Irish pub which spills onto the square on summer evenings. Order at the bar, where foreign bottled beers (including, of course, Guinness) are served, as well as pastas and snacks, and there are regular live bands from 10 or 11pm.

Web Café Via Caronda 166. Lively pub with good range of beers, aged rum, great steaks, regular Latin nights, and 20 computers with Internet access.

The arts... and the Festa di Sant'Agata

To check out all the options, get hold of the free fortnightly **arts and entertainment guide**, *Lapis*, available from and posted outside bars and cafés; it's in Italian, but comprehensive and comprehensible. For more general information about what's on where, get a copy of Catania's daily newspaper, *La Sicilia*, available from kiosks all over the centre, which has city entertainment listings.

As far as cultural entertainment goes, there are occasional open-air jazz and classical **concerts** held in the summer in the Villa Bellini; and the Catania **festival** runs from November to April, with gigs in the Teatro Metropolitan, Via S. Euplio 21 (☎095.322.2323), parallel to Via Etna, next to the Villa Bellini, and Teatro Nuovo, Via Re Martino 195–7 (☎095.493.775; bus #448 from Piazza Stesícoro).

The Cinema King, Via Antonio de Curtis 14, near Corso Sicilia (℡095.530.218), holds foreign **film seasons** in the original language during the winter months. Of the city's **theatres**, the Teatro Mássimo Bellini (℡095.730.6111; see p.255) is the most famous: the opera and concert season usually starts in October and runs through until June. You'll have to go elsewhere to see **plays**: either to the Teatro Stábile Verga, Via Giuseppe Fava 35 (℡095.363.545), or, for more alternative productions, to Teatro Musco, Via Umberto I 312 (℡095.535.514), and Teatro Nuovo – though all performances are in Italian. You might be able to make more of a **puppet-show** performance, but this involves leaving Catania and heading out to Acireale (see p.260), an easy evening's excursion.

The Festa di Sant'Agata

One of Sicily's best festivals, the **Festa di Sant'Agata** takes place in Catania between February 3 and 5. A golden statue of the saint is paraded through the streets, there are fireworks in Piazza del Duomo, special stalls in Via Etnea selling festival nougat and sweets, and the highlight of the event is the procession of the *Cannaroli* – long candles, up to 6m high, carried for hours at a time by groups representing different trades. A prize goes to the group which holds out the longest.

Listings

Airlines Alitalia, at the airport ℡095.746.9418; Air Malta, Corso Mártiri della Libertà 188 ℡095.539.983; Meridiana ℡095.346.966; Transavia ℡095.723.9320; Volare ℡095.340.227.

Airport Fontanarossa ℡095.340.505. Take the Alibus from Stazione Centrale or Via Etnea; departures every 20min, 5am–midnight.

Banks Banco di Sicilia at Corso Sicilia (Mon–Fri 8.30am–1.30pm & 2.45–3.45pm); Banca Etnea Agricola at the airport (Mon–Fri 8.30am–1.30pm & 2.50–3.50pm).

Bus terminals AST, Piazza Giovanni XXIII, opposite Stazione Centrale (℡095.746.1096), for services to Acireale, Caltagirone, Carlentini, Etna (Rifugio Sapienza), Lentini, Nicolosi, Piazza Armerina, Siracusa and Zafferana Etnea; there are timetables pinned to posts and a ticket office at Via L. Sturzo 220, on the east side of the square. Interbus/Etna Trasporti, Via d'Amico 181, at the back of Piazza Giovanni XXIII (℡095.532.716), to Acireale, Caltagirone, Enna, Gela, Giardini-Naxos, Licata, Nicosia, Noto, Pachino, Piazza Armerina, Ragusa, Rome, Siracusa and Taormina; Fratelli Scionti, Stazione Centrale (℡095.354.704), to Augusta; SAIS, Via d'Amico 181, to Agrigento, Enna, Caltanissetta, Naples, Rome, Florence and other mainland destinations (call ℡095.536.201), and to Messina and Palermo (call ℡095.536.168).

Car rental Avis at the airport and Via V. Cagliari 1, premium rate line ℡199.100.133, ⓦ www.avis .co.uk; Sixt at airport and Via Umberto 294b, ℡095.538.831, premium rate line ℡340.252, ⓦ www.sixt.co.uk; Hertz at airport and Via Toselli, premium rate line ℡199 112.211, ⓦ www.hertz .co.uk; Holiday Car Rental at airport ℡095.346.769; Maggiore at airport and Piazza G. Verga, premium rate line ℡848.867.067, ⓦ www.maggiore.com.

Car repairs Automobile Club d'Italia, ℡095.533.380.

Catamaran tickets Virtu Ferries (℡095.316.711) for catamaran services to Malta. Book online at ⓦ www.virtuferries.com, or in person at La Duca Viaggi (see Travel agents, below) or Tropical Travel, Piazza Giovanni XXIII 3, ℡095.532.207; fares are one way €91, return €127, under-25s one way €70, return €109.

Club Alpino Italiano Piazza Scammacca 1, between Piazza dell'Università and Piazza Bellini ℡095.715.3515, for climbing advice, information and maps of Mount Etna.

Emergencies Ambulance ℡118; police ℡113.

Exchange There's an exchange office, Agenzia Cambio, at Via S. Maria del Rosario 2, off Piazza dell'Università (Mon–Fri 9am–1pm & 4–6.30pm, Sat 9am–1pm); one inside Stazione Centrale (daily 7am–9pm), and another at the airport (daily 8am–9pm), where there's also an exchange machine.

Gay information Open Mind, Via Gargano 33 (near the station) ℡095.532.685, ©opencatania@tiscalinet.it (daily 5–8pm).
Hospital Casualty at Ospedale Garibaldi, Piazza S. Maria di Gesù / ℡ 095.759.4368.
Internet access Nievski, Via Alessi 13 (the most central); Web Café, Via Caronda 166 ℡095.437.170; Web Café, Via Etnea 678 ℡095.437.170; and Internet Café, Viale Jonio 71 ℡095.377.080.
Pharmacies Caltabiano, Piazza Stesícoro 36 ℡095.327.647; Croce Rossa, Via Etnea 274 ℡095.317.053; Europa, Corso Italia 111 ℡095.383.536; Cutelli, Via Vittorio Emanuele II 54 ℡095.531.400. The last three are open all night.
Police Emergencies ℡112 or 113; Carabinieri, Piazza Giovanni Verga 8 ℡095.537.822 or Vigili

Urbani, Via Veniero 7 ℡095.531.333. The Questura is in Piazza S. Nicolella 8 ℡095.736.7111.
Post office Main post office and poste restante at Via Etnea 215, close to the Villa Bellini (Mon–Sat 8.15am–6.30pm).
Scooter rental Hollywood Rent, Via L. Sturzo, opposite the train station ℡095.530.594. Mopeds and scooters from €16 per day; mountain bikes also available for €10 per day.
Supermarket SMA supermarket at Corso Sicilia 50.
Swimming Piscina Comunale at Viale Kennedy (near the campsites; bus #4/27L or #D (in summer) from the station or Piazza Borsellino).
Travel agents La Duca Viaggi, Piazza Europa 2 ℡095.722.2295; Elisea, Corso Sicilia 31 ℡095.312.321; and GW Munzone, Corso Mártiri della Libertà 186–88 ℡095.539.983.

North of the city: the coastal route

Although all the good sandy beaches are to the south of Catania, it's the coast **north of the city** that's the most popular holiday area. The lava streams from Etna have reached the sea many times over the centuries, turning the coastline into an attractive mix of contorted black rocks and sheer coves, excellent for swimming. Consequently, what was once a series of small fishing villages, stretching from **Ognina** as far as **Acireale**, is now a fair-sized strip of hotels, lidos and restaurants, idle in the winter but swarming in summer with trippers from the city. It's an appealing coastline, easily reached by AST bus from outside Catania's Stazione Centrale and, while some of the villages – like **Aci Castello** – are really only worth a visit when the summer is well under way, Baroque **Acireale** warrants a day-trip from Catania at any time.

It's an area that has taken well to imaginative interpretation. The nineteenth-century Sicilian novelist, Giovanni Verga, set his masterpiece *I Malavoglia* in and around the village of **Aci Trezza**; and some of the better known of the Homeric myths have been ascribed to this locality. The prefix "Aci", given to a number of settlements here, derives from the local River Aci, said to have appeared following the death of the herdsman Acis at the hands of the giant, one-eyed Polyphemus.

Ognina, Aci Castello and Aci Trezza

Bus #3/34 from Catania's Piazza del Duomo runs right the way to **OGNINA**, a small suburb on the northern outskirts of Catania. Built on lava cliffs formed in the fifteenth century, it's an easy break from the city: there are a few restaurants here, overlooking the little harbour, as well as a campsite.

To go any further north, continue on the #3/34 bus or take one of the frequent AST buses, which run up the coast to Acireale, stopping first in **ACI CASTELLO**, 9km from the city. Here, as the name suggests, there's a **castle** (Tues–Sun: May–Sept 9am–1.30pm & 3.30–7pm; Oct–April 9am–1pm & 3–5pm; €0.60), a lofty thirteenth-century building that rises above the sea in splinters from a volcanic rock crag. It was the base of the rebel Roger di Lauria in 1297 and is remarkably well preserved, despite many volcanic explosions and the destruction wrought by Frederick II of Aragon, who took the castle from Roger by erecting a wooden siege-engine adjacent. In town, there are a couple of small trattorias, handy for lunch, while the ragged coastline to the north is popular for sunbathing and swimming: in summer, a wooden boardwalk is built over the lava rocks here and you pay a small fee to use the changing rooms and showers.

Aci Castello marks the beginning of the so-called Riviera dei Ciclopi, named after the jagged points of the **Scogli dei Ciclopi** that rise from the sea just beyond the town. Homer wrote that the blinded Polyphemus slung these rocks (broken from Etna), at Ulysses as he and his men escaped from the Cyclops in their ships. The three main sharp-edged islets – also known as *faraglioni* – present an odd sight (the largest sticking some 60m into the sky) and it's a good half-day's diversion to get off the bus at Aci Castello, and walk the couple of kilometres north along the rough coast to **ACI TREZZA**. Here, right opposite the rocks, on the lungomare, are a selection of bars, *gelaterie* and fine seafood **restaurants**, including the posh *I Faraglioni* – in an ugly concrete hotel, but with great views and food – and a less expensive place, *Osteria dei Marinai*, with tables outside overlooking the small port. There's nowhere particularly cheap to **stay** in the area, though *I Ciclopi*, Via Provinciale 3 (℡095.276.873; ➎), is reasonably priced with a pool and tennis court.

Acireale

ACIREALE, 16km north of Catania, is marvellously sited high above the rocky shore and the surrounding lemon groves, something best appreciated from the public gardens at the northern end of town: from here you can look right back along the Riviera dei Ciclopi. Known since Roman times as a spa centre, Acireale's **sulphur baths** (Terme di Santa Vénera) are still in use, located on the coastal road, Via delle Terme 47 (Mon–Sat 7am–1pm; ⓦ www .terme.acireale.gte.it), with a range of prices starting from €21 for a mud and baths treatment. Most visitors, though, are more likely to be attracted by the town's striking examples of Sicilian Baroque in the crowded central streets. This, the fourth successive town on the site, was rebuilt directly over the old lava streams after the 1693 earthquake. As in Catania, the result is a planned town centre, which relies on a few grand buildings, a handsome square and some long thoroughfares for its effect.

All the finest buildings are right in the centre, on and around Piazza del Duomo. The restored **Duomo**, with its extravagant tiled spires, still retains a good Baroque portal; it's the larger of the two churches in the open square. Over the way, facing the piazza from Via Romeo, is the long **Municipio**; a little further down Via Ruggero Séttimo, in Piazza Vico, the church of **San Sebastiano** sports an elaborate balustraded facade, decked out with a barrage of statues; and straight up from Piazza del Duomo is the grand **Palazzo Musmeci**, in Piazza San Domenico. It won't take long to whip around this compact enclave of decorative Baroque work, and once you've done that there's little else to detain you in town, though you might derive some small interest from the art and historical collections in the **Pinacoteca Zelantea** (Mon–Fri 10am–1pm & 3–6pm, Sat 10am–1pm; free), just off Piazza San Domenico on Via Marchese di Sangiuliano.

A visit to Acireale really pays dividends if you come during Carnevale (see p.60), when it hosts one of Sicily's best **festivals**, with flower-decked floats and fancy-dress parades clogging the streets for five noisy days. There's more traditional entertainment, too, in Acireale's surviving **puppet theatre**: check out the Teatro dell'Opera dei Pupi, which comprises Turi Grasso, at Via Nazionale 95 (☎095.764.8035), I Paladini, at Via L. Pirandello 25 (☎328.709.2502), and Cooperativa E. Magri, at Corso Umberto 11 (☎095.606.272); or contact the tourist office (see below) for details.

Practicalities

You can get to Acireale by **train**, though the station is well to the south of town, near the sulphur baths, and it's a long walk into the centre along Via Vittorio Emanuele. It's better to arrive by **bus**, either locally from Catania or stopping off on the Interbus Catania–Messina route: local buses stop along the main Corso Umberto or at the ranks outside the public garden, at the end of the corso; the Messina buses pass Piazza del Duomo. If you need information, the **tourist office** is at Via Oreste Scionti 15 (Mon–Fri 8am–2pm, plus Tues & Thurs 4.30–8pm, or 4–7pm mid-Sept to April; ☎095.892.129). With Catania so close, you shouldn't need to **stay** in Acireale, and there are no budget choices in the centre, though if you're stuck the *Hotel delle Terme*, at Via de Gásperi 20 (☎095.604.480; ❹), is relatively good value – turn right out of the station, and right again under the tracks at Via Santa Caterina. Around festival time, everywhere in town will be full. If you're looking for a **meal** in town, head for the *Antica Osteria* at Via Carpinati 34 (off Via Vittorio Emanuele II), an unpretentious trattoria with a good, moderately priced range of pizzas, pastas, meat and fish (closed Mon in winter).

Santa Maria La Scala

From Acireale, it's an easy 2km downhill stroll or drive to the tiny hamlet of **SANTA MARIA LA SCALA**, huddled around a miniscule harbour full of painted fishing-boats, with a tiny church and a beach of lavic, black rock at its southern end. There are also three or four **trattorias** overlooking the small bay, the best of which are *La Grotta* at Via Scalo Grande 46 (turn left at the church), where you're offered spaghetti and then a choice of charcoal-grilled fish or seafood from a tray (closed Tues), and *Al Molino*, at the southern end of the hamlet, away from the harbour, which has an outdoor terrace and more grilled fish (closed Wed).

The walk to Santa Maria takes half an hour from Acireale – down Via Romeo (to the side of the Municipio), across the busy main road and then down the steep rural path to the water: you might find yourself passing a flock of sheep on the way or a donkey being led up or down. You might even fancy the **campsite** nearby, too; *Camping La Timpa* (☎095.764.8155, ⓦwww.campinglatimpa.it), next to the sea at Via Floristella 25.

South: across the Piana di Catania

There's a real paucity of places to stop south of the city, certainly compared to the good day-trips to be made to the north. Partly, this is down to geographical factors, much of the land a vast, largely uninhabited plain – the **Piana di Catania**. A rich, fertile agricultural region, full of citrus trees and other crops, it was known to the Greeks as the Laestrygonian Fields after the Laestrygonians, a race of cannibals who devoured several of Odysseus' crew. You'll head across here on the way to Siracusa, or taking the autostrada to Enna, and it's a pretty enough ride through the windmill-dotted flat fields, but the only features of interest lie on the very fringes of the plain. Closest to Catania are the good sand **beaches** which line the wide Golfo di Catania, reached by taking buses #4/27 or #5/38 from the city; there are also three big campsites here that front the sea (see p.249).

Lentini

Half an hour or so south of Catania, **LENTINI** has a long pedigree that puts it among the earliest of the Greek settlements in Sicily, and the first of all the inland colonies. Established in 729 BC as a daughter city of Naxos, Lentini (Leontinoi) flourished as a commercial centre for two hundred years, before falling foul of Hippocrates of Gela. Later, the city was absorbed by Syracuse, sharing its disasters but never its prosperity. It was Leontinoi's struggle to assert its independence, by allying itself with Athens, that provided the pretext for the great Athenian expedition against Syracuse in 415 BC. Another attempt – this time an alliance with the Carthaginians during the Second Punic War – resulted in the Romans beheading two thousand of its citizens, a measure that horrified the whole island, as no doubt it was intended to do. By the time Cicero got round to describing the city, Lentini was "wretched and empty", though it continued as a small-scale agricultural centre for some time, until the great earthquake of 1693 completely demolished it.

Some of the ancient city survives today as an extensive archeological site, a few kilometres out of the modern town (see below), and Lentini itself has a good collection of finds in the town's **Museo Archeológico** in Piazza del Liceo (Tues–Sun 9am–6pm, Sun 9am–noon; free), though some of the best artefacts have been appropriated by the museums at Catania and Siracusa. All the same, you'll see plenty of examples of the local pottery, a graphic reconstruction of the ancient city's south gate and plans of the site itself. The museum, however, is tricky to find – and defies directions; there are no signposts and no tourist office, so you'll have to be very persistent.

Modern Lentini has little else to recommend it, being a noisy, sprawling town with few redeeming features. The long main Via Garibaldi curves round into what remains of the old town, principally the **Duomo** (often locked) at the head of a reasonably attractive double square.

Practicalities

The **train** station is some way out of the town centre, with no bus connection into town. It's better, therefore, to come here by **bus** from Catania, which drops you at Piazza dei Sostiti, from where it's a ten-minute walk to the Duomo. There's nowhere to stay in Lentini itself, but there is a very nice **agriturismo** 3km out of town at Contrada Piscitello, on the road to Carlentini: *La Casa dello Scirocco* (☎095.783.6120; ❹) is an eighteenth-century *palazzo* built over the remains of some Roman baths, with a swimming pool and restaurant. For **refreshment** in town, try the bar/*pasticceria Navarria*, on Via Conte Alaimo (extending behind the town hall on the main street), which is good for granitas, pastries, ice cream and other snacks. For fuller **meals**, head across the road to *La Maidda*, on the corner of Via Alfieri (closed Thurs), where inexpensive pizzas and local specialities are served in congenial surroundings.

Carlentini and the Zona Archeológica

You wouldn't be missing too much by skipping Lentini altogether and heading straight to the Zona Archeológica, a twenty-minute walk south of the nearby upper town of **CARLENTINI**, which you can reach directly by bus from Catania with AST. Again, there's no real point in getting out at Carlentini itself, though it, too, has a fairly pleasant central square with bars: most buses also stop in Piazza San Francesco on the outskirts of Carlentini, closer to the zone, as do buses #1 or #2 from Lentini's train station. From Piazza San Francesco, there are regular buses back to Catania (Mon–Sat), the last one at 8.30pm.

The **Zona Archeológica** (Mon–Fri 8.30am–1.30pm; free) is then a five-minute signposted walk away, spread over the two hills of San Mauro and Metapíccola. The first of these is the more interesting, holding the ancient town's acropolis and substantial remains of a vast necropolis nearby. You'll see the pincer-style **south gate** immediately, part of a well-conserved system of fortifications that surrounded the ancient town. After about 600 BC, Leontinoi expanded over the opposite hill of Metapíccola, though the remains here are very scanty: the foundations of a Greek temple and some scattered huts belonging to an earlier native village, mentioned by Thucydides. Together, the hills make a good couple of hours' rambling, while a dirt road to the side of the main entrance climbs around the perimeter fence to allow views over the whole site and down to Lentini in the valley below.

Mount Etna

One of the world's largest volcanoes, **MOUNT ETNA** dominates much of Sicily's eastern landscape, its smoking summit a familiar feature when travelling in this area. The main crater is gradually becoming more explosive and more dangerous, as illustrated by the spectacular eruptions of July and August 2001, and October 2002, which far eclipsed those of the preceding decade (in 1992, 1997 and 1998). Regarded as the most complex in the last 300 years, the **2001 eruption** spewed forth from six vents on Etna's northern and southeastern sides and sent vast, fiery fountains of lava to the skies. Drivers found the roads blocked and air passengers were forced to divert to other island airports, while Catania suffered a rain of black ash day and night. In **October 2002**, the eruption was triggered by an earthquake, and lava streams poured down both north and south flanks, destroying restaurants, hotels and a cable car in the ski resort of Piano Provenzana, and threatening the villages of Nicolosi and Linguaglossa below. Emergency teams, however, succeeded in diverting the flow, and the damage was far less than on previous occasions, when Catania was devastated and lava flows reached the sea. Despite the risk of eruptions, the volcano remains a remarkable draw for travellers, and really demands that you set aside at least a day to see it.

If you're pushed for time you'll have to make do with the glimpses of Etna's peak and hinterland from the **Circumetnea railway**, a circular route from Catania to Riposto that provides one of Sicily's most fascinating rides. It passes through some intriguing settlements: medieval **Randazzo** is the only place you might want to stop over, but there's interest in the towns of **Paternò** and **Adrano**, both of which have fine castles, while **Linguaglossa** is the base for Etna's surviving ski resorts. If you're driving, you can follow exactly the same route as the railway, around the volcano: a minor but perfectly adequate road sticking close to the line.

There are interesting villages, too, on the **southeastern** side of Etna, worth stopping in for their proximity to the lower craters: **Nicolosi** is an important ski-centre, and is within walking distance of craters blown open in the seventeenth century. But skirting the foothills of the volcano can only be second-best to **the ascent** to the top, a trip worth the effort, and one made easier – until the repair of the cable car – by a ride on a 4WD minibus. Although you're not allowed to reach the main crater itself, getting to the ones just below is possible, though the level you actually achieve is dictated by current volcanic activity.

⑤ The Circumetnea railway: Catania to Riposto

The **Circumetnea railway** (Ferrovia Circumetnea) is a private line, 114km long, which runs around the base of the volcano through fertile vegetation – citrus plantations, vines and nut trees – and past (often through) the strewn lava of recent eruptions. It's a marvellous ride, across Etna's foothills with endless views of the peak, starting in Catania and circling Etna as far as Riposto on the Ionian coast. There's only 30km between Catania and Riposto if you go on the direct coastal route, which means that you can circumnavigate the volcano and get back to Catania on the same day: if you make the entire trip, allow around three and a half hours to Riposto, plus another half an hour back to Catania on the FS main line. InterRail/Eurail passes are not valid on the Circumetnea, and **tickets** for the route (not including the FS coastal trip back to Catania) cost €5.45 one way: buy them on the train, or visit the Circumetnea office in Catania, at Via Caronda 252 (☎095.541.246); see "Travel details" at the end of the chapter (p.273) for schedules.

Bear in mind that **accommodation** in the towns around Etna is scarce, so if you're going to stop over anywhere, plan (and ring) ahead; see the text for details of hotels.

Catania to Bronte

The first part of the route runs out through Catania's grim suburbs, with **Misterbianco** the first stop. Soon, though, the first of the citrus and olive groves are visible and, by the time you reach **PATERNÒ**, you're well within sight of Etna's southern slopes. A busy town in the valley of the River Simeto, Paternò clusters around its main street, Via Vittorio Emanuele, with the train station at one end and a medieval **castello** at the other. Founded by Count Roger in 1073, the castle is largely thirteenth-century (though much restored) and is worth a look for the view from the terrace at the top – the reason the Germans used it as an observation post during World War II. They proved hard to dislodge, and four thousand people died here during the subsequent aerial bombardment. If you're lucky, you'll find the doors open, in which case don't hesitate to poke your nose inside, and, if at all possible, have a wander.

Paternò's one **hotel**, the echoing *Sicilia*, is near the station at Via Vittorio Emanuele 391 (☎095.853.604, ℱ095.854.742; ❶), about a twenty-minute walk to the old centre, at the other end of Via Vittorio Emanuele. The hotel is rather grumpily run, however, and geared toward the business fraternity, so is best regarded as a fallback if you're stuck.

Biancavilla and Adrano

Ten kilometres further on, Biancavilla was founded by Albanian refugees in 1480. The area around is devoted to growing oranges, and small side roads from here run up through the orchards and onto the higher, southwestern slopes of Etna – a nice little diversion if you're coming this way by car.

ADRANO, close by, is one of the more interesting stops hereabouts, built over the site of ancient Adranon, a town founded by Dionysius the Elder – parts of the Greek lava-built **walls** are still visible in town, though they're barely distinguishable from later fortifications. Much more impressive is the **castello**, another of Count Roger's creations and, like that at Paternò, squat, solid and battlemented. Inside there's a small museum (Mon–Fri 9am–1pm & 4.30–7pm; free), with finds from local sites, including early Bronze Age pottery, but with little information. Take a look, too, in the **Chiesa Madre**, next to the castle, which has some good artwork inside, including sixteenth-century panels by Girolamo Alibrandi in the transepts, though the exterior is disfigured by an unfinished modern campanile. The old centre of Adrano provides a fairly pleasant wander, with its shady gardens and faded churches; sit-down bars offering snacks face the gardens. For **lunch**, wander further down the road to Piazza Duca degli Abruzzi, where the cosy and rustic *Hostaria Bellini* is tucked away next to the derelict Teatro Bellini (closed Mon); the emphasis here is on local ingredients.

If you're driving and fancy a side-trip, you can head 8km west of Adrano, near Cárcaci, to the **Ponte dei Saraceni**, a fourteenth-century bridge that arches over the River Simeto (it's at the end of the first road on the right after Cárcaci; keep to the right).

Bronte and around

Some of the best views of Etna are revealed between Adrano and Bronte, as the railway line and road climb ever closer to the lava flows that have marked the landscape further north. **BRONTE** lies about halfway along the Circumetnea route, its rather shabby, amorphous aspect belying a noble past. The town was founded by Charles V in 1535, and many echoes of its original layout survive, particularly in the numerous battlemented and pointed campanili that top its ageing churches. The town gave its name to the dukedom bestowed upon Nelson, the English admiral, in 1799, and his ducal seat (the Castello Maniace – see below) is a few kilometres north of town. Otherwise, Bronte's sole claim to fame these days is as the centre of Italy's pistachio-nut production: the plantations around town account for 85 percent of the country's output, but are only harvested in the early autumn of odd-numbered years. You'll find some great pistachio ice cream and other sweet goodies in town at *Bar Il Tartufo*, Via Cavalieri di Vittorio Veneto 28, and at the *Caffetteria Luca*, Via Messina 273. Bronte is also a handy jumping-off point for an extended trip into the interior of Sicily, with buses heading to Cesarò, from where a fine route cuts west into the Nébrodi hills – covered in Chapter Seven.

Back on the Circumetnea, the pistachios give way beyond Bronte to walnuts and chestnuts, and the train passes the huge lava flow of 1823 which came close to destroying the town. A little further on, **Maletto** is the highest point on the Circumetnea line. From here, a very minor road leads west to the **Castello Maniace**, founded as a convent in 1174 on the site of a victory over the Arabs by George Maniakes, when he was attempting to regain the island for Byzantium. The 1693 earthquake destroyed much of the building, but the estate was given to Lord Nelson as part of his dukedom, granted by King Ferdinand in gratitude for British help in repressing the Neapolitan revolution of 1799, which had forced the Bourbon court to flee to Palermo. Nelson never got round to visiting his Sicilian estate, though his family, the Bridports, only relinquished control of the property in 1978; it's now owned by the *Comune*.

As you pass through the walls, you'll see the restored thirteenth-century **chapel**, where you'll find an account of the history of the castle in English. Were it not for the beautiful tiled floors, restored to match the original pattern in yellow, rose and blue, the **house** (Tues–Sun 9am–1pm & 3–7pm; €2.60) could easily be mistaken for an English country residence. Its style and furnishings – wallpaper, maritime paintings – were defined by Alexander Hood, one of the Bridports, who lived here for sixty years until the 1930s. The same Englishness is evident in the well-tended garden, planted with box hedges, magnolias and palm trees. The garden, or the grounds outside the gates, would make a pleasant **picnic** spot. On the other side of the river lies the only part of the estate still owned by Nelson's descendants, the English cemetery, its most celebrated occupant the Scottish author William Sharp (1855–1905), who wrote under the name of Fiona Macleod and was a regular visitor here. The other literary connection is the origin of the surname of the literary sisters, Anne, Charlotte and Emily; their father, the Rev Patrick Prunty, harboured such an obsession for Nelson, that he changed his name to Bronte (and added an umlaut).

Randazzo

The closest town to the volcano's summit as the crow flies, **RANDAZZO** is imbued with Etna's presence, the dark medieval town built entirely of lava. Despite the dangerous proximity, it has never been engulfed, though an eruption in 1981 came perilously close; the lava flow is easily visible on the road out of town. Randazzo was also one of the main forward positions of the German forces during their defence of Sicily in 1943, and everything in town was bombed to bits. But the churches and buildings from the wealthy thirteenth- to sixteenth-century period have been meticulously restored, and there's some pleasant rambling to be enjoyed around the lava-clad streets.

In medieval times three churches took it in turns to act as cathedral, a sop to the three parishes in town whose inhabitants were of Greek, Latin and Lombard origin and had little in common. The largest, **Santa Maria** (daily from 10am–noon, and usually for a few hours after 3pm), in the main Via Umberto I, is the modern-day holder of the title, a severe Catalan-Gothic structure incorporating chunks of volcanic rock and a fine carved portal with vine decoration. The interior reveals impressive black lava columns, the capital of one serving as an altar. Further up the road on the northern edge of town, lies the church of **San Martino**, notable for its newly restored fourteenth-century campanile, distinctively fashioned in black and white stone. Across the square, the blackened tower that forms part of the old city walls is all that survives of Randazzo's castle. From the fifteenth century until about 25 years ago, it did duty as a prison; nowadays it holds the **Museo Vagliasindi** (daily 9am–1pm & 3–8pm, closes at 7pm in winter; €1.60), which has a good collection of objects, all on a small scale, mainly from a nearby fifth- to second-century BC Greek necropolis. Best of all are the oinochoe, a wine jug with a face of a woman, and a vessel in the shape of a spunky little rat. Downstairs holds serried ranks of dangling Sicilian puppets (see p.61), variously sporting armour, a velvet cloak or a deer-stalker cap.

Practicalities

Arriving in Randazzo on the **Circumetnea train**, walk straight down the road in front of you to reach the central Piazza Loreto; the medieval town is down Via Umberto I and away to the left. The **bus station** is a couple of blocks back from Piazza Loreto, towards the Circumetnea station (down Via Vittorio Véneto). You'll find plenty of information on Etna at the Parco dei Parchi **tourist office** at Via Umberto I 197 (daily 9am–1pm & 3–7pm; ☎095.799.1611).

If you want to break the journey around Etna, Randazzo is the best place to **eat**. Two good, moderately priced choices are *La Veneziana*, off Piazza Loreto at Via dei Romano 8a (closed Sun evening and Mon), which has excellent local dishes and specializes in mushrooms, and the *San Giorgio e Il Drago*, close to Santa Maria Piazza at San Giorgio 28 (☎095.923.972; closed Tues), an upmarket, reconstructed rustic spot with mood music. In the evening, Randazzo has a lively *passeggiata* up and down Via Umberto I, where you'll also find some nice, old-fashioned bars such as the intricately decorated *Arturo* at no. 75. The only **accommodation** in town is the smart, newly renovated *Scrivano* (☎095.921.126, ℱ095.921.433; ❸) behind the Agip petrol station on Via Regina Margherita, off Piazza Loreto. For more atmosphere, head to the agriturismo *Parco Statella* (☎095.924.036, ⓦwww.parcostatella.com; ❸), 2km out of town along the SS120 to Fiumefreddo, which has rooms and mini-apartments in the various buildings of an old baronial villa, and a restaurant run by the mushroom-loving owner of *Il Veneziano*.

East to Riposto

The lava flows around Randazzo are quite clearly defined, and you'll pass through the midst of great rivers of volcanic rubble cluttering the slopes. Occasionally, all that survives of a former orchard or vineyard is the wall, visible through the wreckage. As you'd expect, the views of Etna are magnificent this close to the summit – just 15km away.

Linguaglossa

Road and rail stick close together around the northernmost stretch of the route, passing the station at Castiglione di Sicilia (a good 5km from the town itself; see p.238) and, shortly after, running into **LINGUAGLOSSA**. The main tourist centre on Etna's north slopes, it had a narrow escape from lava flow during the 2002 eruption, when hotels, restaurants and a ski lift were destroyed at the ski-resort of Piano Provenzana, 15km above. During the summer Linguaglossa is a quiet town with locals' bars lining the cobbled streets, and extensive pine forests out of the centre which are good for a ramble. In winter, however, especially at weekends, it fill up with skiers. There's a very helpful **tourist office**, in Piazza Annunziata (Mon–Sat 9am–1pm & 4–8pm in summer, 3–7pm winter, Sun 9am–1pm; ☎ & ℱ095.643.094, ⓦwww.prolocolinguaglossa.it), who can book taxis up to Piano Provenzana if you don't have your own transport. Behind and above it, a small **museum** displays diverse objects ranging from doorknobs to mushrooms, pickled snakes and lava (same hours as office; free).

If you're going **to stay** in town, it's always worth booking ahead; try the *Happy Day*, 300m to the right of the station at Via Maraneve 9 (☎ & ℱ095.643.484; ❷), whose rooms come equipped with showers, or, on the same road at no. 42, the tidy *Villa Refe* (☎095.643.926; no credit cards; ❷), which offers cooking facilities as well as private parking. There are also several bed and breakfasts, among them *Casa Etna*, Via Trento (☎095.643.184; ❹), with two room/apartments, but no cooking facilities.

It would be hard luck indeed to get stuck here for the night; if you do, head for the inexpensive *Sicilia* (☎095.779.2552, ℱ095.779.2832; ❷), at Via Gallipoli 444, near the mainline station. At the bottom of Corso Italia, around Piazza San Pietro, there are a few bars, a couple of trattorias and views over the working boatyard. Much more attractive, if you're driving, is to head up the coast, 3km north, to Fondachello, where there are two seaside **campsites**, signposted from just about everywhere on this stretch of coast: *La Zagara*, Via Spiaggia 127 (☎095.770.0132; June–Oct), pleasantly sited among trees, and *Mokambo*, Via Spiaggia 211 (☎095.938.731; April–Sept), which has a wide range of facilities. Both also have bungalows available for rent (book ahead in summer; two-berths at ❶–❷, four-berths at ❸).

The volcano: its foothills and the ascent

Although the Circumetnea route takes in some fairly adventurous scenery, you get little impression of Etna as an active volcano other than the sight of the odd solidified lava flow. To really appreciate Etna's might, you'll have to make the effort to roam around the **northern and southeastern foothills**, much closer to the summit than the towns on the Circumetnea route – though without your own transport the effort can be considerable. Still, it's not impossible to get around the foothills and craters by public transport, and there are buses from Catania that link some of the villages, notably **Zafferana Etnea** and **Nicolosi**.

The major attraction, however, is a trip up to the higher reaches of what, at 3323m high, is a fairly substantial mountain – the fact that it's very much an active volcano only adds to its fascination. Etna was just one of the places that the Greeks thought to be the forge of Vulcan, a fitting description of the blustering and sparking from the main crater. The philosopher Empedocles studied the volcano closely, living in an observatory near the summit. This presumably terrifying existence was dramatized by Matthew Arnold in his *Empedocles on Etna*:

Alone! –
On this charr'd, blacken'd melancholy waste,
Crown'd by the awful peak, Etna's great mouth.

Certainly, it all proved too much for Empedocles, who in 433 BC jumped into the main crater in an attempt to prove that the gases emitted would support his body weight. They didn't.

Of the scores of recorded **eruptions** since that of 475 BC (described by Pindar), some have been disastrously spectacular: in 1169, 1329 and 1381 the lava reached the sea, while in 1669, the worst year, Catania was wrecked and its castle surrounded by molten rock. In the twentieth century, the Circumetnea railway line was repeatedly ruptured by lava flows, the towns of the foothills threatened, and roads and farms destroyed. In 1979 nine tourists were killed by an explosion on the edge of the main crater, and though the eruptions in 2001 caused no fatalities, the upper cable-car station was destroyed and the cluster of buildings around the *Rifugio Sapienza* narrowly escaped being engulfed. The 1971 eruption destroyed the observatory supposed to give warning of such an event, and in 2001, the hut that held the

5

Tours are most easily taken from Taormina and are usually full-day affairs, including transport there and back, an accompanied trip up to the craters, and protective clothes and boots. Prices depend on the altitude you decide to go to, from around €28 per person, plus €42.50 for the optional minibus ride from the *Rifugio Sapienza*. Departures depend on weather conditions and generally don't take place at all from September to April. If the rates above are too pricey, then you could try one of the inexpensive excursion buses that leave throughout the year for various points in the foothills, which provide at least a taste of the volcano – this is very much a second-best option, though.

• Of the **agents in Taormina**, SAT, at Corso Umberto I 73 (☎0942.24.653, ⓦwww.sat-group.it), runs daily excursions to the north and south faces, as well as sunset tours (Tues and Thurs); CST, Corso Umberto I 101 (☎0942.626.088), also runs daytime tours; while SAIS, Corso Umberto I 222 (☎0942.625.179), offers various excursions, including an evening sunset tour. The **tourist offices** in Catania, Randazzo and Giardini-Naxos can also advise on Etna tours.

• AST operates a daily bus (8.15am all year) from Catania's Piazza Giovanni XXIII (outside Stazione Centrale) to the *Rifugio Sapienza*, the trip taking two hours. The return bus is at 4.30pm; tickets cost around €5 return.

monitoring live-cam was also engulfed (though the equipment was saved). This unpredictability – the last eruption was expected, but could not be pinpointed to a precise time – means that it's no longer possible to get close to the main crater.

During the 1992 eruption, which engulfed the outskirts of Zafferana Etnea, the American navy joined Italian forces in an attempt to stem the lava flow by dropping reinforced concrete blocks (so-called "Beirut-busters", used to defend military camps) from helicopters into the fissures. In 2001, when the lava flow petered out four kilometres short of Nicolosi, the military helicopters were again in force, this time water-bombing the forest fires and blazing orchards. In 2002, rescue workers dug channels to divert flows away from centres of habitation. Some local villagers, on the other hand, preferred to place their faith in parading statues of the Virgin Mary before the volcano, although the devout were far outnumbered by the flocks of sightseers who made excursions as close as they dared, until curtailed by the authorities.

Access to the summit is by 10km of rough track, a large part of it covered by lava. You'll not be in any danger, provided you stay within the limit that is currently deemed safe to reach.

Approaches: around the northern and southeastern foothills

If you're short on time and don't have your own transport, the easiest way to see the volcano and climb its slopes is by **organized tour** from either Catania or Taormina, or by special **excursion bus** (see box above). Otherwise, with your **own transport** you can take one of the several approaches to the craters: some of the best scenery is on the **north side** (signposted "Etna Nord"), from the road that leads up from Linguaglossa. The road beyond Piano Provenzana is carefully and strictly controlled, and even with a four-wheel-drive, you will be strongly encouraged to leave your vehicle, and take an organized jeep trip (see p.272).

By **public transport**, the only practicable routes into the foothills are on the **south side** of Etna ("Etna Sud"); frequent buses run out of Catania to the nearby villages.

The north side

From Linguaglossa (see p.267), a tortuous fifteen-kilometre road corkscrews up past the skiing pistes of **Piano Provenzana** and the tourist village of Mareneve, still being reconstructed after the last eruption. Without your own transport, you'll need to take a taxi from Linguaglossa (ask at the tourist office) to the Piano, and from here take a four-wheel-drive minibus (called jeeps) to see some of the craters higher up – a round trip of about three hours that costs around €37. The early evening tours are the best – Etna at sunset is a spectacular sight. The minibuses don't run to a fixed timetable – they simply take off when full, and the operation is a more low-key affair than on the southern side. The extent to which you'll be allowed out to explore independently depends on weather conditions – even in August the windchill can make winter clothing advisable and windspeeds can be strong enough to blow children off their feet. Jackets and walking boots can be hired in Piano Provenzana for a few euros. If your budget doesn't stretch to an excursion, there is still interesting walking to be done around the Piano.

You'll find information on local walks and much more at Piano Provenzana's English-speaking **tourist office** (daily: April–Oct 9am–6pm; Nov–March 9am–4pm; ☎095.647.352), while a number of outlets around the resort sell **ski passes** (a one-day pass costs around €12) and **rent out skis** (about €15 per day). If you want to stay, there's a **hostel**, the *Casa Brunek* (☎095.643.015; €26 per person for a dorm-bed, €39 including dinner) in the pinewoods, 5km below Piano Provenzana (follow the road). The only place to **eat** in Piano is at the moderately priced *Ristorante Monte Conca* (☎095.647.968).

A lower, more direct road leads south from Linguaglossa past various old lava flows – of 1852, 1950 and, near Fornazzo, of 1979 – to **MILÒ**, 15km away; here, there are impressive views of the Valle del Bove above (see p.272 for more views of this, from the top). Maps show a road from Milò which climbs northwest, up the volcano to the *Rifugio Citelli*, and back towards Linguaglossa, but frequent landslides often make this route impossible. You should be able to get some of the way up though, for more striking views of the summit and the coastline below.

The south side

Most pleasant of the villages on the south side is **ZAFFERANA ETNEA**, an hour from Catania by bus. It's surrounded by vineyards and citrus groves and is renowned for its honey, the smell of which lingers in the air. Parts of the outskirts were damaged by lava in April 1992, when the village became the operational centre of the effort to halt the flow from the volcano. The centre, however, was untouched and it retains an eighteenth-century air in its buildings and churches, making it a pleasant stop, say for a coffee in the bar on the corner of the elegant central piazza. The previous eruption to threaten Zafferana occurred in 1792, halted on that occasion – according to local tradition – by the intervention of Our Lady of Divine Providence, whose name was again invoked by God-fearing locals during the last volcanic ructions.

Zafferana has acquired a reputation as a low-key hill-resort, and the population of around seven thousand practically doubles at weekends and holidays as the trippers arrive. Certainly, there's some good walking to be done in the green hills behind the village, and if you fancy a longer stay here there's a choice of **hotels**, all sited north of the centre. Try the comfortable and cheerfully furnished *Primavera dell'Etna*, Via Cassone 67 (☎095.708.2348, ☏095.708.1695; ➍), set in its own grounds, or the smaller *Villa Pina*, Via dei Gerani 19 (☎ & ☏095.708.1024, no credit cards, ➌), which is popular with German holiday-makers.

The other easily reached village from Catania is **TRECASTAGNI**, whose main church, the **Chiesa Madre**, is a fine Renaissance building probably designed by Antonello Gagini, and affording marvellous views over the coast from its elevated position. Frankly, though, you're hardly likely to come here for just these; better, if you're driving, to look upon Trecastagni as a coffee-stop.

Nicolosi

A tidy little town just to the west of Trecastagni, **NICOLOSI**, which also had a narrow escape in the 2002 eruption, is a popular winter ski resort and, though rather bland in itself, is probably the best target in the foothills, with several hotels and some good places to eat; it is also well-served by frequent AST buses from Catania. At around 700m, it's pretty brisk in Nicolosi even in summer, and the area around boasts some good walking possibilities. Best of these, certainly if you're going no further, is the hike up to the **Monti Rossi** craters, around an hour each way. Formed in the eruption of 1669, they're the most important of the secondary craters that litter the slopes of the volcano.

Nicolosi is the last main stop before the steeper slopes begin – a good place to pick up information. There's a helpful **information office** at Via Garibaldi 63 (Mon–Fri 8.30am–2pm, 4.30–7pm; ☎095.911.505), on the main road that runs through town. The **hotels** in Nicolosi are a fairly expensive bunch, though there are some exceptions. Best bet is the *Etna Garden*, in the centre of town at Via della Quercia 7 (☎095.791.4686, ☏095.791.4701, ⓦwww .etnagardenostell.com; ➌), which has stylish rooms, a courtyard garden and small museum. It also doubles as a **youth hostel**, with dorm beds (€16 per person). Otherwise, try the *Gemmellaro*, 2km out of town up the hill, at Via Etnea 160 (☎095.911.373, ☏095.911.071; ➋), with bright and modern rooms. Closer to the centre you'll find two reasonably priced **restaurants**: *Al Buongustaio*, Via Etnea 105, specializes in local mushrooms and sausage, while the excellent and popular *Pizzeria Antichi Proverbi*, Via M. Rapisardi 2, serves wood-fired pizzas with wild mushrooms and rocket, in its lively interior or outside in the garden. If you're **camping**, *Camping Etna* (☎095.914.309) is on Via Goethe, signposted from town, just past the hotels.

The ascent

Although there are regular buses to Nicolosi from Catania, only one (early morning, from outside Catania's Stazione Centrale) continues to the mountain refuge/hotel that marks the end of the negotiable road up the south side of Etna. It's a bizarre ride. **Beyond Nicolosi**, the green foothills give way to wooded slopes, then to bare, black-and-grey seas of volcanic debris, spotted with the hardy endemic plants, the yellow-green Spino Santo and Etna violets – the only things to grow on the heights of the volcano. The most recent lava streams lie to the right of the road, where you'll also see earlier spent craters – grass-covered on the lower reaches, and no more than black pimples further up.

Rifugio Sapienza

RIFUGIO SAPIENZA, 1400m below the summit, was the scene of frenetic activity in July and August 2001, when large dams and channels were constructed to contain the molten lava and prevent it from engulfing the tourist complex here. As a result, only the lower cable-car station and the car park were damaged, when the lava eventually spilled down and crossed the road in a broad 500m band. It had another narrow escape at the end of 2002, when lava covered a nearby building, causing it to explode. Thirty two people were injured, but the refuge was untouched. The *Rifugio Sapienza* itself (℡095.915.321; €55 per person half-board) displays graphic photographs of its near escapes, and is the cheapest place to **spend the night**, though it's always wise to ring ahead and book. The alternative is the pricey and newly refurbished *Corsaro* (℡095.914.122, Ⓦwww.hotelcorsaro.it; ❹), set a little apart from the rest of the site and popular with tour groups. Otherwise, arriving on the early-morning bus, you'll have enough time to reach the top and get back for the return bus to Catania – it leaves at 4.30pm from the refuge. Failing that, it's not impossible to cadge a lift down with someone.

Up the volcano

Until the upper **cable-car** station, destroyed in the 2001 eruption, reopens, options of ascending the volcano are limited to going up by foot or taking one of the numerous minibuses (with guide), which leave the cable-car station on demand (April–Oct 9am–5.30pm, weather permitting; €42.50). The route threads through the most recent lava up to the Torre del Filósofo; journey time is around two and a half hours. Otherwise, you can **walk**, though it's not an easy climb, taking around four hours from the *Sapienza*, the return much less. However you go, take warm clothes, a hat, good shoes or boots and – especially if you wear contact lenses – glasses to keep the flying grit out of your eyes. Weather conditions higher up are often different from those at the *Rifugio Sapienza*, so you might want to take advantage of the padded jackets and boots that are available for rent from the minibus guides.

The volcano is a lunar landscape, the ground under your feet alternately black, grey or red depending on the age of the lava. The most recent stuff lies in great folds; below, the red roofs and green fields of the lower hills stretch away to the sea. Even in winter, the snow on the southern side tends to lie only in patches, partly melted by the heat of the rocks. On the northern side, however, hollows in the ground are filled year-round with snow. From here, the ice used to be cut, covered with ash and then transported to the rest of the island, the mainland and even Malta, for refrigeration purposes – a peculiar export that constituted the main source of revenue for the Bishop of Catania, who owned the land until comparatively recently. On the way down, the minibus makes short photo-stops, including the **Valle del Bove**, an enormous chasm almost 20km in circumference, its walls 900m high and streaked with recent lava flows. A massive rent in the side of the volcano, its sunken flank comprises a sixth of the entire surface area of Etna.

Depending on weather conditions and volcanic activity, you should be able to reach the so-called **Torre del Filósofo**, a tower said to have been the home of Empedocles, but more likely a memorial built by the Romans to celebrate the emperor Hadrian's climb to the summit. Beyond, from the turnaround point for the minibus, you look up to the summit, smoke puffing from the **southeast crater** immediately above. It would be foolish to venture any further – gaseous explosions and molten rock are common this far up. Higher still is the **main crater**: depending on the weather conditions you'll see smoke from here too, and, if you're lucky, spitting explosions. Disappointingly, there's often haze or cloud, which can mar the unsurpassed panorama to the sea; for the clearest view, come at sunrise.

Festivals

January
15 Festival of San Mauro in **Aci Castello**.
17 Festival of Sant'Antonio in **Nicolosi**.

February
3–5 Festa di Sant'Agata in **Catania** boisterous street events, fireworks and food stalls, and the procession of the saint's relics.

February/March
Carnevale Five days of floats, flowers and traditional music in **Acireale** – one of Sicily's best annual events. Smaller-scale affair at **Paternò**.

March/April
Easter Good Friday procession in **Acireale** in traditional costume. Easter Sunday ceremony in **Adrano**, the Diavolata – a symbolic display showing the Archangel Michael defeating the Devil.

May
9–10 Traditional high jinks at **Trecastagni**: a pilgrimage by athletic souls who, barefoot and shirtless, run the main road linking Catania to the sanctuary at Trecastagni; as well as costumes, painted carts, etc.

July
19–26 Festival commemorating St Vénera in **Acireale**.
24 Pesce a Mare festival at **Aci Trezza**: a fisherman pretends to be a fish and excitedly the local fishermen catch him. Unmissable.

August
15 Procession of the *vara* in **Randazzo**: an 18m-high column with decorative figures representing the Assumption.

November
11 San Martino's Day celebrations in **Catania**.

December
Christmas week Display of eighteenth-century cribs in **Acireale**.

Travel details

Trains

Catania to: Acireale (1–2 hourly; 10min); Caltagirone (6 daily Mon–Sat, 3 daily Sun; 2hr); Caltanissetta (7 daily; 1hr 50min–2hr 10min); Enna (Mon–Sat 7 daily; 1hr 20min); Gela (6 daily Mon–Sat, 3 daily Sun; 2hr 40min); Giarre-Riposto (1–2 hourly; 30min); Lentini (hourly; 30min); Messina (1–2 hourly; 1hr 30min); Palermo (3 daily; 3hr 45min); Siracusa (hourly; 1hr 30min); Taormina (1–2 hourly; 50min).

Circumetnea trains

Catania to: Paternò, Adrano, Bronte, Maletto, Randazzo (7 daily; 2hr).
Randazzo to: Linguaglossa, Giarre-Riposto (5 daily; 1hr 10min).

Buses

Catania to: Acireale (1–2 hourly; 40min–1hr 15min); Adrano (hourly Mon–Sat; 1hr 35min); Agrigento (12 daily Mon–Sat, 7 daily Sun; 2hr 50min); Augusta (hourly Mon–Sat, 3 daily Sun; 1hr); Caltagirone (19 daily Mon–Sat; 1hr 30min); Enna (12 daily Mon–Sat, 3 daily Sun; 1hr 30min–2hr 25min); Gela (13 daily Mon–Fri, 8 daily Sat, 5 daily Sun; 1hr 45min); Giardini-Naxos (1–2 hourly Mon–Sat, 6 daily Sun; 20–40min); Lentini (1–2 hourly Mon–Sat; 45min–1hr); Messina (1–2 hourly Mon–Sat; 1hr 35min); Nicolosi (hourly; 40min); Nicosia (8 daily Mon–Sat, 2 daily Sun; 2hr–2hr 30min); Noto (7 daily Mon–Sat, 5 daily Sun; 1hr 25min–2hr 15min); Pachino (7–8 daily Mon–Sat, 4 daily Sun; 1hr 50min–2hr 40min); Palermo (hourly; 2hr 40min); Piazza Armerina (3–6 daily Mon–Sat, 2 daily Sun; 1hr 50min); Ragusa (12 daily Mon–Sat, 6 daily Sun; 2hr); Rifugio Sapienza (1 daily; 2hr); Siracusa (1–2 hourly Mon–Sat, 11 daily Sun; 1hr 20min); Rome (2–3 daily; 11hr); Taormina (16 daily Mon–Sat, 6 daily Sun; 1hr 40min); Trecastagni (every 30min Mon–Sat, 2 daily Sun; 40min); Zafferana Etnea (12 daily Mon–Sat, 2 daily Sun; 1hr 15min).
Catania airport to: Agrigento (11 daily Mon–Sat, 7 daily Sun; 2hr 40min); Enna (6 daily Mon–Sat,

3 daily Sun; 1hr 10min); Messina (7–9 daily Mon–Sat, 7 daily Sun; 1hr 50min); Milazzo (1 daily June–Sept; 2hr); Siracusa (11 daily Mon–Sat, 9 daily Sun; 1hr 5min); Taormina (2 hourly Mon–Sat, 16 daily Sun; 1hr 20min).

Lentini to: Catania (1–2 hourly Mon–Sat; 45min–1hr); Siracusa (12 daily Mon–Sat; 40min).

Randazzo to: Bronte (4 daily Mon–Sat; 30min); Cesarò (2 daily Mon–Sat; 1hr); Giardini-Naxos (1 daily Mon–Sat; 1hr); Maletto (3 daily Mon–Sat; 20min); Messina (2 daily Mon–Sat; 1hr 50min).

Catamarans

From Catania to: Malta (3–6 weekly July & Aug, 1–2 weekly March–June & Sept to early Oct; 3hr).

6

Siracusa and the southeast

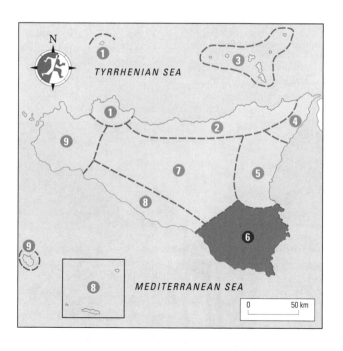

CHAPTER 6

Highlights

✱ **Duomo, Siracusa** A Greek temple transformed into a Baroque cathedral, this ancient building dominates Sicily's most graceful piazza. **p.284**

✱ **Performance in Siracusa's Teatro Greco** Classical dramas and more modern theatrical or musical productions are staged every summer in the city's spectacular Greek theatre. **p.289**

✱ **Pantálica** Spend an entire day exploring the thousands of prehistoric tombs that honeycomb this high ravine. **p.297**

✱ **Noto** The apotheosis of Baroque town planning, Noto offers glorious vistas at every turn, from extravagantly balconied *palazzi* to soaring church facades. **p.302**

✱ **San Giorgio, Ragusa** In a region studded with Baroque masterworks, this church represents the finest of the genre, the work of mastercraftsman Rosario Gagliardi. **p.307**

△ The Duomo, Noto

6

Siracusa and the southeast

Sicily's **southeast** corner is dense with interest, an area whose historic towns and vigorous scenery merit as much time as you can give them. This has always been one of the island's wealthiest enclaves, reflected in the opulence of its building styles, and especially in **Siracusa**, whose long and glorious history outshines all other Sicilian cities. With its streets displaying examples of the architecture of almost every age, Siracusa has managed to survive the earthquakes that have repeatedly afflicted the area, none so destructive as that of 1693, which affected the whole of the region as far north as Catania. This upheaval did, however, produce one positive and lasting effect: where there were ruins, a confident new generation of architects raised planned towns, displaying a noble but vivacious **Baroque style** – of which **Noto**, **Ragusa** and **Módica** are the most outstanding examples.

In contrast to the refinement of its cities, much of the southeastern landscape is rough and wild, cut through by the **Monti Iblei** and riven by

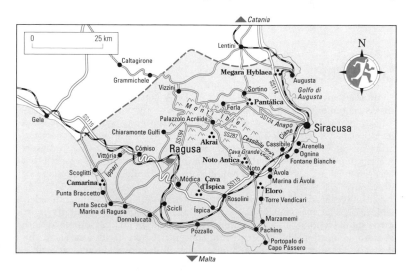

unexpected and often spectacular ravines, or *cave*. Wedged in one of these, **Pantálica**, west of Siracusa, is Sicily's greatest necropolis. Nearby **Palazzolo Acréide** has the best of the classical digs outside Siracusa, while there are several other archeological sites along the coast, often beside uncrowded expanses of sand.

Siracusa and around

Once **Siracusa** was the most important city in the western world. Now, with most of Sicily's business activity located elsewhere and all political power centred on Palermo, the port's only status is that of a mere provincial capital. But although Siracusa retains the intimacy of a small town at its heart, it's charged with historical resonance. There's no shortage of things to see, and it's a useful base for visiting any of the other places mentioned below, all on bus routes and few more than 45 minutes' drive from the city.

Like Siracusa, **Augusta**, to the north, is a port centred on an offshore islet, but the similarity ends there. The coast between the two, the **Golfo di Augusta**, holds Sicily's greatest concentration of industry, a petrochemical nightmare of immense proportions that utterly overwhelms what's left of the old Greek city of **Megara Hyblaea**. Inland, the high mountainous area around **Pantálica**, occupied since the thirteenth century BC, has preserved its ancient necropolis from twentieth-century intrusions, while the nearby town of **Palazzolo Acréide** shelters the site of Greek **Akrai**. You have to head south, though, for the biggest draw in Siracusa's hinterland: the town of **Noto**, whose charms vie with those of the provincial capital but are dedicated to the perfection of just one artistic style, the Baroque.

The coast around here has plenty of good **beaches**, trailing off into a humdrum series of small resorts dotting Sicily's southern cape, **Capo Pássero**.

Siracusa

More than any other Sicilian city, **SIRACUSA** (ancient Syracuse) has a past that is central not just to the island's history, but to that of the entire Mediterranean region. Its greatest splendour belongs to antiquity. Syracuse established its ascendancy over other Sicilian cities for more than five hundred years and at its height was the supreme power in Europe, with at least three times its present population. Its central position on the major trade routes ensured that even after its heyday the port continued to wield influence and preserve its prestige.

All this is reflected in a staggering diversity of monuments, spanning the Hellenic, early Christian, medieval, Renaissance and Baroque eras – the styles are often shoulder-to-shoulder, sometimes in the same building. Combined with its inspired location, and medieval core concentrated on an offshore island, this distracting medley makes Siracusa one of the most enjoyable towns in Sicily.

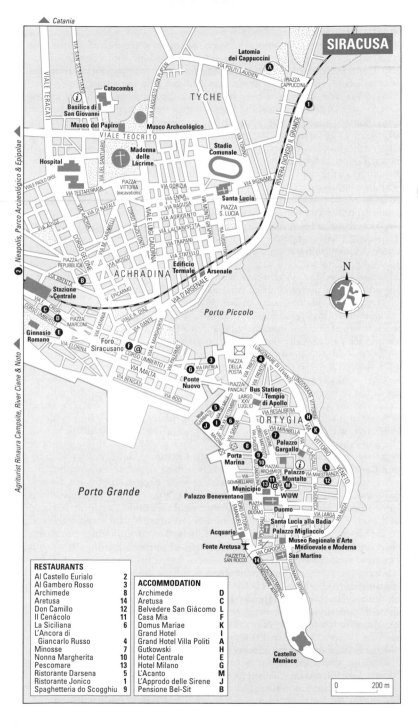

SIRACUSA

Catania

Latomia
dei Cappuccini

PIAZZA
CAPPUCCINI

TYCHE

Catacombs

Basilica di
San Giovanni

Museo del Papiro

Museo Archeológico

VIALE TEÓCRITO

Madonna
delle
Lácrime

Stadio
Comunale

Hospital

PIAZZA
VITTORIA
(excavations)

Santa Lucia

PIAZZA
S. LUCIA

PIAZZA
REPUBBLICA

ACHRADINA

Edificio
Termale

Arsenale

Stazione
Centrale

Porto Píccolo

N

PIAZZA
MARCONI

Ginnasio
Romano

Foro
Siracusano

PIAZZA
DELLA
POSTA

Ponte
Nuovo

PIAZZA
PANCALI

Bus Station

LARGO
XXV
LUGLIO

Tempio
di Apollo

ORTYGIA

Palazzo
Gargallo

Porta
Marina

PIAZZA
ARCHIMEDE

Palazzo
Montalto

W@W

Municipio

Palazzo Beneventano

PIAZZA
DEL
DUOMO

Porto Grande

Duomo

Santa Lucia alla Badia

Acquario

Palazzo Migliaccio

Fonte Aretusa

Museo Regionale d'Arte
Medioevale e Moderna

San Martino

PIAZZETTA
SAN ROCCO

Castello
Maniace

RESTAURANTS
Al Castello Eurialo   2
Al Gambero Rosso   3
Archimede   8
Aretusa   14
Don Camillo   12
Il Cenácolo   11
La Siciliana   6
L'Ancora di
  Giancarlo Russo   4
Minosse   7
Nonna Margherita   10
Pescomare   13
Ristorante Darsena   5
Ristorante Jonico   1
Spaghetteria do Scogghiu   9

ACCOMMODATION
Archimede   D
Aretusa   C
Belvedere San Giácomo   L
Casa Mia   F
Domus Mariae   K
Grand Hotel   I
Grand Hotel Villa Politi   A
Gutkowski   H
Hotel Centrale   E
Hotel Milano   G
L'Acanto   M
L'Approdo delle Sirene   J
Pensione Bel-Sit   B

0   200 m

6

SIRACUSA AND THE SOUTHEAST | Siracusa

279

A brief history

The **ancient city** grew around Ortygia, an easily defensible offshore island with two natural harbours on either side, fresh springs, and access to extensive fertile plains over on the mainland, from which important trade routes weaved inland. These natural advantages couldn't help but attract settlers, and Corinthian colonists arrived here in 733 BC, apparently at the behest of the Delphic oracle. It wasn't until the beginning of the fifth century BC that the city's political position was boosted by an alliance with Greeks at Akragas (Agrigento) and Gela. With the crushing victory of their combined forces over the Carthaginians at Himera in 480 BC (see p.138), and the transfer of Gela's tyrant, **Gelon**, to Syracuse, the stage was set for a century of expansion and the beginning of the city's long supremacy on the island. The grandest monuments you'll see today are from this period, and more often than not were built by slaves provided from the many battles won by Syracuse's bellicose dictators.

Inevitably, the city's ambitions provoked the intervention of Athens, which dispatched one of the greatest fleets ever seen in the ancient world. This **Great Expedition** was scuppered in 413 BC by a mixture of poor leadership and astute defence: "to the victors the most brilliant of successes, to the vanquished the most calamitous of defeats", commented the historian Thucydides. But Syracuse earned the condemnation of the Hellenic world for its seven-year incarceration of the vanquished Athenians – in appalling conditions – in the city's notorious quarries, some of which are still visitable today.

Throughout this period Syracuse was in a state of constant tension between a few overweening but extremely capable rulers, and sporadic convulsions of democracy. Occasionally the tyrants displayed a yearning for cultural respectability that sat uncomfortably beside their shrewd power-seeking. **Hieron I** (478–466 BC), for instance, described by the historian Diodorus as "an utter stranger to sincerity and nobility of character", invited many of the luminaries of the age to his court, including **Pindar**, and **Aeschylus** – who possibly witnessed the production of his last plays, *Prometheus Bound* and *Prometheus Released*, in the city's theatre. **Dionysius the Elder** (405–367 BC) – "cruel, vindictive and a profane plunderer of temples" and responsible for the first of the **Euryalus** forts – comically harboured literary ambitions to the extent of regularly entering his poems in the annual Olympic Games. His works were consistently rejected, until the Athenians judged it politic to give him the prize, whereupon his delirious celebrations were enough to provoke the seizure which killed him. His son **Dionysius II** (367–343 BC) dallied with his tutor **Plato**'s "philosopher-king" theories until megalomania turned his head and Plato fled in dismay. Dionysius himself, recorded Plutarch, spent the end of his life in exile "loitering about the fish market, or sitting in a perfumer's shop drinking the diluted wine of the taverns, or squabbling in the streets with common women".

Rarely, the rulers themselves initiated democratic reforms – men such as **Timoleon** (343–337 BC), who arrived from Corinth to inject new life into all the Sicilian cities, and **Hieron II**, who preserved Syracuse's independence from the assertions of Rome by a novel policy of conciliation, abandoning expansion in favour of preserving the status quo. His long reign (265–215 BC) saw the construction of such monuments as the **Ara di Ierone II**, and the enlargement of the **Teatro Greco** to more or less its existing proportions.

With the death of Hieron, Syracuse, along with practically every other Sicilian city, sided with Carthage against Rome in the Second Punic War. For two years the city was besieged by the Romans, who had to contend with all the ingenious contrivances devised for its defence by **Archimedes**, though

Syracuse eventually fell in 211 BC, an event that sent shock waves rippling around the classical world. The city was ransacked, and Archimedes himself – the last of the great Hellenic thinkers – was hacked to death, despite the injunctions of the Roman general Marcellus.

Syracuse languished under Roman rule and shared in the general despoliation of Sicily carried out by the governor Verres. Its trading role still made it the most prominent Sicilian city, and it became a notable centre of early Christianity, as attested by its extensive **catacombs**. The city briefly became the capital of the Byzantine empire when Constans moved his court here in 663 AD, but otherwise Syracuse was eclipsed by events outside its control and played no active part against all the successive waves of Arab, Norman and other medieval conquerors. The **Castello Maniace**, erected by Frederick II, survives from this period, along with some other important vestiges of fourteenth- and fifteenth-century building that help to give Ortygia its lavish appearance today. The 1693 earthquake laid low much of the city, but provided the impetus for some of its Baroque masterpieces, notably the creations of the great Siculo-Spanish architect Giovanni Verméxio, who contributed an imposing facade to the **Duomo** – a building that encapsulates the polyglot character of modern Siracusa.

Modern Siracusa: orientation

Siracusa today has kept the same general arrangement as it had two and a half millennia ago, with the city divided between its ancient hub, the island of Ortygia, and the four mainland quarters of Achradina, Tyche, Neapolis and – further west – Epipolae. You'll spend much of your time on **Ortygia**, still the heart and soul of Siracusa, and predominantly medieval and Baroque in appearance. Across the Ponte Nuovo, the main bridge linking the island with the mainland, the modern city is centred on **Achradina**, now, as in Greek times, the busy commercial centre, traversed by the main street of **Corso Gelone**. North of Achradina, the old residential quarter of **Tyche** holds Siracusa's **catacombs** and its celebrated **Museo Archeológico**, while **Neapolis** is the site of a **Parco Archeológico**, containing remains of the Greek city's theatres and some extensive quarries. Spread over the ridge to the west of town, **Epipolae** holds the old defensive walls and the solid remnants of the **Euryalus fort**.

Arrival, getting around and information

The **train station** (for information call the premium rate line ☎892.021) is on the mainland at the end of Via Francesco Crispi. The **bus station** is on Piazza della Posta (also known as Riva della Posta), just over the Ponte Nuovo in Ortygia, and is where AST (☎0931.462.711) has its office and operates its city and regional buses. You'll find the Interbus ticket office and regional buses at Via Trieste (☎0931.66.710), round the corner from Piazza della Posta. For departure points and destinations out of Siracusa, see "Listings".

Although much of Siracusa is easy enough to see on foot, you can always avail yourself of the orange AST **city buses** if the sightseeing begins to take its toll. Tickets are on sale at the booth on Piazza della Posta and from *tabacchi*, and the tourist office has a bus map and timetables. The main stops on Ortygia are in Piazza della Posta and Piazza Pancali/Largo XXV Luglio; on the mainland, they are along Corso Umberto. One ride costs €0.80, and relevant routes are specified in the text. As for **taxis**, there are ranks in Piazza Pancali (☎0931.60.980), Via Ticino (☎0931.64.323), and at the train station (☎0931.69.722).

For good free maps, accommodation listings and other information, visit the main **tourist office** on Ortygia, at Via Maestranza 33 (summer Mon–Sat

8.30am–2pm & 4.30–7pm; winter Mon–Fri 8.30am–2pm & 3–5.30pm, Sat 8.30am–2pm; ☎0931.464.255). There's another office on the mainland which covers the whole province, at Via San Sebastiano 43–45 (Mon–Fri 8.30am–1.30pm & 3–6pm, Sat 8.30am–1pm; ☎0931.67.710, ⊛www.apt-siracusa.it).

Accommodation

Siracusa's **accommodation** choices cover the full range for price and comfort, though in high season you should check in early or reserve in advance. Most of the city's cheaper hotels are on the mainland, within walking distance of the train station (where there's no problem parking), but the hotels and B&Bs on Ortygia are preferable for atmosphere and proximity to the best bars and restaurants – and are worth reserving in advance.

The nearest **campsite** to Siracusa, *Agriturist Rinaura* (☎0931.721.224), is four kilometres south of town and two kilometres from the sea, just off the Noto road (turn right after the junction for Arenella). If you bus it (#21, #22, #23 and #24 from Corso Umberto or Piazza della Posta), you'll have to walk the last kilometre to the site. It's a pleasant and friendly place, and has a few **cabins** available for rent (❷), but the best choice for campers is further down the coast at Fontane Bianche (see p.301), close to a first-class beach.

Hotels and B&Bs

L'Acanto Via Roma 15 ☎0931.461.129. Central B&B with quite small but neat en-suite rooms; the one at the front is noisy, others are around a courtyard. ❹

L'Approdo delle Sirene Riva Garibaldi 15 ☎0931.24.857, ⊛www.apprododellesirene.com. A recently opened B&B in a tastefully renovated waterfront building just across the bridge in Ortygia. Great home-made breakfasts are served on a terrace overlooking the sea, and the hotel has a boat for excursions and canoes for hire. You can also borrow bikes free of charge. ❻

Archimede Via Francesco Crispi 67 ☎0931.462.458. Halfway between the station and the Foro Siracusano, this large, old-fashioned hotel is the best-value choice in the area. ❷

Aretusa Via Francesco Crispi 75 ☎ & ☎0931.24.211, ⊛www.hotelaretusa.it. Closer to the station than the *Archimede*, this is a useful if basic hotel for a quick stay. Rooms with bath cost more, and breakfast is optional at €2.60. ❶

Pensione Bel-Sit 4th floor, Via Oglio 5 ☎0931.60.245. The cheapest option in the station area, this is within walking distance of the Neapolis, though less handy for the bars and restaurants of Ortygia. From Foro Siracusano, head up Corso Gelone and take the second left down Via Brenta. Rooms come with or without attached bath and there's a lift. ❶

Belvedere San Giácomo Via Maestranza 111 ☎0931.69.005. Quite a plain and impersonal B&B with smallish rooms except for one – no. 7 – which is much larger with its own bathroom

and a terrace, but the price shifts up to ❻. Some rooms have shared bathrooms, and there are also rooms with three and five beds available. ❷

Hotel Centrale Corso Umberto 141 ☎0931.60.528. On the west side of Piazzale Marconi, quite basic, but very friendly, with good prices; you can even try bargaining them down a little out of season. It's also a home for pigeons, which can be noisy. Rooms with and without bath. ❷ with bath, ❶ without.

Casa Mia Corso Umberto 112 ☎0931.463.349. Though not on Ortygia, this is the nicest of Siracusa's B&Bs, with friendly, attentive service from the couple who run it. Rooms, all en suite, are quiet and furnished with grand old beds, and are separate from the family's living quarters, though there's a shared terrace where breakfast is served. ❹

Domus Mariae Via Vittorio Veneto 76 ☎0931.24.858 or 0931.24.854, ☎0931.24.859, ⊛www.sistemia.it/domusmariae. On Ortygia, efficiently run by nuns and with views to the sea, the fairly swish rooms all have TVs, bathrooms and air-conditioning. There's a solarium, reading room and a chapel, too. ❽

Grand Hotel Viale Mazzini 12 ☎0931.464.600, ☎0931.464.611. This veteran establishment enjoys a prime position in Ortygia, overlooking the Porto Grande. Access to a private beach, lavish furnishings and all the refinements, as you'd expect when the bill comes to a cool €225 per double room. ❽

Grand Hotel Villa Politi Via M. Politi 2 ☎0931.412.121, ☎0931.36.061. North of the centre, in Tyche, this luxury hotel has attracted the rich and famous in the past. Guests enjoy views right into the adjacent Latomia dei Cappuccini. A splendid spot for a splurge. ❽

Gutkowski Lungomare Vittorini 26 ⓣ 0931.465.861, ⓦ www.guthotel.it. Lovely hotel overlooking the sea on Ortygia's east side, with tastefully bare but comfortable rooms and good bathrooms. Room 8 is the biggest, and 11 has a small terrace. Breakfast includes fresh juice from organic oranges, locally made preserves and, in summer, almond granita. ❺

Ortygia

The ancient nucleus of Siracusa, **ORTYGIA** best conserves the city's essential spirit. Here the artistic vestiges of over 2500 years of history are concentrated in a space barely 500m across, 1km in length and all within an easy stroll through quiet streets and alleys. Although parts of Ortygia have been badly neglected in the past, sensitive maintenance in recent years has rescued many of the island's monuments from irreversible damage, helping to restore the old town's lustre.

Across the narrow ribbon of water severing the island from the mainland, the **Tempio di Apollo**, on Largo XXV Luglio, is a case in point. This dignified old ruin is thought to have been the first of the great Doric temples built in Sicily, though not much survives of its seventh-century or early sixth-century BC fabric apart from a couple of columns, fragments of others and part of the south wall of its cella. The arched window in this wall dates from a Norman church that incorporated part of the temple into its structure, and you can make out a dedication inscribed to Apollo on the reconstituted stereobate. However, to get a complete picture of the original temple you'll have to see the scale model in Siracusa's museum (see p.287).

Around Piazza Archimede

Corso Matteotti leads up from Largo XXV Luglio to Ortygia's central **Piazza Archimede**, its centrepiece a twentieth-century fountain depicting the nymph Arethusa (the symbol of Ortygia) at the moment of her transformation into a spring. The square has a couple of bars with outdoor seating, from which you can survey the Catalan-Gothic *palazzi* around its sides, a common architectural style in Ortygia.

Take a look, too, around the corner from Piazza Archimede, down the claustrophobic Via Montalto, where the **Palazzo Montalto** is sadly shored up, though you can still admire its facade, graced by immaculate double- and triple-arched windows, and with an inscription dating the building's construction to 1397. This is one of the few surviving examples of the style favoured by the powerful Chiaramonte dynasty, more of which can be seen from the derelict courtyard at the back, where a loggia still stands.

Piazza del Duomo

Ortygia's most impressive architecture, however, belongs to its Baroque period, and nowhere does this reach such heights as in the city's loveliest square, the elongated **Piazza del Duomo** – a traffic-free space surrounded by a range of seventeenth- and eighteenth-century buildings, including the **Municipio**, on the corner of Via Minerva, which displays a fancy Rococo carriage from 1763 just inside the entrance. Opposite here, **Palazzo Beneventano** has an attractive eighteenth-century facade, while further down the piazza, the southern end is marked by the late seventeenth-century church of **Santa Lucia alla Badia**, finishing point of the procession of Santa Lucia in December. The church's upper storey was a later, mid-eighteenth-century addition; the building is only open for the occasional concert or exhibition these days.

The highlight of the piazza, however, is the **Duomo** itself (daily 8am–noon & 4–8pm, closes at 6pm in winter). To get an idea of the great age of this cathedral, walk round to the side on Via Minerva to see not just the battlemented west wall added by the Normans, but also the stout Doric columns that form the skeleton of the structure, part of an earlier Greek temple. Although these bones were fleshed out by later builders, they still provide the church's main proportions and set a tone of dark antiquity.

The site was already a sacred one when the Greeks started work on an Ionic temple to Athena here in about 530 BC, though this was abandoned when a new temple was begun in thanksgiving for the victory over the Carthaginians at Himera. The extravagant decoration that adorned this building spread its fame throughout the ancient world, and tantalizing details of it have come down to us through Cicero, who visited Syracuse in the first century BC and listed the temple's former contents as part of his prosecution of the Roman praetor and villain Verres, who appeared to have walked off with a good proportion of them – part of the booty he plundered from many Sicilian temples. The doors were of ivory and gold, and its walls painted with military scenes and portraits of various of Syracuse's tyrants – claimed to be the earliest examples of portraiture in European art. On the temple's roof stood a tall statue of the warrior-goddess Athena carrying a golden shield which, catching the sun's rays, served as a beacon for sailors out at sea.

Although all this rich decoration has vanished, the main body of the temple was saved further despoliation thanks to its conversion into a Christian church, which was elevated to cathedral status in 640 AD. A more drastic overhaul was carried out after the 1693 earthquake, when the Norman facade collapsed and was replaced by the present formidable Baroque front, with statues by Marabitti. This is in sharp contrast to the more muted **interior**, in which it's the frame of the ancient temple that is still prevalent. The aisles are formed by the massive Doric columns, while the cella walls were hacked through to make the present arched nave. There's also evidence of the temple in the apse at the end of the north aisle, where you can make out the columned end of the cella wall. This apse is actually the one Byzantine element in the building, and stylistic boundaries are further fudged by the presence here of a good statue, *Madonna of the Snow*, by the Renaissance artist Antonello Gagini. Other statues by the Gagini clan line the north aisle, where the distorted pillars give some inkling of how close the entire structure came to toppling when the seventeenth-century earthquake hit Siracusa. The Duomo's south aisle shows more characteristic Baroque effusion in the series of richly ornate chapels, though the first one – actually the baptistry – is from an earlier age. Enlivened by some twelfth-century arabesque mosaics, it contains a Norman font that was cut from a block still marked with a Greek inscription, and is supported by seven bronze lions.

Palazzo Bellomo and San Martino

Siracusa's tradition of architectural hybridism is again apparent in the **Palazzo Bellomo**, Via Capodieci 14, an interesting mixture of thirteenth- and fifteenth-century features, with a courtyard that has some thirteenth-century arcading and a Spanish-style stairway leading up to the loggia. This and the next-door Palazzo Parisio are the ideal surroundings for the superlative **Museo Regionale d'Arte Medioevale e Moderna** (Tues–Sat 9am–7pm, Sun 9am–2pm; €2.50, or €6 with Museo Archeológico and Parco Archeológico), a small but select display, with mainly sculpture on the ground floor – including some medieval and Renaissance tombs, and the inevitable examples of Gagini expertise – as well as some exceptional paintings on the first floor. Most famous of these is the *Annunciation* by Antonello da Messina, rescued from a state of advanced decay in a church at Palazzolo Acréide (see p.299). The decision to transfer the painting from wood to canvas attracted much controversy, but it remains an absorbing image despite the considerable damage. You can also find Caravaggio's sombre *Burial of St Lucy* here, a local favourite.

Around the corner in Via San Martino, take a look at the church of **San Martino** – one of Siracusa's oldest churches. Originally a sixth-century basilica, it was rebuilt in the fourteenth century and smartened up with a good-looking rose window and Gothic doorway. If you can get in (it's usually closed except for ceremonies and concerts), its dusky interior is a treat – plain stone columns leading to a tiny mosaic half-apse with a fifteenth-century triptych to the right of the choir.

The Fonte Aretusa and medieval Ortygia

Walk east down Via Capodieci to the seafront, where the **Fonte Aretusa** spreads serenely below the small piazza Largo Aretusa. Mentioned in the original Delphic directions that brought the first Greek settlers here, the number of myths associated with this freshwater spring underlines the strong sentimental links that continued to bind the colonists to their motherland. This was where the nymph Arethusa rose after swimming across from the Peloponnese, having been metamorphosed into a spring by the goddess Artemis to escape the attentions of the predatory river-god Alpheus; all in vain, though, for the determined Alpheus pursued her here to mingle with her in a watery form. Other legends declared that the spring's water would stain red at the time of the annual sacrifices at the sanctuary of Olympia, and that a cup thrown into the river there would rise here in Ortygia. More recently, and less apocryphal, Admiral Nelson took water supplies on board here on his way to the Battle of the Nile. Now that the spot has been planted with papyrus, and filled with bream below the water and ducks above, it's a compulsory stop on the evening *passeggiata*, and the piazza is furnished with a nice selection of cafés. There's also an **acquario** here, discreetly tucked away in the trees behind the pool (daily 10am–8.30pm; €2.50). Its three rooms – one Mediterranean and two tropical – hold sharp-toothed piranhas among other familiar and more unusual fish, and there's a good collection of shells.

At the end of the dangling limb of land south of here sits the stout **Castello Maniace**, a defensive bulwark erected around 1239 by Frederick II, but named after George Maniakes, the Byzantine admiral who briefly reconquered Syracuse from the Arabs in 1038. Unfortunately the solid square keep still retains its military function as a barracks and access isn't allowed.

Back below the Fonte Aretusa is a small garden; from here the main procession of promenaders takes off, extending all the way along the tree-lined **Foro Vittorio Emanuele II**, with rows of bars on one side and the odd millionaire's yacht on the other. The vast, still pool of the **Porto Grande** spreads out beyond, dotted with fishing-boats, liners and tankers. At the end of the avenue, to the right, the **Porta Marina** is a remnant of the city's medieval walls, a fifteenth-century gateway surmounted by a curlicued Spanish heraldic device.

If you've walked around the sights in a fairly disciplined order, it's well worth taking a couple of hours to do some aimless wandering around the less immediately obvious parts of Ortygia: typically, you'll run across a clutch of good-looking *palazzi* from different epochs, spread all over the island. The best of these are from the spate of building that took place under the aegis of the Aragonese, such as the **Palazzo Gargallo** (in Via Gargallo, north off Via Maestranza), with a Catalan outer stair, and the **Palazzo Migliaccio** in Via Pichcrali (off Piazza del Duomo, close to the Fonte Aretusa), its white marble terrace adorned with black lava chevrons. But look out too for the later Baroque constructions, notably on **Via Maestranza** itself and **Via Vittorio Véneto**, on the eastern side of the island. Connecting this last street with Largo XXV Luglio, **Via Resalibera** is also worth a stroll, squeezing the occasional church between its tangled rows of houses, or a solitary bar – usually just a room full of wine barrels and old men, both half full of the stuff.

Achradina

Modern development in the central mainland quarter of **ACHRADINA** makes it difficult to picture the ancient city that Plutarch wept over when he heard of its fall to the Romans. Much of the new building dates from World War II, when Siracusa was bombed twice over – once by the Allies, then, after its capture, by the Luftwaffe in 1943. But you're likely to be staying in one of the hotels scattered around this part of town, or will pass through on the way to the archeological museum and park, so you could well drop in on some of these lesser sites en route.

You'll certainly become familiar with the rather shabby park area known as the **Foro Siracusano**. Site of the old town's *agora*, it holds a few paltry columns in a landscaped garden, and is not improved by the grotesque war memorial towering above, a Fascist monument from 1936. On Via Elorina, to the west, there's a much more interesting relic, the little-visited **Ginnasio Romano** (Mon–Sat 9am–1pm; free). This was never actually a gymnasium but a small Roman theatre, probably built in the first century AD when the ancient city's much grander Greek theatre was requisitioned for blood sports. A well-tended lawn surrounds the rectangular *cavea*, with the remains of a portico behind it; this once enclosed a small shrine, part of which is still visible. These days the theatre's orchestra is flooded from an underground cistern, hindering further excavation, though if anything this enhances the appeal of this forgotten, mossy site.

Eastern Achradina

Over on the eastern edge of Achradina, close by the crowded huddle of boats in the **Porto Píccolo**, you'll find a much less recognizable ruin, the **Arsenale**, by the railway line, which is fenced off to the public. As its name suggests, it was a provisions centre, where ships were refurbished, hoisted up from the port by devices that clamped into the ground – and the slots that engaged them are about the only thing to look at here. Adjacent is another low-key sight, the **Edificio Termale**, a Byzantine bathhouse claimed to be the very same one in which, in 668 AD, the Emperor Constans was assassinated, knocked on the head by a servant wielding a soap dish. It's under a modern block of flats and about the only thing visible are a few piles of stones.

North: Santa Lucia

Via Fuggetta leads up to the modern city's most pleasant square, Piazza Santa Lucia, a huge space planted with an arcade of trees around three sides. It takes its name from the church of **Santa Lucia** (daily 9am–noon & 4–6pm), lying at its northern end, built in 1629 and supposedly marking the spot where St Lucy, Siracusa's patron saint, was martyred in 304 AD. Today the church has been methodically stripped of all the treasures that once made it an essential item on tourist itineraries, though it does retain its fine wooden ceiling and

Norman tower. You can still visit Giovanni Verméxio's octagonal chapel of **San Sepolcro** outside in the piazza – ask inside the church. The mortal remains of the saint were originally preserved below this chapel, before being carried off to Constantinople by the Byzantine admiral Maniakes in 1038, and later shipped to Venice as part of the spoils plundered by the Venetian "crusaders" in 1204.

The real disappointment, though, is the lack of access to the extensive network of **catacombs** lying beneath this site. After the ones in Rome, Siracusa's catacombs constitute the largest system of subterranean tombs in Italy, and are the oldest in Sicily.

Tyche

The entire district of **TYCHE**, which stretches north from Santa Lucia, is riddled with more of these catacombs, on account of the Roman prohibition of Christian burial within the city limits (Siracusa having by then shrunk back to its original core of Ortygia). The warrens were hewn out of the rock and often followed the course of underground aqueducts, disused since Greek times. All are now inaccessible, apart from those below the **Basilica di San Giovanni** (Tues–Sun 9am–1pm & 2.30–6pm), which lies opposite the tourist office at Via San Sebastiano, off Viale Teócrito, and has been in ruins since 1693. Fronted by a triple arch, the church's nave is now open to the sky and the interior overgrown, but you can still admire the seventh-century apse and a medieval rose window. Once the city's cathedral, it was built over the crypt of St Marcian, first bishop of Siracusa. Steps lead down to the pillar where he was flogged to death in 254; his tomb is here too, along with a modern altar marking the spot where St Paul is supposed to have preached, stopping in the city as a prisoner on his way to Rome.

It's an unnerving experience walking through the gloomy, labyrinthine system of **catacombs** (tours €3.50) underneath the church. Numerous side-passages lead off from the main gallery (*decumanus maximus*), often culminating in *rotonde*, or round caverns used for prayer; other passages are forbiddingly dark and closed off to the public. Entire families were interred in the thousands of niches hollowed out of these walls and floors, anxious for burial close to the tomb of St Marcian. Most of the treasures buried with the bodies have been pillaged, though the robbers overlooked one – an ornate sarcophagus unearthed from just below the floor in 1872 and now on show in Siracusa's archeological museum.

Round the corner in Viale Teócrito, the small **Museo del Papiro** (Tues–Sun 9am–1pm; free) is worth a visit to see papyrus art, ancient and modern, including models of boats and even sandals made of the stuff, and there's a video showing how papyrus is grown and processed.

The Museo Archeológico

Aside from the catacombs, the **Museo Archeológico**, also on Viale Teócrito (Tues–Sat 9am–2pm, Sun 9am–1pm, usually opens all day in summer, but phone ☎0931.6022 to check; last entry 1hr before closing; €4.50, or €6 with Museo Regionale and Parco Archeológico), forms Tyche's main attraction. From Ortygia, buses #4, #12 and #15 for the museum leave from Largo XXV Luglio and run up Corso Gelone and along Viale Teócrito. Purpose-built in the grounds of the Villa Landolina, and a bit of a maze, the museum contains Sicily's most wide-ranging collection of antiquities, worth a prolonged browse to view the almost indescribable wealth disgorged from archeological sites throughout the province and beyond. Near the entrance, an explanatory diagram colour-codes the three main sections into which the exhibits are arranged: prehistoric (section A); items from Syracuse, Megara Hyblaea and the Chalcidinian colonies (B); and finds from Gela, Agrigento, Syracuse's sub-colonies and the indigenous Sikel centres, including copious material from the sites of Pantálica and Castelluccio (C). The information in English on the cases peters out after a while; the leaflet provided by Le Carte (see "Basics", p.59), on sale at the desk, is useful.

Displayed in section B, the museum's most celebrated exhibit is the **Venus Anadiomene**, also known as *Landolina*, after the archeologist who discovered her in 1804. *Anadiomene* means "rising from the sea", which describes her coy pose: with her left hand she holds a robe, while studs show where her broken-off right arm came across to hide her breasts. Probably Roman-made in the first century AD, from a Greek model, the headless statue has always evoked extreme responses, alternately exalting the delicacy and naturalism of the carving, and condemning her "immodest modesty", her knowing sensual attitude that symbolized the decline of the vigorous classical age and the birth of a new decadence. By the statue's feet, the dolphin, Aphrodite's emblem, is the only sign that this was a goddess.

Among the earlier Hellenic pieces, the museum also has some excellent *kouroi* – toned, muscular youths, one of which (in section B), from Lentini, is one of the most outstanding fragments still extant from the Archaic age of Greek art – around 500 BC. Of the same period, from the colony of Megara Hyblaea, there is a striking image of a mother/goddess in the act of suckling twins, its absorbed roundness expressing a tender harmony as close to earth and fertility rites as the *Venus Landolina* is to the cult of sensuality. The huge burial urns (*pithoi*) from the seventh century BC are impressive; look out also for the gruesome theatrical masks and, in the museum's central area, the superb *Sarcófago di Adelfia*: a finely worked fourth-century marble tomb from the catacombs below San Giovanni. It held the wife of a Roman official, the couple prominently depicted and surrounded by reliefs of scenes from the Old and New Testaments.

Santuario della Madonna delle Lácrime

Opposite the museum, across Viale Teócrito, stands the monolithic **Santuario della Madonna delle Lácrime** (daily 7am–12.30pm & 4–7pm), completed in 1994 to house a statue of the Madonna that allegedly wept for five days in 1953 (*delle Lácrime* means "of the tears"). Designed to resemble a giant teardrop, the monument is the most prominent addition to the city's skyline and, some would say, the least harmonious. Typically for Siracusa, the newest architecture appears next to some of the oldest: just to the south, in Piazza della Vittória, fenced-off (but visible) **excavations** have revealed extensive Greek and Roman houses and streets.

Neapolis and the Parco Archeológico

NEAPOLIS was the district containing most of the ancient city's social and religious amenities – theatres, altars and sanctuaries – and was thus never inhabited. Today it's encompassed by Siracusa's large **Parco Archeológico** (Tues–Sun 9am–2hr before sunset; €4.50, or €6 with Museo Regionale and Museo Archeológico), accessible on foot in about twenty minutes from Foro Siracusano, or on buses #4, #8, #11, #12 or #15 from Piazza della Poste to Corso Gelone/Viale Teócrito. The entrance is hidden behind a tawdry parade of souvenir stalls and ice-cream stands, catering to the busloads of tourists which arrive every few minutes in the summer.

On your way to the ticket booth, you'll pass the ruined base of the **Ara di Ierone II**, a 200-metre-long altar erected by Hieron II in the second half

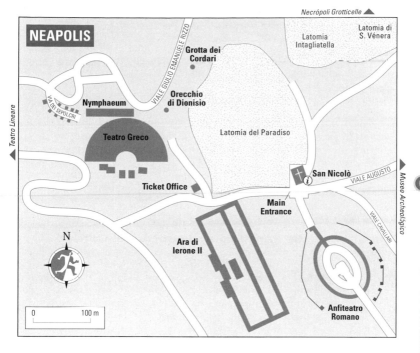

of the third century BC. Built in honour of Zeus Eleutherios, "the giver of freedom", it commemorated the achievements of Timoleon, who liberated the city from tyranny and decline, and was the biggest construction of its kind in all Magna Graecia. It was also the venue for some serious sacrificing: Diodorus records that 450 bulls were led up the ramps at either end of the altar to be slaughtered in the annual feast. Now railed off to the public, little is left standing above plinth level, though the sheer dimensions of the structure still retain their impact.

The Teatro Greco

At the end of the lane is the ticket office and entrance to the **Teatro Greco**, Siracusa's most spectacular monument. One of the biggest and best-preserved Greek auditoriums, its site has been home to a theatre since at least the fifth century BC, though it was frequently modified and added to at different periods. Most of what you see today is owed to Hieron II, who expanded it to accommodate 15,000 people, in nine sections of 59 rows (of which 42 remain). The inscriptions around the top of the middle gangway on the west side of the theatre – faint but still visible – date from the third century BC, giving the names of the ruler and his family, with Zeus Olympios in the middle.

Most of the alterations carried out by the Romans were made to adapt the arena for gladiatorial combat, and included extending the orchestra by cutting back the first rows of seats. They also installed some marble-faced seats for privileged spectators, and the seventeenth row was removed, possibly to segregate the classes. Nowadays the theatre is used for a milder form of entertainment: **concerts** and **Greek dramas**, performed every May and June – though not staged early in the morning, as were the original productions; ask at the ticket office for details. Note that on performance days, the theatre closes for visits at 5pm (last entry at 4.30pm), though you can still see quite a bit from the top.

Walk up through the theatre and the high terrace above contains the **Nymphaeum**, a large artificial grotto (fed by water from an ancient aqueduct) where a number of statues were found, all now displayed in the museum. To the left of here, the **Via dei Sepolcri** (Street of the Tombs) is deeply rutted by the carts that plied to and fro, and is flanked by more votive niches. It's mostly closed to the public and overgrown by fig trees nowadays, but you can get a fair view of it from the barrier.

Below the Greek theatre, in the trees behind the stage, sits a smaller structure, known as the **Teatro Lineare** due to its simple, straight design – you can get the best view of it from outside the archeological park, about 500m up the road that climbs up the hill behind the Greek theatre. Nearby are the scant remains of one of the site's most venerated spots, the **Santuario di Apollo**, which once contained a huge bronze statue of the god before this was carried off to Rome by the Emperor Tiberius.

The Latomie del Paradiso and Grotta dei Cordari

At the entrance to the theatre, another path descends to the largest of Siracusa's huge *latomie* (pits), from which the rock for the city's multifarious monuments was excavated. These wide, vertically walled **quarries** also provided a harsh but effective prison for the 7000 Athenian prisoners of war following the fiasco of the Great Expedition. Most were probably kept in the lusciously overgrown Latomia dei Cappuccini, across on Siracusa's eastern seafront in Tyche – now a garden for the Capuchin monks and closed until the collapsing walls can be bolstered. But here in Neapolis, the **Latomia del Paradiso** is well worth a look in its own right, mainly for the remarkable cavern known as the **Orecchio di Dionisio**. Over 60m long and 20m high, it owes its name (Ear of Dionysius) to the painter Caravaggio, who noted its resemblance to a human ear, while the association with Dionysius derives from a story that the tyrant used the cavern's acoustic qualities to overhear the conversations of suspected conspirators. In fact, Dionysius probably had far more efficient means of extracting information, though the sound-enhancing effect is still there and can be tested by anyone.

A second cave, the geometrically shaped **Grotta dei Cordari**, was used as a work space by the ancient city's ropemakers, who found that the damp air prevented rope strands from breaking under stress: it's possible to make out the grooves worn into rock by the twined rope, though the cave remains closed indefinitely to visitors. There are two other quarries here, the **Latomia Intagliatella**, with a tall rocky pillar in the centre amid the lemon trees, and the niched **Latomia di Santa Vénera**, from where a precipitous passage leads off to the **Necrópoli Grotticelle**. This Greco-Roman burial ground includes one grave with a Doric pediment, dubiously imagined to be the tomb of Archimedes.

The Anfiteatro Romano

Keep hold of your ticket for entry to the **Anfiteatro Romano**, through a gate on the right as you leave the park: a large elliptical arena built in the third century AD to satisfy the growing lust for circus games. One hundred and forty metres long – one of the largest of its kind anywhere – it's encircled by a parapet inscribed with the names of some of the leading citizens of the time, though you're unlikely to get near enough to see this, as the interior is out of bounds (unless you're here for a performance; see p.295). The rectangular tank in the centre of the arena is too small to have been used for aquatic displays, and is more likely to have been for draining the blood and gore spilled in the course of the combats. But not before the spectators had had their fill: at the end of the contests the infirm, ill and disabled would apparently attempt to suck warm blood from the bodies and take the livers from the animals, in the belief that this would speed their recovery.

Out from the city: Epipolae, the Ciane River and Siracusa's beaches

If you're beginning to wilt under the combined onslaught of heat and crowds, Siracusa offers some good possibilities for **half-day trips** out of the centre. Each is a bus ride away, or, in the case of the Ciane River, a boat ride – though this last also makes a decent walk, once you get off the main road.

Epipolae and the Castello Eurialo

The outlying area of **EPIPOLAE**, 7km west of the city, holds ancient Siracusa's inland military and defensive works. To get here from the centre, take bus #11, #25 or #26 from Ortygia (#11 and #25 also from Corso Gelone outside the Parco Archeológico), to the village of **Belvedere**, a twenty-minute ride.

These heights were first fortified by Dionysius the Elder in about 400 BC, after the Athenians had come so close to taking the city by occupying them a few years previously. Constantly modified and extended over a couple of centuries, what remains today consists of a great wall, which marked the city's western limit, and the **Castello Eurialo** (daily 9am–1hr before sunset; free), just before the village on the right. The Euryalus castle is the major Greek fortification in the Mediterranean that's still standing, most of it dating from Hieron II's time, when **Archimedes**, as his General of Ordnance, must have been actively involved in its renovation. Despite the effort and ingenuity that went into making this site impregnable, the castle has no very glorious history: ignored altogether by the attacking Carthaginians, it surrendered without a fight to the Roman forces of Marcellus in 212 BC.

Assailants had to cope with three defensive trenches, designed to keep the new artillery of the time at bay, as well as siege-engines and battering rams. The first of the trenches (approached from the west, where you come in) was just within range of catapults mounted on the five towers of the castle's most impressive remain, the **keep**, while in the trench below the keep you can see the high piers supporting the drawbridge that once crossed it. All around here, long galleries burrow beneath the walls into the keep, serving as supply and escape routes, and also enabling the defenders to clear out (by night) the material thrown in by attackers during the day. Chambers were also dug out of the rock for use as storerooms and stables.

Behind the keep is a long, wedge-shaped fortification, to the north of which is the main gateway to the western quarter of the city. This, the **Epipolae gate**, was built indented from the walls, allowing the defenders to shower attackers with missiles, and is reminiscent of the main gate at Tyndaris (see p.151), a city that shared the same architects. The longest of the underground passages surfaces here, stretching 180m from the defensive trenches. From the gate, you can stroll along Dionysius' extensive walls, looking down over the oil refineries and tankers off the coast north of the city, and back over Siracusa itself, with Ortygia clearly visible pointing out into the sea.

Ciane and the Olympieion

Just south of the city, the **Ciane River** offers a good rustic excursion. The river's source is only 10km inland, forming a pool said to have been created by the tears of the nymph Cyane when her mistress Persephone was abducted into the underworld by Hades. The pool and the river banks are overgrown by thickets of **papyrus**, apparently the gift of Ptolemy Philadelphus of Egypt to Hieron II, making this the only place outside North Africa where the plant grows wild. Indeed, there's still a thriving papyrus industry in Siracusa, with gift shops on Ortygia selling painted scrolls and pictures.

You can get to the pool from Siracusa **by car**, taking the road for Canicattini Bagni at the end of Viale Paolo Orsi, and following the signs for about 5km. But if you want to make the trip **on foot**, following the lush river banks along a good path, take the #21, #22 or #23 from Piazza della Posta, getting off where the SS115 crosses the Ciane River (immediately after the Ánapo River, which runs parallel). It takes just over an hour from the main road, and this route allows you to drop in on the scant but evocative remains of the **Olympieion**, or Tempio di Giove Olimpico, a Doric temple built in the first half of the sixth century BC, of which only two columns and the stylobate remain. The hillock the ruin stands on was a vital strategic point in classical times and was often occupied by Siracusa's enemies when the city was under attack. The pestilential air of the Lysimelia marshes below saved the day on more than one occasion, infecting the hostile armies with malaria.

The most laid-back way to see both temple and pool is on one of the **boat cruises** which operate between early March and mid-November from the bridge over the Ciane, a couple of kilometres south of town, and reachable by car on the SS115 or on buses #21, #22 or #23 from Pizza della Posta. Just turn up at any time between 9.30am and 4.30pm for departures, or call ⓣ368.729.6040 or 0931.69.076. Tickets for the one-hour trip cost around €8 per person.

The beaches

Since the coast north of Siracusa has become an evil depository for noxious chemicals, the city's main **beaches** all lie to the south. **Bus** #23, from Piazza della Posta in Siracusa, goes direct to **ARENELLA**, the first of the beach resorts and the only sandy stretch in the area, though most of it consists of private lidos, and all can get horribly crowded. You might prefer the less populous stretches of rock further south, where the inlets create clear pools that are good for snorkelling. You can walk to these easily enough from Arenella, or else drive down the coast (or take bus #21, also from Piazza della Posta) to **OGNINA**, where there's a small fishing port and marina, and walk back a little way.

If you want to be sure of beautiful surroundings, though, it would be worth heading down a bit further south, to Fontane Bianche, 20km south of Siracusa; see p.301 for details.

Eating and drinking

There's no shortage of opportunities to spend money in Siracusa, either in the many sit-down bars with outdoor seating, or at a choice of **trattorias** and **restaurants**. Prices here are higher than in much of the rest of Sicily, but there's a great deal to be said for paying a little more to sit outside in a medieval street or courtyard and while the evening away over a beer or a pizza. On the whole, Ortygia has the best choice of eating places, many offering tourist menus at around €13 excluding drinks; every restaurant listed below, except *Al Castello Eurialo*, *Ristorante Jonico* and *Al Gambero Rosso*, is on the island. **Bars** are rather more widely scattered, though again, most of the best are on Ortygia: the main focus of evening drinking is little Piazzetta San Rocco and the streets around it.

Meal prices

The restaurants listed are graded according to the following price categories:
Inexpensive: under €15
Moderate: €15–30
Expensive: €30–50
Very expensive: over €50
These prices reflect the per person cost of a full meal including wine and cover charge; see p.53 for more details.

Inexpensive and moderate restaurants

L'Ancora di Giancarlo Russo Via Perno 7. Reasonable prices for excellent-quality fish – try the raw shrimp marinated in orange juice and onion, or *spaghetti ai ricci di mare*. Closed Mon. Moderate.

Archimede Via Gemmellaro 8. Signposted off the Piazza Archimede. A restaurant on one side of the street, a pizzeria on the other, with pizzas served in the restaurant as well (ask to see the menu). Provides good basic dishes, especially fish, and game when in season, to visitors and locals alike. Wash it all down with Corvo. Closed Sun. Moderate.

Aretusa Lungomare Alfeo. Slightly chaotic but good-humoured and reasonably priced seafood restaurant where you can sit outside with views across the Porto Grande. Also has an entrance on Via Castello Maniace, where it's called *Da Pasqualino*. Moderate.

Al Castello Eurialo Viale Epipoli 286. Busy and spacious *ristorante*-pizzeria out at Belvedere that attracts crowds of Siracusani every night during the summer, and has indoor and outdoor seating. It's by the entrance to the castle; take buses #11, #25 or #26 from Ortygia, a 20min ride. Closed Tues. Moderate.

Il Cenácolo Via del Consiglio Reginale 9–10. Signposted everywhere, this restaurant is north of Piazza del Duomo, down Via Landolina and off to the right, 100m or so down, set back in a little square. It's worth the effort to find since you can sit outside in the calm piazzetta, and there are tasty pizzas and a good choice of risottos. Grainy old pictures of Siracusa inside. Closed Wed. Moderate.

Al Gambero Rosso Via Eritrea 2. Excellent fish – and the meat's good too – on the very edge of the modern town just over the bridge from Ortygia. Moderate.

Pescomare Via Landolina 6. Just off Piazza del Duomo (the northern end), this offers succulent giant clams and other excellent fish and shellfish meals in an atmospheric, plant-filled old courtyard in summer, though the interior is rather less alluring in cooler periods. Closed Mon. Moderate.

La Siciliana Via Savoia 17. A no-frills pizzeria with a wood-fired oven and a choice of over fifty tasty pizzas from around €3.50, including the speciality *Siciliana*, a closed and fried variation of *calzone*. There are tables outside but the crawling lines of traffic are too close for comfort. No credit cards. Closed Mon. Inexpensive.

Spaghetteria do Scogghiu Via Domenico Scina 11. On an alley close to Piazza Archimede, this popular place has a long list of excellent, very reasonably priced and very generous plates of spaghetti, and a shorter menu of fish and meat dishes to follow. Service is fast and evenings can be rowdy. No smoking. No credit cards. Closed Mon. Inexpensive.

Expensive restaurants

Ristorante Darsena Riva Garibaldi 6 ℡0931.66.104. Overlooking the fishing-boats at the northwestern end of Ortygia, this fish restaurant is a popular Sunday-lunch spot, with a large, conservatory-like dining room. The *spaghetti alla vongole*, with fresh clams, is excellent, or you can eat more expensively from the fish and shellfish on display at the front of the restaurant. Closed Wed. Expensive.

Don Camillo Via della Maestranza 96. Refined restaurant in the fifteenth-century vaults of a former convent, serving wonderful seafood. Try the exemplary *consommé di pesce*, or, if there are enough of you, a whole fish baked inside a crust of golden bread (order in advance). Popular with local politicos from the nearby *Comune*. Has Siracusa's finest wine cellar as well. Closed for a week or so in July. Very expensive.

Ristorante Jonico Riviera Dionisio Il Grande 194 ℡0931.655.40. Siracusa's best restaurant, perched above the sea in the Santa Lucia district, north of Ortygia. The menu is written entirely in dialect, but the owner speaks enough English to guide you through the superb Sicilian specialities

– pasta with fresh tuna, or, a specifically Siracusan dish, spaghetti with dried breadcrumbs, olive oil and parsley. Grilled fish and local desserts complete the meal, which – if you eat your way through the menu – will cost up to €40, though you could eat well enough for around €30. It's best to reserve a table before trekking out here: take bus #2 or #3 from Piazza della Posta to the *Villa Politi* hotel, from where it's a 3min walk, or it's a 25min walk up the Riviera from the Foro Siracusano. Closed Tues. Expensive.

Minosse Via Mirabella 6 ☏ 0931.66.366. In a narrow street off the Corso Matteotti, and once visited by the pope (as advertised by photos on the walls), this place provides deferential service and ample portions; try the seafood salad (*insalata di mare*). Closed Mon in winter. Expensive.

Bars and cafés

Bar Bonomo Corso Gelone 48. Announced by the smell of fresh bread, this bar on the way to Neapolis has its own bakery making fresh rolls, *arancini*, pizza and cakes; the ice cream is also good.

Bar Ortigia Largo Aretusa 2–3. A large bar-*gelateria* right by the fountain with video games, cocktails, good ice cream and snacks. Seats outside in the square, too.

Bar Viola Corso Matteotti 51. Small bar, set apart from other buildings on this main Ortygia street, serving famous ice cream (with optional extra cream), as well as cakes, sweets and pastries. Closed Mon.

Biuo Via delle Vergine 16. Commercial house and pop, for a young and (as the name implies) noisy set. Round the corner from Piazzetta San Rocco.

Doctor Sam Piazzetta San Rocco 4. The Piazzetta is at the hub of Ortygia's night-scene and this pub, universally known as *Lele's*, is a popular hangout for classic rock fans. Nice food at lunchtime, with tables outside.

La Piazza Duomo Piazza del Duomo. Bar-cum-*gelateria*-cum-*pasticceria* with a daunting array of free nibbles and low prices that belie the superb location.

Les Crêpes Via Castello Maniace 9. Off Largo Aretusa, an intimate pub with wooden tables and an assortment of bottled and draught beers. You can munch on salads, panini, bruschetta and (of course) crêpes.

Lungo la Notte Lungomare Alfeo. Just off Largo Aretusa, this modish wine bar and restaurant attracts an elegant clientele, but is magnificently sited overlooking the harbour. It's only open in the evening.

Minerva Via Minerva 13. Facing the side of the Duomo, this is a good place for coffee or cocktails, with tables outside.

Pub San Rocco Piazzetta San Rocco 6. Chillout music and house, DJs at weekends and tables outside all week on one of the most atmospheric – and liveliest – piazzas in town.

Sale Corte dei Bottai, Via della Amalfitania. Elegant and relaxed wine bar in a lovely old courtyard in the heart of Ortygia. Also owned by Lele of *Doctor Sam* fame.

Spizzica Via Castello Maniace 8. In a prime position close to the Fonte Aretusa, it does a mean *latte di mandorla*, as well as food. Closed Mon.

Voglia Matta Corso Umberto 34. A superb *gelateria* near the Ponte Nuovo, with an incredible range of ice cream, and usually buzzing with contented customers. Closed Thurs.

Entertainment: puppet shows, theatre and concerts

If you're looking for other evening diversions in Siracusa, look for posters or enquire at the tourist office about **puppet shows**, in which you can follow the swashbuckling adventures of Orlando and his pals. The performances generally take place in summer only, in piazzas or small theatres on Ortygia. Fans can also see the collection of puppets, props and various related articles at Via Giudecca 17, off Via Maestranza, the stock in trade of the Vaccaro family, Siracusa's puppeteers; it's usually open in the evenings, and mornings in summer too.

The tourist office can also fill you in on the possibility of seeing **Greek plays** staged by the venerable Istituto Nazionale Dramma Antico at the Teatro Greco (early May to June Tues–Sun only) in the Parco Archeológico, one of Sicily's finest venues; tickets start at around €15 for whatever bench-space you can find at the back, increasing to €25 for numbered seats, and €35 for seats right in front of the action, though look out for special reductions on specified days. For more information or to buy tickets in advance, go to ⓦwww.indafondazione.org. Throughout July and August **concerts** are also held in the Anfiteatro Romano, including jazz, opera and ballet, often attracting big names, with seats at €8–15. For further information about what's on in and around Siracusa, pick up the listings pamphlet *Zero* from bars around town.

Listings

Banks Banco di Sicilia, Piazza Archimede; Banca Nazionale del Lavoro, Corso Umberto; Banca Commerciale Italiana, Via Savoia. All change travellers' cheques and cash, have cashpoints (ATMs), and open roughly Mon–Fri 8.30am–1.30pm & 2.45–3.45pm.

Boat trips Daily in summer around the city's harbours on the boat *Selene*: departures are from Ortygia's Riva della Posta, and trips cost €5.20 per person. Call ⓣ368.317.0/11 for more info, or visit ⓦ www.ortigiatour.cjb.net.

Buses AST, at Piazza (or Riva) della Posta ⓣ0931.464.820 (for Augusta, Lentini, Catania, Cómiso, Íspica, Módica, Noto, Palazzolo Acréide, Ragusa, Sortino and Vittória); Interbus, at Via Trieste 28 ⓣ0931.66.710 (for Catania, Noto, Pachino, Palermo and Taormina).

Car rental Bingo Viaggi, Via Maestranza 37 ⓣ0931.468.022; Maggiore, Via Pausania 6 ⓣ0931.66.548.

Car repairs ACI, Foro Siracusano 27 ⓣ0931.66.656.

First aid Call ⓣ113.

Hospital Ospedale Civile, Via Testaferrata ⓣ8000.130.09.

Internet access Adelph bookshop, Corso Umberto 106 (Mon–Sat 9am–8.30pm, also Sun 3–9pm in summer); L'Antico Mercato di Ortygia, Via Trento 2 (ⓣ0931.449.201; Mon–Wed

11am–3pm, Thurs–Sun 11am–3pm & 6.30–11pm) also has free left luggage, bar, *gelateria* and food; and W@W, Via Roma 16 (daily 10am–10pm).

Left luggage There's an office at the train station (daily 7am–11pm). See also above.

Market There's a general market every morning from Monday to Saturday, at Via Trento near the Tempio di Apollo; it merges with the food market at Via de Benedictus.

Pharmacies Farmacia Centrale, Via Maestranza 42 (ⓣ0931.65320); and Gibiino, Via Roma 79 (ⓣ0931.65760).

Police The Questura is north of the centre at Viale Scala Greca 248 ⓣ0931.495.144.

Post office The main post office is at Piazza delle Poste 15 (Mon–Sat 8am–7.30pm).

Supermarkets Linguanti, Corso Umberto 1; or Famila, at Viale Teracati 34, which takes credit cards.

Telephones The main Telecom Italia office is at Viale Teracati 42, close to the Parco Archeológico (8am–midnight). At night (8pm–8am), use the phones at the *Bar Bel Caffè*, Piazza Marconi 18.

Train information ⓣ892.021.

Travel agents Paparoni-Lacagnina, Corso Umberto 76 ⓣ0931.463.588; Zuccalà, Viale Epipoli 136 ⓣ0931.740.732.

North: the coast to Augusta

The coast **north of Siracusa**, the **Golfo di Augusta**, has been defaced by some of the ugliest industry you'll see in Sicily, filling the air with acrid fumes and the sea with chemicals. These mammoth plants employ one-tenth of Siracusa's population, but the scale of this industrial zone – one of the largest concentrations of chemical plants in Europe – has effectively obliterated the coast from any other point of view. Oil tankers hover offshore, while people living in some of the coastal villages have been evacuated and their houses destroyed, their places taken by a mesh of pipes and containers that will seem all too close if you're travelling this route by train. It casts a foul shadow (and smell) over the area's ancient sites: the Bronze Age tombs of Thapsos on the besieged peninsula of Magnisi are closed off now, and the extensive remains of **Megara Hyblaea** are hidden behind a barrage of alien development, though you can still fight your way through to visit them. Beyond, **Augusta** thrives as an industrial port but preserves a fine Baroque centre, with beaches to the north just out of reach of the emissions. If you're using **public transport**, you'll find that Augusta is easily reachable by bus or train, but you'll need your own vehicle to get to Megara Hyblaea, or take a taxi (25min out of Siracusa; around €40).

Megara Hyblaea

Although the earliest settlers of the site of **Megara Hyblaea** were Neolithic, it was as a Greek colony that the town prospered, after the Sikel king of Hybla had granted land alongside his own to Greeks from Megara (near Athens). By the mid-seventh century BC, the population had done so well out of trade and their high-quality pottery that they were able to found some minor colonies of their own, including Selinus (see p.421), though their city was eventually submerged by Syracusan ambitions and destroyed by Gelon in 482 BC. In the middle of the fourth century BC, the site was resettled and the town flourished again, until it was finally levelled by the Romans in the same avenging campaign that ended Syracuse's independence in 214 BC.

Most of the ruins you'll see at the **site** (daily 9am–1hr before sunset; free) belong to the fourth-century revival, but the fortifications were erected a century later, interrupted by the Romans' arrival. Various buildings – temples, baths, the marketplace – lie confusingly scattered over a wide area, though this is considered to be the most complete model of an Archaic city still surviving. All the finds, however, including some marvellous examples of statuary, are in Siracusa's Museo Archeológico (see p.287).

Augusta and its beaches

Despite **AUGUSTA**'s superficial resemblance to Siracusa – its old centre detached from the mainland on its own islet, surrounded by two harbours – the port has never attained the same importance and didn't even exist until 1232. Frederick II, who founded the town, characteristically stamped his own personality on it in the form of a castle, though everything else of the medieval town was entirely destroyed by the 1693 earthquake. What's left is a handsome – though crumbling – Baroque centre with several restaurants and a decent hotel; a relief after the rampant industrialization all around.

You can't miss the **castello** that dominates the causeway leading onto the island, though you're unlikely to get inside: used for years as a prison, it's now awaiting conversion into a war museum. The **Villa Comunale** below is a shady public garden through which all traffic is channelled, including the promenaders who overflow into here from the long and narrow main street, Via Príncipe Umberto. On both sides of the gardens are views out to sea: on one side over the port and tankers; on the other, to the headland. A few blocks down Via Príncipe Umberto is a piazza holding the eighteenth-century Duomo (now shored up by scaffolding) and a solemn **Palazzo Comunale**, its facade crowned by Frederick II's imperial eagle.

The beaches: Monte Tauro and Brúcoli

If you've got time to explore the **coast to the north**, you'll come across resorts with some decent swimming and a couple of **campsites**. The nearest of these is *A'Massaria* (☎0931.983.078; May–Oct), in **MONTE TAURO**, reachable by hourly bus from Augusta's Villa Comunale. Much nicer, though, and open all year, is the *Baia del Silenzio* (☎0931.981.881), a little further on and overlooking a pretty bay: take the Brúcoli bus (also from the Villa Comunale), get off at the signpost before the town and walk the 2km to the site. **BRÚCOLI** itself is a small resort with a restored fifteenth-century castle and ominous "Bathing prohibited" signs on account of a nearby sewage outflow. It's a good spot for lunch, though, with an amenable fish **restaurant**, *Al Castello*, right on the sea (closed Wed except in summer).

Practicalities

From Augusta's train station, it takes fifteen minutes to walk to the castle and town centre. If you want to stay over, the best-value hotel is the *Villa Marina*, 2km from the town centre on the road to Monte Pergola (℡0931.983800; ❸), close to the sea; take any bus marked Villa Marina.

Augusta has a poor selection of **restaurants**. There are some bars and touristy trattorias with outdoor seating on Piazza Castello, but you can eat better in a couple of places off Via Umberto, which leads off from here: turn left at Via San Lorenzo for good pizzas and other basic dishes at the inexpensive *Pizzeria Poiana* (closed Tues & Aug), or turn right a little further down at Via Roma for *I Siciliani*, a smarter trattoria with tasty antipasti and other moderately priced local dishes (closed Fri). Otherwise, take your choice among a crop of drinks bars, mostly on or around Via XIV Ottobre (parallel to Via Umberto), where you can find panini and chips to go with your beers. The same road, incidentally, behind the Duomo, holds Augusta's daily morning **market**, where you can pick up bread, fruit and veg. For breakfast, the bar-*pasticceria* at the bottom of Via Umberto is a good bet, opposite the Villa Comunale.

Inland: Pantálica and Palazzolo Acréide

These are two separate day-trips you can make **inland from Siracusa**, both lying in the folds of the **Monti Iblei**. This is a dramatic landscape, crossed by dry-stone walls and dotted with small villages springing the odd surprise – a crumbly church or an inviting trattoria. Whatever time you spend at the necropolis of **Pantálica** will be mainly taken up by wandering the deep gorge through which the Ánapo River runs. The refreshing walks hereabouts draw strollers and weekend picnickers from all over the region, though the chief interest is the presence of several thousand tombs hollowed out of the valley sides. A short ride southwest of here, **Palazzolo Acréide** is a mainly Baroque town with a compact Greek and Roman site lying just outside, one of the most interesting of the province's classical sites.

Pantálica

Around 40km west of Siracusa, **PANTÁLICA** is Sicily's greatest necropolis, first used between the thirteenth and the tenth century BC by Sikel refugees from the coast. After the eighth century BC, this plateau is thought to have been the site of Hybla, whose king invited Megarian Greeks to colonize first Thapsos and then Megara Hyblaea; there are visible remains from this era, but all pale into insignificance in contrast to the five thousand or so tombs hewn out of the gorge below. Several skeletons were found in each tomb, suggesting that a few thousand people once lived in the vicinity.

The plateau rises between the River Ánapo and its northern tributary, the Calcinara, and can be approached on foot from either end of the gorge. The **approaches** are from the villages of Sortino, 5km from the gorge, or Ferla, 9km away. Both places are linked to Siracusa by **bus**, though Sortino has far more connections, with a last departure back to Siracusa at 6.30pm.

Getting there: from Sortino

AST buses to **SORTINO** (daily except Sun) leave Siracusa from Piazza della Posta and the journey takes around an hour; the earliest departures are at 7am, 8.15am and 10am. You're dropped on, or close to, the central Piazza G. Verga and signs throughout the sprawling village point towards Pantálica. Your best bet is first to find an **alimentari** and get a sandwich made up: there's nowhere on the way to buy anything to eat or drink. Even without the sun, you'll get through a litre of **water** walking both ways: in the height of summer, take as much water as you can carry. Once you're clear of Sortino (about 5min), the road drops steeply downhill, passing the roofless fifteenth-century ruin of Santa Sofia after 1km, and then climbing across the valley to the gorge. It takes around an hour to reach the end of the road and the entrance to the gorge – about twenty minutes from the entrance, you'll have your first view over the rock-cut tombs. If you're driving, you can park just before the site entrance.

The site

At the **entrance** (always open; free) an obvious path leads through the gorge, around the **northern cemetery**, down to the river and up the other side. You'll soon see the **tombs**, first just dotting the walls of the valley in clusters and finally puncturing the whole cliff face; at times the tombs are very close to the path. They were dug out of the vertical cliff walls, and the sheer number of them creates an eerie impression. In some were found the traces of several separate skeletons, probably of the same family, and others show evidence of habitation – though much later, when the Syracusans themselves were forced to flee inland from barbarian incursions. The atmosphere is primeval and almost sinister – for Vincent Cronin, even something terrifying: "Here is Sicily of the stone age, intent on nothing higher than the taking of food and the burial of its dead." For Cronin, the free play of nature in this ravine embodied Sicily's own particular contribution to the man-made wonders bestowed later by the island's conquerors, and as such – symbolized by a honeycomb he came across in one of the caves – the object of the quest described in his book, *The Golden Honeycomb*.

From the Sortino side it takes thirty minutes to walk through this stretch of the gorge: there are superb views from the higher reaches and the path and rock-cut steps remain good all the way. Once across the river and up the other side of the gorge, the road begins again and runs west, all the way to Ferla (see below). Even if you're planning to return to Sortino, continue along the road for a while. It climbs up past the remains of a Villagio Bizantino (there's nothing to see) and a lookout point across the section you've just walked; after 25 minutes or so, on top of the plateau, a side road leads off to the left to the rectangular foundations of a building from ancient Hybla: the **Anaktoron**, or prince's palace, with a few stretches of wall nearby. There's a signposted path, below the Anaktoron, leading back into the gorge, to the **south cemetery**, a 1.5-kilometre walk with more visible rock tombs at the end as your reward.

Returning to the road, you can then either head on to Ferla (around 8km to the west), or **return to Sortino**. If the latter is your plan, reckon on it taking three hours from the Anaktoron back to Sortino, aiming for the last return bus to Siracusa at 6.30pm. Note that buses from Sortino's Piazza G. Verga also run twice daily to Catania (not Sun).

Ferla

FERLA is prettier than Sortino, possessing a good **trattoria**, *Dell'Arco*, with a terrace at the back, in its Piazza San Sebastiano, as well as a stately church nearby – overrun with weeds – and surroundings planted with fruit trees. It also has a **B&B**, *Pantálica*, close to the Porta di Pantálica (☎0931.870.147; ❷), where you'll have to stay if you're relying on public transport, as the AST bus leaves Siracusa at 2pm, and doesn't return until 6.55am the following morning. The owners of the B&B can also arrange transport to Pantálica for a small charge. For more help and information call in at the **tourist office**, Via Gramsci 13 (☎338.245.0898). From Ferla there are two roads into the gorge, though the lower road is closed to all private traffic. Along the upper road, the basic *Ristorante Pantálica* sells a map of Pantálica.

Palazzolo Acréide

Lying on a hill some 18km south of Ferla, **PALAZZOLO ACRÉIDE** is the modern successor of the Greek colony of Akrai, founded in the middle of the seventh century BC by Syracuse in its first drive inland. The remains of the ancient town lie just outside the modern settlement, a twenty-minute walk. Both occupy the higher slopes of a promontory once strategically commanding routes inland, now somewhat stranded from the main road and rail links crossing the province. It's a good excursion, though, enabling you to wander the town's knot of small Baroque streets before visiting the site.

Palazzolo's main square, **Piazza del Pópolo**, is the heart of the Baroque town, two sides dominated by the handsome church of San Sebastiano and the town hall. From here lanes radiate down past opulent facades and gargoyled balconies, eventually leading to a trio of fine Baroque churches, the Chiesa Madre, San Paolo and the Annunziata. But the main focus of interest in this part of town – at least for anyone curious about the roots of Sicilian culture – is the **Casa-Museo di Antonino Uccello** (daily 9am–1pm & 3.30–7pm; free), tucked away in an old house at Via Machiavelli 19. The fruit of one man's thirty-year obsession to root out and preserve the traditions of rural Sicily, this varied collection of 5000 objects constitutes eastern Sicily's most important documentation of folk art, showing trousseaux, ceramics, olive presses, puppets,

reconstructions of houses and stables, and anything else judged by Uccello to be in danger of extinction. There's lots more scattered about the rambling rooms, though without some knowledge of Italian, the labelling and guide's explanations won't mean much.

Akrai: the ancient city

Syracuse chose the site of **Akrai**, its first inland colony, well; it dominated the trade routes into the interior, particularly the Via Selinuntina to Akragas. The city thrived during the peace and security that characterized Hieron II's reign in the third century BC, though it declined under the Romans, later re-emerging as an important early Christian centre (as shown by the number of rock-cut tombs in the area), only to be eventually destroyed by the Arabs.

Of the ancient city's visible remains at the **Zona Archeológica** (daily 9am–1hr before sunset, but sometimes also closed at lunchtime; free), most complete is the small **Teatro Greco**, built towards the end of Hieron's reign and modified by the Romans. A perfect semicircle, the theatre held six hundred people and retains traces of its scene-building. Behind the theatre to the right is a small **senate-house**, or *bouleuterion*, a rectangular construction that was originally covered. Beyond is a 200-metre stretch of *decumanus* that once connected the two gates of the city (Porta Siracusana and Porta Selinuntina). Crossed at regular intervals by junctions and paved in lavic rock, it's in better condition than many of the more recent roads in the area.

The rest of the site isn't as clearly defined and other remains give little impression of their former grandeur. You'll have a job identifying the excavated Roman **Tempio di Persefone**, above the theatre, an unusually round chamber that was formerly covered by a cupola. Equally fragmentary is the much older **Tempio di Afrodite**, sixth- or fifth-century BC, lying at the head of what was the *agora*. From here you can look straight down into one of the two quarries from which the stone to build the city was taken. Later they were converted into Christian burial chambers, and in the first of them, the **Intagliata**, you can plainly see the recesses in the walls: some of them catacombs, others areas of worship, the rest simply rude dwellings cut in the Byzantine era. The narrower, deeper quarry below it, the **Intagliatella**, has more votive niches and a relief cut from the rock-face, over 2m long, that combines a typically Greek scene – heroes banqueting – and a Roman one of heroes offering sacrifice. It's thought to date from the first century BC.

There are more niches and chambers in a lower quarry, the **Templi Ferali**, though you'll have to ask the custodian to let you see this, along with the much more interesting **Santoni** further down (a 15min walk from the site). If it's a slack day and he can't be bothered to make the trip, you may well be told that they are "closed". It's a shame, since these twelve rock-cut sculptures are of a fertility goddess, Cybele, a predominantly eastern deity whose origins are steeped in mystery. Certainly there's no other example of so rich a complex relating to her worship, and the local name tagged to these sculptures – *santoni*, or "great saints" – suggests that the awe attached to them survived until relatively recently. Carved no later than the third century BC, the rough, weathered images are protected in individual locked shelters; they represent the Magna Mater seated, attended by priests, lions and other deities.

Practicalities

Buses from Siracusa pull up in the main square, Piazza del Pópolo, across from which – next to the church – the *Bar Canguro* is handy for snacks and drinks. There are plenty of good **places to eat** in town, including the *Barocco*, at Via

Duca d'Aosta 27 (closed Wed), just down from the piazza. If you fancy a quiet alternative to staying in Siracusa – and Palazzolo can be dead as a doornail at night – there's a good **hotel**, the simple *Santoro*, just below Piazza del Pópolo at Via San Sebastiano 21 (℗0931.883.855; ❷). Alternatively, if you have your own transport, try the agriturismo *Fattoria Giannavi* (0931.881.776; ❷), 8km from Palazzola in Contrada Giannavi, a farm with rooms and a restaurant serving home-grown, home-cooked food.

South: to Fontane Bianche and Ávola

It's not until you reach **FONTANE BIANCHE**, 20km south of Siracusa, that the coast comes into its own: the wide arc of sand here provides some of the best swimming on this part of the coast. Buses #21 and #22 leave Piazza della Posta in Siracusa every hour or so (last one at around 8.15pm) for the thirty-minute journey. Along with a number of bars and pizzerias, this popular resort has a good **campsite**, *Fontane Bianche* (℗0931.790.333; May–Oct), just a short walk from the beach, though surprisingly there are no hotels. The superb beaches get very crowded in July and August, but don't expect a lot of action here outside that period. There is one free public beach (signposted *spiaggia libera* near the car park), but all the others are private lidos, which charge around €2.50 per day in summer and at weekends, plus extra for renting deck chairs, parasols and pedalos. In summer, pop concerts take place on a stage at the southern end of the beach.

Slightly inland of here, and about 4km to the north on the SS115, the non-descript town of **Cassíbile** is known to Italians as the place where, in an olive yard on September 3, 1943, generals Bedell-Smith and Castellano signed the armistice that took Italy out of the Axis alliance in World War II.

Ávola

The main road (and railway) continues on another 10km south to **ÁVOLA**. This agricultural town has an old Baroque centre, partly reconstructed on a hexagonal design after earthquake damage. An idea of its erstwhile proportions can be gleaned in the huge central Piazza Umberto, the square and long main Corso Vittorio Emanuele lined with forlorn *palazzi*, slowly crumbling away. There's a small **Museo Cívico** at Piazza Umberto 17, containing finds from Thapsos, Pantálica and the pre-earthquake town – if you're lucky, you'll get in, though it's been closed for "renovations" for as long as anyone can remember.

The **train station** is at the top of the corso; **buses** drop you halfway down, on Piazza Vittorio Véneto, with Piazza Umberto another five minutes' walk down the corso. Glinting in the distance is the sea and the seaside settlement of **ÁVOLA MARINA**, a two-kilometre walk straight downhill from the square. Most **eating places** down here are seasonal, though one of the best is open all year, *La Ola*, a large bar-restaurant right on the beach with a very good-value tourist menu: turn left when you reach the water and it's about 700m along.

If you're driving, you can reach the magnificent gorge and nature reserve of the **Cava Grande** by following the main road north out of Ávola for about 15km, past the signpost marked "Convento di Ávola Vecchia". Look out for signs for the belvedere along this road, where you can park and either just admire the circling birds of prey, or follow the footpath down to the pool below; here the path will take you alongside the River Cassíbile for most of the gorge's 11km (allow 3hr for the return trip).

Noto

Six kilometres beyond Ávola, and the same distance inland, **NOTO** represents the apogee of the wholesale renovation that took place following the cataclysm of 1693, a monument to the achievement of a few architects and planners whose vision coincided with the golden age of Baroque architecture. Although there existed a town called Noto, or Netum, in this area for centuries, what you see today is in effect a "New Town", conceived as a triumphant symbol of renewal.

Noto was flattened on January 11, 1693, and a week later its **rebuilding** was entrusted to a Sicilian-Spanish aristocrat, Giuseppe Lanza, Duke of Camastra, on the strength of his work at the town of Santo Stéfano di Camastra, on the Tyrrhenian coast. Lanza visited the ruins, saw nothing but "un montón de pie-dras abandonadas" (a mountain of forsaken rocks), and quickly decided to start afresh, on a new site 16km to the south. In fact, the ruins weren't abandoned; the city's battered population was already improvising a shantytown, and even held a referendum when Lanza's intentions became known, rejecting the call to relocate their city. But partly motivated by the prestige of the undertaking, partly by the need to refurbish the area's defences, Lanza ignored the local feel-ing, even pulling down their new constructions and the old town's remaining church. With the help of the Flemish military engineer Carlos de Grunemburg, Lanza devised a revolutionary new plan, based on two quarters – one for the political and religious establishment, the other for the people – which were to be almost completely separated from each other. The best architects were to be used: Vincenzo Sinatra, Paolo Labisi and the master craftsman Rosario Gagliardi – not innovators, but men whose enthusiasm and experience enabled them to concoct a graceful synthesis of the latest architectural skills and forms. Their collaboration was so complete that it's still difficult to ascribe some buildings to any one person. Within an astonishingly short time the work was completed: a new city, planned with the accent on symmetry and visual harmony, from its simple street plan to the lissom figures adorning its buildings. It's easily the most successful post-earthquake creation and, for a time, in the mid-nineteenth century, the new Noto replaced Siracusa as the region's provincial capital.

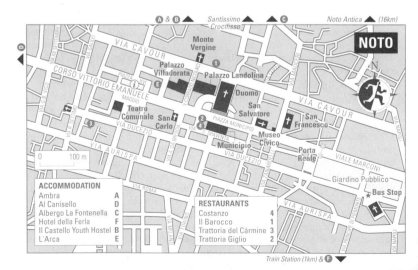

The twentieth century saw a deterioration of the town, mainly due to the traffic that thunders through. The local Iblean stone, so workable and suitable for delicate carving, is also highly fragile; but it was not until 1987 that belated restoration work was begun: heavy traffic was diverted round the outskirts of town and corroded ornamentation subjected to a thorough cleaning. Long before this was complete, however, a new disaster afflicted the Duomo, when the cupola suddenly collapsed in March 1996. The whole building is likely to be sheathed in scaffolding for years to come, and many of the other buildings are also subject to intermittent renovation work – a tragedy in a city where the visual aspect is so important – but it's still worth the visit.

Around the town

The centre is best approached through the monumental **Porta Reale**, built in 1838 and topped by the three symbols of the town's allegiance to the Bourbon monarchy: a dog, a tower and a pelican (respectively, loyalty, strength and sacrifice). The **Corso Vittorio Emanuele**, which leads off from here, runs through the heart of the lower, patricians' quarter and is lined with some of Sicily's most captivating buildings. All are a rich honey colour – starting with Vincenzo Sinatra's formal-looking church of **San Francesco** (1704), to the right, its facade rather dulled by the more flamboyant **Convento del Santíssimo Salvatore** next door. Part of this convent houses the **Museo Cívico**, on the corner, containing finds from Greek coastal sites and material from Noto Antica, but it's been closed for years and is unlikely to open in the near future.

A little way up is what is arguably Sicily's finest piazza. Perfectly proportioned, the tree-planted **Piazza del Municipio** is the elegant heart of the town and contains its noblest buildings. Unfortunately, its centrepiece, the imposing twin-towered **Duomo**, is still under long-term repair after the collapse of its dome. This was precipitated by a heavy thunderstorm, but was really the cumulative result of inadequate repair work in the past and the soft quality of the stone. Completed in 1776, it's said to have been inspired by models of Borromini's churches in Rome, but now it's a good example of the inadequacy of the Italian bureaucratic system; with delays in even the first stages of the restoration work, no one can venture a guess as to when it will be back to its former glory. Opposite, the **Municipio** (or Palazzo Ducezio) is again the work of Vincenzo Sinatra, flanked by its own green spaces, the arcaded building presenting a lovely, convex front of columns and long stone balconies. To the west of the Duomo, on Via C. Nicolaci, the **Palazzo Villadorata** is an eccentric piece of work. Onto a strictly classical front six extravagant balconies were grafted, supported by the last word in sculpted buttresses – a panoply of griffins, galloping horses and bald and bearded figures with fat-cheeked cherubs at their bellies. The *palazzo* is open for guided visits (daily 10am–1pm & 3–7pm; €3), though there is just one room, the Salone delle Feste, where the faded scraps of wallpaper begin to hint at its one-time splendour; this also offers stunning views over the town. The rest of the tour comprises the cellars where you can see traces of the local settlement which pre-dated eighteenth-century Noto. If this fails to inspire, you can savour even better panoramic views from the top of the belltower of the church of **San Carlo**, back on the corso at the bottom of Via Nicolaci (daily 9am–1pm & 4–8pm or 3–7pm in winter; €1.50).

There's a lot more pleasure to be had out of Noto by straying off into the side streets on either side of Corso Vittorio Emanuele, or down the corso to Piazza XVI Maggio and Noto's food **market** (Mon morning, plus first and third Tues of the month 8.30am–1.30pm). The square is also the home of

Noto's **Teatro Comunale** (☎0931.896.655; daily 8.30am–1.30pm & 3–8pm; €1), which you can peek into if there are no rehearsals or evening performances underway to admire its richly decorated auditorium, dating from 1860. It's most impressive when it's full of people, for which you'd have to come to a play or concert (Oct–April).

Don't leave without visiting the upper part of town, filled with massive monastic houses and the dwellings of Noto's poorer eighteenth-century citizens. They had their own church, Gagliardi's **Santíssimo Crocifisso**, in Piazza Mazzini. Never completed, the church preserves some treasures from the old town, including a magnificent pair of Romanesque lions, and *Madonna of the Snow*, carved in 1471, the only statue in Sicily actually signed by the master sculptor Francesco Laurana (it's behind the altar on the right-hand side). The church is currently closed for restoration work.

Noto Antica

If you've got a car, you could venture out to see the sparse remains of **NOTO ANTICA**, 16km northwest of town, up the SS287. Until finally abandoned in 1693, the town had several times been a significant historical stronghold – one of the few Sicilian towns to resist the looting of the Roman praetor Verres and the last bastion of Arab Sicily before the Normans arrived. After passing the convent of Santa Maria delle Scale, turn left and pass through the gate of a castle. The visible remnants of the old town are confined to bits of wall and the bric-a-brac held in a makeshift museum at the **Éremo della Madonna della Providenza**. There should be someone around to let you in; it's free, but not very exciting.

Practicalities

From Siracusa, it's around half an hour's journey to Noto by hourly buses or (less frequently) by train. The **bus** will drop you at the Giardino Púbblico at the eastern end of town, close to the Porta Reale; the **train station** is ten minutes' walk away down Via Príncipe di Piemonte; the bus for Pachino (see p.306) leaves from outside Noto's train station. Get free maps and information from the **tourist office** in Piazza XVI Maggio, behind the Hercules fountain (April–Sept Mon–Fri 8am–2pm & 3.30–6.30pm, Sat 9am–noon & 3.30–6.30pm; ☎0931.836.744).

First choice for **accommodation** is the charming *Albergo della Fontanella*, Via Pilo Rosolino 3 (☎0931.894.724, ⓦwww.albergolafontanella.it; ❺), in a restored nineteenth-century *palazzo* on the edge of the old town. If it is full, try the pristine, modern *Hotel della Ferla*, Via Gramsci 5 (☎0931 576.007; ❻), on the edge of the old town, or ask the tourist office about **rented rooms** (around €65 per night for two people), some of which have private bathrooms and cooking facilities. The most convenient options are the friendly and cheerfully furnished *L'Arca*, in the centre of the town at Via Rocco Pirri 14, off Corso Vittorio Emanuele (☎0931.894.202, ⓕ0931.573.360, ⓦwww.notobarocca .com/arcarooms); *Al Canisello* at Via Cesare Pavese 1 (☎0931.835.793); and *Ambra* at Via Francesco Giantommaso 14 (☎0931.835.554) – the last two are about a fifteen-minute walk from the centre. There is also a **youth hostel**, *Il Castello*, housed in a renovated *palazzo* in the upper town, at Via Fratelli Bandiera (☎0931.571.534). Its facilities are pristine, and there are large, clean dormitories, excellent showers and wonderful views over the town. Dorm beds cost €14.50 with breakfast, €13 without. It's accessible from the centre in a few minutes up signposted steps from Via Cavour, behind the Duomo (drivers must work their way round from Via Coffa, off Via Cavour). Alternatively, you could stay at Noto Marina, a small coastal resort 8km to the southeast, where there are several holiday hotels, though these may be booked up in summer; check with the tourist office about vacancies.

If you want a **meal**, *Trattoria Giglio*, in the corner of Piazza del Municipio, is a cheap and cheerful place for lunch, with dishes such as clam and mussel soup; while the small, excellent-value *Trattoria del Cármine*, Via Ducezio 1 (closed Mon), serves popular *cucina casalinga* including twenty different types of vegetable. Behind the Duomo, at Via Cavour 8, *Il Barocco*, housed in an old stables, is also a decent choice, with a small internal garden and a tourist menu for €8. Just down the steps from the *Giglio*, behind the Municipio at Via Silvio Spaventa 7–11, *Costanzo* is a famous **bar**-*gelateria*, known for its locally made sweets and pastries.

For **renting bikes** (€8 a day) or **scooters** (€25 a day), try Allakatalla, Largo Porta Reale (℡0931.836.021, ✉info@allakatalla.it), who also offer **guided tours** and **left luggage**.

The coastal route to Sicily's southern cape

Trains no longer run south from Noto, and if you're travelling **down the coast** you'll have to take the hourly Interbus bus from Siracusa/Noto to Pachino. It's quite easy to reach Eloro by foot from Noto Marina, to which there are frequent buses; otherwise you'll have to go by taxi. If you have a car, though, you'll be able to stop off at some of the more remote beaches along the way.

Eloro and Torre Vendícari

First stop out of Noto, 8–9km to the southeast, are the seaside ruins of Helorus, or **Eloro** (daily 9am–1.30pm; free). This Syracusan colony, founded in the seventh century BC at the mouth of the Tellaro River, is still being excavated, but the small site can be viewed quite easily through the fence even when closed. There are some city walls, a small theatre and a sanctuary dedicated to Demeter and Kore, with the remains of a *stoa*, or portico. It's all very ramshackle, and made all the more attractive by its position right on the rocky shore. The broad expanse of sand alongside also offers **good swimming**, though access is tricky from the site: best option for drivers is to take the next road along that leads directly to the beach.

If you're driving, there's another secluded **beach** 5–6km further south, at the **Torre Vendícari**, an abandoned Norman tower overlooking a crescent of sand that's hidden behind some disused saltpans. It's signposted off the new road running down the coast to Pachino: turn left over a narrow railway bridge and keep an eye open for the tower. A nature reserve here preserves the area from development, though there is one first-class place to **stay** here, *Il Roveto* (℡0931.66.024, 🌐www.roveto.it; ❹), a beautifully restored old farmhouse offering agriturismo in self-contained apartments sleeping up to six people (the rate above is for two). It's very close to the pristine beach, and can provide fruit, vegetables, wine and excellent olive oil produced on the farm. Connections are good, too – buses between Noto and Pachino stop about 400m away. On the minus side, it's usually booked up in summer, and there's a three-night minimum stay; however, even if you're not staying, you can try out its good **restaurant**.

Pachino and the cape

The lowlands south of here are best reached from the area's main town, **PACHINO**. It's a pleasant enough place, with an outsized central piazza that's lined with bars, and there are regular local buses from here to various coastal resorts. One, **MARZAMEMI** (4km northeast), is a low-key resort-cum-fishing port, with an old Arab feel to it and a couple of **hotels**: the slightly bizarre-looking *Celeste*, Viale del Lido 7 (℡0931.841.244; ❷), and the more central *Conchiglietta*, Via Regina Elena 9 (℡0931.841.191; ❸). Each has a **restaurant** – and the *Conchiglietta*'s has a terrace overlooking the sea – but the best eating choice around here is *L'Acquario*, on the lungomare near the *Conchiglietta*, where you can preview your supper swimming around in two great tanks near the entrance. Pizzas are also on offer.

Seven kilometres south of Pachino is the larger town of **PORTOPALO DI CAPO PÁSSERO**. In summer it's a fairly lively place, with several bars and discos along the main street and three or four reasonable **hotels**, including *El Condor*, Via Vittorio Emanuele 38 (℡0931.842.016; ❹), which has a lively garden pizzeria in summer. If you want to **eat**, you could also try the *La Giara* down by the harbour (closed Mon), where you'll find fresh seafood at reasonable prices, or light snacks. You might be able to persuade someone to row you over to the little islet lying just offshore, complete with a seventeenth-century castle. Otherwise, there's a pleasant day's moseying around to be done in the area: the flat land here is market-garden country, the fields and greenhouses sheltering tomatoes, strawberries and artichokes; the coast – when you can get to it along dusty, unmade tracks – rough and seaweed-scattered, and often edged with high bamboo.

There are two **campsites** along the road that leads to the cape, both with cabins and adjacent beaches. The first of these is only a kilometre away, the *Capo Pássero* (℡0931.842.333; two-berth bungalows ❹, four-berth ❻), though it can get fairly crowded; if you can face the hike, you'd do better to go a bit further, to the southeastern point of **Isola delle Correnti**, where the clean and well-equipped *Captain* campsite (℡0931.842.595; May–Oct; two-berth cabins at ❶) sits in happy isolation behind its own unspoiled sandy bay. You're on the southernmost tip of Sicily here, with nothing between you and Africa.

Ragusa and the Baroque southeast

Aside from the much-vaunted Noto, the best of the Baroque in Sicily's southeast is in the **province of Ragusa** – less visited, but providing surprising pockets of grandeur amid the bare hills and deep valleys of the region. The most congenial base for any exploration of the area is **Ragusa**, a busy provincial capital not especially interesting in itself but with two or three hotels and a pleasant, atmospheric old town. From here, it's easy to reach the other

Baroque towns by train or bus: **Módica** to the south, **Cómiso** and **Vittória** to the west, with smaller examples closer to the coast – like **Scicli** or **Íspica**. This last town is at the end of one of the best **walks** in the region, through the **Cava d'Íspica**, a gorge lined with rock-cut tombs. The **coast** south of Ragusa has a string of small-scale holiday towns and a couple of ancient sites, interspersed with good **beaches**.

Ragusa

The 1693 earthquake destroyed many towns and cities that were then rebuilt in a different form, but the unique effect on **RAGUSA** was to split the city in two. The old town of Ragusa Ibla, on a jut of land above its valley, was comprehensively flattened, and within a few years a new town emerged, on the higher ridge just to the west. Unlike Noto Antica, Ibla was stubbornly rebuilt, though retaining its medieval appearance, while its new neighbour, known simply as Ragusa, developed along planned lines. Rivalry between the two was commonplace, until 1926 when both towns were nominally reunited, a move which proved to be the kiss of death for Ragusa Ibla. It rapidly became depopulated, with all the business and industry relocated to the prosperous upper town, where oil is the latest venture – derricks are scattered around modern Ragusa's higher reaches. Ibla meanwhile has benefited from European funding to tidy up its streets, giving its central core a gleaming tourist-friendly veneer, though at the cost of losing its old ramshackle charm. Even so, it's far enough off the beaten track to escape reckless commercialization, and since no one stays in Ragusa, the streets here are usually deserted after dark.

Ragusa: the upper town

You'll arrive in the **upper town**, buses and trains dropping you a five-minute walk from the exposed **Ponte Nuovo**. The bridge spans a huge cleft in the ridge, and what there is of interest lies across the far side of this. Via Roma runs right into the heart of modern Ragusa, the gridded town slipping off to right and left on either side of the steeply sloping Corso Italia. Just around the corner, above Piazza San Giovanni, stands the **Duomo**, conceived on an imposing, symmetrical scale. Finished in 1774, its tapered columns and fine doorways are a fairly sombre background to the vigorous small-town atmosphere around.

Close by, beneath the supermarket at the Ponte Nuovo, there's an important **Museo Archeológico** (daily 9am–1pm & 4–7.30pm; €2). Aside from the usual exhibits – prehistoric flints to late Roman mosaics – the museum mainly houses finds from the Greek site of Kamarina (sixth-century BC), on the coast to the southwest (p.315). Especially interesting are the necropolis reconstructions, amplified by photos, and a restored potter's kiln (from a site at Scornavacche), the neat little terracotta figures found around it displayed in separate cases. There are plans to relocate the museum to an old church in Ragusa Ibla; call ☎0932.622.963 for the latest news.

As far as Ragusa goes, that's about it. Although the new Baroque town received its share of good-looking buildings (like the few grand *palazzi* down Corso Italia), most of the architects' efforts seem to have gone into keeping the streets as straight as possible, and the town's most striking vistas are where this right-angled order is interrupted by the gorge, exposing the bare rock on which the city was built (best appreciated from the motor-free **Ponte dei Cappuccini**). Otherwise the liveliest scenes in this predominantly commercial town are around Piazza San

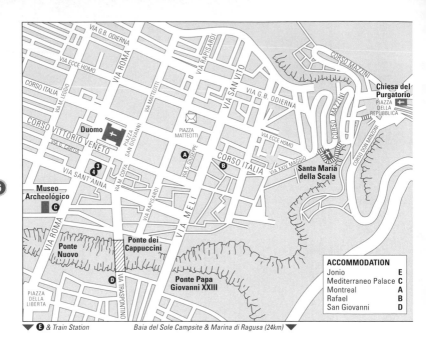

ACCOMMODATION

Jonio	E
Mediterraneo Palace	C
Montreal	A
Rafael	B
San Giovanni	D

E & Train Station   Baia del Sole Campsite & Marina di Ragusa (24km) ▼

Giovanni and the main streets at *passeggiata* time. Via Roma is packed shoulder to shoulder with milling people by 6pm, the cars forced off the roads for an hour or two while everyone circulates among the bars and cake shops.

Ragusa Ibla

It's in **RAGUSA IBLA**, the original, lower town, that you'll probably while away much of the day. It's by far the most interesting part of Ragusa, its tortuous stepped streets lined with locked and shuttered buildings exuding atmosphere, and interspersed with pockets of architectural exuberance and occasional panoramic views. If it's hot, you'll probably want to take advantage of the shuttle bus (*bus navetta*) which plies between the upper and lower towns every thirty minutes or so: catch it from just about anywhere in the new town, and get off in Largo Camarina, near the central San Giorgio. Otherwise you can walk in about half an hour, heading down Corso Italia and the narrow Via XXIV Maggio: from the terrace by the restored fifteenth-century church of **Santa Maria della Scala** (which features the remains of an unusual exterior pulpit), Ragusa Ibla lies beyond and below. It's a mighty view, the weather-beaten roofs straddling the outcrop of rock, rising to the prominent church dome of San Giorgio, which fronts the town like the prow of a ship.

Walking, it'll take about another twenty minutes to descend to Ragusa Ibla itself, following the steps from Santa Maria down beneath the winding road, to the **Chiesa del Purgatorio**. Although there are quicker routes into the centre, it's an idea to follow Via del Mercato, which hugs the edge of the spur on which the town rests, so that you can look out over the grey valley before cutting back through Largo Camarina. This is the best approach for entering Piazza del Duomo, for the first excellent views of **San Giorgio**, stridently placed at the top of the square. One of the masterpieces of Sicilian Baroque,

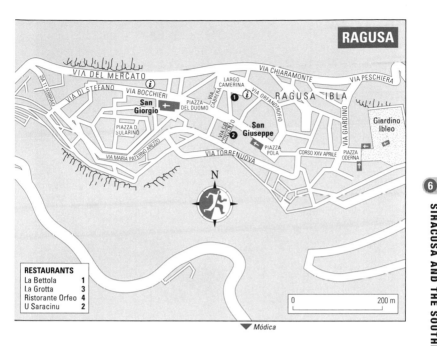

RAGUSA

RESTAURANTS
La Bettola	1
La Grotta	3
Ristorante Orfeo	4
U Saracinu	2

0   200 m

▼ *Módica*

the church was designed by Rosario Gagliardi – one of Noto's chief architects – and took nearly forty years to complete. The sloping piazza, split by six palms, ends in impressive wrought-iron fencing, beyond which broad steps lead to the church set slightly at an angle. Its three-tiered facade, sets of triple columns climbing up the wedding-cake exterior to a balconied belfry, is an imaginative work, though typically not matched inside. As with Gagliardi's other projects, all the beauty is in the immediacy of the powerful exterior; nonetheless, you shouldn't miss taking a look inside (enter from the side-door to the right of the facade), where the tall nave walls are festooned with theatrical red drapery.

The whole town is ripe for aimless wandering. Gagliardi gets another credit for the elegant rounded facade and bulging balconies of **San Giuseppe** in Piazza Pola, a few steps below San Giorgio, while Corso XXV Aprile continues down past abandoned *palazzi* to the **Giardino Ibleo** (daily 8am–8pm, stays open later in summer). The violet-strewn flowerbeds here set off the remains of three small churches, abandoned in the grounds; and to the right of the garden's entrance there's the surviving Gothic portal of the shattered old church of San Giorgio Vecchio, the badly worn stone centrepiece depicting a skeletal St George killing the dragon. The shady benches in the gardens make good picnic or siesta spots.

Practicalities

All **buses** stop outside the **train station** in the upper town: bus departure schedules are posted on the wall by the bus park, and in the *Bar Salinitro* over the road (at Via Dante 94). There are two **tourist offices**, both in Ragusa Ibla: at Via Capitano Bocchieri 33 (daily 8.30am–2pm, Tues also 4–6pm; ☏0932.221.511, Ⓦwww.ragusaturismo.it), with information covering the whole province, and the more local Pro Loco in Largo Camerina (May–Sept Tues–Sun 9am–1pm & 4–8pm; Oct–April Sat & Sun 9am–1pm & 3–7pm; ☏0932.244.473).

△ Ragusa

Accommodation

Accommodation is limited to a few **hotels** in the upper town, most of them fairly colourless. Best-value and most convenient is the *San Giovanni*, Via Traspontino 3 (ⓣ0932.621.013, ⓕ0932.621.294; ❶), just off the Ponte dei Cappuccini; rooms have TV and central heating (those with bath fall into the next category up), and there's a bar downstairs. If you want to stay near the station, try the uninspiring, 1950s-period *Jonio*, 50m to the right from the station at Via Risorgimento 49 (ⓣ0932.624.322, ⓕ0932.654.530; ❷). Far better alternatives, however, are more centrally located: the *Rafael* at Corso Italia 40 (ⓣ0932.654.080; ❺) and, just up the street (but with the entrance on Via San Giuseppe), the *Montreal* (ⓣ0932.621.133, ⓔhotelmontreal@sprintnet.it; ❺); both are elegant if somewhat bland places, with comfortable facilities. And if you want to really treat yourself, the glitzy *Mediterraneo Palace* beckons just over the Ponte Nuovo on the way into town from the station, at Via Roma 189 (ⓣ0932.621.944, ⓕ0932.623.799, ⓦwww.mediterraneopalace.it; ❼). It has superb views and marble everywhere, though you'll be rubbing shoulders predominantly with business types.

The nearest **campsite**, *Baia del Sole* (ⓣ0932.239.844), is 24km south at Marina di Ragusa (see p.315), near the sea on Lungomare Andrea Doria, with hotel rooms available too (❸). There are buses every hour in summer from Ragusa (less frequent in winter).

Eating and drinking

There's rather more choice when it comes to **eating** and drinking. In the new town, the *Ristorante Orfeo*, Via Sant'Anna 117 (closed Sun), is a really good, inexpensive place serving delicious stuffed sardines and bean soup, washed down with the local wine. For **pizza**, visit *La Grotta*, Via G. Cartia, off Via Roma (closed Wed), with draught beer and cheap prices. A much greater range of slightly pricier restaurants can be found in Ragusa Ibla, two of the best being *U Saracinu* (closed Wed) at Via del Convento 9, opposite the church of San Giorgio, and *La Bettola* in Largo Camerina (closed lunchtime & Mon), with outside tables in summer.

Ragusa also has some surprisingly good **bars**, mostly along Via Roma and the surrounding streets. *Caffè Roma*, Via Roma 158, has Art Nouveau fittings and good cakes and savoury snacks. The swisher *Caffè Italia*, below the Duomo on Piazza San Giovanni, does a decent line in savouries, too, and has a full range of pastries and tables on the square in summer.

South: Módica and around

The wild countryside continues to impress as you head beyond Ragusa. The route to **Módica**, half an hour's drive to the south, is a case in point. As the bus swirls down past Ragusa Ibla and climbs through some rugged hills, all the vegetation seems to have been pulled into the valleys below, the tiered slopes bare and rocky – the effect only spoiled by the siting of an asphalt works right on the top, disfiguring the stark hills. Beyond Módica, the train ambles south towards the coast, passing other small Baroque towns like **Scicli**, before reaching **Íspica**, base for an exploration of its gorge.

Módica

MÓDICA is an enjoyable place to spend half a day. A powerful medieval base of the Chiaramonte family, the **upper town** (Módica Alta) is watched over by the magnificent eighteenth-century facade of **San Giorgio**, a worthy rival to the church of the same name in Ragusa Ibla. It's thought that Gagliardi was responsible for this, too: the elliptical facade is topped by his trademark, a belfry, while the approach is characteristically daring – twin flights of stairs zigzag up across the upper roads of the town, ending in a terrace before the church. From here, or better still from the tight streets above San Giorgio, you can look back over the grey-tiled roofs and balconies of the town, built up two sides of a narrow valley. The **lower town** (Módica Bassa) lies in the valley cleft, traced by the main Corso Umberto I and home to *palazzi* whose balconies are buttressed by gargoyles, twisted heads and beasts – and to a crop of battered churches.

It's worth making the journey from Ragusa to Módica by **bus** if you can – the train route isn't half as spectacular. Buses pull up on Corso Umberto I, and just down the street, on the left, a side street flanking San Pietro church leads up to the steps which rise to San Giorgio. To get into the town centre from the **train station**, walk to the right and, at the ornamental fountain, bear left for the corso.

Practicalities

There's a **tourist office** in Piazza Monumento, Corso Umberto I (daily: summer 9am–1pm & 4–8pm; winter 9am–1pm & 3.30–7.30pm; ℡0932.753.324, Ⓦwww.turismodica.com), which can supply a good map and other local information. The best of Módica's **accommodation** options is *I Tetti di Siciliando* at Via Cannata 24, in a narrow passage off Corso Umberto (℡0932.942.843, Ⓦwww.siciliando.it; ❹), where the atmospheric rooms have balconies with great views, and there's a small garden. Breakfast is eaten in a room with a vaulted frescoed ceiling, and art and craftwork courses are held here; bikes are available to rent. The only alternative is the large and somewhat pricey *Hotel Bristol* (℡0932.762.890, Ⓕ0932.763.330; ❺) at Via Risorgimento 8; it's just over 2km south of the centre in the Sacro Cuore district, on the road in from Íspica (you might want to take a taxi if you're not driving).

Módica has one of the classiest **restaurants** in the region in the *Fattoria delle Torri* at Vico Napolitano 14 (signposted across the corso from Piazza Matteotti): a cool interior with choice local dishes. Set menus are not exactly economical at €39 and €46.50, and you won't find anything on the enormous wine list for under €10, but it's a memorable gastronomic experience for which booking is advised (℡0932.751.286; closed Sun eve & all Mon). More realistically, try *La Contea*, Via Grimaldi 15 (opposite San Domenico church), a moderately priced restaurant serving a range of pizzas and pastas, or the good, basic trattoria, *L'Arco*, beyond the fountain on Piazza Corrado Rizzone, next to the Esso petrol station off Corso Umberto (closed Mon), offering home-made ravioli and tagliatelle. If you're spending the evening in Módica, you might head a little further up this alley to the friendly **birreria** at Via Pozzo Barone 22, which has a little courtyard and sells crêpes (closed Mon).

Scicli, Pozzallo and Íspica

SCICLI, just 10km south of Módica (buses and trains from Ragusa and Módica), is dramatically pitched against the bottom of a knobbly bluff, its air of faded grandeur reinforced by the almost exclusively geriatric population; indeed the only sounds you're likely to hear are prayers for the dead seeping out of shuttered windows. Perhaps because it's off the tourist track, Scicli's profusion of pale-yellow eighteenth-century churches, balconied *palazzi* and spacious, empty squares is being allowed to slip into terminal neglect, though it still retains the graceful lines and tones typical of the region's post-quake towns.

Just off the main Piazza Italia, the crumbling **Palazzo Beneventano** features some spectacularly ugly eighteenth-century exterior decoration: manic grinning faces with lolling tongues and bald heads tucked under the balconies and clinging to the walls. From the *palazzo*, it's worth the trek uphill to the terrace by the empty church of **San Matteo** (now fenced off) to enjoy grand views over Scicli below. Take Via Matrice and then, to the right of Via San Matteo, the cobbled steps, which in turn become an overgrown path; you'll see an abandoned shell of a chapel on your way. At the church, the track leads to the remains of a lookout tower; walk a little way beyond here, to the top of the ridge, and you're standing right above a series of abandoned **cave-dwellings** that litter the hills around, used from Neolithic times until fairly recently. From the vantage-point you can make out bricked-up entrances, caves and doorways in the tree-dotted cliffs below.

The **tourist office** (Mon–Sat 9am–1pm & 4–8pm; ☎0932.932.782) is off Piazza Italia at Via Castellana 2. You'll find a decent **restaurant**, *Tre Cantoni*, on Via Pluchinotta (closed Mon), where you can eat well for around €15; otherwise, there's panini and pizzas at *Fuori Orario*, in Piazza Italia, or ice cream at the next-door *Café Italia*.

Pozzallo

From Scicli the train forges a devious route south, to the coast at **POZZALLO**, a small port with a nice beach and a tangled industrial complex close by. British troops, led by Montgomery, landed here in 1943, joining with the Americans, who had landed further west, to take Gela – the first European ground to be recaptured by the Allies in World War II.

Unless you're taking the catamaran to Malta (see p.316), there's not a lot of reason to spend much time in Pozzallo, but if you need a **hotel** here, the only choice is the smart, modern *Villa Ada* (☎ & ☎0932.954.022; ❺), centrally located on Corso Vittorio Véneto, with TVs in the rooms, and a restaurant. There's also a fully equipped **campsite** called *The King's Reef*, a little way out in Contrada Scaro (☎0932.957.611). **Catamarans to Malta** leave year-round from Pozzallo's port, at the western end of town: once or twice weekly in winter, when there's a passenger-only service, and up to twice daily for cars and passengers in August (see "Travel details", p.316, for frequency and journey time). Tickets, costing up to €104 return (less outside the peak season), and €73 day-return, are available from Via Studi 80 (☎0932.954.062, ⊛www .virtuferries.com), off Via Lungomare Raganzino, about 500m beyond the *Villa Ada* hotel. Note that the catamarans aren't the most comfortable of vessels, the ride is often nauseatingly rough and departures are sometimes cancelled.

Íspica

Another ten minutes on, **ÍSPICA** lies at the head of a wide gorge riddled with more Neolithic tombs and cave-dwellings, later used by Sikels, Greeks and early Christians to bury their dead. The gorge, the **Cava d'Íspica**, stretches for 12km to the northwest, and the whole length can be walked without too much hardship. Rock-cut **dwellings** and **tombs** are scattered along the entire route, starting with the **Zona Sud**, nearest Íspica (daily 9am–1.45pm & 3–6.45pm; free), but perhaps more impressive are the set at the other, northwestern, end of the gorge, the so-called **Lato Nord-Ovest** (summer daily 9am–6.30pm; winter Mon–Sat 9am–1.30pm; free). If you have transport and want to head directly to these, they're roughly halfway between Módica and Íspica, 6km up a minor road signposted off the main SS115.

Chiaramonte, Cómiso, Vittória and the southern coast

Chiaramonte Gulfi, situated to the north of Ragusa, merits a visit chiefly for its far-reaching views across Sicily and has a great lunch-spot. Cómiso and Vittória, west of Ragusa, are strictly for passing through, though, only of interest to lovers of Baroque or students of small-town life. Both are on the main train line from Ragusa to Gela, while a regular bus service links Chiaramonte to Ragusa: each place could be seen in half a morning if you time the transport connections right. The coast is considerably more difficult to see without your own vehicle; to be frank, you're not missing a great deal if you move on to pastures new.

Chiaramonte Gulfi

Twenty kilometres north of Ragusa, CHIARAMONTE GULFI is one of several places dubbed "balcony of Sicily", on account of its stupendous views, stretching west towards Gela and north to Etna. Though hazy in summer, the panorama embraces dun-coloured farmland interspersed with solitary villages – a still, silent scene, but for the occasional dog's bark or the whine of a Vespa. There are some nice old buildings here, too, and one excellent restaurant, *Majore*, on Via Mártiri Ungheresi 12, off Piazza Duomo (closed Mon and July), which specializes in pig meats – the area is famous for its salamis and cured hams, which you can buy to take away at the restaurant shop.

Cómiso

The journey to CÓMISO is worth making by bus or car if you can, crossing a barren 600-metre-high plateau that looks away to the distant sea and down to the massive domes dominating the town's skyline. Although the Chiaramonte and other noble families filled Cómiso with a wealth of architecture during the Middle Ages, it is the Baroque spirit which infuses the place, most prominent in the two major churches, the Chiesa Matrice and the nearby Santíssima Annunziata. Both are post-1693 products and overwhelm everything else within reach of their ponderous shadows. A relief, then, to wander up Via Virgilio (or, from the Annunziata, Via degli Studi) to gaze on a much more modest affair, the thirteenth-century church of San Francesco, to which a rich Renaissance chapel was added in 1517 to house the tombs of the powerful Naselli family. You can see their restored castello near the centre of town, at the end of Via San Biagio.

Cómiso was the birthplace of both the painter and sculptor Salvatore Fiume (1915–97) and his friend, the writer Gesualdo Bufalino (1920–96). The main body of Fiume's paintings, chiefly figurative in style, can be seen in the Vatican museums, but he also designed sets for opera houses and worked on architectural projects. Bufalino's career was a more curious one. He began his first book in 1950, having spent three years in a Palermitan sanatorium, but declined to let it be published until 1981, when he was finally satisfied with it. After that he picked up steam and wrote several novels and short stories, including the respected *Night's Lies*, which won Italy's most prestigious literary award, the Strega Prize, in 1988.

Vittória

Another ten minutes beyond Cómiso by train, VITTÓRIA lies at the centre of a rich wine district. Founded in 1607 by Vittória della Colonna, daughter of the Spanish viceroy and wife of the Count of Módica, it differs from other hillside towns in the region in its location on the plain west of the Monti Iblei – a setting reflected in its flat and regular street plan. You can confine your visit here to the two principal squares, Piazza del Pópolo and Piazza Ricca, the first graced by the curved facade of the church of **Madonna della Grazia** and the later Neoclassical Teatro Comunale. The smaller Piazza Ricca lies in the lee of the church of **San Giovanni Battista**, its interior dripping with gilt.

Along the coast

The coast – and the start of the so-called "riviera", which extends as far as Gela (p.351) – is only 10km southwest of Vittória, at Scoglitti. Three kilometres south of here, just beyond the mouth of the River Ípari, lie the desolate remains of ancient **Kamarina** (also spelt Camerina), a Syracusan colony founded in 599 BC, several times devastated in the conflicts with nearby Gela and eventually destroyed by Rome in 258 BC. Only accessible by bus from Ragusa, this dispersed area lies on a headland overlooking beaches on either side, though an **Antiquarium** (daily 9am–1pm & 3–8pm; €2.60) marks the site's centre, containing everything that hasn't already been appropriated by Ragusa's museum. Behind the antiquarium is all that's left of a fifth-century BC **Tempio di Atena**, surrounded by the rubble of city walls. West of it lie the various ruins of the Hellenistic-Roman city, accessible from separate entrances along the road, each keeping the same hours as the antiquarium.

At the bottom of steep cliffs south of here is a swish *Club Med* complex, while 5km further down the coast, at **PUNTA BRACCETTO**, are a clutch of **campsites**, most open only in the summer, though the *Baia dei Coralli* (☎0932.918.192) stays open all year round and has a pool, pizzeria and shop (all closed in winter). Carry on down to the next point, **PUNTA SECCA**, to see another minor archeological site, Byzantine **Caucana**. There are traces of a fourth- to sixth-century harbour here, and the remains of a basilica, though nothing very thrilling. You might be more engaged by one of the area's most fashionable sandy **beaches** nearby.

The coast stretches further east dotted by a series of minor resorts and attendant bars and hotels. None of it is overdeveloped, and some of the small towns – **MARINA DI RAGUSA** and **Donnalucata** – are quite appealing, if rather dismal out of season. Marina di Ragusa is probably the best target, with frequent buses running from Ragusa in summer. There are campsites here (see "Ragusa", p.301), as well as some decent ice-cream bars and a couple of popular "pubs".

Without your own transport, the only way to reach the coast is **by bus**, from Ragusa to Marina di Ragusa or Kamarina, or from Scicli to Donnalucata. There's a coastal road that connects them all, though there is little or no transport service between.

Festivals

April

Last Sunday St George's Day celebrations in **Ragusa Ibla**: statues paraded through the streets and a costumed procession.

May

1 Procession in **Siracusa**, with the statue of St Lucy carried around town.

May /June

Classical drama festival at **Siracusa**, events taking place in the Greek theatre.

August

First Sunday Boat race (*palio*) round Ortygia island in **Siracusa**, in which the five traditional quarters of the city compete with raucous enthusiasm.

27–29 Festivities in **Ragusa** to mark the city's

patron St John the Baptist; more processions and statues.

29 Start of Madonna delle Lácrime festival (devoted to the "weeping" Madonna) in **Siracusa**; runs until September 3.

Last Sunday Festival of St Corrado in **Noto**.

December
13 Festival of St Lucy in **Siracusa**: a procession to the church of Santa Lucia.

Travel details

Trains

Ragusa to: Cómiso (5 daily; 30min); Gela (5 daily; 1hr 20min); Íspica (5 daily; 1hr 10min); Licata (2 direct and 2 via Gela daily; 1hr 35min–2hr 30min); Módica (8 daily Mon–Sat, 6 daily Sun; 20min); Noto (5–6 daily; 1hr 30min); Pozzallo (5–6 daily; 1hr); Scicli (5–6 daily; 35min); Siracusa (5–6 daily; 2hr); Vittória (5–6 daily; 40min).

Siracusa to: Augusta (10–11 daily; 30min); Catania (10 daily; 1hr 25min); Gela (6–7 daily; 3hr 35min); Lentini (10 daily; 55min); Messina (9 daily; 3hr); Módica (9 daily Mon–Sat, 6 daily Sun; 1hr 50min); Noto (9 daily Mon–Sat, 6 daily Sun; 30min); Ragusa (4 daily; 2hr 10min); Taormina (10 daily; 2hr 30min).

Buses

Módica to: Catania (10 daily Mon–Sat, 6 daily Sun; 2hr); Catania airport (10 daily Mon–Sat, 6 daily Sun; 1hr 45min); Íspica (13 daily Mon–Sat, 3 daily Sun; 20min–1hr); Pachino (Mon–Sat 2 daily; 1hr 20min); Palermo (5 daily Mon–Sat, 2 daily Sun; 4hr); Pozzallo (11 daily Mon–Sat, 1 daily Sun; 20–40min); Ragusa (hourly Mon–Sat, 2 daily Sun; 25min); Scicli (14 daily Mon–Sat, 2 daily Sun; 30–40min); Siracusa (8 daily Mon–Sat, 3 daily Sun; 2hr–2hr 30min).

Noto to: Ávola (19 daily Mon–Sat, 5 daily Sun; 15min); Eloro (Mon–Sat 4 daily; 20min); Íspica (12 daily Mon–Sat, 8 daily Sun; 50min); Siracusa (7 daily Mon–Sat, 3 daily Sun; 55min).

Pachino to: Marzamemi (Mon–Sat 11 daily until 2pm; 10min); Portopalo di Capo Pássero (Mon–Sat 11 daily; 15min); Siracusa (8 daily Mon–Sat, 3 daily Sun; 1hr 30min).

Ragusa to: Kamarina (Mon–Sat 9 daily; 1hr); Catania (12 daily Mon–Fri, 5–6 daily Sat & Sun; 2hr); Catania airport (12 daily Mon–Fri, 5–6 daily Sat & Sun; 1hr 45min); Chiaramonte Gulfi (Mon–Sat 7 daily; 55min); Gela (Mon–Sat 2 daily; 1hr 40min); Íspica (Mon–Sat 7 daily; 1hr); Marina di Ragusa (hourly; 30min); Módica (12 daily Mon–Sat, 3 daily Sun; 30min); Noto (10 daily Mon–Sat, 1 daily Sun; 1hr 50min); Palermo (4 daily Mon–Sat, 2 daily Sun; 4hr); Pozzallo (9 daily Mon–Sat, 3 daily Sun; 1hr); Scicli (9 daily Mon–Sat, 2 daily Sun; 40min); Siracusa (Mon–Sat 9 daily; 2hr 15min).

Siracusa to: Augusta (Mon–Sat 9 daily; 40min); Ávola (9 daily Mon–Sat, 3 daily Sun; 40min); Caltagirone (Mon–Sat 1 daily; 2hr); Catania (16 daily Mon–Sat, 4 daily Sun; 1hr 20min); Catania airport (6–7 daily; 1hr); Ferla (Mon–Sat 1 daily; 1hr 30min); Lentini (Mon–Sat 12 daily; 55min); Módica (8 daily Mon–Sat, 3 daily Sun; 2hr); Naples (1 daily and 3 weekly; 10hr); Noto (12 daily Mon–Sat, 4 daily Sun; 40min); Pachino (8 daily Mon–Sat, 3 daily Sun; 1hr 30min); Palazzolo Acréide (16 daily Mon–Sat, 8 daily Sun; 1hr); Palermo (6 daily Mon–Sat, 3 daily Sun; 3hr 15min); Piazza Armerina (Mon–Sat 1 daily; 2hr 30min); Ragusa (Mon–Sat 5 daily; 2hr 15min); Rome (1 daily and 3 weekly; 13hr); Sortino (Mon–Sat 9 daily; 1hr 15min).

Sortino to: Catania (Mon–Sat 3 daily; 1hr 30min); Siracusa (Mon–Sat 10 daily; 1hr 15min).

Catamarans

Catania to: Malta (Feb–April & Oct 1 weekly; May, June, July & Sept 3 weekly; Aug 6 weekly; 3hr).

Pozzallo to: Malta (June, July & Sept 8–11 weekly; Aug 2 daily; Oct–May 1–3 weekly; 1hr 30min).

7

The interior

7

THE INTERIOR

TYRRHENIAN SEA

MEDITERRANEAN SEA

0   50 km

CHAPTER 7

Highlights

✳ **Enna** Spend a day exploring the old town and museums of this ancient hill-town and take in the view from Castello di Lombardia that extends to Etna. **p.321**

✳ **Driving the SS120** This picturesque road wends its way through some gorgeous landscape and makes a wonderful jumping-off point for a leisurely drive, cycle or hike through the heart of Sicily. **p.327**

✳ **Petralia Sottana** High up in the Madonie National Park, the small and beautifully preserved and sited town is a great place to base yourself for walks. **p.329**

✳ **Villa Romana del Casale, Piazza Armerina** One of the foremost sights of the island, the scale, diversity and vitality of the Roman mosaics near Piazza Armerina should not be missed. **p.336**

✳ **La Scala, Caltagirone** In this town famed for its ceramics, these 142 steps are adorned with beautiful patterned tiles. **p.344**

△ Hunting scene mosaic, Pizza Amerina, Villa Romana del Casale

The interior

... for the last five hours all they had set eyes on were bare hillsides flaming yellow under the sun ... They had passed through crazed-looking villages washed in palest blue; crossed dry beds of torrents over fantastic bridges; skirted sheer precipices which no sage and broom could temper. Never a tree, never a drop of water; just sun and dust.

Giuseppe di Lampedusa, *The Leopard*

Sicily's slow cross-country trains and the limited-exit autostrada (the A19) do little to encourage stops in the island's vast and mountainous **interior**, but it's only here that you really begin to get off the tourist trail. It's an intensely rural region, with just two or three decent-sized towns, bunched together almost in the dead centre of the island. Outside these, much of the land is burnt dry during the long summer months, the cracked fields and shrivelled plantations affording a meagre living to the sparse population. Unlike other parts of Italy, those who cultivated the land here (if it was cultivable) actually travelled to work from their towns and villages rather than living on site. Now thoroughly depleted by mass emigration, the countryside is empty and you're unlikely to see many signs of life outside the small hill-top towns. But these settlements, though often moribund, occasionally possess an exuberance and vitality that's in startling contrast to the stillness of the interior's rolling hills.

Travelling in the interior can get monotonous, as much of the land is given over to extensive cornfields – a feature of the Sicilian landscape since Greek times – but there are compensations for coming this far off the beaten track. Some of the minor inland routes give fascinating glimpses of a life that's all but disappeared in the rest of Sicily (indeed Italy), and there are some of the finest routes and views on the island, as well as some of its most curious towns. A blustery mountain settlement dominating the dry hills below, **Enna** is as central as you can get, and makes a good starting point for trips to the untouched towns and villages of the **northeastern interior**, of which **Nicosia** is the main attraction. The biggest town in the region, **Caltanissetta** is also the most disappointing, largely modern and devoid of charm. But, with your own transport, the region beyond it – the little-visited **western interior** – makes an absorbing journey, stretching to **Corleone**: an agricultural centre that, like so many in the neighbourhood, is tainted by its Mafia associations.

Although the Arabs settled the centre of the island, leaving their mark in a number of place names and warren-like towns, the Greeks and Romans tended to leave Sicily's interior alone. Nevertheless, the **southern interior** boasts some unexpected ancient gems, not least **Piazza Armerina** and its fabulous

southern interior boasts some unexpected ancient gems, not least **Piazza Armerina** and its fabulous

319

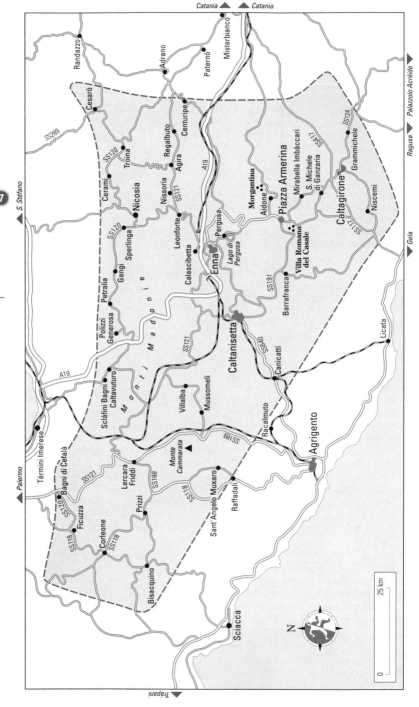

Roman mosaics, and the nearby excavations at **Morgantina**. And there's interest, too, in ceramic-studded **Caltagirone**, a handy departure point for the Baroque towns of the southeast.

Practicalities

Getting around the interior can be tricky. Public transport is patchy at best, though you can easily reach all the important centres – Enna, Caltanissetta, Piazza Armerina and Caltagirone – by bus or train. It's more difficult to travel into the mountains: most accessible are the hill-top towns of the northeast, with **buses** running out of Enna and along the two major routes. The towns and villages west of Caltanissetta are virtually impossible to reach without your **own transport**, and a car would make visiting the rest of the region a lot easier, too. You should plan ahead if you want to stay the night anywhere, as good **accommodation** is scarce; most of the options are detailed in the text, but it's worth noting that there are *no* official **campsites**.

7

THE INTERIOR | Enna

Enna and the northeastern interior

Despite its stranded mountain-top position and frontier feel, there's no great effort involved in getting to **Enna** these days: there are regular buses and trains from Catania and Palermo. But without your own transport you'll usually have to be prepared to spend the night, certainly if you intend to move further into the **northeastern interior** to some of the least-developed parts of the island. Fairly frequent **buses** leave Enna for towns along the eastbound **SS121**, which eventually runs to Catania. From **Leonforte**, first stop on this route, there are buses north to **Nicosia**, which sits in the middle of a second route, the **SS120**. Eastward, this runs to **Cesarò** and on into the foothills of Etna, though it's fairly hard to travel this section by public transport; heading west to **Polizzi Generosa** is an easier choice, as all the towns are connected by bus. A few places along the SS120 (east and west) can also be reached from towns on the Tyrrhenian coast, cutting across dramatic tracts of the Nébrodi and Madonie mountains.

Enna

From a bulging V-shaped ridge almost 1000m up, **ENNA** lords it over the surrounding hills of central Sicily. One of the most ancient towns on the island, Enna has only ever had one function: Livy described it as "inexpugnabilis" and, for obvious strategic reasons, the town was a magnet for successive hostile armies, who in turn besieged and fortified it. The Arabs,

321

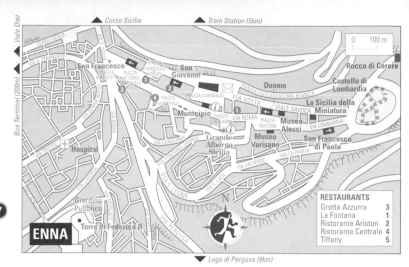

Corso Sicilia   Train Station (5km)

0   100 m

San Francesco

San Giovanni

Rocco di Cerere

Duomo

Castello di Lombardia

La Sicilia della Miniatura

Municipio

Museo Alessi

Grande Albergo Sicilia

Museo Varisano

San Francesco di Paola

Hospital

Giardino Pubblico

Torre di Federico II

ENNA

RESTAURANTS
Grotta Azzurra   3
La Fontana   1
Ristorante Ariston   2
Ristorante Centrale   4
Tiffany   5

Lago di Pergusa (9km)

for example, spent twenty years trying to gain entrance to Enna and eventually, in 859, resorted to crawling in through the sewers. The approach to this mountain stronghold is still formidable, the road climbing slowly out of the valley and looping across the solid crag to the summit and the town. Enna remains medieval at heart, as any foray into its densely packed streets shows, and even the modern development echoes the town's defensive past, its office buildings and apartment blocks rising like so many watchtowers from a distance.

The very distinct hill-town atmosphere here is worth staying overnight for. Summer evenings in Enna are among the most enjoyable in Sicily, watching the sun set from some of the finest vantage-points imaginable. Come in winter and you should expect snow, the wind blowing hard through the streets, and white slopes blending with the anaemic stone buildings.

The Town

Despite the numerous wars that have touched the town over the years, most of Enna's remains are medieval and in good condition, prize exhibit being the thirteenth-century **Castello di Lombardia** (summer daily 8am–11pm; winter 9am–1pm & 3–5pm; free) dominating the easternmost spur of town. Built by Frederick II, it's a mighty construction with its strong walls complete, guarding the steep slopes on either side of town. Six surviving towers (out of an original twenty) provide lookouts and the tallest, the Torre Pisana, is worth climbing for great views of Enna itself, the rugged countryside in all directions, and across to Mount Etna. Back down, it's a good spot to lounge about with a picnic.

A road to the side of the castle climbs a little way further to the **Rocca di Cerere**, an exposed outcrop where some scattered foundations are presumed to be the remnants of a temple erected by Gelon in 480 BC. Enna was the centre of the Greek cult of Demeter, the fertility goddess (her Roman counterpart was Ceres, hence the rock's name), and the most famous of the myths associated with the goddess – the carrying off of her daughter, Persephone, to the underworld – is supposed to have taken place just a few kilometres away, at Lago di Pergusa.

Attractive chunks of the **old town** survive intact too, though much worn by the brisk winds that scurry across the squares and streets, even in summer. Tightly packed houses hug the two ridges that divide Enna, occasional gaps revealing swirling drops down into the valleys. Though it's fun to wander through the crumbly southern and eastern sections of Enna, virtually all the accredited sights lie stretched out along and around the narrow, better-preserved **Via Roma**, a continuation of Via Lombardia which descends from the castle. First stop down is **La Sicilia delle Miniature** at Via Roma 533 (daily except Mon 9am–1pm & 3–7pm; €2), with its tiny examples of Sicilian architecture – cottages, stable, church and quarry – all well-made in original materials. The street carries on, interrupted by small piazzas, one of which fronts the hemmed-in **Duomo** (daily 9am–noon & 4–7pm), dating in part from 1307. Rebuilt several times since, its long medieval wall, which has Gothic touches, is hardly complemented by the Duomo's thin Baroque facade, while the spacious sixteenth-century interior, whose every surface is ornamented, features huge supporting dark-grey columns, the bases of which are carved with grotesques – manic heads with human hands and snake bodies, snarling mouths and dome-like pates.

Outside, the **Museo Alessi** (daily except Mon 9am–9pm; €2.60) fields the impressive contents of the cathedral's own treasury, including a tall eighteenth-century wooden cabinet which opens to reveal a silver throne. Some of the handiwork on display is remarkable: a seventeenth-century gold and crystal crown is decorated with minute scenes from the life of Christ, picked out with studded jewels. There's a rich collection of local church art too, downstairs, and cases of old coins on the floor above. A second archeological museum, equally good, lies at the back of the Piazza Mazzini, opposite the cathedral – the **Museo Varisano** (daily 8am–7pm; €2), which covers Neolithic to Roman times; all the exhibits, which include a fine series of painted Greek vases, were dug up in the locality.

Via Roma continues down past the Catalan-Gothic **Palazzo Pollicarini**, opposite the *Grande Albergo Sicilia*. The *palazzo* has now been turned into apartments, but if you peek into the courtyard you can see the typical medieval Catalan exterior staircase climbing up to the first floor. Just to the west of here, in Piazza Coppola, the tower of the church of **San Giovanni** is crowned by a little cupola. It's one of the few surviving relics of the Arab occupation of Enna, though the town's winding central streets suggest an Eastern influence too.

The western extremity of Via Roma is marked by the sloping, rectangular **Piazza Vittorio Emanuele**, focal point of the evening *passeggiata*. Off here, a long cliff-edge promenade looks out to the little rust-coloured village of Calascibetta over the valley. The plain, high wall of the church of **San Francesco**, which flanks the piazza, has a massive sixteenth-century tower, previously part of the old town's system of watchtowers which linked the castle with all Enna's churches.

One of the watchtowers, the **Torre di Federico II**, still stands in isolation in the **Giardino Púbblico** in the largely modern south of the town. An octagonal tower, 24m high, it's a survivor of the alterations to the city made by Frederick of Aragon, who added a (now hidden) underground passage connecting the tower to the castle. Provided there's no scaffolding around the tower, you can climb to the top for more great views.

Practicalities

All long-distance and most local buses use the **bus terminal** on Viale Diaz in the new town – turn right out of the terminal, right again down Corso

Sicilia, and it's around a ten-minute walk to Piazza Vittorio Emanuele. The **train station**, however, is 5km below town, a long and dauntingly steep walk: a local bus runs roughly hourly to the town centre (less frequently on Sunday), and a taxi into town costs around €8. For train information, call the station (☏0935.500.910 or 848.888.088), or pick up a timetable from one of the tourist offices.

You can reach everywhere in Enna itself very easily on foot, though #5 **buses to Pergusa** (Mon–Sat 6.55am–10pm, Sun 9am–10pm) leave hourly from Piazza Matteotti, outside San Francesco church; you'll need a ticket (€0.80) before you get on, bought from *tabacchi* and valid for one hour. **Taxi** ranks are along Viale Diaz, near the bus terminal, on Via Pergusa and at Piazza Vittorio Emanuele; alternatively, call ☏0935.500.905.

Information on Piazza Armerina (see p.336), as well as a good free **map** of Enna, is available from the **tourist office** at Via Roma 413 (Mon–Sat 9am–1pm & 3–7pm; ☏0935.528.828 or 800.221.188, ⓦwww .vivienna.it); and there's a smaller office in Piazza Colaianni (Mon–Fri 8am–2pm, Wed 8am–6.15pm; ☏0935.500.875), next to the *Grande Albergo Sicilia*.

Accommodation

There's only one **hotel** in Enna, and if it's full (or too expensive), you'll have to stay in nearby Pergusa instead, where there are several cheaper possibilities, or try Calascibetta (see opposite). The dead-central *Grande Albergo Sicilia* is in Piazza Colaianni (ⓦwww.hotelsiciliaenna.it; ☏0935.500.850, ⓕ0935.500.488; ❹); its brutalist exterior hides an Art Deco lobby and nicely refurbished rooms kitted out with hand-painted furniture and fine art; breakfast is included, and you might even swing a discount if they're not full.

Eating and drinking

There's considerably more choice when it comes to **eating and drinking**. For moderately priced pizzas and regular Italian dishes from €5–8, *Tiffany*, Via Roma 487 (closed Thurs), is handily placed, just down from the cathedral. There are a couple of reasonably priced trattorias, including the little *Ristorante Centrale*, Piazza VI Dicembre 9, off Via Roma at Piazza Umberto, which attracts a local crowd with its bright interior and offers a full Sicilian menu for €19 (closed Sat in winter). Run for forty-plus years by the charming Giuseppe and Maria, the cool and lovely *Grotta Azzurra* (☏0935.24.328; closed Sat off season) serves the cheapest meals in town: €2.50 for *primos* and €4 for *secondos*. It is just down the hill on Via Colaianni (between Piazza Matteotti and Piazza Vittorio Emanuele): follow the signs up the alley. Alternatively, the friendly *La Fontana*, Via Vulturo 6 (closed Fri in winter), has good meat specialities and some outdoor tables near a spouting fountain; a full meal costs around €18. Considerably grander is the *Ristorante Ariston*, Via Roma 353 (closed Sun), specializing in fresh pasta and good Sicilian dishes; expect to pay €25–30 a head for a full meal with wine.

For a good **bar**, try the *Caffè Italia*, on Piazza Garibaldi, which serves tasty snacks, drinks and light meals, while *Bar Azimut*, just inside the castle grounds, is also a good spot for a shady drink. There are many other appealing *pasticcerie*-bars in town, most stretched along Via Roma; one of the nicest is the *Gran Caffè Roma*, Via Roma 312 (closed Mon), down by Piazza Vittorio Emanuele, which serves wine by the glass and has tables at the back.

Listings

Bank Banco di Sicilia, Via Roma 367; Banca d'Italia, Piazza Garibaldi 4.
Bus companies Both are at the bus terminal: SAIS ☏0935.500.902 (for Calascibetta, Caltanissetta, Catania, Catania airport, Messina, Palermo and Piazza Armerina); Interbus ☏0935.502.390 (for Catania, Leonforte and Nicosia).
Cinema Cinema Arena Pergusa, on the road just out of Pergusa towards Enna, has outdoor screenings in June and July ☏335.772.9664.

Hospital Ospedale Umberto I, Contrate Ferrante in Enna Bassa on the road to Pergusa ☏0935.516.111.
Pharmacies Librizzi, Piazza Vittorio Emanuele 20 ☏0935.500.908; Farmacia del Centro, Via Roma 315 ☏0935.500.650.
Police Questura at Via San Giuseppe 2 ☏0935.501.289.
Post office Via A. Volta, off Piazza Garibaldi.

Around Enna: Calascibetta and the Lago di Pergusa

Close to Enna, on a lower hill to the north across the valley, the small town of **CALASCIBETTA** hints at what Enna would be like without the tower blocks. Once a Saracen town, it was fortified by Count Roger in his successful attempt to take Enna in 1087, and the brooding atmosphere in its tangled streets seems straight from that age. Tightly packed red-stone buildings are perched above a sheer drop on the eastern side, rising to the restored Chiesa Madre at the very top. There are frequent buses to Calascibetta from Enna's bus terminal (or every couple of hours from Enna's train station). The pleasant *Da Pietro*, Contrada Longobardi (☏0935.33.647 or 0340.276.5763; ❷), is on the lower edge of town, and surrounded by a garden: it's signposted "Bed and Breakfast".

Lago di Pergusa

Nine kilometres south of Enna (and served by regular buses; see p.348), the **Lago di Pergusa** is the legendary site of Hades' abduction of Persephone to the underworld. The story has it that Persephone, surrounded by nymphs, was gathering flowers on the lush banks of the lake when Hades emerged from a chasm beneath the water and spirited her away. Demeter searched in vain for her daughter, and her grief at the loss of Persephone prevented the corn from growing. To settle the matter, Zeus ruled that Persephone should spend half the year as Queen of the Underworld, living for the other six months in Sicily with her mother as one of the island's goddesses. In her gratitude, Demeter, as goddess of grain and agriculture, made the corn grow again – a powerful symbol in a traditionally fertile land.

Today, the lake is encircled by a motor-racing track, and despite the wooded banks beyond the water it's difficult now to imagine a less romantic spot. Mary Taylor Simeti's journal, *On Persephone's Island*, labels the lake "a brilliant example of the Sicilians' best efforts to ruin their landscape", and while the woods here are pleasant enough, it's not worth coming for any glimpse of the truth behind the legend, though it is a possible base near Enna. Alongside the lake there are several modern **hotels**: best value on the Enna road is the *Miralago* (☏0935.541.272; no credit cards, ❶); its unprepossessing exterior reveals attractive en-suite rooms. Overlooking the lake, on Via Autodroma Pergusa, the *Riviera* (🌐www.rivierahtl.it, ☏0935.541.267, 🅕0935.541.260; ❺) has a swimming pool; when there are no race meetings, it's a peaceful place. If you don't want to go back into Enna, there are plenty of places to **eat** at reasonable prices, including the pizzeria at the *Miralago*, or the *Trattoria Al Carretino* further down on the opposite side of the main road, whose local pasta speciality (*Cavatelle al Carretino*) is both excellent and cheap (€5.50). The café opposite, *La Paglia*, serves good after-dinner *gelato* and granita.

The SS121: Enna to Centúripe

Out of Enna, and beyond Calascibetta, it's around forty minutes by bus to **LEONFORTE**. In many ways, it's typical of the many small towns you'll come across east of Enna, quaint and almost sleepy, with its roots firmly in the seventeenth century. Leonforte's attractive central square sprouts bars in profusion, and besides the impressive Duomo there's also great interest in the domineering Palazzo Baronale, whose bulky facade is recognizable from way outside town. However, the most notable sight here is **La Gran Fonte**, built in 1651, less a fountain than a row of 24 waterspouts set in a sculpted facade of embossed roses and figures. It's about 300m on foot down from the Chiesa Madre overlooking the hills on the edge of town. If you're driving, you'll see the sign for it as you enter the town, but it involves a hefty doubling back on yourself along the one-way system. The fountain has recently been well restored, and is a good place to fill water bottles; there's a little bar opposite for a drink with a view. If you were going to stop anywhere along the SS121, this is perhaps the place; you'll find a couple of reasonable trattorias up in the town centre.

The bus from Enna steers a course further east through attractive **Nissoria**, whose central leafy street is lined with bars occupied by old men shooting the breeze across the moving traffic. It's another 7km on to **AGIRA**, again, well located on the brow of a hill. From a distance, its buildings form a perfect cone, with the ruins of its much-neglected medieval castle prominent atop the peak. Agira is also the only place on this route for an **overnight stop**, at the tidy if worn *Albergo Aurora*, Via Annunziata 6 (T0935.691.416; no credit cards, ❷). There's also a decent selection of places to **eat and drink**, including a trio on Via Vittorio Emanuele, the main road through town: *Ristorante al Capriccio*, at no. 323, has great views and inexpensive prices; *Al Muretto* at no. 343, is good for a quick pizza and drink; while steps away at no. 334, the pub-like *De Paris* makes a nice stop for a drink. Just down from the castle at Via Rametta 27, the *Belvedere* serves good pasta dishes (from €5) and has a terrace with superb panoramas of the lake and hills. There are several daily **buses** from here north to Troina – useful if you want to get to the SS120 (see opposite).

The SS121 continues through tiny **Regalbuto** and eventually to Catania, a journey that strikes through land fiercely contested during the short Sicilian campaign of World War II. The hills between Agira and the western slopes of Etna saw most of the heaviest fighting. Just out of Agira, close to the **Lago di Pozzillo**, there's a poignant **war cemetery** sited on a gentle hillside, the resting place of 490 Canadian soldiers killed in July 1943.

Centúripe

Some 15km on from Regalbuto, a minor road leads south for 8km through orange and olive groves to the isolated outpost of **CENTÚRIPE**, which faces Etna across the Simeto River valley, giving it a strategic importance that accounts for its various power struggles over the centuries. Several medieval campaigns destroyed the town, while the last great battle in August 1943 dislodged Hermann Goering and his forces. Modern Centúripe is an uneasy mix of new building and an untouched central piazza, near which a terrace provides the outstanding views that earned Centúripe the tag "balcony of Sicily". After gazing at the views, you'll exhaust the town's possibilities in around two minutes flat – perhaps ten, if you stop for a drink at one of the three bars in the central square.

The towns beyond Centúripe, on and off the SS121, are covered in the section on the Circumetnea railway; see p.264.

Across the mountains: the SS120

Before the Palermo–Messina coastal road was constructed, traffic between the two cities passed inland, on a long mountainous route that took in some of the island's most impressive scenery. Today, free of the traffic that clogs the coast, the **SS120** makes an attractive trans-island alternative, across some of the remoter stretches of the Madonie and Nébrodi mountains. Make sure you reserve accommodation in advance, though, as the few hotels tend to fill up quickly.

Nicosia

The biggest town on this stretch, and best base for excursions east and west, is **NICOSIA**, a basically medieval, convoluted mass of cracked *palazzi* topped by the remains of a Norman castle; it's reachable by buses from Leonforte, Palermo, Términi Imerese and Santo Stéfano Mistretta. In the cramped town centre, the chatter-filled Piazza Garibaldi is the site of Nicosia's lovely old cathedral, **San Nicola** (daily 8–10.30am), a stately construction with a fourteenth-century facade and belltower, and a sculpted Gothic portal.

Behind the cathedral, Via Salomone rises steeply to the former Saracen district of the town, a jumble of streets occupying one of the four hills on which Nicosia is built. At the top, **Santa Maria Maggiore**, founded in 1267 but rebuilt after an eighteenth-century landslide, has the bells from its campanile piled up outside – they fell down after another earthquake and the sound of them is now electrically reproduced. Inside, amid "No Spitting" notices, there's an impressive marble polyptych by Antonello Gagini and a throne used by Charles V when he passed through here in 1535, on the way back from his Tunisian crusade. The views from outside encompass the town's other three promontories, on the highest of which sits the ruined **castello**.

Buses leave Nicosia from Piazza Marconi, at the bottom of Via Vittorio Emanuele. There's only one **place to stay** in town, the central *Umberto I* (☎0935.631.135 or 347.153.53.82; ❷), a tiny five-roomed bed and breakfast at Via Umberto I 34. If you're driving, you could stay at the comfortable *Vigneta* (☎0935.646.074; ❷), in Contrada San Basilio, about 7km out of town, though it's a somewhat characterless, modern hotel; to find it, follow signs to Mistretta. Having your own transport will also enable you to seek out *La Cirata* **restaurant**, about 5km towards Enna on the SS117 (closed Mon & Nov), for dishes based on local produce; it's a vast place, catering mainly to passing coach groups and quite pricey, but makes a good alternative to the few basic places in the centre. For a nightcap or ice cream at any

to be found in churches all over southern Italy. From the edge of the village you get a long view over the Madonie and Nébrodi mountains and, if you're westward bound, a last dim sight of Etna.

Polizzi Generosa and Caltavuturo

Minor roads connect the Petralias with the lovely Madonie mountain region to the north centred on Piano Battáglia (p.139), though there's no bus this way. The service along the SS120 branches off for **POLIZZI GENEROSA**, half an hour west and right in the heart of the Monti Madonie. Stop here to see the grand old **Chiesa Matrice**, containing the area's greatest work of art: a triptych of the *Madonna and Child* flanked by saints; attributed to a mysterious fifteenth-century Fleming known only as the "Maître au Feuillage brodé", it's reckoned to be his best work. There's a decent **restaurant** just up from here in Piazza Castello – *U Bagghiu* (closed Tues) with a great seasonal speciality, *Pennerette Bagghiu* (cheesy penne with tomato and garlic), for €5; it also runs a basic agriturismo, just south of the town, in C. da Santa Venera (ⓣ & ⓕ0921.649.421, ⓦwww.santavenera.com; ❶). Alternatively, *Orto dei Cappuccini* (closed Mon), Via Cappuccini 3, on a side street off the road up to town, is highly recommended, with its nice cloistered garden, and creative fish and meat dishes from €8.50. If you just want an ice cream or home-made pastries, the *Pasticceria Al Castello* in Piazza Castello will serve.

From Polizzi, a daily bus crosses the autostrada and heads to **CALTAVU-TURO**, a predominantly Baroque town despite its Saracen castle and Arabic name. Nearby, smaller **SCLÁFANI BAGNI** also attests to its former importance as a fief of the Scláfani family by notching up two fourteenth-century castles and a cathedral. These, though, are minor diversions, and you might as well sit tight in Polizzi Generosa and await the onward bus to the Tyrrhenian coast, or to Palermo, an hour and a quarter away. If you're driving from Polizzi Generosa to the A19, take the access road that heads north; it's much more scenic than the southern route, and has been recently resurfaced, making for a rare smooth ride through the hillside.

Caltanissetta and the western interior

With twice as many inhabitants as Enna, **Caltanissetta** is easily the largest town in the interior, though there's little else that's remarkable about it. Beyond lie the rolling expanses of Sicily's **western interior**, the rural heart of the island. The towns and villages you'll pass through are uniformly poor and raddled; at times, positively ghostlike. Many, like **Corleone**, have names that have become familiar through their Mafia associations, but few are worth even a coffee-stop. The only place that merits more than a cursory glance is the village of **Sant'Ángelo Muxaro**, whose 3000-year-old tombs dot the hill below.

Access **by public transport** is very awkward: you can get to Caltanissetta easily enough, but otherwise you're unlikely to be able to see much more of the region than what you can glean from a bus window on the fast route between Agrigento and Palermo. From Caltanissetta, the railway line meanders northwest (ultimately to Palermo), past a series of empty upland plains occasionally pocked by unexpected crags and gullies, one of the most desert-like of Sicilian journeys.

Caltanissetta and around

Despite the modern sheen that marks out **CALTANISSETTA** from other inland towns, this provincial capital is immersed in the same listless torpor that you find throughout Sicily's interior. Consequently, it's not exactly the most exciting place to end up. If you find yourself changing transport here, you may as well take a look at Caltanissetta's one worthy attraction, the **Museo Archeológico** (daily Mon–Sat 9am–1pm & 3.30–7pm; €2), on Via Napoleone Colajanni, close to the train station, which contains some of Sicily's earliest finds, including vases and Bronze Age sculpted figures. Otherwise, with time to kill, you could

strike out to one of the island's stranger castle sites. The **Castello di Pietrarossa** lies at the town's eastern extremity, though within easy walking distance from Caltanissetta's centre, Piazza Garibaldi. Improbably balanced on an outcrop of rock, the castle – of Arab or Norman origin – looks like it should have fallen down years ago, and you get the feeling that no one would notice if it did.

Back in the centre of town, take a spin round the sagging walls of the seventeenth-century **Palazzo Moncada**, off Corso Umberto I, an aristocratic mansion belonging to one of Sicily's great feudal dynasties; there's an impressive row of waterspouts. For views and fresh air in this traffic-drowned town, stroll down Viale Regina Margherita (a continuation of Corso Umberto I), where there's a park and belvedere.

As well as these meagre attractions, the outskirts of Caltanissetta hold a restored twelfth-century abbey, the **Badia di Santo Spírito**, which drivers en route to Enna might find worth a stop. Lying about 3km north of town, on a left turn off the SS112 (signposted "Santa Caterina Villarmosa"), the abbey was founded by Count Roger and – a rare thing in Sicily – is purely Norman in form. On the outside, the plain structure is only enlivened by three tiny apses at the back, though the interior has more distraction in the form of a fifteenth-century fresco over the central apse and a twelfth-century font. If the church is locked, ring at the door on the right (home of the parish priest).

Practicalities

Train travellers **heading to Enna** would be advised to take a bus instead from Caltanissetta, as Enna's train station is a long way out of town (see p.324). To get to Caltanissetta's **bus station**, head up from Via Kennedy from the tourist office, turn right at Piazza Don Sturzo, left at Via Salemi: the bus station is at Piazza Repubblica, off Via Turati, which begins at the end of Via Salemi (it's about a 25min walk). The two **tourist offices** (Mon–Fri 8am–2pm & 2.45–6.15pm, Wed until 8pm) are at Corso Vittorio Emanuele 109 (☎0934.530.440, ⓦwww.aapit.cl.it), and at Viale Testasecca 20 (☎0934.421.089), at the junction of Via Kennedy and Viale Testasecca.

If you want to **stay** in Caltanissetta, the least expensive choice is the rather swanky *Plaza*, Via Gaetani 5 (☎ & ⓕ0934.583.877; ❸), off Corso Vittorio Emanuele, decorated in restful dark blue colours. The only other central option is the *Hotel San Michele* on Via Fasci Siciliani (☎0934.553.750, ⓕ0934.598.791, ⓦwww.hotelsanmichelesicilia.it; ❼), off Via della Libertà, near the Campo Sportivo at the end of Via Rosso di San Secondo, which is reasonably priced for its four-star rating, with a pool.

One of the best places for a **meal** in Caltanissetta is *Il Ruscello*, on Piazza Trento (up Via Rosso di San Secondo and right at the second set of lights), where around €23 will get you a full spread at this superb traditional restaurant (closed Tues). Closer to the centre, at Via Palmieri 10, *L'Archetto* is an informal pizzeria/*ristorante* that does a couscous paella (closed Tues). For **snacks**, the *RaiR* bar on Corso Umberto I has great almond biscuits (the local speciality), *cannoli* and other ricotta delights, as well as *arancini* and pizza slices (closed Tues).

Seven kilometres west of town, in the village of **San Cataldo**, *U'Anzalone*, on the main corso, is an inexpensive and very traditional *osteria* specializing in such local delicacies as snails, tripe and calves' hooves. It's a good place to visit during the Easter celebrations, when the trial and crucifixion of Christ are re-enacted: Caltanissetta's tourist office has details.

Towards Agrigento: Canicattì and Racalmuto

Buses run southwest down the SS640 from Caltanissetta, reaching Agrigento in around an hour and a quarter. It's more fun to do the same journey by **train**, though, steering out of Caltanissetta through wooded hills and up through almond- and olive-planted slopes into higher, craggy country.

At **CANICATTÌ** the line splits, trains running south to Licata on the coast, or continuing for another hour southwest to Agrigento. Canicattì itself is intriguingly referred to by Italians as their equivalent of Timbuktu, a reference to the town's supposed remoteness. It's actually just a dull market town, not all that remote and barely worth venturing off the train for.

The train route to Agrigento (or a 5km diversion off the main road by car) also runs through **RACALMUTO**, a similarly minor fly-blown town, distinguished only by the fact that it was the birthplace of **Leonardo Sciascia** (1921–89), perhaps the greatest of all modern Sicilian writers (see p.478); he's buried here, too.

Into the western interior

Unless you're driving, the only part of the **western interior** you'll see much of is along the train or bus route between Agrigento and Palermo. The quickest route between the two places – and the path that the direct Agrigento–Palermo bus takes – is following the **SS189**. But if you've the time, you might consider driving along the less-used **SS118**, which passes through some of the remoter inland towns and villages. Either way, there are several short detours worth doing. Both the routes below are described heading north from Agrigento.

The SS189

Around 40km north of Agrigento, a side road off the main **SS189** turns east up to **MUSSOMELI**. On the other side of the town is the extraordinary, crag-perched castle of **Castello Manfredónico**, erected in the fourteenth century by the powerful Chiaramonte family. It makes a vivid impression on the unsuspecting traveller, tilting over its tall rocky base as if lashed by a strong wind.

About 10km west of the SS189, **Monte Cammarata** (1578m) was a key point of the Axis defences in World War II, an impregnable redoubt that was expected to seriously delay the American advance to Palermo in 1943. In the event it was taken without a shot being fired, apparently due to pressure exerted on the Italian soldiers by Calógero Vizzini (Don Calò), head of the island's Mafia.

Back on the main road, halfway between Agrigento and Palermo, **LERCARA FRIDDI**'s claim to fame is as the birthplace of the Sicilian-American gangster Lucky Luciano, freed from a thirty- to fifty-year prison sentence (convicted on 62 counts of "compulsory prostitution") in the US, to be sent to Sicily. Like Don Calò, Luciano was enlisted by the Americans in their Sicilian campaign, which was fully backed by the Mafia in its desire to end the Fascist rule.

A few kilometres north of Lercara, you pick up the SS121, which winds across the entire length of Sicily from Catania and finishes its run in Palermo. Twenty-five kilometres north of the junction at **BAGNI DI CEFALÀ**

– signposted just off the SS121 – are some eleventh-century Arab baths, flowing with thermal waters, which the locals use for washing clothes, though you can swim here too. There are few other examples of Arab architecture in such good condition in Sicily.

The SS118: Sant'Ángelo Muxaro and Corleone

Taking the alternative **SS118**, a minor road that wriggles all the way to Palermo, turn off 30km north of Agrigento at Raffadali for **SANT'ÁNGELO MUXARO**, another 15km along. This small agricultural centre in the middle of the steeply sloping Plátani River valley boasts a number of local *tholos* (tombs) hollowed out of the rock in dome-shaped caves. The earliest date from the eleventh century BC, but most are from around the eighth to the fifth century BC, and recall Minoan and Mycenaean examples in design. You'll spot them as you approach the bare hillside on which the village stands: the road leads up past a ramshackle brick wall, beyond which a path heads along the sheer rock to the "beehive" caves. At the bottom, the largest is known locally as the **tomba del Príncipe**: later converted into a Byzantine chapel, it's half-hidden by overhanging trees and you may have to backtrack to get inside. Like all the others, it's empty now, the finds scattered in various museums around Europe.

You can get to Sant'Ángelo by **bus** from Agrigento with the Lattuca line, leaving from outside Agrigento's Astor cinema on Piazza Vittorio Emanuele (daily at 9am & 2pm); the last bus back leaves at 4pm. Alternatively, you can **spend the night** at *Val di Kam*, just off the town's main piazza at Via Libertà 1 (☎0922.919.670 or 339.530.5989, ⓦwww.valdikam.it; ❶). This family-run bed-and-breakfast outfit also organizes inexpensive hiking, caving and archeological trips around Sant'Ángelo, and is a mine of useful information on the area.

Corleone

The best countryside begins past Alessandria della Rocca, the road climbing up to 1000m at Prizzi, from where there are occasional bus services down to **CORLEONE**, a fairly large town for these parts, squeezed between a couple of rocks with a craggy column at its centre. The only tourists who pass this way come on the scent of the Mafia. Especially in the immediate postwar years, statistics showed the town to have one of the highest murder rates in the world, with 153 violent deaths (out of a population of 18,000) in the four years between 1944 and 1948. One of the men who met a violent end in this period was the trade union leader **Plácido Rizzoto**, who took advantage of the Mafia's internal preoccupations to do the unthinkable and manoeuvre a left-wing town council into power. Two years after his disappearance in 1948, the fire brigade hauled out his dismembered corpse from a ninety-foot crevice near Corleone, along with sackfuls of other bodies of Mafia victims. His killers were eventually acquitted for lack of evidence, the most common end to murder charges brought against mafiosi.

The town's notoriety has been fuelled since it lent Mario Puzo's fictional Godfather, Don Corleone, his adopted family name (though it is also the real-life name of Sicily's most notorious Mafia clan). Fact and fiction merged in January 1993 when Corleonese clan leader, **Salvatore Riina** (see box) – the alleged supreme Sicilian Mafia boss – was arrested on the outskirts of Palermo, having apparently lived in Corleone with his family for over twenty years. The town has little to see, besides the **Museo Anti-Mafia**, Via Orfanotriofo 7 (☎091.846.12.55; Tues–Sun 9am–1pm & 3.30–7.30pm;

Corleone and the Mafia

Mario Puzo chose the name **Corleone** for his central character in *The Godfather* with good reason: for over fifty years it's been the stamping ground of some of the most feared – and respected – Mafia leaders. Many of the so-called *capo di tutti capi* (literally "boss of all the bosses"), who have held sway over an international network of crime and corruption, came originally from the town, including **Luciano Liggio** (imprisoned in 1974) and his effective successor **Salvatore Riina**, who was captured by the Carabinieri in early 1993. Recognized by most Mafia families, and by the authorities, as the present *capo di tutti capi*, Riina's arrest came as a complete surprise – informed on by his driver, a native of San Giuseppe Iato, to the northwest of Corleone, Riina was picked up as he was being driven through Palermo. He was the most-wanted man in Italy, allegedly responsible for ordering at least 150 murders, 40 of which he's said to have committed himself; the authorities also hold him responsible for the murders of anti-Mafia investigators Giovanni Falcone and Paolo Borsellino, both killed in Palermo in 1992.

Once he was under arrest, the political fallout began, since it became clear that for over twenty years Riina had lived with his family openly in Corleone, registering his children at local schools and hospitals, and coming and going pretty much as he pleased. This, it's said with some justification, could only have been the case if Riina had enjoyed some variety of high-level protection; and, if so, who had been responsible for shielding one of the Mafia's most notorious leaders? The arguments that this arrest in particular have provoked will doubtless continue to rumble on. Meanwhile, at the time of writing, Riina is firmly ensconced in prison and declining to say anything; his wife and family have disappeared behind closed doors in Corleone; and his driver – also under arrest – doubtless fears the revenge of Riina's associates. More members of the Corleonese clan have been put away since Riina's arrest, which may yet end the hegemony of this sleepy inland town, though one Bernardo Provenzano – known as "the Tractor" on account of his brutal methods – remains at loose, and may be behind a regrouping of the Cosa Nostra after its recent setbacks.

free), which houses a collection of photographs illustrating the Mafia's violent history, and a few rather old-fashioned bars clustered around the centre. However, it does have one of the area's few **hotels**, the modern and clean *Belvedere* (☎091.846.4964; ❸), on the southern approach road to the town, with views over Corleone from some rooms. Further up the hill, there's a **trattoria** under the same management, *A'Giarra*, a popular place for pizzas and local dishes, with outdoor tables.

Ficuzza

From Corleone, regular buses run through the hills to Palermo, 60km away. If you're driving, though, you could stop at **FICUZZA**, around 25km north, backed by the wooded heights of Rocca Busambra (1613m), which is crisscrossed by a network of mountain paths. The tiny hamlet was once a hunting centre and it's still dominated by Ferdinand III's hunting lodge, the stately **Palazzina Reale** (daily 10am–7pm; free). There's not a great deal of interest inside – Mussolini's troops burnt most of the palace – though the Sala da Pranzo survives, decorated with hunting scenes, as does the queen's bidet. You could have **lunch** in one of the trattorias in the piazza, before heading on to the hills around Piana degli Albanesi, 25km from Palermo (p.123).

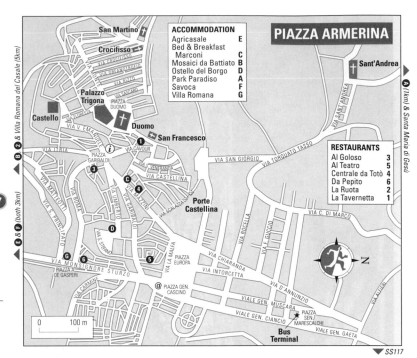

ACCOMMODATION
Agricasale — E
Bed & Breakfast
 Marconi — C
Mosaici da Battiato — B
Ostello del Borgo — D
Park Paradiso — A
Savoca — F
Villa Romana — G

RESTAURANTS
Al Goloso — 3
Al Teatro — 5
Centrale da Totò — 4
Da Pepito — 6
La Ruota — 2
La Tavernetta — 1

Narrow alleys lead down from the terrace of Piazza del Duomo into the older parts of town: an endearing jumble of cobbled flights of steps and faded grandeur, oddly adapted to the modern age. Just behind the cathedral, on a spur off Via Cavour, the seventeenth-century church and former convent of **San Francesco** is now in use as a hospital; at the bottom of a steep street nearby, Via Castellina, the surviving medieval town wall has had a rough arch hacked through it for traffic access; and there's someone living in the adjacent watchtower. The other way, down Via Floresta (to the side of Palazzo Trigona), leads to the closed and tumbledown **castello**, built at the end of the fourteenth century and surrounded by once-rich *palazzi* in a similar state of decay. Best route, though, is down the steep **Via Monte**, once the medieval town's main street. Just east of the Duomo, the adjacent **Piazza Europa** and **Piazza General Cascino** are lively, grassy pedestrian walks teeming with activity, and great spots for people-watching.

The town is compact enough for you to get out fairly easily into the fields and slopes beyond. It's only a kilometre's walk to the twelfth-century Norman church of **Sant'Andrea**, north of town and still impressive despite its simple proportions. Another kilometre or so down the same road, through orchards and gardens, is the sixteenth-century church and convent of **Santa Maria di Gesù**, a low building, gently set amid green hills.

Practicalities

Most **buses** will drop you off at Piazza Senatore Marescalchi, on the main road, Viale Generale Muscara, in the lower, modern town. The old town is further up the hill, centred around Piazza Garibaldi: the **tourist office** is just off here

at Via Cavour 15 (Mon–Fri 9am–1pm & 3–7pm; ℡0935.680.201, @www
.piazza-armerina.it), though it has little information in English.

For **bus information and tickets** to Aidone, Caltagirone and Dittaino
(the nearest train station to Piazza Armerina, 35km north), ask in the *Bar della
Stazione* in Piazza Sen. Marescalchi, or the AST office next door. If you're driving, free **parking** can be found at Piazza Garibaldi and Piazza Duomo, though
you'll have to get there early in the morning to find a space. There's a **taxi** rank
in Piazza Generale Cascino, while **banks** are found either along Via Generale
Ciancio, which runs between piazzas Generale Cascino and Marescalchi, or in
Piazza Garibaldi in the old town. International Point, 30 Piazza Gen. Cascino,
offers **Internet** and **phone** services (daily 9am–1pm & 3–9pm; Internet €4.15
per hour), though its computers are very slow.

Accommodation

There are only two **hotels** in Piazza Armerina itself, one of which is way out
of the centre and decidedly pricey. However, there is a good central **hostel**
and a few peaceful **agriturismo** places just out of town. For all these, it's best
to book ahead.

The only central choice is the rather unattractive and noisily situated *Villa
Romana*, Via A. de Gasperi 18 (℡0935.682.911, ℱ0935.682.912, @www
.piazza-armerina.it/hotelvillaromana; ❸); it's on the southern edge of town, at
the signposted route to the mosaics. For a slightly younger crowd, head for the
Ostello del Borgo (℡0935.687.019, ℱ0935.686.943, @www.ostellodelborgo
.it; ❷), a refurbished fifteenth-century monastery at Largo San Giovanni 6, at
the southern end of Via Umberto; a bed in their dorm-style rooms costs €15,
and they also offer inexpensive Internet access for guests. In a similar price
range, *Bed & Breakfast Marconi* (℡0935.682.989; ❶), Via Marconi 26, offers
several clean, but fairly ordinary rooms. Piazza's top hotel is the *Hotel Park
Paradiso* (℡0935.680.841, ℱ0935.683.391; ❺), 1km beyond the church of
Sant'Andrea and only really of use if you're driving; it's signposted from just
about everywhere in town.

Four kilometres out of town, at the turn-off to the Villa Romana, the *Mosaici
da Battiato* in Contrada Paratore (℡ & ℱ0935.685.453; no credit cards; ❶), is
a friendly enough place, with smart rooms and an outdoor terrace. Taxis here
won't be prohibitively expensive, while the bus to the mosaics passes right by.
Immediately across the roundabout from here, a little way down the road to the
Villa Romana, *La Ruota* restaurant (℡0935.680.542) has space for **camping**,
though it's not an official campsite. Signposted everywhere by a red fox, the
great-value *Agriturismo Agricasale* (℡ & ℱ0935.686.034, @www.agricasale.it; ❸),
5km south of Piazza Armerina, has peaceful rooms and a huge swimming pool,
with a vast multicourse dinner included in the price. Slightly quieter and more
neighbourly, *Savoca* in Contrada da Polleri, 3km south of Piazza Armerina on
the Mirabella Imbáccari road and on the Palermo/Enna/Caltagirone bus route
(℡ & ℱ0935.683.078, @www.agrisavoca.com; ❷) is also a pleasant spot with a
pool, run rather idiosyncratically by a kind man and his teenage sons; go for the
nicer rooms in the main block rather than those beneath the swimming pool.

Eating and drinking

In town, *La Tavernetta*, Via Cavour 14 (closed Sun), is reasonable value for
money, with fish specialities from €8–13, though it offers little atmosphere.
Alternatively, *Da Pepito*, Via Roma 140 (closed Tues in winter), opposite the
park, has a tourist menu featuring some great Sicilian dishes, such as baked
lasagne for €6; in summer there's karaoke on Thursday and Sunday. The

trattoria *Al Goloso* (closed Wed in winter), on Via Garao near Piazza Garibaldi, is also good value, with a nice terrace in front; the rabbit in mushroom sauce goes for €8. Between Piazza Europa and the Duomo, Via Mazzini holds the *Centrale da Totò* (closed Mon), with fine staple dishes and wines, decent prices and local atmosphere; the house speciality *Bocca di Lupo* is a delicious steak dish with prosciutto, aubergine and mozzarella (€8). For close on thirty different types of pizza, try *Al Teatro* (closed Mon in winter), on Via del Teatro, where the outside tables have nice views of the upper town.

Out of town, the *Agricasale* (see above) serves plentiful portions of great home-grown organic food and is open to non-residents; the almond wine is recommended. At the Villa Romana, there are two moderately priced options: the *Mosaici* hotel (see above), which specializes in grills, but is subject to an influx of tour groups at lunch times; and *La Ruota*, across the way (☎0935.680.542), an attractive rustic spot with shaded outdoor seating, and excellent home-made pasta.

Piazza Armerina's **nightlife** is based around the cafés and bars that line piazzas Europa and General Cascino: *Break Coffee*, just in front of the Villa Garibaldi, is one of the most popular.

Villa Romana del Casale

Built on terraces in the rolling countryside that surrounds Piazza Armerina, the **Villa Romana** (daily 8.30am–1hr before sunset; €4.50) at the otherwise virtually uninhabited hamlet of **Casale**, is a confusing swatch of rooms and corridors, built and decorated with pictorial mosaics on a sumptuous scale. There are conflicting theories about its function, though the most convincing explanation of its location in the middle of deserted slopes and woods is that the villa was an occasional retreat and hunting lodge; a theory supported by the many mosaics of animals and birds, including two specific hunting scenes. Dating from the early fourth century AD (though built over an earlier structure), it was used right up until the twelfth century when a mudslide largely covered it until comprehensive excavations began in the 1950s. It's been covered again, more recently, to protect the mosaics, a new roof and walls added to indicate the original size and shape, while walkways lead visitors through the rooms. If you're here in summer, try coming early or late in the day in order to avoid the heat and crowds, as it's rather like being in a greenhouse.

Getting there

From Piazza Armerina, a **bus** (Line B; May–Sept) leaves Piazza Senatore Marescalchi for the Villa Romana at 9am, 10am, 11am, 1pm, 4pm and 5pm; the return service is on the half-hour, starting at 9.30am. Otherwise you'll have to **walk**: head down Via Matteotti or Via Principato and follow the signs – it takes around an hour on foot and is an attractive and enjoyable stroll, though you should avoid doing it in the heat of the sun. If you're pushed for time, a **taxi** from Piazza Generale Cascino in Piazza Armerina costs around €10 one way. There are good illustrated guidebooks in English on sale from the stalls at the entrance. As for food, you can either take your own or head for the adequate bar-restaurant at the site.

Daily buses leave **Caltanissetta** at 6am, 8.15am and 12.15pm (Sun 8.25am only) and arrive at Piazza Armerina an hour later, with return trips at 1.15pm, 3.15pm and 6pm (Sun 1.15pm & 6pm). These buses stop in **Enna** roughly 30 minutes after departure from Caltanissetta; call ☎0934.573.315 to confirm departure times, as schedules sometimes change slightly. Bear in mind that you'll still have to get from Piazza Armerina itself to the site.

The Villa Romana

It's immediately clear from the extent of the uncovered remains that the Villa Romana belonged to an important owner, possibly Maximianus Herculeus, co-Emperor with Diocletian between 286 and 305 AD. The villa is made up of four separate groups of buildings, built on different levels of the hillside and connected by passageways, doors and courtyards. Nearly all of what you see would have been occupied by the family it was built for, though the slaves' housing, presumably also fairly extensive, and other outbuildings, are still to be excavated properly. Yet it's not the building that's the main attraction – although there are few enough surviving examples of such splendid Imperial Roman wealth – so much as the unrivalled interior decoration. The floors of almost the entire building are covered with bright **mosaics** of excellent quality, stylistically belonging to an early fourth-century Roman-African school, which explains many of the more exotic scenes and animals portrayed. Their design also contains several hints as to their period and patron, though given their extent they're likely to have taken fifty or sixty years to complete.

What's left of the villa's **main entrance** gives one of the best impressions of its former grandeur, the approach leading through the remains of a columned

arch into a wide courtyard. Today's site entrance, though, is through the adjacent **thermae** (or baths): a typical arrangement of dressing/massage rooms and plunge-baths around an octagonal **frigidarium**, its central mosaic a marine scene of sea nymphs, tritons, and little cherubs rowing boats and spearing fish. A walkway leads out of the baths and into the villa proper, to the massive central courtyard or **peristyle**. This is where guests would have been received, and the vestibule displays a badly fragmented mosaic depicting a formal welcome by an attendant holding an olive branch. The corridor around the four sides of the courtyard is covered with a series of animal-head medallions: snarling tigers, yapping dogs and unicorns. Just off here, a balcony looks down upon one of the villa's most vivid pictures, a boisterous circus scene showing a chariot race. Starting in the top right-hand corner, the variously coloured chariots rush off, overtaking and crashing at the turns, until finally there's victory for the green faction. The next room's mosaic shows a family attended by slaves on their way to the baths. Period detail – footwear, hairstyles and clothes – helped archeologists to date the rest of the mosaics.

Small rooms beyond, on either side of the peristyle, reveal only fragmentary geometric patterns, although one displays a **small hunting scene**, an episodic adventure ending in a peaceful picnic in the centre. Another room contains what is probably the villa's most famous image, a two-tiered scene of **ten girls**, realistically muscular figures in Roman "bikinis", taking part in various gymnastic and athletic activities. One of the girls, sporting a laurel wreath and a palm frond, is clearly the winner of the competition.

The peristyle is separated from the private apartments and public halls beyond by a long, covered corridor, which contains the best of the villa's mosaic works. The **great hunting scene** sets armed and shield-bearing hunters against a panoply of wild animals, on sea and land. Along the entire sixty-metre length of the mosaic, tigers, ostriches, elephants and even a rhino, destined for the games back in Rome, are pictured being trapped, bundled up and down gangplanks and into cages. The caped figure overseeing the operation is probably Maximianus himself. Much of the scene is set in Africa, Maximianus's main responsibility in the Imperial Tetrarchy, while an ivy-leaf symbol on the costume of the attendant to his right is that of his personal legion, the Herculiani.

Family apartments and public halls beyond are nearly all on a grand scale. A large courtyard, the **xystus**, gives onto the **triclinium**, a dining room with three apses, whose mosaics feature the labours of Hercules. One bloody scene portrays his fight against the giants, all stuck by arrows, who writhe and wail with contorted faces. A path leads around the back to the **private apartments**, based around a large basilica, with mosaics echoing the spectacular scenes of the main building: a **children's circus**, where the small chariots are drawn by colourful birds, and a **children's hunt**, the tiny tots being chased and pecked by the hares and peacocks they're supposed to snare.

Aidone and the site of Morgantina

Fifteen kilometres northeast of Piazza Armerina, there's more classical interest in the extensive remains of the Greek city of **Morgantina**, at its height in the fourth century BC. The site's hard to reach without your own transport, though there are several **buses** daily from Piazza Armerina (from Piazza Senatore Marescalchi) to **Aidone**, a fifteen-minute ride. The site is a long, hot walk away, another 5km beyond the village, along the minor SS288. If you're driving, turn off the SS117 for Aidone at the crossroads known as Madonna della Noce, where there's a large **restaurant-pizzeria**; it's then a gorgeous seven-kilometre ride through the trees to the village.

Aidone

AIDONE itself is a charming little spot, its quiet central square and most of its inhabitants laid-back to the point of being comatose. There are a couple of nice bars, a crumbly church and – signposted in the upper part of the village – the **Museo Archeológico** (daily 8am–6.30pm; €3), an indispensable preliminary to seeing the site itself. Housed in an ex-Capuchin monastery, the museum gathers together all the removable bits and pieces from the ancient city: ceramics, statuettes and third-century BC busts, as well as some domestic artefacts, all imaginatively displayed, while aerial photos and plans of the excavations provide a useful idea of Morgantina's layout.

Morgantina

The **site of Morgantina** (daily 9am–1hr before sunset; €3) occupies two quiet, dusty hillsides. There's a car park close to the west hill (the first you reach), though it's best to continue down the rough track to a second car park near the main entrance under the east hill, opposite which is a **bar-restaurant**, serving decent spaghetti, grilled meats and local wine.

After its demise, the city became buried and forgotten for almost two thousand years, and even after the site's discovery it wasn't identified as Morgantina until 1957. To date, only a fifth of the city has been excavated, but the finds have shed much light on the island's pre-Hellenic Sikel population, who inhabited central Sicily from the ninth century BC. In the sixth century BC, Chalcidian Greeks settled here and lived in harmony alongside the Sikels until the city became the centre of a revolt led by the Sikel leader Ducetius, who destroyed it in the late fifth century BC. Swiftly rebuilt on a grid-plan with walled and towered defences, Morgantina reached its apogee in the fourth and third centuries BC under the protection of Syracuse, and many of the surviving buildings date from this period. A couple of hundred years later the city was in decline and soon after was abandoned altogether.

From the main entrance a path (straight ahead) leads directly onto Morgantina's most distinctive ruin, the **agora**, bounded by three stepped sides, used as seats for public meetings. The small **teatro** to its right was built in the third century BC, but reconstructed in Roman times. Performances of Greek plays are sometimes held here in the summer: check with the site office (☎0935.86.777) or the tourist office in Enna (see p.324). Immediately in front is a Roman building, behind which (next to the *agora*) is a fourth-century BC **santuario** of Demeter and Kore. On the level ground behind the *agora* is a granary and square slaughterhouse, beyond which stretches the 100-metre-long **east stoa**. Further up the hillside stand the ruins of some Hellenic **houses**, with two mosaic floors. One, the "House of Ganymede", has an illustration of the youth Ganymede being carried away to Olympus by Zeus's eagle to become the cupbearer of the gods.

Excavations on the **west hill**, a twenty-minute walk across the site, are less revealing, but you'll come across the fairly substantial remains of houses, some with mosaics, roads and walls, in what was once a residential area of the ancient city. In recent years, the remains of a second temple and a spring and aqueduct have been unearthed, though these aren't open for public viewing yet.

South to Caltagirone

Around 16km south of Piazza Armerina, the minor SS124 breaks east off the Gela road and heads for Caltagirone, passing through fine farming country, at its best around the village of **SAN MICHELE DI GANZARIA**. There's no particular reason to break your journey here, though you might be tempted by *Pomara*, at Via Vittorio Véneto 84 (℡0933.976.976, 🅦www.hotelpomara.com; ❻), a surprisingly fine hotel for the sticks with a large pool and excellent views, and the village's couple of pizzerias. The bus from Piazza Armerina also comes this way, though diverting first to the even tinier **Mirabella Imbáccari**, just to the north. All told, it's just under an hour from Piazza Armerina to the heights of Caltagirone.

Caltagirone

There were settlers in **CALTAGIRONE** well before the Greeks, making it one of the most ancient of Sicilian towns, but the present name derives from the Arabic (*kalat*, "castle" and *gerun*, "caves"). Nothing from these periods survives, and the dominant impression of the town is Baroque. Its central swath of monumental buildings date from the rebuilding after the 1693 earthquake that flattened the area. Well before that, though, Caltagirone had acquired a reputation for the excellence of its **ceramics**, an industry given an added dimension with the arrival of the Arabs, who introduced local craftsmen to the glazed polychromatic colours – in particular, blues and yellows – which have subsequently become typically Sicilian in execution. Up until the great earthquake, the town supported a population of around 20,000, of whom perhaps five percent were actively engaged in the tiled decoration of churches and public buildings. The Baroque rebuilding saw a further burst of creative construction; later, in the nineteenth century, came the principal period of ceramic figurative work (excellent examples are on display in the town museum); while today, Caltagirone's traditional industry is flourishing again, with over seventy ceramicists displaying work at galleries across the town.

The Town

The old **upper town** has great public edifices, decorative churches and public gardens spread across three hills, the effect lightened by tiled decoration found in nooks and crannies everywhere; with recent renovations, a good selection of shops and general activity, it has an upbeat feel.

Most effective decorations are the ceramic flowers and emblems flanking both sides of the **Ponte San Francesco** on the way into the centre from the train station. The grandest statement, though, is undoubtedly made by the 142 steps of **La Scala**, which cut right up one of Caltagirone's hills to the sorely neglected church of Santa Maria del Monte at the top. The risers in between each step are covered with a hand-painted ceramic pattern, no two the same. It's a tough climb, but the views from the top are magnificent, across town to the distinctive spire of the Sicilian Baroque church of San Francesco all'Immacolata, with the plain stretching away into the distance beyond. The staircase was originally conceived at the turn of the seventeenth century as a road between the Santa Maria del Monte church, then the town cathedral, and the Senatorial Palace below; the steps were added once it was clear that the incline was too steep, but the majolica-tile risers are a much more recent addition, in place only since 1954. On July 24 and 25 every year, the steps are lit by thousands of coloured paper lamps as part of the celebrations for the feast of St James (San Giácomo).

On either side of the staircase, all the way up, are some of the **workshops** and galleries of today's ceramicists, all worth venturing inside even if you're not

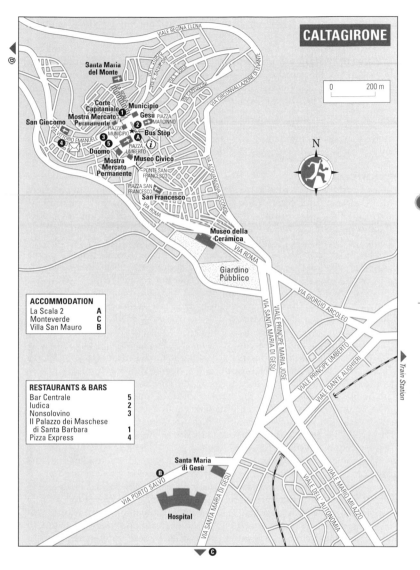

ACCOMMODATION
La Scala 2	A
Monteverde	C
Villa San Mauro	B

RESTAURANTS & BARS
Bar Centrale	5
Iudica	2
Nonsolovino	3
Il Palazzo dei Maschese di Santa Barbara	1
Pizza Express	4

▶ *Train Station*

planning to buy. The **Museo della Cerámica**, in the large public garden off Via Roma (daily 9am–6.30pm; €2.50), is stuffed full of original ceramicware, while the **Mostra Mercato Permanente** (Mon–Sun 9am–8pm), with venues on both Via Vittorio Emanuele, just to the right at the bottom of La Scala, and Piazza Umberto, is the best place to see and buy modern ceramics made by local artists.

At the top of La Scala, the church of **Santa Maria del Monte** itself holds little of interest beyond a venerated image from the thirteenth century, the *Madonna dei Conadomini*, and a belltower which, when open, affords excellent views over the town. There are several more striking buildings in the upper town, however, including (beyond Piazza Umberto and the restyled **Duomo**), the seventeenth-century **Corte Capitaniale**, a sturdy, long and low building decorated by the Gagini family and used today for temporary exhibitions. Back below Piazza Umberto, the solid square-built block with grilled windows and spike-studded metal doors was once an eighteenth-century Bourbon prison, and now houses the **Museo Cívico** (Mon–Fri 8am–2pm & 3.30–7.30pm, Sat & Sun 9am–1pm & 3.30–7.30pm; €2.50). This has a small display of modern ceramics, as well as a collection of local curios – architectural fragments, paintings by the Vaccaro family who renovated the cathedral in the nineteenth century, and a gilded, sixteenth-century processional cart.

Practicalities

Buses nearly all stop first in Piazza Municipio in the upper town, where you should get off if you're only looking around for the day. If you're planning on staying, stay on until the new town, a couple of kilometres below, which is home to the **train station** and Caltagirone's only accommodation. When **leaving town**, Pitrelli buses to Ragusa depart from Viale Príncipe Umberto 215, and AST services leave from outside the Metropol cinema further up the road – though again they should all call at Piazza Municipio in the upper town on the way. The helpful **tourist office** (Mon–Sat 9am–7pm, Sun 9am–1pm & 3–7pm; ☎0933.53.809) is in the upper town, down an alley (Via Volta Libertini) just off Piazza Umberto, while Link di Cusumano Desirée, Via A. Manzoni 46 in the new town, provides decent **Internet** access.

Accommodation in the centre is rather limited, but *La Scala 2* (☎0933.57.781 or 335.768.18.67; ❷) has **rooms** to rent right in the main square at Piazza Umberto I 1, with shared bathrooms and a degree of noise from the piazza; book in advance in summer or drop in at the *La Scala* restaurant (see below). The hotel *Monteverde* (☎0933.53.682; ❸), south of town at Via delle Industrie 11, is comfortable with a good restaurant, and if you're driving it's a better bet than the expensive and ugly *Villa San Mauro*, at Via Porto Salvo 18 (☎0933.26.500, ⓦwww.framonhotels.com; ❻).

Perhaps the nicest **place to eat** in the upper town is the excellent *Il Palazzo dei Marchese di Santa Barbara*, located within a cavernous ex-residence of the aristocracy, at the foot of La Scala; they serve an upmarket menu at good prices (€5–7 for firsts – try the Marchese pasta) and are usually packed in the summer, especially on the terrace; there's a pianist at weekends. Also good value is *Nonsolovino*, on Via Vittorio Emanuele at Piazza Municipio (closed Mon), with an average tourist menu at around €15, while *Iudica* on Discesa Collegio, in front of the Gesù church, is a good *távola calda*, with an outdoor terrace. On Via Vittorio Emanuele, the friendly *Pizza Express*, at no. 121 (no credit cards), serves *Braccio di Ferro* (with spinach) and *Da Francesca* (with sausage and mushroom) pizzas alongside its regular choices, while the *Bar Centrale*, at no. 23, has indoor and outdoor seating and serves sandwiches and great ice cream. There's a daily food **market** in the mornings on Piazza Marcinnò, behind and below the Gesù church.

Around Caltagirone: Grammichele and Monte San Mauro

Just ten minutes **east** of Caltagirone by train, **GRAMMICHELE** is one of the most ambitious of the new towns built after the 1693 earthquake. The best place to appreciate its hexagonal design would be from the air – failing that, position yourself at the dead centre of the town's imposing central piazza to see the six radial streets reaching out, each bisected by secondary piazzas. The shape's no longer entirely perfect, due to a surfeit of new streets around the station at the southern edges of town, but it makes for an intriguing couple of hours' stroll, with all the streets in each segment corresponding exactly to their neighbours in dimension and appearance. Despite the grand design, Grammichele is a rather tatty, predominantly rural-looking town – be prepared to meet a donkey in the road, or see chickens cooped up in a basement, and farms near the train station. **Piazza Carafa**, the main square, has a handful of old-fashioned **bars** where most of the town's over-60s gather. For a bit more life, head down Corso Vittorio Emanuele, past *Bar Sinatra*, to Piazza Dante, where the *Bar Iudia*, with outdoor seating, has sandwiches and snacks as well as pastries and ice cream. There's nowhere to stay in town, but for **pizzas** and beer, there's *Michelangelo*, on the corner of Corso Vittorio Emanuele and Via Garibaldi.

If you're driving or travelling by train **south** of Caltagirone, look out for the hill of **Monte San Mauro**, halfway to Niscemi, which was the scene of the one battle that could be called a separatist uprising in Sicily. At the end of 1945, Concetto Gallo, lawyer, landowner and commander-in-chief of the Separatist army (EVIS), led 58 men in a last stand against a force of five thousand Italian troops commanded by three generals. Gallo's inevitable defeat signalled the effective end of the Separatist movement in Sicily.

Festivals

March/April
Easter Holy Week celebrations in **Enna**; including processions, special Masses and the parade of saintly relics. Running all week from Palm Sunday to Easter Sunday, the best day is Good Friday, when thousands march in silent procession dressed in the white-hooded costumes of the medieval fraternities. More costumed processions can be seen at **Caltagirone**, **Troina** and at **Caltanissetta** (best days Maundy Thursday and Good Friday), with processional carts (the *misteri*) and monks. **Prizzi**, in the western interior, is a good place to be on Easter Sunday, when giant statues of Christ and the Virgin Mary are taunted by masked figures representing Death and the Devil, to whom onlookers are forced to give money.
The **motor racing** season starts at the Autodromo di Pergusa, around the **Lago di Pergusa**, running until September.

May
Sagra del Lago Throughout the month at **Lago di Pergusa**, with folk events and fireworks, singing competitions and games.
Penultimate Sunday Festa dei Rami at **Troina**, in which laurel branches are carried to the tomb of St Silvester.

July
Estate Ennese Beginning of a series of concerts and opera in the open-air theatre at the castle in **Enna**. Runs until end of August.
24–25 Festival of San Giácomo in **Caltagirone**, when the La Scala steps are illuminated.

August
13–14 Il Palio dei Normanni in **Piazza Armerina**, a medieval pageant commemorating Count Roger's taking of the town in the eleventh century. Processional entry into town on the thirteenth, ceremonial joust on the fourteenth, along with costumed parades and other festive events. There are similar events around the same time in a number of surrounding towns, though Piazza's is by far the largest.

September
Festival of Madonna dell'Alto in **Petralia Sottana**, with a nocturnal procession on horseback and a maypole dance known as the Ballo della Cordella.

December
Annual exhibition of terracotta sculpted cribs in **Caltagirone**.

Travel details

Trains

Caltagirone to: Catania (7–9 daily Mon–Sat; 1hr 40min–2hr); Gela (8–10 daily Mon–Sat, 5 daily Sun; 35min); Grammichele (7–9 daily Mon–Sat, 2 daily Sun; 15min).

Caltanissetta to: Agrigento (8 daily; 1hr 20min); Canicattì (10 daily; 30min); Gela (9 daily; 2hr); Licata (9 daily; 1hr 20min).

Enna to: Caltanissetta (8 daily Mon–Sat, 7 daily Sun; 1hr); Catania (7 daily; 1hr 20min); Palermo (5 daily; 2hr 20min).

Buses

Agira to: Troina (4 daily Mon–Sat, 1 daily Sun; 50min).

Caltagirone to: Catania (11 daily Mon–Sat, 4 daily Sun; 1hr 25min); Gela (5 daily Mon–Sat; 1hr 25min); Grammichele (2 daily Mon–Sat; 30min); Piazza Armerina (6 daily Mon–Sat; 45min–1hr 20min); Ragusa (4 daily Mon–Sat; 1hr 30min).

Caltanissetta to: Agrigento (6–8 daily Mon–Sat, 7 daily Sun; 1hr 15min); Caltagirone (1–2 daily; 2hr 10min); Canicattì (5–8 daily Mon–Sat, 7 daily Sun; 35min); Catania (5–8 daily Mon–Sat, 7 daily Sun; 1hr 35min); Enna (4 daily Mon–Sat; 40–55min); Piazza Armerina (5 daily; 1hr 20min).

Cesarò to: Giardini-Naxos (1 daily Mon–Sat; 2hr 20min); Randazzo (1 daily Mon–Sat; 45min); Sant'Agata (1 daily; 1hr 30min).

Enna to: Agira (6 daily Mon–Sat; 1hr); Calascibetta (12 daily Mon–Sat, 2 daily Sun; 30min); Caltanissetta (5 daily Mon–Sat; 40–55min); Catania (8–11 daily Mon–Sat, 3 daily Sun; 1hr 20min); Gela (1 daily Mon–Sat; 1hr 20min); Leonforte (7–10 daily Mon–Sat; 35min); Palermo (3 daily Mon–Sat, 2 daily Sun; 1hr 45min–2hr); Pergusa (hourly Mon–Sat, 6 daily Sun; 20min); Piazza Armerina (7 daily Mon–Sat, 2 daily Sun; 40min); Regalbuto (4 daily Mon–Sat; 1hr 30min).

Gangi to: Enna (1 daily Mon–Sat; 1hr 45min); Palermo (1–2 daily Mon–Sat, 1 daily Sun; 3hr); Sperlinga (1 daily Mon–Sat; 20min).

Leonforte to: Catania (10 daily Mon–Sat, 2 daily Sunday; 1hr 40min); Enna (16 daily Mon–Sat, 2 daily Sun; 35min); Nicosia (6 daily Mon–Sat, 1 daily Sun; 45min).

Nicosia to: Agira (1 daily Mon–Sat; 50min); Catania (6 daily Mon–Sat; 2hr 15min); Gangi (4 daily Mon–Sat, 2 daily Sun; 45min); Leonforte (5–6 daily Mon–Sat; 40min); Petralia Soprana (4 daily Mon–Sat, 2 daily Sun; 1hr 20min); Petralia Sottana (4 daily Mon–Sat, 2 daily Sun; 1hr 30min); Polizzi Generosa (2 daily; 2hr); Sperlinga (2 daily; 15min); Palermo (6–8 daily Mon–Sat, 2 daily Sun; 2hr 40min).

Piazza Armerina to: Aidone (8 daily Mon–Sat, 2 daily Sun; 15min); Caltagirone (2 daily Mon–Sat, 1 daily Sun; 45min); Enna (7 daily Mon–Sat, 1 daily Sun; 40min); Gela (5 daily Mon–Sat, 2 daily Sun; 40min); Palermo (5–6 daily Mon–Sat, 3 daily Sun; 2hr 15min).

Polizzi Generosa to: Caltavuturo (1 daily Mon–Sat; 35min); Palermo (Mon–Sat 5 daily, 2 daily Sun; 1hr 15min); Términi Imerese (2 daily Mon–Sat; 1hr 30min).

Troina to: Agira (4 daily Mon–Sat, 2 daily Sun; 50min).

8

The south coast

N

TYRRHENIAN SEA

1

3

1

2

4

9

7

5

8

6

9

8

MEDITERRANEAN SEA

0   50 km

CHAPTER 8

Highlights

* **Museo Archeológico, Gela** Stunning painted vases were a speciality of Greek Gela, and the town's museum holds scores of fine examples. **p.353**

* **Tempio della Concordia, Agrigento** This simple, elegant temple provides the backdrop for an atmospheric walk in the past. **p.360**

* **Eraclea Minoa** A superb sandy beach overlooked by the impressive remains of a Greek city. **p.365**

* **Sciacca** Medieval buildings and quirky stone heads at Castello Incantato make underrated Sciacca a worthwhile stop. **p.366**

* **Lampedusa** The rocky shore, cliffs and grottoes of Lampedusa are best seen on a boat tour of the island. **p.371**

△ Isola dei Conigli, Lampedusa

8

The south coast

The long south coast, from Gela to Sciacca, should be one of the most attractive parts of Sicily. Sparsely developed, there are good beaches and some low-key Mediterranean ports and resorts which are barely known to Italians, let alone other tourists. Nevertheless, sporadic but spectacularly ugly coastal industrial development conspires to put off many people. The sea is heavily polluted in some areas, particularly around **Gela**, a large port and petrochemical town. But to give this coast a miss would be to ignore some of the most important sights on the island. Gela itself retains its extensive Greek fortifications, while further west the hill-top town of **Agrigento** overlooks a series of splendid ancient temples, unrivalled in extent and preservation outside Greece.

On either side of Agrigento, isolated sandy **beaches** – packed with locals on summer weekends – warrant the occasional trip off the busy main road, the SS115. One of the best lies just below another Hellenic site, **Eraclea Minoa**, while the port of **Licata** has a few old-town diversions to go with its beach. Of the other coastal towns, **Sciacca** is perhaps the most enjoyable, a fishing port and summer resort with amazing cliff-top views, and from here you can make a couple of detours into the tall and craggy mountains that back this part of the coast. Or you might consider heading out to the **Pelágie Islands**: these barren spots in the Mediterranean are closer to Africa than Europe, but are connected by regular ferry and hydrofoil with **Porto Empédocle**, near Agrigento.

Regular **train** and **bus** services link the coastal towns and villages, while there are less frequent services to the inland towns. **Hotel** accommodation is limited outside the major settlements, but there are plenty of opportunities to **camp** at sites along the coast.

Gela

GELA couldn't present a worse aspect as the train edges into town through a mess of futuristic steel bubbles and pipes – the city is known locally as "Beirut". Despite a few fine dune-backed beaches in the vicinity, you wouldn't come here to bathe as there are serious doubts about the cleanliness of the water, and there's often a chemical tang to the air. It was not always so. Gela was one of the most important of Sicily's Greek cities, founded in 688 BC, and under Hippocrates in the fifth century BC it rivalled even ancient Syracuse as the island's political hub. Its artistic eminence attracted literary stars, most notably the dramatist Aeschylus, who left his mark on the city (literally) when felled by a tortoise dropped by an eagle, which – the tale relates – mistook

Catánia

Ragusa

Palermo

Palermo

Palermo

Santa Margherita di Bélice

Castelvetrano

25 km

0

Piazza Armerina

Enna

Mazzarino

Caltagirone

Caltanissetta

SS117

Butera

Il Castelluccio

SS191

Gela

SS115

Ravanusa

Falconara Sicula

Manfria

Canicattì

Campobello di Licata

Palma di Montechiaro

Licata

SS640

Favara

Naro

SS115

V. Mosè

Sant'Angelo Muxaro

Raffadali

SS118

Marina di Palma

Cattólica Eraclea

Agrigento

San Leone

Montallegro

Porto Empédocle

To Pelágie Islands

Ribera

SS115

Eraclea Minoa

Caltabellota

Monte San Calógero (388m)

Sambuca di Sicila

SS188

SS115

Sciacca

Menfi

Porto Palo

N

PELÁGIE ISLANDS

Linosa

Linosa

To Porto Empédocle

Pelágie Islands

Lampedusa

Lampedusa

Lampione

his bald head for a stone on which to dash its prey. However, Gela's heyday was short-lived. Hippocrates' successor, Gelon, transferred his power and half the city's population east to Syracuse in 485 BC, the deep-water harbour there being more to the tyrant's liking. Gela was subsequently smashed by the Carthaginians and the Mamertines, its walls razed in the third century BC and abandoned to the encroaching sands. Modern Gela was the first Sicilian town to be liberated by the Allies in 1943, but otherwise – beyond an excellent archeological museum and a fine set of Greek defensive walls – is almost entirely without interest.

Gela's Greek remains

There's really no need to stay longer than half a day in Gela, time enough to see the only two sights, which lie at either end of the town's main Corso Vittorio Emanuele. At its eastern end, a twenty-minute walk from the centre, Gela's **Museo Archeológico** (daily 9am–1pm & 3–7pm; €3, includes entry to Greek fortifications) is notable largely for its important collection of painted vases upstairs. Mainly seventh- to fifth-century BC, the black and red jugs and beakers were Greek Gela's speciality: most major world museums tend to feature one or two, but the bulk are here. Other impressive finds include an animated sculpture of a horse's head (sixth-century BC) and the remains of necropoli from Geloan dependencies. Outside the museum, a small **acropolis** has been uncovered, consisting of a few walls and a single temple column from the fifth century BC, though the small site loses all its romance to the brooding, dirty industrial plant that dominates the beach below.

There are more archeological remains at **Capo Soprano**, at the western end of town. Head along the corso and take a left fork (Via Manzoni), which runs parallel to the sea as far as the red gates of the site, a three- to four-kilometre walk. The **Greek fortifications** here (daily 9am–1hr before sunset; €3, includes entry to Museo Archeológico) date from the fourth century BC. Preserved by the sand dunes under which they were discovered, the walls stand nearly 8m high in parts, made up of perfectly fitted stone blocks topped by a layer of brick and now covered in protective glass panels. It's a beautiful site, and you're free to wander around the line of the walls: in some places you can make out the remains of watchtowers and gateways, while waves crash onto a duned stretch of beach below. If you've come this far out of town, you may as well nip around the corner (back towards the centre and left, by the hospital), to Via Europa, to see the remains of Gela's fourth-century BC **public baths**, the only ones from Greek times discovered in Sicily and still equipped with their original seats.

Practicalities

Driving into town, simply follow the signs for museum and fortifications – it's slow going on the SS115, which cuts right through the centre. **Buses** leave from directly outside the **train station** (tickets and information from the Autolinee office, across the square): there are regular departures to nearby towns, including Licata and Agrigento, Vittória, Caltanissetta and Siracusa. From the station, turn right down the main road and, at the junction, bear right for the town centre and Corso Vittorio Emanuele.

Information can be obtained at the **tourist office** at Via Palazzi 211, further up Via Europa and then right, on the corner with Via Francia (Mon–Fri 8am–2.30pm & Wed 4–7pm; summer also Sat & Sun 8am–2.30pm; ☎0933.911.509).

You won't want **to stay** in Gela, though if you get stuck, the *Sole* isn't bad, on Via Mare 32 (☎0933.925.292; no credit cards, ❹).

Around Gela

With your own transport, you can pay a quick visit to Gela then strike off inland to the medieval town of Butera or west along the coast to find a beach. Gela's surroundings don't improve until you're a good few kilometres out of town in any direction. Best for scenery are the two **inland** routes north: either up the SS191 to the hill-town of Butera, or northeast along the scenic SS117, which swoops towards Caltagirone/Piazza Armerina, following the line of the fertile Gela valley; by car, you can be in either within the hour, the road taking you through rolling cornfields and vineyards. For the coast to the **west of Gela**, stick to the main SS115, which runs through town.

Inland to Butera

Around 8km out of Gela on the SS117, at a small road junction, a forlorn Norman keep – **Il Castellúccio** – sticks out on a hillock, in the middle of land keenly contested at the start of the Allied landings in Sicily in 1943. Defensive concrete pillboxes still stud the dirt-brown hillsides on either side of the keep.

From Il Castellúccio, a minor road runs 7km west to join the rather more direct SS191 from Gela, which runs to **BUTERA** in twenty winding kilometres. An important sixteenth-century town, under the control of the Barresi princes, Butera today idles along in its lofty, remote way, pulling in the occasional stray driver to Caltanissetta, another 50km north. It's a pretty little place, with the drive up alone revealing why Butera was once coveted by medieval overlords – the town sits on an impregnable crag, overseeing a patchwork of walled fields, burnt hillsides, bare peaks, regimented rows of vines and tomato plantations.

All traffic (including buses from Gela and Caltanissetta) pulls into Piazza Dante, the main square, from where Via Aldo Moro leads up in five minutes to the **Castello dei Normanni**, a yellowing pile of which one battlemented wall and the central keep survive, incongruously tucked between modern apartment blocks. From the terrace beyond are tremendous views, to Gela and the coast.

Back in Piazza Dante, you can get a drink while contemplating the next move. *La Lanterna* has outdoor seats, and doubles as an inexpensive pizzeria-restaurant, while both *Big Ben* and the adjacent *Britannia* bars are as oddly named a pairing as you'll come across in Sicily.

West along the coast to Falconara Sicula

The long, empty coastline to the west of Gela is dotted by more pillboxes left behind after the war. Following the SS115 from Gela, there's a decent sand **beach** at **MANFRIA**, just off the main road, although you won't get to stop here if you're travelling by train, as it loops inland soon after Gela and doesn't stop until **FALCONARA SICULA**, a few kilometres beyond. There's little at either place apart from their respective beaches, though Falconara boasts a fourteenth-century castle – the private property of Palermitan aristocrats – and a local **campsite**: the *Due Rocche* (☎0934.349.006), with a **hotel** attached, the *Lido degli Angeli* (☎0934.349 054; no credit cards, ❹).

Licata and around

Ten kilometres further along the coast, the port of **LICATA** is the only other worthwhile coastal stop before Agrigento, though there's not much here that can't be seen in an hour or so. There's certainly nothing left of ancient Phintias, the settlement founded here in 280 BC by Greeks from Gela whose own city had been destroyed in successive attacks. Instead, the centre of Licata is largely Baroque in character, with a lower town split into two distinct halves: pavement cafés line the two wide corsos that form an L-shape at the heart of town, while behind here, the narrow crisscrossed alleys of the old town reach back to the harbour. There's a lido and **beach** just up from the harbour, though as Licata is still a working port, full of maritime hardware, it's hardly attractive. For a view over the harbour, climb up to the top of the town from the main Corso Roma and then work your way round the hill to reach an imposing sixteenth-century **castello**. Other strolls can take in the lively old-town **market** (over by 2pm), held in the cobbled square in front of the church, and some of Licata's good *palazzi*, the most prominent being the gargoyle-studded **Palazzo Canarelli** on Corso Roma. The **Museo Cívico** in Piazza Linares, off Corso Umberto (Tues–Sat 9am–12.30pm & 4–7pm; free), displays a good deal of local prehistoric and Greek material.

Practicalities
Buses pull up on Corso Roma, right in the centre; the bar at no. 36 posts timetables and sells tickets for departures to Agrigento, Gela, Catania and Palermo. The **train station** is five minutes' walk away: go back down the corso to the church, turn right down Via Giovanni Amendola, left at the bottom and then take the fifth right, down a little street called Via Stazione.

There are a couple of **hotels**, though neither are terribly alluring: try the simple *Roma*, Corso Serrovira 54 (☎0922.774.075; no credit cards, ❷); walk down Corso Roma to Piazza Progresso, turn left down Corso Umberto, and after 200m take a left again onto Corso Serrovira. Alternatively, the *Al Faro*, Via Dogana 6 (☎0922.775.503, ☏0922.773.087; ❺ including breakfast), by the port and near the lido, has its own decent restaurant, though the surroundings are nothing special. Licata's **dining** choices are limited: there are a few pizza joints by the lido, or you could try *Pizza Pizza* at 109 Corso Umberto, though you'll be lucky to get anything more than a reheated slice of *margarita*. Alternatively, there's the basic *Il Veliero*, Via Dessié 12 – from the piazza make a right off Corso Umberto at the IP petrol station and then a second right – an ordinary trattoria with moderate prices.

Around Licata: Palma di Montechiaro and Naro

If you're heading straight for Agrigento, it's quicker to pick up a direct bus at Licata than stick with the train, which swoops inland to Canicattì before doubling back to the coast. If you're driving, though, there are a couple of stops you could make along the way.

From Licata, it's 20km to shabby **PALMA DI MONTECHIARO**, which lies just off the SS115; the Agrigento–Licata bus passes this way too. This was once the seat of the Lampedusa family, the last of whom – **Giuseppe Tomasi di Lampedusa** – wrote the acclaimed novel, *The Leopard*. He died in 1957 (*The Leopard* was published a year later), though the palace in Palma had lain derelict for a long time before that. Indeed, far more resonant for *Leopard* fans are the ruins in the western Sicilian town of Santa Margherita di Belice (see p.425). Today, the only echoes of the great feudal family recorded in the novel are to be found in Palma's imposing seventeenth-century **Chiesa Matrice**, built by one of Lampedusa's ancestors and approached by a wide flight of crumbling steps, and the ruined site of the **Castello di Palma**, a few kilometres to the west of town at the end of a small track. Four kilometres south of town, on the coast, **MARINA DI PALMA** has a strip of beach, mobbed by locals at weekends in summer.

North of Palma, the road climbs 17km up to medieval **NARO**, whose thirteenth- and fourteenth-century buildings merit a look if you have time on your hands; there are SAIS **bus** services here from Agrigento (4 daily, last one returning at 3.30pm; call ☎0922.595.933 for up-to-date schedules). The best of the buildings are the Chiaramonte **castello** at Naro's highest point, and the nearby ruins of the old cathedral; other churches in this walled and battlemented town are emphatically Baroque. Architecturally harmonious though Naro is, the real attraction is less the end destination and more the drive itself, from Palma and Agrigento, which is rewarded by extensive sweeping views down to the coast.

Agrigento

No one comes to **AGRIGENTO** for the town, though its worn medieval streets and buildings soak up thousands of tourists every year. The interest instead focuses on the substantial remains of Akragas, Pindar's "most beautiful city of mortals", a couple of kilometres below. Strung out along a ridge facing the sea, its series of Doric temples are the most captivating of Sicilian Greek remains and are unique outside Greece.

In 581 BC, colonists from nearby Gela and Rhodes founded the city of Akragas between the rivers of Hypsas and Akragas. It was the concluding act of expansion that had seen Geloans spread west along the high points of their trade routes, subduing and Hellenizing the indigenous populations as they went. They surrounded the new city with a mighty wall, formed in part by a higher ridge where they placed the acropolis (and where, today, the modern town stands). The southern limit of the ancient city was a second, lower ridge and it was here, in the so-called **Valle dei Templi** (Valley of the Temples), that the city architects erected their sacred buildings during the fifth century BC. They were – and are – stunning in their effect, reflecting the wealth and luxury of ancient Agrigento: "Athens with improvements", as Henry Adams had it in 1899.

But, as so often, Agrigento's Hellenic pre-eminence was no buffer against the cruel tide of Sicilian history. Conquered and sacked by successive waves of Carthaginians, Romans (twice), Saracens and Normans, the ancient city lost its status and many of its finest treasures. In a way, Agrigento never really

AGRIGENTO

N

RESTAURANTS & CAFÉS
Atenea	2
Caffeteria Nobel	7
Chez Jean 2	1
Concordia	4
L'Ambasciate di Sicilia	6
La Corte degli Sfizi	3
Manhattan	5
Trattoria Caico	9
Trattoria dei Templi	8

ACCOMMODATION
Amici	E
Bella Napoli	A
Belvedere	C
Camere a Sud	B
Collaverde Park	F
Del Viale	D
Pirandello Mare	H
Villa Athena	G

Casa Pirandello

Porto Empèdocle (9km)

San Leone, campsites, **H** & **9**

San Leone

Villaggio Mosè, Lìcata & Gela

8

THE SOUTH COAST | Agrigento

recovered, and despite the undoubted modern pulling-power of the temples which fills the town with tourists throughout much of the year, there's little sense of purpose here. Ugly modern suburban building and road flyovers on the coast below town lack all sense of proportion and are creeping ever closer to the temples themselves. Meanwhile, government statistics show Agrigento to be one of Italy's poorest towns; consequently it comes as no surprise to learn that the Mafia has an undue local influence. Speculative building projects aside, Agrigento crime families are generally reckoned to be heavily involved in trafficking cocaine from South America.

Arrival, getting around and information

Coming by public transport, you'll arrive in the centre of town. While you could easily jump straight on a bus to the **Valle dei Templi** archeological site, **the town** itself is worth exploring and has some decent accommodation options. Six kilometres south of Agrigento, the resort of **San Leone** has several hotels and restaurants, two campsites and a decent beach, while 6km southwest of town, **Porto Empédocle** is the departure-point for ferries to the Pelágie Islands, Lampedusa and Linosa.

Trains arrive at the edge of the old town at Stazione Centrale, with a beautiful garden and a number of luggage lockers (€2 for 12 hours) – don't make the mistake of getting out at Agrigento Bassa, 3km north of town. **Buses** arrive at the terminal in Piazza Roselli, near the post office a few minutes' walk to the north. If you're **driving** into Agrigento, be warned that the one-way system in the old town is a nightmare. Some hotels are signposted, but you may well not be able to **park** anywhere near where you're staying. You can usually bag a space on Viale della Vittória or Via F. Crispi, but make sure you don't leave anything visible in the car.

City transport and information

The old town stretches west of the three main interlocking squares, piazzas Marconi, Aldo Moro and Vittorio Emanuele. Via Atenea is Agrigento's principal artery, running west from Piazza Aldo Moro. **City buses** (€0.90 for 90 minutes) leave from outside the train station on Piazza Marconi to the temples and the beach at San Leone; buses to Porto Empédocle for the Pelágie Islands leave from Piazza Roselli. You need to buy bus tickets before your journey from kiosks or *tabacchi*, not on the bus. There's a kiosk on either side of Piazza Marconi, though they're not always open on Sundays. **Taxi** ranks are at Piazzale Aldo Moro and outside the train station (phone numbers for taxi firms are given in "Listings", p.364).

There are various **tourist offices** in Agrigento, with the main one being the friendly office in the Prefettura building at the back of Piazza Vittorio Emanuele (Mon–Fri 8am–2pm & 2.30–7pm; ☎800.236.837 or 800.315.555, ⓦwww.provincia.agrigento.it), which hands out useful maps and brochures. There's a less helpful branch at the eastern end of Via Atenea, at Via Cesare Battisti 15 (Mon–Sat 8.30am–1pm; ☎0922.20.454), and a kiosk at the Valle dei Templi car park (same hours as the site).

Accommodation

Finding **accommodation** in Agrigento itself is rarely a problem, although in peak season the nearby coastal resorts fill fast. All the budget choices, primarily small family-run establishments, are in the old town above the temples. Tour groups tend to stay in the grander hotels a few kilometres east of town at **Villaggio Mosé**, on the coast road into Agrigento. The hotels themselves, three- and four-star palaces, are fine, but it's a horrible traffic-choked suburb lined with stores, garages, furniture shops and apartment blocks. The nearest **campsites**, the *Nettuno* (☎0922.416.268) and the *San Leone* (☎0922.416.121), are 6km south of town at the coastal resort of San Leone: both are near the beach, and open all year. Take bus #2 from outside the train station (every 30min until 9pm), and the sites are a one-kilometre hike along the coast at the other end.

Amici Via Acrone 5 ☎0922.402.831, ⓦwww .hotelamici.com. Just across from the train station, the smart, bright, air-conditioned rooms here have TVs, tiled floors and gleaming bathrooms. Some sleep three, and are the size of small apartments; those on the ground level are smaller but have great coastal and valley views (especially room 1) and balconies. Super-friendly staff, breakfast included, plus parking. ❹

Bella Napoli Piazza Lena 6 ☎ & ⓕ0922.20.435, ⓔhotelbellanapoli@tin.it. A reasonable budget choice at the far western end of the old town, with a cheery owner: rooms facing the square can be noisy, though with French windows and balconies they have the most light. The lobby is classy, but the rooms are in dire need of decoration. It's off Via Bac Bac, and if you're lucky you'll be able to park in the square outside. ❷

Belvedere Via San Vito 20 ⊤ & ⓕ0922.20.051.
On the east side of the main squares, across from
the old town – climb the vast flight of steps (signposted) opposite Banco di Sicilia or follow the sign
at the back of Piazza Vittorio Emanuele by road.
Room 30 has an enormous balcony (though not
much of a view); others (with and without private
bathroom) are trim and clean without being exciting. No fan or air-conditioning available: breakfast
is €3 extra. ❷
Camere a Sud Via San Vito 20 ⊤349.638.4424,
ⓦwww.camereasud.it. A real find, this new B&B
off Via Atenea has three modish rooms (and more
in the works) and a roof terrace for breakfasts; one
room has private bath, the other two share. ❸
Collaverde Park Passeggiata Archeológica
⊤0922.29.555, ⓕ0922.29.012,
ⓦwww.colleverde-hotel.lt. Halfway to the archeological zone, with parking, English-speaking staff
and beautiful gardens. It's quite pricey, even given
the location and facilities; you'll pay most for the
valley-facing rooms, but there are a few cheaper

town-facing rooms available too. Worth bargaining
if they're not full. ❽
Hotel Costazzurra Via delle Viole 2, San Leone
⊤0922.411.222, ⓕ0922.414.040, ⓦwww
.hotelcostaazzurra.com. A five-minute walk from
the beach in San Leone, 6km south of town (bus
#2 from outside the train station), this family-run
hotel offers quiet, modern rooms and a good
restaurant. ❹
Del Viale Via del Piave 12 ⊤0922.20.063,
ⓕ0922.20.194. A good mid-range choice, a little
way along Viale della Vittória (signposted off Piazza
Cavour, behind an apartment block), with clean,
comfortable air-conditioned rooms with TV. Breakfast available for an extra charge. ❹
Villa Athena Località Templi ⊤0922.596.288,
ⓕ0922.402.180. Located in the Valle dei Templi,
this lovely villa sits in landscaped grounds overlooking the Concordia temple, in some of Sicily's
most prized real estate. It has a pool, but is surprisingly small, so book ahead if you fancy a night
of luxury. ❽

The town

It would be a mistake not to scout around the modern **town of Agrigento**.
Modern only in comparison with the temples, it's thoroughly medieval at its
heart. After the mean streets of some Sicilian towns, the long, main drag, **Via
Atenea**, is something of a revelation, flaunting a run of quality jewellers, trendy
boutiques, bookshops and *pasticcerie* – closed to traffic in the late afternoon,
it's a positive pleasure to window-shop here. The streets off both sides revert
to type, however, harbouring ramshackle *palazzi* and minuscule *cortili* (courtyards), and, while just ambling around here is entertainment enough, there are
a couple of specific buildings worth seeking out. North of Via Atenea, **Santo
Spírito**, at the end of Via Foderà, was built for Cistercian nuns in 1290, and
you can usually find someone to show you round the church, in return for a
small tip. Inside, florid early eighteenth-century monochrome stuccoes by Serpotta sprawl over the walls and trompe l'oeil domed ceiling. Upstairs, there's
a small **folk museum** (Mon–Sat 9am–1.30pm; €4.50) with some decorative
nineteenth-century pictures of angels and saints inlaid with mother-of-pearl
just before the entrance; the museum itself contains local artefacts, including
Toby jugs. From here there are marvellous views of the temples across the
fields. Back downstairs, if you ring the bell marked "*monastero*" and ask for "*dolci
di mandorla*", a nun will bring you a tray of almond cakes, which are expensive,
chewy, and worth the experience.

Via Atenea cuts right through the oldest part of town, at its most grand at
the western end, around the **Municipio**, in Piazza Sinatra, housed inside a
seventeenth-century convent. The narrowest and steepest of the streets spread
up the hill from here, passing the church of **Santa Maria dei Greci**, built over
a Greek temple of the fifth century BC. The flattened columns can be seen
in the nave and, outside (visible from an underground tunnel in the flower-
filled courtyard), the stylobate and column stumps are incorporated into the
church's foundations. Inside are the remains of Byzantine frescoes; if the church
is closed, you can get a key from the guardian at Via Santa Maria dei Greci 15,

opposite. Just up from here, Via Duomo leads past a line of decrepit *palazzi* to the massive **Duomo**, set on a terrace at the top of the hill and fronting a spacious piazza below (daily except Fri 9.30am–12.30pm & 4–6pm).

The Valle dei Templi

A road winds down from Agrigento to the **Valle dei Templi**, buses (#1, #2 or #3) from outside the train station dropping you at a car park between the two separate sections of archeological remains, the eastern and western zones. You'll pass Agrigento's Museo Archeológico on the way and, if you're intent upon doing the ancient site and museum in one go, you'll need a full day here: take a picnic, or use the bar-*távola calda* at the car park. Entrance to both the eastern and western temple sites costs €4.50, or €6 including the museum (July–Sept 8.30am–9.30pm; Oct–June 8.30am–7.30pm). Guided tours are sometimes offered in English – ask at the information kiosk in the car park for details.

The eastern zone

The **eastern zone** is the more popular, and is at its least crowded in the early morning or late at night when floodlit in striking amber light. A path climbs up to the oldest of Akragas's temples, the **Tempio di Ércole** (Herakles). Probably begun in the last decades of the sixth century BC, it's a long structure, nine of the original 38 columns re-erected, everything else scattered around like a half-finished jigsaw puzzle.

Retrace your steps, back over what remains of a deep, wheel-rutted Greek street, and the main path continues up past the site of the city's ancient necropolis to the **Tempio della Concordia** (Concord), dating from around 430 BC. Perfectly preserved and beautifully situated, with fine views to the city and the sea, the tawny stone lends the structure warmth and strength. It's the most complete of the temples, and has required less renovation than the others, mainly due to its conversion in the sixth century AD to a Christian church. Restored to its (more or less) original layout in the eighteenth century, the temple has kept its simple lines and slightly tapering columns, although sadly it's fenced off from the public. Circle the temple at least once to get a decent view, and stand well back to admire its elegant proportions.

The path continues, following the line of the ancient city walls which hug the ridge, to the **Tempio di Giunone** (Juno, or Hera), an engaging structure, half in ruins, standing at the very edge of the spur on which the temples were built. A long altar has been reconstructed at the far end of the temple; the patches of red visible here and there on the masonry denote fire damage, probably from the sack of Akragas by the Carthaginians in 406 BC.

The western zone

The **western zone**, back along the path and beyond the car park, is less impressive, though still archeologically engaging – a vast tangle of stone and fallen masonry from a variety of temples. Most notable is the mammoth pile of rubble that was the **Tempio di Giove** (Jupiter, or Zeus). The largest Doric temple ever known, it was never completed, left in ruins by the Carthaginians and further damaged by earthquakes and the removal of stone to build the port of Porto Empédocle to the south. Still, the stereobate remains, unnaturally huge in scale, while on the ground, face to the sky, lies an eight-metre-high telamone: a supporting column sculpted as a male figure, arms raised and bent to bear the temple's weight. As excavations continue, **other scattered remains** litter the area, not least piles of great

△ Fallen telamon, Valle dei Templi

column drums marked with a U-shaped groove, which enabled them to be lifted with ropes.

Beyond, behind the excavated gates and walls of the Greek city, is the earliest sacred site, the Sanctuary of the Chthonic Deities, marked by two altars (one square and fire-reddened, the other round), dating from the seventh century BC, before the official foundation of the colony. This is also the site of the so-called **Tempio dei Dioscuri** (Castor and Pollux), rebuilt in 1832, its columns and corner-work actually made up of unrelated pieces from the confused debris on the ground.

The Museo Nazionale Archeológico

The road that leads back to town from the car park, Via dei Templi, runs past the excellent **Museo Nazionale Archeológico** (Tues–Sat 9am–7pm, Mon & Sun 9am–1pm; €4.50), outside which buses will stop on request. It's an extraordinarily varied collection, devoted to finds from the temples, the ancient city and the surrounding area. There are brief notes in English throughout, and it can occupy a good couple of hours when you combine it with seeing the remains of the residential area of the old city, just over the road. During the summer there are informal weekly evening jazz and classical music concerts inside the museum's main hall: phone ☎0922.200.014 for details of the programme.

Unusually for an archeological museum, there's much here that's of artistic merit as well as historical interest. You could skip most of the initial local prehistoric and Bronze Age finds, though in **room 1** look out for the gold signet rings, engraved with animals. **Rooms 3 and 4** feature an outstanding vase collection, beguiling sixth- to third-century BC pieces, one of which depicts the burial of a warrior. The highlight is a stunningly detailed white-ground *krater* from 440 BC portraying a valiant Perseus freeing Andromeda. But it's the finds from the temples themselves that make this collection come alive: leaving **room 4**, you'll pass a series of sculpted lion's-head water-spouts, a common device for draining the water from the roofs of the city's temples, while **room 6** is given over to exhibits relating to the Tempio di Giove, with three enormous stone heads from the temples sitting in the recessed wall. Some useful wooden model reconstructions help to make sense of the disjointed wreckage on the ground, although the prime exhibit is a reassembled telamon stacked against one wall: all the weather damage can't hide the strength implicit in this huge sculpture. The finest statue in the museum is in **room 10**, where the Ephebus, a naked Greek youth – displays a nerveless strength and power that suggests that the model was probably a soldier. Rooms beyond hold coins, inscriptions and finds from local necropolises; typical is an alabaster child's sarcophagus in **room 11** showing poignant scenes from his life, which was cut short by illness. The last couple of rooms contain finds from the rest of the province, one of which, in **room 15**, is the equal of anything that's gone before: a fifth-century BC *krater* displays graphic red figures hacking and slicing away in the Battle of the Amazons, amply demonstrating the famed Geloan skill as masters of vase-ware.

In the grounds of the museum, look out for the Gothic doorway of the adjacent church of **San Nicola**. There's an invigorating view from the terrace outside over the temple valley, while just beyond is a small odeon (third-century BC) used for public meetings, during which the participants stood rather than sat in the narrow rows. Nip over the road on the way out of the museum, too: the **Hellenistic-Roman quarter** opposite (daily 9am–1hr before sunset; free) contains rows of houses, inhabited (on and off) until the fifth century AD, many with mosaic designs still discernible.

Other archeological remains

You could see everything already described in four or five hours, but without your own transport the archeological park's remaining sights mean a lot of extra walking. The quickest way to reach the most distant is to climb over the wall to the side of the Tempio di Concordia and scramble down through the field to the road. Here, at the end of a dusty track, stands the undersized **Tempio di Esculapio** (Asclepius), with solid walls instead of a colonnade. Nearby, back along the main road and close to the crossroads, is a large two-storeyed Roman tomb (75 BC), the **Tomba di Terone**, mistakenly named by historians after the Greek tyrant Theron. The road then heads up, past the car park and museum, where a right fork followed by another right turn (Via Demetra) leads to the tiny church of **San Biagio**, a 3km walk. A Norman chapel, this was built over the visible remains of a temple, contemporary with the ones below on the ridge. It's currently closed for restoration, but hang around and a custodian will lead you down the cliff behind the chapel to the eerie **Santuario di Demetra** (be prepared to tip). A stone-built chambered shrine hides two dingy caves that stretch 20m into the hillside. The thin corridor between building and caves has a sort of vestibule with niches for water so that worshippers could wash themselves. It's the most ancient of Agrigento's sacred sites, once devoted to the cult of Demeter and Persephone and in use even before Akragas was founded. A mysterious and evocative place, it's at its best as the sun sets, with shadows flitting across the dark and silent caves.

Caos and the Casa Pirandello

Just **out of Agrigento** (at the end of the flyover leading out towards Porto Empédocle; bus #1 hourly from the train station), the suburb of **Caos** was the birthplace of **Luigi Pirandello**, and the inspiration for the Taviani brothers' film, *Kaos*, based on four of his short stories. One of the greats of twentieth-century Italian literature, Pirandello is best known for his dramatic works, such as *Six Characters in Search of an Author* and *Henry IV*, though his 1934 Nobel Prize was awarded as much for his novels and short stories. He had a tragic life: his wife was committed to an asylum having lapsed into insanity following the ruin of her family and the birth of their third son, and for much of his life Pirandello was forced to write to supplement his frugal living as a teacher. His drama combines elements of tragedy and comedy with keenly observed dialogue, and the nature of identity and personality, reality, illusion and the absurd are all recurring themes. Pirandello's ideas – and innovations – formed the blueprint for much subsequent twentieth-century drama.

Although he left Agrigento while still young, Pirandello spent time here every summer at the **Casa Natale di Luigi Pirandello**, Contrada Caos just off the SS115, past the Valle dei Templi (daily 9am–1pm & 2–7pm; €2), and you can see the study where he wrote, crammed with foreign editions of his works. As well as a couple of murals he painted, there are stacks of photos, including one sent by George Bernard Shaw, and a fifth-century vase, depicting a bearded man attacking a young woman, that was formerly used as an urn for Pirandello's ashes. After seeing the house, with its bamboo and daub interior, you can wander down through the grounds to where the writer's ashes are interred, though the views he once enjoyed over the sea are now ruined by a patch of industrial horror.

Eating and drinking

There's a fairly good choice of **restaurants** in Agrigento, many clustered around Via Atenea and offering some kind of *menù turistico*. They tend to be a bit touristy, though prices are reasonable. Only two or three places in town offer pizzas – most **pizzerias** are at Villaggio Mosé, east of town, below the temples, or at the coastal resort of San Leone.

There are two distinct areas for **cafés and bars**. The town-centre *passeggiata* focuses on Via Atenea, and once the shops re-open in the late afternoon the whole street is packed. To watch the action, choose a seat at one of the little bars in Piazzale Aldo Moro, a nice place to sit in the early evening, despite the occasional burst of organ music from a local crooner. For sunsets and views, stroll along Viale della Vittória to the park: four or five cafés along here cater more to a local family crowd.

L'Ambasciate di Sicilia Via Giambertoni 2 ☎0922.20.526. Fairly standard food in folksy surroundings, though tables on the outdoor terrace provide one of the few good views in town. The house pasta and fresh fish are the things to choose. Closed Mon. Moderate.

Atenea Via Ficani 12 ☎0922.412.366. Family-run budget restaurant, set in a quiet courtyard with outdoor tables in summer. Expect simple, no-frills pasta, meat and fish dishes of variable quality, or try the €14.50 tourist menu with wine. No credit cards. Closed Sun. Inexpensive.

Caffeteria Nobel Viale della Vittória 11 ☎0922.24.562. A good place for an ice cream, cool drink, snack or a beer, under the shady trees of the avenue. It stays open late too, until midnight or so. Inexpensive.

Chez Jean 2 Via Cicerone ☎0922.29.651. Simply a wood-fired pizza oven with seats and an outside deck, this place serves the best pizza in town. Choose from Italian (with mozzarella) or French (mozzarella and Swiss cheese); appetizers are chips or ricotta-stuffed *focacce*. Fantastic. No credit cards. Inexpensive.

Concordia Via Porcello 8, opposite Via Atenea 61 ☎0922.22.668. Tourist prices and tourist clientele but nice food, a chatty *padrone*, and an air-conditioned dining room with a bit of exposed ancient wall – in summer, you can eat outside in a private courtyard across the way. Spaghetti (*alla sarde*, pesto, or with prawns) or grilled fish are the best choices, and there are two tourist menus for around €11 (wine extra). Closed Sundays off-season. Moderate.

La Corte degli Sfizi Cortile Contarini, opposite Via Atenea 169. Little trattoria with a summer walled courtyard where you can eat tasty pasta (like *cavatelli* with aubergines), or dishes such as grilled sausage or swordfish. Also does pizza in the evenings. Nice staff and very reasonable food for the price. Closed Tues. Moderate.

Manhattan Alita Madonna degli Angeli 9, just up from where Via Atenea begins. A popular recent addition to Agrigento's outdoor alleyway trattorias, serving a host of fresh pastas, nearly all €7. The menu is pretty standard, but the food is nicely prepared. Usually busy at lunchtime. Moderate.

Trattoria Caico Via Nettuno 35, San Leone ☎0922.412.788. The local choice in San Leone, in business for half a century. Try the *cavatelli alla Siciliana* (pasta with tomato and aubergine), spaghetti vongole or grilled meats and fish on the vine-shaded patio, or dig into evening pizzas from the wood-fired oven. Closed Tues and Nov. Moderate.

Trattoria dei Templi Via Panoramica dei Templi 15 ☎0922.403.110. Fresh seafood in a traditional restaurant halfway between town and the Valle dei Templi. The €14 *fettuccini all'aragosta*, pasta served with a chunk of lobster, is a good example of their ample fish dishes. Closed Sun in summer, Fri rest of the year. Moderate.

Listings

Banks and exchange ATMs at Banco di Credito Siciliano, Via Atenea 15; Banco Populare Sant'Ángelo, Piazza Vittorio Emanuele 23; Banco di

Sicilia, Piazzale Aldo Moro 1, which also changes travellers' cheques for a small commission. There's an exchange office at the post office, and at the information kisok at the Valle dei Templi (open same hours as the site).

Buses The bus terminal at Piazza Roselli is little more than a bus park, with timetables posted on stands in front of the various companies' stops. Services include: Autoservizi Cuffaro to Palermo; SAL to Licata, Gela, Palma di Montechiaro and Porto Empédocle; SAIS to Caltanissetta, Canicattì, Catania and Naro; Salvatore Lumia to Castelvetrano, Marsala, Mazara, Montallegro, Ribera, Sciacca and Trápani; Fratelli Camilleri to Raffadali and Palermo. There's an SAIS bus ticket/information office in the corner of the piazza ☎0922.595.933; for buses to Palermo, ring ☎0922.596.490. Otherwise, buy tickets on the bus.

Car rental Avis, Piazza San Colaggero near the Stazione Centrale ☎0922.26.353; and Hertz, Via Imera 209 ☎0922.403.091.

Car repairs ACI, Via Matteo Cimara ☎0922.604.284.

Cinema Cine Astor, Piazza Vittorio Emanuele.

Hospital Ospedale Civile San Giovanni, Contrada Consolida, just outside town ☎0922.401.344.

Internet Internet Train, Cortile Contarini, opposite *La Corte degli Sfizi* (Mon–Sat 10am–1pm & 4–8pm; €5 per hour).

Pharmacies Camilleri, Via Atenea 385 ☎0922.25.832; Maria Teresa Indelicato, Piazza Vittorio Emanuele 13 ☎0922.23.889.

Police Questura at Piazza Vittorio Emanuele ☎0922.483.111; Carabinieri at Piazzale Aldo Moro 2 ☎0922.596.322.

Post office The circular building in Piazza Vittorio Emanuele (Mon–Sat 8.30am–6.30pm).

Taxis Ranks at Piazzale Aldo Moro (☎0922.21.899) and outside the train station (☎0922.26.670).

Telephones Make calls from Telecom Italia, Via Atenea 96 (Mon 4–7.30pm, Tues–Sat 9am–1pm & 4–7.30pm).

Travel agents For ferry tickets to the Pelágie Islands and other services: Edrega Viaggi, Via Atenea 21 ☎0922.594.155; Trasportaereo, Via Imera 23 ☎0922.596.333; Ulisse, Via Atenea 138 ☎0922.26.333.

Eraclea Minoa

Thirty-five kilometres along the coast northwest of Agrigento is the region's other important Greek site, **ERACLEA MINOA**. According to the historian Diodorus, this was originally named Minoa after the Cretan king Minos, who chased Daedalus from Crete to Sicily and founded a city where he landed. The Greeks settled here in the sixth century BC, later adding the tag Heraklea. A buffer between the two great cities of Akragas, 40km to the east, and Selinus (Selinunte), 60km west, Eraclea was dragged into endless border disputes, but flourished nonetheless: most of what's left dates from the fourth century BC, the city's most important period, three hundred years or so before it fell into decline.

It's an almighty effort to **reach the site** without your own transport – impossible really in summer when it's too hot to walk. If you have no choice, catch any bus between Agrigento and Sciacca and ask the driver to put you off at the turning, 5km west of Montallegro, on the SS115; the site is 3.5km from there, with the beach another 1km below. **Heading on** west from the site turn-off, you should be able to flag down a bus en route to Sciacca.

The site

The **site** (daily 9am–7pm; €2) sits on a ridge high above a beautiful arc of sand, with the mouth of the River Plátani on the other side. It's one of the most attractive of all Greek sites in Sicily, occupying a headland of which only around a third has so far been excavated. What there is to see is the fruit of successive (and continuing) excavations by foreign universities, who, together with the local *Comune*, have landscaped the remains to good effect. Don't stray too far off the paths, though, as snakes lurk in the undergrowth.

Apart from the city **walls**, once 6km long and with a good part still standing, the most impressive remains are of the sandstone **theatre**. Now restored to its former glory, the theatre is protected from the worst of the elements by a plastic roof, after years of deterioration of the seats, which are made of very soft stone: unfortunately, access to the theatre itself is closed.

Above the theatre, excavations have also revealed tombs and traces of a Greco-Roman temple, while below are the ruins of a grand house, with fragments of Roman mosaics, though these are currently covered and inaccessible. Many of the finds are displayed in a small on-site **museum** (free), which one of the custodians should open up for you.

The beach

While you're here, you'll be hard put to resist a trip down to the **beach**, one of the best on Sicily's southern coast, backed by pine trees and chalky cliffs, and supporting ranks of holiday homes. It's hideously busy in July and August; unless you get here early, you'll never find a space to park. A couple of **bar-restaurants** sit right on the beach, where you can rent chairs and sunshades; the *Sabbie d'Oro* stays open all year and the food is reasonably priced (€9–15 for fish dishes), while next door *Jammin Beach* has all-night DJ sounds. Set back a bit from the beach, *Lido Gabbiano* is a fast-food joint with a few **rooms** (℡339.813.7907; ❷), or try any of those advertised in the houses and villas, though in high season you'll need to have booked way in advance. Alternatively, the *Eraclea Minoa Village* (℡0922.847.310 or 0922.846.023; open May–Sept) has two-bedroom cabins (❸), a **campsite**, plus a bar-restaurant. There's also a small supermarket, 200m or so up from the *Sabbie d'Oro*.

Sciacca and around

Just over 30km further up the coast from Eraclea Minoa, **SCIACCA** comes as a welcome surprise after the ugly industry around the southern coast's other towns. Although not immediately attractive – it is, after all, a working fishing port – it does have a good-looking upper town that's virtually untouched by tourism. A spa town for nearby Selinus in ancient times, it enjoyed great prosperity under the Arabs, from whom its modern name is thought to derive (the Arabic *xacca* meaning "from the water"). The town was at the centre of a feud between Catalan and Norman families that simmered on for a century, resulting in the deaths of a good half of the local population. Despite the destruction, Sciacca preserves some notable buildings, which infuse its agreeable Mediterranean air with more than a passing historical interest and make for some pleasant strolling through the weaving streets. With a car you could use the town as a base for a day's circular drive, taking in a few minor **inland towns**, including the superbly sited village of **Caltabellotta**.

The Town

The upper town is still walled, entered through one of five grand gates, the westernmost of which, **Porta San Salvatore**, leads onto the **Chiesa del Cármine**, whose facade is lent a skewwhiff air by an off-centre Gothic rose window. Past the church, up Via P. Gerardi, the fifteenth-century **Palazzo Steripinto** is even more ungainly, its embossed exterior only partially offset by some slender arched windows.

From here, Sciacca's main street, **Corso Vittorio Emanuele**, runs right the way down to the lovely **Piazza A. Scandaliato**, a large terrace with some

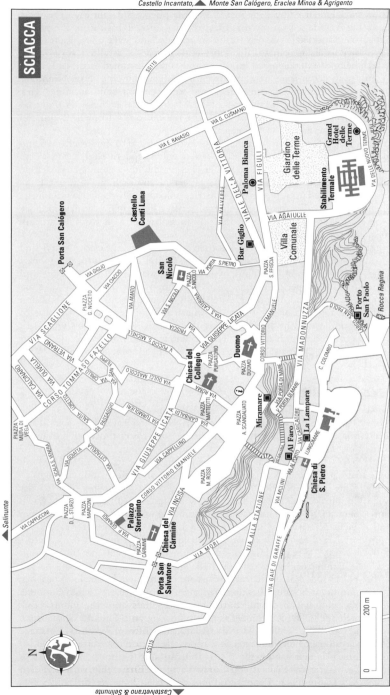

SCIACCA

SS115

VIA E. RAVASIO

VIA G. CUSMANO

Porta San Calógero ⚜

VIA GIGLIO

VIA CACCIO

Castello
Conti Luna

Paloma Bianca

VIA FIGULI

Giardino
delle Terme

Grand
Hotel
delle Terme

Stabilimento
Termale

VIA DELLE NUOVO TERME

PIAZZA
G. NOCETO

VIA AMATO

San
Nicolò

PIAZZA
S. NICOLÒ

VIA S. NICOLÒ

VIA PORTA
S. PIETRO

Bar Giglio

VIA VALVERDE

VIAGAIULLE

VIA S. CATERINA

VIA PUCCIO S. MICHELE

VIA FRISCIA

VIA DULCI MASCOLO

VIA OMILLO

VIA FILIPPO

VIA GIUSEPPE LICATA

PIAZZA
PURGATORIO

Duomo ✝

PIAZZA
DUOMO

Villa
Comunale

PIAZZA
S. FRISCIA

CORSO VITTORIO EMANUELE

VIA MADONNUZZA

LARGO SAN PAOLO

Porto
San Paolo ⚓

Rocca Regina

VIA SCAGLIONE

VIA VETRANO

VIA OLIVELLA

VIA CALCINARO

VIA TOMMASO FAZELLO

Chiesa del
Collegio ✝

PIAZZA
ROMA

ℹ

PIAZZA
MATTEOTTI

Miramare

VIA PORTA DI MARE

PORTA DI MARE

VIA CABRICATORE

C. COLOMBO

PIAZZA
MURA DI
VEGA

VIA SCALA S. VENERA

VIA GOATTA

VIA CITADELLA

SALITA GABELLO

VIA PASSAGGIO

VIA TURBAMOLITERI

VIA GARIBALDI

PIAZZA
A. SCANDALIATO

Al Faro 🍴

VIA ALBERTO

VIA PORTA DI MARE

La Lampara 🍴

LUNGOMARE

PIAZZA
D. L. STURZO

PIAZZA
MARCONI

CORSO VITTORIO EMANUELE

VIA GIUSEPPE LICATA

VIA CAPPELLINI

PIAZZA
M. ROSSI

VIA MILLINI

🏛

VIA P. GERARDI

Palazzo
Steripinto

Chiesa del
Cármine ✝

VIA INCISA

VIA MORI

VIA ALLA STAZIONE

Chiesa di
S. Pietro ✝

PIAZZA
CARMINE

Porta San
Salvatore ⚜

VIA CAPPUCCINI

VIA GAIE DI GARAFFE

SS115

▲ Selinunte

N

200 m

0

▲ Castelvetrano & Selinunte

THE SOUTH COAST | Sciacca and around

good cafés, enhanced by wide views over the port and distant bays. The most enduring Arab legacy in town is the street layout and, back from the piazza, above the **Duomo**, a Moorish knot of passages and steep alleys leads up to the rather feeble remains of the fourteenth-century **Castello Conti Luna**, which belonged to one of the feuding families that disrupted medieval Sciacca. A little way down from here, the twelfth-century church of **San Nicolò** is a tiny construction with three apses and some elegant blind arcading. Back up beyond the Duomo, at the end of Via Madonnuzza, are Sciacca's **thermal baths** (*Stabilimento Termale*; Mon–Fri 8am–noon; from €10), where you can take a cleansing dip in the therapeutic waters.

From Piazza Scandaliato, steps lead down the cliffside to the lower town and **port**, whose most distinctive feature is a steepled modern church. Just north of the church you'll see steps, each riser decorated with contemporary ceramic tiles, some depicting sea life, some just patterned, and each one different. Fishing vessels lie tied up at the quayside, lorries unload salt by the bucketful for the anchovy- and sardine-processing that takes place here, and repairmen, foundry workers and chandlers go about their business, breaking off work for a drink in one of the scruffy portside bars.

Just outside town, a couple of kilometres to the east of Sciacca, you'll find a garden full of thousands of stone heads at **Castello Incantato**, Via Ghezzi (Tues–Sat 10am–noon & 4–8pm; free); it's on bus routes #1 or #4. Carved in naive style over a period of fifty years by Filippo Bentivegna, their faces are serious, beautiful and disturbing. After being rejected by his girlfriend, beaten up and left for dead on the streets of America, Bentivegna returned home to Sciacca and devoted his life to carving these heads, symbols of his imaginary enemies, until his death in 1967. The eccentric artist would walk the streets of Sciacca with a short stick and a sceptre, and liked to be addressed as "Your Excellency".

Practicalities

Buses pull up on Via Figuli at the Villa Comunale (the town gardens), at the eastern end of Sciacca. Bus tickets to Agrigento and Trápani are sold at the *Bar Giglio* on Viale della Vittória. There are two **tourist offices** (Mon–Sat 8am–2pm & 4–6pm) along Corso Vittorio Emanuele, one at no. 127 (℡0925.87.012), and one at no. 84, on the first floor (℡0925.21.182): both have maps, public transport timetables, hotel lists and information in English.

There are just a couple of **hotels** in the centre of town. Close to the Villa Comunale, the *Paloma Bianca*, at Via Figuli 5 (℡0925.25.130; ❸), is only adequate for the money, though some rooms do have little balconies and a view. Alternatively, if you fancy a thermal spa treatment, there's the upmarket *Grand Hotel delle Terme*, Viale delle Nuove Terme 1 (℡0925.23.133, ℻0925.87.002, ⓦwww.grandhoteldelleterme.com; ❼), on the cliffs beyond the Villa Comunale, set in its own park and with superb views out to sea. Other resort-style hotels and **campsites** are out of town by the local beaches: nearby Contrada Sovareto has three or four expensive resorts, while Contrada Makauda, 9km east of town, has the more reasonably priced *Torre Makauda* (℡0925.968.500, ℻0925.968.905; ❻), with a pool. The *Makauda Beach Residence* (℡0925.997.001, ⓦwww.makaudabeach.com), also in Contrada Makauda and right on the beach, is a good, safe choice of campsite.

The best places to eat are the fish **restaurants** at the port, down the steps from the main piazza. When you reach the modern church, turn left (a sign points to "Trattoria") and you'll find *Al Faro*, Via al Porto 25 (℡0925.25.349;

closed Sun; no credit cards), with moderate prices and local wine; in August, fixed-price menu only. The nearby *La Lampara*, Via Caricatore, is slightly pricier but better quality, with *pasta con sarde* for €6.20 (closed Mon). Further along the quayside, at Largo San Paolo 1, the pricey *Porto San Paolo* (☎0925.27.982; closed Wed), serves delicious dishes such as seafood risotto and lobster fettuccine on its terrace overlooking the sea: you can also get pizza in the evening, and it's advisable to book in summer. Back up in town, the *Miramare* on Piazza Scandaliato also has a terrace with excellent panoramas and serves pizzas from €5.50. There are a couple of other decent pizza places in the upper town, along Viale della Vittória and Corso Vittorio Emanuele.

Around Sciacca

The easiest side-trip from Sciacca is to the vaporous caves at **Monte San Calógero** (388m), 8km north of town. Bus #5 runs here in ten minutes, every ninety minutes from Sciacca. Excavations and finds have shown that the site has been used as a place of healing since antiquity, though the mountain takes its contemporary name from the saint whose sanctuary is at the summit, near some natural caves.

Alternatively, take a day's drive through Sciacca's hinterland, visiting small towns en route, such as **RIBERA**, 25km east of Sciacca. Known as the "*città d'arancia*" for the expansive orange groves that surround it, it's the birthplace of statesman and former Italian Prime Minister Francesco Crispi (1818–1901), who was born in a house on Via Crispi.

Further inland is the cloud-swathed village of **CALTABELLOTTA**, magnificently perched on three jutting fangs of rock, from which tremendous views stretch out on all sides. On the highest of these pinnacles, you can pass through the solitary surviving entrance of the Norman castle that once stood here, and climb up some rock-cut steps to the very top, from which the village below appears as a patchwork of grey roofs. The castle itself, ruined by an earthquake, was where the Angevins and Aragonese signed the peace treaty ending the Wars of the Vespers. Immediately below sit the Norman **Chiesa Madre** and the Gothic **Chiesa di San Salvatore**, both wonderfully sited against a rocky backdrop. The village is 20km northeast of Sciacca and there's a direct route from town; SAIS buses run here three times a day (Mon–Sat), the last one back leaving in the mid-afternoon – an impressive ride, past sparkling fresh streams and jagged outcrops of rock.

Continue north from Caltabellotta onto the SS386, and turn west at Chiusa Sclafani for the little town of **SAMBUCA DI SICILIA**, on a hill west of the Arancio lake. Sambuca has an Arab past – just about discernible in its convoluted old-town layout – and a sixteenth-century church in Piazza della Vittória, the **Chiesa del Cármine**, home of a statue that's reputed to be by Antonello Gagini. You can **eat** in Sambuca at one of two or three very cheap trattorias, or detour 10km north to see the low-key excavations (always open; free) at **Monte Adranone**, a Greek city of the sixth century BC which fell to Carthage in the fourth.

Ten kilometres west of Sambuca you join the main SS188 which sweeps back to Sciacca, though there are a couple of other diversions before that: either head north for 6km to Santa Margherita di Belice (see p.425), or south for 9km to **MENFI**, planned in the eighteenth century but devastated by an earthquake in 1968. Today Menfi presents a very mean aspect: lacerated churches on derelict central streets, a jumble of untidy prefab housing – still being used – and bland rebuilding on the outskirts. If this is all a bit depressing, things improve when you drive on 7km to the coast at **PORTO PALO**, a fishing village and summer resort with a nice beach and one simple **hotel**, the *Miramare*, Via Piamonte 34 (☎0925.78.211; ❷), with a beachside restaurant. Back at Menfi, it's just 20km to Sciacca, either along the minor road or the faster SS115.

The Pelágie Islands

The remote **Pelágie Islands** (Isole Pelágie) are little more than dry rocks, even further south than Malta and bang in the middle of the Mediterranean. Throughout history they've been neglected, often abandoned or uninhabited, and only occasionally has their strategic importance been recognized. In 1943 the Allies bombed the main island, Lampedusa, prior to springing into Sicily; and Colonel Gaddafi of Libya nearly gave a repeat performance in 1987 when he retaliated against the American bombing of Tripoli by targeting missiles at the US base on Lampedusa. Italian troops were mobilized and Sicily was on a virtual war-footing for three days, though in the event the missiles dropped into the sea short of the island.

The largest island, **Lampedusa** attracts Italians in ever-increasing numbers, and it's pretty jam-packed in July and August, but it does offer good scuba diving and snorkelling in the wonderfully clear waters. The smaller, volcanic **Linosa**, is much quieter, generally hotter and less breezy than Lampedusa, while the tiniest islet, **Lampione**, is uninhabited and rarely visited.

Getting there

There are direct **flights** to Lampedusa from Palermo, Trápani and Rome, though most visitors still get to the islands by **ferry** from the depressing town of **Porto Empédocle**, 6km southwest of Agrigento. It's a large oily port dominated by an enormous cement works, with a popular beach west of the town centre. If you're waiting for a ferry, there's a pleasant enough stroll along the central pedestrian walkway in town. Buses leave for the port from Agrigento every thirty minutes or so from outside the train station (a 10min journey), dropping you in Piazza Italia, one block from the waterfront; the last bus from Agrigento leaves at 8.30pm. A taxi costs around €25.

By ferry and hydrofoil

Daily **ferries** leave Porto Empédocle at midnight in summer, six weekly in winter (not Fri), calling at Linosa (5hr 45min) and Lampedusa (8hr 15min). **Tickets** can be bought from the Siremar office (☎0922.636.683 or 0922.636.685), right on the quayside in Porto Empédocle, or from travel agents in Agrigento (see p.365). A one-way ticket is around €30 to Linosa, or €35 to Lampedusa; returns cost double. It's worth reserving either a **couchette** (€12), a bed (€15) or a reclining chair (€5), rather than bending yourself round a couple of chairs in the grimy TV lounge. Bring your own **food**, as the on-board restaurant is expensive and unimaginative.

Ústica Lines **hydrofoils** run six times a week (not Wed) from May to October. They leave Porto Empédocle at 4pm, arriving in Linosa at 7.30pm and Lampedusa at 8.30pm. **Tickets** (€36 to Linosa, and €53 to Lampedusa oneway) are sold from the Ústica Lines office right by the dock (☎0922.636.110, ⓦwww.usticalines.it).

There's no point taking a car to the islands: leave yours in the Stagno **garage** (☎0922.636.029; from €5 per day) down at the port, at the end of

Via Roma. If it's full, you should be able to leave your vehicle inside the port itself, preferably near the *Dogana* (customs) or anywhere else where it may be glanced at now and again by official eyes; enter by the eastern entrance and drive through.

By plane

You can **fly from Palermo** several times a day direct to Lampedusa with Meridiana (☎091.652.5020, ⓦwww.mediriana.it; 1hr), or **from Trápani** (1hr) and **Rome** (summer only; 2hr) with AirOne (☎199.207.080 or 848.848.880, ⓦwww.flyairone.it). Flights from Palermo and Trápani start at €26 one-way if you buy enough in advance, and can be booked on the Internet, or at a local travel agent (see "Listings" in Palermo, p.112).

Linosa

Northernmost of the islands, **LINOSA** is the tip of a submerged volcano, with four extinct craters to poke around, some laval beaches and not much else in the way of sights. A haven for pirates in the sixteenth century, the small island (five square kilometres) wasn't really settled until the mid-nineteenth century, and even now the only village has just a few hundred inhabitants, rather fewer cars and a minimal road system. It exudes tranquillity, with the only exciting events to disturb it being when the government in Rome regularly sent their latest star Mafia prisoner to be detained on the island pending trial, and even this practice has been suspended since the tourist trade picked up. If you take the tracks that lead away from either side of the port, you can clamber around the cliffs and coves, and reach the couple of black-sand beaches with crystal clear water.

From May to the end of October you can see the island on a **day-trip** from Lampedusa, only an hour away by Ústica Lines hydrofoil (departing from Lampedusa daily at 9.30am and 5.30pm, returning at 10.45am and 6.45pm; one-way tickets €17): see Lampedusa's "Listings" (p.376) for ticket details.

Linosa has no hotels, but there are a number of **rooms** you can rent: the *Ristorante-Bar Errera*, Via Scalo 1 (☎0922.972.041; ❷), has a few, while both the Linosa Diving Centre, Via Príncipe Umberto 13 (☎0922.972.061, ⓦwww.linosadivingcenter.it), and Mare Nostrum, Via Re Umberto 84 (☎0922.972.042 or 328.169.8697, ⓦwww.marenostrumdiving.it; open June–Sept), can arrange rooms as well as **scuba-diving** trips. There's also a **bank** on the island, the Banco di Sicilia, with limited opening hours.

Lampedusa

LAMPEDUSA, 50km south of Linosa and 205km from Porto Empédocle, is the last inhabited vestige of Italy. Originally a fragment of the African continent, and lying further south than Tunis, it's much bigger than Linosa (23 square kilometres) and is the centre of more activity. Around 5000 people live here, mostly in the town of the same name, the majority making their living from fishing and tourism; increasing numbers of tourists, the vast majority Italian, arrive every year, especially in July and August.

Historically, however, Lampedusa has been as neglected as the other Mediterranean islands off Sicily. In 1667 it passed into the hands of the **Tomasi** family (as in Giuseppe Tomasi di Lampedusa, of *The Leopard* fame), one of whose descendants attempted to sell the island to Queen Victoria in 1839 when it still had only twenty or so inhabitants. The queen lost out on the sale, at a cost of twelve million ducats, to Ferdinand II, the Neapolitan king, who

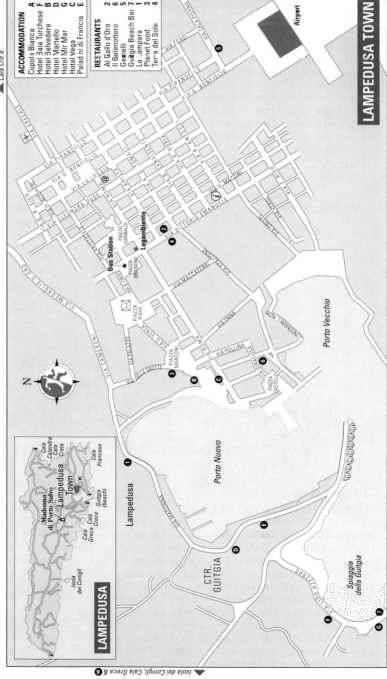

▲ Cala Francese

▲ Cala Crea

LAMPEDUSA TOWN

ACCOMMODATION
Cupola Bianca   A
Hotel Baia Turchese   F
Hotel Belvedere   B
Hotel Martello   D
Hotel Mir Mar   G
Hotel Vega   C
Paladini di Francia   E

RESTAURANTS
Al Gallo d'Oro   2
Il Balenottero   6
Gemelli   5
Guitgia Beach Bar   7
La Lampara   1
Planet Food   3
Terra del Sole   4

Airport

VIA CALABASSINA
VIA GRECALE
VIA PIRANDELLO
VIA G. BONFIGLIO
VIA PIRANDELLO
VIA G. BONFIGLIO
VIA LEONORA DUSE
VIA LA LOGGIA
VIA ROMA
VIA VARSINO
VIA D'ORIA
VIA TARESSINI
VIA ANFOSSI
VIA CAVOUR
VIA MAZZINI
VIA TERRA NOVA
VIA PISA
VICO ALFIERI
VIA G. BUSSA
VIA CALABRESE
VIA CAMERONI
VIA MEDAGLIE D'ORO
VIA DELLE GROTTE
VIA PALAZZO
VIA G. VERGA
VIA MACCAFERRI
VIA ROMA
VIA ENNA
VIA SAN VITO
VIA POLLINA
VIA SIRACUSA
LUNGOMARE L. RIZZO
VIA VITTORIO EMANUELE

Bus Station
★ PIAZZA
BRIGNONE
PIAZZA
GARIBALDI
Legambiente @
PIAZZA
PIAVE
PIAZZA
MARCONI
PIAZZA
CASTELLO

Porto Vecchio
Porto Nuovo

Lampedusa

CTR.
GUITGIA

VIA LIDO AZZURRO

Spiaggia
della Guitgia

N

LAMPEDUSA

Cala
Calandra
Cala
Creta
Cala
Francese
Cala
Greca
Cala
Croce
Guitgia
(beach)
Madonna
di Porto Salvo
Lampedusa
Town
Isola
dei Conigli

▲ Isola dei Conigli, Cala Greca & A

was no doubt aghast at the prospect of losing such a scraggy but strategically important island.

The island is long, thin, flat and dry, the main attraction being the **beaches** and the sea. For years the pristine water has offered some of the best swimming and diving in the Mediterranean, with an abundance of fish life; you might also see dolphins, or even, in March, the **sperm whale migration**. But a myopic attitude for most of this century has meant that Lampedusa has been practically stripped of its natural vegetation – the resulting soil erosion accounting for the arid state of the land. Recently, however, a programme of reforestation in a couple of the shallow valleys has been started, thus encouraging the regrowth of pine and mastic trees, and germander (from the mint family). At Cala Galera, look out for the Phoenician juniper, and carob and wild olive trees, all survivors of the original blight. **Rare plants**, too, can be seen here, including the *caralluma europa*, a cactus-like plant with star-shaped flowers, and the *centaurea acaulis*, from the centaury family. During mid-May, the **flowers** really come into their own as squills, irises, crocuses, orchids, echinops and thyme are all part of a vibrant display. Along the roads you'll see more common tall cacti, which rival the telegraph poles in height: poles that only arrived in 1963, when the telephone system was installed.

Apart from the sun, sea and sand, the island's attractions are low-key: there's a religious sanctuary in the middle of the island, an offshore nature reserve where turtles come to lay their eggs, and some good cliff-walks to divert you from your tan. And, for the views of the cliffs and grottoes alone, it's worth taking a boat trip around Lampedusa. Remember that it's a small, exposed island, so evenings are cooler than on the mainland; it's not really somewhere you'd want to holiday in winter, when the wind whips across the barren landscape.

Arrival and information

The **airport** practically sits in the town, and most hotels and campsites arrange courtesy buses for guests. Arriving by ferry at the **harbour** (Porto Vecchio), it's a ten-minute walk up to town, or a twenty-minute walk west to the larger harbour of Porto Nuovo, which is home to the pleasure- and fishing-boats, as well as the main beach and the bulk of the hotels. A minibus meets the ferry in summer, and for a small charge will take you wherever you want to go, or you can jump in a taxi.

If you're lucky, the Pro Loco **tourist office** (April–Oct, erratic hours; ☎0922.971.390), at Via V. Emanuele 87, will be open. If not, the friendly environmental agency, Legambiente, Via V. Emanuele 27 (daily 9am–2pm; ☎ & ℻0922.971.611), can provide information in English on excursions around the island. For **online information**, ⓦ www.lampedusa.to has useful listings and links to accommodation and other services.

Transport and tours

The **bus station** is right in the centre of the town in Piazza Brignone, off Via Roma; hourly buses go to the south-coast beaches in summer. The town itself is easily explored on foot, but for the rest of the island you're better off **renting** a **bike** (€6 a day), a **scooter** (€15–20), or a mini-moke or **car** (€25–30): see "Listings" on p.376 for rental shops.

You can do a complete circuit of the island in a day by bicycle, and even in the hottest months a refreshing breeze blows constantly. The cliff road along the north coast is rough and stony, as are the roads that cross the island – they deteriorate the further west you go – but the south coast road is easier. Take provisions (there are no shops along the way) and insect repellent.

Numerous people on the quayside at the port offer **boat tours** around the island – reckon on paying about €12 per person for a half-day trip (around €24 for a full day with lunch).

Accommodation

The season on Lampedusa runs from Easter to November, and for most of that time there'll be no problem finding a **hotel**. During July and August, however, booking is essential and there's often a minimum stay of three nights, with full- or half-board compulsory. **Rooms** can be rented (usually ❷–❸) from Servizi Mikael, Via Tacceri 24 (☎0922.973.571, ⓦwww.servizimikael.com), or Greco Ettore, Via Sanvisente (☎0922.970.456), either in town or along the coast, though, again, you must book in advance in July and August. Alternatively, you can stay in a modern version of a traditional **dammusi**: these shepherds' huts, found only in Sicily and North Africa, are small, stone buildings with domed roofs that stay cool in summer, and most of the ones here have kitchenettes too. Both *I dammusi dell'Imbriacola*, Contrada Imbriacola 56, on the way to Isola dei Conigli (☎0922.773.9034, ⓕ0922.973.612, ⓔidammusilampedusa @virgilio.net), and the more upmarket *Villaggio Albergo i Dammusi di Borgo*, Cala Creta (☎0922.970.394, ⓕ0922.970.590, ⓦwww.calacreta.com) have nice sites.

Finally, there are two official **campsites**: *La Roccia* (☎0922.970.055, ⓦwww.laroccia.net), at Cala Greca, 3km from the town, with its own beach and a few bungalows; and the slightly nearer *Lampedusa*, at Cala Francese (☎0922.970.720). Both are open from June to September.

Hotels

Baia Turchese Via Lido Azzurro ☎0922.970.455, ⓕ0922.970.098, ⓦwww.guitgia.com. Spacious, comfortable and only 30m from the beach. The pastel-coloured rooms are all air-conditioned, but if you want a view you'll pay more. Umbrellas and sun loungers are provided. Half-board compulsory (❹ per person) in July & Aug. ❻

Belvedere Piazza Guglielmo Marconi 4 ☎0922.970.188. Adequate accommodation overlooking the harbour – you're more likely to find room-only rates here, and singles are relatively cheap. It is sometimes block-booked by municipal workers for the season, so call ahead to check if there's room. ❷

Cupola Bianca Via Madonna ☎ & ⓕ0922.971.274, ⓦwww.hotelcupolabianca.it. A luxury outfit 2km out of town, with plush standard rooms as well as luxury *dammusi*-style accommodation. ❼

Martello Salita Medusa ☎0922.970.025, ⓕ0922.971.696, ⓦwww.hotelmartello.it. A comfortable modern hotel near the harbour, whose restaurant has panoramic sea views: can also arrange diving and boat trips. Half-board compulsory in July and Aug (❼ per person). ❺

Mir Mar Contrada Guitgia ☎0922.970.093. The cheapest hotel on the island for singles, and one of the few places offering room-only in summer. It's right on the beach; the nine rooms are basic, but all have showers. No credit cards. ❻

Paladini di Francia Via Alessandro Volta (in the southwest corner of Porto Nuovo) ☎0922.970.550, ⓦwww.paladinidifrancia.com. Lampedusa's newest addition, with four of the twelve neat rooms having views right onto the port. It also has an upmarket, prix-fixe restaurant and is popular with tour groups, so book well in advance. ❻

Vega Via Roma 19 ☎0922.970.099, ⓦwww.lampedusa-hotelvega.it. One of the few hotels in the town itself, at the harbour end of the main street. Smaller than most, it provides good and friendly service. ❹

Around the town and island

The gridded system of streets in the upper part of **LAMPEDUSA TOWN** funnels down to the harbour, from where a gentle walk westwards brings you to the busy beach, **Spiaggia della Guitgia**, around which the main cluster of hotels is sited. The town's activity centres on Via Roma, which turns pedestrian in the evenings for the *passeggiata*. Lining the pavements are the usual souvenir shops selling beach paraphernalia and fruits of the sea, especially sponges, as well as hand-crocheted Arab caps that the women make in between serving customers.

There'll be no problem finding spots to **swim** away from the port (though in season you'll never be alone on the beaches), and there are plenty of opportunities for diving and snorkelling. You can hire gear fairly easily in town (see "Listings" below for addresses; expect to pay around €35 for a dive, and €18 for full equipment rental), and there's good fish-watching only a few metres away from the beaches. If you don't fancy the small main beach, try **Cala La Croce**, the next bay west of Spiaggia della Guitgia, or the rockier **Cala La Francese**, a ten-minute walk east of town. Less busy are the rocks, up the east coast at **Cala La Calandra** – but watch out for tar. Nearby Cala Creta is home to the World Wildlife Fund's **Centro Recupero Tartarughe Marine** (summer Mon–Sat 6–8pm; ☏338.219.8533, ⊛www.isolablu.org), a museum and infirmary where you can visit turtles who have been injured by fishing nets or plastic flotsam; ask about their *liberazioni tartarughe* (turtle emancipations) held at Calamadonna beach every week in summer, where the healthy turtles are released back into the sea. There's nowhere to swim on the north side of the island, other than from a boat – it's mostly sheer cliffs, which tier down like a wedding cake.

A further 7km west along the south coast is the popular **Isola dei Conigli** (Rabbit Island), accessible by hourly bus from town. If you've got your own transport, leave it at the top of the cliff and clamber down the jagged path to a stretch of fine, white sand – arguably Lampedusa's best – and gorgeous aquamarine waters. There are no facilities here, so bring your own umbrella and picnic. Just offshore is the little island itself, which you can reach either on foot or by swimming, depending on the tide. A **nature reserve** (open at all times; free), it's the only place in Italy where you can see the turtle *Caretta Caretta* laying its eggs. During summer evenings, the turtles deposit between 100 and 150 eggs in deep holes, which the babies stagger out from after sixty days. The nests are individually fenced off, but that doesn't help protect them from the peregrine falcons which also nest here. Organized trips to the island are advertised along Via Roma, back in town, or contact Legambiente (see "Arrival and information", p.373). The Centra Ricerca Delfini, Lungomare Luigi Rizzo 157 at Porto Vecchio (summer Mon–Sat 9.30am–1pm, 4–8pm & 10pm–midnight), also displays information on marine life local to these waters.

There's not a great deal to see inland, apart from a stream of boy racers zapping around on scooters. Off the main road west out of town, the church of the **Madonna di Porto Salvo** can be appreciated for its scenic location, its white steeple set in a little wooded valley, flowers and bougainvillea abounding in the garden in front. There's a pilgrimage here every September, commemorating a sixteenth-century Italian slave, captured by Saracens, who was shipwrecked on the island and made his way to the sanctuary here. Afterwards, he used the image of the Madonna on the sail of his makeshift raft to safely return to Liguria.

Lampione

Lampedusa is also the starting point for trips to the third island, **LAMPIONE**, a mere speck of land to the west. Starkly vegetated and uninhabited, the island offers spectacular diving and wonderful offshore fishing – you should be able to persuade someone to take you in their boat from Lampedusa Town, or contact the Mediterraneo Immersioni Club diving centre (see "Listings" p.376), which organizes frequent diving trips to the reefs around the island; it's around an hour's crossing and you'll pay about €30 for a day's trip.

Eating and drinking

There's no shortage of eating places in Lampedusa, and while prices tend to be a little higher than on the mainland, you'll still find plenty of inexpensive tourist menus. Fish, of course, is a speciality, along with couscous, either as a main dish or an antipasto. At night the whole of the Via Roma becomes one long lively café, with chairs and tables sprawling on the pavements; the *Café Royal* does great ice cream. Other places to try are the *Bar del Amicizia*, Via Vittorio Emanuele 34, where you can get a deliciously light *latte di mandorla* or granita; or, if you're heading to the beach, stop at the *Trattoria e Bar del Porto*, for a snack and a *tè freddo*. Most places are closed in winter but open daily in season.

Il Balenottero Via Sbarcatoio 40, Porto Vecchio ☎0922.970.830. A cool, quiet family-style restaurant in the old port with good seafood dishes. Less crowded than the more central places, and with a fairly laid-back atmosphere. Moderate.

Al Gallo d'Oro Via Vittorio Emanuele 45. Cheap, cheerful and friendly, though the service can be slow. They have a good tourist menu of fish and occasionally dish up a fine couscous. Inexpensive.

Gemelli Via Cala Pisana 2 ☎0922.970.699. Off the Via Bonfiglio, on the airport side of town, and worth the few minutes' walk for Arab specialities as well as *bouillabaisse*, paella and *crespelle di pesce* (fish pancakes). A quiet spot, where oil lamps on the tables and Arab decoration add to the ambience. Booking essential in Aug. Closed Mon. Expensive.

Guitgia Beach Bar and Spaghetteria Via Lido Azzurro. If you're on the beach, use this as a

pit-stop for good sandwiches (try the unleavened bread). At night, sit under bamboo thatch by candlelight and enjoy the lapping of the waves. Standard food, but excellent location. Inexpensive.

La Lampara Via Madonna. Watch the evening *passeggiata* of mobile phones and Vespas along the harbourside as you sample the local fish, spicy couscous and sweet tomatoes. Moderate.

Planet Food Via della Grotte. Just up from the harbour on the edge of the town, what it lacks in atmosphere it makes up for with its huge selection of pizzas. Inexpensive.

Terra del Sole Via Vittorio Emanuele 30. Full of interesting seafood dishes like *crepes frutti di mare* and *ravioli di cernia* (a local fish), this fine restaurant is right in the centre but has a very quiet garden at the back to escape the crowds. Moderate.

Listings

Airport Information ☎0922.970.006.

Banks ATMs at Banco di Sicilia, Via Roma 123; and Banco Populare di Sant'Ángelo, Via Roma 50; both exchange cash for a €4 commission.

Car and bike rental Autonoleggio di d'Agostino, Via N. Bixo 1 ☎0922.970.755; Di Manzo, Via E. Duse ☎0922.970.529; Edonoleggio, Via Cortile Caltanissetta ☎0922.970.265; Licciardi, Via Siracusa ☎0922.970.768.

Diving centres Lo Verde Diving, Via Roma 118 ☎0922.971.986; Mediterraneo Immersioni Club, Via A. Volta 8 ☎0922.971.526, ⍟www .mediterraneoimmersionclub.it; Blue Dolphins Diving Centre, Via A. Volta 18 ☎0922.971.606, ⍟www.bluedolphins.it. Many hotels also offer equipment, excursions and boats at reduced rates.

Ferry/hydrofoil tickets Siremar (☎0922.971.964) at the harbour; departure to Linosa/Porto Empédocle daily at 10.15am (not Sat; Oct–May); one-way ticket to the mainland around

€30). For Ústica Lines hydrofoil to Linosa, buy tickets at Agenzia Maríttima Strazera, Lungomare Rizzo 1 ☎0922.970.003 or at the Ústica Lines kiosk right by the boat (☎0923.33.300, ⍟www .usticalines.it); departures (May to end of Oct) at 9.30am and 5.30pm; one-way tickets €18.

Hospital Via Grecale ☎0922.970.604.

Internet L'Edicola, Via Roma 150 (summer 8am–11pm; winter hours variable; €5 per hour).

Pharmacy Dottore Inglisa, Vittorio Emanuele at Via Roma (Mon–Fri 8.30am–1pm & 5–9pm, Sat 8.30am–1pm; ☎0922.970.195).

Police Carabinieri, Via Roma 37 ☎0922.970.001 or ☎112.

Post and telephone office At Piazza Piave, just west of the bus station.

Supermarket Supermercato Sferlazzo, Via Roma 38.

Travel agents Agenzia Maríttima Raccomandataria, Lungomare Luigi Rizzo ☎0922.971.964; La Pelágie, Via Roma 155 ☎0922.970.170.

Festivals

February
First/second week Almond-blossom festival, the Sagra del Mandorlo in Fiore, at **Agrigento**: events take place in the Valle dei Templi – costumes, music and processions.

February/March
Carnevale at **Sciacca**, with participation of the entire town in five days of parades and competitions.

March/April
Easter Holy Week processions at **Agrigento**.

June
27–29 Sagra del Mare at **Sciacca**: a statue of St Peter is paraded on a boat at sea; there's a big fish fry-up and maritime-themed games at the port.

July
First/second Sunday Festival at **Agrigento** in honour of St Calógero.
Pirandello week Plays and concerts held at Pirandello's house at **Caos**, near **Agrigento**.

September
22 Pilgrimage and religious procession at **Lampedusa**, in honour of the Madonna di Porto Salvo.

Travel details

Trains

Agrigento to: Caltanissetta (10 daily; 1hr 30min); Canicattì (10 daily; 45min); Enna (5 daily; 2hr 40min); Palermo (10 daily; 2hr).
Gela to: Caltagirone (11 daily; 40min); Canicattì (10 daily; 1hr 30min, change at Canicattì for the 10 daily service to Agrigento); Licata (10 daily; 30min); Ragusa (8 daily Mon–Sat, 5 daily Sun; 1hr 20min); Vittória (8 daily; 40min).

Buses

Agrigento to: Caltanissetta (14 daily Mon–Sat, 7 daily Sun; 1hr 15min); Canicattì (14 daily; 40min); Catania (14 daily Mon–Sat, 5 daily Sun; 2hr 50min); Gela (3 daily; 1hr 30min); Licata (every 30–60min; 1hr); Montallegro (for Eraclea Minoa, hourly Mon–Sat, 2 daily Sun; 30min); Palermo (4 daily; 2hr); Palma di Montechiaro (every 30–60min; 30min); Porto Empédocle (every 30min until 8.30pm; 20min); Ribera (for Eraclea Minoa, hourly Mon–Sat, 2 daily Sun; 1hr); Sant'Ángelo Muxaro (3 daily Mon–Sat; 1hr); Sciacca (11 daily Mon–Sat, 3 daily Sun; 2hr); Trápani (4 daily Mon–Sat; 3hr 30min).
Gela to: Agrigento (3 daily; 1hr 30min); Caltagirone (5 daily Mon–Sat; 1hr 25min); Caltanissetta (4 daily Mon–Sat, 2 daily Sun; 2hr); Catania (5–9 daily Mon–Sat, 4 daily Sun; 1hr 45min); Enna (1–2 daily; 1hr 40min); Licata (3 daily Mon–Sat; 45min); Palermo (3–4 daily; 3hr); Piazza Armerina (5 daily Mon–Sat, 2 daily Sun; 40min); Siracusa (2 daily Mon–Sat, 1 daily Sun; 2hr); Vittória (6 daily Mon–Sat; 50min).
Sciacca to: Agrigento (11 daily Mon–Sat, 3 Sun; 2hr); Caltabellotta (4 daily Mon–Sat, 3 daily Sun; 25min); Castelvetrano (3 daily; 1hr 30min); Menfi (7 daily; 35min); Palermo (10 daily Mon–Sat, 5 daily Sun; 2hr 30min); Trápani (9 daily Mon–Sat, 4 daily Sun; 3hr).

Ferries

Porto Empédocle to: Linosa/Lampedusa (June–Oct daily at midnight; Nov–May daily except Fri at midnight; 5hr 45min/8hr 15min).
Lampedusa/Linosa to: Porto Empédocle (June–Oct daily at 10.15am/12.15pm; Nov–May daily except Sat 10.15am/12.15pm; 8hr 15min).

Hydrofoils

Lampedusa to Linosa: daily service from mid-June to end Sept; from Lampedusa at 9.30am and 5.30pm; from Linosa at 10.45am and 6.45pm; journey time 1hr.

Planes

Palermo to: Lampedusa (3 daily; 1hr).
Lampedusa to: Palermo (3 daily; 1hr).

Trápani and the west

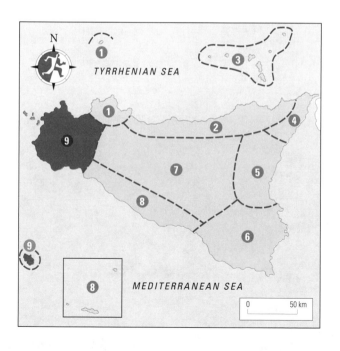

CHAPTER 9

Highlights

* **Riserva Naturale dello Zíngaro** Hike the footpaths or swim from isolated pebble coves within Sicily's most beautiful nature reserve. **p.387**

* **The procession of the Misteri, Trápani** Trápani's annual Good Friday celebrations see life-sized wooden statues, representing scenes from the Passion, paraded through the old-town streets. **p.393**

* **Égadi Islands** From tuna fishing to prehistoric cave paintings, the three Égadi Islands offer a unique Sicilian perspective. **p.402**

* **Selinunte** Perhaps the most romantic of all Greek sites on the island – and the only one with a lively beach resort attached. **p.418**

* **Pantelleria** It takes some effort to get here, but up-and-coming Pantelleria is Sicily's most fashionable offshore retreat. **p.425**

△ Punte Lunge Harbour, Favignana

9

Trápani and the west

Closer to North Africa than the Italian mainland, Sicily's western reaches are traditionally poor and remote, the economy dependent on fishing and small-scale farming. Since the opening of the A29 auto-strada, the region has become more integrated with the rest of Sicily than it has ever been, although even today, public transport links to the rest of the island are limited. Indeed, much of the appeal of the area lies in the fact that it's still very different from the rest of the island. Historically, the region has always been distinct, influenced by a strong **Phoenician** and **Arab** culture rather than the prevailing Greek and Norman tradition elsewhere in Sicily. The Arab influence can still be tasted in its food – couscous is a local favour-ite – and visually too, the flat land, dotted by white cubic houses, is strongly reminiscent of North Africa.

On the northern coast, the **Golfo di Castellammare** is only an hour's train ride from Palermo, and though there are patches of industrial development along the gulf it still manages to offer some empty beaches and a couple of unspoiled villages at its western end. In particular, the coastline between the old tuna-fishing village of **Scopello** and the resort of **San Vito Lo Capo** encompasses Sicily's first and most beautiful nature reserve, the **Zíngaro**. The capital of the province that embraces almost this entire area, **Trápani** is a con-genial port town within sight of the flat saltpans on which its wealth was based. It is also a departure point for the **Égadi Islands**, and makes a good base for visiting the mountain town of **Érice** – originally a centre of Punic influence, though diverging from the region's dominant trend in its uniform Norman and medieval character. The pattern re-establishes itself a little way down the coast at **Mózia**, Sicily's best example of a Phoenician site, while further south the Moorish imprint is discernible in the secretive alleys and courtyards of **Marsala** and **Mazara del Vallo**.

Although the Greeks never wielded much influence in the area, the Hellenic remains at **Segesta** and **Selinunte** (Selinus) count among the island's most stunning. Between the two, the Valle del Belice delineates the region struck by an earthquake in 1968, which left a trail of destruction still visible in many towns and villages. This is most notable at **Gibellina**, abandoned in its ruined state as a powerful reminder, and at the little town of **Santa Margherita di Belice**, whose once-proud palace and church were immortalized in that quintessential Sicilian novel, *The Leopard*. There could be no greater contrast to this disorder than the peaceful island of **Pantelleria**, a distant outpost, much nearer to Africa than Europe, mountainous and wind-blown, and visited mainly by birds as a stop on their long migrations.

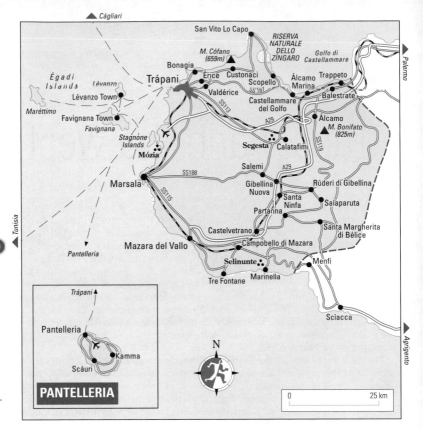

You'll find **getting around** the coast a simple matter, as frequent buses and trains cover the short distances between all the towns and villages. There's much less public transport, though, if you strike off **inland**: what interior bus services there are depart from Marsala or Castelvetrano. If you're driving, apart from the two arms of the A29 autostrada there are only two other main roads, the SS115 between Trápani and Mazara and the inland SS188 between Marsala and Salemi.

The Golfo di Castellammare

Backed by a forbidding wall of jagged mountains, the wide bowl of the **Golfo di Castellammare** is almost entirely made up of small holiday towns, sometimes uncomfortably close to industrial plants, though these disappear as you progress west. The main train line from Palermo (and the SS187 road) skirts the bay from Trappeto to Castellammare del Golfo, but despite the ease of access and the consequent development the resorts have not entirely shrugged off their original role as fishing villages – though they have completely lost the mean look they had when fishing was the only source of income. If you're after a beach, some of these would make a reasonable morning's halt, though be warned that in July and August it's slow going on the roads and the sands are packed. Otherwise, the train ride is as fair an entertainment, hugging the coast at the base of massive wedges of rock, often of a raw red colour, echoed by smaller, weathered nuggets poking out of the sea.

Trappeto, Balestrate and Álcamo Marina

Today, the two villages of **TRAPPETO** and **BALESTRATE**, just 5km apart (and each on the train line), have a tidy sense of wellbeing in sharp contrast to the poverty that Danilo Dolci found when he came to the region in 1952. His *Sicilian Lives* records his first impressions of Trappeto: "Coming from the North, I knew I was totally ignorant. Looking all around me, I saw no streets, just mud and dust. Not a single chemist – or sewer. The dialect didn't have a word for sewer." Nowadays, things have dramatically improved, and the beaches on either side of the villages, backed by orange groves, are regularly visited by Palermitan holiday-makers. There are popular summer pizzerias in both places, and even a couple of hotels, though there's no real reason to stay: in summer it's just too busy and in winter too funereal. There's more of the same 10km further west at **ÁLCAMO MARINA**, where a few more bars and restaurants provide some sweeping views of the gulf.

Inland: Álcamo

Inland, and just inside the Trápani provincial boundary, **ÁLCAMO** itself is the only large town hereabouts, founded by Frederick II in the early thirteenth century and spread across a low hill overlooking the sea. Good wine is made from Álcamo grapes, but other than that the town will only be of interest to fans of **Mary Taylor Simeti** – much of whose book *On Persephone's Island* (see p.473) is set hereabouts – or ecclesiastical architecture, with its largely Baroque **churches** all found along and around the old town's lengthy main street, Corso VI Aprile. The Chisea Madre on the corso is typical, with its bold frescoes and elaborate sculptures by members of the Gagini family. There's an impressive fourteenth-century castle too, just up from the central Piazza Ciullo.

It's not really practical to arrive by train, since the **train station** (Álcamo Diramazione) lies 5km below town, off the main SS113. **Buses** run four times a day (not Sun) from Trápani and take about an hour and a half, but are scheduled to benefit Álcamo's commuters, with the only returns from Álcamo being early in the morning. In fact, there is little point coming without a car, not because it's easy to drive around (the confusing one-way system and narrow streets put paid to that) but because most of the other things to see and do are out of town.

If you decide to stay over, Álcamo has a recently refurbished **hotel**, the *Miramare*, Corso Médici 72 (☎0924.21.197; ❸), on the edge of town at the end of the main street away from the central square; all rooms have bathrooms and air-conditioning. Otherwise there's the new *La Principessa*, Via Canape 5 (☎0924.507.789, ⓦwww.albergolaprincipessa.it; ❸), all of whose simple rooms have bath, air-conditioning, mini-bars and TV; it also has some apartments to rent. The *Bar Grazia*, Corso VI Aprile 388, close to the market, is good for a snack, while there's a couple of decent, moderately priced **restaurants**: the *Salsaparigua*, at Via Libertà 1, and *La Funtanazza*, a few kilometres south of town in the woods on Monte Bonifato (signposted).

Monte Bonifato (825m) is worth the 5km drive out of town for the panoramic views from the top: the route up a corkscrew road is well signposted from town. The other local attraction is the **Stabilimento Termale Gorga** (℡0924.23.842; no credit cards, ❶), a thermal spa where you can bathe in the exquisitely hot pool for €5, or take other treatments, such as a mud bath (€11), or a sauna (€10). You can also stay here − all rooms have bath and phone. It's just a couple of hundred metres along the right-hand dirt track from the train station (don't go down under the bridge). There's a second spa, **Terme Segestane** (℡0924.530.057), five to ten minutes' drive to the west, where mud treatments cost €18 and entrance to the pool €5.

Castellammare del Golfo

CASTELLAMMARE DEL GOLFO is the last coastal stop on the gulf before the train line winds inland to Trápani. It's the biggest of the local fishing ports, entirely surrounded by high hills and built on and around a hefty rocky promontory, which is guarded by the squat remains of an Aragonese castle. Beneath the castle walls, on the harbourside, a run of café-restaurants face the fishing-boats, a nice place to kill time and eat lunch. There's a scrappy sand beach at the harbour, though you may prefer the fine sands 2km east of the centre, between the town and train station.

Castellammare's incredible pedigree of bloodshed once gave it one of the worst reputations in Sicily for Mafia violence. Maxwell claimed that in the late 1950s eighty percent of the town's adult males had served prison sentences, and one in three had committed murder: coupled with this are the official statistics for the same period that classify one family in six as destitute. Needless to say, all of this is extremely hard to believe today: strolling down the sloping Corso Garibaldi towards the castle and harbour, past handsome *palazzi* interspersed with bars and shops selling beach gear, it seems a most benign place.

If you want to stay, the **hotel** *Al Madarig*, Piazza Petrolo 7 (℡0924.33.533, ℻0924.33.790; ❺), is a stylish choice on one side of a wide piazza, with cool, sea-view rooms and a summer-dining *terrazza* in the square: breakfast is included. Alternatively, try the new *Cala Marina*, Via Don Leonardo Zangara 1 (℡0924.531.841, ⓦwww.hotelcalamarina.it; ❺) − ask for one of the three smart, bright rooms with sea views. Above town on the main SS187, the *Belvedere* (℡ & ℻0924.33.330, ⓦwww.hotelbelvedere.net; ❹) has even better views − all rooms have a terrace and there's a restaurant (handy, as it's too far to walk into town). The pinewood slopes of Monte Inici behind the hotel are a popular picnic and viewpoint spot and there's another pizzeria-restaurant here, *Quetzal*, with tables under the trees. The local **campsite**, *Nausicaa* (℡0924.33.030; open May–Sept), is 3km east of Castellammare and handy for the beach. For a **meal** in town, *L'Approdo* down at the harbour is a relaxing place to sit − not too pricey and serving good pizzas in the evening − or try a speciality *cuscus a pesce* at any of the other three or four moderately priced places here. There's also the inexpensive *La Muciara* (closed Mon), just down the steps from the town gardens.

The local **train station** is 4km east of town; a bus meets arrivals (more or less) and shuttles you into Castellammare, passing the campsite on the way. It drops you at the **bus station** in the upper part of the town on Via della Repubblica, which runs off Via Segesta. From here there are regular services **to Scopello** (Mon–Sat at 7.10am, 9am, 1.30pm, 4pm and 6.30pm) and to the beach ("Spiaggia"), as well as to San Vito, Palermo, Trápani, Álcamo and Calatafimi/Segesta. Note that the only buses on Sunday run to Palermo.

You'll find the **tourist office** (Mon–Fri 8am–2pm, Tues & Thurs also 3–6pm; ☎0924.592.111) up the steps at Via A. de Gasperi 6, opposite the gardens in Corso Bernardo Mattarella, with friendly and enthusiastic English-speaking staff. Other offices are on the outskirts of the town, at Viale Umberto I 3 (daily 9am–1pm & 4–8pm; ☎0924.31.320), and in the castle (Mon–Fri 9am–1pm & 4–8pm). **Banks** are on the main Corso Garibaldi.

Scopello and Zíngaro

The coastline northwest of Castellammare is perhaps the most beautiful in the whole of Sicily, with no shortage of unspoiled coves and gravel beaches, connected by paths to the road above. It culminates in the area around **Scopello**, 10km from Castellammare, a tiny hamlet a little way inland that once serviced an old tuna fishery (*tonnara*) on the coast below. The swimming here is terrific, while the road itself stops 3km beyond Scopello *tonnara*, at a nature reserve, the **Riserva Naturale dello Zíngaro**, where you can proceed on foot through pristine country and past more extremely beautiful coves and beaches. It's not exactly unknown territory, since hundreds of Palermitani descend on Scopello and its surroundings on summer weekends, but at other times – and especially out of season – it's one of the most tranquil places in Sicily. In addition, since the whole area is regulated by building restrictions which actually seem to be enforced, the water quality – and consequently the swimming – is excellent.

The Tonnara di Scopello

The road to Scopello from Castellammare forks just before the village, with one strand running the few hundred metres down to the coast and to the **TONNARA DI SCOPELLO**, set in its own tiny cove. This old tuna fishery and its associated outhouses were where the writer Gavin Maxwell lived and worked in the 1950s, basing his *Ten Pains of Death* on his experiences there. It's almost too picturesque to be true – not least the row of abandoned buildings on the quayside, fronted by lines of rusting anchors, and the ruined old watchtowers tottering on knobbly columns of rock above the sea. From the shore, it's still precisely as Maxwell described it forty years ago: "a sea of purple and blue and peacock green, with a jagged cliff coastline and great *faraglioni* [rock towers] thrusting up out of the water as pinnacle islands, pale green with the growth of cactus at their heads". The *tonnara* remained in intermittent use until the 1980s, but although it's still privately owned the gate is always open (free) to allow visitors to wander around the quayside and – more to the point – swim off the tiny shingle **beach** in the most crystal clear of waters. It's a thoroughly enjoyable spot, made more so by the fact that visitors are tolerated provided they don't bring with them a whole host of proscribed items – dogs, radios, chairs, sunshades "and anything else that would disturb the tranquillity of the place". An injunction like this is usually as a red rag to a bull to your average Sicilian, to whom disturbing tranquillity comes as second nature; here, amazingly, peace and quiet appears to hold sway.

Scopello

The road past the *tonnara* runs onto Zíngaro (see opposite), with a loop heading back to the village of **SCOPELLO DI SOPRA** – or simply Scopello – which perches on a ridge a couple of hundred metres above the coastline. This is little more than a paved square and a fountain, off which run a couple of alleys; on one side of the square sits the gateway and enclosed courtyard of the village's eighteenth-century **baglio**, or manor house, now the focus of local life. In here – centred on a huge eucalyptus tree – the courtyard buildings harbour a ceramicist's workshop, artist's studio, craft shop, a couple of bars and a pizzeria-restaurant. With the lights on and the wind rustling the leaves, it's a magical place at night, though in July and August – when every bar table is full and queues develop at the pizzeria – you could be forgiven for wishing for more solitude. That you'll get if you come anytime other than high summer, when traditional village life is more to the fore: men playing cards at the tables, people gossiping around the fountain and neighbours helping out in each other's fields.

Scopello can be rather an exclusive retreat, given the building restrictions which limit the accommodation choices. In summer, you should book well in advance if you want to stay here, and be prepared to accept half-board terms in the *pensioni* (which matters little since there's hardly anywhere else to eat anyway). Out of season you'll be able to pick and choose, and the prices drop a little too.

Practicalities

The **bus** from Castellammare drops you in the square, by the fountain; there are four services a day (Mon–Sat) back to Castellammare, the last at 4.40pm. Elsewhere in the village (you won't have to look far to find everything) there's an *alimentari*, a bakery, butcher's shop, a couple of bars, a post office, and phones by the fountain.

You might be lucky and find some **rooms to rent**; try asking around in the bars and shops. Otherwise, all the official **places to stay** and eat are within a thirty-second walk of the square – official street names are a bit pointless, but are given in case you want to write and book. *La Tranchina*, at Via A. Diaz 7 (℡ & ℻0924.541.099; ❹), is run by a friendly family that includes an English speaker, and has comfortable modern rooms with decent plumbing and an open fire in winter (when the nights can get chilly); dinner is served here, too. *La Tavernetta*, next door at no. 3 (℡ & ℻0924.541.129; ❺), has similarly pleasant rooms, some with distant sea views. The food here isn't bad either, with pasta, fresh fish, local wine and fruit running to around €20, though you could eat for less. The best **food** in the village is at the wonderful *Torre Benistra*, just around the corner at Via Natale di Roma 19 (℡ & ℻0924.541.128; no credit cards): at the time of writing it was closed for refurbishment, but as the owner Lucina is a wonderful cook, it's worth calling to see if she's re-opened. There are two other places to eat in the village: *Il Baglio*, in the *baglio* courtyard, an extremely popular place for **pizzas** at the weekend, with attractive outdoor seating and a full menu; and the moderately priced *Al Cantuccio*, on the main road, which serves meat, fish and crêpes.

The nearest **campsite** is *Baia di Guidaloca* (℡0924.541.262; April–Sept), 3km south of Scopello and a stone's throw from the lovely bay of **Cala Bianca**, where there's good swimming; the bus from Castellammare passes right by.

The Riserva Naturale dello Zíngaro

The southern entrance to the **Riserva Naturale dello Zíngaro** is just 2km from Scopello village, along a road affording wonderful views of the *tonnara's* towers and the gulf beyond, passing reasonably discrete holiday homes, fields of vines and grazing horses.

The Zíngaro was the first nature reserve to have been established in Sicily and comprises a completely unspoiled seven-kilometre stretch of coastline backed by steep mountains. Its genesis was the proposal to force a coast road through from Scopello to San Vito, an idea that horrified environmentalists, who persuaded six thousand supporters to march in protest in May 1980. The road was scrapped and the reserve established, following which great efforts have been made to attract sympathetic visitors to the site. Most, it's true, come for the isolated cove **beaches**, which provide scintillating swimming, but since there's no vehicle access beyond the entrances it's not hard to escape the crowds by simply walking further into the reserve. There's a network of **paths**, the easiest and best-maintained running close to the coast, though the mid- and high-mountain routes are popular with well-prepared walkers and ornithologists. Around forty different **bird species** nest and mate here, and apart from the wide variety of flora there's also great archeological interest in an area that supported some of Sicily's earliest prehistoric settlements.

At the Scopello entrance, there's a car park and an **information hut** (daily: summer 7.30am–8pm; winter 8am–5pm), where you can pick up a simple map showing the trails through the reserve. If you're heading off from the coastal path, treat the map with some scepticism and make sure you carry plenty of water. There's a water fountain at the information hut and, in summer, a van selling ices and drinks.

It's less than twenty minutes to the first beach, **Punta della Capreria**, which means it can be crowded at weekends and in July and August. When it's not, it's perfect: a tiny cove of white pebbles, azure water, shoals of little fish nibbling at the edge and baby squid darting in and out. There's a **Museo Naturalistico** (daily 10am–5pm; free) and visitors' centre (same hours) just above the beach. Sticking with the coastal path, it's 3km to the successive coves of **Disa**, **Berretta** and **Marinella**, which should be a little more secluded, and 7km in total to the **Tonnara dell'Uzzo**, just beyond which is the northern, San Vito Lo Capo, park entrance. If you're walking on to San Vito, note it's another 11km from the entrance, and there's no public transport or facilities of any kind along the way.

Segesta and around

Around 15km south of Castellammare del Golfo (and 30km east of Trápani), the remains of the ancient city of **Segesta** are among the most inspiring on the island. Set amid deserted green countryside, all that still stands is a Doric temple and a brilliantly sited theatre, relics of a city whose roots – like Érice's – lay back in the twelfth century BC. Unlike Érice, though, ancient Segesta was eventually Hellenized and spent most of the later period disputing its border with Selinus. The temple dates from a time of prosperous alliance with Athens, but it was never finished – work on it being abandoned when a new dispute broke out with Selinus in 416 BC.

If you're driving, it's easiest to see the site en route between Palermo and Trápani, since it lies just off the motorway. By public transport, the best approach is by bus from Trápani. However you arrive, the only possibility of an overnight stop in these lovely surroundings is the small hotel at **Calatafimi**, the nearest town to the ruins.

The site

The site of **SEGESTA** (daily 9am–1hr before sunset; €4.50) is best seen early or late in the day when not only are visitor numbers fewer but the light less blanching in its effect. The **temple** itself, started in 424 BC, crowns a low hill beyond the café and car park. From a distance you could be forgiven for thinking that it's complete: the 36 regular stone columns, entablature and pediment are all intact, and all it lacks is a roof. However, get closer (and for once you're allowed to roam right inside) and you see just how unfinished the building is: stone studs, always removed on completion, still line the stylobate, the tall columns are unfluted and the cella walls are missing. In a way, this only adds to the natural grandeur of the site, and it's not too fanciful to imagine that the temple simply grew here – a feeling bolstered by the birds nesting in the unfinished capitals, the lizards scampering over the pale yellow stone, and the pitted and sun-bleached interior.

From the main entrance, a road winds up through slopes of wild fennel to a small **theatre** on a higher hill beyond; if you don't relish the twenty-minute walk you can use the half-hourly summer **bus service**. The view from the top is terrific, across green slopes and the plain to the sea, the deep blue of the bay a lovely contrast to the theatre's white stone – the panorama not much damaged by the motorway snaking away below. Behind the theatre, **excavations** (explained by information boards) have revealed the foundations of a mosque and Arab-style houses. These were pulled down in the thirteenth century when a Norman castle was erected on the high ground – though this itself lasted less than a hundred years, as political forces on the island waxed and waned. There are also the remains of a late medieval church, built for local shepherds and landholders and used, in one form or another, until the nineteenth century. Thus it is a site of enormous significance and utility used over the generations.

In odd-numbered years, summer **concerts and plays** are staged at the theatre. Ask at the tourist offices in Palermo and Trápani for details of these, or consult Ⓦ www.calatafimisegesta.it. Special excursion buses leave from both cities to coincide with the performances, and tickets for the various productions cost €15–20.

Practicalities

Coming from Trápani or Palermo by car, the easiest way to Segesta is to take the A29 autostrada. Near the signposted turn-off there's a café-restaurant, which – apart from the small café and shop at the site – is the only other nearby place for refreshments. Otherwise, you'll have to take one of the **buses** from Piazza Malta in Trápani, which leave Monday to Saturday at 7.10am, 8am, 10am, 2pm and 5pm, returning at 1.10 pm, 4.10pm and 6.35pm. The only reasonable Sunday departure is at 10am, returning at 1.10pm. The **train** from Trápani to Álcamo/Palermo stops at Segesta-Tempio; it's a twenty-minute walk uphill to the site from here, with the temple up on the right. Services are infrequent, though, and to return to Trápani by train you'll probably have to walk from the site car park to the train station of Calatafimi (see below), signposted a couple of kilometres to the east, from where there are trains back to Trápani roughly every two hours throughout the day.

Calatafimi

The small town of **CALATAFIMI** lies 4km south of its train station, so it's better to come by bus – there are four services daily here from Trápani. Defended by a castle (hence the Arabic *kalat* of its name) whose remnants top a wooded hill, the town gained fame as the site of the first of Garibaldi's victories against the Bourbon forces in 1860, which opened the way to Palermo and hence the rest of Sicily. The battle took place on the Salemi road, around 1km south of Calatafimi and then 3km up a hill, the summit marked by a white obelisk. It's signposted "Ossario di Pianto Romana" and named as such since the bones of the fallen from the battle are collected here. They used to be on display in cases for the edification of the local population; now they're hidden behind commemorative tablets underneath an Italian flag. The custodian might attempt an explanation of the history if your Italian is up to it – a tip wouldn't go amiss. The views outside, to Calatafimi itself, Érice and the Castellammare gulf, are magnificent.

The old town isn't much more than a strip of development along a single main street, at the top of which stands the church and, just beyond, the only hotel, the *Mille Pini*, at Piazza F. Vivona 2 (℡0924.951.260, ℻0923.950.223, Ⓔmillepini@tin.it; ❶). This has half a dozen simple rooms with balconies and valley views, and a restaurant where you can eat well for around €15 – overall, it's a very nice place for a quiet night in the sticks.

Trápani

TRÁPANI is the first of three major towns on Sicily's western edge, and, although predominantly modern, has an elegant old centre squeezed into a narrow arm of land pointing out to sea. Lent an end-of-the-line feel by its port, the town's inconspicuous monuments give no great impression of its long history. Nonetheless, Trápani flourished as a Phoenician trading centre and as the port for Eryx, modern Érice, profiting from its position looking out towards Africa. As an important stopover on the sea routes linking Tunis, Naples, Anjou and Aragon, the town was ensured an enduring role throughout the Middle Ages, when Europe's crowned heads virtually passed each other on the quayside. The Navarrese king Theobald died here of typhoid in 1270; two years later Edward I of England touched down after a Crusade to learn he'd inherited the throne, while Peter of Aragon arrived in 1282 to claim the Sicilian throne, following the expulsion of the Angevin French. The city's growth over the last century has been founded on the development of salt, fishing and wine industries, though severe bombardment during World War II has given rise to miles of dull postwar building around the outskirts.

Still, as a **touring base** for the rest of the west, Trápani can't be beaten. There are a good few accommodation possibilities, all in the old-town area, regular trains south to nearby Marsala and Mazara del Vallo, buses to Érice, the resort of San Vito Lo Capo and the more distant site of Segesta, and the nearest of the Égadi Islands is only twenty minutes away by hydrofoil.

Museo Regionale Pépoli, Santuario dell'Annunziata & Youth Hostel

Égadi Islands, Pantelleria, Ústica & Naples

Égadi Islands, Pantelleria, Cagliari & Tunis

TRÁPANI

RESTAURANTS

Ai Lumi	2
Angelino	8
Calvino	4
Cantina Siciliana	3
Da Peppe	6
Da Salvatore	5
La Bettolacca	2
P & G	1
Trattoria del Porto	7

ACCOMMODATION

Ai Lumi	D
Cavallino Bianco	A
Maccotta	F
Messina	D
Moderno	C
Nuovo Russo	E
Vittoria	B

N

200 m

0

Train Station

Bus Station

Hydrofoil Port

Stazione Marittima

Molo di Sanità

Questura

Villa Margherita

San Domenico

Palazzo della Giudecca

Santa Maria di Gesù

Sant'Agostino

Collegio

Cattedrale

Chiesa del Purgatorio

Market

Torre di Ligny

Lazzaretto

Villino Nasi

PIAZZA MALTA
PIAZZA UMBERTO I
PIAZZA VITTORIO EMANUELE
PIAZZA VITTORIO VENETO
PIAZZA "JOLANDA"
PIAZZA GEN. SCIO

VIA S. VULPITTA
VIA MUSICA
VIA NAUSICA
VIA XX SETTEMBRE
VIA S. BASSI
VIA ORLANDINI
VIA ERRANTE
VIA LIVIO
VIA PASSO ENZA
VIA G. B. FARDELLA
VIA MARINO TORRE
VIA VESPRI
VIA PASSENETO
VIA NISO
VIA VIRGILIO
VIA DIDONE
VIA ANCHISE
VIA MAZZINI
VIA TREMITI
VIA PALMIEFI
VIA SARACENI
VIA TORRE PALI
VIA BISCOTTAI
VIA AMMIRAGLIO STAITI
VIA SPALTI
VIA OSORIO
VIA SCONTRINO
VIA F. CRISPI
VIA SCUDANIGLIO
VIA S.G. BOSCO
VIA BELLINI
VIA PALMERIO ABATE
VIA XXX GENNAIO
CORSO ITALIA
VIA DELLA GIUDECCA
VIA MERCÉ
VIA BADIELLA
VIA SAN MICHELE
VIA SAN PIETRO
VIA SAN AGOSTINI
VIA TURRETTA
VIA ROMA
VIA LIBERTÀ
CORSO VITTORIO EMANUELE
VIA TINTORI
VIA TORRE ARSA
VIA GARIBALDI
VIA SERISSO
VIA SAN FRANCESCO D'ASSISI
VIA SAN NASI
VIA G. G. BARTAGLIA
VIA CASSARETTO
VIA CARTAGLIA
VIA REGINA ELENA
LUNGOMARE DANTE ALIGHIERI
VIA MURA DI TRAMONTANA OVEST
VIALE DELLE SIRENE
VIALE DUCA D'AOSTA
VIA DEI RANUNCOLI
VIA CAPPUCCINI
VIA CAROLINA
VIA C. COLOMBO
VIA TORRE DI LIGNY

The best time to visit Trápani itself is at **Easter**, to see the famous procession of the **Misteri** – eighteenth-century wooden images arranged in scenes
representing the last days of Christ's life. If you're aiming to be here then, make
sure of a hotel room in advance, though you should have no problem finding
space at any other time.

Arrival, orientation and information

The **train station** and main **bus station** (for regional buses) are at the edge
of the modern part of town, in Piazza Umberto and the adjacent Piazza Malta
(also known as Piazza Montalto) respectively. **Buses from Palermo and
Agrigento** drop you either at the bus station or at the **hydrofoil** dock on Via
Ammiraglio Staiti, or the **Stazione Maríttima** at Molo di Sanità, from where
there are **ferries** to the Égadi Islands, Pantelleria, Ústica, Naples and Cágliari
(Sardinia). Trápani's **airport** has connecting flights to the major Italian cities
and Pantelleria, and is 15km south of the city at Birgi: AST buses connect with
flights and run into the centre (20min). There's also a once daily Segesta service
from Palermo airport direct to Trápani (1hr 10min). See "Listings" (p.395)
for all ticket office addresses and "Travel details" (p.434) for full schedules.

The **old town**'s narrow and irregular layout occupies around a square
kilometre at Trápani's western end, centred on the main **Corso Vittorio
Emanuele**, which is about a fifteen-minute walk from the train station.
Everything in the old town is easily reachable on foot, though you'll need to
catch a **city bus** to visit Trápani's museum, in the new part of the city: most
routes depart from Piazza Vittorio Emanuele. Tickets are available from *tabacchi*,
and are valid for one hour. During the day, there are usually **taxis** outside the
train station – just make sure they switch on the meter or you could be in for
a surprise. For numbers of local companies, see "Listings", p.434.

Despite the unhelpful staff, the **tourist office**, at Piazzetta Saturno in the old
town (July & Aug Mon–Sat 8am–2pm & 2.30–8pm, Sun 9am–1pm; Sept–June
Mon–Sat 8.30am–1.30pm & 2.30–7.30pm, Sun 9am–noon; ☏0923.29.000,
ⓦwww.apt.trapani.it), has plenty of information in good English, accommodation listings and free maps.

Accommodation

Trápani's cheaper accommodation is all in the old town, though driving and
parking here can be difficult. Outside Easter, finding somewhere to stay is
usually no problem. The nearest (summer-only) campsite is up the coast from
Trápani, near Bonagia (see p.399), though there is a local **youth hostel**, the
Ostello per la Gioventù, Contrada Raganzili (☏0923.552.964), hidden away
3km out of town and open only after 6pm each day. Take bus #21 from the
station, or bus #23 from Piazza Vittorio Emanuele II, three blocks right of the
station, and get off at the Ospedale Villa dei Gerani, a 15min ride; from the
stop, take the second on the right and walk 600m uphill. Drivers should take
the road to Valderice and follow signs. Bed and breakfast costs €15.

Ai Lumi Corso Vittorio Emanuele 71
☏0923.872.418. Entered through a lovely arcaded
courtyard filled with potted plants, this bed and
breakfast has five small but pristine rooms and
apartments, as well as a fine trattoria a couple of
doors along the street. ❷
Cavallino Bianco Lungomare Dante Alighieri
☏0923.21.549, ⓕ0923.873.002. On a

rather forsaken stretch of the coast, a couple of
kilometres out of the centre along the
lungomare. No problem parking, and you do
get a balcony and a sea view, but it's a bit
isolated and rather overpriced for the
standard. ❺
Maccotta Via degli Argentieri 4 ☏0923.28.418,
ⓕ0923.437.693, ⓔalbergo-maccotta@comeg.

it. Clean and friendly place behind the Palazzo Senatorio, with spacious, fairly modern rooms; the cheapest share a separate bathroom. You can even use the Internet if you can rouse the *signora* into action. ❸

Messina Corso Vittorio Emanuele 71 ☎0923.21.198. Occupies the first floor of the eighteenth-century Palazzo Bernardo Ferro, and entered through the same grand courtyard as *Ai Lumi* (see above). The rooms are less impressive, though, and some of the staff smoke, but it's clean and the cheapest option in the city: advance reservations are recommended. No en-suite bathrooms or credit cards. ❶

Moderno Via Ten. Genovese 20 ☎0923.21.247, ☏0923.23.348. As you might imagine, it's no such thing, though it does have more character than some, housed in an old building with an internal courtyard. Simple rooms have French windows opening onto little balconies over the street. ❷

Nuovo Russo Via Tintori 4 ☎0923.22.166, ☏0923.26.623. Best choice in the old town for comfort at moderate prices. Bright rooms with tiled floors and coordinated colours, and good bathrooms with decent water pressure. Front rooms face the cathedral and its bells (mercifully, silent at night) and have tiny terraces for corso views. Breakfast and air-conditioning available for small extra charge. ❺

Vittória Via Francesco Crispi 4 ☎0923.873.044, ☏0923.29.870. Facing Trápani's only real open space and not far from the bus and train stations, this is the most reasonably priced new-town option. All rooms are en suite, the views are good from the upper floors, and there's parking available. ❺

The City

Almost everything of interest in Trápani is found in the **old town**, west of the Villa Margherita gardens. There's been some renovations of churches and palaces over the years, but off the main corso and away from the central shopping streets there's a scruffy, tatty air to much of Trápani, with litter blowing down the alleys and *palazzi* crumbling under the onslaught of years of accumulated grime.

You don't see any of this if you stick to the **Corso Vittorio Emanuele**, the old town's pedestrianized main street, dominated at its eastern end by the pinkish marble front of the **Palazzo Senatorio**, the seventeenth-century town hall. With its twin clocks separated by an imperious eagle, it adds a touch of grandeur to the thin promenading strip, otherwise hemmed in by balconied *palazzi*, a couple of Baroque churches, and the **Cattedrale** on the right, with its Baroque portico, cupolas and vast interior. Dedicated to San Lorenzo, and now a glorious sandy hue following restoration, there's a *Crucifixion* inside, attributed to Van Dyck.

The corso runs to the very tip of the curving promontory from which the town took its Phoenician name of Drepanon (sickle), ending at the seventeenth-century **Torre di Ligny**, an old Spanish fortification with a squat tower. This holds Trápani's collection of prehistoric finds, as well as photographs of drawings from the Grotta del Genovese on the island of Lévanzo, but has been closed for some time. On the way back into town, a walk down the north side of the promontory will show you what's left of the medieval city wall, the *bastione*, breached by the thirteenth-century **Porta Botteghelle**.

Back at the eastern end of the corso, **Via Torrearsa** is one of the old town's main shopping streets. At its northern end there's a good daily morning **market** in the arcaded Piazza Mercato di Pesce: fish, fruit and vegetables, local tuna products, olives, capers and cheeses are all on sale, and many can be sampled. The other way along the street, on Piazzetta Saturno, the church of **Sant'Agostino** (adjacent to the tourist office) has a pretty fourteenth-century rose window of interlocking stone bands; the church is occasionally used as a concert hall (details of performances from the tourist office). Architecturally more appealing is the sixteenth-century church of **Santa Maria di Gesù**, on Via San Pietro to the east, whose two doors display a diversity characteristic of the town, the right-hand one Gothic, the other defiantly Renaissance, and there's a good relief in the architrave. Step inside, and at the end of the nave there's a terracotta *Madonna degli Ángeli* by Andrea della Robbia, sheltered beneath a graceful marble canopy carved by Antonello Gagini.

There's little more to see in this part of town apart from a few unusual facades, one of them buried in the wedge of hairline streets and alleys north of Corso Italia, at Via della Giudecca 43, where the sixteenth-century **Palazzo della Giudecca** sports a plaque-studded front and some Spanish-style Plater-esque windows. The building lies at the heart of Trápani's old **Jewish quarter**, an area dating from Trápani's medieval heyday at the centre of Mediterranean trade. From here, it's not far to the **Villa Margherita**, the shady town gardens (open dawn to dusk) where summer concerts are held (more info available from the tourist office; see p.391).

The Misteri

Trápani's most rewarding church is the **Chiesa del Purgatorio** (daily 4–6.30pm, though in practice it's often locked) on Via Generale Domenico Giglio, south of the main corso and close to the port. It's the home of the **Misteri**, extraordinary life-sized wooden statues depicting scenes from the Passion. Sculpted from cypress wood and cork in the eighteenth century, each of the twenty groups of chocolate-brown figures is associated with one of the town's trades – fishermen, saltworkers, etc – whose representatives undertake to main-tain them and, draped in cowls and purple robes, carry them shoulder-high every Good Friday through Trápani's streets. It's one of Sicily's most evocative religious processions, held since the seventeenth century. If the church is open, there's usually a priest around to explain which of the trades are responsible for each of the sculpted groups, and what the particular figures represent – though most of the scenes are familiar enough. If it's locked, try asking about arranging admission at the tourist office.

The Santuario dell'Annunziata and the Museo Regionale Pépoli

The only incentive to set foot in the **modern city** is to visit Trápani's most lavishly decorated monument, the **Santuario dell'Annunziata** (daily: sum-mer 7am–noon & 4–6pm; winter 7–10am & 4–7pm, Sun 7am–1.30pm & 4–7pm; free), a fourteenth-century convent and church whose cloisters also incorporate the town's main museum. Take bus #24, #25 or #30 from Piazza Vittorio Emanuele and get off at the park, **Villa Pépoli**, which is just in front of the building.

The sanctuary was rebuilt in 1760 and only the facade, with its Gothic portal and magnificent rose window, is original. Inside (entrance on Via Pépoli), there are a series of sumptuous **chapels**, two dedicated to Trápani's fishermen and seamen – one echoing the facade's shell motif around the sides of the room – and, best of all, the **Cappella della Madonna**, containing Trápani's sacred idol: the beautiful, smiling *Madonna and Child*, attributed to Nino Pisano in the fourteenth century. Responsible for a host of miracles, the statue is housed under a grandiose marble canopy sculpted by Antonello Gagini and surrounded by polychrome marble – and generally by a crowd of hushed worshippers.

The **Museo Regionale Pépoli** (Tues–Sat 9am–1.30pm, Sun 9am–12.30pm; €2.50) is adjacent, entered through the Villa Pépoli. Although the museum was designed by one of Italy's foremost architects in the field, it's equipped with abysmal lighting, as it was intended that the exhibits should be seen in full daylight; come early, preferably in the morning. The wide-ranging collection takes in everything from exemplary Gagini statuary to seventeenth-century coral craftwork. Highlights downstairs include a little bronze horse and rider by Giacomo Serpotta and a sixteenth-century marble doorway by Berrettaro Bartolomeu, taken from the old church of San Giuliano, which, though badly worn in parts, displays a lively series of tableaux. Downstairs, too, bizarrely, is a grim wooden guillotine from 1789 with a basket for the head, and a coffin at the ready. The museum houses a good **medieval art** section – including a powerful *Pietà* by Roberto Oderisio, and a couple of fine fifteenth-century triptychs by the anonymous *Maestro del Políttico di Trápani* (presently under restoration). Other displays include a coin collection, with Greek, Roman, Arab and Italian examples; an eighteenth-century majolica-tiled scene of La Mattanza (tuna slaughter; see p.404), with the fishermen depicted corralling the fish in their boats; a small archeological section with a few finds from Selinunte and Mózia, though nothing outstanding; and some intricate coral work, including crib scenes with alabaster and shell decoration.

Eating and drinking

Eating out in Trápani is one of the city's better attractions – although that should probably be "eating in", since there are very few places where you can sit outside, Mediterranean-style, other than a couple of pavement cafés along the recently pedestrianized Via Garibaldi. Nonetheless, you can get fresh fish and couscous almost everywhere, while the local pasta speciality, *alla Trápanese*, is terrific – either spaghetti or home-made *busiate* served with a pesto of fresh tomato, basil, garlic and almonds, sometimes accompanied by fried potatoes. There are quite a few lively **bars** around, too, good for breakfast and snacks and bustling at night with people stopping off from the rowdy *passeggiata* that fills Via Torrearsa and the bottom end of the corso. The daily **market** is at the northern end of Via Torrearsa. For an explanation of the restaurant price categories, see p.53.

Restaurants

Ai Lumi Corso Vittorio Emanuele 75
☎0923.872.418. Well-regarded local taverna with regional dishes, such as *ghiotta di pesce* (seafood soup), home-made pasta, grilled meats and simple grilled fish. Closed Sun. Moderate.
Angelino Via A. Staiti 87 ☎0923.26.922. Examine the mouthwatering displays in this fashionable *pasticceria-távola calda*, order at the bar, grab a table in the conservatory and tuck in. You're spoiled for choice – *involtini* of aubergine rolled around spaghettini, stuffed sardines, rosemary-roast potatoes, lasagne and *foccacia*, all served at the table with wine by the glass, and coffee and cake to follow if you wish. Closed Sun & Mon lunch. Inexpensive.
La Bettolacca Via Gen. Enrico Fardella 25
☎0923.21.695. Friendly, informal *osteria* known for its excellent risotto and a short list of locally inspired pastas and fish dishes, such as oven-baked bucatini with sardines. It's just off the corso, round the corner from the *Messina* hotel. Moderate.

Calvino Via N. Nasi 77 ☎0923.21.464. An excellent back-street pizzeria, parallel to the corso, the *Calvino* has some Moorish-style cubbyhole rooms at the back where you can eat superb hot pizza on squares of greaseproof paper, washed down with cold beer. Try the *Rianata*, made with fresh oregano, tomato, garlic, anchovies and pecorino cheese – a local speciality. No credit cards. Closed Tues. Inexpensive.
Cantina Siciliana Via Giudecca 32
☎0923.28.673. In what was once the old Jewish quarter, this serves reasonably priced, traditional Sicilian food as well as a fish couscous. It's nice and cosy for a romantic dinner. Moderate.
P&G Via Spalti 1 ☎0923.547.701. A smart restaurant with a great chef who lays on a fine antipasto selection and good fresh fish or grilled meats. Try the garlicky *spaghetti alla Trápanese*, with fried potatoes, or home-made *busiate* served with a pesto of anchovy, garlic, pine nuts and tomato. Closed Sun. Expensive.
Da Peppe Via Spalti 52 ☎0923.28.246. The food's good – from *busiate* with sardines and a

fish couscous to grilled sea bass and baked tuna – and it's popular with the locals, but service can be a bit brusque and the atmosphere a little stuffy. Go elsewhere for a riproaring night out. Closed Mon. Expensive.

Trattoria del Porto Via A. Staiti 45 ☎0923.547.822. Family-run trattoria (also known locally as *Da Felice*) opposite the port with painfully slow service, but good food and nice outdoor tables under the arches. Top choices are the spaghetti marinara, fish couscous, roast squid or grilled *spigola* (sea bass), and there's an excellent-value *menù turistico* at €20, which includes wine and fruit. Moderate.

Da Salvatore Via N. Nasi 19. A trattoria of the old school, TV blaring away, paper tablecloths and voluble locals. The food's not great, but it's perfectly adequate – a plate of pasta *alla Trápanese*, a slice of grilled fish, a bit of fruit, some rough local wine – and very cheap. Inexpensive.

Bars, birrerias and cafés

Bar Tritone Piazza Vittorio Emanuele 38. There's not many places in town with any kind of view – here, you can sit among the palm trees, sip a drink or munch on *gelato* and wonder exactly what

kind of bird it is that the statue of King Vittorio Emanuele has on his head.

Birreria Italia Via Torrearsa 5–7. One of several bars at this end of town, the boisterous *Italia* has bottled beer, snacks and cakes, and streetside tables for *passeggiata*-watching. There's pizza by the slice, too, over the way at *Passa a Taglio*. Closed Sun.

Colicchia at the corner of Via delle Belle Arti and Via Carosio, just off Via Torrearsa. Fine bar-*pasticceria* with a super array of cakes; a good place to sample a granita. No seats.

Garibaldi Via Garibaldi s/n. Nicest of the Via Garibaldi cafés, and worth a visit just for the joy of sitting outside on a traffic-free road lined with grand Baroque churches and palaces. It serves the usual stuff – toasted sandwiches, pizzette, etc – but is really a place to come for an evening *aperativo* and nibbles. Closed Sun in high summer.

Gelateria Sebastiano Via Roma 15. Make a bee-line here for excellent home-made ice cream. The opening hours are erratic, but the official closing day is Tuesday.

Poldo Piazza Gen. Alberto della Chiesa 9. A noisy birreria and *panineria*, busy at night, serving good hot sandwiches and big mugs of beer.

Listings

Airline tickets from Agenzia Salvo (see above).
Airport information For Trápani airport flight info, call ☎0923.842.502 or 0923.843.136.
Airport transport Agenzia Salvo, Corso Italia 52 (☎0923.545.0111), offer their customers a free bus service to the airport or there's an AST bus from Piazza Malta. There's also a direct bus from Trápani bus station to Palermo airport daily at 9am.
Banks Cashpoints (ATMs) at Banca Populare S. Angelo, Piazza Umberto I 45; Banca di Roma, Corso Italia 38; Banco di Sicilia, Via Garibaldi 9; and at the Stazione Maríttima.
Buses Autoservizi Segesta ☎0923.21.754, from Piazza Garibaldi (for Palermo and Palermo airport); AST ☎0923.23.222, from Piazza Malta (for destinations within the province, including Érice, Marsala, Mazara del Vallo, Castelvetrano, Gibellina, San Vito Lo Capo, Salemi, Valderice and the airport); S. Lumia ☎0922.20.414, from Piazza Malta (for Agrigento and Sciacca); Tarantola ☎0924.31.020, from Piazza Malta (for Segesta).
Car rental Sixt, Via Virgilio 37 ☎0923.54.234 or 0923.24.388, ⓦ www.sixt.com; Serse, Via Passo Enea 30 ☎0923.21.843; Europcar at Stazione Maríttima ☎0792.76075, ⓦ www.europcar.com.

Car repairs ACI at Via Virgilio 75 ☎0923.27.292.
Ferry tickets Siremar ☎0923.545.455, ⓦ www .siremar.it (for the Égadi Islands and Pantelleria); Tirrenia ☎0923.21.896, ⓦ www.tirrenia.it (for Cágliari); Med Mar ☎081.551.3352 (for Tunis); Grimaldi ☎081.496.111 (for Tunis). All the ferry companies have offices at the Stazione Marittima, Molo di Sanità, Via A. Staiti.
Garages Bulgarella, Via Mazzini 17 ☎0923.547.022. €8 per day.
Hospital Ospedale S. Antonio Abate, Via Cosenza ☎0923.809.111; 24hr emergency first-aid ☎0923.809.450.
Hydrofoil tickets Siremar ☎0923.545.455 (for the Égadi Islands); Ústica Lines ☎0923.22.200 (for the Égadi Islands, Naples and Pantelleria). Both companies have ticket offices on the dockside, open 15min before departures.
Internet Access Piazza Garibaldi 28 (Mon–Sat 9am–1pm & 4–11pm, Sun 4–11pm), with Internet access for €1/10min, €5/hour; fax, phones and mobile phone charge-cards as well. M Point, Corso Vittorio Emanuele 17 (Mon–Sat 9am–1pm & 4.30–8pm), with Internet access at €3 per hour; also fax, photocopying, and left luggage.

Pharmacies Rizzi, Via G.G. Fardella 136; Vivona, Corso Vittorio Emanuele 211; and Zichichi, Via N. Nasi 27.

Police Questura at Piazza Vittorio Véneto ☎0923.598.111; Carabinieri, Via Orlandini ☎0923.27.122.

Post office At Piazza Vittorio Véneto, at the bottom of Via Garibaldi. Mon–Fri 8am–7pm, Sat 8am–1pm.

Taxis Ranks at Piazza Umberto ☎0923.22.808, and at the hydrofoil dock on Via A.

Staiti (☎0923.21.088, 368.734.0893 or 347.682.2137).

Train information FS information line is ☎89.20.21.

Travel agents CTS Viaggi, Piazza Umberto I 39, ☎0923.546.444; Agenzia Salvo, Corso Italia 52 ☎0923.871.242; Egatour Viaggi, Via A. Staiti 13 ☎0923.21.754. All agents can provide information and tickets for getting to Pantelleria, plus all other hydrofoil and ferry tickets, and bus tickets to Catania and Agrigento.

Érice

Although only a forty-minute bus ride from Trápani, **ÉRICE** couldn't be further away in spirit. It's a walled mountain town – almost 800m above sea level – with powerful associations; thoroughly medieval, with its creeping hillside alleys, grey stone buildings and silent charm, but boasting a truly ancient lineage. Founded by Elymians, who claimed descent from the Trojans, the city was known to the ancient world as Eryx, and a magnificent temple, dedicated to Aphrodite Erycina, Mediterranean goddess of fertility, once topped the mountain and was big enough to act as a landmark to sailors. According to legend, it was here that Daedalus landed, unlike his son Icarus who flew too near the sun, after fleeing from Minos; he presented the temple with a honeycomb

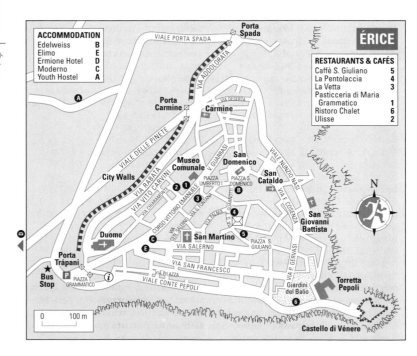

made of gold as his gift to the goddess. Even though the city was considered impregnable, Carthaginian, Roman, Arab and Norman armies all forced entry over the centuries, but all respected the town's sanctity, the Romans rebuilding the temple and setting two hundred soldiers to serve as guardians of the shrine. Later, the Arabs renamed the town Gebel-Hamed, "Mohammed's mountain", while Count Roger called it Monte San Giuliano, a name that stuck until Mussolini returned its ancient moniker in 1934. Nowadays it's a centre for scientific conferences, and you're as likely to see as many foreigners with labels on their lapels as you are tourists.

The only blots in the town's otherwise homogeneous aspect are twentieth-century ones: the pylons towering above the grey walls, and the tourists, though as people have always come to Érice to sightsee and worship, it seems churlish to resent these. In any case, there are enough cobbled alleys and quiet spots to enable you to avoid the tour groups, and the views from Érice's terraces are superb, taking in Trápani, the Égadi Islands and even (allegedly) distant Cape Bon in Tunisia.

Érice is only a small town, with a population of a few hundred, though this multiplies considerably in summer – in **August** the streets are busy until late at night as trippers and holiday-home owners negotiate the polished cobblestones. **Easter** is another popular time to visit, when the *Misteri* sculptures representing the Stations of the Cross are paraded through the streets on Good Friday.

The Town

There's nothing specific to see in Érice and you'll soon get lost in the winding alleys, but the most convoluted of routes is only going to take a couple of hours and every aspect is delightful. The houses, square and solid from the outside, hide pretty courtyards, and while most of the churches are locked, there's usually something to admire – a carved door, a cupola or a belltower. The number of tourists means a fair amount of tat in the souvenir shops, from tea towels to puppets, but **traditional industries** still flourish here, in particular the making of ceramics, tapestries and *dolci di badia* (almond-paste sweets).

You enter through the Norman **Porta Trápani**, at the southwestern edge of town. Just inside is the battlemented fourteenth-century campanile of the battered stone **Duomo** (summer daily 10am–7pm/midnight; winter daily 10.30am–12.30pm), which did service as a lookout tower for Frederick III of Aragon. From here the main Corso Vittorio Emanuele climbs steeply past houses, shops and *pasticcerie* to the pretty **Piazza Umberto I**, whose cafés strew tables adventurously across the sloping cobbles. The small **Museo Comunale** (Mon–Fri 8am–2pm, Mon & Thurs also 2.30–5pm; free) here boasts a good *Annunciation* by Antonello Gagini and the pick of the local archeological finds. Further north, the medieval **Porta Cármine** marks the other end of town, from where the line of ancient **city walls** leads back to the Duomo.

Heading east instead from the Porta Trápani, along Viale Conte Pepoli, you get the best of the views across the plains and out to sea. You'll eventually come to the ivy-clad, twelfth-century **Castello di Vénere** (daily 9am–6pm; free), built on the site of the famed ancient temple of Aphrodite, chunks of which are incorporated into the walls. The castle is built on the most precarious of crags, offering grand views in all directions, while stuck in the middle of the public garden below is a restored fifteenth-century tower, the **Torretta Pépoli**, lived in until the turn of this century. From here, you can wind towards Piazza Umberto I, perhaps passing clifftop **San Giovanni Battista** and its distinctive dome before eventually negotiating the minuscule **Piazza San Domenico**, whose church and palace facade is one of the town's most harmonious sights. The *Antica Pasticceria del Convento* on one corner of the square does a fierce trade in locally produced sweets and pastries.

Practicalities

Buses from Trápani stop outside the Porta Trápani, where there's also a handy **car park**. Don't even think of taking your car into the old-town streets. The helpful **tourist office** (Mon–Fri 9am–2pm; ☎0923.869.388) is just up Viale Conte Pépoli from the gate. The **post office** is on Via G.F. Guarnotti (and has an ATM), and there's a **bank** at the top of the corso, by Piazza Umberto I.

Accommodation

It's relatively expensive to stay the night in Érice, and in summer, or at Easter and Christmas, you'd do well to book in advance. If you stay in the old town you'll have to park outside Porta Trápani and carry your luggage up. There is a **youth hostel**, at Viale delle Pinete (☎0923.567.888; €16 per person for a dorm bed), a good kilometre outside the town walls, though this is only open from July to September, and is often booked up by groups, so check first. The other option is to stay in Valderice (see below), about twenty minutes' drive back down the mountain.

Edelweiss Cortile Padre Vincenzo 5 ☎0923.869.420, ℱ0923.869.158, ℮edelweiss@libero.it. The cheapest (and smallest) place in town, tucked up a cobbled alley off Piazza San Domenico. Thirteen smallish modern rooms, all with shower. ❹

Elimo Corso Vittorio Emanuele 75 ☎0923.869.377, ℱ0923.869.252, ℮ elimoh@comeg.it. Beautifully restored building with a little courtyard garden and characterful rooms. Some have super views – as does the restaurant where you take breakfast (included in the price). ❽

Ermione Via Pineta Comunale 43 ☎0923.869.138, ℱ0923.869.587, ⓦwww .ermionehotel.com. Five minutes' walk below the Porta Trápani, this gruff building (think 1970s Soviet Union) improves dramatically inside – an interior brightened by wall paintings and prints, nice staff, reasonably spacious rooms with huge views (those on the third floor have balconies) and a pool (though rarely in use given the stiff clifftop wind). Breakfast included; parking available. ❺

Moderno Corso Vittorio Emanuele 63 ☎0923.869.300, ℱ0923.869.139, ℮modernoh@tin.it. Best aspect is the roof terrace which offers sweeping views; the rooms aren't so terrific, at least not for the price, though rates drop a category out of season. ❻

Eating and drinking

Prices are a good bit higher in Érice, though you can still eat at a reasonable price if you stick to pizza and avoid the expensive fish dishes. Bring a picnic and you can sit in the gardens, or there's a *panineria* on Corso Vittorio Emanuele.

Restaurants

La Pentolaccia Via G.F. Guarnotti 17 ☎0923.869.099. Housed in an old monastery, this is a popular restaurant specializing in home-made *busiate* with aubergine, basil, pine nuts and ricotta salata. Couscous is good too, or there are simple grills and cheap local wine. Closed Tues. Moderate.

Ulisse Via Chiaramonte 45 ☎0923.869.333. Reached down the stepped Vico San Rocco, just off the main square, and with a nice courtyard-garden. The pizzas here are the best in town (and Sundays sees a queue form early), while the regular menu is good too, if on the pricey side. Closed winter & Thurs. Moderate for pizza, otherwise expensive.

La Vetta Via G. Fontana ☎0923.869.404. Signposted off Piazza Umberto (and also called *Da Mario*), this is the place for evening pizzas and standard trattoria meals. Outdoor tables in the alley in summer. Closed Thurs. Inexpensive.

Cafés and bars

Caffè S. Giuliano Via G.F. Guarnotti 11. When the wind blows, hide in this stone-walled bar, sip a marsala and play the pinball machine.

Pasticceria di Maria Grammatico Corso Vittorio Emanuele 14. Famous speciality cake

shop/café selling marzipan fruits, *amaretti* and the like.
Ristoro Chalet del Balio in the gardens near the Torretta Pépoli. This little sun-shaded café-terrace off Viale Conte Pépoli is about the only place in town you can sit with a coffee or ice cream and soak up the views to Trápani and the Égadi Islands. Particularly pleasant at sunset.

North to Custonaci

North of Trápani, the main attraction is the resort town of San Vito Lo Capo (see below), though with a car you could explore the rugged coastline en route. Between Trápani and the cape, 40km away, two wide gulfs – Bonagia and Cófano – are backed by holiday homes and small plantations, overlooked both by the heights of Érice and by its lower neighbour **VALDERICE**, a ribbon development occupying a prominent ridge. The buses from Trápani to Érice come this way. There's no real reason to stop, save for the coastal views from Valderice's belvedere, although there are a couple of **hotels**, both under the same ownership. The *Érice Valle*, Via del Cipresso 1 (T0923.891.133, F0923.833.178; ❺), is a modern hotel at the southern (Trápani) end of the main road, whose rooms open on to a Mediterranean garden. Five kilometres out of Valderice on the SS187 (and signposted), the *Baglio Santa Croce* (T0923.891.111, F0923.891.192; ❻) is a glorious renovation of an old, seventeenth-century stone-built estate, whose 25 rooms have beamed ceilings, exposed walls, tiled floors and iron bedsteads. There's a lovely pool and superb views to the coast, and the restaurant is locally renowned.

From Valderice, a minor road winds 5km down to the coast at **BONAGIA** where the old tuna fishery has been transformed into a luxurious, stylish hotel, the *Tonnara di Bonagia* (T0923.431.111, Wwww.framon-hotels.com; open April–Oct only; ❻). Boats bob around here in the small harbour, overlooked by a couple of fairly smart restaurants. The swimming, though, isn't much good given the swathes of kelp which infest the coast – perhaps why the only other hotel here, also on the harbour, the smart *Saverino* (T0923.592.727, F0923.592.388; ❻), is relatively reasonably priced. Trápani's nearest **campsite**, *Lido Valdérice* (T0923.573.477; June–Sept), is also in the Bonagia locality; there are up to nine buses a day (not Sun) out this way from the Trápani bus terminal, a twenty-minute ride. From Bonagia, the coastal road runs the 12km back into Trápani, past a couple more hotels and some less attractive bits of coastline.

On from Bonagia, the road weaves under some of the gigantic outcrops of rock characteristic of Sicily's west, most spectacular of which is **Monte Cófano** (859m). The village of **CUSTONACI**, 20km from Trápani, nestles under here, slightly inland, famous as a marble-cutting centre. The road then plunges east and inland – passing through purgatory (well, the settlement of Purgatorio) – to re-emerge beside sparkling clear water and more rocky beaches leading up to the San Vito cape, 40km from Trápani.

San Vito Lo Capo and around

With its dense ranks of trattorias, hotels and bars, **SAN VITO LO CAPO** is geared to consumers, yet its comparative remoteness has helped to stave off the worst pressures of the tourist industry, even in high season; in winter you won't find a soul. It's a small town, clustered around one of Sicily's finest **beaches** – a wide, curving stretch of white sand – framed by the looming cliffs behind and overlooked by jagged slabs of rock. The visitors here are mainly Italian.

San Vito is really just one long shop- and restaurant-lined main strip, **Via Savoia**, which runs at right angles from the beach. It's largely closed to traffic and is the focus of the evening *passeggiata*, with its shops staying open late in summer. There are only two things to see: the squat honey-coloured **church** (concerts are held outside in summer; check posters around town), and a little further up Via Savoia at no. 57, the small **Museo del Mare** (inside the tourist office; same hours; free), though the marine exhibits inside won't grab your attention.

A pleasant promenade backs the beach, which stretches to the east of town, while in the other direction, past the harbour, it's a twenty-minute walk to the point of **Capo San Vito** itself – a rocky and windswept plain adorned with a fenced-off lighthouse. For views you need to climb above the town (bear left on the way out to the lighthouse), up a steep road leading to the top of the high cliffs and looking down over the Golfo di Castellammare. The other local walk is east to the Riserva Naturale dello Zíngaro, a nature reserve, covered in more detail on p.385.

Arrival, information and excursions

Regular daily **buses** run from Trápani's bus terminal and from Palermo's Piazza Marina, stopping on Via P. Matarella, close to the seafront; the central Via Savoia is three blocks to the right. The last bus back to Trápani leaves at 8pm; it's a bit too far for a day-trip from Palermo.

The **tourist office** is in the Museo del Mare, Via Savoia 57 (summer approx daily 9am–1pm and 8pm–midnight). The Banco di Sicilia, at 80 Via Savoia, has an ATM, with the **post office** a few doors down.

Best place for information about **fishing trips** and **boat excursions** is the tourist office, where schedules are posted for summer services. The glass-bottom *Nautilus* makes twice daily four-hour cruises to Zíngaro and Scopello (☎347.576.6391 or 393.905.9655; €15), while the *Leonardo da Vinci* runs twice daily in July and August with lunch on board to Zíngaro (☎0924.34.222; €23). **Divers** can contact *Argonauta*, based in the summer at the port in San Vito (☎0923.972.888, ⑩www.argonauta.it).

Accommodation

Accommodation is plentiful, with most options on and around Via Savoia. As with all resorts, the nearer the sea, the more expensive the room. It's worth noting that in July and August prices virtually double in many places – you don't exactly get value for money, you'll almost certainly have to agree to half-board terms, and you're unlikely to find anything suitable without an advance reservation. In winter, you won't find many places open; ask around the bars in the centre if you get stuck.

There are several **campsites** in the area. Most central is *La Fata*, Via P. Matarella (☎348.000.0303), right in town, just up from the bus stop, while *La Pineta* (☎347.786.6827, ⑩www.campinglapineta.it) is twenty minutes' walk from town along the seafront (towards Scopello); here, there's also a bar, pizzeria and rooms to rent. *El Bahira* (☎0923.972.577; April–Sept), 4km south of town, is in a dramatic coastal location at Contrada Macari. The "No camping" signs on the town beach should be heeded.

Bougainvillea Via Mulino 51 ☎ &
ⓕ 0923.972.207. Quite a walk from the beach –
500m down Via Savoia, past the Municipio, and on
the left. It's a friendly place with climbing plants,
five decent rooms and a spiral staircase leading to
a roof terrace. No credit cards. April–Oct. ❷
Capo San Vito Via S. Vito 1 ☎ 0923.972.1220,
ⓕ 0923.972.559, ⓦ www.caposanvito.it. Right
on the beach, at the end of Via Savoia, this comfortable hotel (top-of-the-range in town) has 35
air-conditioned rooms. Those at the front have terraces and sea views (and are a bit pricier); a small
garden gives on to the beach and meals (half-
board only June–Sept at ❺ per person) are taken
in the terrace restaurant. Breakfast is included in
room rates. ❽
Costa Gaia Via Savoia 123 ☎ 0923.972.268,
ⓦ www.albergocostagaia.com. A good, central first
choice, though with only eight en-suite rooms this
little *pensione* fills quickly. Half-board only in July
and August (❷ per person). Breakfast is included
in the room rates. ❺
Eden Via Mulino 62 ☎ 0923.972.460. Probably the
cheapest place in town, with a selection of clean,
reasonably spacious rooms with and without bathroom. Simply furnished but perfectly adequate,
though a ten-minute walk from town centre and
beach. No credit cards. ❷

Egitarso Via Lungomare 54 ☎ 0923.972.111,
ⓕ 0923.972.062, ⓦ www.hotelegitarso.it. A low
block right on the beach, offering bright air-conditioned rooms with balconies and fine views,
and a few apartments. There's a buffet breakfast
included, plus 24hr bar and beachside service.
Half-board only June–Sept (❹ per person), though
good off-season discounts. ❺
Pocho Contrada Macari ☎ & ⓕ 0923.972.525.
Making the most of its coastal location, 4km south
of town (near *El Bahira* campsite), this small (nine-
room) hotel-restaurant has a pool on a cliffside
terrace – a nice base for anyone with transport. ❺
Poseidon Via P. Matarella 22 ☎ 0923.972.444,
ⓦ www.poseidonresidence.com. Good for families,
these stylish one- and two-room apartments have
kitchenette and shower. No views on the ground
floor; more light and space higher up, though you
pay more. Available by the week only. ❹
Sabbia d'Oro Via Santuario 49 ☎ 0923.972.508,
ⓕ 0923.621.163, ⓦ www.hotelsabbiadoro.com.
Popular with families, as they're close to the
beach (behind the church), the simple, central,
air-conditioned rooms with TV are either here or
around the corner in the associated *Ocean View*.
You're encouraged to take half-board though B&B
is available – breakfast and meals are taken in a
little internal tropical garden. ❼

Eating and drinking

Via Savoia and the lungomare are lined with possibilities: bars, ice-cream
parlours, pizzerias and fish restaurants. Most stay open throughout the winter
too.

Bar Cusenza Via Savoia, beside the church.
Best place for breakfast, with outdoor tables in
the square, and good cakes and pastries. Try
the *torrone* ice cream. Closed Thurs in winter.
Inexpensive.
Delfino Via Savoia 13. A pizzeria-trattoria on the
main street with smoked-fish antipasti, fresh
home-made pasta and a short list of decent pizzas to eat in or take away. Closed Mon in winter.
Inexpensive–moderate.
Mediterraneo Via Faro 37. Five minutes out
of town (on the road to the lighthouse), this is
the place for *forno a legna* pizzas which come
bubbling from the oven, served (if you get there
early enough and beat the crowds) in an
attractive tiled garden. Also a short menu of
other dishes and a small but tasty antipasto
selection. Pizzas to take away as well.
Moderate.
Santareddu Piazza Marinella 3 ☎ 0923.974.350.
Small, blue and cluttered, this is popular with

locals and always busy. It's best known for
its couscous, prepared by hand using the traditional Arab method (rather than using the
pre-cooked stuff you dunk in boiling water),
and laced with almonds and cinnamon. The
antipasti are abundant and the fish, which
depends on the catch of the day, is always
fresh. Booking essential. Closed Wed.
Moderate.
La Sirenetta Via Savoia, corner of Via Faro.
Gelateria overlooking the beach and port – a
choice of twenty ice creams and a summer
shaded terrace to enjoy them in. Specialities
are *gelsomino* (jasmine flower) and *torrone*.
Inexpensive.
Thaam Via Duca degli Abruzzi 32–36
☎ 0923.972.836. Elaborately decorated
restaurant with a marked Tunisian influence
– *merguez*, kebabs and couscous alongside more
mainstream Italian dishes. Booking advised in
summer. Moderate.

Getting to Zíngaro

The **northern entrance** to the isolated **Riserva Naturale dello Zíngaro** (for full details, see p.385) is 11km southeast of San Vito. Accessible by your own transport or on a boat-trip from San Vito Lo Capo (see p.399), it's also a fine walk, initially following the road along the lungomare from San Vito and across the flat headland, before winding up into the mountains. In the higher reaches, the views are exhilarating, with the surrounding scenery almost alpine in character – fir trees, flowers flanking the road, and the clank of bells from goats roaming the hillsides. It's a secluded and dramatic landscape, though sadly with few opportunities for descending from the road to the alluringly deserted coves below.

The **access road** to the reserve is signposted just before the ruined Torre dell'Impiso, around a three-hour walk from San Vito. From the sign to the park entrance itself is about another 1km, following a gravel track and then a path, which runs down into the reserve, past the Tonnara dell'Uzzo. At the San Vito **entrance** there's a car park, hiking information, a beautiful little cove-beach below, translucent water, and glorious peace and quiet all around.

Various well-marked **trails** run through the reserve, with water taps and shelter periodically available. Scopello (see p.400) is a ten-kilometre walk south from the San Vito entrance, though hikers should note that there are no shops, bars or restaurants along the road from San Vito, at the park entrance or in the park itself: take all your own supplies – and take away all the empties.

The Égadi Islands

Moored off the western coast, the three **Égadi Islands** (Isole Égadi) are the easiest of Sicily's offshore islands to visit – something that accounts for the summer crowds swarming over Favignana, the nearest of the Égadis to the Sicilian mainland. The other islands are much less affected, however, and if you come out of season things are noticeably quieter everywhere.

Before the advent of tourism, the economic success of the islands was largely based on a historical relationship with the northern Italian city of Genova, whose sailors plied the trading routes on which the Égadis stood throughout the Middle Ages; the seal was formalized in the middle of the seventeenth century, when the Bourbon king Philip IV sold all the islands, in lieu of a debt, to Genovese businessmen. Then, as now, the major element in the local economy was the **tuna fish**, which congregate here to breed at the end of

---

Getting there

Ferries (Siremar) and **hydrofoils** (Siremar and Ústica Lines) depart several times daily from Trápani, are more frequent between June and September, and most frequent in July and August. They generally call at Favignana, Lévanzo and Maréttimo, in that order, though there are occasional exceptions, and sometimes services don't run as far as Maréttimo. Ferries **depart** from the Stazione Maríttima in Trápani, and hydrofoils from further east along Via A. Staiti; you can buy **tickets** at booths on the dockside. Ferries are less frequent than hydrofoils and take around twice as long, but they're roughly half the **price**. One-way ferry tickets to Favignana and Lévanzo cost around €3.50, and to Maréttimo around €7; one-way hydrofoil tickets are around €6 and €12 respectively; all return tickets cost exactly twice as much. See "Travel details" (p.434) for frequencies and journey times.

spring. Channelled through the straits between the two main islands during their migrations around the Sicilian coast, they are systematically slaughtered in an age-old rite known as **La Mattanza**.

Favignana, the biggest island and site of the main fishery, is only 25 minutes away from Trápani by hydrofoil. The Genovese link is most apparent in the island of **Lévanzo**, across the strait, which is named after a quarter in the city of Genova and shelters the **Grotta del Genovese**, a cave in which a rich bounty of prehistoric cave paintings was discovered. These days, with the annual tourist influx, the greatest hope for peace and quiet lies in the furthest island, **Maréttimo**, whose rugged coasts are indented with a succession of coves, ideal for clean and secluded swimming. The island also offers a choice of **hikes** across its interior and along the rocky coasts.

You could easily see any of the islands as a **day-trip** from Trápani; seeing two on the same day is fairly simple too. If you want to stay longer, be warned that **accommodation** is extremely limited, and in summer you should phone ahead to reserve a room. It's certainly worth staying over, though you should also bear in mind that, in general, **prices** for rooms and food are higher than on the mainland.

Favignana

The main island, **Favignana**, has progressed over the years from prison to tuna centre, and now tourist resort. Looking like a lopsided butterfly, the island is almost split in two, its narrow "waist" holding the port and most of the population. To the east are Favignana's best swimming spots, the water accessible from a succession of rocks and inlets, while the western half of the island is only reachable along the southern coastal road, which tunnels through Favignana's sole hill, **Monte Santa Caterina** (300m). Its peak is topped by an abandoned castle, floodlit at night, and reached by a crazy-paved stairway. The castle, though, is in such a parlous state and so full of rubbish that it's far nicer to follow the lower path over the mountain to a crest with views to Maréttimo. The path down the other side, however, is hard to follow and you may end up scrambling over walls and through fields to reach the road.

The port, **FAVIGNANA TOWN**, is the focus of most of the tourist traffic. As the archipelago's only town, it holds the island's main services and best choice of accommodation and restaurants, but otherwise there's no particular reason to hang around. The only distinctive feature is the imposing building near the port, the **Palazzo Florio**. Now the town hall, this was built by Ignazio Florio, an entrepreneur who took over the islands in 1874 and revitalized the fisheries; there's a statue of him in nearby Piazza Europa. His tuna fishery, **Stabilimento Florio**, is similarly impressive, its vaulted nineteenth-century buildings a solid counterpoint across the bay. It is currently being restored and is due to re-open as a complex of artisan studios and shops. Otherwise, all there is to do is window-shop in the many places selling "tipici" products – tinned tuna, of course, as well as *bottarga*, oil, local dried herbs, wine and bloody postcards of *la mattanza*.

The **rest of the island** is tidily cultivated, pitted with square white houses built from **tufa** quarried from curious pits all over the island – an export that has historically provided Favignana with a second source of cash (after fishing). One of the old quarries, behind the town church by the decrepit chapel of Santa Anna, has been landscaped and turned into an interesting sunken garden.

La Mattanza

For centuries each May and June, Favignana has witnessed the bloody spectacle of **La Mattanza**, the slaughter of the local tuna catch. Usually the killings take place two or three times a week, presided over by a *Rais* – a title handed down from the Arabs. The huge fish are surrounded, netted, impaled, dragged aboard and bludgeoned to death. Most of the meat is sold to the vast Japanese vessels that call in at fishing ports all over the Mediterranean; they transport the cargo back to Japan, where it's put into cans and re-exported back to Europe, although there are still a couple of small canning factories in the Trápani area. There's also a tuna artisan on Favignana itself, Alessandro Sammartano (at Favonia, Via Garibaldi 16, Favignana Town), who prepares *bottarga* (salted and dried tuna roe) and other traditional tuna products by hand.

In recent years the slaughter has become something of a tourist attraction, though in 2004, infighting among the *tonnaroti* (tuna fishermen), bureacratic foot-dragging, and the alleged over-fishing of tuna around the Straits of Gibraltar resulted in La Mattanza being cancelled. Check with the tourist office in Favignana about its future prospects.

You can swim at the beach near the town, but better is the sandy beach at **Lido Burrone**, on the island's south side, where there's a friendly restaurant-bar; otherwise just follow the coast roads and plunge in off the rocks, or settle down on one of the tiny handkerchiefs of sand. Call in at **Cala Azzurra**, below the lighthouse at the island's eastern end, where there's a beautiful blue bay, but little sand, or, just north of here, the spectacular **Cala Rossa**, where you can swim off rocks at the base of towering tufa cliffs. Its name – Red Cove – is said to derive from the blood washed ashore after the Roman defeat of the Carthaginians in a fierce sea battle in 241 BC. The road to Cala Rossa in particular is noted for its tufa quarries – just before the cove itself is a huge quarry with stacks of tufa and unexcavated pillars rising high from the gloomy depths. On the other side of the mountain, the best beach is at **Cala Rotonda**, where, local legend would have it, Odysseus washed up before being attacked by the Cyclops.

Arrival, information and transport

From the port, you can see the dome of the church: aim for that and you'll reach the main square, Piazza Madrice, with the **tourist office** at no. 8 (Mon–Sat 9am–1pm & 4.30–8.30pm, Sun 9.30am–1pm; stays open till midnight in August and closes earlier in winter; ☎0923.921.647). Everything else is contained in the short streets between here and the nearby Piazza Europa. The Banco Nuova, Via Catania 5, in Piazza Europa, and the Banco di Sicilia in Piazza Madrice both have **ATMs**; there's an English-speaking **pharmacy**, Dottore Abramo, on Piazza Europa, and another, Rizza, in Piazza Madrice; while the **ticket offices** for ferries and hydrofoils are down at the port.

The best way to **get around the island** is by bike, since the flat terrain and good road surfaces enable you to see the whole of Favignana in an afternoon. There are **bike rental** shops all over town, including down at the port – look for the words "*noleggio bici*". Isidoro, at Via Mazzini 40, stays open all year; expect to pay about €5 a day. There's also a summer **bus service** (June–Aug) which leaves from down by the port and makes circuits on three routes, calling at all parts of the island. Departures are roughly hourly during the day. **Boat tours** (from €10 per person) of the island's offshore grottoes are offered by fishermen down at the port – there's always someone around in summer though you may have to ask in town at other times.

Accommodation

Favignana's most striking accommodation is at the designer *Hotel Le Cave*, at Zona Cavallo (℡0923.925.423, ℱ0923.925.424, ⓦwww.hoteldellecave .it; ❻). Built on the lip of an abandoned quarry with gardens and a restaurant inside the quarry itself, it has just nine rooms. Closer to town, you'll find the new and very pleasant *Hotel Favignana*, Contrada Badia 8 (℡0923.925.449, ⓦwww.favignanahotel.com; ❺), and the small *Égadi*, Via Cristóforo Colombo 17 (℡ & ℱ0923.921.232; no credit cards, ❼), off Piazza Madrice, down a narrow street to the right of the church, with modern, comfortable rooms. Other town-centre possibilities include the *Bougainville*, Via Cimabue 10 (℡0923.922.033, ℱ0923.922.649; ❹), and the very nice *Aegusa*, at Via Garibaldi 11 (℡0923.922.430, ℱ0923.922.440; ❺). Out-of-town accommodation is resort-style, pick of the lot being the *Approdo di Ulisse* at Cala Grande (℡0923.922.525, ℱ0923.921.511; May–Sept; ❽) on the western wing of the island.

Campsites lie out of town, an easy walk and well signposted from the port: to the east, there's the *Camping Egad* (℡0923.921.555), and, more expensive and much larger, the *Miramare* (℡0923.921.330; April–Oct), with a playground, kids club and decent restaurant, at Località Costicella to the west of town. Both have cabins available.

Eating and drinking

Piazza Madrice, Piazza Europa and the surrounding streets are where you'll find Favignana's **bars and restaurants**. The family-run *Pizzeria Da Salvador* on Via Nicotera serves good pizza, as well as local specialities like couscous, and in summer has plenty of seating outside. For fish, *La Tavernetta* (℡0923.921.639), across from the church at Piazza Madrice 54, is pretty and cool, and you can sit outside in summer; there's no menu but the prices are decent. For ice cream and almond goodies try *Bar Albatros*, or join the locals sitting on rows of chairs either side of the street at *Grammatico*, on Via Pilota di Garibaldi, just off Piazza Europa. Restaurant prices on the island tend to be high, so you may prefer to pick up an excellent pizza from the wood-fired oven of *Arte Pizza*, just off Piazza Madrice at Via Mazzini 16, and **picnic** on the town beach. There are also excellent slices of pizza, *schiacciata* and the like just up the hill from Piazza Madrice at the bakery *Costanza* on Via Roma, while for picnic provisions, carry on up the hill to the SMA supermarket, where the deli counter has local ricotta and a good range of cheeses and hams. If you're looking for **nightlife** there are two out-of-town options, *Zazzamita Café* at Zona Cavallo, with a cool, leafy garden (open in the daytime as well), and *Sotto Le Stelle*, an open-air pub with simple food off the coast road leading to Punta Lunga.

Lévanzo

Lévanzo, 4km north of Favignana, is the smallest of the three main islands, most of it used to pasture sheep and goats and, with its turquoise seas and white houses, having very much the feel of a Greek island. Its population is concentrated in **LÉVANZO TOWN**, little more than a cluster of square houses and holiday homes around a tiny port, where you'll find the island's two hotels, a bar and a couple of restaurants.

Lévanzo's main attraction is its prehistoric cave paintings in the Grotta del Genovese. The coastline is rocky and largely inaccessible, but you can get around on foot by following the dirt paths along the shore and over the hills. Following the only road twenty minutes west of the port, you'll come to a rocky spire sticking out of the sea – the Faraglione – beyond which there's a rocky path north up the coast to the **Grotta del Genovese** itself. The cave is best approached, though, by following an inland route, shorter and prettier, along a path through the valley in the centre of the island. It's impossible to find on your own and you'll have to ask the official custodian, Signor Natale Castiglione, who lives at Via Calvario 11 (T0923.924.032), near the hydrofoil quay. Rates are negotiable, depending on how many you are, and whether you go on foot, by jeep or by boat, but you shouldn't have to pay more than €15 each; the round trip is roughly 10km and takes about two hours by jeep, one and a half by boat. Note that in winter tours generally take place only on weekends, and it's always best to telephone ahead.

The cave's walls display some remarkable Paleolithic **incised drawings**, discovered in 1949, as well as later Neolithic pictures; they're mostly of animals, and are between 6000 and 10,000 years old. Despite their age, the evocative drawings retain their impact, drawn by prehistoric man in an attempt to harness and influence the power of nature: one lovely picture of a deer, kept behind glass near the entrance, dates from when the island was still connected to the Sicilian mainland. The later Neolithic sketches are easy to pick out too; less well drawn, more stylized representations of men and even of tuna fish.

Many of the other grottoes on the island were once used by locals to hide from the corsairs who regularly called on raiding missions. To see some of them, you might bargain for a **boat rental** at the port; again, prices are very flexible. If you want to stretch your legs in the island's lovely **interior**, walk west along the road from the port (towards the Faraglione), turning right up the steep tarmacked road. It becomes a stone and dirt track once it reaches the upper part of the valley and, if you keep to it, it's around an hour to the lighthouse at **Capo Grosso** at the northeastern point of the island. On your way to the cape, you can swim at the lovely white **Tramontana bay**: just before you reach an old metal gate, a track leads down the red-earth mountainside, ending in an acute concrete slope, which you can just about slither down, though scrambling back up is hard work.

Practicalities

The **port** is just below the island's only road, Via Calvario. In summer both Siremar and Ùstica Lines have ticket booths at the port; in winter, they move into the town, out of reach of stormy waves. Precise locations vary from year to year, so check with the ferry or hydrofoil crew before landing. For **boat excursions** around the island, call T339.736.7785.

There are just two **hotels** with a total of 25 rooms, so booking ahead is advisable; ask around, though, and you may find someone who'll rent you a **room**. Closest to the port, next to the bar, is *Pensione Paradiso* (T0923.924.080; ❷), with a terrace-restaurant and marvellous views over the sea. Just behind, the *Pensione Dei Fenici* (T0923.924.083; no credit cards, ❸) is a little fancier and with the same good views. In summer, both hotels will usually only take you on half-board terms (€60 per person), though as the only other options for food on the island are two bars, an *alimentari* and a bakery, which doubles as the island's Internet café, this is no hardship. In any case, the food is good at both places.

Maréttimo

Wildest and furthest out from Trápani, **Maréttimo** was claimed by Samuel Butler, in his *The Authoress of the Odyssey*, as the original Ithaca, home of Odysseus; more far-fetched, Butler also thought that Homer himself was the princess Nausicaa of ancient Trápani. These theories aside, there are compelling reasons to come to Maréttimo. Its spectacular fragmented coastline is pitted with rocky coves sheltering hideaway beaches, and there are numerous walks to be done which will take you all over the island. Even in high season, you're likely to have much of Maréttimo to yourself, as few tourists can be bothered to visit a place with limited accommodation and no more than half a dozen trattorias. That said, there are signs of heightened interest these days in the shape of a sprinkling of new holiday homes, while EU money has gone towards paving a couple of sections of track. However, such "improvements" are still fairly low-key and, at least for now, the island retains its off-the-beaten-track air.

As you pull into port and explore its few streets, **MARÉTTIMO TOWN** appears almost North African in character, with its flat-roofed cube houses with blue shutters and painted tiles and alleys full of tumbling bougainvillea. There's one main street, a little square and church, and a second harbour, the

---

Maréttimo hikes

To the Case Romane

The simplest walk takes you to some old Roman defensive works, still in quite good condition. Climb up the road to the side of *Caffè Tramontana* and, at the top, scout around to the left and then right to find the signpost for the start of the walk. The remains are half an hour on, sitting next to a small and dilapidated church that shows marked Arab characteristics but is thought to have been built by Byzantine monks in the twelfth century.

To Cala Sarde and Cala Nera

Follow the road south of Maréttimo port, turning inland after about 1km where the path divides. There's a steep climb, with the town's cemetery below you, rising to about 300m. After about half an hour, you'll pass a pine forest and a small outhouse, looking out on views towards Tunisia; below is the Cala Sarde, a small bay reachable along a smaller path to the left in another half an hour.

Instead of descending to the bay, continue for about an hour on the main path along the island's rocky west coast. You'll pass a lighthouse and a route down to Cala Nera, where you can swim off the rocks in perfect isolation.

To the castle at Punta Troia

This walk follows the footpath all the way to the northeastern tip of the island, a hike that should take you around three hours; you'll need a head for heights in certain stretches. Go past the fishing harbour with the sea on your right, and keep to the coast along the path for about ten minutes, until the terrace wall on your left stops. A sign here ("Castello Punta Troia") points to the left where you cut up to find the main path on a small spur above you. This stretches along the whole length of the island about 100m above the sea, ending at some concrete steps that descend to a lovely secluded beach and the foot of the castle, perched on an impregnable rocky crag. This precipitous fortification was originally built by the Saracens, enlarged by Roger II, and further extended by the Spanish in the seventeenth century, when it became a prison, acquiring a dire reputation for cruelty.

fishing port, just along from the main harbour. Two of the island's popular bathing spots are conveniently close, one near the main harbour, one near the fishing harbour, but you'll find other places on the way to destinations further afield – at Cala Sarde and Cala Nera on the south coast, or at the Saracen castle at the northeastern point of the island (see box opposite). None of the walks are particularly onerous, though you might have to scramble at times   and you should take water with you in the summer if you're planning to stay away from the village for any length of time (around three litres a day per person minimum). Alternatively, you could take a three-hour **boat tour** of the island (a "*giro dell' isola*") from the main harbour, letting you see Maréttimo's entire rocky coastline and dive into otherwise inaccessible waters, which are clean and clear and a joy for snorkellers. You'll doubtless be offered a tour on arrival at the port; expect to pay around €10 per person.

Practicalities

Maréttimo's main street and square is about a minute's walk from the harbour where the ferries and hydrofoils dock. There's a **bank** with an ATM here, and a Siremar **ticket agency**; the Ústica Lines agency is in a little shop further along the street. Walk up and down for a few minutes and you'll find all the other services: a pharmacy, an *alimentari*, bakery and fresh fish shop. **Boat trips** can be organized from *Rosa dei Venti* (see below), and various options are possible: around the island to Cala Bianca for swimming costs €12 per person, or the same with a picnic, including home-cured fish, and local cheeses and wines is €20 per person. On either, you can be left at a cove to swim and collected an hour or so later.

To organize **rooms** before you come, call *Rosa dei Venti* (℡0923.923.249, 368.768.1571 or 333.675.8893; ❷), which has half a dozen rooms with bathrooms, as well as apartments with cooking facilities. Alternatively, *Maréttimo Residence* (℡0923.923.202, Ⓦwww.marettimoresidence.it; ❸) is a little resort-cluster of cottages above a stony beach south of the main port – demand is so high that in summer you'll probably have to stay for a week. Otherwise, rented rooms do exist, although nobody advertises them – you'll have to ask around in the restaurants.

There's a decent selection of **places to eat**, though prices are a little higher than on the mainland, given the cost of shipping-in ingredients. Not all the places listed below stay open throughout the year, though there's always something open. *Il Veliero*, a trattoria by the fishing harbour, has good *cucina casalinga* and a summer cane-and-fishing-trap-bedecked terrace. *Il Pirata* (℡0923.923.027), nearby, is similarly sited, while on the road above the fishing harbour, *Caffè Tramontana* has the best sea views. All the other places are on and just off the main street: *La Hiera* (℡0923.923.017) is good for pizzas; *La Scaletta*, overlooking the main port, for ice cream; and *Il Timone*, up Via Garibaldi (℡0923.923.142), a little trattoria with a terrace out back.

Mózia and around

Fifteen kilometres down the coast from Trápani, the uninhabited **Stagnone Islands** (Isole dello Stagnone) have been given over mostly to salt extraction since the fifteenth century. On the mainland opposite, several windmills still stand near the surviving **saltpans**, which form a crystalline patchwork between Trápani and Marsala. Offshore, the long, thin Ísola Grande shelters the only one of the Stagnone group that you can visit: San Pantaleo, in the middle of a shallow lagoon, holding the site of the ancient Phoenician settlement of Motya (or **Mózia** in Italian). Along with Palermo and Solus (Solunto), Motya was one of the three main Phoenician bases in Sicily, settled some time in the eighth century BC and completely razed to the ground by Dionysius I in 397 BC. It's the only one of the three sites that wasn't subsequently built over, though it remained undiscovered until the seventeenth century, and wasn't properly excavated until Joseph "Pip" Whitaker (amateur archeologist and member of one of the marsala wine dynasties) bought the island in the late nineteenth century and began digging it up.

You reach the island site and its archeological museum by short ferry ride from the mainland, a trip that's become quite popular in summer with Italian holidaymakers. Although the linguistic link between the islands' name (Stagnone) and our "stagnant" is not entirely coincidental, it doesn't seem to stop them from wading into the lagoon on the mainland side or crossing to Mózia in beachwear. The island museum, at least, has had enough and won't allow entry to anyone who's not properly clothed

The island: the remains of Motya

Flat, cultivated and only 2.5km in circumference, **Motya** is one of the most manageable of Sicily's ancient sites, with the unique Phoenician ruins spread across the whole island. You could circle the perimeter in an hour or so, but it's more enjoyable to make a day of it and bring a picnic. There's a little kiosk by the island jetty which sells water and cold drinks (summer only).

You buy **entrance tickets** (daily: April–Oct 9am–7pm; Nov–March 9am–noon; €5.50) on the way up the path to Joseph Whitaker's house – once incongruously furnished in Edwardian style and now converted to use as the **Museo Whitaker**. Outside there's an aristocratic bust of its founder, "Giuseppe" Whitaker, and a shaded picnic area under the trees nearby. You might as well call in to the museum first to see the finds from the island, its cool rooms packed with a beautiful collection of jewellery, arrowheads, terracotta figurines and domestic artefacts, the earliest pieces dating from the eighth century BC. Pride of place goes to the magnificent fifth-century BC marble sculpture of a youth, *Il Giovanetto di Mozia*: sensual and self-assured in pose, the subject's identity is unknown, but he was likely to have been a high-ranking official, suggested by the subtle indentations round his head, indicating some kind of crown or elaborate headwear.

The remains on the ground start immediately outside the museum. In front and 100m to the left is the **Casa dei Mosaici**, two houses containing some faded black-and-white mosaics made from sea pebbles. One, probably belonging to a patrician, shows animal scenes; the other, thought to be a craftsman's, yielded numerous shards of pottery. Further along the path you come to the **cothon**, a small artificial boat dock built within the ancient town's walls and similar in style to a much larger one at Carthage itself.

The other way, back past the museum, leads along the rough tracks, set amongst flowering cacti and vine plantations, that were once the city's main thoroughfares, most of which end at one of the gates on Motya's formerly well-fortified shore. The once-strong **north gate**, now a ragged collection of steps and ruined walls – up beyond the museum and right – lies at the head of a causeway built by the Phoenicians in the sixth century BC connecting the island with the mainland (and a necropolis) at Birgi, 7km to the north: the road is still there, although these days it's submerged under the water. Left along the shore from the gate is the **Tophet** burial ground. Most of the information about day-to-day life in Motya has come from here, the sanctuary revealing a number of urns containing the ashes of animals and people – mainly children

– sacrificed to the Phoenician gods, chiefly Baal Hammon. A remarkable series of inscribed votive stele from the Tophet is on display in the museum. Just inland of the gate, the **Cappiddazzu** site shows the foundations of a large building, probably a temple, while between gate and Cappiddazzu is a Punic **industrial zone** which was dedicated to the production of pottery and ceramics. This was where the famous marble sculpture was found, probably hidden by the city's inhabitants as the Greeks stormed the island.

The saltpans and salt museum

Glistening in the shallows between Trápani and Marsala are a series of **saltpans** that have been worked since Phoenician times. Barechested men toil with shovels, carting full wheelbarrows across from the pans to a rising conveyor belt which dumps two-metre-high mounds of white salt along the banks. At different times of the day, as the light changes, there's a pink tint to the saltpans, while Maréttimo rises in the distance through the haze. On the mainland, just opposite Mózia, one of three windmills has been turned into a showroom, the **Salina Ettore e Infersa** (9.30am–6pm: March–Oct daily; Nov–Feb Sat & Sun only). It's free to enter if you just want to browse the locally produced foods and crafts, or you can pay €3 for an instructive guided tour of the whole salt-making process.

Practicalities

From Marsala, take the local AST bus from Piazza del Pópolo (Mon–Sat, every 60–90min from 8am to 6.15pm; 25min) to the Mózia ferry-landing; in summer a special bus, Linea D, runs far more frequently. Return buses are on a similar schedule; there are only four services a day in either direction on a Sunday. **From Trápani**, you'll have to take the bus or the train first to Marsala.

    Ferries out to the island are run by Arini & Pugliese (☎0347.779.0218). You'll always be able to get a ferry when the island is open to visitors (daily: April–Oct 9am–12.30pm & 3–6.30pm; Nov–March 9.30am–3.30pm; 20min), and in summer, a steady flow of visitors means that there's usually a ferry waiting; tickets are €3 return. In winter, the schedules are much reduced, and you should ring first to check before setting out. The ferries depart 500 metres along the shore from the **bar-restaurant** *Mamma Caura*, by the windmill and saltpans; it has rooms (❷) and canoes to rent if you'd like to weave your way around the saltpans. There's also **parking** available.

Marsala

When the island-city of Motya had been put to the sword by the Syracusans, the survivors founded Lilybaeum (modern **MARSALA**), 10km to the south. The main city of the Phoenicians in Sicily, and the only one to resist the Greek push westwards, Lilybaeum finally succumbed to Rome in 241 BC, and not long after was used as a springboard for an attack against the Carthaginian heartland itself. The town's position at Sicily's western tip later made it the main Saracenic base on the island, and it was renamed Marsah Ali, Arabic for the "port of Ali", son-in-law of the Prophet, from which its modern name derives.

△ Fish market, Marsala

The town scored a place in modern Italian history for its role in the saga of the **Risorgimento**, the struggle for Italian unity in the nineteenth century. It was here that Garibaldi kicked off his campaign to drive out the Bourbons, in the company of his red-shirted "Thousand". Until a planned Garibaldi museum on Marsala's eastern seafront (on Via Scipione Africano) gets round to opening, memorials to the swashbuckling freedom-fighter are confined to a few statues and street names, and the nearby Porta Garibaldi, at the end of Via Garibaldi, which recalls the hero's entry into the town. Local enthusiasts clad in red shirts parade through the gate each year on May 11th, in commemoration of the exploits of the "Thousand".

The Town

The town centre is a mainly Baroque assortment of buildings, though there are hints of the older town's layout in the narrow, largely traffic-free streets around the central **Piazza della Repubblica**. The square's elegance is due to its two eighteenth-century buildings: the arcaded **Palazzo Comunale**, and the **Chiesa Madre** – dedicated to San Tommaso di Canterbury, patron saint of Marsala – from which four statues peer loftily down. In the church's large but rather disappointing interior, there are a number of Gagini sculptures, and a plaque near the door commemorating a returned emigrant's donation of funds in 1956 for the completion of the facade.

Behind the Duomo, at Via Garraffa 57, the sole display at the **Museo degli Arazzi** (Tues–Sun 9am–1pm & 4–6pm; €1.50) is a series of eight enormous hand-stitched wool and silk tapestries depicting the capture of Jerusalem. Made

The Baglio Anselmi, in which Marsala's archeological museum is housed, is one of a number of old *bagli*, or warehouses, conspicuous throughout this wine-making region. Many are still used in the making of the famous dessert wine that carries the town's name. It was an Englishman, John Woodhouse, who first exploited the commercial potential of **marsala wine**, when he visited the town in 1770. Woodhouse soon realized that, like port, the local wine could travel for long periods without going off, when fortified with alcohol. Others followed: Ingham, Whitaker, Hopps and many more whose names can still be seen on some of the warehouse doors. Interestingly, it was the English presence in Marsala that persuaded Garibaldi to launch his campaign here rather than Sciacca (his first choice), judging that the Bourbon fleet wouldn't dare to interfere so close to Her Majesty's commercial concerns.

Marsala owes much of its current prosperity to the marketing of its wine, still a thriving industry, though no longer in British hands. You can visit some of the *bagli* and sample the stuff for free: try the **Stabilimento Florio** (Mon–Fri 10am–1pm & 3.30–6pm; call ☎ 0923.969.667 to arrange a guided tour), on Lungomare Mediterraneo, to the south of town beyond the port. For enthusiasts, there's also an **Enomuseum** (daily 8.30am–1pm & 3–7pm; free) at Contrada Berbaro (3km along the road to Mazara del Vallo), where you can look over the old apparatus and techniques for wine-making. Otherwise, you'll find marsala or the sweeter marsala all'uovo (mixed with egg yolks) in every bar and restaurant in town.

in Brussels in the sixteenth century, they were the gift of the Spanish ambassador, who doubled as the archbishop of Messina, and are beautifully rich, in burnished red, gold and green. Threading up from Piazza della Repubblica, Via XI Maggio is lined with smart shops and has some pretty courtyards, most impressive being the **Complesso San Pietro** (Mon–Sat 9am–1pm & 4–8pm; €2), a fifteenth-century monastery now fully restored as a cultural centre. The facade on Via XI Maggio holds the town library; elsewhere inside are the video and newspaper archives, civic collections, a courtyard for open-air performances and café-bar.

At the far end of Via XI Maggio, through the eighteenth-century **Porta Nuova**, Piazza della Vittória has a couple of good bars and a gate into the municipal gardens. Beyond the piazza lies **Capo Boeo**, the westernmost point of Sicily that was the first settlement of the survivors of annihilated Motya. All the town's major antiquities are concentrated here, including the old **Insula Romana**, closed to the public at present, but normally accessible from Via Vittório Véneto. The site contains all that's been excavated so far of the city of Lilybaeum, though most of it is third-century BC Roman, as you might guess from the presence of a *vomitarium*, lodged in the most complete section of the site – the **edificio termale**, or bathhouse. There's some good mosaicwork here: a chained dog at the entrance and, much better, a richly coloured **hunting scene** in the atrium, showing a stag being savaged by a wild beast.

From Piazza della Vittória, Viale N. Sauro leads to the church of **San Giovanni**, under which is a grotto reputed to have been inhabited by the sibyl Lilibetana, endowed with paranormal gifts. There's another slice of mosaic here, and a well whose water is meant to impart second sight. There's a pilgrimage here every 24 June.

The Museo Archeológico

Beyond the church, in one of the stone-vaulted warehouses that line the promenade, is the **Museo Marsala** (Mon, Tues & Thurs 9am–1.30pm, Wed, Fri, Sat

& Sun 4–7pm; €2), most of whose space is given over to a surprisingly well-preserved example of a warship from the classical period. Displayed under a heat- and humidity-regulated plastic tent, it ranks as the only extant *liburnian*, a specifically Phoenician or **Punic warship**, probably sunk during the First Punic War in the great sea battle off the Égadi Islands that ended Carthage's rule of the waves. Brought here in 1977, after eight years of underwater surveying by an English team working under the archeologist Honor Frost, the vessel – originally 35m long and rowed by 68 oarsmen – has been the source of much detailed information on the period, including what the crew ate and the stimulants they chewed to keep awake. Scattered about the museum is a medley of items found in or around the ship: heaped amphorae and anchors, and various photographs and explanations of the ship's retrieval from the sea. Other rooms have a variety of more mundane finds from Motya and ancient necropoli in the neighbourhood, as well as some colourful examples of Italian and North African pottery.

Practicalities

From Trápani particularly, there are quicker, more frequent services to Marsala by train than by bus. The **train station** is at the southeastern edge of town on Via A. Fazio, a fifteen-minute walk from the centre. **Buses** arrive centrally at Piazza del Pópolo (also known as Piazza Marconi), near Porta Garibaldi. Between June and September, there's a useful **hydrofoil** link to the Égadi Islands: Ústica Lines (☎348.357.9863) services dock down at the harbour, fifteen minutes' walk from the centre – you can buy tickets on the dockside.

There's a **tourist office** at Via XI Maggio 100, off Piazza Repubblica near the Chiesa Madre (Mon–Sat 8am–8pm, Sun 9am–noon; ☎0923.714.097, Ⓦwww.prolocomarsala.org), and most of the town's sites have informative notices posted in English. You'll find a **post office** at Via Garibaldi, and a **bank** with an ATM, the Banco di Sicilia, at Via XI Maggio 83, plus others along Via Roma. The library on Via XI Maggio has **Internet** access (Mon–Fri 8am–2pm, Sat 8am–1pm). For general groceries, there is a lively daily **market** just inside the Porta Garibaldi, spilling over into the adjacent Piazza del Pópolo.

Accommodation

Marsala has little budget accommodation, though it does have a fine selection of mid- and upper-range hotels, any of which make a nice base for exploring the region.

Baglio Vajarassa Contrada Spagnola ☎ & Ⓕ0923.968.628. You'll need a car to stay at this old manor house, 6km north of town on the way to Mózia. Just a few well-kept rooms are available, with hearty local meals on offer too. ❹

Garden Via Gambini 36 ☎ & Ⓕ0923.982.320. The cheapest hotel in town, this is behind the train station, right over the level crossing and right again. It's not great, but it's modern and clean enough, and has small discounts outside high season. It only has nine rooms, so ring ahead. ❹

New Palace Lungomare Mediterraneo ☎0923.719.492, Ⓕ0923.719.496. Four-star opulence overlooking the tourist harbour, just out of the centre. Surprisingly, there's no pool. ❽

President Via Nino Bixio 1 ☎0923.999.333, Ⓕ0923.999.115. Spacious rooms and comfortable beds in this solid business-travellers' hotel. Best of all is the swimming pool in a sunken garden, shrouded by flowering capers – some rooms at the back have balconies overlooking this. It's a 20min walk from the centre, about half that to the nearest restaurant. ❻

Villa Favorita Via Favorita 27 ☎0923.989.100, Ⓕ0923.980.264. This beautiful, secluded villa on the outskirts of town is set in its own gardens and has a pool and charming restaurant. Book in advance since the value-for-money prices mean it's often full. It's 2km from the centre (and signposted). ❻

Eating and drinking

In the centre at least, which empties of life after 9pm, **restaurants** can be hard to come by. The couple of **bars** in Piazza della Repubblica are good for a *tè freddo alla pesca* (peach tea), accompanied by earnest discussion of lottery numbers. After dinner, finish off with a beer or an ice cream at one of the bars outside the Porta Nuova, where you can sit and admire the austere Art Deco front of the Cine Impero, so out of keeping with the Baroque arch opposite. To sample some **marsala wine**, visit either the *Enoteca Sombrero*, Via Garibaldi 32, or one of two adjacent *enoteca*-souvenir shops in Via Lungomare Boeo, by the archeological museum.

Caffè Millennium Piazza F. Pizzo. This is the best place for breakfast (and handy for anyone in the *President* or *Garden* hotels) – grilled sandwiches, *cornetti*, *arancini*, and good coffee. There are lunch specials too, and it stays open late at the weekends. Closed Wed. Inexpensive.

Capo Lilybeo Via Lungomare Boeo 40 ✆0923.712.881. Housed in a restored warehouse near the archeological museum, the food here is great – try the home-made *busiate alla Marsigliese* (with shrimp and lobster ragù). It's also renowned for its fish couscous (served on Fridays), and there are pizzas in the evenings. Closed Mon. Moderate.

E&N Via XI Maggio 30. The self-styled "taste experts", this classy *pasticceria* and *gelateria* has seats outside. Inexpensive.

Nashville Piazza F. Pizzo 24 ✆0923.951.826. Very nice pizzas served on a summer terrace in the square, and a standard Sicilian menu that won't break the bank either. Inexpensive.

Trattoria Garibaldi Piazza Addolorata 5 ✆0923.953.006. Cosy, upmarket trattoria in the centre. Fish is the speciality, though you'll eat for less if you choose grilled meat. Closed Mon. Moderate.

Mazara del Vallo

The North African element in Sicily's cultural melange is strongest at the major fishing port of **MAZARA DEL VALLO**, 22km and a thirty-minute train or bus ride down the coast from Marsala. Under the Muslims, Mazara was one of Sicily's most prosperous towns and capital of the biggest of the three administrative districts, or *walis*, into which the island was divided – hence the "del Vallo" tag. The first Sicilian city to be taken by the Arabs, and the last they surrendered, Mazara's prosperity lasted for 250 years, coinciding with the height of Arab power in the Mediterranean. Count Roger's anxiety to establish a strong Norman presence in this Muslim powerbase ensured that Mazara's importance lasted long after his conquest of the city in 1087, and it didn't give up its rank as provincial capital until Trápani took over in 1817.

The Arab links have revived since the port became the prime Sicilian destination for Tunisian immigrants flocking across the sea to work in the vast fishing fleet – one of Italy's biggest. Indeed, wandering through Mazara's casbah-like back-streets, there are moments when you could imagine yourself to be in North Africa, passing Tunisian shops and a café plastered with pictures of the Tunisian president, and Arab music percolating through small doorways. There's also talk of building a mosque for the families who have stayed to make their homes here. For the visitor, the attraction of Mazara is its profusion of fine churches in a slowly reviving – though far from genteel – old town. The tree-shaded lungomare and seafront gardens add another facet to its character, and with a row of sea-view restaurants, Mazara is one of the few towns in the west to make the most of its coastal location.

Hopps Hotel & ▼ Sporting Camping Club

The Town

The **old town**, where all the interest lies, is bordered by the Mázaro River and sea on two sides and the main corsos – Umberto I and Vittória Véneto – on the others. Mazara's principal street, **Corso Umberto I**, ends at Piazza Mokarta and the scant ruins of Count Roger's **castello**, magnificently floodlit at night, when the square is the focus of Mazara's promenading crowds. Fronting the garden to one side of the piazza is the **Duomo**, originally Norman but completely remodelled in the late seventeenth century – though the relief over the main door showing a mounted Count Roger trampling a Saracen underfoot was carved in 1584. Inside there's an almost indigestible profusion of stuccoed and sculptured ornamentation, including, behind the altar, a group of seven marble statues depicting the *Transfiguration*, carved by Antonello Gagini. To the right, a niche reveals a fragment of Byzantine fresco, dating from the end of the thirteenth century, and, through the marble doorway on the right side of the nave, there's some excellently chiselled Roman sarcophagi, with reliefs of a lively hunting scene and a battle, rich with confusion.

Outside the Duomo, **Piazza della Repubblica** heralds a harmonious set of Baroque buildings: the square itself is flanked by the double-storey porticoed facade of the **Seminario** and the **Palazzo Vescovile**, both eighteenth-century. In nearby Piazza del Plebiscito, the fifteenth-century church of Sant'Egido now houses the **Museo del Satiro** (daily 9am–2pm & 3–9.30pm, closes at 7pm in winter; €4.50), whose highlight is a rather risqué fourth-century BC bronze satyr captured in the ecstatic throes of an orgiastic Dionysian dance. It was, quite literally, caught by a Mazara fishing-boat, the *Captain Ciccio*, in the waters between Pantelleria and Cape Bon, Tunisia, in 1998. Sadly, as the fishermen hauled the catch aboard, one of the arms broke off and has yet to be recovered. Opposite the museum, and entered through a rather fine sculpted doorway, the earlier **Collegio dei Gesuiti** houses the tiny **Museo Cívico** (currently closed for restoration; call ☎0923.671.111 for an update), displaying a smattering of minor, mainly Roman, finds from the area. You'll find many other Baroque constructions in the intricate network of streets and squares that makes up Mazara's old town. The church of **Santa Veneranda**, in the square of the same name, is perhaps the most beautiful, its twin belltowers styled with a jaunty twist.

Most of Mazara's churches were built after its teeming Arab population had dwindled to nothing. But it's also in the old town, especially in the old Pilazza quarter, that their descendants have returned, making up a **Tunisian quarter** centred on Via Porta Palermo and nearby Via Bagno. Stroll around here and you'll pass an authentic Tunisian café and shop in Via Goti, and various social clubs resounding to Arab tapes and the clack of backgammon tables. On the edge of the quarter stands the church of **San Nicolò Regale**, a restored Norman church with strong Arab elements – a honey-toned, battlemented exterior, and a simple interior rising to a single cupola.

The church stands on a platform overlooking the Mázaro River, its waters hidden by the hulls of the two hundred or so trawlers that clog Mazara's **port**. Heavy overfishing and the use of illegal explosives (dropped into the sea to stun the fish) have greatly decreased the catch in recent years, but the rich waters above the continental shelf have ensured that there are enough fish left to make it worthwhile for the fishermen to pursue their trade – at least, given the reduced wages that the Tunisians are prepared to accept.

Out of the centre: the beach and Santa Maria della Giummare

Crossing over the bridge further down the river, you can walk past the docks to Mazara's seafront, mostly sandy **beach**, though a good part of it is choked by seaweed. It gets better the further up you go, but bathers might bear in mind that the stretch between Mazara and the Stagnone Islands was recently found to be one of Sicily's most polluted coastlines. If you're looking for a **swim** you'd be better advised to drive or jump on a bus from Mazara's train station to **TONNARELLA LIDO**, 7km south.

There's one more easy excursion out from the centre of Mazara – walkable this time – a couple of kilometres away on the outskirts of town, though drivers could see it on their way in or out by following Via Circonvallazione, the main SS115 running to Marsala. Signposted "Madonna del Alto", the chapel of **Santa Maria della Giummare** sits on a slight elevation on the right-hand side of the road (looking north). Built as a Basilian convent by a daughter of Count Roger's in 1103, its portal also shows a strong Saracen strain.

Practicalities

Buses stop either outside the **train station** or 200m up at Piazza Matteotti. The **tourist office** is in the old part of town, past the Duomo in Piazza S. Veneranda (Mon–Sat 7.45am–2.15pm, Wed also 2.45–6.15pm, Sun 9am–noon; ☎0923.941.727). There's a smaller office (Mon–Sat 9am–12.30pm & 5–8pm, Sun 9am–12.30pm) in Piazza Mokarta, behind the castle ruin. There are **banks** with ATMs on Piazza Mokarta and up Corso Umberto I, and **Internet** access at *Internet Point* on Via S. Caterina.

The most central **hotel** is the *Hopps Hotel*, Via G. Hopps 29 (☎0923.946.133, ℱ0923.946.075; ❼), five minutes' walk down the lungomare from the public gardens. It's a resort-style three-star centred on a palm-fringed pool, and the rooms are spacious if a bit dated. Breakfast by the pool is included in the price and there's parking. All in all it's not a bad base, though a bit noisy in summer when the poolside radio blasts all day and there's singing at night. The local **campsite**, *Sporting Camping Club* (📞0923.947.054), at Località Bocca Arena, a few kilometres out of town (signposted from the lungomare), is resort-like too.

As you might expect in a Sicilian/Tunisian fishing port, you can eat well in Mazara. There's a line of **restaurants** near the public gardens, each offering variations of fish couscous and all with tables outside. Of these, *Lo Scoiattolo* – "The Squirrel" at Via N. Tortorici 9 – has a fine antipasto buffet and daily fish specials, though many locals come here at night for the huge choice of pizzas. *La Béttola* at Via Maccagnone 32, near the train station (closed Wed), is a good place for regional specialities. *Bar Garden* in Piazza della Repubblica faces the town's most harmonious buildings and is a nice place to wait for the sun to set; or there's the *Belvedere Normanno*, by the castle, another good vantage-point for a quiet drink.

Selinunte and around

SELINUNTE, the site of the Greek city of Selinus, lies around 30km east of Mazara del Vallo, stranded on a remote corner of the coast in splendid isolation. It's a crucial sight if you're travelling through the west of Sicily, its series of mighty temples lying in great heaps, where they were felled by earthquakes.

Most westerly of the Hellenic colonies, **Selinus** reached its peak in the fifth century BC. A bitter rival of Segesta, whose lands lay adjacent to the north (see p.387), the powerful city and its fertile plain attracted enemies hand over fist, and it was only a matter of time before Selinus caught the eye of Segesta's ally, Carthage. Geographically vulnerable, the city was sacked by Carthaginians, any attempts at recovery forestalled by earthquakes, which later razed the city. However, people continued to live here until 250 BC, when the population was finally transferred to Marsala before the Roman invasion. The Arabs did occupy the site briefly, but the last recorded settlement at Selinunte was in the thirteenth century, after which time it remained forgotten until rediscovered in the sixteenth century. Despite the destruction, the city ruins have exerted a romantic hold over people ever since.

By **public transport**, it's easiest to approach from Castelvetrano (see p.422), which is a twenty-minute ride from Mazara del Vallo by road or rail. Selinunte is another twenty minutes south from there, via buses that run five times daily (Mon–Sat) from Piazza Regina Margherita (tickets from the *tabacchi* opposite San Domenico church) – the most useful departures are those at 12.30pm and 5.20pm. The archeological site is situated just to the west of the tiny village of Marinella, a far better base than Castelvetrano, and where the buses stop.

Marinella di Selinunte

MARINELLA DI SELINUNTE only has one main road, which winds down to a small harbour where the fishing-boats are hauled up onto the sands by pulleys, and then runs west to the site of Selinunte. The village is no longer the isolated place it once was, with recent buildings in the centre and new side streets off the main road, while the seafront has become top-heavy with trattorias, and shops selling Tunisian carpets, souvenirs and beachwear. But it remains an attractive place, of particular appeal if you're planning to use the fine sand **beach** which stretches west from the village to the ruins. The water

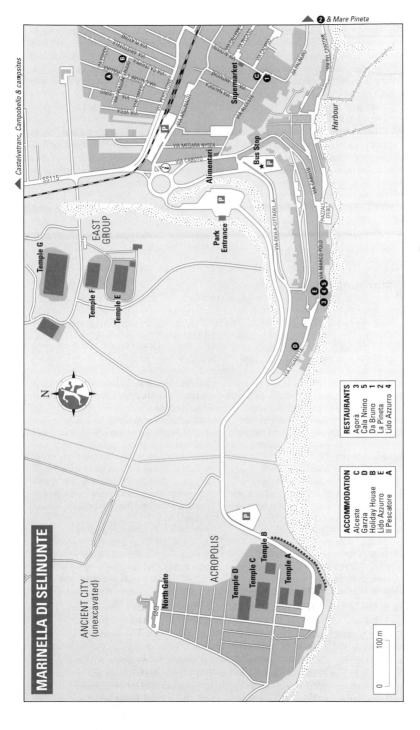

MARINELLA DI SELINUNTE

▲ Castelvetrano, Campobello & campsites

▲ ② & Mare Pineta

SS115

VIA BLATONE
VIA ARISTOFANE
VIA PICASSO
VIA CANOVA

VIA CASSIOPEA E FRONTE QUAGLIA Ⓑ
VIA APOLLONIO FRONTE QUAGLIA Ⓐ
VIA PRASSITELE
VIA NAUSICA
VIA CAPUTO

VIA DEI CANTONE
VIA PALINURO

VIA VEGA
VIA SIRIO
VIA ARGONAUTI

Supermarket
VIA ANTONIO
VIA NAISVEA Ⓒ ①
VIA ALCESTE

VIA MEGARA NYSEA

Harbour

ⓘ
VIA CABOTO
Alimentari

Bus Stop ★ P

Ⓟ
Park Entrance

VIA DELLA CITTADEL A
VIA MARCO POLO
PIAZZALE EFEBO

EAST GROUP

Temple G
Temple F
Temple E

Ⓔ ③④⑤
③
Ⓓ
VIA PIGAFETTA

N

ANCIENT CITY (unexcavated)

ACROPOLIS

North Gate

Temple D
Temple C
Temple A
Temple B

Ⓟ

ACCOMMODATION
Alceste   C
Garzia   D
Holiday House   B
Lido Azzurro   E
Il Pescatore   A

RESTAURANTS
Agorà   3
Cala Nnino   5
Da Bruno   1
La Pineta   2
Lido Azzurro   4

0   100 m

isn't great to swim in, since it's clogged with seaweed at the sand's edge, though this doesn't deter the kids. However, the surfing here is particularly good, and you can rent equipment in the summer, as well as pedalos, chairs, shades and all the usual beach paraphernalia. There's another beach east of the village, the **Mare Pineta**, backed by pine trees stretching into the distance; follow the road beyond the port for ten minutes.

Arrival and information

The **bus station** is south of the entrance to the temple site, though most buses continue to the entrance as well. The small but obliging **tourist office** (Mon–Sat 8am–8pm, Sun 9am–noon & 3–6pm; ☎0924.46.251) is here, but it can get very busy in summer. Just opposite on this road there's an **alimentari** and, beyond it, in the main residential district – where most of the cheap accommodation is – a bigger **supermarket** behind the *Alceste* hotel. The road then descends to the seafront, where a couple of hotels and restaurants are situated, and along which you'll also find **telephones**, an **exchange office**, and a few shops. Note, though, that Marinella has few other facilities: the nearest bank, and other services, are in Castelvetrano, though there is an **ATM** in the entrance lobby of the archeological site.

Accommodation

You may well be offered **rooms** as you get off the bus, which are worth accepting in summer when the hotels and pensions in the village fill rapidly. There are two **campsites** virtually next to each other on the main road, about 1.5km north of the village: the *Athena* (☎0924.46.132), with a ridiculous temple facade and a good pizzeria, and *Il Maggiolino* (☎0924.46.044); the bus to and from Castelvetrano passes right by them.

Alceste Via Alceste 21 ☎0924.46.184, ☏0924.46.143. Friendly place with air-conditioned rooms (sea views from the third floor), good showers and private parking. It's a bit unkempt here and there, but you can forgive the occasional slackness when you get breakfast (included) on the open-air terrace. **⑥**

Garzia Via A. Pigafetta 6 ☎0924.46.660, ☏0924.46.196. The most expensive choice on the seafront road, this Arabic-style building has a variety of rooms, with and without sea views, and its own lido. Half-board is compulsory in July and August (€65–80 per person), though they might do room-only at the back. **④**

The Holiday House (Casa Vacanze) Via Appollonio Rodio 23 ☎0924.46.035. *La signora* maintains four double/twin rooms in a family home, sharing one small but clean bathroom. A couple are largish and have balconies (not that

there's a view), while the furniture and beds are all from the visit-grandma school of comfort. No credit cards. **①**

Lido Azzurro Via Marco Polo 98 ☎ & ☏0924.46.256. A charming villa on the seafront road, with laid-back staff, prints on the walls, rugs on the floors and attractive rooms with sea-facing balconies. The owner speaks good English. The only drawback is that it's liable to be noisy in summer with all the comings and goings from nearby restaurants and bars. Half-board €49 per person in August. **③**

Il Pescatore Via Castore e Polluce 31 ☎0924.46.303. Small "rooms" place which provides a shared kitchen for guests, as well as self-catering apartments. The fresh-fruit breakfast on the terrace with views over to the valley of the temples and the sea (extra charge) is not to be missed. No credit cards. **①**

Eating and drinking

Via Marco Polo, the road above the west beach, is where all the best **eating** and **drinking** places are, starting down at the little harbour where a couple of bars put out tables from where you can watch the sun set and the fishermen argue among themselves. At night in summer, visitors emerge from their holiday homes and the locals come in from the surrounding villages to parade along Via Marco Polo on foot, in cars and on Vespas, with the party chugging along merrily until well after midnight.

Agorà Via Marco Polo 51. Ocean views and magnificent *forno a legna* pizzas, with the honours done by a pizza chef who looks as if he has sampled rather too many of his own products. Also a welcome smattering of Tunisian dishes on the menu – *brik* (fried pastry parcels), oily aubergine salads and couscous. Moderate.

Da Bruno Via Alceste, opposite the *Hotel Alceste*. In the residential district, this place offers crispy pizzas cooked in a wood-burning oven, good antipasti and locally inspired fish dishes, like pasta with tuna and capers. Moderate.

Cala Nnino Via Marco Polo. The speciality of the house is sea urchin, but it also serves plain grilled fish. Moderate.

Lido Azzurro Via Marco Polo, opposite the eponymous hotel. Also known as *Baffo's*, this has a huge open dining-room terrace overlooking the sea and does tasty *fettuccine* dishes. Moderate.

La Pineta on the east beach, Mare Pineta. The beach-bar here has a trattoria at the back (closed in winter) serving fresh fish meals: a real find, it stays open in the evenings during July and August, but take a torch if you do go at night, as the road there is unlit. Moderate.

Selinus: the site

The **ruins** of Selinus are back behind the main part of the village, split into two parts with temples in each, known only as temples A to G and O. The two parts are enclosed within the same site, with the car park and **entrance** (daily: summer 9am–6.30pm; winter 9am–4pm; €4.50) lying through the landscaped earthbanks that preclude views of the east group of temples from the road.

Shrouded in the wild celery which gave the ancient city its name, the **East Group** temples are in various stages of reconstructed ruin. The most complete is the one nearest the sea (Temple E), probably dedicated to Hera (Aphrodite) and re-erected in 1958. A Doric construction, almost 70m by 25m, it remains a gloriously impressive sight, its soaring columns gleaming bright against the sky, its ledges and capitals the resting place for flitting birds. Temple F, behind, is the oldest in this group, from around 550 BC, while the northernmost temple (Temple G) is an immense tangle of columned wreckage, 6m high in places and crisscrossed by rough footpaths. In Sicily, the only temple bigger than this is the Tempio di Giove at Agrigento.

The road leads down from here, across the (now buried) site of the old harbour, to the second part of excavated Selinus, the **acropolis**, where there's another car park for those that can't face the twenty-minute walk. This contains what remains of the other temples (five in all), as well as the well-preserved city streets and massive stepped **walls** which rise above the duned beach below. These huge walls were all constructed after 409 BC – when the city was sacked by the Carthaginians – in an attempt to protect a limited and easily defensible area of the old city.

Temple C stands on the highest point of the acropolis, giving glorious views out over the sparkling sea. Built in the early sixth century BC (and probably dedicated to Apollo), it was from here that the best of the metopes (decorative panels) were removed; they're now on show in Palermo's archeological museum (see p.96). Its fourteen standing columns were re-erected in the 1920s; other fallen columns here, and at the surrounding temples, show how they were originally constructed – the drums lying in a line, with slots and protrusions on either side which fitted into each other. The buildings immediately behind temples C and D were shops, split into two rooms and with a courtyard each; while at the end of the main street beyond is the **north gate** to the city – the high blocks of stone marking a gateway that was 7m high. Behind the north gate stood the rest of the **ancient city**, still largely unexcavated, though crisscrossed by little paths through the undergrowth. The agora was probably sited here, as was a necropolis further to the north, though there's no contemporary evidence of either.

Campobello and the Cave di Cusa

If you've got your own transport, it makes some sense to call in at the quarries where the stone for the building of Selinus was extracted in the fifth century BC. They're 3.5km south of the scruffy town of **CAMPOBELLO DI MAZARA**, deep in olive country. From Selinunte, it's a lovely twenty-kilometre drive along country roads lined with olive groves and vines: when you reach Campobello, follow the signs ("Cave di Cusa") and keep your fingers crossed.

At the site of the **Cave di Cusa** (always open; free), a path leads into a bucolic setting that owes more to English Romanticism than to ancient Greece. In early summer, workers fork hay into piles in between the rock ledges and tended shrubs, while behind them stretch shaded groves of olives. Everywhere, you can see the massive column drums and stumps lying randomly about, quarried and chiselled into shape here before being dragged to the ancient city on wooden carts, where they formed part of the great temple complex. There are examples of all the various stages of the process, with unfinished pieces poignantly abandoned, the work interrupted when Selinus was devastated in 409 BC. The most impressive pieces are those stone drums and column sections still in place where they were being excavated: a couple are 6m high and 2m across, with a narrow groove dug all the way around in which the stonemasons had to work – the reflected heat must have been appalling. Other rock sections indicate clearly where drums have already been cut – parts of the site look as though someone has been through with a giant pastry-cutter.

Tre Fontane

It's only another 5km or so south from the quarries to the coast at **TRE FONTANE**. The beach here stretches east and west of the road, a long, long sandy stretch with beach-bars, umbrellas, shades and extremely shallow water – you can get 20m out and still only be up to your knees. The small resort itself is basically one long strip of family villas, and not terribly engaging, though there are plenty of "*affitasi*" ("to rent") signs around should you fancy renting a villa, and a **campsite**, *Il Sombrero* (☎0924.80.300), 1km before the village.

Castelvetrano and around

It's hard to recommend a visit to **CASTELVETRANO**, 15km inland, for any reason other than getting the bus straight out again. A depressed town, it's lightened only marginally by an elegant if traffic-choked centre, where the **Teatro Selinus** – looking rather like a copy of a Greek temple – boasts a proud plaque commemorating Goethe's visit in 1787. Just around the corner is a good-looking **Chiesa Madre** from the sixteenth century. The church's finely engraved doorway leads into an interior warmly illuminated by stained-glass windows – a rare thing in Sicily – and ornamented by a number of stuccoes by Serpotta and Ferraro. Off the adjacent square, Piazza Garibaldi, it's a short walk down to Via Garibaldi 50 and the **Museo Cívico** (daily 9am–1pm & 3–6pm; €2.50), home of the bronze *Efébo di Selinunte*, a statue of a young man from the fifth century BC.

From behind the church, Via Vittorio Emanuele leads down towards Piazza Matteotti and the train station. Piazza Matteotti marks the end of Via Serafino Mannone, where aficionados of banditry can visit the courtyard in which the body of the island's most notorious outlaw, **Salvatore Giuliano** (see p.449), was found on July 5, 1950. The courtyard is between Via Mannone 92 and 100, though it's a rather less appealing spot than its legend might suggest.

Santíssima Trinità di Delia

Three and a half kilometres west **out of Castelvetrano** is a twelfth-century Norman church that makes a pleasant rural excursion for anyone not in a blazing hurry. Head down Via R. Séttimo from Piazza Umberto, along a country lane fringed by vineyards, keeping left where the road forks. The domed church, **Santíssima Trinità di Delia**, is signposted before you arrive at the artificial lake of Lago Trinità: ring the bell to the right of the church for the key. The small, square building, its four slender columns and triple apse reminiscent of Saracenic styles, was meticulously restored by two brothers, whose mausoleum the church has become. Their tombs, dominating the small interior, rival those of the Norman kings in Palermo for splendour.

Practicalities

To **get to Selinunte** from Castelvetrano, take the bus for Marinella from outside the train station – there's a timetable posted inside the station – or from Piazza Regina Margherita in town.

To reach the town centre from the **train station**, in Piazza Améndola, walk up to the main road and turn left: it's just a few minutes to Piazza Matteotti, from where Via Vittorio Emanuele – the main shopping street – leads all the way to the rear of the church. **Buses** from Marsala and Trápani stop outside the *Bar Selinus* on Via Selinunte. There's a basic **tourist office** (Mon–Sat 8am–8pm, Sun 9am–noon; ☎0924.904.932) in the museum on Via Garibaldi.

Inland: Salemi, Gibellina and Santa Margherita di Belice

The interior – north of Castelvetrano, east of Marsala – is intensely rural, its few small towns little changed by the coming of the A29 autostrada, which cuts across the region. The whole area is green and highly fertile, mainly given over to vine-growing; indeed, the wine around the **Salemi** district is some of Sicily's best. But, hard though it is to believe, the entire region still hasn't recovered from the **earthquake** of 15 January 1968, which briefly spotlighted western Sicily, sadly more for the authorities' inadequate response to it than for the actual loss of life. Four hundred died and a thousand were injured, no great number by Sicilian standards, but it was the 50,000 left homeless that had the most lingering impact on this already depressed part of the island, and the earthquake's effects are still evident everywhere. Ruined buildings and ugly temporary dwellings being used four decades later testify to the chronically dilatory response to the disaster, aggravated by private interests and particularly by Mafia contractors capitalizing on the catastrophe. Even where rebuilding went ahead, such as in the new town of **Gibellina**, it's still possible to see the dread hand of inertia.

It goes without saying that this is a little-visited area of Sicily, but it's intriguing nonetheless. This is, after all, the part of the world known best to Giuseppe di Lampedusa, whose classic novel, *The Leopard*, is partly set in the little town of **Santa Margherita di Belice** – also badly damaged in 1968 but emerging slowly from the doldrums, and an essential stop for anyone who's read the book. There are local buses to all the towns in the region but it's impossible to construct any kind of sightseeing itinerary using them – you have to have your own car, not least to avoid the possibility of getting stuck in backwaters with no accommodation.

Salemi

The town of **SALEMI**, 20km north of Castelvetrano and 30km east of Marsala, oddly enjoyed the privilege of being the first capital of a united Italy in 1860, albeit for only three days, as a plaque in front of its thirteenth-century **castello** records. Another plaque marks Garibaldi's declaration of a dictatorship, asserting that "in times of war, it's necessary for the civilian powers to be concentrated in the hands of one man" – namely Garibaldi himself, though King Vittorio Emanuele still gets a mention. Many treasures from various local churches – including the cathedral destroyed in the earthquake – have found their way into the town's **Museo Cívico** in the former Collegio dei Gesuiti on Via d'Aguirre (Mon–Sat 9am–2pm & 3–7pm; free), where you'll also find assorted pieces of "Garibaldini" – letters, documents and arms connected with the town's finest hour.

Gibellina

Salemi escaped the earthquake lightly, even though a third of the population had to abandon their shattered homes. Other towns, like Gibellina, were completely flattened, the population moved en masse to a site close to Santa Ninfa. This is **GIBELLINA NUOVA**, a modern town which has become a symbol of progress in the region, with innovative buildings that deliberately diverge from old styles: weird shapes and forms abound, designed by a handful of modern architects with big budgets. There's a vast stainless-steel star astride the motorway where you exit for Gibellina, as well as huge white spheres, and giant ploughs, snails and much besides – 47 constructions in all, with a few in the Egyptian style still to come. Many buildings are apparently crumbling already, and the designs themselves are embarrassingly frozen in the images of what appeared modern in the 1970s. The town, meanwhile, bakes in the summer sun, since all the modern piazzas are vast concrete spaces with little shade. You can get a taste of what it's all about by driving to the main square – Piazza XV Gennaio 1968, in case there was any doubt about whose fault all this was – where the arcaded City Hall is fronted by some particularly abstract examples. Staff at the **tourist office** here (Mon–Sat 8am–2pm; ☎0924.67.877) will probably have a fit at the sight of a tourist, but recover enough to hand over a map showing where everything is. There's a local museum with separate archeological and anthropological sections, a modern art gallery and even a botanical garden, though it's a dedicated visitor who takes in any of these. For a **lunch** stop, look no further than *La Massara*, Viale dei Vespri Siciliani 41, an inexpensive trattoria ten minutes' walk from the piazza, whose very filling house pasta is made with aubergines, tomato and mozzarella.

Eighteen kilometres east along the SS119 (through Santa Ninfa), the old town of **RÚDERI DI GIBELLINA** complements the new: a mountain of rubble from which smashed and mutilated houses poke out, strewn over a green hillside. On the way into town, you'll pass what is ironically its best-preserved fragment: a shady cemetery stretching down the side of the valley. Further down, modernism has left its mark here too, in the form of a wide, white mantle of concrete, **Il Cretto**, poured over one slope, and carved through by channels that recall the previous layout of streets. But everything else is as it was after the earthquake struck: only a church has since been restored, and a jumble of scaffolding on a hummock cradles a stage where the new town's inhabitants are supposed to return every year to remember the catastrophe.

In reality, though, the stage has been co-opted to entice tourists to a very remote spot of the Sicilian countryside to watch a series of classical dramas, concerts and events, known as the **Orestiadi**. As well as works by Euripides, Sophocles and others, there are modern interpretations by the likes of Jean Cocteau, Stravinsky and John Cage, and a full programme of exhibitions and cinema. Performances (July to October) take place in both old and new Gibellinas – more details are available from the tourist office at Gibellina Nuova.

Santa Margherita di Belice

Often cited as one of the finest of all historical novels, Giuseppe di Lampedusa's *The Leopard* ("Il Gattopardo" in Italian) is a masterpiece of manners and morals, written by a Sicilian prince who only ever completed this one work. Set in 1860s Sicily, it draws heavily on Lampedusa's own experiences, not least the summers he used to spend in his grandmother's palace in **SANTA MARGHERITA DI BELICE**, a small village 35km east of Castelvetrano. This is the Donnafugata of the book – the fictional prince's summer home, a place cherished for the "sense it gave him of everlasting childhood". The 1968 earthquake, unfortunately, completely wrecked the seventeenth-century palace and church described so intently in the novel, though fragments of the palace have been incorporated in a gleaming new Town Hall (Municipio). This, with its cool internal courtyards and lovely garden to the side, at least echoes the spirit of the original; more poignant is all that's left of the adjacent Chiesa Madre – a two-storey corner open to the elements, displaying its elegant marble tracery and painted medallions to the birds. Having paid your literary dues, it's a quick matter to look around the rest of Santa Margherita, which shows a few signs of revival these days – there's a thoroughly modern church with a space-rocket spire, new extensions grafted onto older, damaged buildings, and a traffic-free stretch of street where you can grab a cold drink in the *Caffè Gattopardo*.

Pantelleria

With the exception of Malta, **PANTELLERIA** is the biggest of the islands surrounding Sicily. Forty kilometres nearer to Tunisia than to Sicily, the island has been occupied since early times by whichever power controlled the central Mediterranean. By the time of the Phoenicians, who colonized the island in the seventh century BC, it was called Hiranin, "island of the birds", after the birds who still stop over here on their migratory routes; for the Greeks, it was Kossyra, or "small". But its present name probably derived from the Arabic *bint al-rion* ("daughter of the winds"), after the restless breezes that blow around the island's rocky shores. Pantelleria has always attracted its fair share of famous visitors, and former aficionados like Truman Capote and Aldous Huxley have been replaced in time by the current celebrity A-list, with Madonna and Sting both enamoured of its charms. Parts of *Il Postino* (*The Postman*) were filmed here, too.

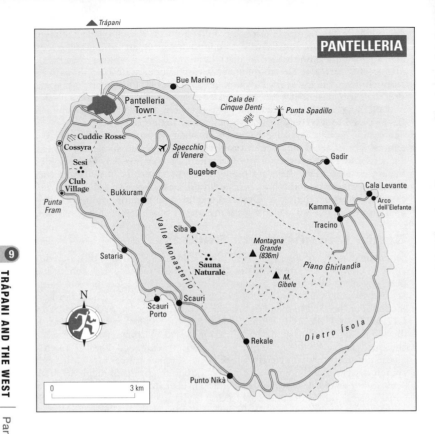

There are no beaches of any kind in Pantelleria, its rough black coastline consisting mainly of jagged rocks, but the swimming is still pretty good in some exceptionally scenic spots. Inland, the largely mountainous country offers plenty of rambling opportunities, all an easy moped or bus ride from the port, where most of the accommodation options are. If you're spending any length of time on Pantelleria, one novel option is to rent one of the local *dammuso* houses: their strong walls and domed roofs keep the temperature down indoors.

The main drawback to spending time on Pantelleria is the **cost of living**: there are only a few pricey hotels, while food (and water) is mostly imported and therefore relatively expensive. The island does offer some unique gastronomic experiences, though, including what are touted as the best capers in the Mediterranean. At some point, you ought to sample the locally produced ricotta-type cheese known as *tumma*, which is one of the ingredients of *ravioli con menta e ricotta*, a slightly bitter but fresh-tasting dish for which Pantelleria is famous. Pasta often comes served with *pesto pantescho*, a rough sauce of tomatoes, garlic and basil; while an *insalata pantescha* utilizes tomatoes, onions, cubes of boiled potato, and local capers and herbs. The **wine** is well thought of too, made from the *zibbibo* grapes that grow well in this volcanic soil. The day-to-day drinking stuff – *vino pantescho* – is mostly white, with a nice fruity fragrance, while for something considerably stronger try the fortified *Moscato*, a sweet, amber-coloured dessert wine. Even better is the raisin wine, known generically as *passito*, which has a rich golden colour and a dry and heady flavour – the best known variety is *Tanit*.

Despite the expense, a few days spent here will probably leave you wanting more. Best times are May/June or September/October, to avoid the summer's ferocious heat; try and book your accommodation before you arrive.

Getting to Pantelleria

You can reach Pantelleria by (year-round) ferry or (summer-only) hydrofoil services from Trápani. Flights are from Trápani or Palermo and are, obviously, much quicker – a far better use of your time if you only have a couple of days to see the island.

Siremar **ferries** do the journey in around five hours (June–Sept daily; Oct–May daily except Sat), leaving Trápani at midnight, for a deck-class fare of around €25 one way (slightly cheaper in low season). For around €5 you can reserve a reclining chair (a *poltrona*), an expense worth considering since the regular seats are difficult to sleep in and uncomfortably close to the TVs; or there are couchette-cabins for around €20 per person. **Tickets** are on sale in the Siremar office at the Stazione Maríttima in Trápani (☎0923.545.455, ⓦ www.siremar.it), right up until departure.

In addition, Ústica Lines (☎0923.22.200, ⓦ www.usticalines.it) runs a daily **hydrofoil service** from Trápani to Pantelleria, from June to September, taking about two and a half hours; tickets are around €35 one way. Note that, even in summer, hydrofoil sailings are sometimes cancelled at the last minute because of poor weather conditions.

Pantelleria is just a thirty-minute **flight** from Trápani (1–2 flights daily) with Gandalf Airlines (☎035.322.369, ⓦ www.gandalfair.com), or a forty-minute flight from Palermo (1–2 flights daily) with Air Sicilia (☎800.412.411, ⓦ www .airsicilia.it). Between April and September, there are also direct flights from Milan, Rome and Venice. One-way tickets start at €70, but special deals are sometimes on offer, especially if you can book some time in advance. Contact the airlines direct or travel agents in Trápani or Palermo (listed on p.396 and p.112).

Pantelleria Town

The only settlement of any size on Pantelleria, **PANTELLERIA TOWN** is hardly your idyllic island port: most of it was flattened during the last war when Allied bombers pulverized what had become one of the main German bases in the Mediterranean. The scars are still evident, and the numbered blocks of concrete destined for the rebuilding of the harbour are still waiting outside the port.

Consequently, much of the town has a homogenous, modern appearance, its buildings mainly consisting of low-rise concrete cubes spread back two or three streets deep from the harbour. The only building here that predates the war is the morose, black **Castello Barabacane** on the far side of the harbour, a legacy of the Spaniards. The partly restored interior is open in summer (check at the tourist office for hours) and for occasional art exhibitions. In case you'd forgotten you're still in Sicily, a plaque on the harbour-facing wall honours assassinated anti-Mafia judge Paolo Borsellino and his five bodyguards.

Yet to call the town unattractive and devoid of interest, as many do, would be to miss the point. It might be small and remote, but it's not as unsophisticated as the other offshore islands – it's long been on the African shipping route

Map labels:

A & Siba Airport ▲   ▲ Scauri

PANTELLERIA TOWN

Amil Patente (Shop)   Ceramic Shop   Agip Service Station

Not to scale

VIA CATANIA

① Banco Nuova **②**   **③** **④**   **G** **B**

VIA   BORGO   ITALIA

Air Sicilia (Ústica Lines)   Bakery   Agenzia Rizzo (Siremar)   Cossira (Alitalia & Siremar)

Valentim (Tabacchi)   Castello Barabacane

& Market

Alimentari Ugo

Bakery

VIA ROMA

PIAZZA CAVOUR

Harbour

Ferry & Hydrofoil Dock

⑥ Pharmacy

ⓘ   Banco di Sicilia

VIA VERDI

⑦

RESTAURANTS & BARS	
Café Aurora	4
Il Cappero	6
Cicci's Bar	7
Il Dammuso	1
Goloso	3
La Risacca	5
Tikirriki	2

ACCOMMODATION	
Khamma	B
Miryam	D
Port	C
La Perla Rosa	A

9

Hospital, Kamma & Tracino

and has a distinct liveliness to it, seen best at 6am, when the ferry disgorges its passengers, or at 8pm, when the traffic starts to circle the harbour and the harbourside café-bars fill with perambulating locals. Indeed, arriving here at dawn is rather romantic, as the town lights flick off to reveal a spread of white-painted cubes which – only close up – emerge as modern rather than medieval. Throughout the day delivery vessels and fishing smacks come and go, while the marina sees the manoeuvrings of some uncommonly flash yachts and even the odd schooner or two.

Arrival, information and transport

The **airport** is 5km southeast of town; a bus connects with flight arrivals and drops you in the central Piazza Cavour (a 15min journey). **Arriving by sea**, you'll disembark right in the centre of town, just a short walk from most of the bars, restaurants and hotels. In bad weather, you may be deposited instead at Scauri, a smaller port on the island's southwestern side, from where a bus takes foot passengers into town. Both Siremar and Ústica Lines agencies are along Via Borgo Italia on the harbourfront.

There is a **tourist office** (June–Sept Mon–Sat 9am–12.30pm & 6–8pm; ☎0923.911.838) on the main square, Piazza Cavour, or you can usually pick up a rough island **map** and ask the odd question at Agencia Rizzo (the Siremar office), on Via Borgo Italia. There's also a useful local **website**: ⓦwww .pantelleria.it.

The little local **buses** leave from Piazza Cavour, with regular departures to all the main villages on the island – there are no services on Sundays. Buy tickets in advance from any *tabacchi*, not on the bus. For more independence, you might also consider **renting a car or moped**; see "Listings" (opposite) for details.

Accommodation

The town itself has limited accommodation, though other **hotels** can be found at Cuddie Rosse, Punta Fram and Bue Marino. During July and August, some places impose a minimum stay of three days or even a week – at other times of the year, prices drop considerably. There's no **campsite** on the island, and camping rough is impractical given the terrain and the lack of water. To

TRÁPANI AND THE WEST | Pantelleria

rent one of the idiosyncratic **dammuso** houses dotted around the island, go to ⓦ www.pantelleriatravel.com, or check the notices in the bars, hotels and restaurants for local contact numbers. Alternatively, try one of the following **agencies**: Call Tour, Via Cágliari 14 (☎0923.911.065); Dammusi di Rukia (☎335.120.6226, ⓔinfo@pantelleria.com); or Agenzia Rizzo, Via Borgo Italia 12 (☎0923.911.120). Most *dammusi* are in the ❻, ❼ or ❽ accommodation price category – though a week's minimum rental is usual – and you'll really need a car to get to and from them.

Khamma Via Borgo Italia 24 ☎0923.912.680, ⓕ0923.912.570. Immediately at the end of the dock, on the harbourfront, this offers three-star comforts at fairly reasonable rates. Free pickup from the airport. ❻

Miryam Corso Umberto I ☎0923.911.374, ⓕ0923.911.777. At the far end of the port, near the castle, this is the cheapest option in town and, despite rather glum external appearances, is bright and pleasant inside. Try to get a room with a sea-facing balcony. Breakfast included. ❺

La Perla Rosa Via Dante Alighieri, Contrada Itria ☎0923.912.181, ⓕ0923.912.166, ⓦwww .porthotel.pantelleria.it. Sixteen little one- and two-bedroom apartments, 500m from town,

sharing a pool, garden, BBQ facilities and parking. You can use the bar, restaurant and other facilities at the *Port* hotel. Rooms are air-conditioned and have TV. Minimum stay is one week, though this may be flexible in winter. One-bedroom ❼, two-bedroom ❽

Port Via Borgo Italia 16 ☎0923.911.299, ⓕ0923.912.203, ⓦwww.porthotel.pantelleria.it. Next to the *Khamma* and rather flashier, with a nice covered esplanade-bar overlooking the harbour. The 43 rooms have air-conditioning and satellite TV; the best have a sea-view balcony. Half- or full-board is required in Aug. The hotel also has *dammuso* accommodation available elsewhere on the island. ❻

Eating and drinking

There are several **restaurants and trattorias** in town – all rather flash, though not unaffordable. Most double as pizzerias – and good ones too – so you don't need to spend a fortune every night. If you're **self-catering**, you can buy your own food in the Alimentari Ugo (8am–1pm & 5.30–8.30pm; closed Wed afternoon & Sun), which sells local cheese, among other things. There's a fruit and vegetable shop and a bakery, respectively on and just off the main Piazza Cavour.

For drinking, the **bars** on the harbourfront are where all the action is, starting at 6am (when they open their doors for the arriving ferry passengers) and finishing any time between midnight and 2am depending on season and inclination. They all have outdoor esplanades (where prices are higher), the nicest belonging to *Goloso*, whose evening drinks come with a dish of olives and other nibbles. *Tikirriki* has good pastries and ice cream, while *Café Aurora* has another fine esplanade. Off Piazza Cavour, *Cicci's Bar* also has a lively evening crowd, and you can pick up good snacks here.

Il Cappero Via Roma 31. Just off the main piazza, this is probably the best place to eat in town (if not the island), serving the local ravioli stuffed with *tumma*, fresh fish (including large tuna steaks) and popular pizzas. There's a good antipasto table too. Saturday night is very busy. No credit cards. Closed Mon in winter. Moderate.

Il Dammuso Via Borgo Italia. Trendy little joint that's the best-placed trattoria in town (near the *Miryam*), with windows opening onto the harbour. There's a long menu, including great fish and pizzas; for dessert, try the *tumma* cheese served here with local capers and olive oil. Moderate.

Franco Castiglione Via Borgo Italia 24. Sleek, air-conditioned restaurant that's part of the *Khamma* hotel. Dip into the excellent (mostly veggie) anti-pasto table, and follow it with pizza and local wine and you'll escape lightly; full meals are pricier. Closed Fri. Moderate.

La Risacca Via Padova 66. Under the same management as *Il Cappero*, and with similar food and prices, but further out from the centre. This place also serves pizzas and has outdoor seating. No credit cards. Closed lunchtime in summer & Wed in winter. Moderate.

Listings

Airport enquiries ☎ 0923.111.398.
Banks ATMs at both Banco di Sicilia, Piazza Cavour, and Banco Nuova, Via Catania 5.
Car and bike rental Autonoleggio Policardo, Via Messina 31 ☎ 0923.912.844.
Ferries and hydrofoils The ferry back to Trápani leaves at noon (June–Sept daily and Oct–May Fri & Sat), and at 10am (Oct–May Sun–Thurs). Hydrofoils back to Trápani leave daily at 8.30am (June–Sept).
Hospital For first-aid and medical matters, go to the Ospedale, Via Almanza ☎ 0923.911.110.
Market Every Tuesday and Friday morning on Via San Leonardo. Fresh fish is sold at stalls on the road to the hospital and the lighthouse, on the far side of the harbour from the dock.
Pharmacy Farmacia Greco on Piazza Cavour (Mon–Fri 8.30am–1pm & 4.30–8.30pm).

Police Carabinieri, Via Trieste 13 ☎ 0923.912.883.
Post office The island's main post office is off Piazza Cavour on Via Verdi (Mon–Sat 8am–1.20pm).
Shopping There are a couple of good ceramicists working on Pantelleria, and shops at the harbour sell decent stuff. For local wines, capers, home-made marmalade, olive paste, preserved seaweed, pasta sauces and much more, visit Amil Patente, a store also marked "Prodotti locali", on Via Catania.
Taxi Call Consolo, Piazza Castello ☎ 0923.912.716.
Travel agencies Cossira, Via Borgo Italia 19 ☎ 0923.911.078 (for airline and Siremar tickets). Siremar tickets are also sold by Agenzia Rizzo, Via Borgo Italia 12 ☎ 0923.911.120; further along the harbour, the Air Sicilia office sells Ústica Lines hydrofoil tickets before every departure.

Around the island

Surprisingly, most of Pantelleria's population of 8500 are farmers rather than fishermen: with a soil nourished by frequent past eruptions (the last in 1831), the islanders traditionally preferred tilling to risking life and limb in a sea swarming with pirates on the prowl. There are, however, problems relating to farming in Pantelleria, not least the numerous chunks of lava and basalt in the earth that preclude mechanical ploughing, not to mention the incessant wind, scorching sun and almost complete lack of water. But the islanders have evolved methods of minimizing these disadvantages by some ingenious devices that would bring a gleam to an ecologist's eye. The prolific *zibbibo* vines are individually planted in little ridges designed to capture the precious rainwater; and the famous *giardini arabi* – high walls of stone built round orange trees and other plants – give protection from the wind and the salt it carries with it. All over the island, various **co-operatives** (often signposted from the road) sell local produce to visitors and locals – capers, wine, jojoba oil, honey and candles. If you want to buy, look for the words "*azienda agricola*".

Otherwise, it's a blackened landscape, thick with volcanic debris, in which the local **dammuso** houses, when whitewashed, provide some visual relief. Unembellished, these sombre cubic dwellings, unique to the island, blend in perfectly with their environment. These, too, are examples of technological adaptation, the thick walls and shallow-domed roofs designed to maintain a cool internal temperature, while ridges in the roofs catch the rain.

It's easy enough to get around the island by bus or bike, though to visit the isolated coves of the southeastern Dietro Ísola, and other good swimming spots, you'll need to **rent a boat**. There are notices in the agencies along the harbour, in every hotel, and on the boats themselves. If you don't want to navigate yourself, it's not hard to track down someone willing to give you a tour, though you'll get a better deal if you can get a small group together.

Along the southwest coast

There are seven daily buses along the **southwest coast** to both Scauri and Rekale. If you intend to walk any stretch of this, you're advised to take the bus first to Scauri (25min) and then walk back as far as the Sesi (see below), which, at a couple of hours or so, is more than enough for most people.

The route south of town is initially very unpromising, through an industrial wasteland of noisome and noisy factories, abandoned farmhouses and past a military barracks. Things pick up after a couple of kilometres at the **Cuddie Rosse**, volcanic red rocks that mark the site of a prehistoric cave settlement. There's nothing much to see, though the rocks are overlooked by the good-value *Cossyra Hotel* (℡0923.911.154, ℻0923.911.026; ❺), with a pool: half-board is obligatory in July and August (€70 per person).

Fifteen minutes' walk further on, a signposted track on the left leads up 300m to the first of the island's strange **Sesi**, massive black Neolithic funeral mounds of piled rock, with low passages leading inside; a second one lies further up to the left. They're thought to be products of Pantelleria's first settlers, possibly from Tunisia. The main one here is 6m high, a striking sight, completely at one with its lunar-like environment. There must have once been scores of these dotting the island, satisfying some primeval fears and beliefs. That so few survive is not so hard to understand when you take a look around at the regular-shaped stones from which the local *dammuso* houses are built – centuries of plunder have taken their toll.

Beyond the Sesi, at **Punta Fram**, the island's poshest resort, the *Club Village Punta Fram* (℡0923.918.075, ℻0923.918.244; June–Sept; ❽), has a tennis court, a fine outdoor swimming pool and steps leading down to its own little rocky cove, where you can swim happily. There's public access to the coast here, just back down the road a little way towards the Sesi; look for a footpath, marked "*Discesa a mare*", opposite a side road to a little tower.

On foot, it's just over an hour all told from the Sesi to **SATARIA**, where concrete steps lead down to a tiny square-cut sea-pool, ideal for splashing around in. In the cave behind are more pools where warm water bubbles through, reputed to be good for curing rheumatism and skin diseases: there's usually a handful of people jumping from pools to sea. There's room on the concrete apron around the pool to lay out a towel, and it's the only place for kilometres around with any shade; a nice place to eat your picnic.

From the port at **SCAURI**, 2km (30min on foot) further on, you can see Cape Mustafa in Tunisia on a clear day. There's a highly rated **restaurant** here, *Zabib* (℡0923.916.617), with a wide terrace right on the portside, though it's only open on summer evenings. The village itself is a steep twenty-minute walk above its harbour, and consists of no more than a minuscule church perched on a shelf of land, surrounded by a cluster of houses; there's a bakery and pharmacy, and an *alimentari* that does decent panini.

From here, the only other stop (and end of the bus line) is **REKALE**, an even smaller and more remote hamlet, beyond which the extensive southeastern segment of the island, the **Dietro Ísola**, curves round. There are more hot springs at **Punto Nikà**, which – although you can get there on foot – are more easily reached by boat.

The northeast coast

There are six daily buses along the northeast coast to both Kamma and Tracino, the latter village marking the end of the line, a 25-minute ride from town.

Very early on you'll pass **Bue Marino**, which, though not the most striking part of this coast, has reasonable swimming from the rocks, and accommodation in the shape of the *Turistico Residenziale* (℡0923.911.054, ℻0923.911.680; ❻), and *Bue Marino* (℡0923.912.715; June–Sept; ❺), whose eight self-contained studio apartments have sea-facing balconies, though rental is by the week only. The best swimming is actually a little further on, from the flat rocks below the road junction to Bugeber.

At the **Cala dei Cinque Denti**, fantastic-shaped rocks jut out of the sea like monstrous black teeth, hence its name, "Bay of the Five Teeth" – though the rocks are really best seen from the sea. Just beyond, a minor road cuts away to the lighthouse at **Punta Spadillo**, the cliff edges here covered with a carpet of surprising greenery that's somehow taken hold in the volcanic rocks.

There's a fork further on in the road, where the bus can drop you at the top of the smartly engineered route down into **GADIR**, one of the most perfect spots on Pantelleria. It's a small anchorage, with just a few houses hemmed in by volcanic pricks of rock, which – when the wind is up – can be battered and lashed by violent waves. At other times, people lay about on the flat concrete harbourside, splashing in the small thermal pools hereabouts.

The lower road from Gadir to Tracino is one of the loveliest on the island, along slopes that are terraced and corralled behind a patchwork of stone walls. Vines grow in profusion, with capers and blackberry bushes in the hedgerows. It's an easy, fairly flat hour's stroll to the charming **CALA LEVANTE**, a huddle of houses around another tiny fishing harbour. There's a bar here, the *Oasi* (erratic hours) and – provided the sea's not too rough – good swimming from the rocks. Where the road peters out, beyond the *Oasi*, bear right along the path at the second anchorage and keep along the coast for another five minutes until the **Arco dell'Elefante**, or "Elephant Arch", hoves into view, named after the lovely hooped formation of rock that resembles an elephant stooping to drink. Again there's no beach, but it's a good place to swim anyway.

From the harbour, a stupendously steep road climbs all the way up to **TRACINO** in around twenty minutes, passing old *dammusi*, newer holiday homes, and striking gardens of vines and flowers. The top of the road marks the centre of Tracino, where there's a small square, a bar-restaurant, and a parked van selling *tutto per la casa*. There's also a second **restaurant**, *I Mulini* (☎0923.915.398): ask for the *bacci* – waffles wedged together with cream and sugar. It's difficult to see where Tracino ends and adjacent **KAMMA** starts, though this matters little once you're on the bus back to town.

Keen **hikers** make Tracino the start of their route into the pretty **Piano Ghirlandia**. The road runs out the other side of Tracino and soon becomes a track, which continues all the way down to meet the road on the south coast near Rekale.

The Specchio di Vénere and Bugeber

From the first road junction on the northwest coast, it's a ten-minute walk up and around for the initial stunning views of the island's small lake, **Specchio di Vénere** (Venus Mirror), shimmering below in a former crater. It glistens aquamarine in the middle, though has a muddy-brown edge, deposits of which you're supposed to apply to your body and let bake hard in the sun; then dive in and swim, washing all the mud off in the pleasantly warm water. A path skirts the edge of the lake, around which horse races take place every August as part of the ferragosto celebrations.

There's a trattoria by the lake shore, *Da Pina*, beyond which the road climbs up for another 2km to the hamlet of **BUGEBER**, set amid tumbling fields of vines and craggy boulders. Just past the white chapel, another **trattoria**, the *Bugeber* (☎0923.914.009; closed Tues in winter), is signposted to the left – it's the house immediately on the left, with panoramic veranda views. The bus back to town runs past here twice a day; alternatively, walk the 3km past the lake back to the main road, where you can pick up any of the buses from Tracino.

Siba and the Montagna Grande

The other inland destination is up to Pantelleria's main volcano, the Montagna Grande, whose summit is the island's most distinctive feature seen from out at sea. Buses (4 daily) run from the port, turning sharp left past the airport for the crumbly old village of **SIBA**, perched on a ridge below the volcano, with views over the terraced slopes and cultivated plains to the sea. Few of the ancient *dammusi* here are so much as whitewashed, let alone bristling with mod cons; outside, large wooden water barrels sit on the mildewed dry-stone volcanic walls; while the hamlet's only services are an *alimentari* and a *tabaccaio*. If time hasn't exactly stood still here, it's in no great hurry to get on with things either.

To climb the peak of **Montagna Grande** (836m), keep left at the telephone sign by the *tabaccaio* here, and strike off the main road. The mountain's slopes afford the best views on the island, and are pitted by numerous volcanic vents, the **Stufe de Khazen**, marked by the escaping threads of vapour.

From Siba, another (signposted) path – on the left as you follow the road through the village – brings you in around twenty minutes to a natural sauna, **Sauna Naturale** (or Bagno Asciutto), where you can sweat it out for as long as you can stand. It's little more than a slit in the rock-face, where you can crouch in absolute darkness, breaking out into a heavy sweat as soon as you enter. It's coolest at floor-level; raising yourself up is like putting yourself into a pizza oven, while the ceiling is so hot it's impossible to keep the palm of your hand pressed flat against it. Ten minutes is the most you should attempt the first time – emerging into the midday sun is like being wafted by a cool breeze. Bring a towel.

The road through Siba degenerates into a track which descends back down towards the coast, midway between Scauri and Rekale, running through the so-called **Valle Monastero**. Even locals describe the road as "*brutissima*", but if you're carrying enough water, and tackling the hike early enough in the day, it's a lovely route, past the abandoned monastery that gives the valley its name.

Festivals

February
3 Festival of St Biagio in **Salemi**, with pasta figures given to children and a slippery-pole competition.

March
19 Festival of St Joseph at **Salemi**, with poetry recitals and sculptures of Jesus, Mary and Joseph made out of bread.

March/April
Good Friday Procession of the Misteri in **Trápani** and **Érice**.
Easter Thursday Enactment of the Passion in **Marsala**, in brightly jewelled processions with gorgeous finery.
Easter Sunday Symbolic meeting of statues of Christ and Mary in **Mazara del Vallo**.

May/June
La Mattanza tuna slaughter in **Favignana**, though check first with the tourist office in Favignana (see p.404).

June
19–21 Festival of Santa Maria dei Mirácoli at **Álcamo**, with a pilgrimage to Monte Bonifato.
29 Feast of SS Peter and Paul in **Pantelleria**.

July
Music festival in **Trápani** at the Villa Margherita.
10–13 Feast of the Three Maries in **Pantelleria**.

August
Festival of modern Italian art in **Marsala**.
15 Horse race around Specchio di Vénere lake in **Pantelleria**.

September
International couscous festival at **San Vito Lo Capo**.

December
24 Procession of characters from the Nativity story in **Salemi**.

Travel details

Trains

Castelvetrano to: Marsala (15 daily; 45min); Mazara del Vallo (15 daily; 20min); Palermo (7 daily; 2hr 15min); Trápani (15 daily; 1hr 10min).

Marsala to: Castelvetrano (15 daily; 45min); Mazara del Vallo (15 daily; 25min); Ragattisi (14 daily; 10min); Trápani (15 daily; 35min).

Mazara del Vallo to: Campobello di Mazara (14 daily; 10min); Castelvetrano (14 daily; 20min); Marsala (12 daily; 25min); Trápani (15 daily; 50min).

Trápani to: Álcamo (15 daily; 40min); Castelvetrano (10 daily; 1hr 10min); Marsala (10 daily; 35min); Mazara del Vallo (10 daily; 50min); Palermo (15 daily; 2hr–3hr 30min); Ragattisi (13 daily; 20min); Segesta-Tempio (3 daily; 20min).

Buses

Castellammare del Golfo to: Álcamo (12 daily Mon–Sat, 2 daily Sun; 25min); Calatafimi (3 daily Mon–Sat, 1 daily Sun; 30min); Palermo (9 daily; 1hr 30min); San Vito Lo Capo (2 daily Mon–Sat; 1hr); Scopello (4 daily Mon–Sat; 30min); Segesta (5 daily Mon–Sat; 30min); Trápani (4 daily Mon–Sat; 1hr).

Castelvetrano to: Agrigento (4 daily Mon–Sat; 2hr); Gibellina (6 daily Mon–Sat; 1hr); Marinella (for Selinunte, 5 daily Mon–Sat; 20min); Marsala (8 daily Mon–Sat; 55min–1hr 20min); Mazara del Vallo (8 daily Mon–Sat; 30min); Palermo (8 daily Mon–Sat, 2 daily Sun; 1hr 40min); Salemi (2 daily Mon–Sat; 35–45min); Sciacca (3 daily Mon–Sat, 1 daily Sun; 1hr 5min–1hr 40min); Trápani (8 daily Mon–Sat, 1 daily Sun; 1hr 15min–1hr 55min).

Érice to: Trápani (11 daily Mon–Sat, 4 daily Sun; 40–50 min).

Marinella/Selinunte to: Castelvetrano (summer 5–7 daily, fewer in winter; 20min).

Marsala to: Agrigento (3 daily Mon–Sat, 1 daily Sun; 3hr 25min); Castelvetrano (8 daily Mon–Sat; 45min–1hr 10min); Campobello (5 daily Mon–Sat; 55min); Mazara del Vallo (17 daily Mon–Sat, 2 daily Sun; 45min); Mózia (13 daily Mon–Sat, 4 daily Sun; 25min); Palermo (15–17 daily Mon–Sat, 5 daily Sun; 2hr 35min); Trápani (8 daily Mon–Sat; 55min).

Mazara del Vallo to: Agrigento (3 daily Mon–Sat, 1 daily Sun; 3hr); Marsala (approx hourly Mon–Sat, 2 daily Sun; 25min); Palermo (11 daily Mon–Sat, 2 daily Sun; 2hr); Trápani (7 daily Mon–Sat,; 1hr–1hr 30min).

Pantelleria Town to: Bugeber (2 daily Mon–Sat; 15min); Kamma (4 daily Mon–Sat; 20min); Rekale (4 daily Mon–Sat; 30min); Scauri (4 daily Mon–Sat; 25min); Siba (3 daily Mon–Sat; 20min); Tracino (4 daily Mon–Sat; 25min).

San Vito Lo Capo to: Palermo (winter 2 daily, summer 4 daily; 2hr–3hr); Trápani (7 Mon–Sat; 1hr 20min).

Scopello to: Castellammare del Golfo (4 daily Mon–Sat; 30min).

Trápani to: Álcamo (Mon–Sat 4 daily; 1hr–1hr 30min); Agrigento (3 daily Mon–Sat, 1 Sun; 2hr–3hr); Bonagia (9 daily Mon–Sat; 20min); Castellammare del Golfo (4 daily; 1hr); Castelvetrano (6 daily Mon–Sat; 1hr 30min); Érice (11 daily Mon–Sat, 4 daily Sun; 40–50min); Marsala (4 daily; 55min); Mazara del Vallo (3 daily; 1hr 30min); Palermo (hourly; 1hr 50min–2hr 10 min); Palermo airport (1 daily; 1hr 10min); San Vito Lo Capo (8 daily Mon–Sat, 4 daily Sun; 1hr 20min); Segesta (4 daily Mon–Sat, 2 daily Sun; 1hr).

Ferries

Pantelleria to: Trápani (1 daily; 5hr).

Trápani to: Cágliari (1 weekly; 10–11hr); Favignana (1 daily; 55min); Lévanzo (3 daily June–Sept, 1 daily Oct–May; 1hr 40min); Maréttimo (1 daily; 2hr 50min); Pantelleria (midnight daily June–Sept, midnight Mon–Sat Oct–May; 5hr 45min); Tunis (1–3 weekly; 7hr 30min).

Hydrofoils

Castellammare del Golfo to: Favignana (July & Aug 3 weekly; 1hr 30min);

Marsala to: Favignana (3 daily Oct–May, 5 daily June–Sept; 35min); Maréttimo (2 daily June–Sept;1hr 5min).

Pantelleria to: Trápani (June–Sept 1 daily; 2hr 10min–2hr 40min).

Trápani to: Favignana (approx hourly; 25min); Lévanzo (approx hourly; 20–35min); Maréttimo (3 daily; 1hr 5min); Naples (3 weekly June–Sept; 6hr 45min); Pantelleria (June–Sept 1 daily; 2hr 10min–2hr 40min); Ústica, via Lévanzo and Favignana (4 weekly June–Sept; 2hr 30min).

Planes

Pantelleria to: Palermo (1–2 daily; 40min); Trápani (1–3 daily; 30min).

Trápani to: Pantelleria (1–3 daily; 30min).

Contexts

Contexts

Sicily's history

Sicily has a richer and more eventful past than any of the other islands dotted around the Mediterranean. Its strategic importance made it the constant prey of conquerors, many of whom, while contributing a rich artistic heritage, also turned Sicily into one of the most desolate war zones in Europe, their greed utterly transforming its ecology and heaping misery onto the vast majority of its inhabitants.

Early times

There are numerous remains of the **earliest human settlements** in Sicily, left mainly along the coast by people originally from mainland Europe. The most interesting of these are the cave paintings in Addaura, on the northern face of Monte Pellegrino, and those in the Grotta del Genovese, on Lévanzo in the Égadi Islands, which give a graphic insight into late Ice Age **Paleolithic** culture, from between 20,000 and 10,000 BC.

In the later **Neolithic period**, between 4000 and 3000 BC, there was a new wave of settlers from the eastern Mediterranean, landing on Sicily's east coast and in the Aeolian Islands. Examples of their relatively advanced Stentinello culture – incised and patterned pottery and simple tools – are displayed in the museum on Lípari in the Aeolians. Agricultural advances, the use of ceramics and the domestication of animals, as well as the new techniques of metalworking imported by later waves of Aegean immigrants in the **Copper Age** (3000–2000 BC), permitted the establishment of fixed farms and villages. In turn, this caused an expansion of trade, and promoted greater contact with far-flung Mediterranean cultures. The presence of Mycenaean ware, from the Greek mainland, became more noticeable in the **Bronze Age** (2000–1000 BC), a period to which the sites of Capo Graziano and Punta Milazzese on the Aeolian Islands belong. In about 1250 BC, there were further population movements, this time from the Italian mainland: the Ausonians settled in the Aeolians, and the **Sikels** in eastern Sicily, pushing the indigenous tribes inland. It was the Sikels, from whom Sicily takes its name, who are thought to have first excavated the vast necropolis of Pantálica, near Siracusa. At about the same time, the Sicans, a people thought to have originated in North Africa, occupied the western half of the island. Not much more is known about another tribe in western Sicily, the **Elymians**, who claimed descent from Trojan refugees: their chief city, Segesta, was alleged to have been founded by Aeneas' companion, Acestes.

The Carthaginians and the Greeks

After about 900 BC, Mycenaean and Aegean trading contacts began to be replaced by **Carthaginian** ones from North Africa, particularly in the west of the island. The Carthaginians – originally Phoenicians from the eastern

Mediterranean – first settled at Panormus (modern Palermo), Solus (Solunto) and Motya (Mózia), during the eighth and seventh centuries BC, their arrival coinciding with the establishment of **Greek colonies** in the east of Sicily. As was the case in previous migrations, the Aegean Greeks who colonized Sicily's eastern coast were driven by a shortage of cultivable land back home. The first Greek settlements had already been made on the Italian mainland in Tuscany and around the bay of Naples, and the colonization of **Naxos** in 734 BC was undertaken primarily for strategic reasons. The possibilities for expansion soon became apparent and the Chalcidinians and Naxians who founded this colony were quickly followed by Megarians at **Megara Hyblaea**, north of Siracusa, Corinthians at **Ortygia** in Siracusa itself, and Rhodians, Cnidians and Cretans in **Gela**. These cities, while continuing to have close links with their original homes, became independent city-states and founded subcolonies of their own, most important of which were **Selinus** (Selinunte) and **Akragas** (Agrigento). Along with the Greek colonies on the Italian mainland, these scattered communities came to be known as Magna Graecia, "Greater Greece", whose wealth eventually overtook that of Greece itself.

The settlers found themselves with huge resources at their disposal, not least the island's fertility, which they quickly exploited through the widespread cultivation of corn – so much so that Demeter, the Greek goddess of grain and fecundity, became the chief deity on the island: the lake at Pergusa, near Enna, was claimed to be the site of the abduction of her daughter, Persephone. The olive and the vine were introduced from Greece, and commercial activity across the Ionian Sea was intense and profitable. The magnificence of the temples at Syracuse and Akragas often surpassed that of the major shrines in Greece. But the settlers also imported their native rivalries, and the history of Hellenic Sicily is one of almost uninterrupted warfare between the cities, although they generally joined forces in the face of common foes such as the Carthaginians. It was the alliance against Carthage of Gela, Akragas and Syracuse, and the resulting Greek victory at **Himera** in 480 BC, that determined the ascendancy of **Syracuse** in Sicily for the next 270 years. The defeat, in about 450 BC, of a rebellion led by **Ducetius**, a Hellenized Sikel, extinguished the remnants of any native resistance to Greek hegemony, and the following century has been hailed as the "Golden Age" of Greek Sicily.

The accumulation of power by Syracusan **tyrants** attracted the attention of the mainland Greek states; Athens in particular was worried by the rapid spread of Corinthian influence in Sicily. In 415 BC, Athens dispatched the greatest armada ever to have sailed from its port. Later known as the **Great Expedition**, the effort was in response to a call for help from its ally, Segesta, while at war with Syracuse-supported Selinus. By 413 BC Syracuse itself was under siege, but the disorganization of the attacking forces, who were further hampered by disease, led to their total defeat, the execution of their generals and the imprisonment of 7000 soldiers in Syracuse's limestone quarries, many of whom were destined for slavery. This victory represented the apogee of Syracusan power. Civil wars continued throughout the rest of the island, attracting the attention of the Carthaginian **Hannibal**, who responded to attacks on his territory by sacking in turn Selinus, Himera, Akragas and Gela. A massive counterattack was launched by the Syracusan tyrant **Dionysius I**, or "the Elder" (405–367 BC), which culminated in the complete destruction of the Phoenician base at Motya, its survivors founding a new centre on the western tip of the island at Lilybaeum – modern Marsala.

The general devastation in Sicily caused by these wars was to some extent reversed by **Timoleon** (345–336 BC), who rebuilt many of the cities and re-established democratic institutions with new injections of settlers from Italy and Greece. But the carnage continued under the tyrant **Agathocles** (315–289 BC), who was unrivalled in his sheer brutality. Battles were fought on the Italian mainland and North Africa, and the strife he engendered back in Sicily didn't end until **Hieron II** (265–215 BC) opted for a policy of peacekeeping, and even alliance, with the new power of the day, Rome. The **First Punic War** that broke out in 264 BC – when the mercenary army in control of Messina, the **Mamertines**, appealed to Rome for help against their erstwhile Carthaginian protectors – left Syracuse untouched, though again it led to the ruin of much of the island, before the final surrender of the Carthaginian base at Lilybaeum in 241. For Syracuse and its territories, though, this was a period of relative peace, and Hieron used the breathing space to construct some of the city's most impressive monuments.

Roman Sicily

Roman rule in Sicily can be said to have begun with **the fall of Syracuse**, a momentous event that became inevitable when the city, whose territory was by now the only part of Sicily still independent of Rome, chose to side with Carthage in the **Second Punic War**, provoking a two-year siege that ended with the sacking of Syracuse in 211 BC. For the next seven hundred years, Sicily was a province of Rome, though in effect a subject colony, since few Sicilians were granted citizenship until the third century AD, when all inhabitants of the Empire were classified as Romans. Much of the island's present appearance was determined during this period. Large parts of the remaining forests were cut down to make way for the grain cultivation that was to become Sicily's major function. The island was Rome's granary or, as Cato had it, "the nurse at whose breast the Roman people is fed". The land was apportioned into large units, or *latifondia*, which became the basis for the vast agricultural estates into which Sicily is still to a certain extent divided. Conditions on these estates were so harsh that the second century BC saw two **slave revolts**, in 135–132 BC and 104–101 BC, involving tens of thousands of men, women and children, most of whom had been Greek-speaking citizens from all over Rome's newly won Mediterranean and Asian empire. Far more damaging to the island, however, was the **civil war** between Octavian, the future Emperor Augustus, and Sextus Pompey, who seized Sicily in 44 BC. For eight years the island's crucial grain exports were interrupted, and the final defeat of Sextus – in a sea battle off Mylae, or Milazzo – was followed by harsh retribution against the island.

These were isolated incidents, however, and on the whole Sicily benefited from the relative calm bestowed by the Romans. But little of the heavy tribute exacted by Rome was expended on the island itself and, though a degree of local administration existed, all important decisions were taken by the Roman Senate. It was represented on the island by two tax collectors, or quaestors, stationed in Syracuse and Lilybaeum, and a governor (praetor), who normally spent his year-long term extracting as much personal profit from the island as he could. The praetor **Verres** used his three terms of office, from 73 to 71 BC, to strip the countryside and despoil a large part of the treasure still held in the island's lavish temples. **Cicero**'s prosecution of Verres, though undoubtedly exaggerated, constitutes our main source of information on Sicily under the

Roman Republic. It gives some idea of the extent of the ruination wreaked by the unscrupulous praetor: "When I arrived in Sicily after an absence of four years, it seemed to me a land in which there had been fought a prolonged and cruel war. Those fields and hills which I had seen bright and green I now saw devastated and deserted, and it seemed as if the land itself wept for its ancient farmers."

With Octavian instated as emperor in 27 BC, Sicily entered a more peaceful period of Roman rule, with isolated instances of imperial splendour, notably the extravagant villa at Casale, near Piazza Armerina. The island benefited especially from its important role in Mediterranean trade, and Syracuse, which handled much of the passing traffic, became a prominent centre of **early Christianity**, supposedly visited by SS Peter and Paul on their way to Rome. Here, and further inland at Akrai, catacombs were burrowed from the third century AD onwards – and in caves throughout Sicily, Christian sanctuaries took their place alongside the shrines of the dozens of other cults prevalent on the island.

Barbarians, Byzantines and the Arabs

Rome fell to the Visigoths in 410 AD, though Sicily became prey to another Germanic tribe, the **Vandals**, who launched their invasion from the North African coast. The island was soon reunited with Italy under the Ostrogoth Theodoric, though the barbarian presence in Sicily was only a brief interlude, terminated in 535 AD when the **Byzantine** general Belisarius occupied the island. Although a part of the population had been Latinized, Greek remained the dominant culture and language of the majority, and the island willingly joined the Byzantine fold. In 663, Syracuse even became the centre of the eastern empire for a short time, possibly for political reasons but no doubt partly with an eye to the reconquest of barbarian lands and the ultimate revival of the Roman Empire.

But Constantinople was never able to give much attention to Sicily, and the island was perpetually harried by piratical attacks, particularly from North Africa, where the Moors had become the most dynamic force in the Mediterranean. In around 700, the island of **Pantelleria** was taken, and it was only discord among the Arabs that prevented Sicily itself from being next. In the event, trading agreements were signed, Arab merchants settled in Sicilian ports, and it was not until 827 that a fully fledged **Arab invasion** took place, when a Byzantine admiral rebelled against the emperor and invited in the Aghlabid Emir of Tunisia. Ten thousand Arabs, Berbers and Spanish Muslims (known collectively as **Saracens**) landed at Mazara del Vallo, and four years later Palermo fell, though it wasn't until 965 that the invading forces reached the Straits of Messina. As with the Roman invasion, however, the turning point came with the fall of Syracuse in 878, its population massacred and the city plundered of its legendary wealth.

Palermo became the capital of the **Arabs in Sicily**, under whom it grew to become one of the world's greatest cities, wholly cosmopolitan in outlook, furnished with gardens, mosques (more than anywhere the traveller Ibn Hauqal had seen barring Cordoba) and luxurious palaces. The Arabs brought great benefits to the rest of the island, too, resettling rural areas, renovating and extending the irrigation works, breaking down many of the unwieldy *latifondia* and introducing new crops, including citrus trees, sugar cane, flax, cotton, silk, melons and date palms. Mining was developed, the salt industry greatly expanded and commerce improved, with Sicily once more at the centre of a flourishing trade network. Many Sicilian place names testify to the extent of the Arab settlement of the island, with prefixes such as *calta* (castle) and *gibil* (mountain) plentiful; while other terms still in use indicate their impact on fishing, such as the name of the swordfish boats prowling the Straits of Messina (*felucca*), or the tuna-fishing terminology of the Égadi Islands. Taxation was rationalized and reduced, and religious tolerance was greater than under the Byzantines, though non-Muslims were subject to a degree of social discrimina-tion – a factor that probably helped to persuade a large number of Christians to adopt the Muslim faith.

The Arabs were prone to divisive feuding, however, and when in the tenth century the Aghlabid dynasty was toppled in Tunisia and their Fatimid suc-cessors shifted their capital to Egypt, Sicily lost its central position in the Arab Mediterranean empire and was left vulnerable to external attack. In 1038, the Byzantine general **George Maniakes** attempted to draw the island back under Byzantine sway, but he was unable to extend his occupation much beyond Syracuse. The real threat came from western Europe, particularly from the **Normans**, some of whom had accompanied Maniakes and seen for them-selves the rewards to be gained. One of these, William "Bras de Fer" ("Iron Arm"), who had earned his nickname by his slaying of the Emir of Syracuse with one blow, was the eldest of the Hauteville brothers, whose exploits were soon to change the map of southern Europe.

The Normans

The **Hauteville brothers** had long been active in southern Italy by the time the youngest of them, Roger, seized Messina in 1061 in response to a call for help by one of the warring Arab factions. It took another thirty years to take control of the whole island, in a series of bloody and destructive campaigns that often involved the enlistment of Arabs on the Norman side. In 1072 Palermo was captured and adopted as the capital of **Norman Sicily**, and was subsequently adorned with palaces and churches that count among their most brilliant achievements.

The most striking thing about the Norman period in Sicily is its brief span. In little more than a century, five kings bequeathed an enormous legacy of art and architecture that is still one of the most conspicuous features of the island. When compared with the surviving remains of the Byzantines, who reigned for three centuries, or the Arabs, whose occupation lasted roughly two, the Norman contribution stands out, principally due to its absorption of previous styles: the best examples of Arab art to be seen in Sicily are elements incorporated into the great Norman churches. It was this fusion of talent that accounted for the great success of Norman Sicily, not just in the arts but in administration, justice and religious tolerance.

The policy of acceptance and integration was largely determined by force of circumstances: the Normans could not count on having adequate numbers of their own settlers, or bureaucrats to form a governmental class, and instead were compelled to rely on the existing framework. They did, however, considerably streamline and centralize administration, and gradually introduced a Latinized aristocracy and clerical hierarchy from northern Italy and France, so that the Arabic language was largely superseded by Italian and French by 1200.

The first of the great Sicilian-Norman dynasty, **Count Roger**, or Roger I, sustained his power in accordance with Byzantine notions of absolutism and through his retention of a permanent mercenary army and strong fleet. He was a resolute and successful ruler, marrying his daughters into two of the most powerful European dynasties, one of them to the son of the western emperor Henry IV. Roger's death in 1101, followed soon after by the death of his eldest son, left Sicily governed by his widow Adelaide as regent for his younger son, who in 1130 was crowned **Roger II**. This first Norman king of Sicily was also one of medieval Europe's most gifted and charismatic rulers, who consolidated his father's gains by making the island a great melting pot of the most vigorous and creative elements in the Mediterranean world. He spoke Greek, kept a harem and surrounded himself with a medley of advisers, notably **George of Antioch**, his chief minister, or Emir of Emirs. As well as being a patron of the arts, Roger extended his kingdom to encompass all of southern Italy, Malta and parts of North Africa, and more enduringly drew up the first written code of law in the island.

His son, William I (1154–1166) – "**William the Bad**" – dissipated these achievements by his enthusiasm for pleasure-seeking and his failure to control the barons, who exploited racial tensions to undermine the king's authority. During the regency that followed, the Englishman Walter of the Mill had himself elected Archbishop of Palermo and dominated the scene for some twenty years, along with two other Englishmen: his brother Bartholomew and Bishop Palmer. This triumvirate preserved a degree of stability, but also encouraged the new king William II (1166–1189), "**William the Good**", to establish a second archbishopric and construct a cathedral at **Monreale** to rival that of Palermo, just 10km away. The period saw a general consolidation of Christianity and a shift away from Muslim influence, though Arabs still constituted the bulk of the rural population and William himself resembled an oriental sultan in his style and habits, building a number of Arab-style palaces.

The death of William, aged only 36 and with no obvious successor, signalled a crisis in Norman Sicily. The barons were divided between **Tancred**, William's illegitimate nephew, and **Constance**, Roger II's aunt who had married the Hohenstaufen (or Swabian) Henry, later to become the emperor Henry VI. Tancred's election by an assembly was the first sign of a serious erosion of the king's authority: others followed, notably a campaign in 1189 against Muslims living on the island, which caused many of them to flee; and a year later the sacking of **Messina** by the English Richard I, on his way to join the Third Crusade. Tancred's death in 1194 and the succession of his young son, **William III**, coincided with the arrival in the Straits of Messina of the Hohenstaufen fleet. Opposition was minimal, and on Christmas Day of the same year Henry crowned himself king of Sicily. William and his mother were imprisoned in the castle at **Caltabellotta**, never to be seen again.

Hohenstaufen and the Angevins

Inevitably, Henry's imperial concerns led him away from Sicily, which represented only a source of revenue for him on the very outer limits of his domain. A revolt broke out against his authoritarian rule, which he repressed with extreme severity, but in the middle of it he went down with dysentery, died, and the throne passed to his three-and-a-half-year-old son, who became the emperor Frederick II, **Frederick I** of Sicily.

At first the running of the kingdom was entrusted to Frederick's mother Constance, but there was little stability, with the barons in revolt and a rash of race riots in 1197. Frederick's assumption of the government in 1220 marked a return to decisive leadership, with an immediate campaign to bring the barons to heel and eliminate a Muslim rebellion in Sicily's interior. The twin aims of his rule in Sicily were to restore the broad framework of the Norman state, and to impose a more authoritarian and imperial stamp on society, indicated by his fondness for classical Roman allusions in his promulgations and coinage. He allowed himself rights and privileges in Sicily that were impossible in his other possessions, emphasizing his own authority at the expense of the independence of the clergy and the autonomy of the cities. As elsewhere in southern Italy, strong **castles** were built, such as those at Milazzo, Catania, Siracusa and Augusta, to keep the municipalities in check. When the most progressive of these, Messina, rebelled in 1232, the port was ruthlessly punished.

A unified legal system was drawn up, embodied in his *Liber Augustales*, while his attempts to homogenize Sicilian society involved the harsh treatment of what had now become minority communities, such as the Muslims. He encouraged the arts, too, championing Sicilian vernacular poetry, whose pre-eminence was admitted by Petrarch and Dante. A multitalented ruler, Frederick acquired the name "**Stupor Mundi**" ("Wonder of the World"), reflecting his promotion of science, law and medicine, and the peace that Sicily enjoyed during the half-century of his rule.

However, Frederick's mounting preoccupation with his other territories was to the detriment of the island. The balance of power he achieved within Sicily laid the foundations for many of the island's future woes – for example, the weakening of the municipalities at a time when most European towns were increasing their autonomy. His centralized government worked so long as there was a powerful hand guiding it, but when Frederick died in 1250, decline set in, despite the efforts of his son **Manfred**, who strove to defend his crown from the encroachments of the barons and the acquisitiveness of foreign monarchs. New claimants to the throne were egged on by Sicily's nominal suzerain, the pope, anxious to deprive the Hohenstaufen of their southern possession, and he eventually auctioned it, selling it to the king of England, who accepted it on behalf of his 8-year-old son, Edmund of Lancaster. For ten years Edmund was styled "King of Sicily".

But a new French pope deposed Edmund, who had never set foot in Sicily, and gave the title instead to **Charles of Anjou**, brother of the French king, "St" Louis IX. In 1266 the Angevin forces beat the Hohenstaufen army in a battle on the Italian mainland, in which Manfred was slain, and in 1268 another battle resulted in Manfred's 14-year-old nephew, his heir Conradin, being publicly beheaded. Backed by the papacy and with a degree of popular support, Charles of Anjou embarked on a punitive campaign against the majority of the Sicilian population, who had supported the Hohenstaufen, plundering land to give to his followers and imposing a high level of taxation to recoup the cost of the recent war. The nobility, too, were affected by Charles's draconian measures and some began negotiating with the Ghibelline anti-papal faction in Aragon, where the king, Peter, had become the champion of the Hohenstaufen cause by marrying Manfred's daughter. But in the end it was a grassroots revolt that sparked off the **Sicilian Vespers**, an uprising against the French that began on

Easter Monday 1282; it is traditionally held to have started after the bell for evening services, or Vespers, had rung at Palermo's church of Santo Spirito. The incident that sparked it all off was an insult to a woman by a French soldier, which led to a general slaughter in Palermo, soon growing into an island-wide rebellion against the French. It was the one moment in Sicilian history when the people rose up as one against foreign oppression – though in reality it was more an opportunity for horrific butchery and the settlement of old scores than a glorious expression of patriotic fervour.

The movement was given some direction when a group of nobles enlisted the support of Peter of Aragon, who landed at Trápani five months after the initial outbreak of hostilities and was acclaimed king at Palermo a few days later. The ensuing **Wars of the Vespers**, fought between Aragon and the Angevin forces based in Naples, lasted for another 21 years, mainly waged in Spain and at sea, while, in Aragonese Sicily, people settled down to over five centuries of Spanish domination.

The Spanish in Sicily

Sicily's new orientation towards Spain and its severance from mainland Italy meant that it was largely excluded from all the great European developments of the fourteenth and fifteenth centuries. There was no liberation from feudalism, and little impact was made by the Renaissance. Rather, the feudal bonds were reinforced at the expense of social mobility, with the granting of large portions of land to a Spanish aristocracy in return for military service, while intellectual life on the island was suffocated by the strictures of the Spanish Inquisition.

Although Peter of Aragon insisted that the two kingdoms of Aragon and Sicily should be ruled by separate kings after his death, his successor James ignored this and even reopened negotiations with the Angevins to sell the island back to them. His younger brother Frederick, appointed by James as Lieutenant of Palermo, convened a "parliament", which elected him king of an independent Sicily as **Frederick II** (1296–1337). As a result of the barons' support for him, Frederick was obliged to increase their feudal privileges, to the detriment of his own. Factions arose, growing out of the friction between Angevin and Aragonese supporters and fuelled by Angevin Naples. Open warfare followed until 1372, when the independence of Sicily – or Trinacria ("three-cornered"), as it was known under the terms of the subsequent treaty, an ancient name revived to distinguish the island from the mainland Regnum Siciliae, ruled by the kingdom of Naples – was guaranteed by Naples in return for an annual tribute and the recognition of the suzerainty of the pope.

It was the populace that suffered most from this feuding, since the policy of both sides was to avoid pitched battles and strike instead at the food sources in the country. This, combined with the effects of the Black Death, led to the interior of Sicily becoming depopulated and unproductive. The feudal nobility spent time mainly in the **towns**, and here at least there is some evidence of wealth in the mansions constructed during this period, in the **Chiaramonte** or the later, richly ornate **Catalan-Gothic** styles. A tradition of artistic patronage grew up, though most of the artists operating in Sicily came from elsewhere – for example, Francesco Laurana and the Gagini family were originally from northern Italy. A notable exception was **Antonello da**

Messina (1430–1479), who soaked up the latest Flemish techniques on his continental travels. With the closing off of the eastern Mediterranean by the Ottoman Turks in the fifteenth century, Sicily was isolated from everywhere except Spain – from which, after 1410, it was ruled directly. The ports of Palermo and Messina continued to do a certain amount of business, but most of the merchants were from Genova, Pisa and Lucca. Sicily found itself on the very fringes of Europe, an Aragonese outpost in the firing line from Turkish incursions and raids from North Africa. The unification of Castile and Aragon in 1479, followed soon after by the reconquest of the whole Spanish peninsula from the Moors, meant that Sicily's importance to its Spanish monarchs declined even more, and the island soon became of most use as a source of cash, crucial for the financing of the Reconquista and the wars against the Turks.

Although **Alfonso II** (1416–1458) made the island the base for his expansion to Naples, the two territories were separated again after his death, and Sicily came under the rule of a succession of **viceroys**, who were to wield power for the next four hundred years. Few of these were Sicilian (none at all after the first fifty years), while the only Spanish king to visit the island during the whole viceregal period was Charles V, on his way back from a Tunisian crusade in 1535.

Little else of note happened in the **sixteenth century**, though the curse of piracy was partially removed by the victory of the combined fleets of Spain, Venice and the Vatican against the Ottomans in 1571, at the Battle of Lépanto. But with the Spanish centres of power removed from the Mediterranean, and mercantile and imperial interest focused instead on the Atlantic, the period saw the utter **stagnation** of Sicily. The island's close bond to Spain meant that its degeneration deepened alongside Spain's decline in the **seventeenth and eighteenth centuries**. The aristocracy maintained their power and privileges while they were being eroded everywhere else in Europe, and corruption thrived in the viceroy's court, with offices being bought and sold and political patronage the order of the day. Throughout this period, Sicily still had a parliament, though it was largely symbolic. More far-reaching was the influence of **the Church**, one of the main pillars of the State and mainly non-Sicilian at its highest levels. This was bolstered by the wide powers of **the Inquisition**, both institutions playing a great part in creating and enforcing a sense of loyalty to, and even veneration of, the Spanish Crown, though the overall effect was a docile acceptance of the status quo on the part of Sicilians. Certainly there were few serious attempts at rebellion during this period, apart from a couple of isolated and short-lived uprisings in Sicily's two major towns, Palermo and Messina. There were, too, occasional revolts against the excesses of the zealous Inquisition, though on the whole discontent manifested itself in a resort to **brigandage**, for which the forest and wild *maquis* of Sicily's interior provided an ideal environment. The mixed fear and respect that the brigand bands generated played a large part in the future formation of an organized criminal class in Sicily.

Already burdened by the ever-increasing taxes demanded by Spain to finance its remote religious conflicts (principally, the 1618–1648 Thirty Years' War), the misery of the Sicilians was compounded by sporadic outbreaks of **plague**, and at the end of the seventeenth century by two appalling natural disasters. The **eruption of Etna** in 1669 devastated a large part of the area around Catania, while the **earthquake** of 1693 – also in the east of the island – flattened whole cities, killing around five percent of the island's population. These disasters did at least provide an opportunity for Sicilian craftsmen to show off the latest

Baroque building techniques when called upon to repair the damage. With the death of Charles II of Spain in 1700 and the subsequent Wars of the Spanish Succession, the island once more took a back seat to mainland European interests, was bartered in the **Treaty of Utrecht** that negotiated the peace, and given to the northern Italian House of Savoy, only to be swapped for Sardinia and given to Austria seven years later.

The **Austrian government** of the island – as usual administered through viceroys – lasted only four years, cut short by the arrival of another Spaniard, Charles of Bourbon, who claimed the throne of the Two Sicilies (the title of the combined southern Italian possessions of the Spanish and Bourbon kings of Naples) for himself. Though he never visited Sicily again after his first landing, **Charles III** (1734–1759) brought a refreshingly constructive air to the island's administration, showing a more benevolent attitude towards his new subjects, to whom he granted significant tax concessions. But, with his succession to the Spanish throne in 1759 and the inheritance of the Neapolitan crown by his son, **Ferdinand IV**, it was back to the bad old days. Any meagre attempts at reform made by his viceroys were opposed at every turn by the reactionary aristocracy, who were closing ranks in response to the progress of the Enlightenment and the ideas unleashed by the French Revolution. In the ensuing **Napoleonic Wars** which wracked Europe, Sicily, along with Sardinia, was the only part of Italy unconquered by Napoleon, while the Neapolitan *ancien régime* was further buttressed by the decision of Ferdinand (brother-in-law of Marie Antoinette) to wage war against the revolutionary French. He was supported in this by the British, who sustained the Bourbon state, so that when Ferdinand and his court were forced to flee Naples in 1799 it was **Nelson**'s flagship they sailed in, accompanied by the British ambassador to Naples, Sir William Hamilton, and his wife Lady Emma. Nelson was rewarded for his services by the endowment of a large estate at Bronte, just west of Etna.

Four years later, Ferdinand was able to return to Naples, though he had to escape again in 1806 when Napoleon gave the Neapolitan crown to his brother Joseph. This time he had to stay longer, remaining in Palermo until after the defeat of Napoleon in 1815 – a stay that was accompanied by a larger contingent of British troops and a heavy involvement of British capital and commerce. **Liberalism** became a banner of revolt against the king's continuing tax demands, and Ferdinand's autocratic reaction provoked the British commander William **Bentinck** to intervene. Manoeuvring himself into a position where he was the virtual governor of Sicily, Bentinck persuaded the king to summon a new parliament and adopt a **constitution** whereby the independence of Sicily was guaranteed and feudalism abolished.

Although this represented a drastic break with the past, the reforms had little direct effect on the peasantry, and, following the departure of the British, the constitution was dropped soon after Ferdinand's return to the mainland. He now styled himself "Ferdinand I, King of the Two Sicilies" and repealed all the reforms previously introduced. Renewed talk of independence in Sicily spilled over into action in 1820, when a rebellion was put down with the help of Austrian mercenaries. The **repression** intensified after Ferdinand I's death in 1825, and the island's fortunes reached a new low under Ferdinand II (1830–59), nicknamed Re Bomba for his five-day **bombardment of Messina** following major insurrections there and in Palermo in 1848–49. Another uprising in Palermo in 1860 proved a spur for Garibaldi to pick Sicily as the starting point for his unification of Italy.

Unification and two world wars

On May 11, 1860, five weeks after the Palermo revolt, **Giuseppe Garibaldi**, a professional soldier and one of the leading lights of **Il Risorgimento**, the movement for Italian unification, landed at Marsala with a thousand men, with whom he intended to liberate the island from Bourbon rule, in the name of the Piedmont House of Savoy. His skill in guerrilla warfare, backed by an increasingly cooperative peasantry, ensured that the campaign progressed with astonishing speed. Four days after disembarking, he defeated 15,000 Bourbon troops at **Calatafimi**, closely followed by an almost effortless occupation of Palermo. A battle at **Milazzo** in July decided the issue: apart from Messina (which held out for another year), Sicily was free of Spain for the first time since Peter of Aragon acquired the crown in 1282.

A **plebiscite** was held in October, which returned a 99.5 percent majority in favour of union with the new kingdom of Italy under Vittorio Emanuele II. The result, greeted by general euphoria, marked the end of Garibaldi's five-month dictatorship, and the official **annexation** of the island to the Kingdom of Savoy. Later, however, many began to question whether anything had been achieved by this change of ruler. The new **parliamentary system**, in which only one percent of the island's population was eligible to vote, made few improvements for the majority of people, with political patronage, as ever, determining voting tendencies. Attempts at opposition – and local uprisings such as that at Palermo in 1866 – were met with ruthless force, sanctioned by a distant and misinformed government convinced that the island's problems were fundamentally ones of law and order. Sicilians responded with their traditional defence of *omertà*, or silent non-cooperation, along with a growing **resentment** of the new Turin government (transferred to Rome in 1870) that was even stronger than their distrust of the more familiar Bourbons.

A series of reports made in response to criticism of the Italian government's failure to solve what was becoming known as "**the southern problem**" found that the lot of the Sicilian peasant was, if anything, worse after Unification than it had been under the Bourbons. Power had shifted away from the landed gentry to the *gabellotti*: the middlemen to whom they leased the land. These men became increasingly linked with the **Mafia**, a shadowy, loosely knit criminal association that found it easy to manipulate voting procedures, while simultaneously posing as defenders of the people. Everywhere, liberal programmes of reform were similarly subverted by the deep-rooted power relationships of the rural society onto which they had been grafted. But at the end of the nineteenth century a new, more organized opposition appeared on the scene in the form of **fasci** – embryonic trade-union groups demanding legislation to protect peasants' interests. Violence erupted and, when landowners called for repressive measures, the Italian prime minister, **Francesco Crispi** – a native Sicilian who had been one of the pioneers of the Risorgimento – dispatched a fleet and 30,000 soldiers to put down the "revolt", making use of an armoury of autocratic measures in the process, such as closing newspapers, censoring postal services and detaining suspects without trial. But, just as rashly, he soon followed repression with a radical series of reforms designed to effect a fairer and more efficient distribution of the land. These proposals, and others to grant partial autonomy to the region, were rejected by conservative Sicilians, who complained of interference in their affairs.

Although there were some signs of progress by the **end of the nineteenth century**, in the formation of worker co-operatives and in the enlightened land-reform programmes of individuals such as **Don Sturzo**, mayor of Caltagirone, the overwhelming despair of the peasantry was expressed in **mass emigration**. Despite their intimate attachment to the land and their close-knit family structure, one and a half million Sicilians decided to leave in the years leading up to 1914, most going to North and South America. Many of these were people who had been left homeless in the wake of the great **Messina earthquake** of 1908, in which upwards of 80,000 lost their lives. The high rate of emigration was a crushing indictment of the state of affairs on the island, though it had many positive effects for those left behind, who became the beneficiaries of huge remittances sent back from abroad and of the wage increases that resulted from labour shortages.

But any advantages were offset by Italy's military adventures. The **conquest of Libya** in 1912 was closely followed by **World War I**, and both were heavy blows to the Sicilian economy. In 1922 **Mussolini** gained power in Rome – largely without Sicilian support – and dispatched **Cesare Mori** to solve "the southern problem" by putting an end to the Mafia. Free of constitutional and legal restrictions, Mori was able to imprison thousands of suspected *mafiosi*. But the effect was only to drive the criminal class deeper underground, while the alliance he forged with the landed classes to help bring this about dissolved all the gains that had been made against the ruling elite, setting back the cause of agrarian reform. In the **1930s** Mussolini's African concerns and his drive for economic and agricultural self-sufficiency gave Sicily a new importance for Fascist Italy, the island now vaunted as "the geographic centre of the empire". In the much-publicized "**Battle for Grain**", wheat production increased, though at the cost of the diversity of crops that Sicily required, resulting in soil exhaustion and erosion. Mussolini's popularity on the island is best illustrated by his order, in 1941, that all Sicilian-born officials be transferred to the mainland, on account of their possible disloyalty.

In **World War II**, Sicily was the first part of Europe to be invaded by the Allies, when, in July 1943, Patton's American Seventh Army landed at Gela and Montgomery's British Eighth Army came ashore between Pachino and Pozzallo further east. This combined army of 160,000 men was the biggest ever seen in Sicily, but the campaign was longer and harder than had been anticipated, with the Germans mainly concerned with delaying the advance until they had moved most of their men and equipment over the Straits of Messina. Few Sicilian towns escaped **aerial bombardment**, with Messina itself the most heavily bombed of all Italian cities before it was taken on August 18.

Modern times

The **aftermath** of the war saw the most radical changes in Sicily since Unification, and a series of intense and convoluted struggles between competing interests. With anarchy and hunger widespread, a wave of banditry and crime was unleashed, while the **Mafia** were reinstated in their behind-the-scenes role as adjudicators and power-brokers, now allied to the landowners in the face of large-scale land occupations by a desperate peasantry. **Separatism** became a potent rallying cry for protesters of all persuasions, who believed that Sicily's ills could best be solved by cutting its links with the mainland, and a Separatist army was formed, financed by some of the gentry, though lacking the organization or resources to make any great impact. It was largely in response to this call for independence that, in 1946, Sicily was granted **regional autonomy**, with its own assembly and president – its status comparable to that of Scotland in the UK. The same year saw the declaration of a republic in Italy, the result of a popular mandate.

Autonomy failed to heal the island's divisions, however, and brute force was used by the Mafia and the old gentry against what they perceived as the major threat to their position – **communism**. The most famous bandit of the time, **Salvatore Giuliano**, who had previously been associated with the Separatists, was enlisted in the anti-communist cause, organizing a campaign of bombings and assassinations, most notoriously at the 1947 May Day celebrations at **Portella della Ginestra**, a mountain pass near Palermo. Giuliano's betrayal and murder in 1950 was widely rumoured to have been carried out to prevent him revealing who his paymasters were, though it all helped to glorify his reputation in the popular imagination.

By the **1950s**, many saw the **Christian Democrat** party, Democrazia Cristiana, as the best hope to defend their interests. Along with the emotional hold it exerted by virtue of its close association with the Church, the DC could draw on many of the Sicilians' deepest fears of change. It became especially important after **Fanfani**'s revitalization of the party after 1954, with Sicily holding about a third of his supporters country-wide. But the party was too closely involved with business and the land-owning classes to have any real enthusiasm for reform. All attempts at enterprise were channelled through the party's offices, and favours were bought or bartered. Cutting across party lines, political patronage, or **clientelismo**, grew to be stronger than ever, still affecting people's lives on all levels today, especially in the field of work – from finding a job to landing a contract. The favours system was also evident in the workings of the island's sluggish **bureaucracy**, considered even more contorted than the mainland's, so that the smallest reforms proved complicated to put into practice, often taking years to effect. In 1971 a law was passed to improve the functioning of the bureaucracy, but, though progress has been made, the essential problem is unchanged, with the elaborate machinery of the civil service often exploited to accumulate and dispense personal power.

One area that managed to avoid bureaucratic control or planning of any sort was **construction** – one of Sicily's greatest growth industries, the physical evidence of which is one of the visitor's most enduring impressions of the island. The building boom was inextricably connected with the Mafia's involvement in land speculation, and boosted by the phenomenal rate of **urban growth** all over Sicily. But in both the towns and rural areas, the minimum safety standards were rarely met, as highlighted by the **1968 earthquake**, in which 50,000 were made homeless along the Valle di Belice in the west of the island, although the quake was seismically quite small. But, while large expanses of the countryside have been blighted by rapid and often unsafe development, other areas are badly neglected, for instance Palermo, where, in some areas, bomb damage is still unrepaired after more than fifty years, though recent years have seen marked improvements.

Industry, too, has been subject to mismanagement, and, apart from isolated cases, has rarely fulfilled the potential it promised after the discovery of oil near Ragusa and Gela in the 1950s, and the development of refineries and petrochemical plants on the Golfo di Augusta. Despite the huge resources allocated to them, other projects have failed miserably. **Agriculture**, on the other hand, has been deprived of both funds and attention, though investment and the better use of land can produce outstanding results, as shown by the success of citrus cultivation in the north and east of the island, and the draining of the Piana di Catania. Substantial subsidies have helped in these programmes, mainly through a financial agency called the Cassa del Mezzogiorno, set up in 1950 but discontinued in 1983, and from the **European Union**, which Italy joined in 1958.

Subsidy and support, meanwhile, have not prevented Sicilians from complaining of being left out of Italy's great "economic miracle". While Italy claims to be in the "top ten" of western economies, it is the great urban centres in the north that flaunt their prosperity, while the south of Italy, known as Il Mezzogiorno, is left far behind. The other side of the coin is that the huge financial concessions made to the island have provoked resentment from Italy's more self-sufficient regions, for whom the failure of land-reform programmes and industrial development is chiefly due to corruption and incompetence in the island itself. Few Sicilians would wholly deny this; a longer view, however, points to Sicily's disadvantages being derived principally from the past misuse of resources, coupled with a culture and mentality that have never given much credence to collectivist ideals. But **progress** has been made, and the manifold increase of per capita income in the last fifty years is reflected in greater numbers of newer and bigger cars jamming the island's roads every year, while laws passed relating to land distribution and reform of the bureaucracy show a greater commitment to change. There is more awareness, too, on the part of the state that the fight against **organized crime** requires more than moralistic speeches. Indeed, in **1992**, following the murders of anti-Mafia investigators Falcone and Borsellino (see p.455), the Chief of Police of Palermo was sacked, while 7000 troops were sent to the island to patrol prisons and search towns with a known Mafia presence. There have been significant breakthroughs, though these are mostly connected with a change in the public attitude towards criminality, resulting in part from a campaign to reform Sicily's dilapidated **education** system, itself often a victim of Mafia corruption. In the 1990s, a campaign of anti-Mafia education began in Sicilian schools, with the aim of cutting the secondary-school drop-out rate, still reaching over forty percent in some regions, by encouraging children away from the traditional path of corruption, crime and Mafia involvement.

But despite such superficial improvements, the deep problems that have always bedevilled Sicily remain in some form. Unemployment, still high at fifteen to twenty percent, is not helped by the fewer outlets available for **emigration**, though a million still managed to escape the island between 1951 and 1971, along with the majority of Sicily's most outstanding artists and writers. Ironically, the late 1990s saw the problem of **immigration** hitting the agenda for the first time in several centuries, as economic refugees from North Africa arrive by regular boatloads on the island's southern littoral, particularly the two southernmost islands of Lampedusa and Pantelleria. The *extracomunitari* (literally, "those from non-EU countries") are routinely rounded up and sent to crowded processing centres, where they languish for months, almost all eventually being returned to their countries of origin. Others slip through and join the already strained jobs market. Harsh anti-immigration legislation introduced by **Silvio Berlusconi**'s right-wing Forza Italia! party, has resulted in a forty percent drop in illegal immigrants landing on Italian shores in recent years, but it remains to be seen whether the trend will continue.

Berlusconi, who came to power in 1994 and again in 2001 – the second time, surprisingly, with the backing of the majority of Sicilians – has divided the island with his proposal for a 3km-long **bridge** across the Straits of Messina connecting Sicily to the Italian mainland. The multibillion-euro construction project, scheduled to begin in late 2005, would doubtless profit the Mafia, but ordinary Sicilians are divided on whether the island itself would reap any benefit. In the long run, perhaps the greatest hope for Sicily lies in the exploitation of **tourism**: the annual deluge of mainly French, Swiss and Germans is growing in numbers and impact, while more and more Italians are discovering the island's holiday potential, especially its outdoor attractions and wildlife – though the benefits for the island are chiefly concentrated in specific areas so that most Sicilians are missing out.

The Mafia in Sicily

I n Sicily, there is "mafia" and there is "the Mafia". Mafia refers to a criminal mentality, the Mafia to a specific criminal organization. In Italy's deep south, where a man can look mafioso, or talk like a mafioso, meaning he has the aura, or stench, of criminality about him, mafia values are woven into the very fabric of society. The Mafia, on the other hand, operates outside society, and even transcends state boundaries. And, while notions of family solidarity and the moral stature of the outlaw mean that mafia can never be completely extirpated from Sicilian society, the Mafia is an entity whose members can be eliminated and its power emasculated.

What has always prevented this from happening is the shadowy nature of the organization, protected by the long-standing **code of silence**, or *omertà*, that invariably led to accusations being retracted at the last moment, or to crucial witnesses being found dead with a stone, cork or a wad of banknotes stuffed into their mouths, or else simply disappearing off the face of the earth. As a result, many have doubted the very existence of the Mafia, claiming that it's nothing more than the creation of pulp-thriller writers, the invention of a sensationalist press and the fabrication of an Italian government embarrassed by its inability to control an unusually high level of crime in Sicily.

But in 1982, proof of the innermost workings of the Mafia's organization emerged when a high-ranking member, **Tommaso Buscetta**, was arrested in Brazil, and – after a failed suicide attempt – agreed to prise open the can of worms. His reason for daring this sacrilege, he claimed, was to destroy the Mafia. In its stampede to grab the huge profits to be made from the international heroin industry, the "Honoured Society" (La Società Onorata) had abandoned its original ideals: "It's necessary to destroy this band of criminals", he declared, "who have perverted the principles of Cosa Nostra and dragged them through the mud." He was doubtlessly motivated by revenge: all of those he incriminated – Michele Greco, Pippo Calò, Benedetto Santapaola, Salvatore Riina and many others – were leaders of, or allied to, the powerful Corleone family who had recently embarked on a campaign of terror to monopolize the drugs industry, in the process eliminating seven of Buscetta's closest relatives in the space of four months, including his two sons.

The background

Buscetta's statements to Giovanni Falcone, head of Sicily's anti-Mafia "pool" of judges, and later to the Federal Court in Manhattan, were the most important revelations about the **structure** of Cosa Nostra since Jo Valachi – a prominent member of the New York Genovese family – provided the first inside view in 1962. Mafia "families" are centred on areas, he revealed: villages or quarters of cities from which they take their name. The boss (*capo*) of each group is chosen by election, and appoints a lieutenant (*sottocapo*) and one or more *consiglieri*, or counsellors. Larger groups also have officers known as *capodecini*, each in command of ten men. Above the families is the *cupola*, or **Commission**, a governing body that includes representatives from all the major groupings. Democracy and collective interest, Buscetta claimed, had been replaced in the Commission by the greed and self-interest of the individuals who had gained control. Trials of strength alone now decided the leadership, often in the form of bitter feuds between rival factions – or *cosche* (literally, "artichokes", their form symbolizing solidarity).

The existence of the Commission sets the Mafia apart from the normal run of underworld gangs, for without a high level of organization the international trafficking in heroin which they engage in would be inconceivable. The route is a circuitous one, starting in the Middle and Far East, moving on to the processing plants in Sicily, and ending up in New York, where American Mafia channels are said to control sixty percent of the heroin market. This multimillion-dollar racket – known in the US as the "**Pizza Connection**", because Sicilian pizza parlours were used as covers for the operation – was blown apart chiefly as a result of Buscetta's evidence, and led to the trial and conviction of the leading members of New York's Mafia Commission in September 1986. The trial introduced a significant new note in Mafia cases when the defence lawyers stated at the outset that their clients were self-confessed members of Cosa Nostra – making the issue more one of whether the Mafia was necessarily a *criminal* organization; with most of the American drug profits safely invested in legitimate gambling, construction and high finance, there was little to distinguish it from any other business cartel.

The history

The Mafia has certainly come a long way since its rustic beginnings in feudal Sicily. Although Buscetta denied that the word "Mafia" is used to describe the organization – the term preferred by its members is "Cosa Nostra" – the word has been in currency for centuries, and is thought to derive from the Arabic, *mu'afah*, meaning "protection". In 1863, a play entitled *Mafiusi della Vicaria*, based on life in a Palermo prison, was a roaring success among the high society of the island's capital, giving the word its first extensive usage: when the city rose against its new Italian rulers three years later, the British consul described a situation where secret societies were all-powerful: "*Camorre* and *maffie*, self-elected juntas, share the earnings of the workmen, keep up intercourse with outcasts, and take malefactors under their wing and protection."

Previously, *mafiosi* had been able to pose as defenders of the poor against the tyranny of Sicily's rulers, but in the years immediately following the toppling of the Bourbon state in Italy *mafiosi* were able to entrench themselves in Sicily's new power structure, acting as intermediaries in the gradual redistribution of land and establishing a modus vivendi with the new democratic representatives. There is little or no documentary proof of the rise to power of the "Honoured Society", but most writers agree that between the 1890s and the 1920s its undisputed boss was **Don Vito Cascio Ferro**, who had close links with the American "Black Hand", a Mafia-type amalgam of southern Italian emigrants. Despite numerous homicide charges brought against him, the only man whom Ferro admitted to shooting was an American detective, Jack Petrosino, killed on the same day he docked at Palermo to investigate links between the Sicilian and American organizations.

Ferro's career ended with Mussolini's anti-Mafia purges, instigated to clear the ground for the establishment of a vigorous Fascist structure in Sicily. **Cesare Mori**, the Duce's newly appointed Prefect of Palermo, arrived in the city in 1925 with the declared aim of "clearing the ground of the nightmares, threats and dangers which are paralysing, perverting and corrupting every kind of social activity". This might have worked, but the clean sweep that Mori made of the Mafia leaders (in all, 11,000 cattle rustlers, thieves and "conspirators" were jailed in this period, often on the basis of flimsy hearsay) was annulled after World War II when the prisons were opened and Mafia leaders, seen as unjustly jailed by the Fascist regime, returned to their regular operations. In the confusion that reigned during Italy's reconstruction, crime flourished throughout the south, and criminal leagues regrouped in Naples (the Camorra) and Calabria (*'ndrángheta*), controlling the black market and smuggling rackets. In Sicily, men such as **Don Calógero Vizzini** were the new leaders, confirmed in their power by the brief Anglo-American postwar administration, in return for their contribution towards the smooth progress of the Allied landings and occupation. One of them, **Lucky Luciano**, a founder member of the American Commission, was even flown out from prison in America to facilitate the invasion. Later he was alleged to be responsible for setting up the Sicilian-American narcotics empire, taken over at his death in 1962 by **Luciano Liggio**, who subsequently manoeuvred himself into the leadership of the Corleone family (though he was jailed in 1974).

The new Mafia

The cycle by now was complete: the Mafia had lost its original role as a predominantly rural organization, and had transformed itself by its postwar "Americanization" through transferring its operations to the cities and moving into entrepreneurial activities like construction, real estate and, ultimately, drug smuggling. With the growth of the heroin industry, the stakes were raised immensely, as shown by the vicious feuds fought over the division of the spoils, and the struggle for control of narcotics trafficking played a key role in the consolidation of power within the Mafia. The Italian State responded with an **anti-Mafia Parliamentary Commission** that sat from 1963 to 1976, and posed enough of a threat to the underworld to provoke a change of tactics by the Mafia, who began to target important state officials in a sustained campaign of terror that continues to this day. In 1971, Palermo's chief public prosecutor, Pietro Scaglione, became the first in a long line of "**illustrious corpses**" – *cadáveri eccellenti* – which have included journalists, judges, lawyers, police chiefs and left-wing politicians. A new peak of violence was reached in 1982 with the ambush and murder in Palermo's city centre of **Pio La Torre**, Regional Secretary of the Communist Party in Sicily, who had proposed a special government dispensation to allow lawyers access to private bank accounts.

One of the people attending La Torre's funeral was the new Sicilian prefect of police, **General Dalla Chiesa**, a veteran in the state's fight against the Brigate Rosse, or Red Brigades, and whose dispatch promised new action against the Mafia. The prefect began investigating Sicily's lucrative construction industry, which provided an efficient means of investing drug profits. His scrutiny of public records and business dealings threatened to expose one of the most enigmatic issues in the Mafia's organization: the extent of corruption and protection in high-ranking political circles, the so-called "**Third Level**". But, exactly 100 days after La Torre's death, Dalla Chiesa himself was gunned down, together with his wife, in Palermo's Via Carini. The whole country was shocked, and the murder revived questions about the depth of government commitment to the fight. In his engagement with the Mafia, Dalla Chiesa had met with little local cooperation, and had received next to no support from Rome, to the extent that Dalla Chiesa's son had accused the mandarins of the Christian Democrat party – former prime minister Andreotti among them – of isolating his father. Nando Dalla Chiesa refused to allow many local officials to his father's funeral, including Vito Ciancimino, former mayor of Palermo and a Christian Democrat. Later, Ciancimino was accused, not just of handling huge sums of drug money, but of actually being a sworn-in member of the Corleone family. Those who were present at the funeral included the Italian president and senior cabinet ministers, all of them jeered at by an angry Sicilian crowd and pelted with coins – an expression of disgust that has since been repeated at the funerals of other prominent anti-Mafia fighters.

To ward off accusations of government inertia or complicity, the law that La Torre had demanded was rushed through Parliament soon afterwards, and was used in the **super-trials**, or *maxiprocessi*, arising from the confessions of Buscetta and the other *pentiti* (penitents) who had followed his lead. The biggest of these trials, lasting eighteen months, started in February 1986, when 500 *mafiosi* appeared in a specially built maximum-security bunker adjoining the Ucciardone prison in the heart of Palermo. The insecurity felt by the Mafia was reflected in continuing bloodshed in Sicily throughout the proceedings, but the worst was to come after the trial closed in December 1986, starting right on the steps of the courthouse with the murder of one of the accused *mafiosi* – many of whom were freed after they had squealed on their accomplices. Of those that were convicted, 19 received life sentences, and 338 others sentences totalling 2065 years.

Contemporary events

The **1990s** saw the violence reach a new level of ferocity, starting in 1992 when a wave of assassinations of high-profile figures splashed over the headlines. In March, Salvatore Lima, a former mayor of Palermo who later became a Euro MP, was shot outside his villa in Mondello. Lima didn't have police bodyguards because he didn't believe he needed them; he had, in fact, been in the Mafia's pocket throughout his political career. His "crime" was his failure to fix the Supreme Court, which had gone ahead and confirmed the convictions of scores of *mafiosi* who had been incriminated in the super-trials of the 1980s.

This murder was followed by two more atrocities in quick succession: in May, the best-known of Sicily's anti-Mafia crusaders, **Giovanni Falcone**, was blown up by half a tonne of TNT on his way into Palermo from the airport, together with his wife and three bodyguards, and two months later his colleague, **Paolo Borsellino** (and five of his police guards), was the victim of a car-bomb outside his mother's house, also in Palermo. These two were the more visible half of the so-called "four musketeers" – judges who refused to be intimidated by death threats routinely made against anti-Mafia investigators. As ever, public opinion was divided over what it all meant. There were those who claimed that these murders were public gestures, while others saw in them increasing evidence of the panic percolating through the Mafia's ranks in the face of the growing number of defections of former members who were turning *pentiti*. The carnage certainly mobilized public opinion, and propelled the state into action that saw positive results shortly afterwards, with a dramatic breakthrough: the arrest, in January 1993, of **Salvatore Riina**, the so-called

Boss of all the Bosses, and the man held ultimately responsible for Falcone's murder. During his televised trial, it emerged that Riina had been ensconced in his native village of Corleone for most of the 24 years that he had been on the run, coming and going pretty much as he liked. Throughout Sicily, there was fury at the political complicity and protection that – presumably – allowed him to remain free, despite being the most wanted man in Europe. For more on Riina, see p.335.

Evidence for the postwar alliance between Italy's former leading party and organized crime had already come to light after November 1991, when Tommaso Buscetta began to implicate politicians for the first time, at last convinced of the state's sincerity in wanting to investigate itself. Allegations inexorably focused on the very highest levels of government, and specifically on the relationship of Mafia stooge Salvatore Lima to his protector, the Christian Democrat leader **Giulio Andreotti**. Italy's most successful postwar politician, Andreotti stepped down as prime minister in 1992 after 45 years in government, during which he had occupied every major position in the cabinet. Formerly considered untouchable, he finally bowed to increasing pressure to relinquish the parliamentary immunity that had hitherto blocked any serious investigation into his role; in September 1995, aged 75, he went on trial in Palermo for complicity and criminal association. Much fuss was made of the famous *bacio*, a kiss he was reported to have symbolically exchanged with Riina, according to *pentiti* revelations in 1994. However, the fact that most of the charges levelled against Andreotti were based on the testimony of Mafia informers (and therefore unreliable witnesses) led to Andreotti's complete acquittal in 1999, even if, for many, the result was less a vindication of the political stalwart himself than of his famous cunning and survival skills, which have given him the nickname "the fox".

Statements by *pentiti* and others accused of Mafia associations were also at the bottom of investigations into the business dealings of prime minister **Silvio Berlusconi** and his Fininvest consortium. This time they were considered serious enough to warrant a raid on Berlusconi's Milan headquarters by an elite anti-Mafia police unit in July 1998, and a hasty dash to Sicily by Berlusconi to defend himself against charges of money-laundering for Cosa Nostra, though he has just as often exercised his right to silence when confronted with other Mafia-related accusations. Despite these whiffs of scandal, the interminable delays and legal niceties of the trials that, after all, mainly concern past events, have caused many Italians to lose interest in the outcome, and revelations of endemic corruption in northern Italian cities such as Milan and Venice have switched attention away from specifically Sicilian criminality. Since 1992, in the wake of the mass arrests of politicians, businesspeople and crooked contractors, and the resulting confrontation between government and judiciary, nothing in Italy has seemed stable or predictable any more, and anything is believable, from the detention of the country's top fashion designers to rumours of Mafia infiltration in far-off Brussels and Strasbourg. The very concept of Mafia involvement has become increasingly irrelevant with each new report of political and business corruption, which dominated public life in Italy throughout the 1990s; as the mayor of Venice remarked, in response to whispers of Mafia involvement in the fire that destroyed La Fenice opera house in 1996, "Claiming it was burnt by the Mafia is about as useful as saying it was attacked by alien spacecraft."

In Sicily itself, however, the war goes on. In Palermo, **Leoluca Orlando**, the mayor of the city who was forced out of office by his own Christian Democrat party in 1990, has spent the last decade establishing an independent power base from which he has risen to the national stage on an anti-Mafia ticket, at the head of his own Rete (Network) party. Most significantly, Orlando succeeded in dislodging the Christian Democrats and their Partito Popolare heirs as the principal party in Palermo, and regained his post as mayor, since when he and La Rete have polled consistently highly in local elections, though Orlando lost to Berlusconi's candidate for the Sicilian presidency in 2001's regional elections. Some notable coups against leading Mafia figures have been made: **Leoluca Bagarella**, Riina's successor and brother-in-law, and the convicted killer of the chief of the Palermo Flying Squad in 1979, was captured in 1995 (Bagarella's hideout turned out to be a luxury apartment overlooking the heavily guarded home of two of the judges who had helped catch him), and the following year, another of the Corleone family, **Giovanni Brusca**, was arrested, a particularly gratifying coup for the anti-Mafia forces as Brusca was one of the organization's most ruthless killers. The mastermind behind Falcone's assassination, he was also believed responsible for the strangling of an informant's 11-year-old son, whose body was then disposed of in a vat of acid. This atrocity had provoked general outrage and a demonstration in the Mafia-ridden town of Altofonte, and popular anger resurfaced when it emerged that Brusca was being given special treatment and a monthly income as a *pentito*. Elsewhere on the island, **Natale D'Emanuele**, alleged to be the financial wizard behind the Mafia in Catania, was arrested and charged with trafficking arms throughout Italy, using hearses and coffins to transport them in a throwback to 1930s Chicago. Two other bosses, **Vito Vitale** and **Mariano Troia**, were netted in 1998. On the minus side, January 1999 saw one of the worst Mafia massacres in the last half-century, when five people were gunned down in a bar in Vittória, a town little known for Mafia violence. There is also evidence that, as in other Mafia groups (notably the Neapolitan Camorra), women have moved into the top jobs while their husbands and sons languish in gaol: in December 2000, police arrested twelve women alleged to be the leading figures in Siracusa's Corsi drugs clan.

The violence has for the most part calmed down since the turn of the millennium, and while killings still occur, few political figureheads are targeted today, perhaps because fewer are willing to take the visible risks that sealed the fate of crusaders like Falcone and Borsellino. In the last decade, the Palermo anti-Mafia magistrate repossessed over €6 billion in assets, largely from the real estate and construction industries, to which the Mafia has responded by diversifying its assets abroad and selling off a large chunk of its property holdings. In the immediate future, Cosa Nostra is sure to benefit from planned EU subsidies and Berlusconi's proposed Messina Straits bridge. In Italy's May 2001 elections, Berlusconi's coalition won a surprising 61 out of 61 Sicilian electoral seats for the Senate and Lower House of Parliament, and the leading Sicilian members of Forza Italia! and allied parties are routinely under investigation for ties to the Mafia. Mafiosi recognize that their success relies on an ability to permeate the democratic process, and it is precisely because the Italian state has so often fallen victim to its own corruption that the Mafia, much more organized and steadfast than local government, is able to prosper so easily. Meanwhile, a number of recent legislative proposals, including outlawing certain types of phone taps and allowing politicians a larger voice in Mafia investigations seem to be backward steps that will no doubt lead to more corruption and collusion. And in a case of crime imitating art, during the 2004 filming of the Steven Soderbergh film *Ocean's 12* in Sicily, several known Mafiosi were observed mingling with stars George Clooney and Catherine Zeta-Jones and were later suspected of trying to extort money from Soderbergh's production company.

It is a claim the producers deny but one which nevertheless shows the Mafia's undying interest in having a finger in every pie. Even today, most Sicilians who are victims of burglary still run to the Mafia, rather than the police, and it is estimated that some eighty percent of stores in Catania and Palermo still pay a *pizzo*, or protection money.

The most important development, however, has been the growth of a new open attitude towards the Mafia, in contrast to the previous denial and *omertà*. One of the most watched TV programmes in Italy in recent years has been *La Piovra* ("The Octopus"), a drama series along the lines of *The Sopranos*, while in Corleone, an anti-Mafia museum has opened to educate both foreigners and Sicilians alike. Sicilians themselves are now bolder than ever in their public demonstrations of disgust at the killings and intimidation, as witnessed by the angry scenes at the funerals of Falcone and Borsellino. There have been notable individual acts of courage, too, such as that of the wife of one "illustrious" victim, Judge Cesare Terranova (killed in 1979), who has led a women's movement against the Mafia. "If you manage to change the mentality," she has said, "to change the consent, to change the fear in which the Mafia can live – if you can change that, you can beat them."

The strongest weapon in the Mafia's armoury is precisely that element of "consent" among ordinary Sicilians. The product of fear, it is the foundation of the Mafia's existence, bolstered by an attitude that has traditionally regarded the *mafioso* stance as a revolt against the State, justified by centuries of oppression by foreign regimes. This historical dichotomy is perhaps best expressed by one of Sicily's greatest writers, Leonard Sciascia, who proclaimed, "It hurts when I denounce the Mafia because a residue of Mafia feeling stays with me, as it does in any Sicilian. So in struggling against the Mafia I struggle against myself. It is like a split, a laceration." Yet, while the corrupt government of foreigners and their acolytes has historically forfeited any deep respect for the law in Sicily, the knowledge that those very authorities have been clinched in a sinister embrace with the Mafia has stirred up general outrage. And it is this, sustained by the revelations of Andreotti's trial, that has damaged the organization where it is most vulnerable: in the public mind.

In the long run, however, no matter how many politicians and businessmen are uncovered for their Mafia associations – and Andreotti's defenders have pointed out that it is impossible for anybody in Italian political life *not* to have had contacts with organized crime – it is the changing attitudes of people at ground level that are more likely to signal the end of the Mafia's hold on Sicilian life. One risk is of Mafia-fatigue in the public mind, bordering on resignation – an attitude which appears to be supported by recent signals from Berlusconi's new government, which include an off-the-cuff remark by his interior minister in 2001 that the Mafia will never be defeated. ("We have got to learn to live with this reality".) This may be another way of saying that the fight against organized crime has taken a back seat, since Sicilians have always had to live with its constant shadowy presence. At least now the problem is being confronted, the payment of *pizzo* is openly acknowledged, and few Sicilians now hold any illusions about the true nature of the Mafia, shorn of its one-time altruistic ideals – if they ever existed. Most importantly, the myth of the Mafia's invincibility has been irreparably dented.

Sicilian Baroque

M ost of the church and civic architecture you'll come across in Sicily is Baroque in style, certainly in the east of the island. More particularly, it's of a type known as Sicilian Baroque, and this is a brief introduction to the subject, designed to serve as a handy reference for some of the more important aspects of the style mentioned in the text. It will at least explain the hows and whys of Baroque architecture in Sicily with respect to some of the major towns and sights.

Origins

The qualities that attract art historians to the Sicilian Baroque – the "warmth and ebullience", "gaiety", "energy", "freedom and fantasy"– to some extent typify all **Baroque** architecture. The style grew out of the excesses of Mannerism, a distorted sixteenth-century mode of painting and architecture which had flourished in Italy in reaction to the restraint of the Renaissance. The development of a full-blown, ornate Baroque style followed in the late sixteenth century, again originating in Italy, and it quickly found a niche in other countries touched by the Counter-Reformation. The Jesuits saw in Baroque art and architecture an expression of a revitalized Catholicism, its particular theatrical forms involving the congregation by portraying spiritual ecstasy in terms of physical passion.

The origin of the word "Baroque" is uncertain: the two most popular theories are that it comes either from the seventeenth-century Portuguese *barroco*, meaning a misshapen pearl, or the term *barocco*, used by philosophers in the Middle Ages to mean a contorted idea. Whatever its origins, it was used by contemporary critics in a derogatory sense, implying odd or extravagant shapes, as opposed to the much-vaunted Classical forms of the Renaissance.

Although Baroque was born in Rome, the vogue quickly spread throughout Europe. Everywhere, the emphasis was firmly on elaborate ornamentation and spectacle, something that reflected the growing power of the aristocracy, who had begun to challenge the established wealth and tradition of the Church. Civic architecture gained in importance, at the expense of formerly pre-eminent religious buildings. The motivating force behind the decoration of the buildings was primarily the need to impress the neighbouring gentry; building to the glory of God came a poor second.

Some of the finest (though least-known) examples of Baroque architecture are to be found in Sicily, although there's some debate as to the specific origins of the **Sicilian Baroque** style. During the eighteenth century alone, Sicily was conquered and ruled in turn by the Spanish Habsburgs, the Spanish Bourbons, the House of Savoy, the Austrian Habsburgs and the Bourbons from Naples, lending a particularly exuberant flavour to its Baroque creations – which some say was borrowed from Spain. Others argue that the dominant influence was Italian: Sicilian architects tended to train and to travel in Italy, rather than Spain, and brought home what they learned on the mainland, adapting prevalent Roman Baroque ideas to complement peculiarly Sicilian architectural traditions. Both theories contain an element of the truth, though perhaps more pertinent is Sicily's unique long-term history: two and a half millennia of invasion and domination have produced a very distinct culture and society – one that is bound to have influenced, or even produced, an equally distinct architectural form.

Baroque towns

Sicily's seismic instability has profoundly affected its architectural history. The huge **earthquake of 1693** that almost flattened Catania, and completely destroyed Noto, Ragusa, Ávola and Módica, provided a fantastic opportunity for local architects, who began massive rebuilding programmes in the southeast corner of Sicily. To them, as to all contemporary Baroque planners, a **Baroque town** aspired to be, and should have been seen to be, a centre of taste and sophistication: they designed their new towns to please and delight their citizens, to encourage the participation of passers-by and to impress outsiders, with long vistas contriving to focus on the facade of a church or a palace, or an unexpected view of the sea. To enhance the visual effect even more, a building was designed to have multiple, changing views from different angles of approach. This way, a completed plan might include all the buildings in a square or series of squares, and the experience of walking from place to place through varied but harmonious spaces was considered as important as the need to arrive at a destination. Moreover, as much of eighteenth-century Sicilian town-life took place outside, the facade of a building became synonymous with the wealth and standing of its occupant. External features became increasingly elaborate and specialized, and some parts of buildings – windows and staircases, for example – were often merely there for show. Invariably, what seem to be regular stone facades have been cosmetically touched up with plaster to conceal an asymmetry or an angle of less than ninety degrees: a self-conscious approach to town planning that can sometimes give the impression of walking around a stage set. Interestingly, this approach remained confined to the south and east of Sicily; outside the earthquake zone, in the west of the island, local architectural traditions continued to dominate in towns which hadn't had the dubious benefit of being levelled and left for the planners.

Ideally, where there was scope for large-scale planning, an entire city could be constructed as an aesthetic whole. As early as 1615 the Venetian architect and theorist **Vincenzo Scamozzi** published a treatise, *Dell'Idea dell'architettura universale*, in which he stated that the architectural harmony of the ideal city should reflect the perfect relationship between the prince, the judiciary, the Church, the marketplace and the populace.

Noto (p.302) is an almost perfect example of Scamozzi's ideal city. After the 1693 earthquake, the old town was so devastated that it was decided to move its site and rebuild from scratch. The plan that was eventually accepted was nearly an exact replica of Scamozzi's. Noto is constructed on a grid-plan, traversed from east to west by a wide corso crossing a main piazza, which is itself balanced by four smaller piazzas. The buildings along the corso show remarkable balance and grace, while the attention of the Baroque planners to every harmonious detail is illustrated by the use of a warm, golden stone for the churches and *palazzi*.

Neighbouring towns in the southeast were also destroyed by the earthquake and rebuilt along similar lines, utilizing wide squares and thoroughfares, designed with the possibility of future tremors in mind. **Ávola** (p.301) and

Grammichele (p.346) were both moved from their hill-top positions to the coastal plain, and their polygonal plans were similarly influenced by Scamozzi. Grammichele, particularly, retains an extraordinary hexagonal layout, unique in Sicily. **Ragusa** (p.307) is more complex, surviving today as two towns, the medieval Ragusa Ibla, which the inhabitants rebuilt after the earthquake, and the Baroque upper town of Ragusa, which is built on a sloping grid-plan, rather similar to Noto. Although Ibla isn't built to any kind of Baroque pattern, it does lay claim to one of the most spectacular of Sicilian Baroque churches (p.308).

Catania (p.243), unlike the other southeastern towns, was not completely destroyed by the earthquake, and was rebuilt over its old site. New, broad streets were built to link existing monuments and to facilitate rescue operations in case of another earthquake. The city is divided into four quarters by wide streets meeting in Piazza del Duomo, and wherever possible these spaces are used to maximize the visual impact of a facade or monument. The main piazza was conceived as a uniform set piece and, although several different architects collaborated, their intention was to produce a homogenous ensemble. They also went a step further in utilizing the city's natural assets: the main street, Via Etnea, cuts a swath due north from Piazza del Duomo, always drawing the eyes to the volcano, Mount Etna, smoking in the distance.

Over on the other side of the island, Baroque **Palermo** (p.74) evolved differently, without the impetus of any one great natural disaster. There's no comparable city plan, Palermo's intricate central layout owing more to the Arabs than to seventeenth- and eighteenth-century designers; what Baroque character the city possesses is almost entirely to do with its highly individual churches and palaces. They were constructed in a climate of apparent opulence but encroaching bankruptcy; as the Sicilian aristocrats were attracted to Palermo to pay court to the Spanish viceroy, they left the management of their lands to pragmatic agents, whose short-sighted policies allowed the estates to fall into neglect. This ate away at the wealth of the gentry, who responded by mortgaging their lands in order to maintain their living standards. The grandiose palaces and churches they built in the city still stand, but following the damage caused during World War II many are in a state of terrible neglect and near collapse; wild flowers grow out of the facades and chunks of masonry frequently fall into the street below. Renovation work is hampered by the local Mafia, and minor earthquake tremors always ensure that the need for repair is one step ahead of the builders, though EU funding and the initiatives of Palermo's mayor Leoluca Orlando have made a big impact in recent years.

Specific features

Eighteenth-century aristocrats in Palermo felt the need for **summer villas** outside the city, to which they could escape in the hottest weather, and many of these still survive around Bagheria (p.122). The villas tend to be quite small and simply designed, but are bedecked with balconies and terraces for afternoon strolling, and were approached by long, impressive driveways. Above all, they are notable for their **external staircases**, leading to the main entrance on the first floor (the ground floor usually contained the kitchen and servants' quarters). It's typical of the Baroque era that an external feature should take on such significance in a building – and that they should show such a remarkable diversity, each reflecting the wealth of the individual owners. Beyond the fact that they were nearly always double staircases, symmetrical to the middle axis of the facade, each one was completely different and, though external staircases can be found elsewhere on mainland Europe, they're rarely of such imaginative construction as in Sicily.

Balconies had always been a prominent feature of Sicilian domestic architecture, but during the eighteenth century they became prolific. The balcony supports, or buttresses, were elaborately carved: manic heads, griffins, horses, monsters and mythical figures all featured as decoration, fine examples of which survive at Noto's **Palazzo Villadorata** (p.303), as well as in Módica (p.311) and Scicli (p.312). The wrought-iron balustrades curved outwards, almost like theatre boxes, to allow room for women's billowing skirts; they still afford the best views of street processions and other festivities at Carnevale.

Church building, too, flourished during this period. Baroque architects could let their imaginations run wild: the facade of the **Duomo** at Siracusa (p.284) was begun in 1728, based on designs by Andrea Palma of Palermo, and the result is highly sophisticated and exciting. Other designs adapted and modified accepted forms for church architecture, as well as inventing new ones. In Palermo especially, typically Sicilian elements – like central circular windows – were used to great effect.

It was in the church **interiors**, however, that Sicilian Baroque came into its own, with tomb sculpture ever more ostentatious and stucco decoration abundant. Inlaid marble, a technique introduced from Naples at the beginning of the seventeenth century, became *de rigueur* for any self-respecting church. It reached its prime in the second half of the century, when whole walls or chapels would be decorated in this way. Palermo fields some of the best examples of all these techniques, most impressive the church of **San Giuseppe dei Teatini** (p.88), designed by Giacomo Besio, a Genovese who lived most of his life in Sicily. For real over-the-top detail, though, the churches of **Santa Caterina** (p.88) and **Il Gesù** (p.90), also in Palermo, conceal a riot of inlaid marble decoration.

Palermo is also distinguished by a series of highly decorative **oratories**, built in the late seventeenth and early eighteenth centuries, when the Spanish viceroys placed much of the city's power in the hands of the local aristocrats, who could afford to endow monasteries with new funds. Much was spent on small private chapels, where local sculptors had the chance to shine. The master of the genre was Giacomo Serpotta (see opposite), and his best works are in the oratories of **Santa Zita** (p.97), **San Domenico** (p.95) and **San Lorenzo** (p.98), though he left his mark over much of the west of the island.

Architects and sculptors

Rosario Gagliardi was responsible for much of the rebuilding of Noto and Ragusa, and became known as one of the most important architects in southeast Sicily. Born in Siracusa in 1698, he worked in Noto as a carpenter from the age of 10, and was first acknowledged as an architect in 1726. Between 1760 and 1784 he was chief architect for the city of Noto, and during this time also worked on many different projects in Ragusa and Módica. As far as is known, he never travelled outside Sicily, let alone to Rome, yet he absorbed contemporary architectural trends from the study of books and treatises, and reproduced the ideas with some flair.

Gagliardi's prime interest was in facades, and his work achieved a sophisticated fusion of Renaissance poise, Baroque grandeur and local Sicilian ornamentation. He had no interest, however, in spatial relationships or structural innovation, and the interiors of his buildings are disappointing when compared to the elaborate nature of their exteriors. Perhaps his most significant contribution was his development of the belfry as a feature. Sicilian churches traditionally didn't have a separate belltower, but incorporated the bells into the main facade, revealed through a series of two or three arches – an idea handed down from Byzantine building. Gagliardi extended the central bay of the facade into a tower, a highly original compromise satisfying both the local style and the more conventional notions of design from the mainland. The belfry on the church of **San Giorgio** in Ragusa Ibla (p.308) is an excellent example of this and is Gagliardi's masterpiece.

Giovanni Battista Vaccarini was the principal architect working on the design and rebuilding of Catania after the 1693 earthquake. He was born in Palermo in 1702, but trained in Rome and embraced the current idiom, working with such illustrious figures as Alessandro Specchi (who built the papal stables) and Francesco de Sanctis (designer of the Spanish Steps). In 1730 he arrived in Catania, having been appointed as city architect by the Senate, and at once began work on finishing the Municipio (p.249); the lower two floors had been designed by a local architect, but Vaccarini completely ignored the original plan and transformed the building by redesigning the *piano nobile* in the Roman style. Outside it he placed a fountain, whose main feature is an obelisk supported by an elephant, the symbol of Catania – reminiscent of Bernini's elephant fountain in Rome.

Giacomo Serpotta, master of the Palermitan oratories, was born in Palermo in 1656. He cashed in on the opulence of the Church and specialized in decorating oratories with moulded plasterwork in ornamental frames. He would include life-sized figures of Saints and Virtues, surrounded by plaster draperies, trophies, swags of fruit, bouquets of flowers and other extravagances much beloved of the Baroque. One of the most remarkable of his works is the Oratory of the Rosary in the church of **Santa Zita** (p.97), where the end wall is a reconstruction of the Battle of Lépanto. Three-dimensional representation is taken to an extreme here, and actual wires are used as rigging.

Other Baroque architects are less well known, but influential in Sicily all the same. **Giacomo Amato** (1643–1732) was a monk, sent to Rome in 1671 to represent his Order, where he came into contact with the works of Bernini and Borromini. Dazzled by what he'd seen, he neglected his religious duties after his return to Palermo in order to design some of the city's most characteristic churches, **Sant'Ignazio all'Olivella** (p.96) and **San Domenico** (p.95) among them. **Vincenzo Sinatra** had a more traditional career, starting as a stonecutter before working with Gagliardi in the 1730s as his foreman. In 1745 he married Gagliardi's niece, a move which did him no harm at all, since by 1761, when Gagliardi had a stroke, Sinatra was managing all his affairs. For ten years he directed the construction of Noto's Municipio, and during the rest of his life Sinatra worked in collaboration with the other city architects on a variety of projects – a respectable career, but one which makes it difficult to trace any personal architectural method. More important, and certainly with an identifiable style, was **Giovanni Vermexio**, who was working in Siracusa at around the same time. His work graces the city's Piazza del Duomo, notably the **Palazzo Arcivescovile**, while he gets a couple of ornate-interior credits, too, in the shape of one of the Duomo's chapels, and the octagonal **Cappella di San Sepolcro** in the church of Santa Lucia in the Achradina quarter of Siracusa (p.286).

Sicily in fiction

Some of the most respected modern Italian authors are Sicilian. Extracts from the work of just three – Lampedusa, Vittorini and Sciascia – are reprinted below, and although each author has his own particular viewpoint and style, there's a similarity apparent too: each of the extracts touches upon a different aspect of the same theme, namely the intricacies of Sicilian life and the unique problems of the island.

The Leopard

Perhaps the best-known Sicilian novel, The Leopard is a towering record of a nineteenth-century aristocrat's reactions to the old order crumbling around him as the Bourbon state of Naples and Sicily draws to a close, to be replaced by a new unified Italy. It was the posthumously published masterpiece of Giuseppe Tomasi di Lampedusa (1896–1957), himself from a Sicilian aristocratic family that claimed descent from a commander of the Imperial Guard of the sixth-century Byzantine emperor Tiberius. Certainly Lampedusa would have had some considerable understanding of the emotions felt by the prince, Don Fabrizio, as he contemplates the destruction of the traditional values he cherishes. The Leopard appeared in 1958 to immediate critical acclaim, although Lampedusa wrote little else of note. In the extract below, the prince is out hunting at his country estate with his retainer, Don Ciccio, shortly after the Plebiscite on unification.

"And you, Don Ciccio, how did you vote on the twenty-first?"

The poor man started; taken by surprise at a moment when he was outside the stockade of precautions in which, like each of his fellow townsmen, he usually moved, he hesitated, not knowing what to reply.

The Prince mistook for alarm what was really only surprise, and felt irritated. "Well, what are you afraid of? There's no one here but us, the wind and the dogs."

The list of reassuring witnesses was not really happily chosen; wind is a gossip by definition, the Prince was half Sicilian. Only the dogs were absolutely trustworthy and that only because they lacked articulate speech. But Don Ciccio had now recovered; his peasant astuteness had suggested the right reply – nothing at all. "Excuse me, Excellency, but there's no point in your question. You know that everyone in Donnafugata voted 'yes'."

Don Fabrizio did not know this; and that was why this reply merely changed a small enigma into an enigma of history. Before this voting many had come to him for advice; all of them had been exhorted, sincerely, to vote "yes". Don Fabrizio, in fact, could not see what else there was to do: whether treating it as a *fait accompli* or as an act merely theatrical and banal, whether taking it as a historical necessity or considering the trouble these humble folk might get into if their negative attitude were known. He had noticed, though, that not all had been convinced by his words; into play had come the abstract Machiavellianism of Sicilians, which so often induced these people, with all their generosity, to erect complex barricades on the most fragile foundations. Like clinics adept at treatment based on fundamentally false analyses of blood and urine which they are too lazy to rectify, the Sicilians (of that time) ended by killing off the patient, that is themselves, by a niggling and hair-splitting rarely connected with any real understanding of the problems involved, or even of their interlocutors. Some of these who had made a visit *ad limina leopardorum* considered it impossible for a Prince of Salina to vote in favour of the Revolution (as the recent changes were still called in these remote parts), and they interpreted his advice as ironical, intended to effect a result in practice opposite to his words. These pilgrims (and they were the best) had come out of his study winking at each other – as far as their respect for him would allow – proud at having penetrated the meaning of the princely words, and rubbing their hands in self-congratulation at their own perspicacity just when this was most completely in eclipse.

Others, on the other hand, after having listened to him, went off looking sad and convinced that he was a turncoat or half-wit, more than ever determined to take no notice of what he said but to follow instead the age-old proverb about preferring a known evil to an untried good. These were reluctant to ratify the new national reality for personal reasons too; either from religious faith, or from having received favours from the former regime and not being sharp enough to insert themselves into the new one, or finally because during the upsets of the liberation period they had lost a few capons and sacks of beans, and had been cuckolded either freely like Garibaldini volunteers or forcibly like Bourbon levies. He had, in fact, the disagreeable but distinct impression that about fifteen of them would vote "no", a tiny minority certainly, but noticeable in the small electorate of Donnafugata. Taking into consideration that the people who came to him represented the flowers of the inhabitants, and that there must also be some unconvinced among the hundreds of electors who had not dreamt of setting foot inside the palace, the Prince had calculated that Donnafugata's compact affirmative would be varied by about forty negative votes.

The day of the Plebiscite was windy and grey, and tired groups of youths had been seen going through the streets of the town with bits of paper covered with "yes" stuck in the ribbons of their hats. Amid waste paper and refuse swirled by the wind they sang a few verses of *La Bella Gigugin* transformed into a kind of Arab wail, a fate to which any gay tune in Sicily is bound to succumb. There had also been seen two or three "foreigners" (that is from Girgenti) installed in *Zzu* Menico's tavern where they were declaiming Leopardi's lines on the "magnificent and progressive destiny" of a renovated Sicily united to resurgent Italy. A few peasants were standing listening mutely, stunned by overwork or starved by unemployment. These cleared their throats and spat continuously, but kept silent; so silent that it must have been then (as Don Fabrizio said afterwards) that the foreigners decided to give Arithmetic precedence over Rhetoric in the Quadrivium arts.

The Prince went to vote about four in the afternoon, flanked on the right by Father Pirrone, on the left by Don Onofrio Rotolo; frowning and fair-skinned, he proceeded slowly toward the Town Hall, frequently putting up a hand to protect his eyes lest the breeze loaded with all the filth collected on its way should bring on the conjunctivitis to which he was subject; and he remarked to Father Pirrone that the health-giving gusts did seem to drag up a lot of dirt with them. He was wearing the same black frock coat in which two years before he had gone to pay his respects at Caserta to poor King Ferdinand, who had been lucky enough to die in time to avoid this day of dirty wind when the seal would be set on his own incapacity. But had it really been incapacity? One might as well say that a person succumbing to typhus dies of incapacity. He remembered the king busy putting up dykes against the flood of useless documents: and suddenly he realised how much unconscious appeal to pity there was in these unattractive features. Such thoughts were disagreeable, as are all those which make us understand things too late, and the Prince's face went solemn and dark as if he were following an invisible funeral car. Only the violent impact of his feet on loose stones in the street showed his internal conflict. It is superfluous to mention that the ribbon on his top hat was innocent of any piece of paper; but in the eyes of those who knew him a "yes" and "no" alternated on the glistening felt.

On reaching a little room in the Town Hall used as the voting booth he was surprised to see all the members of the committee get up as his great height filled the doorway; a few peasants who had arrived before were put aside, and so without having to wait Don Fabrizio handed his "yes" into the patriotic hands of Don Calogero Sedàra. Father Pirrone, though, did not vote at all, as he had been careful not to get listed as a resident of the town. Don 'Nofrio, obeying the express desires of the Prince, gave his own monosyllabic opinion about the complicated Italian question; a masterpiece of concision carried through with the good grace of a child drinking castor oil. After which all were invited for a "little glass" upstairs in the mayor's study; but Father Pirrone and Don 'Nofrio put forward good reasons, one of abstinence, the other of stomach-ache, and remained below. Don Fabrizio had to face the party alone.

Behind the Mayor's writing desk gleamed a brand new portrait of Garibaldi and (already) one of King Victor Emmanuel hung, luckily, to the right: the first handsome, the second ugly; both, however, made brethren by prodigious growths of hair which nearly hid their faces altogether. On a small low table was a plate with some ancient biscuits blackened by fly droppings and a dozen little squat glasses brimming with *rosolio* wine: four red, four green, four white, the last in the centre: an ingenious symbol of the new national flag which tempered the Prince's remorse with a smile. He chose the white liquor for himself, presumably because it was the least indigestible and not, as some thought, in tardy homage to the Bourbon standard. Anyway, all three varieties of the *rosolio* were equally sugary, sticky and revolting. His host had the good taste not to give toasts. But, as Don Calogero said, great joys are silent. Don Fabrizio was shown a letter from the authorities of Girgenti announcing to the industrious citizens of Donnafugata the concession of 2,000 lire towards sewage, a work which would be completed before the end of 1961 so the Mayor assured them, stumbling into one of those *lapsus* whose mechanism Freud was to explain many decades later; and the meeting broke up.

Before dusk the three or four easy girls of Donnafugata (there were some others there too, not grouped but each hard at work on her own) appeared on the square with tricolour ribbons in their manes as protest against the exclusion of women in the vote; the poor creatures were jeered at even by the most advanced liberals and forced back to their lairs. This did not prevent the *Giornale di Trinacria* telling the people of Palermo four days later that at Donnafugata "some gentle representatives of the fair sex wished to show their faith in the new and brilliant destinies of their beloved Country, and demonstrated in the main square amid great acclamation from the patriotic population".

After this the electoral booths were closed and the scrutators got to work; late that night the shutters on the balcony of the Town Hall were flung open and Don Calogero appeared with a tricolour sash over his middle, flanked by two ushers with lighted candelabra which the wind snuffed at once. To the invisible crowd in the shadows below he announced that the Plebiscite at Donnafugata had the following results:

Voters, 515; Voting, 512; Yes, 512; No, zero.

From the dark end of the square rose applause and hurrahs; on her little balcony Angelica, with her funereal maid, clapped lovely rapacious hands; speeches were made; adjectives loaded with superlatives and double consonants reverberated and echoed in the dark from one wall to another; amid thundering of fireworks messages were sent off to the King (the new one) and to the General; a tricolour rocket or two climbed up from the village into the blackness towards the starless sky. By eight o'clock all was over, and nothing remained except darkness as on any other night, always.

From *The Leopard* by Giuseppe Tomasi di Lampedusa, translated by Archibald Colquhoun.

© Giangiacomo Feltrinelli Editore 1958, © in the English translation Harvill 1961.

Reproduced by permission of The Harvill Press.

Conversations in Sicily

Elio Vittorini (1908–1966) was born in Siracusa, a staunch anti-Fascist whose first novel was censored under Mussolini. His best work, Conversations in Sicily, written in 1937, initially managed to escape the same fate, as Vittorini wrapped his simple, taut story of a man's visit to his mother in an abstract, almost poetic style. The book deals with the return to Sicily, after fifteen years, of an emigrant who now lives in the industrial – and comparatively wealthy – north of Italy. The "conversations" are the emigrant's encounters with fellow travellers and villagers in Sicily – encounters that lead him to rediscover a humanity in their otherwise downtrodden, despairing existence. The extract reprinted below follows his approach to his former home, a route that today is still redolent with the flavours that Vittorini records.

Toward midnight I changed train at Florence, then again about six in the morning at the Termini station in Rome, and about midday I reached Naples. There it was not raining, and I sent off a telegraphic money-order of fifty lire to my wife. I wired to her: "Returning Thursday."

Then I took the train for Calabria. It began raining again, and night came on. It all came back to me, the journey, and I as a child on my ten flights from home and Sicily, travelling back and forth through a countryside of smoke and tunnels, the rending whistles of the train halted by night in the jaws of a mountain or by the sea, and the names – Amantea, Maratea, Gioia Tauro – evoking dreams of ancient times. And so, suddenly, the mouse within me was no longer a mouse, but scent, savour, and the heavens, and the pipe no longer played mournfully, but merrily. I fell asleep, awoke, fell asleep again, and awoke once more, until at last I found myself on board the ferry-boat for Sicily.

The sea was black and wintry. Standing on that high plateau of the top deck, I saw myself once again as a boy breathing the air, gazing hungrily at the sea, facing towards the one coast or the other, with all that garbage of coastal town and village heaped at my feet in the rain-swept morning.

It was cold, and I remembered myself as a boy feeling cold yet remaining obstinately on that elevated windy platform, with the sea speeding swiftly by below.

We were a tight fit. The boat was full of little Sicilians travelling third-class, hungry, frozen, without overcoats, yet mild-looking, jacket lapels turned up and hands dug into trouser pockets. I had bought some food at Villa San Giovanni, some bread and cheese, and I was munching away on deck at the bread, raw air, and cheese, with zest and appetite, because I recognized the old tang of my mountains, and even their odours – herds of goats and wormwood – in that cheese. The little Sicilians, bowed with backs to the wind and hands in pockets, watched me eat. They had dark, but mild faces, with beards four days old. They were workers, labourers from the orange groves, and railwaymen wearing grey caps with the thin red piping of the labour gangs. Munching, I smiled at them, and they looked back at me unsmiling.

"There's no cheese like our own," I said.

No one replied. They all stared at me, the women in their voluminous femininity seated on their great bags of belongings, the men standing, small and as if scalded by the wind, hands in pockets.

Again I said: "There's no cheese like our own."

Because I felt suddenly enthusiastic about something – that cheese, its savour in my mouth, with the bread and the sharp air, its flavour clear but acrid, and ancient, its grains of pepper like sudden embers on the tongue:

"There's no cheese like our own," I said for the third time.

Then one of the Sicilians, the smallest and gentlest and darkest of the lot, and the most scalded by the wind, asked me:

"But are you a Sicilian?"

"Why not?" I replied.

The man shrugged his shoulders and said no more. He had what looked like a little girl with him, sitting on a bag at his feet. He bent over her, and taking a great red hand out of his pocket, he seemed to touch her caressingly while he adjusted her shawl to keep her warm.

Somehow this gesture made it clear that she was not his daughter but his wife. Meanwhile Messina drew near, and it was not a heap of garbage on the sea's edge, but houses and moles, white tramcars and rows of dark-hued wagons in the railway sidings. The morning seemed wet, though it was not raining. Everything on the top of the deck was moist, the wind blew moist, the sirens from the ships sounded moist, and the railway engines ashore whistled with a moist note; but it was not raining. And suddenly we saw the lighthouse sailing by in the wintry sea, very high, heading for Villa San Giovanni.

"There's no cheese like our own," I said.

All the men, who were standing, pressed toward the deck rail to gaze at the city, and the women too, seated on their bags, turned their heads. But no one made a move towards the lower deck to be ready to disembark. There was still time. From the lighthouse to the jetty, I remembered, took fifteen minutes or more.

"There's no cheese like our own," I said.

Meanwhile I finished eating. The man with the wife who looked like a child bent down once again: in fact, he knelt; he had a basket at his feet and, watched by her, he began to busy himself with it. It was covered by a piece of wax-cloth sewn with string at the edges. Very slowly he undid a bit of the string, dug his hand under the wax-cloth, and produced an orange.

It wasn't big or very luscious or highly tinted, but it was an orange, and without a word, without rising from his knees, he offered it to his baby wife. The baby looked at me; I could discern her eyes inside the hood of the shawl; and then I saw her shake her head.

The little Sicilian seemed desperate, and remained on his knees, one hand in his pocket, the other holding the orange. Then he rose again to his feet and stood with the wind flapping the soft peak of his cap against his nose, the orange in his hand, his coatless diminutive body scalded by the cold, and frantic, while immediately below us the sea and the city floated by in the wet morning.

"Messina," said a woman mournfully. It was a word uttered without reason, merely as a kind of complaint. I observed the little Sicilian with the baby-wife desperately peel his orange, and desperately eat it, with rage and frenzy, without the least desire; then without chewing he gulped it down and seemed to curse, his fingers dripping with the orange juice in the cold, a little bowed in the wind, the peak of his cap flapping against his nose.

"A Sicilian never eats in the morning," he said suddenly. "Are you American?" he added.

He spoke with desperation, yet gently, just as he had always been gentle while desperately peeling the orange and desperately eating it. He spoke the last three words excitedly, in a strident tense voice, as if it were somehow essential to the peace of his soul to know if I were American.

I observed this, and said: "Yes, I am American. For the last fifteen years."

Reprinted from *Conversations in Sicily* by Elio Vittorini, translated by Wilfrid David (Canongate Books).

The Day of the Owl

Widely regarded as one of Italy's finest writers, Leonardo Sciascia (1912–1991), from the southwest of Sicily, used the island as a backdrop in all his work – as what he called a "metaphor of the modern world". Both the novels and short stories provide keen insights into the world of the Mafia, the Church in Sicily, the mores of the people and the island's tortuous history – all touched by the same wit and sharp, perceptive characterization. The Day of the Owl is at heart a crime story: a Carabinieri inspector arrives from the mainland to investigate a Mafia murder, described below in the book's opening pages.

The bus was just about to leave, amid rumbles and sudden hiccups and rattles. The square was silent in the grey dawn; wisps of cloud swirled round the belfry of the church. The only sound, apart from the rumbling of the bus, was a voice, wheedling, ironic, of a fritter-seller; fritters, hot fritters. The conductor slammed the door, and with a clank of scrap-metal the bus moved off. His last glance round the square caught sight of a man in a dark suit running towards the bus.

"Hold it a minute," said the conductor to the driver, opening the door with the bus still in motion. Two ear-splitting shots rang out. For a second the man in the dark suit, who was just about to jump on the running-board, hung suspended in mid-air as if some invisible hand were hauling him up by the hair. Then his brief-case dropped from his hand and very slowly he slumped down on top of it.

The conductor swore; his face was the colour of sulphur; he was shaking. The fritter-seller, who was only three yards from the fallen man, sidled off with a crab-like motion towards the door of the church. In the bus no one moved; the driver sat, as if turned to stone, his right hand on the brake, his left on the steering wheel. The conductor looked round the passengers' faces, which were blank as the blinds.

"They've killed him," he said; he took off his cap, swore again, and began frantically running his fingers through his hair.

"The *carabinieri*," said the driver, "we must get the *carabinieri*."

He got up and opened the other door. "I'll go," he said to the conductor.

The conductor looked at the dead man and then at the passengers. These included some women, old women who brought heavy sacks of white cloth and baskets full of eggs every morning; their clothes smelled of forage, manure and wood smoke; usually they grumbled and swore, now they sat mute, their faces as if disinterred from the silence of centuries.

"Who is it?" asked the conductor, pointing at the body.

No one answered. The conductor cursed. Among the passengers of that route he was famous for his highly skilled blaspheming. The company had already threatened to fire him since he never bothered to control himself even when there were nuns or priests on the bus. He was from the province of Syracuse and had had little to do with violent death: a soft province, Syracuse. So now he swore all the more furiously.

The *carabinieri* arrived; the sergeant-major, with a black stubble and in a black temper from being woken, stirred the passengers' apathy like an alarm-clock: in the wake of the conductor they began to get out through the door left open by the driver.

With seeming nonchalance, looking around as if they were trying to gauge the proper distance from which to admire the belfry, they drifted off towards the sides of the square and, after a last look around, scuttled into alley-ways.

The sergeant-major and his men did not notice this gradual exodus. Now about fifty people were around the dead man: men from a public works training centre who were only too delighted to have found such an absorbing topic of conversation to while away their eight hours of idleness. The sergeant-major ordered his men to clear the square and get the passengers back onto the bus. The *carabinieri* began pushing sightseers back towards the streets leading off the square, asking passengers to take their seats on the bus again. When the square was empty, so was the bus. Only the driver and the conductor remained.

"What?" said the sergeant-major to the driver. "No passengers today?"

"Yes, some," replied the driver with an absent-minded look.

"Some," said the sergeant-major, "means four, five or six … I've never seen this bus leave with an empty seat."

"How should I know?" said the driver, exhausted from straining his memory. "How should I know? I said 'some' just like that. More than five or six though. Maybe more; maybe the bus was full. I never look to see who's there. I just get into my seat and off we go. The road's the only thing I look at; that's what I'm paid for … to look at the road."

The sergeant-major rubbed his chin with a hand taut with irritation. "I get it," he said, "you just look at the road." He rounded savagely on the conductor. "But you, you tear off the tickets, take money, give change. You count the people and look at their faces … and if you don't want me to make you remember 'em in the guardroom, you're going to tell me now who was on that bus! At least ten names … You've been on this run for the last three years, and for the last three years I've seen you every evening in the Café Italia. You know this town better than I do … "

"Nobody would know the town better than you do," said the conductor with a smile, as though shrugging off a compliment.

"All right, then," said the sergeant-major, sneering, "first me, then you … But I wasn't on the bus or I'd remember every passenger one by one. So it's up to you. Ten names at least."

"I can't remember," said the conductor, "by my mother's soul I can't remember. Just now I can't remember a thing. It all seems a dream."

"I'll wake you up," raged the sergeant-major, "I'll wake you up with a couple of years inside …" He broke off to go and meet the police magistrate who had just arrived. While making his report on the identity of the dead man and the flight of the passengers, the sergeant-major looked at the bus. As he looked, he had an impression that something was not quite right or was missing, as when something in our daily routine is unexpectedly missing, which the senses perceive from force of habit but the mind does not quite apprehend; even so its absence provokes an empty feeling of discomfort, a vague exasperation as from a flickering light-bulb. Then, suddenly, what we are looking for dawns on us.

"There's something missing," said the sergeant-major to *Carabiniere* Sposito, who being a qualified accountant was the pillar of the *Carabinieri* Station of S., "there's something or someone missing."

"The fritter-seller," said *Carabiniere* Sposito.

"The fritter-seller, by God!" The sergeant-major exulted, thinking: "An accountant's diploma means something."

A *carabiniere* was sent off at the double to pick up the fritter-seller. He knew where to find the man, who after the departure of the first bus, usually went to sell his wares at the entrance of the elementary schools. Ten minutes later the sergeant-major had the vendor of fritters in front of him. The man's expression was that of a man roused from innocent slumber.

"Was he there?" the sergeant-major asked the conductor.

"He was," answered the conductor gazing at his shoe.

"Well now," said the sergeant-major with paternal kindness, "this morning, as usual, you came to sell your fritters here … As usual, at the first bus for Palermo …"

"I've my licence," said the fritter-seller.

"I know," said the sergeant-major, raising his eyes to heaven, imploring patience. "I know and I'm not thinking about your licence. I want to know only one thing, and, if you tell me, you can go off at once and sell your fritters to the kids: who fired the shots?"

"Why," asked the fritter-seller, astonished and inquisitive, "has there been shooting?"

Reprinted from *The Day of the Owl* by Leonardo Sciascia, translated by

Archibald Colquhoun and Arthur Oliver (Granta Books).

Books

There are only a few modern writers who have travelled in and written about Sicily, though the island has provided the inspiration for some great literature, by both Sicilians and European visitors. Most of the books listed below are in print and those that aren't shouldn't be too difficult to track down (out-of-print books are indicated by "o/p"). Wherever a book is in print, the UK publisher is listed first, with a semicolon separating this from the publisher in the US, which follows. If the title is available in one country only, we've specified the country; or if the UK and US editions are the same, we've given the publisher's name only once. Where paperback editions are available, these are listed in preference to hardcover. The book symbol marks titles that are particularly recommended.

Travel and general

★ **Luigi Barzini** *The Italians* (Penguin; Atheneum). Long the most respected work on the Italian nation, and rightly so. Barzini leaves no stone unturned in his quest to pinpoint the real Italy.

Anthony Blunt *Sicilian Baroque* (Weidenfeld & Nicolson UK, o/p). The only book specifically on the subject, this contains everything you ever wanted to know about Sicilian Baroque. It's very readable and anecdotal, with pages of black-and-white photos. Out of print in the US, but should be available in large public libraries.

★ **Vincent Cronin**, *The Golden Honeycomb* (Harvill; Rupert Hart-Davis, o/p). Disguised as a quest for the mythical golden honeycomb of Daedalus, this is a searching account of a sojourn in Sicily in the 1950s. Although overwritten in parts, it manages to combine colourful descriptions of Sicily's art, architecture and folklore with a knowing and erudite commentary.

Duncan Fallowell *To Noto* (Gibson Square Books, UK). Details a trip from London to Baroque Noto in an old Ford – an erudite travelogue, seeping with wit and pithy observations on Sicily and the Sicilians.

Francis M. Guercio *Sicily: the Garden of the Mediterranean* (Faber, o/p). Fairly comprehensive but dated (prewar) introduction to the island, and with more than a passing sympathy for Mussolini. Interesting as a period piece, though, and the history and archeological site accounts are sound.

Russell King *Sicily* (David & Charles; Stackpole Books, o/p). One of the *Islands* series, this is an informed and comprehensive read, with chapters on archeology, industry, bandits, the Mafia, and volcanoes and earthquakes. If you can't track down a copy you'll usually find it in public libraries.

★ **Norman Lewis** *In Sicily* (Cape, UK). A broad contemporary portrait of the island which Lewis came to know through his wife and her family, and to which he returns frequently. Subjects range from reflections on Palermo's ruined *palazzi* to the impact of immigration, and there's plenty on the Mafia.

Theresa Maggio *Mattanza: Love and Death in the Sea of Sicily* (Perseus). A first-hand observation and explanation of the rituals of the annual trapping and killing of bluefin tuna off the island of Favignana.

Awesome, fascinating and often gruesome, the account extends to the islanders and the author's relationship with the fishermen.

Daphne Phelps *A House in Sicily* (Virago; Carroll & Graf). An Englishwoman inherits a grand *palazzo* in Taormina and turns it into a guesthouse to make ends meet. This allows vignettes of eminent guests – Bertrand Russell, Tennessee Williams, Roald Dahl – as well as of the locals, though her patronizing take on some of these, including the local Mafia don, grates, and her anglocentric, provincial style are off-putting.

Fiona Pitt-Kethley *Journeys to the Underworld* (Chatto & Windus, o/p).

English poet searches Italy for the Sibylline sites, a good third of her time spent in Sicily – though Pitt-Kethley's salacious appetite for sexual adventure often distracts from the real interest.

 Mary Taylor Simeti *On Persephone's Island: a Sicilian Journal* (Bantam; Vintage). Sympathetic record of a typical year in Sicily by an American who married a Sicilian professor and has lived in the west of the island since the early 1960s. Full of keenly observed detail about flora and fauna, customs, the harvests, festivals and – above all – the Sicilians themselves. Also see "Cuisine" (p.479) for her splendid book on Sicilian food.

Specific guides

Paul Duncan *Sicily: a Travellers' Guide* (John Murray, o/p). Useful guide that's strong on architecture in general and Palermo in particular.

 Gillian Price *Walking in Sicily* (Cicerone Press). Forty-two

walks throughout the island are detailed here – along the coasts, over mountains and up Etna. Somewhat crude maps, photos and good local background enhance this superb hiking guide.

History, politics and archeology

David Abulafia *Frederick II: a Medieval Emperor* (Pimlico; Oxford UP). Definitive account of the Hohenstaufen king, greatest of the medieval European rulers, with much on his reign in Sicily as well as elsewhere in Europe. It's a reinterpretation of the usual view of Frederick, revealing a less formidable king than the omnipotent and supreme ruler usually portrayed. For more on Sicily, see the same author's *Italy, Sicily and the Mediterranean, 1100–1400* (Variorum).

Aziz Ahmad *A History of Islamic Sicily* (Columbia University Press; Edinburgh University Press). Though written in the 1970s, this gives a

solid, if slightly academic, overview of the role of Islam in the development of modern Sicily. It includes an interesting account of the controversial connection between Dante's *Divine Comedy* and similar Islamic works that preceded it.

Brian Caven *Dionysius I: Warlord of Sicily* (Yale UP). Detailed but readable account of the life of Dionysius I by a historian who sees him not as a vicious tyrant but as a valiant crusader against the Carthaginians.

M.I. Finley, D. Mack Smith & C.J.H. Duggan *A History of Sicily* (Chatto & Windus, UK, o/p). An updated abridgement of the trilogy first published in 1968 by Finley and Mack Smith, this is concise but readable and informative, skipping fast from the Stone Age to the early 1980s.

Margaret Guido *Sicily: an Archaeological Guide* (Faber, o/p). Indispensable and approachable account of Sicily's prehistoric and Roman remains and the island's Greek sites, comprehensive and with good site-plans. One reservation is that it's not been revised since 1977 – which means there are a few gaps and the practical information is out of date.

John Haycraft *Italian Labyrinth: Italy in the 1980s* (Penguin, o/p). Fine, rambling study of modern Italy, its customs, politics, social problems, economy and arts. There's much on Sicily, with interesting insights into the Church, the Mafia, and corruption in Palermo.

Christopher Hibbert *Garibaldi and His Enemies* (Penguin, o/p; Plume, o/p). A popular treatment of the life and revolutionary works of Giuseppe Garibaldi, thrillingly detailing the exploits of "The Thousand" in their lightning campaign from Marsala to Milazzo.

R. Ross Holloway *The Archaeology of Ancient Sicily* (Routledge). Accessible and comprehensive introduction to the wealth of ancient monuments and artefacts discovered in Sicily,

from the Paleolithic to the later Roman period.

★ **John Julius Norwich** *The Normans in Sicily* (Penguin). Published together for the first time under one title, J.J. Norwich's *The Normans in the South* and *Kingdom in the Sun* are the accessible, well-researched story of the Normans' explosive entry into the south of Italy, dealing with their creation, in Sicily, of one of the most brilliant medieval European civilizations. Full of fascinating anecdotes and background to Sicily's glittering eleventh and twelfth centuries.

Steven Runciman *The Sicilian Vespers* (Cambridge UP). The classic account of Sicily's large-scale popular uprising in the thirteenth century. More entertaining is Runciman's *A History of the Crusades: 1, 2 & 3* (Penguin; CUP), complete with full details of the Norman kings of Sicily, as well as of the crusading Frederick II himself. An essential read if you want to unravel all the intricacies of the period.

★ **Gaia Servadio** *Motya* (Phoenix, UK). On one level, an account of Phoenician history and culture as they relate to the excavated ruins of Motya – but in truth, so much more than that, as Servadio explores the fabric of Sicily and its people in uncompromising, enlightening detail.

Crime and society

Pino Arlacchi *Mafia Business* (Oxford Paperbacks, UK; Oxford UP, o/p). Dry and academic account of how the Mafia moved into big business, legal and illegal, its argument summarized by the book's subtitle *The Mafia Ethic and the Spirit of Capitalism*. The author has served on the Italian government's Anti-Mafia Commission, which makes him

supremely qualified to accurately judge the Mafia's cutting edge.

John Dickie *Cosa Nostra* (Coronet Books; Hodder & Stoughton). Dickie, an Italian professor at University College London, has been researching the Mafia and its role in Sicilian society for over 20 years. This new work provides a very in-depth look at the secret workings of the Mafia, from its early days in the mid-1800s to its current relationship with Berlusconi's government.

Danilo Dolci *Sicilian Lives* (Writers and Readers, o/p; Random House). Dolci's formidable record of the lives of the Sicilians he met when he moved to Trappeto in the early 1950s. Short accounts told in their own words provide at once a moving and depressing document.

Christopher Duggan *Fascism and the Mafia* (Yale UP; Yale UP, o/p). Well-researched study of how Mussolini put the Mafia in their place. Duggan uses this account to expound his theory that there's no such thing as the Mafia, that it was simply dreamed up by Italians seeking a scapegoat for their inability to control the delinquent society.

Giovanni Falcone *Men of Honour* (Warner, UK, o/p). Judge Falcone's compelling account of what he found out about the Mafia during his time as chief investigator, knowledge that ultimately led to his murder in May 1992. Essential reading for those who still question the existence of the Mafia, or anyone interested in its labyrinthine organization and why the State has failed to curb it, complete with "Commission" membership lists.

Norman Lewis *The Honoured Society* (Eland; o/p in US). Famous account of the Mafia, its origins, personalities and customs. Certainly the most enjoyable introduction to the subject available, though much of it is taken up with banditry – really a separate issue – and the lack of accredited sources leaves you wondering how much is conjecture.

Clare Longrigg *Mafia Women* (Vintage, UK). Fascinating look at the new active role of women within organized crime in the 1990s, mainly in Naples and Sicily. Intimidation and fear are shown to be

the oil that turns the Mafia wheels, with the supreme place of the family appearing to justify almost any outrage or amount of complicity.

★ **Gavin Maxwell** *The Ten Pains of Death* (Alan Sutton, o/p; Dutton, o/p). Maxwell lived in Scopello in the 1950s, recording the lives of his neighbours in their own words. There's much on Sicilian small-town life and poverty, and sympathetic portraits of traditional festivals and characters. His *God Protect Me from My Friends* (o/p) is a good and sympathetic biography of the notorious bandit Salvatore Giuliano, ripe with intrigue and double-dealing, though its evasiveness about its bloody death begs more questions than it answers.

★ **Peter Robb** *Midnight in Sicily* (Panther; Vintage). The Australian Robb spent fifteen years in the Italian south tracing the contorted relations between organized crime and politics. Here, he focuses on the structure of the Mafia, the trials of the bosses in the 1980s, the high-profile assassinations that ensued, and the trial of Andreotti, in a thorough, fast-paced study that provides deep insights into the dynamics of Sicily's society and an authentic portrait of Palermo.

Tim Shawcross & Martin Young *Men of Honour: the Confessions of Tommaso Buscetta* (HarperCollins, UK, o/p). An account of the Sicilian and American Mafia's move into the international narcotics trade, based on the evidence of Buscetta (a former high-ranking Cosa Nostra lieutenant), which kick-started the 1990s' fightback and saw several leaders imprisoned. The various relationships and feuds are contorted enough to require a family tree (which the book lacks) but it's a good, penetrating yarn, if sometimes carelessly constructed. See also Tim Shawcross's *The War Against the Mafia*

(Mainstream, UK), an informative background on the ways and workings of the Mafia and the attempts to contain it.

Renate Siebert *Secrets of Life and Death: Women and the Mafia*, translated by Liz Heron (Verso). History and analysis of the patriarchal nature of Mafia organizations, which are held to be the apotheosis of the masculine society of Italy's south. Poignant first-person narratives give background to the account, exploding the myth of the Mafia as protecting the weak and defending women, who continue to be used as drugs mules and decoys. The author is a German-born professor of sociology at the University of Calabria.

Carl Sifakis *The Mafia Encyclopedia* (Facts on File; Checkmark Books). An A to Z of organized crime in the United States. All the big Sicilian names are here, alongside intriguing entries for Frank Sinatra, George Raft and a host of other hangers-on.

Claire Sterling *The Mafia* (HarperCollins; Acacia in US, where title is *Octopus: The Long Reach of the International Sicilian Mafia*). Thorough piece of Mafia scholarship, showing, to a disturbing degree, just how little Mafia power has been eroded by the State's onslaught of recent years.

Alexander Stille *Excellent Cadavers* (Vintage). An important book tracing the modern fight against the Mafia as led by Giovanni Falcone and Paolo Borsellino, both of whom were assassinated in 1992. But, as Stille shows, the work they started led eventually to the imprisonment of Salvatore Riina (see p.455).

Novels about Sicily

Allen Andrews *Impossible Loyalties* (Deutsch, UK, o/p). Fast-moving, if unevenly paced, narrative of an Anglo-Sicilian family caught up in the turmoil of World War II, containing an authentic portrait of pre-war Messina society.

Tahar Ben Jelloun *State of Absence* (Quartet; Quartet, o/p). The French-Moroccan author visited southern Italy and Sicily in 1990, fashioning his notes about daily life into a provoking, realistic novel about the effect of the Mafia on the people of the south.

Norman Lewis *The March of the Long Shadows* (Secker & Warburg, UK, o/p). An affectionate novel set in postwar Sicily, dealing with the Separatist movement, the bandit Giuliano and a whole cast of endearing characters. Good location-writing, too, detailing the countryside around Palermo. *The Sicilian Specialist* (Penguin, o/p; Critic's Choice, o/p) is a Mafia thriller, full of authentic Sicilian background, which flits from the island to the US to Cuba on the trail of a Mob assassin.

★ **Dacia Maraini** *The Silent Duchess* (Peter Owen; Feminist Press). The work of a Florence-born author, but with a Sicilian mother, this is one of the most successful Italian novels of recent years, set in eighteenth-century Sicily. It's a tale of a noble family seen through the eyes of a young duchess; beautifully written and dripping with authentic detail, particularly about the lot of women in those times. *Bagheria* (Peter Owen; Dufour), by the same author, is a delightfully engaging memoir of her childhood in the town of the title, entwining criticism of local corruption with a historical awareness of events and people which figured in her earlier work.

Lily Prior *La Cucina* (Black Swan; Ecco Press). Subtitled a "novel of rapture", this chronicles the romance between a spinster librarian from Castiglione and an enigmatic English chef. Drawn into the plot are the Mafia, copious recipes, and the convolutions of Sicilian family life.

★ **Mario Puzo** *The Godfather* (Arrow; Signet). The New York Godfather – Don Corleone – was born in Sicily (see p.335) and the book touches on all things Sicilian. In Francis Ford Coppola's three-part film, the first to rehabilitate the Mafia in American eyes, Marlon Brando played an old Don Corleone. The book's a great read, even if you've seen the films (which are pretty faithful to Puzo's novel). Also by Puzo is *The Sicilian* (Arrow in UK,

o/p; Ballantine Books), a novelized life of the bandit Salvatore Giuliano, and the basis of an uninspiring 1988 film starring Christopher Lambert. Better, if you're interested, is to try and catch Francesco Rosi's 1962 film, *Salvatore Giuliano*.

Ann Radcliffe *A Sicilian Romance* (Oxford UP). Early Gothic novel, written in 1790, telling of supernatural events haunting an aristocratic family, with much purple description of the Sicilian landscape.

Peter Vansittart *A Choice of Murder* (Peter Owen; Dufour). Clever novelized account of the life of Timoleon of Siracusa, based on Plutarch's history of the same. A gripping view of the ancient Greek world in Sicily and beyond.

Sicilian literature and biography

Gesualdo Bufalino *The Plague Sower* (Eridanos Press), *Blind Argus* (Harvill in UK, o/p), *The Keeper of Ruins* (Harvill, UK), and *Night's Lies* (Harvill). "Discovered" by Sciascia, Bufalino arrived late on the literary scene, publishing his first novel, *The Plague Sower*, in his sixties. Subsequent publications enhanced the reputation made by this remarkable debut, notably *Night's Lies*, which won Italy's most respected literary award, the Strega Prize, in 1988. Bufalino himself – seeking to explain the Sicilian character – commented, "Don't forget that even our most obscene vices nearly always bear the seal of sullen greatness."

Andrea Camilleri *The Shape of Water, Voice of the Violin* (Penguin; Viking). Born in Agrigento, Camilleri is one of Italy's favourite modern authors, though he writes in Sicilian dialect that not all Italians can understand. His paced, thoughtful, and often quite vulgar and graphic crime novels, featuring Inspector

Montalbano, are set deep in the folds of Sicilian crime culture, and have become hugely popular all over Europe.

David Gilmour *The Last Leopard: A Life of Giuseppe di Lampedusa* (Harvill, o/p). First biography in English of Lampedusa, though frankly no more than a readable account of the life of rather a dull man – to whom nothing very much happened except the publication (after his death) of one remarkable novel.

Maria Grammatico & Mary Taylor Simeti *Bitter Almonds: Recollections and Recipes from a Sicilian Girlhood* (Vintage Departures, US, o/p). Maria Grammatico was raised in a convent, where she learned the pastry-cooking skills that she employs in her outlets in Érice. The book, co-authored by Mary Taylor Simeti (see "Cuisine," p.479), relates her life with the nuns, and includes some of her famous recipes.

★ **Giuseppe di Lampedusa** *The Leopard* (Harvill; Pantheon). The most famous Sicilian novel, written after World War II but recounting the dramatic nineteenth-century years of transition from Bourbon to Piedmontese rule from an aristocrat's point of view. A good character study and rich with incidental detail, including some nice descriptions of the Sicilian landscape, which was put to great effect in Visconti's epic 1963 film.

Luigi Pirandello *Six Characters in Search of an Author* (Penguin), *Henry IV* (Methuen, o/p; Players Press), *The Late Mattia Pascal* (Dedalus), *Short Stories* (Quartet, o/p; Dover). His most famous and accomplished work, *Six Characters …* , written in 1921, and his *Henry IV*, written a year later, contain many of the themes that dogged Pirandello throughout his writing career – the idea of a multiple personality and the quality of reality. *The Late Mattia Pascal* is an early novel (1904), entertainingly written despite its stylistic shortcomings; while the collection of short stories is perhaps the best introduction to Pirandello's work you can buy: abrasive stuff, the dialogue possessing an assured comic touch.

Salvatore Quasimodo *Complete Poems* (Random House, US, o/p), *Collected Poems* (Penguin, UK). Born in Syracuse in 1901, Quasimodo was a founder of Italy's hermetic school of poets. His earliest poems were rather abstruse and metaphysical, while his later work addressed more mundane themes like sociality and mortality. He was awarded the Nobel Prize for Literature in 1959.

Carmelo Samona *Brothers* (Carcanet, UK). Palermo-born author of only two novels, Samona here investigates the fraught relationship of two brothers – an eerie work.

★ **Leonardo Sciascia**, *Sicilian Uncles* (Granta; Carcanet,

o/p), *The Wine-Dark Sea* (Granta; New York Review of Books Classics), *Candido* (Adelphi; Harcourt Brace, o/p), *The Knight and Death* (Carcanet, UK), *Death of an Inquisitor* (Carcanet), *The Day of the Owl* (Granta; published as *Il Giorno della Civetta* in the US, by Manchester UP), *Equal Danger* (Granta; Godine, o/p). Economically written, Sciascia's short stories and novellas are packed with incisive insights into the island's quirky ways, and infused with the author's humane and sympathetic view of its people. The first to describe the Mafia in Italian literature, he wrote metaphysical thrillers in which the detectives often turn out to be the hunted; the best known is *The Day of the Owl*, an extract from which appears on p.469.

Giovanni Verga *Short Sicilian Novels* (Dedalus), *Cavalleria Rusticana* (Penguin), *Maestro Don Gesualdo* (Dedalus), *I Malavoglia* or *The House by the Medlar Tree* (Dedalus), *A Mortal Sin* (Quartet, UK), *La Lupa* (Methuen) and *Sparrow* (Dedalus; Italica Press). Born in the nineteenth century in Catania, Verga spent several years in various European salons before coming home to write his best work. Much of it is a reaction against the pseudo-sophistication of society circles, stressing the simple lives of ordinary people, though they're occasionally bestowed with a heavy smattering of "peasant passion", with much emotion, wounded honour and feuds to the death. D.H. Lawrence's translations are suitably vibrant, with excellent introductions. *Sparrow* is a doomed love story set in cholera-ravaged mid-nineteenth-century Sicily, and filmed by Zeffirelli in 1993.

Elio Vittorini *Conversations in Sicily* (Canongate). A Sicilian emigrant returns from the north of Italy after fifteen years to see his mother on her birthday. The conversations of the title are with the people he meets on the way, local villagers and his mother, and reveal a prewar Sicily that is poverty- and disease-ridden – though affectionately drawn. An extract is printed on p.467. A Vittorini omnibus containing the novels *In Sicily*, *The Twilight of the Elephant* and *La Garibaldina* is published by New Directions in the US, and Vittorini's *Men and Not Men* is published by Marlboro Press in the UK and US.

Cuisine

Antonio Carluccio *Southern Italian Feast* (BBC; West One Hundred Seventy Five). Glossy TV tie-in by Britain's avuncular Italian master, particularly good on Sicilian fish and snacks – his *arancini* recipe is definitive.

Elizabeth David *Italian Food* (Penguin). First published in 1954, this was the book that introduced Mediterranean flavours to a UK ravaged by postwar shortages. Although a learned and entertaining stroll through the whole canon of Italian cooking, there are plenty of Sicilian dishes covered. The 1998 edition includes original illustrations by Renato Guttuso.

Valentina Harris *Southern Italian Cooking* (Trafalgar Square, US, o/p). Excellent book with a chapter on Sicilian cooking, including several of the classic recipes. Also covers the related cuisine of Calabria and other southern regions.

Anna Tasca Lanza *The Flavors of Sicily* (Ici LA Press, US). Sicilian summer cooking from the respected owner of a cooking school established at her family estate on the island. An anecdotal trawl through the classics and the lesser-known dishes, including several from out-of-the-way places like Pantelleria and Strómboli. Look out too for her *Heart of Sicily: Recipes and Reminiscences of Regaleali, a Country Estate* (Clarkson Potter).

Anna Pomar *La Cucina Tradizionale Siciliana* (Brancato); and **Silvia Trombetta**, *Dolci Tradizionali Siciliani* (Brancato). Published in Italy (in Italian), you'll see these complementary books on sale throughout Sicily. They're extremely comprehensive, the first book detailing recipes from every Sicilian region, the second a wealth of recipes for desserts, sweets and festival food.

★ **Mary Taylor Simeti** *Sicilian Food* (Grub Street; published as *Pomp and Sustenance* in US by Ecco Press). Everything a book on food should be: historically and culturally informed, and packed with recipes and fascinating detail about life and food on the island. Thoroughly recommended.

★ **Wanda Tornabene, Giovanna Tornabene & Michele Evans** *La Cucina Siciliana di Gangivecchio* (Knopf). A collection of over 200 sophisticated dishes, each with a *nouveau* slant on Sicilian cuisine, though there's little Arab influence and virtually no fish recipes.

Films

Though Sicily doesn't yet have its own motion picture industry, the island's stunning scenery has been used as a backdrop to a number of very successful films. The Aeolian and Pélagie islands, in particular, have proved popular settings for some interesting films, a few of them now classics of Italian cinema.

Michelangelo Antonioni
L'Avventura (1960). Shot on the barren rocks of Panarea's Lisca Bianca, this film notes the beginning of a marked change in postwar Italian social mores. When a group of friends get together for a day out in the islands, one of them gets lost, and the relationships between those remaining begin to fracture. Here, Antonioni focuses ingeniously on the internal responses of those affected.

Emanuele Crispalese *Il Respiro* (2002). Filmed on the southern island of Lampedusa, this is a timeless, well-constructed look at how an eccentric mother is misunderstood by other islanders. Crispalese's second film, it addresses the overwhelming patriarchy of Italian families and the sexual tension latent between family members.

Francis Ford Coppola *The Godfather* (1971). Mario Puzo's brilliant screenplay tells the story of how Don Vito Corleone, *capo* of the New York Sicilian Mafia, tries to maintain his hold on the family business and his old-world values, despite his renegade son Michael. Since the town of Corleone itself was far too developed for the period filming, much of it was shot in Savoca and Forza d'Agro, outside Taormina.

Pietro Giermi *Divorzio alla Siciliana* (1961). Proof that not all Sicilian films need be deep or cinematic, this is a hilarious and pointed satire of Italian marital conventions. Marcello Mastroianni plays a Sicilian nobleman trying to prove his wife

unfaithful so he can kill her and marry his younger cousin. Known as *Divorce Italian Style* in English, it was filmed in Ispica near Ragusa, and got Giermi nominated for a Best Director Oscar.

Nanni Moretti *Dear Diary* (1994). Moretti plays himself as he tours Italy on a Vespa, visiting all the Aeolian Islands, showing how the inhabitants of each differ in mentality and lifestyle. Mostly comic, but a real downer at the end.

Michael Radford *Il Postino* (1994). An international favourite, featuring a postman who learns to love poetry after befriending Pablo Neruda, who was recently exiled to a small island. The film was shot in the town of Pollara on Salina, leading to a dramatic increase in tourists to the region.

Roberto Rossellini *Strómboli: Terra di Dio* (1949). Starring Ingrid Bergman as a tormented young refugee who marries an Italian to escape the war, this is a sad story of solitude and cynicism, that received little praise in its home country. The real star, however, is the volcano itself, whose brooding presence undermines the illusion of an idyllic, happy island.

Giuseppe Tornatore *Cinema Paradiso* (1988). Though declaimed by critics for its saccharine storyline, this Oscar-winning film by Sicilian director Tornatore received popular acclaim the world over. Shot around Cefalù, it follows the friendship between a young boy and the local cinema projectionist, and is in many ways an homage to cinema itself.

Language

Language

Italian

The ability to speak English confers enormous prestige in Sicily, but though there's no shortage of people willing to show off their knowledge, particularly returned *emigrati*, few outside the tourist resorts actually know more than some simple words and phrases – more often than not culled from pop songs or films.

Some tips

You'd do well to master at least a little **Italian**, a task made more enjoyable by the fact that your halting efforts will often be rewarded by smiles and genuine surprise that an English-speaker should stoop to learn Italian. In any case, it's one of the easiest European languages to learn, especially if you already have a smattering of French or Spanish, both extremely similar grammatically. The best **phrasebook** is Rough Guide's own *Italian Phrasebook* (Penguin), while Collins publishes a comprehensive series of **dictionaries**.

Easiest of all is the **pronunciation**, since every word is spoken exactly as it's written, and usually enunciated with exaggerated, open-mouthed clarity. The only difficulties you're likely to encounter are the few **consonants** that are different from English:

c before **e** or **i** is pronounced as in church, while **ch** before the same vowels is hard, as in cat.

sci or **sce** are pronounced as in sheet and shelter respectively. The same goes with **g** soft before **e** and **i**, as in gentle; hard when followed by **h**, as in garlic.

gn has the **ni** sound of our onion.

gl in Italian is softened to something like **li** in English, as in vermilion.

h is not aspirated, as in hour.

When **speaking** to strangers, the third person is the polite form (ie *Lei* instead of *Tu* for "you"); using the second person is a mark of disrespect or stupidity. It's also worth remembering that Italians don't use "please" and "thank you" half as much as we do: it's all implied in the tone, though if you're in doubt, err on the polite side.

All Italian words are **stressed** on the penultimate syllable unless an **accent** denotes otherwise, although accents are often left out in practice. Note that the ending **–ia** or **–ie** counts as two syllables, hence *trattoria* is stressed on the i. We've put accents in, throughout the text and below, wherever it isn't immediately obvious how a word should be pronounced: for example, in *Maríttima*, the accent is on the first **i**; conversely *Catania* should theoretically have an accent on the second **a**. Other words where we've omitted accents are common ones (like *Isola*, stressed on the I), some names (*Domenico*, *Vittorio*), and words that are stressed similarly in English, such as *Repubblica*.

None of this will help very much if you're confronted with a particularly harsh specimen of the **Sicilian dialect**, which virtually qualifies as a separate

For political reasons, all regional languages in Italy are considered dialects of Italian, though in reality they each have their own histories and influences and the majority of them are, linguistically speaking, separate languages. During the 600-year-long Roman occupation of Sicily, Vulgar Latin became the lingua franca for the entire island, though it was highly influenced by close contacts with Arabic, Norman and Spanish languages. The grammar, lexicon and phonology of Sicilian thus differs immensely from modern standard Italian – so much so that during the 1980s American Mafia trials, the FBI had to enlist special agents fluent in Sicilian to translate the conversations of Mafiosi based in New York. The Sicilian language even has its own regional dialects (*parrati*), though in general these are understood by all Sicilians.

Today nearly all Sicilians speak and understand standard Italian, though, unlike numerous other dialects spoken throughout Europe, the language is in no danger of extinction: in most towns, the younger generation prefers Sicilian to Italian, and almost everyone speaks Sicilian at home. Though Sicilians are well known for using their hands and arms as much as their vocal cords to communicate, their language is rich in idioms and sayings. Below is a sample of some favourite Sicilian proverbs:

Si vo' passari la vita cuntenti, statti luntanu di li parenti.
If you want quiet, stay away from relatives.

Sciarri di maritu e mugghieri, duranu finu a lu lettu.
Quarrels between wives and husbands always end in the bed.

Cu'arrobba pri manciari, nun fa piccatu.
He who steals to eat is no sinner.

Cu'asini caccia e fimmini cridi, faccia di paradisu nun ni vidi.
He who seeks girls and asses will never reach heaven.

Camina chi pantofuli finnu a quannu non hai i scarpi.
Walk with your slippers until you find your shoes (ie make the best of a bad situation).

Cu' va a Palermu e nun va a Murriali, si nni parti sceccu e torna maiali.
He who visits Palermo and not Monreale arrives an ass and returns a pig.

language (see below). However, television has made a huge difference and almost every Sicilian can now communicate in something approximating standard Italian.

A language guide

Basics

Good morning	**Buon giorno**	Hello/goodbye	**Ciao** (informal; when
Good afternoon	**Buona sera**		speaking to
/evening			strangers use the
Good night	**Buona notte**		phrases above)

Goodbye	Arrivederci (formal)	Now	Adesso
Yes	Sì	Later	Più tardi
No	No	Wait a minute!	Aspetta!
Please	Per favore	In the morning	Di mattina
Thank you	Grázie	In the afternoon	Nel pomeriggio
(very much)	(molte/mille grazie)	In the evening	Di sera
You're welcome	Prego	Tonight	Stasera
Alright/that's OK	Va bene	Here/there	Qui/là
How are you?	Come stai/sta?	Good/bad	Buono/cattivo
(informal/formal)		Big/small	Grande/píccolo
I'm fine	Bene	Cheap/expensive	Económico/caro
Do you speak English?	Parla inglese?	Early/late	Presto/ritardo
I don't speak Italian	Non parlo italiano	Hot/cold	Caldo/freddo
I don't understand	Non capisco	Near/far	Vicino/lontano
I haven't understood	Non ho capito	Vacant/occupied	Líbero/occupato
I don't know	Non lo so	Quickly/slowly	Velocemente
Excuse me/sorry	Scusa		/lentamente
(informal)		Slowly/quietly	Piano
Excuse me/sorry	Mi scusi/Prego	With/without	Con/senza
(formal)		More/less	Più/meno
Excuse me	Permesso	Enough/no more	Basta
(in a crowd)		Mr...	Signor...
I'm sorry	Mi dispiace	Mrs...	Signora...
I'm here on holiday	Sono qui in vacanza	Miss...	Signorina...
I live in...	Abito a...	(il Signore, la Signora, la Signorina	
Today	Oggi	when speaking about someone else)	
Tomorrow	Domani	First name	Primo nome
Day after tomorrow	Dopodomani	Surname	Cognome
Yesterday	Ieri		

Accommodation

Hotel	Albergo	How much is it?	Quanto costa?
Is there a hotel	C'è un albergo qui	It's expensive	È caro
nearby?	vicino?	Is breakfast included?	È compresa la
Do you have a room...	Ha una cámera...		prima colazione?
for one/two/three	per una persona,	Do you have anything	Ha niente che costa
people	due/tre persone	cheaper?	di meno?
for one/two/three	per una notte, due	Full-/half-board	Pensione completa/
nights	/tre notti		mezza pensione
for one/two weeks	per una settimana,	Can I see the room?	Posso vedere la
	due settimane		cámera?
with a double bed	con un letto	I'll take it	La prendo
	matrimoniale	I'd like to book a room	Vorrei prenotare una
with a shower/bath	con una doccia un		cámera
	bagno	I have a booking	Ho una prenotazione
with a balcony	con una terrazza	Can we camp here?	Possiamo fare il
hot/cold water	acqua calda/fredda		campeggio qui?

Is there a campsite nearby?	C'è un camping qui vicino?	Cabin	Cabina
Tent	Tenda	Youth hostel	Ostello per la gioventù

Questions and directions

Where?	Dove?	lift to...?	passaggio a...?
(Where is/are...?)	(Dov'è/Dove sono?)	Can you tell me when to get off?	Può dirmi quando devo scendere?
When?	Quando?	What time does it open?	A che ora apre?
What?	Cosa?		
(What is it?)	(Cos'è?)	What time does it close?	A che ora chiude?
How much/many?	Quanto/Quanti?		
Why?	Perché?	How much does it cost	Quanto costa?
It is/There is	È/C'è		
(Is it/Is there...?)	(È/C'è...?)	(...do they cost?)	(Quantocostano?)
What time is it?	Che ora è?/Che ore sono?	What's it called in Italian?	Come si chiama in italiano?
		Left/right	Sinistra/destra
How do I get to...?	Come arrivo a...?	Go straight ahead	Sempre diritto
How far is it to...?	Quant'è lontano a...?	Turn to the right/left	Gira a destra/sinistra
Can you give me a	Mi può dare un		

Transport matters

Aeroplane	Aeroplano	What time does it leave?	A che ora parte?
Bus	Autobus/Pullman	When is the next bus/train/ferry to...?	Quando parte il próssimo pullman /treno/traghetto per...?
Train	Treno		
Car	Mácchina		
Taxi	Taxi		
Bicycle	Bicicletta		
Ferry	Traghetto	Where does it leave from?	Da dove parte?
Ship	Nave		
Hydrofoil	Aliscafo	Which platform does it leave from?	Da quale binario parte?
Hitch-hiking	Autostop		
On foot	A piedi	Do I have to change?	Devo cambiare?
Bus station	Autostazione	How many kilometres is it?	Quanti chilómetri sono?
Train station	Stazione ferroviaria		
Ferry terminal	Stazione maríttima	How long does it take?	Quanto ci vuole?
Port	Porto		
A ticket to...	Un biglietto a...	What number bus is it to...?	Que número di autobus per...?
One way/return	Solo andata/andata e ritorno	Where's the road to...?	Dov'è la strada a...?
Can I book a seat?	Posso prenotare un posto?	Next stop, please	La próssima fermata, per favore

Some signs

Entrance/exit	**Entrata/uscita**	Platform	**Binario**
Free entrance	**Ingresso líbero**	Cash desk	**Cassa**
Gentlemen/ladies	**Signori/signore**	Go/walk	**Avanti**
WC	**Gabinetto/bagno**	Stop/halt	**Alt**
Vacant/engaged	**Líbero/occupato**	Customs	**Dogana**
Open/closed	**Aperto/chiuso**	Do not touch	**Non toccare**
Arrivals/departures	**Arrivi/partenze**	Danger	**Perícolo**
Closed for restoration	**Chiuso per restauro**	Beware	**Attenzione**
Closed for holidays	**Chiuso per ferie**	First aid	**Pronto soccorso**
Pull/push	**Tirare/spingere**	Ring the bell	**Suonare il campanello**
Out of order	**Guasto**		
Drinking water	**Acqua potabile**	No smoking	**Vietato fumare**
To let	**Affítasi**		

Driving

Parking	**Parcheggio**	Road closed/up	**Strada chiusa /guasta**
No parking	**Divieto di sosta/ Sosta vietata**	No through road	**Vietato il transito**
One way street	**Senso único**	No overtaking	**Vietato il sorpasso**
Both sides of the street	**Ambo i lati**	Crossroads	**Incrocio**
		Speed limit	**Límite di velocità**
No entry	**Senso vietato**	Traffic light	**Semáforo**
Slow down	**Rallentare**		

Numbers and days of the week

1	**Uno**	20	**Venti**
2	**Due**	25	**Venticinque**
3	**Tre**	30	**Trenta**
4	**Quattro**	40	**Quaranta**
5	**Cinque**	50	**Cinquanta**
6	**Sei**	60	**Sessanta**
7	**Sette**	70	**Settanta**
8	**Otto**	80	**Ottanta**
9	**Nove**	90	**Novanta**
10	**Dieci**	100	**Cento**
11	**Undici**	1000	**Mille**
12	**Dodici**	Monday	**Lunedì**
13	**Tredici**	Tuesday	**Martedì**
14	**Quattordici**	Wednesday	**Mercoledì**
15	**Quindici**	Thursday	**Giovedì**
16	**Sedici**	Friday	**Venerdì**
17	**Diciassette**	Saturday	**Sabato**
18	**Diciotto**	Sunday	**Domenica**
19	**Diciannove**		

Sicilian food terms

Basics and snacks

Aceto	Vinegar	Pane	Bread
Aglio	Garlic	Pane integrale	Wholemeal bread
Biscotti	Biscuits	Panino	Bread roll
Burro	Butter	Patatine	Crisps/potato chips
Caramelle	Sweets	Patatine fritte	Chips/French fries
Cioccolato	Chocolate	Pepe	Pepper
Focaccia	Oven-baked snack	Pizzetta	Small cheese-and-tomato pizza
Formaggio	Cheese		
Frittata	Omelette	Riso	Rice
Gelato	Ice cream	Sale	Salt
Grissini	Bread sticks	Uova	Eggs
Maionese	Mayonnaise	Yogurt	Yoghurt
Marmellata	Jam	Zúcchero	Sugar
Olio	Oil	Zuppa	Soup
Olive	Olives		

Antipasti and starters

Antipasto misto	Mixed cold meats and cheese (plus a mix of other things in this list)	Melanzane alla parmigiana	Fried aubergine in tomato sauce with parmesan cheese
Caponata	Mixed aubergine, olives and tomatoes	Mortadella	Salami-type cured meat with white nuggets of fat, often with pistachios
Caprese	Tomato and mozzarella cheese salad		
Insalata di mare	Seafood salad (usually squid, octopus and prawn)	Pancetta	Italian bacon
		Peperonata	Grilled green, red or yellow peppers stewed in olive oil
Insalata di riso	Rice salad	Pomodori ripieni	Stuffed tomatoes
Insalata russa	"Russian salad": diced vegetables in mayonnaise	Prosciutto	Ham
		Salame	Salami
		Salmone/tonno /pesce spada /affumicato	Smoked salmon/tuna /swordfish

Pizzas

Biancaneve	"Black and white": mozzarella and oregano	Capricciosa	"Capricious": topped with whatever they've got in the kitchen, usually including baby artichoke, ham and egg
Calzone	Folded pizza with cheese, ham and tomato		

L

LANGUAGE | Sicilian food terms

488

Cardinale	Ham and olives	Quattro formaggi	"Four cheeses":
Diavolo	"Devil": spicy, with hot salami or Italian sausage		usually mozzarella, fontina, Gorgonzola and Gruyère
Funghi	Mushroom: tinned, sliced button mushrooms unless it specifies fresh mushrooms, either funghi freschi or porcini	Quattro stagioni	"Four seasons": the toppings split into four separate sections, usually including ham, peppers, onion, mushrooms, artichokes, olives, egg etc
Frutti di mare	Seafood: usually mussels, prawns, squid and clams	Rianata	Fresh tomato, oregano, garlic and anchovy; a western Sicilian speciality
Margherita	Cheese and tomato		
Marinara	Tomato and garlic		
Napoli/ Napoletana	Tomato, anchovy and olive oil (often mozzarella too)	Romana	Anchovy and olives

The first course (il primo): Soups

Brodo	Clear broth	Pastina in brodo	Pasta pieces in clear broth
Minestrina	Any light soup		
Minestrone	Thick vegetable soup	Stracciatella	Broth with egg
Pasta e fagioli	Pasta soup with beans		

Pasta

Cannelloni	Large tubes of pasta, stuffed	Ravioli	Ravioli (stuffed, square-shaped pasta)
Farfalle	Literally "bow"-shaped pasta; the word also means "butterflies"	Rigatoni	Large, grooved, tubular pasta
		Risotto	Cooked rice dish, with sauce
Fettuccine	Narrow pasta ribbons		
Gnocchi	Small potato and dough dumplings	Spaghetti	Spaghetti
		Spaghettini	Thin spaghetti
Lasagne	Lasagne	Tagliatelle	Pasta ribbons, another word for fettuccine
Maccheroni	Macaroni (tubular pasta)		
		Tortellini	Small rings of pasta, stuffed with meat or cheese
Pappardelle	Pasta ribbons		
Pasta al forno	Pasta baked with minced meat, eggs, tomato and cheese	Vermicelli	Very thin spaghetti (literally "little worms")
Penne	Smaller version of rigatoni		

Pasta sauces (salsa)

Aglio e olio (e peperoncino)	Tossed in garlic and olive oil (and hot chillies)	Panna	Cream
		Parmigiano	Parmesan cheese
		Pesto	Ground basil, pine nut, garlic and pecorino
Amatriciana	Cubed pork and tomato sauce, with onions and hot chillies (originally from Rome)	Pomodoro	Tomato sauce
		Puttanesca	"Whorish": tomato, anchovy, olive oil and oregano
Arrabbiata	Spicy tomato sauce, with chillies	Ragù	Meat sauce
Bolognese	Meat sauce	Trápanese	Cold puréed tomato, garlic and basil
Burro e salvia	Butter and sage		
Carbonara	Cream, ham and beaten egg	Vóngole (veraci)	Clam and tomato sauce (fresh clams in shells, usually served with oil and herbs)
Frutta di mare	Seafood		
Funghi	Mushroom		

The second course (il secondo): Meat (carne)

Agnello	Lamb	Manzo	Beef
Bistecca	Steak	Ossobuco	Shin of veal
Cervello	Brain	Pollo	Chicken
Cinghiale	Wild boar	Polpette	Meatballs
Coniglio	Rabbit	Rognoni	Kidneys
Costolette/cotolette	Cutlets/chops	Salsiccia	Sausage
Fégatini	Chicken livers	Saltimbocca	Veal with ham
Fégato	Liver	Scaloppina	Escalope (of veal)
Involtini	Steak slices, rolled and stuffed	Spezzatino	Stew
		Tacchino	Turkey
Lepre	Hare	Trippa	Tripe
Lingua	Tongue	Vitello	Veal
Maiale	Pork		

Fish (pesce) and shellfish (crostacei)

Note that **surgelato** or **congelato** written on the menu next to a dish means "frozen" – it often applies to squid and prawns.

Acciughe	Anchovies	Déntice	Dentex (like sea bass)
Anguilla	Eel	Gamberetti	Shrimps
Aragosta	Lobster	Gámberi	Prawns
Baccalà	Dried salted cod	Granchio	Crab
Calamari	Squid	Merluzzo	Cod
Céfalo	Grey mullet	Nasello	Hake
Cernia	Grouper	Orata	Gilthead bream
Cozze	Mussels	Ostriche	Oysters
Dattile	Razor clams	Pesce spada	Swordfish

L

LANGUAGE

Sicilian food terms

490

Pólpo	Octopus	Sgombro	Mackerel
Ricci di mare	Sea urchins	Sógliola	Sole
Ricciola	Amberjack	Spígola	Sea bass
Rospo	Monkfish	Tonno	Tuna
Sampiero	John Dory	Tótani	Species of squid
Sarago	White bream	Triglie	Red mullet
Sarde	Sardines	Trota	Trout
Seppie	Cuttlefish	Vóngole	Clams

Vegetables (contorni) and salad (insalata)

Asparagi	Asparagus	Finocchio	Fennel
Basílico	Basil	Funghi	Mushrooms
Broccoli	Broccoli	Insalata verde /mista	Green salad/mixed salad
Cápperi	Capers	Melanzane	Aubergine/eggplant
Carciofi	Artichokes	Orígano	Oregano
Carciofini	Artichoke hearts	Patate	Potatoes
Carotte	Carrots	Peperoni	Peppers
Cavolfiori	Cauliflower	Piselli	Peas
Cávolo	Cabbage	Pomodori	Tomatoes
Ceci	Chickpeas	Radicchio	Red chicory
Cetriolo	Cucumber	Spinaci	Spinach
Cipolla	Onion	Zucca	Pumpkin
Fagioli	Beans	Zucchini	Courgettes
Fagiolini	Green beans		

Deserts (dolci)

Amaretti	Macaroons	Torta	Cake, tart
Cassata	Ice-cream cake with candied fruit	Zabaglione	Dessert made with eggs, sugar and Marsala wine
Gelato	Ice cream		
Macedonia	Fruit salad	Zuppa Inglese	Trifle

Cheese

Caciocavallo	A type of dried, mature mozzarella	Pecorino	Strong-tasting, hard sheep's cheese
Fontina	Northern Italian cheese used in cooking	Provolone	Cheese with grooved rind, either mild or slightly piquant
Gorgonzola	Soft, strong, blue-veined cheese	Ricotta	Soft white cheese made from ewe's milk, used in sweet or savoury dishes
Mozzarella	Soft white cheese, traditionally made from buffalo's milk		
Parmigiano	Parmesan cheese	Vastedda Palermitana	Similar to Caciocavallo, but tastes slightly more acidic

Fruit and nuts

Albicocche	Apricots	Limone	Lemon
Ananas	Pineapple	Mándorle	Almonds
Anguria/coccómero	Watermelon	Mele	Apples
Arance	Oranges	Melone	Melon
Banane	Bananas	Néspole	Medlars
Cacchi	Persimmons	Pere	Pears
Ciliegie	Cherries	Pesche	Peaches
Fichi	Figs	Pignoli	Pine nuts
Fichi d'India	Prickly pears	Pistacchio	Pistachio nut
Frágole	Strawberries	Uva	Grapes

Cooking terms

Affumicato	Smoked	Alla griglia	Grilled
Arrosto	Roast	Al Marsala	Cooked with Marsala wine
Ben cotto	Well done		
Bollito/lesso	Boiled	Milanese	Fried in egg and breadcrumbs
Alla brace	Barbecued		
Brasato	Cooked in wine	Pizzaiola	Cooked with tomato sauce
Cotto	Cooked (not raw)		
Crudo	Raw	Ripieno	Stuffed
Al dente	Firm, not overcooked	Sangue	Rare
Ferri	Grilled without oil	Allo spiedo	On the spit
Al forno	Baked	Stracotto	Braised, stewed
Fritto	Fried	Surgelati	Frozen
Grattugiato	Grated	In úmido	Stewed
		Al vapore	Steamed

Sicilian specialities: starters and pasta

Arancini	"Little oranges": deep-fried rice balls with minced meat, cheese and peas	Pasta con i broccoli arriminati	Pasta cooked with broccoli, anchovy paste, pine nuts and saffron
Caponata	Sautéed aubergine, olives and tomatoes; served cold	Pasta con la mollica	Pasta with oil and toasted bread crumbs
Cozze alla marinara	Mussels in a rich wine-based soup	Pasta con le sarde	Macaroni with fresh sardines, fennel, raisins and pine kernels; a speciality of Palermo
Cozze pepata	Mussels in spicy tomato stock		
Crocchè di patate	Potato croquettes		
Insalata di arance	Orange salad, dressed with oil and parsley	Penne all'arrabbiata	Short tubular pasta with spicy tomato sauce made with chillies (arrabbiata means "angry")
Maccu	Fava-bean (like lima-bean) soup		
Panelle	Chickpea fritters		

Peperonata	Peppers (capsicum) sautéed in olive oil until soft and sweet, either served as antipasto or as a vegetable	Spaghetti alla Norma	Spaghetti with tomato sauce topped with fried aubergine and parmesan or pecorino cheese; a speciality of Catania, named after one of Bellini's operas
Spaghetti alla carrettiera	"Carter's spaghetti", cooked with garlic, oil, pecorino and salt and pepper; a dish traditionally cooked by roving carters, common in Catania province	Spaghetti alla Trápanese	Spaghetti tossed with cold puréed tomatoes, basil and garlic; a pungent dish from Trápani
		Uova/funghi in tegame	Eggs/mushrooms fried in olive oil, served at the table in a little metal pan

Sicilian specialities: main courses

Cuscus	Couscous, usually served with fish and vegetable sauce, sometimes meat; a common dish in western Sicily	Scaloppine di maiale al Marsala	Escalopes of pork cooked in Marsala wine; the most common way of cooking meat with this Sicilian wine
Fritto misto	A standard seafood dish; deep-fried prawns and squid rings in batter	Stocca alla Messinese	Dried cod stewed with potatoes, olives, tomatoes, capers and celery; a speciality of Messina although there are other regional variations
Fritto di pesce	As above but also with other fried fish, like sardines and white bait		
Involtini di pesce spada	Slices of swordfish, stuffed, rolled and fried		
Pesce spada alla Ghiotta	Swordfish cooked in spicy tomato sauce with capers and olives; from Messina	Zuppa di cozze /vóngole	A big dish of mussels /clams in rich wine-based soup
Sarde a beccafico	Sardines stuffed with breadcrumbs, nuts, dried fruit and anchovies; a Palermitan speciality	Zuppa di pesce	As above but usually with pieces of cod, squid and prawns, and served with fried bread

Deserts and festival food

Cannoli	Fried pastry stuffed with sweet ricotta and candied peel; a	Cassata	Carnevale speciality Ice-cream cake with candied fruit

Crispelle di riso	Sweet rice fritters		at the festival of St Joseph (San Giuseppe)
Pasta reale	Almond paste, shaped and coloured to form mock fruit, vegetables, even fish	Torrone di mándorle	Crystallized almonds and sugar, sold at markets around All Saints' Day
Sfinci	Fried pastry stuffed with ricotta; served		

Drinks

Acqua minerale	Mineral water	Succo di frutta	Concentrated fruit juice with sugar
Aranciata	Orangeade		
Bicchiere	Glass	Tè	Tea
Birra	Beer	Tónico	Tonic water
Bottiglia	Bottle	Vino	Wine
Caffè	Coffee	Rosso	Red
Cioccolata calda	Hot chocolate	Bianco	White
Ghiaccio	Ice	Rosato	Rosé
Granita	Iced coffee/fruit drink	Secco	Dry
Latte	Milk	Dolce	Sweet
Limonata	Lemonade	Litro	Litre
Selz	Soda water	Mezzo	Half-litre
Spremuta	Fresh fruit juice	Quarto	Quarter-litre
Spumante	Sparkling wine	Salute!	Cheers!

Glossaries

Artistic and architectural terms

Agora Square or marketplace in an ancient Greek city.

Apse Domed recess at the altar-end of a church.

Architrave The lowest part of the entablature.

Atrium Forecourt, usually of a Roman house.

Bothros A pit that contains votive offerings.

Campanile Belltower.

Capital Top of a column.

Catalan-Gothic Hybrid form of architecture, mixing elements from fifteenth-century Spanish and northern European building styles.

Cavea The seating section in a theatre.

Cella Sanctuary of a temple.

Cupola A dome.

Decumanus The main street in a Roman town.

Entablature The part of the building above the capital on a classical building.

Ex-voto Decorated tablet designed as thanksgiving to a saint.

Hellenistic period 325–331 BC (Alexander the Great to Augustus).

Hypogeum Underground vault, often used as an early Christian church.

Kouros Standing male figure of the Archaic period (700 BC to early fifth century BC).

Krater Ancient conical bowl with round base.

Loggia Roofed gallery or balcony.

Metope A panel on the frieze of a temple.

Naumachia Mock naval combat, or the deep trench in a theatre in which it took place.

Nave Central space in a church, usually flanked by aisles.

Odeon Small theatre, usually roofed, for recitals.

Orchestra Section of the main floor of a theatre, where the chorus danced.

Pantocrator Usually refers to Christ, portrayed with outstretched arms.

Pediment The triangular front part of a building, usually surmounting a portico of columns.

Polyptych Painting or carving on several joined wooden panels.

Portico The covered entrance to a building.

Punic Carthaginian/Phoenician.

Scene-building Structure holding scenery in Greek/Roman theatre.

Stelae Inscribed stone slabs.

Stereobate Visible base of any building, usually a temple.

Stoa A detached roofed porch, or portico.

Stylobate Raised base of a columned building, usually a temple.

Telamon A supporting column in the shape of a male figure.

Thermae Baths, usually elaborate buildings in Roman villas.

Triptych Painting or carving on three joined wooden panels.

Italian words

Aliscafo Hydrofoil.

Anfiteatro Amphitheatre.

Autostazione Bus station.

Autostrada Motorway.

Belvedere A lookout point.

Cappella Chapel.

Castello Castle.

Cattedrale Cathedral.

Centro Centre.

Chiesa Church (main "mother" church, Chiesa Matrice/Madre).

Comune An administrative area; also, the local council or the town hall.

Corso Avenue/boulevard.

Duomo Cathedral.

Entrata Entrance.

Faraglione Obelisk-shaped deposits of volcanic rock rising out of the sea.

Festa Festival, carnival.

Fiume River.

Fumarola Volcanic vapour emission from the ground.

Golfo Gulf.

Lago Lake.

Largo Place (like piazza).

Lungomare Seafront promenade or road.

Mare Sea.

Mercato Market.

Mongibello Sicilian name for Mount Etna.

Municipio Town hall.

Palazzo Palace, mansion or block (of flats).

Parco Park.

Passeggiata The customary early-evening walk.

Pedaggio Toll.

Piano Plain (also "slowly", "gently").

Piazza Square.

Pineta Pinewood.

Santuario Sanctuary.

Sottopassaggio Subway.

Spiaggia Beach.

Stazione Station (train station, stazione ferroviaria; bus station, autostazione, ferry terminal, stazione maríttima).

Strada Road/street.

Teatro Theatre.

Tempio Temple.

Torre Tower.

Traghetto Ferry.

Uscita Exit.

Vícolo Alley

Via Road (always used with name, as in Via Roma).

Zona Zone.

Acronyms

AAST Azienda Autonoma di Soggiorno e Turismo (local tourist office).

ACI Italian Automobile Club.

APT Azienda Provinciale di Turismo (provincial tourist office).

EPT Ente Provinciale di Turismo (provincial tourist office).

DC Democrazia Cristiana; the Christian Democrat Party.

FS Italian State Railways.

IVA Imposta Valore Aggiunto (VAT).

MSI Movimento Sociale d'Italia; the Italian Neo-Fascist party, now called the Alleanza Nazionale.

PDS Partito Democratico della Sinistra; the former Italian Communist Party.

PSI Partito Socialista d'Italia; the Italian Socialist Party.

RAI The Italian state TV and radio network.

SP Strada Provinciale; a minor road, eg SP116.

SS Strada Statale; a main highway, eg SS120.

Rough
Guides
advertiser

Rough Guides travel...

...music & reference

Africa & Middle East
Cape Town
Egypt
The Gambia
Jordan
Kenya
Marrakesh
  DIRECTIONS
Morocco
South Africa, Lesotho
  & Swaziland
Syria
Tanzania
Tunisia
West Africa
Zanzibar
Zimbabwe

Travel Theme guides
First-Time Around the
  World
First-Time Asia
First-Time Europe
First-Time Latin
  America
Skiing & Snowboarding
  in North America
Travel Online
Travel Health
Walks in London & SE
  England
Women Travel

Restaurant guides
French Hotels &
  Restaurants
London
New York
San Francisco

Maps
Algarve
Amsterdam
Andalucia & Costa del Sol
Argentina
Athens
Australia

Baja California
Barcelona
Berlin
Boston
Brittany
Brussels
Chicago
Crete
Croatia
Cuba
Cyprus
Czech Republic
Dominican Republic
Dubai & UAE
Dublin
Egypt
Florence & Siena
Frankfurt
Greece
Guatemala & Belize
Iceland
Ireland
Kenya
Lisbon
London
Los Angeles
Madrid
Mexico
Miami & Key West
Morocco
New York City
New Zealand
Northern Spain
Paris
Peru
Portugal
Prague
Rome
San Francisco
Sicily
South Africa
South India
Sri Lanka
Tenerife
Thailand
Toronto
Trinidad & Tobago

Tuscany
Venice
Washington DC
Yucatán Peninsula

**Dictionary
Phrasebooks**
Czech
Dutch
Egyptian Arabic
EuropeanLanguages
  (Czech, French,
  German, Greek, Italian,
  Portuguese, Spanish)
French
German
Greek
Hindi & Urdu
Hungarian
Indonesian
Italian
Japanese
Mandarin Chinese
Mexican Spanish
Polish
Portuguese
Russian
Spanish
Swahili
Thai
Turkish
Vietnamese

Music Guides
The Beatles
Bob Dylan
Cult Pop
Classical Music
Country Music
Elvis
Hip Hop
House
Irish Music
Jazz
Music USA
Opera
Reggae

Rock
Techno
World Music (2 vols)

History Guides
China
Egypt
England
France
India
Islam
Italy
Spain
USA

Reference Guides
Books for Teenagers
Children's Books, 0–5
Children's Books, 5–11
Cult Fiction
Cult Football
Cult Movies
Cult TV
Ethical Shopping
Formula 1
The iPod, iTunes &
  Music Online
The Internet
Internet Radio
James Bond
Kids' Movies
Lord of the Rings
Muhammed Ali
Man Utd
Personal Computers
Pregnancy & Birth
Shakespeare
Superheroes
Unexplained
  Phenomena
The Universe
Videogaming
Weather
Website Directory

Visit us online

roughguides.com

Information on over 25,000 destinations around the world

- **Read** Rough Guides' trusted travel info
- **Share** journals, photos and travel advice with other readers
- Get exclusive Rough Guide **discounts** and travel **deals**
- Earn membership points every time you contribute to the
  Rough Guide **community** and get **free** books, flights and trips
- Browse thousands of CD reviews and artists in our **music** area

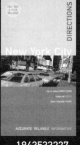

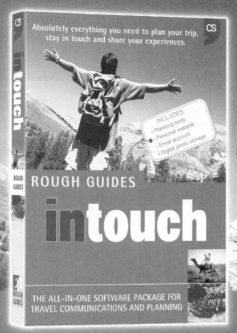

NOTES

Don't bury your head in the sand!

Take cover!

with Rough Guide Travel Insurance

small print and

Index

A Rough Guide to Rough Guides

In the summer of 1981, Mark Ellingham, a recent graduate from Bristol University, was travelling round Greece and couldn't find a guidebook that really met his needs. On the one hand there were the student guides, insistent on saving every last cent, and on the other the heavyweight cultural tomes whose authors seemed to have spent more time in a research library than lounging away the afternoon at a taverna or on the beach.

In a bid to avoid getting a job, Mark and a small group of writers set about creating their own guidebook. It was a guide to Greece that aimed to combine a journalistic approach to description with a thoroughly practical approach to travellers' needs – a guide that would incorporate culture, history and contemporary insights with a critical edge, together with up-to-date, value-for-money listings. Back in London, Mark and the team finished their Rough Guide, as they called it, and talked Routledge into publishing the book.

That first *Rough Guide to Greece*, published in 1982, was a student scheme that became a publishing phenomenon. The immediate success of the book – with numerous reprints and a Thomas Cook prize shortlisting – spawned a series that rapidly covered dozens of destinations. Rough Guides had a ready market among low-budget backpackers, but soon also acquired a much broader and older readership that relished Rough Guides' wit and inquisitiveness as much as their enthusiastic, critical approach. Everyone wants value for money, but not at any price.

Rough Guides soon began supplementing the "rougher" information about hostels and low-budget listings with the kind of detail on restaurants and quality hotels that independent-minded visitors on any budget might expect, whether on business in New York or trekking in Thailand.

These days the guides – distributed worldwide by the Penguin group – offer recommendations from shoestring to luxury and cover more than 200 destinations around the globe, including almost every country in the Americas and Europe, more than half of Africa and most of Asia and Australasia. Our ever-growing team of authors and photographers is spread all over the world, particularly in Europe, the USA and Australia.

In 1994, we published the *Rough Guide to World Music* and *Rough Guide to Classical Music*; and a year later the *Rough Guide to the Internet*. All three books have become benchmark titles in their fields – which encouraged us to expand into other areas of publishing, mainly around popular culture. Rough Guides now publish:

- Travel guides to more than 200 worldwide destinations
- Dictionary phrasebooks to 22 major languages
- History guides ranging from Ireland to Islam
- Maps printed on rip-proof and waterproof Polyart™ paper
- Music guides running the gamut from Opera to Elvis
- Restaurant guides to London, New York and San Francisco
- Reference books on topics as diverse as the Weather and Shakespeare
- Sports guides from Formula 1 to Man Utd
- Pop culture books from *Lord of the Rings* to Cult TV
- World Music CDs in association with World Music Network

Visit **www.roughguides.com** to see our latest publications.

Rough Guide credits

Text editor: Amanda Tomlin
Layout: Amit Verma
Cartography: Karobi Gogoi
Picture research: Harriet Mills
Proofreader: Diane Margolis
Editorial: **London** Martin Dunford, Kate Berens, Claire Saunders, Geoff Howard, Ruth Blackmore, Gavin Thomas, Polly Thomas, Richard Lim, Clifton Wilkinson, Alison Murchie, Sally Schafer, Karoline Densley, Andy Turner, Ella O'Donnell, Keith Drew, Edward Aves, Andrew Lockett, Joe Staines, Duncan Clark, Peter Buckley, Matthew Milton, Daniel Crewe, Nikki Birrell **New York** Andrew Rosenberg, Richard Koss, Chris Barsanti, Steven Horak, AnneLise Sorensen, Amy Hegarty
Design & Pictures: **London** Simon Bracken, Dan May, Diana Jarvis, Mark Thomas, Jj Luck, Harriet Mills, Chloë Roberts; **Delhi** Madhulita Mohapatra, Umesh Aggarwal, Ajay Verma, Jessica Subramanian, Amit Verma
Production: Julia Bovis, Sophie Hewat, Katherine Owers

Cartography: **London** Maxine Repath, Ed Wright, Katie Lloyd-Jones **Delhi** Manish Chandra, Rajesh Chhibber, Jai Prakash Mishra, Ashutosh Bharti, Rajesh Mishra, Animesh Pathak, Jasbir Sandhu, Karobi Gogoi
Online: **New York** Jennifer Gold, Cree Lawson, Suzanne Welles, Benjamin Ross; **Delhi** Manık Chauhan, Narender Kumar, Shekhar Jha, Rakesh Kumar, Lalit Sharma
Marketing & Publicity: **London** Richard Trillo, Niki Hanmer, David Wearn, Demelza Dallow, Kristina Pentland; **New York** Geoff Colquitt, Megan Kennedy, Milena Perez; **Delhi**: Reem Khokhar
Custom publishing and foreign rights: Philippa Hopkins
Finance: Gary Singh
Manager India: Punita Singh
Series editor: Mark Ellingham
PA to Managing Director: Megan McIntyre
Managing Director: Kevin Fitzgerald

Publishing information

This sixth edition published April 2005 by
Rough Guides Ltd,
80 Strand, London WC2R 0RL.
345 Hudson St, 4th Floor,
New York, NY 10014, USA.
14 Local Shopping Centre, Panchsheel Park,
New Delhi 110017, India
Distributed by the Penguin Group
Penguin Books Ltd,
80 Strand, London WC2R 0RL
Penguin Putnam, Inc.
375 Hudson Street, NY 10014, USA
Penguin Group (Australia)
250 Camberwell Road, Camberwell
Victoria 3124, Australia
Penguin Books Canada Ltd,
10 Alcorn Avenue, Toronto, Ontario,
Canada M4V 1E4
Penguin Group (New Zealand)
Cnr Rosedale and Airborne Roads
Albany, Auckland, New Zealand

Typeset in Bembo and Helvetica to an original design by Henry Iles.

Printed in Italy by LegoPrint S.p.A

© Robert Andrews and Jules Brown 2005

520pp includes index
A catalogue record for this book is available from the British Library

ISBN 1-84353-426-6

The publishers and authors have done their best to ensure the accuracy and currency of all the information in **The Rough Guide to Sicily**, however, they can accept no responsibility for any loss, injury, or inconvenience sustained by any traveller as a result of information or advice contained in the guide.

1   3   5   7   9   8   6   4   2

Help us update

We've gone to a lot of effort to ensure that the sixth edition of **The Rough Guide to Sicily** is accurate and up-to-date. However, things change – places get "discovered", opening hours are notoriously fickle, restaurants and rooms raise prices or lower standards. If you feel we've got it wrong or left something out, we'd like to know, and if you can remember the address, the price, the time, the phone number, so much the better.

We'll credit all contributions, and send a copy of the next edition (or any other Rough Guide if you prefer) for the best letters. Everyone who writes to us and isn't already a subscriber will receive a copy of our full-colour thrice-yearly newsletter. Please mark letters: "**Rough Guide Sicily Update**" and send to: Rough Guides, 80 Strand, London WC2R 0RL, or Rough Guides, 4th Floor, 345 Hudson St, New York, NY 10014. Or send an email to **mail@roughguides.com**

Have your questions answered and tell others about your trip at **www.roughguides.atinfopop.com**

Acknowledgements

Roger: Thanks go to Clifton and Amanda for great guidance, patience and in-a-pinch FedEx shipments; Daniele and Rosanna for open-armed welcomes and knowing where all the parties were; Matt and Katrina for timing their wedding perfectly; Rob and Lauren for honeymoon advice; Randi, Roger, Sophie, Andrea, Karyn, Carmelo, Emanuele, Mehdi and Marj; Manuela Tiraboschi D'Ambra for her heart; and Alessandra and Franco Pellizzeri for insight into all things Sicilian.

Ros: Thanks to Loredana from the Messina tourist office, and the tourist offices and pro locos of Bronte, Linguaglossa, Favignana and Siracusa; Beppe and Rosy of the *Favignana Hotel*, who provided Internet access when there was none; Michele and Gemma Bianco for showing me Siracusa nightlife; Rita Piana Kaczynske for guiding me around Catania; Armando La Mattina of the *Hotel Carrubella* in Monreale; and Frank, Ismene and Juno.

Readers' letters

Thanks to all the readers who took the trouble to write in with their comments and suggestions (and apologies to anyone whose name we've misspelt or omitted):

Jane Ackland; Therese Bergman; Dan Bernard; Suzanne Burns; I. Cartwright; Martin Coppen; P. M. Coutts; Dan V. Crowe; Angela and Paul Davis; Crispin Driver; Suzy Gillett; Andor Gomme; Lesley Grayson; Andrew Guest; Robert Hart; Harumi Hotta; Andrew and Julie Howe; Noreen Humble; Patrick Kilbey; Jocelyn Kimmel; Pien van Leeuwen; Helen McConachie; Donal McDonal; Noel McGloin; Stuart McLeod; A. J. Metcalfe; Sue Milliken; Soreen Moore; Carmen Ortega Cortés; Christopher Polkinghorne; Harry Saltzman; Bob & Rose Sandham; Michael Schienke; Dorothy Schulman; Sigurd Solberg; Ben Tichband; Bill Thomas; Mary Tyler; Ruth Wilde; Maya Wolfe; Hans Kleinen Hammans; Dalia Manor.

Photo credits

Cover credits

Main front: Concord, Agrigento © Robert Harding
Small front top picture: Orion Fountain, Messina © Alamy
Small front lower picture: Cefalù © Alamy
Back top picture: Siracusa © Robert Harding
Back lower picture: Cefalù © Alamy

Contents

Interior of Capella Palatina, Palermo
  © John Heseltine/DK Images
Spaghetti alla Norma
  © StockFood/Innerhofer Photodes/Cephas
The Duomo, Siracusa
  © Grazyna Bonati/www.travel-ink.co.uk
Erupting volcano, Stromboli © Peter Wilson
Egadi Islands ferry © Robert Andrews

Introduction

Boats at Cefalu © mediacolor's /Alamy
Lípari coastline © Bowman/Prisma/age footstock/Powerstock
Fiat 500, Sicily © Suzanne Wells
La Santíssima Trinità di Delia, Castelvetrano

© Schütze/Rodemann/Bildarchiv Monheim GmbH/Alamy
Catacombs at the Convento dei Cappuccini, Palermo
  © William A. Allard/National Geographic/ Getty Images
Still from *Il Postino* Dir. Michael Radford
  © Corbis/SYGMA
Temple detail, Segesta, Sicily
  © Roger Wood/Corbis
Painted cart, Via Torres, Palermo
  © John Heseltine/Italian Archive
La Martorana church ceiling, Palermo
  © Mimmo Jodice/Corbis (& repeat on p.3)
Balcony, Noto © Robert Andrews
Tuna Mattanza, Bonagia
  © Tony Gentile/Reuters
Grocery store © Robert Andrews

Things not to miss

01 Diving in Ustica © Courtesy of FOTOTECA/E.N.I.T.
02 Tempio della Concordia, Agrigento
  © Louis-Laurent Grandadam/Impact Photos

SMALL PRINT

SMALL PRINT |

Index

Map entries are in colour.

INDEX

INDEX

Map symbols

maps are listed in the full index using coloured text

– – –	Chapter division boundary	◖	Point of interest
▨▨▨	Motorway	@	Internet café
= = =	Major road	ⓘ	Tourist office
= = =	Minor road	ⓒ	Phone office
———	Viaduct	⊠	Post office
⊞⊞⊞	Steps	⊞	Hospital
}······{	Underpass or long tunnel	◉	Accommodation
▬▬▬	Railway	▣	Restaurant
●- - -●	Cable car	Å	Campsite
- - - - -	Footpath	∴	Ruin
———	River/coastline	ⵟ	Lighthouse
— —	Ferry/hydrofoil	▲	Tower
▬▬▬	Wall	⊤	Gardens
⊠—⊠	Gate	❢	Museum
)(	Bridge	⌖	Church (regional maps)
∧	Mountain range	ṅ	Monastery
▲	Mountain peak	▢	Market
⌐ᴜᴜⁿᴜ	Cliff	▨	Building
⌇	Rocks	⊞	Church
⌇⌇	Gorge	◯	Stadium
⊻	Viewpoint	⊞	Cemetery
✈	Airport	▨	Park
★	Bus stop	▨	Beach
▣	Parking		